T0234026

Lecture Notes in Computer Science   12076

Advanced Research in Computing and Software Science

Subline of Lecture Notes in Computer Science

More information about this series at http://www.springer.com/series/7407

Heike Wehrheim · Jordi Cabot (Eds.)

Fundamental Approaches to Software Engineering

23rd International Conference, FASE 2020
Held as Part of the European Joint Conferences
on Theory and Practice of Software, ETAPS 2020
Dublin, Ireland, April 25–30, 2020
Proceedings

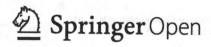

Editors
Heike Wehrheim (iD)
University of Paderborn
Paderborn, Germany

Jordi Cabot (iD)
ICREA
Open University of Catalonia
Barcelona, Spain

ISSN 0302-9743   ISSN 1611-3349   (electronic)
Lecture Notes in Computer Science
ISBN 978-3-030-45233-9   ISBN 978-3-030-45234-6   (eBook)
https://doi.org/10.1007/978-3-030-45234-6

LNCS Sublibrary: SL1 – Theoretical Computer Science and General Issues

This Springer imprint is published by the registered company Springer Nature Switzerland AG
The registered company address is: Gewerbestrasse 11, 6330 Cham, Switzerland

ETAPS Foreword

Welcome to the 23rd ETAPS! ETAPS 2020 was originally planned to take place in Ireland in its beautiful capital Dublin. Because of the Covid-19 pandemic, this was changed to an online event on July 2, 2020.

ETAPS 2020 is the 23rd instance of the European Joint Conferences on Theory and Practice of Software.

ETAPS is an annual federated conference established in 1998, and consists of four conferences: ESOP, FASE, FoSSaCS, and TACAS.

Each conference has its own Program Committee (PC) and its own Steering Committee (SC).

The conferences cover various aspects of software systems, ranging from theoretical computer science to foundations of programming language developments, analysis tools, and formal approaches to software engineering.

Organizing these conferences in a coherent, highly synchronized conference programme, enables researchers to participate in an exciting event, having the possibility to meet many colleagues working in different directions in the field, and to easily attend talks of different conferences.

On the weekend before the main conference, numerous satellite workshops take place that attract many researchers from all over the globe. Also, for the second time, an ETAPS Mentoring Workshop is organized.

This workshop is intended to help students early in the program with advice on research, career, and life in the fields of computing that are covered by the ETAPS conference.

ETAPS 2020 received 424 submissions in total, 129 of which were accepted, yielding an overall acceptance rate of 30.4%.

I thank all the authors for their interest in ETAPS, all the reviewers for their reviewing efforts, the PC members for their contributions, and in particular the PC (co-) chairs for their hard work in running this entire intensive process.

Last but not least, my congratulations to all authors of the accepted papers!

Because of the change to an online event, most of the original ETAPS program had to be cancelled. The ETAPS afternoon featured presentations of the three best paper awards, the Test-of-Time award and the ETAPS PhD award. The invited and tutorial speakers of ETAPS 2020 will be invited for ETAPS 2021, and all authors of accepted ETAPS 2020 papers will have the opportunity to present their work at ETAPS 2021.

ETAPS 2020 originally was supposed to place in Dublin, Ireland, organized by the University of Limerick and Lero. The local organization team consisted of Tiziana Margaria (UL and Lero, general chair), Vasileios Koutavas (Lero@UCD), Anila Mjeda (Lero@UL), Anthony Ventresque (Lero@UCD), and Petros Stratis (Easy Conferences). I would like to thank Tiziana and her team for all the preparations, and we hope there will be a next opportunity to host ETAPS in Dublin.

ETAPS 2020 is further supported by the following associations and societies: ETAPS e.V., EATCS (European Association for Theoretical Computer Science),

EAPLS (European Association for Programming Languages and Systems), and EASST (European Association of Software Science and Technology).

The ETAPS Steering Committee consists of an Executive Board, and representatives of the individual ETAPS conferences, as well as representatives of EATCS, EAPLS, and EASST.

The Executive Board consists of Holger Hermanns (Saarbrücken), Marieke Huisman (Twente, chair), Joost-Pieter Katoen (Aachen and Twente), Jan Kofron (Prague), Gerald Lüttgen (Bamberg), Tarmo Uustalu (Reykjavik and Tallinn), Caterina Urban (INRIA), and Lenore Zuck (Chicago).

Other members of the steering committee are:

Armin Biere (Linz)
Jordi Cabot (Barcelona)
Jean Goubault-Larrecq (Cachan)
Jan-Friso Groote (Eindhoven)
Esther Guerra (Madrid)
Jurriaan Hage (Utrecht)
Reiko Heckel (Leicester)
Panagiotis Katsaros (Thessaloniki)
Stefan Kiefer (Oxford)
Barbara König (Duisburg)
Fabrice Kordon (Paris)
Jan Kretinsky (Munich)
Kim G. Larsen (Aalborg)
Tiziana Margaria (Limerick)
Peter Müller (Zurich)
Catuscia Palamidessi (Palaiseau)
Dave Parker (Birmingham)
Andrew M. Pitts (Cambridge)
Peter Ryan (Luxembourg)
Don Sannella (Edinburgh)
Bernhard Steffen (Dortmund)
Mariëlle Stoelinga (Twente)
Gabriele Taentzer (Marburg)
Christine Tasson (Paris)
Peter Thiemann (Freiburg)
Jan Vitek (Prague)
Heike Wehrheim (Paderborn)
Anton Wijs (Eindhoven), and
Nobuko Yoshida (London)

I'd like to take this opportunity to thank all authors, attendants, organizers of the satellite workshops, and Springer-Verlag GmbH for their support.

I hope you all enjoyed the ETAPS 2020 afternoon.

July 2020   Marieke Huisman
                                                             ETAPS SC Chair
                                                             ETAPS e.V. President

Preface

This volume contains the papers presented at the 23rd International Conference on Fundamental Approaches to Software Engineering (FASE 2020). FASE 2020 was organized as part of the annual European Joint Conferences on Theory and Practice of Software (ETAPS 2020).

FASE is concerned with the foundations on which software engineering is built. The papers submitted covered topics such as requirements engineering, software architectures, specification, software quality, validation, verification of functional and non-functional properties, model-driven development and model transformation, software processes, security, and software evolution. In particular, the 2020 edition of FASE saw an increased number of papers with empirical studies.

FASE 2020 had no separate abstract submission deadline and we received 81 submissions on the paper deadline with 5 tool papers, 4 empirical evaluation papers and 72 research papers. The submissions came from the following countries (in alphabetical order): Argentina, Australia, Austria, Belgium, Canada, China, Colombia, Denmark, Estonia, Finland, France, Germany, Greece, Hungary, India, Iran, Italy, Japan, Luxembourg, Macedonia, Netherlands, New Zealand, Norway, Portugal, Russia, Singapore, South Korea, Spain, Sweden, Switzerland, the UK, and the USA. Out of these submissions, we accepted 23 papers (28% acceptance rate) after the review and discussion phases with the Program Committee (PC) members plus 63 additional external reviewers. FASE again used a double-blind reviewing process. We thank the PC members and reviewers for doing an excellent job!

This volume also contains an invited paper by our keynote speaker Willem Visser. It complements his talk on "The Magic of Analyzing Programs".

For the first time, FASE hosted the International Competition on Software Testing (Test-Comp 2020), chaired and organized by Dirk Beyer. Test-Comp 2020 is the second edition of an annual competition for testing tools providing a comparative evaluation of different tools. This edition contained 10 participating tools, from academia and industry. These proceedings contain papers of six tools, having participated in the competition, as well as a summary by the competition organizer Dirk Beyer. The tool papers were reviewed and selected by a separate PC: the Test-Comp 2020 jury. Each Test-Comp paper was assessed by at least three reviewers.

We thank the ETAPS 2020 organizers, in particular, Tiziana Margaria, the general chair, and Vasileios Koutavas, Anila Mjeda, Anthony Ventresque, and Petros Stratis. We also thank Marieke Huisman, the ETAPS Steering Committee (SC) chair, for managing the whole process, and Gabriele Taentzer, the FASE SC chair, for swift feedback on several questions.

We hope that you will enjoy reading this volume.

February 2020

Jordi Cabot
Heike Wehrheim

Organization

FASE – Program Committee

Amel Bennaceur	The Open University, UK
Jordi Cabot	ICREA - UOC (Internet Interdisciplinary Institute), Spain
Yu-Fang Chen	Academia Sinica, Taiwan
Maria Christakis	MPI SWS, Germany
Vittorio Cortellessa	Universita' dell'Aquila, Italy
Jin Song Dong	National University of Singapore, Singapore
Neil Ernst	University of Victoria, Canada
Esther Guerra	Universidad Autónoma de Madrid, Spain
Reiko Heckel	University of Leicester, UK
Soichiro Hidaka	Hosei University, Japan
Rob Hierons	The University of Sheffield, UK
Jennifer Horkoff	Chalmers and the University of Gothenburg, Sweden
Marieke Huisman	University of Twente, The Netherlands
Reiner Hähnle	TU Darmstadt, Germany
Marie-Christine Jakobs	TU Darmstadt, Germany
Einar Broch Johnsen	University of Oslo, Norway
Marjan Mernik	University of Maribor, Slovenia
Arend Rensink	University of Twente, The Netherlands
Augusto Sampaio	Federal University of Pernambuco, Brazil
Ina Schaefer	TU Braunschweig, Germany
Ana Sokolova	University of Salzburg, Austria
Perdita Stevens	The University of Edinburgh, UK
Marielle Stoelinga	University of Twente, The Netherlands
Gabriele Taentzer	Philipps-Universität Marburg, Germany
Wil van der Aalst	RWTH Aachen University, Germany
Heike Wehrheim	Paderborn University, Germany
Manuel Wimmer	Johannes Kepler University Linz, Austria
Tao Yue	Nanjing University of Aeronautics and Astronautics and Simula Research Laboratory, China

Test-Comp – Program Committee and Jury

Dirk Beyer (Chair)	LMU Munich, Germany
Marie-Christine Jakobs (CoVeriTest)	TU Darmstadt, Germany
Lucas Cordeiro (ESBMC)	University of Manchester, UK
Sebastian Ruland (HybridTiger)	TU Darmstadt, Germany

Martin Nowack (KLEE)　　Imperial College London, UK
Gidon Ernst (Legion)　　LMU Munich, Germany
Hoang M. Le (LibKluzzer)　University of Bremen, Germany
Thomas Lemberger　　LMU Munich, Germany
 (PRTest)
Marek Chalupa (Symbiotic)　Masaryk University, Czech Republic
Joxan Jaffar (Tracer-X)　　National University of Singapore, Singapore
Raveendra Kumar　　Tata Consultancy Service, India
 Medicherla (VeriFuzz)

Additional Reviewers

Ahrendt, Wolfgang
Alqahtani, Abdullah Q. F.
Antonino, Pedro
Bacci, Giorgio
Bankhammer, Gregor
Barros, Flavia
Basciani, Francesco
Berardinelli, Luca
Bill, Robert
Bliudze, Simon
Bride, Hadrien
Bubel, Richard
Cerna, David
Di Pompeo, Daniele
Dillmann, Stefan
Dong, Naipeng
Fila, Barbara
Franzago, Mirco
Gerhold, Marcus
Ghaffari Saadat, Maryam
Gheyi, Rohit
Haas, Andreas
Heydari Tabar, Asmae
Hoare, Suchismita
Janků, Petr
Kamburjan, Eduard
Katsaros, Panagiotis
Klikovits, Stefan
Knüppel, Alexander
Könighofer, Bettina
Le, Hoang M.
Leroy, Dorian

Lima, Lucas
Lin, Hsin-Hung
Lin, Shang-Wei
Lin, Yun
Lombardi, Tiziano
Lukina, Anna
Mauro, Jacopo
Nieke, Michael
Ölveczky, Peter
Pierantonio, Alfonso
Ponce De León, Hernán
Pun, Ka I.
Quanqi, Ye
Resmerita, Stefan
Ruijters, Enno
Runge, Tobias
Rutle, Adrian
Saivasan, Prakash
Sanan, David
Steffen, Martin
Steinhöfel, Dominic
Stolz, Volker
Summers, Alexander J.
Tapia Tarifa, Silvia Lizeth
Teixeira, Leopoldo
Thüm, Thomas
Tucci, Michele
Turrini, Andrea
van der Wal, Djurre
Wally, Bernhard
Wasser, Nathan
Wolny, Sabine

Contents

Test-Comp Contributions

Invited Talk

Improving symbolic automata learning
with concolic execution *

Donato Clun[1]©, Phillip van Heerden[2]©, Antonio Filieri[1]©, and Willem
Visser[2]©

[1] Imperial College London
[2] Stellenbosch University

Abstract. Inferring the input grammar accepted by a program is central for a variety of software engineering problems, including parsers
verification, grammar-based fuzzing, communication protocol inference,
and documentation. Sound and complete active learning techniques have
been developed for several classes of languages and the corresponding automaton representation, however there are outstanding challenges that
are limiting their effective application to the inference of input grammars.
We focus on active learning techniques based on L^* and propose two extensions of the *Minimally Adequate Teacher* framework that allow the
efficient learning of the input language of a program in the form of symbolic automata, leveraging the additional information that can extracted
from concolic execution. Upon these extensions we develop two learning
algorithms that reduce significantly the number of queries required to
converge to the correct hypothesis.

1 Introduction

Inferring the input grammar of a program from its implementation is central
for a variety of software engineering activities, including automated documentation, compiler analyses, and grammar-based fuzzing.

Several learning algorithms have been investigated for inferring a grammar
from examples of accepted and rejected input words, with active learning approaches achieving the highest data-efficiency and strong convergence guarantees. Active learning is a theoretical framework enabling a *learner* to gather
information about a target language by interacting with a *teacher* [1]. A minimally adequate teacher that can guarantee the convergence of an active language
learning procedure for regular language is an oracle that can answer membership
and equivalence queries. Membership queries check whether a word indicated by
the learner is accepted by the target language and equivalence queries can confirm that a hypothesis language proposed by the learner is equivalent to the
target language, or provide a counterexample word otherwise.

---

* This work has been partially supported by the EPSRC HiPEDS Centre for Doc-
toral Training (EP/L016796/1), the DSI-NRF Centre of Excellence in Mathematical
and Statistical Sciences (CoE-MaSS), and a Royal Society Newton Mobility Grant
(NMG\R2 \170142).

H. Wehrheim and J. Cabot (Eds.): FASE 2020, LNCS 12076, pp. 3–26, 2020.
https://doi.org/10.1007/978-3-030-45234-6_1

However, when learning the input language accepted by a program from its code implementation, it is unrealistic to assume the availability of a complete equivalence oracle, because such an oracle would need to check the equivalence between the hypothesis language and arbitrary software code.

In this paper, we explore the use of concolic execution to design active learning procedures for inferring the input grammar of a program in the form of a symbolic finite automaton. In particular, we extend two state of the art active learning frameworks for symbolic learning by enabling the teacher to 1) provide more informative answers for membership queries by pairing the accept/reject outcome with a path condition describing all the input words that would result in the same execution as the word indicated by the learner, and 2) provide a partial equivalence oracle that may produce counterexamples for the learner hypothesis. The partial equivalence oracle would rely on the exploration capabilities of the concolic execution engine to identify input words for which the acceptance outcome differs between the target program and the learner's hypothesis. To guarantee the termination of the concolic execution for equivalence queries, we set a bound on the length of the inputs the engine can generate during its exploration. While necessarily incomplete, such equivalence oracle may effectively guide the learning process and guarantee the correctness of the learned language for inputs up to the set input bound. Finally, we propose a new class of symbolic membership queries that build on the constraint solving capabilities of the concolic engine to directly infer complete information about the transitions between states of the hypothesis language.

In our preliminary evaluation based on Java implementations of parsers for regular languages from the Automatark benchmark suite, the new active learning algorithms enabled by concolic execution learned the correct input language for 76% of the subject, despite the lack of a complete equivalence oracle and achieving a reduction of up to 96% of the number of membership and equivalence queries produced by the learner.

The remaining of the paper is structured as follows: Section 2 introduces background concepts and definitions concerning symbolic finite state automata, active learning, and concolic execution. Section 3 describes in details the data structures and learning algorithms of two state of the art approaches – Λ^* [11] and MAT* [3] – that will be the base for active learning strategies based on concolic execution formalized in Section 4. Section 5 will report on our preliminary experiments on the effectiveness and query-efficiency capabilities of the new strategies. Finally, Section 6 discusses related work and Section 7 presents our concluding remarks.

2 Preliminaries

2.1 Symbolic finite state automata

Symbolic finite state automata (SFA) are an extension of finite state automata where a transitions can be labeled with a predicate identifying a subset of the input alphabet [28]. The set of predicates allowed on SFA transitions should constitute an *effective Boolean algebra* [3], which guarantees closure with respect to boolean operations according to the following definition:

Definition 1. *Effective Boolean algebra [3].* An *effective Boolean algebra $\mathcal{A}$ is a tuple $(\mathcal{D}, \Psi, [\![\_]\!], \bot, \top, \vee, \wedge, \neg)$ where $\mathcal{D}$ is the set of domain elements; Ψ is the set of predicates, including $\bot$ and $\top$; $[\![\_]\!] : \Psi \to 2^{\mathcal{D}}$ is a denotation function such that $[\![\bot]\!] = \emptyset$, $[\![\top]\!] = \mathcal{D}$, and for all $\phi, \psi \in \Psi$, $[\![\phi \vee \psi]\!] = [\![\phi]\!] \cup [\![\psi]\!]$, $[\![\phi \wedge \psi]\!] = [\![\phi]\!] \cap [\![\psi]\!]$, and $[\![\neg \phi]\!] = \mathcal{D} \setminus [\![\phi]\!]$.*

Given an effective Boolean algebra $\mathcal{A}$, an SFA is formally defined as:

Definition 2. *Symbolic Finite Automaton (SFA) [3].* A *symbolic finite automaton $\mathcal{M}$ is a tuple $(\mathcal{A}, Q, q_{init}, F, \Delta)$ where $\mathcal{A}$ is an effective Boolean algebra, called the* alphabet; *Q is a finite set of states; $q_{init} \in Q$ is the* initial state; *$F \subseteq Q$ is the set of* final states; *and $\Delta \subseteq Q \times \Psi_{\mathcal{A}} \times Q$ is the transition relation* consisting *of a finite set of* moves *or* transitions.

Given a linearly ordered finite alphabet Σ, through the rest of the paper we will assume $\mathcal{A}$ to be the Boolean algebra over the union of intervals over Σ, with the canonical interpretations of union, intersection, and negation operators. With an abuse of notation, we will write $\psi \in \mathcal{A}$ to refer to a predicate ψ in the set Ψ of $\mathcal{A}$. A *word* is a finite sequence of alphabet symbols (*characters*) $w = w_0 w_1 \ldots w_n$ ($w_i \in \Sigma$), whose *length* $len(w) = n - 1$. We indicate with $w[: i]$ the prefix of w up to the i element excluded, and with $w[i :]$ the suffix of w starting from element i. We will use the notation w_i and $w[i]$ interchangeably. The language accepted by an SFA $\mathcal{M}$ will be indicated as $L_{\mathcal{M}}$, or only L when the SFA M can be inferred by the context. For an SFA $\mathcal{M}$ and a word w, $\mathcal{M}(w) = true$ if $\mathcal{M}$ accepts w; $false$ otherwise.

Similarly to finite state automata, SFAs are closed under language intersection, union, and complement, and admit a minimal form [3]. Compared to non-symbolic automata, SFAs can produce more compact representations over large alphabets (e.g., Unicode), allowing a single transition predicate to account for a possibly large set of characters, instead of explicitly enumerating all of them.

2.2   Active learning and minimally adequate teachers

Active learning encompasses a set of techniques enabling a learning algorithm to gather information interacting with a suitable oracle, referred to as *teacher*. Angluin [1] proposed an exact, active learning algorithm for a regular language L named L^*. In L^* the learner can ask the oracle two types of queries, namely *membership* and *equivalence* queries. In a membership query, the learner selects a word $w \in \Sigma^*$ and the oracle answers whether the $w \in L$ (formally, the membership oracle is a function $\mathcal{O}_m : \Sigma^* \to \mathbb{B}$, where $\mathbb{B} = \{true, false\}$). In an equivalence query, the learner selects an hypothesis finite state automaton (FSA) $\mathcal{H}$ and asks the oracle whether $L_{\mathcal{H}} \equiv L$; if $L_{\mathcal{H}} \not\equiv L$, the oracle returns a *counterexample*, i.e., a word w in which L differs from L_H (formally, the equivalence oracle is a function $\mathcal{O}_e : FSA \to \Sigma^* \cup \{true\}$). A teacher providing both $\mathcal{O}_m$ and $\mathcal{O}_e$, and able to produce a counter example as result from $\mathcal{O}_e$ is called a *minimally adequate teacher*. Given a minimally adequate teacher, L^* is guaranteed to learn the target language L with a number of queries polynomial in the number of states of a minimal deterministic automaton accepting L and in the size of the largest counterexample returned by the teacher [1].

Discovering FSA states. Consider an FSA $\mathcal{M}$. Given two words u and v such that $\mathcal{M}(u) \neq \mathcal{M}(v)$ (i.e., one accepted and one rejected), it can be concluded that u and v reach different states of $\mathcal{M}$. Moreover, if u and v share a suffix s (i.e., $u = a.s$ and $v = b.s$ with $a, b, s \in \Sigma^*$ and the dot representing word concatenation), a and b necessarily reach two different states q_a and q_b of $\mathcal{M}$. The suffix s is a *discriminator suffix* for the two states because its parsing starting from q_a and q_b leads to difference acceptance outcomes. The words a and b are instead *access words* of q_a and q_b, respectively, because their parsing from the initial state reaches q_a and q_b. This observation can be generalized to a set of words by considering all the unordered pairs of words in the set. Because $\mathcal{M}$ is a finite state automaton, there can be only a finite number of discriminable words in Σ^* and, correspondingly, a finite number of distinct access string identifying the automaton's states.

State reached parsing a word. For a word w, consider a known discriminator suffix s and access word a. If $\mathcal{O}_m(w.s) \neq \mathcal{O}_m(a.s)$, the state reached parsing w cannot be the one identified by a. Throughout the learning process, it is possible that none of the already discovered access words identifies the state reached by w. In this case, w would be a suitable candidate for discovering a new FSA state as described in the previous paragraph.

Discovering FSA transitions. For each access string a and symbol $\sigma \in \Sigma$, a transition should exist between the states reached parsing a and $a.\sigma$, respectively.

2.3   Concolic execution

Concolic execution [14,27] combines concrete and symbolic execution of a program, allowing to extract for a given concrete input a set of constraints on the input space that uniquely characterize the corresponding execution path. To this end, the target program is instrumented to pair each program input with a symbolic input variable and to record along an execution path the constraints on the symbolic inputs induced by the encountered conditional branches. The conjunction of the constraints recorded during the execution of the instrumented program on a concrete input is called *path condition* and characterize the equivalence class of all the inputs that would follow the same execution path (in this paper, we focus on sequential program, whose execution is uniquely determined by the program inputs).

Explored path conditions can be stored in a prefix tree (*symbolic execution tree*), which captures all the paths already covered by at least one executed input. A concolic engine can traverse the symbolic execution tree to find branches not yet explored. The path condition corresponding to the selected unexplored branch is then solved using a constraint solver (e.g., an SMT solver [26]) generating a concrete input that will cover the branch. The traversal order used to find the next branch to be covered is referred to as *search strategy* of the concolic executor.

2.4   From path conditions to SFA

In this paper, we consider only terminating programs that can either accept or reject a finite input word $w \in \Sigma^*$ (e.g., either parsing it correctly or throwing a parsing exception). Furthermore, we assume for a given input word w, the resulting path condition to be expressible using a subset of the string constraint language defined in [5]. This allows the translation of the resulting path condition into a finite state automaton [5]. The adaptation of this translation procedure to produce SFAs is straightforward. In particular, we will focus on constraints F recursively defined as:

$$F \rightarrow C \mid \neg F \mid F \wedge F \mid F \vee F$$
$$C \rightarrow E \ O \ E \mid len(w) \ O \ E \mid w[n] \ O \ \sigma \mid w[len(w) - n] \ O \ \sigma$$
$$E \rightarrow n \mid n + n \mid n - n$$
$$O \rightarrow < \mid = \mid >$$

with $n \in \mathbb{Z}$ is an integer constant and $\sigma \in \Sigma$. Informally, the path condition corresponding to processing a symbolic input word w should be reducible to a combination of interval constraints on the linearly ordered alphabet Σ for each of the symbols $w[i]$ composing the input. Despite its restriction, this constraint language is expressive enough to capture the path conditions obtained from the concolic execution of a variety of programs that accept regular languages (which will be described in the evaluation section). The extension to support the entire string constraint language proposed in [5] is left as future work.

3   Active learning for SFA

Several active learning algorithms have been defined for SFAs. In this section, we recall and formalize the core routines of two extensions of L^* proposed in [11] and [3], named Λ^* and MAT^*, respectively. We will then extend and adapt these routines to improve their efficiency and resilience to incomplete oracles based on partial concolic execution.

Running example. To demonstrate the functioning of the algorithms discussed in this section and their extensions later one, we introduce here as running example the SFA accepting the language corresponding to regular expression `.*\w[^\w]\d[^\d].*`, where `\w` matches any letter, digit, or underscore (i.e., `[a-zA-Z0-9_]`), `\d` matches any digit, and `.*` matches any sequence of symbols. The regular expression is evaluated over the 16bit unicode symbols. The corresponding SFA is represented in Figure 1, where transitions are labeled by the union of disjoint intervals and each interval is represented as $\sigma_i - \sigma_j$, or σ if it is composed by a single element; intervals are separated by a semicolon.

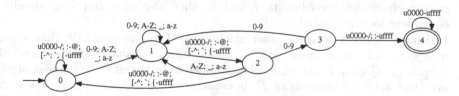

Fig. 1. SFA accepting the language for the running example.

This example highlights the conciseness of symbolic automata. It was chosen because the benefits of the methodologies discussed in this paper increase as the transitions are labeled with predicates representing larger set of characters, and the intervals used in this example are representative of commonly used ones.

3.1 Learning using observation tables

Λ^* is an adaptation of L^* for learning SFAs. In both algorithms, the learner stores and process the information gathered by the oracle in an *observation table* (we adapt here the notation defined in [11]):

Definition 3. *Observation table [11]. An observation table T for an SFA $\mathcal{M}$ is a tuple (Σ, S, R, E, f) where Σ is a potentially infinite set called the alphabet; $S, R, E \subset \Sigma^*$ are finite subsets of words called, respectively, prefixes, boundary, and suffixes. $f : (S \cup R) \times E \rightarrow \{true, false\}$ is a Boolean classification function such that for word $w \in (S \cup R)$ and $e \in E$, $f(w.e) = true$ iff $\mathcal{M}(w.e)$. Additionally, the following invariants hold: (i) $S \cap R = \emptyset$, (ii) $S \cup R$ is prefix-closed, and the empty word $\epsilon \in S$, (iii) for all $s \in S$, there exists a character $\sigma \in \Sigma$ such that $s.\sigma \in R$, and (iv) $\epsilon \in E$.*

Figure 2a shows an example observation table (**T**) according to the notation in [11]. The rows are indexed by elements of $S \cup R$, with the elements of S reported above the horizontal line and those of R below it. The columns instead are indexed by elements of E. An element in $s \in S$ represent the access word to a state q_s, i.e., the state that would be reached by parsing s from the initial state. Elements in the boundary set R provide information about the SFA transitions. The elements of $e \in E$ are discrimination suffixes in that, if there exist $s_i, s_j \in S$ and $e \in E$ such that $f(s_i.e) \neq f(s_j.e)$, s_i and s_j reach different states of $\mathcal{M}$. The cell corresponding to a row index $w \in S \cup R$ and column index $e \in E$ contains the result of $f(w.e)$, which, for compactness, is represented as $+$ or $-$ when the f evaluates to *true* or *false*, respectively. For an element $w \in S \cup R$, we use $row(w)$ to indicate the vector of $+/-$ in the row of the table indexed by w.

An observation table is: *closed* if for each $r \in R$ there exists $s \in S$ such that $row(r) = row(s)$; *reduced* if for all $s_i, s_j \in S$, $s_i \neq s_j \Rightarrow row(s_i) \neq row(s_j)$; *consistent* if for all $w_i, w_j \in S \cup R$ and $\sigma \in \Sigma$, if $w_i.\sigma, w_j.\sigma \in S \cup R$ and $row(w_i) = row(w_j)$ then $row(w_i.\sigma) = row(w_j.\sigma)$; *evidence-closed* if for all $e \in E$ and $s \in S$, $s.e \in S \cup R$. An observation table is *choesive* if it is closed, reduced, consistent, and evidence-closed. Informally, closed means that every element of R corresponds to a state identified by an element of S; reduced, that every state is identified by a unique access string in S; consistent, that if two words w_i and w_j are equivalent according to f and E, then also $w_i.\sigma$ and $w_j.\sigma$ should be equivalent for any symbol $\sigma \in \Sigma$.

Induced SFA. A cohesive observation table **T** induces an SFA that accepts or reject words consistently with its classification function f. Such induced SFA $\mathcal{M}_{\mathbf{T}} = (\mathcal{A}, Q, q_{init}, F, \Delta)$, where $\mathcal{A}$ is assumed to be the effective Boolean algebra over the union of intervals of Σ, is constructed as follows. For each $s \in S$ a corresponding state $q_s \in Q$ is defined, with the initial state q_{init} being q_ϵ. The final states F are all the states q_s such that $f(s) = true$. Since **T** is cohesive, a function $g : S \cup R \rightarrow S$ can be defined such that $g(w) = s$ iff $row(w) = row(s)$. Given g, for $w \in \Sigma^*$ and $\sigma \in \Sigma$, if $w.\sigma \in S \cup R$ then $(q_{g(w)}, \sigma, q_{g(w.\sigma)}) \in \Delta$. However, this intuitive construction of the transition relation Δ would result in

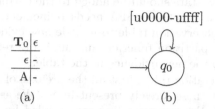

Fig. 2. Example of a cohesive observation table and its induced automata.

the construction of a FSA, where each transition is labeled with a single element $\sigma \in \Sigma$. To obtain an equivalent SFA, an additional step is required to learn the transition predicates of the SFA $\mathcal{M}_{\mathbf{T}}$.

Transition predicates. Given a Boolean algebra $\mathcal{A}$ with domain $\mathcal{D} = \Sigma$, a *partition function* can be defined that generalizes the concrete evidence for a transition of the induced automaton into a predicate of $\mathcal{A}$. Intuitively, the resulting predicate for a transition from state q_i to state q_j should evaluate positively for all the elements $\sigma_j \in \Sigma$ that would label a transition from q_i to q_j according to the function g defined in the previous paragraph, and negatively for all the elements σ_k that would label a transition from q_i to a state other than q_j. Because the function g is by construction a partial function (defined only for words $w.\sigma \in S \cup R$), the partition function can arbitrarily assign the symbols σ not classified by g. This produces a natural generalization of the induced SFA from an observation table.

In this paper, we assume $\mathcal{A}$ to be the Boolean algebra over the union of intervals over Σ, with Σ being a linearly ordered finite alphabet, such as the ascii or unicode symbols. For this algebra, a partition function can be trivially defined by constructing for each transition an interval union predicate characterizing all the concrete evidence symbols that would label the transition according to g. Then, for a given state, the symbols for which g is not defined can be arbitrarily added to any of the predicates labeling an outgoing transition. A more efficient definition of a partition function for this algebra is beyond the scope of this section. The interested reader is instead referred to [11].

The introduction of a partition function to abstract concrete transition symbols into predicates of a Boolean algebra is the key generalization of Λ^* over L^* that allow learning SFAs instead of FSA. Going back to the observation table in Figure 2a, the induced SFA is shown in Figure 2b. The observation table provides concrete evidence for labeling the transition from ϵ to itself with the symbol A. The partition function generalized this concrete evidence into the predicate [u0000-uffff], which assigned all the elements of the unicode alphabet to the sole outgoing transition from q_0.

Learning algorithm. Initially, the learner assumes an observation table corresponding to the empty language, with $S = E = \{\epsilon\}$ and $R = \{\sigma\}$ for an arbitrary $\sigma \in \Sigma$, like the one in Figure 2a. The corresponding induced SFA $\mathcal{M}_{\mathbf{T}}$ is the hypothesis the learner proposes to the equivalence oracle $\mathcal{O}_e$. If the hypothesis does not correspond to the target language, the equivalence oracle returns a counterexample $c \in \Sigma^*$. There are two possible reasons for a counterexample: either a new state should be added to the current hypothesis or one of the predicates in the hypothesis SFA needs refinement. Both cases will be handled updating the observation table to include new evidence from the counterexample c, with the partition function automatically refining the transition predicates according to the new evidence in the table.

To update the observation table, first all the prefixes of c (including c itself) are added to R, except those already present in S. (We assume every time an element is added to R, the corresponding row is filled by issuing membership queries to determine the value of $f(r.e)$, $e \in E$, for each cell.) If for a word $r \in R$ there is no word $s \in S$ such that $row(r) = row(s)$, the word r identifies a newly discovered state and it is therefore moved to S; a word $r.\sigma$ for an arbitrary $\sigma \in \Sigma$ is then added to R to trigger the exploration of outgoing transitions from the newly discovered state. To ensure the updated observation table is evidence-closed, for all $s \in S$ and $e \in E$ $s.e$ and all its prefixes are added to R, if not already present. Finally, the observation table should be made consistent. To this end, if there exist and element $\sigma \in \Sigma$ such that $w_i, w_j, w_i.\sigma, w_j.\sigma \in S \cup R$ with $row(w_i) = row(w_j)$ but $row(w_i.\sigma) \neq row(w_j.\sigma)$, then w_i and w_j should lead to different states. Since $row(w_i.\sigma) \neq row(w_j.\sigma)$, there exist $e \in E$ such that $f(w_i.\sigma.e) \neq f(w_j.\sigma.e)$. Therefore, $a.e$ can discriminate between the states reached parsing w_i and w_j and as such $a.e$ should be added to E. The observation table is now cohesive and its induced SFA can be checked against the equivalence oracle, repeating this procedure until no counterexample can be found.

Running example. We demonstrate the first three iterations of the Λ^* learning procedure invoked on the automaton in Figure 1. The initial table (Figure 2a) is cohesive, so an SFA is induced (Figure 2b) and an equivalence query is issued. The oracle returns the counter example $A!0B$. The counter example and its prefixes are added to the table (Figure 3a), and the table becomes open. The table is closed (Figure 3b), and becomes cohesive. An SFA is induced (Figure 3.1), and the equivalence query returns the counter example B. The counter example is added to the evidence (Figure 3c), and the table becomes consistent but open. The table is closed (Figure 3d), and becomes cohesive.

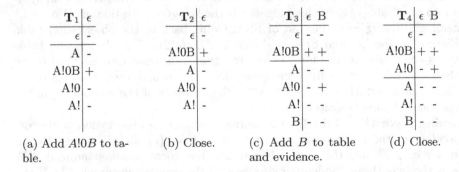

$\mathbf{T_1}$	ϵ
ϵ	-
A	-
A!0B	+
A!0	-
A!	-

$\mathbf{T_2}$	ϵ
ϵ	-
A!0B	+
A	-
A!0	-
A!	-

$\mathbf{T_3}$	ϵ	B
ϵ	-	-
A!0B	+	+
A	-	-
A!0	-	+
A!	-	-
B	-	-

$\mathbf{T_4}$	ϵ	B
ϵ	-	-
A!0B	+	+
A!0	-	+
A	-	-
A!	-	-
B	-	-

(a) Add $A!0B$ to table.   (b) Close.   (c) Add B to table and evidence.   (d) Close.

Fig. 3. Observation tables for two iterations of Λ^*.

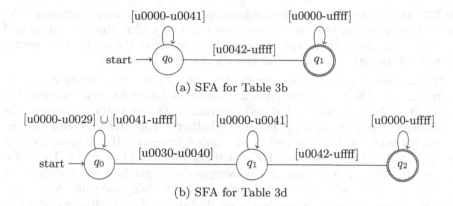

(a) SFA for Table 3b

(b) SFA for Table 3d

Fig. 4. Hypothesis automata for the learning iterations in Figure 3.

3.2 Learning using discrimination trees

A discrimination tree (DT) is a binary classification tree used by the learner to store the information gathered from the teacher. Introduced in [23], it is the core data structure of several learning algorithms, including TTT [20] and MAT^* [3]. We formalize its structure and main routines that will be the baseline for extensions presented in the next section.

Recalling from Section 2.2, each state q_a of an SFA $\mathcal{M}$ is identified by the learner using a unique *access word* $a \in \Sigma^*$. Given two states q_a and q_b, $s \in \Sigma^*$ is a *discriminator suffix* for q_a and q_b if parsing s starting from the two states leads to different outcomes (accept or reject). In terms of the state access words, this is equivalent to stating $\mathcal{M}(a.s) \neq \mathcal{M}(b.s)$. A discrimination tree stores the access words and discriminator suffixes learned for an SFA as per the following definition:

Definition 4. *Discrimination tree (adapted from [3]). A discrimination tree $\mathcal{T}$ is a tuple (N, L, T) where N is a set of nodes, $L \subseteq N$ is a set of leaves, and $T \subset N \times N \times \mathbb{B}$ is the transitions relation. Each leaf $l \in L$ is associated with a corresponding access word ($aw(l)$). Each internal node $i \in N \backslash L$ is associated with a discriminator suffix $d(i)$. For each element $(p, n, b) \in T$, p is the parent node of n and if $b = true$ (respectively $b = false$) we say that n is the accept (respectively, reject) child of p.*

For a leaf $l \in L$ and inner node $n \in N \backslash L$, if l is in the subtree of n rooted in its accept child, then $\mathcal{M}(aw(l).d(n)) = true$. Similarly, if l is in the reject subtree of n, $\mathcal{M}(aw(l).d(n)) = false$. In other words, the concatenation of $aw(l)$ with the discriminator suffix of any of its ancestor nodes is accepted iff l is in the accept subtree of the ancestor node. For any two leaves $l_i, l_j \in L$ let $n_{i,j}$ be their lowest common ancestor in the DT. Then the discriminator suffix $d(n_{i,j})$ allows to discriminate the two states corresponding to l_i and l_j since $\mathcal{M}(aw(l_i).d(n_{i,j})) \neq \mathcal{M}(aw(l_j).d(n_{i,j}))$, with $aw(l_i).d(n_{i,j})$ being the accepted word if l_i is in the accept subtree of $n_{i,j}$, or the rejected word otherwise.

Learning algorithm. We will here refer to the functioning of MAT^* [3], although the main concepts apply to DT-based learning in general. To initialize the DT, the learner performs a membership query on the empty string ϵ. The initial discrimination tree will be composed of two nodes: the root and a leaf node, both labeled with ϵ. Depending on the outcome of the membership query, the leaf will be either the accept or the reject child of the root.

Given a word $w \in \Sigma^*$, to identify the state reached by parsing it according to the DT, the learner performs an operation called *sift*. Sift traverses the tree starting from its root r. For each internal node n it visits, it executes the membership query $\mathcal{O}_m(w.d(n))$ to check whether w concatenated with the discriminator suffix of d is accepted by the target language. If it is accepted, sift continues visiting the accept child of n, and the reject child otherwise. If a leaf is reached, the learner concludes that parsing w the target SFA reaches the state identified by the leaf's access word. If instead the child node sift should traverse next does not exist, a new leaf is created in its place with access word w. Membership queries of the form $a.\sigma$, where a is an access string in the DT and $\sigma \in \Sigma$ are then issued to discover transitions of the SFA, possibly leading to the discovery of new states.

Induced SFA. A discrimination tree DT induces an SFA $\mathcal{M}_{DT} = (\mathcal{A}, Q, q_{init}, F, \Delta)$. In this paper, we assume $\mathcal{A}$ to be the Boolean algebra over the union of disjoint intervals over Σ. Q is populated with one state q_l for each leaf $l \in L$ of DT. The state q_ϵ is the initial state. If $\mathcal{O}_m(aw(l)) = true$, then $q_l \in F$ is a final state of $\mathcal{M}_{DT}$. To construct the transition relation Δ, sifts of the form $aw(l).\sigma$ for $\sigma \in \Sigma$ are issued for the states q_l and the concrete evidence for a transition between two states q_i and q_j is summarized into a consistent predicate of $\mathcal{A}$ using a partition function, as described for Λ^*.

Counterexamples. The equivalence query $\mathcal{O}_e(\mathcal{M}_{DT})$ will either confirm the learner identified the target language or produce a counterexample $c \in \Sigma^*$. As for Λ^*, the existence of c implies that either a transition predicate is incorrect or that there should be a new state. To determine the cause of c, the first step is to identify the longest prefix $c[: i]$ before the behavior of the hypothesis SFA diverged from the target language. To localize the divergence point, the learner analyzes the prefixes $c[: i]$ for $i \in [0, len(c)]$. Let a_i be the access string of the state of $\mathcal{M}_{DT}$ reached parsing $c[: i]$. If $\mathcal{O}_m(a_i.w[i :]) \neq \mathcal{O}_m(c)$, i is the divergence point, which implies that the transition taken from q_{a_i} is incorrect. Let q_j be the state corresponding to the leaf reached when sifting $a_i.c[i :]$. The predicate guarding the transition between q_{a_i} and q_j is incorrect if $c[i]$ does not satisfy the corresponding transition predicate. This is possible because the partition function assigns the symbols in Σ for which no concrete evidence is available to any of the outgoing transitions of q_{a_i}. In this case, the transition predicates should be recomputed to account for the new evidence from c. If instead $c[i]$ satisfies the transition predicate between q_{a_i} and q_j, a new state should be added such that parsing $c[i]$ from q_{a_i} reaches it. To add the new state, the leaf labeled with a_i is replaced by a subtree composed of three nodes: an internal node with discriminator suffix $c[i :]$ having as children the leaf a_i and a new leaf labeled by the access string $j.c[i]$, where j is the access string of the state q_j obtainened by sifting $a_i.c[i :]$. This procedure is called *split* (for more details, see, e.g., [3]). The updated DT will then be the base for the next learning iteration.

Running example. A DT corresponding to the running example introduced in Section 3 is shown below. While the specific structure of the learned DT depends on the order in which words are added to it, all the DT resulting from the learning process induce the same classification of the words $w \in \Sigma^*$, being them consistent representations of the same target language.

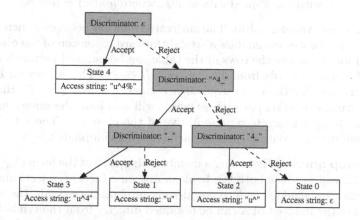

Fig. 5. Discrimination tree learned for the example of Section 3.

4   Active learning with concolic execution

The state-of-the-art active learning algorithms formalized in the previous sections are of limited use when trying to infer (an approximation of) the input language accepted by a program. Their main limitation is the reliance on a complete equivalence oracle, which is unavailable in this case.

In this section, we will propose several extensions of the Λ^* and MAT^* algorithms formalized in Sections 3.1 and 3.2 that make use of a concolic execution engine to 1) gather enhanced information from membership queries thanks to the path condition computed by the concolic engine, and 2) mitigate the lack of an equivalence oracle using the concolic engine to find counterexamples for a hypothesis. While it is usually unrealistic to assume a complete concolic execution of a large program (which would per se be sufficient to characterize the accepted input language), the ability of the concolic engine to execute each execution path only once brings significant benefits in our preliminary evaluation. Additionally, because the concolic engine can ask a constraints solver to produce inputs with a bounded length, it can be used to prove bounded equivalence between the learned input SFA and the target language. Finally, the availability of a partial symbolic execution tree and a constraint solver enables the definition of more effective types of membership queries.

4.1   Concolic learning with symbolic observation tables

Given a program $\mathcal{P}$ its concolic execution on a word $w \in \Sigma^*$ produces a boolean outcome (accept/reject) and a path condition capturing the properties of w that led to that outcome. In particular, we assume the path condition to be reducible to the constraint language defined in Section 2.4, i.e., the conjunction of interval predicates on the elements w_i of w and its length $len(w)$. Under this assumption, the path condition is directly translatable to a word w_Ψ over the predicates Ψ of the Boolean algebra $\mathcal{A}$ over the union of intervals over Σ. We will therefore refer to the path condition produced by the concolic execution of a word $w \in \Sigma^*$ with the Ψ-predicate as w_Ψ, where $len(w) = len(w_\Psi)$.

Symbolic observation table. The surjective relation between concrete words w and their predicates w_Ψ enables a straightforward extension of the observation table used for Λ^*, where the rows of the table can be indexed by words $w_\Psi \in \Psi^*$ instead of concrete words from Σ^*, i.e., $S \cup R \subset \Psi^*$. This allows for each row index to account for the entire equivalence class of words $w \in \Sigma^*$ that would follow the same execution path (these words will also have the same length). We describe as $[\![w_\Psi]\!]$ a concrete representative of the class w_Ψ. The set of suffixes $E \subset \Sigma^*$ will instead contain concrete elements of the alphabet.

Membership queries. Executing a membership query of the form $\mathcal{O}_m([\![w_\Psi]\!].\sigma)$, with $\sigma \in \Sigma$, will produce both the boolean outcome (accept/reject) and a word over Ψ^* that can be added to R, if not already present. As a result, the transition predicates of the induced SFA can be obtained directly from the symbolic observation table, avoiding the need for a partition function to synthesize Ψ-predicates from the collected concrete evidence, as required in Λ^*. The transition relation is then completed by redirecting every $\sigma \in \Sigma$ that does not satisfy any of the discovered transition predicates to an artificial sink state. The induced SFA is then used as hypothesis for the next equivalence query.

Equivalence queries. Because a complete equivalence oracle for the target language is not available, we will use concolic execution to obtain a bounded equivalence oracle comparing the hypothesis SFA induced by the symbolic observation table with the program under analysis. To this end, we translate the hypothesis SFA into a function in the same programming language of the target program $\mathcal{P}$ that takes as argument a word w and returns true (respectively, false) if the hypothesis SFA accepts (respectively, rejects) the word. We assume $\mathcal{P}$ to be wrapped into an analogous boolean function. We then write a program asserting that the result of the two functions is equal and use the concolic engine to find an input word that violate the assertion. If such word can be found, the counterexample is added to the symbolic observation table and the learner starts another iteration. If the concolic execution terminates without finding any assertion violation, it can be concluded that the hypothesis SFA represent the input language of $\mathcal{P}$. However, it is usually unrealistic to assume the termination of the concolic execution. Instead, we configure the solver to search for counterexamples up to a fixed length n. Assuming this input bounded concolic execution terminates without finding a counterexample, it can be concluded that the hypothesis is equivalent to $\mathcal{P}$'s input language for every word up to length n. Notably, this implies that if the target language is actually regular and the corresponding minimal automata has at most n states, the hypothesis learned the entire language.

Running example. A symbolic observation table inducing the SFA for the example introduced in Section 3 is shown in Figure 6. The use of Ψ predicates to index its rows significantly reduces the size of the table, since each row index accounts for a possibly large number of concrete elements of Σ.

T	ε	_$1)	$1)	1)	)
ε	-	+	-	-	-
0-9; [-^; 0-9; :-\uffff	+	+	+	+	+
0-9; [-^; 0-9	+	+	-	-	+
0-9; [-^	-	+	-	+	-
0-9	-	+	+	-	-
a-z; a-z	-	+	+	-	-
-; '; {-\uffff	-	+	-	-	-
-; [-^	-	+	-	+	-
0-9; 0-9	-	+	+	-	-
a-z; :-@	-	+	-	+	-
-; [-^; [-^	-	+	-	-	-
A-Z; A-Z	-	+	+	-	-
\u0000-/	-	+	-	-	-
[-^	-	+	-	-	-
A-Z; -; {-\uffff; 0-9	-	+	+	-	+
0-9; :-@; 0-9; 0-9	-	+	+	-	-
A-Z; \u0000-/; :-@	-	+	-	-	-
0-9; [-^; \u0000-/	-	+	-	-	-
A-Z; :-@	-	+	-	+	-
a-z	-	+	+	-	-
A-Z; _	-	+	+	-	-
-; '	-	+	-	+	-
-	-	+	+	-	-
0-9; :-@; 0-9	-	+	+	-	+
A-Z; :-@; A-Z	-	+	-	-	-
'	-	+	-	-	-
A-Z; '; 0-9; :-\uffff	+	+	+	+	+
:-@	-	+	-	-	-
0-9; {-\uffff	-	+	-	+	-
{-\uffff	-	+	-	-	-
A-Z; \u0000-/	-	+	-	+	-
A-Z; -; {-\uffff; 0-9; \u0000-/	+	+	+	+	+
-; [-^; a-z	-	+	+	-	-
A-Z	-	+	+	-	-
A-Z; '; 0-9; :-\uffff; \u0000-\uffff	+	+	+	+	+
A-Z; :-@; '	-	+	-	-	-
a-z; :-@; _	-	+	+	-	-

Fig. 6. Symbolic observation table for the example of Section 3.

4.2   Concolic learning with a symbolic membership oracle

In the previous section, we used the concolic engine to extract the path conditions corresponding to the execution of membership queries produced by the learner. This enabled reducing the number of queries – each query gathering information about a set of words instead of a single one – and keeping the observation table more compact. In this section, we introduce an oracle that answers a new class of *symbolic membership queries (SMQs)* using the constraint solving capabilities of the concolic engine to directly compute predicates characterizing all the accepted words of the form $p.\sigma.s$, where $p, s \in \Sigma^*$ and $\sigma \in \Sigma$. This oracle will enable a more efficient learning algorithm based on an extension of the discrimination tree data structure.

Definition 5. *Symbolic Membership Oracle* $(\mathcal{O}_s)$. *Given a Boolean algebra $\mathcal{A}$ with predicate set Ψ, a symbolic membership oracle $\mathcal{O}_s : \Sigma^* \times \Sigma^* \to \Psi$ takes as input a pair (p, s) and returns a predicate $\psi \in \Psi$ such that for a symbol $\sigma \in \Sigma$,* *the target program accepts p.σ.s iff σ ⊨ ψ. p and s are called* prefix *and* suffix, *respectively.*

An SMQ query can be solved by issuing a membership query for each $\sigma \in \Sigma$. However, this operation would be costly for large alphabets, such as unicode. On the other hand, the concolic execution of $w = p.\sigma.s$ for a concrete symbol σ returns via the path condition the entire set of symbols that wold follow the same execution path, in turn leading to the same execution outcome. A constraint solver can then be used to generate a new concrete input outside of such set, which is guaranteed to cover a new execution path. This procedure is summarized in Algorithm 1, where we use *pathCondition*[σ] to represent the projection of the path condition on the element of the input string $w = p.\sigma.s$ corresponding to the position of σ.

Input: SMQ $Q = (p, \psi, s)$; *concolic* : $\Sigma^* \to$(accepted, pathCondition)
Result: ψ such that $\forall \sigma \in \Sigma : p.\sigma.s$ is accepted iff $\sigma \models \psi$

$\psi \leftarrow \bot$;
unknown $\leftarrow \Sigma$;
while *unknown* $\neq \emptyset$ **do**
    $\sigma \leftarrow$ pickElementFrom(*unknown*);
    accepted, pathCondition $\leftarrow$ concolic(p.σ.s);
    if *accepted* **then**
        | $\psi \leftarrow \psi \vee pathCondition[\sigma]$;
    end
    unknown $\leftarrow$ *unknown* $\wedge \neg$ *pathCondition*[σ];
end
return ψ;

Algorithm 1: Answering SMQ queries.

Learning transition predicates with $\mathcal{O}_s$. Consider the learning algorithm using discrimination tree introduced in Section 3.2, MAT^*. After each iteration, the discrimination tree DT contains in its leaves all the discovered states (identified by the respective access words) and organized according to their discrimination suffixes (labeling the internal nodes of DT). To construct the transition relation of the induced SFA, the algorithm executes for each leaf l and $\sigma \in \Sigma$ a sift operation to determine the state reached when parsing $aw(l).\sigma$. Each such sift operation requires as many membership query as the depth of the reached state to be determined. Therefore, the number of sift operations needed to construct the complete transition relation is proportional to the number of states times the size of the input alphabet, with each sift operation issuing a number of membership queries proportional to the depth of DT.

Using the symbolic membership oracle, we can instead define a procedure that traversing DT directly synthesize the transition predicate between a source state q_s and a destination state q_t of the induced SFA. This procedure is formalized in Algorithm 2.

Input: $DT = (N, L, T)$; $\mathcal{O}_s : \Sigma^* \to \psi$; source state q_s; target state q_t
Result: The transition predicate π between q_s and q_t
$n \leftarrow$ root of DT;
$\pi \leftarrow \top$;
while $n \in N \backslash L$ **do**
    $\psi \leftarrow \mathcal{O}_s(aw(q_s), d(n))$;
    if q_t *in the accept subtree of* n **then**
        $\pi \leftarrow \pi \wedge \psi$;
        $n \leftarrow acceptChild(n)$;
    else
        $\pi \leftarrow \pi \wedge \neg\psi$;
        $n \leftarrow rejectChild(n)$;
    end
end
return π;

Algorithm 2: Learning transition predicates with $\mathcal{O}_s$.

Algorithm 2 allows to construct the induced SFA by computing for each ordered pair of leaves of DT the transition predicate of the corresponding transition. This results in the direct construction of the complete transition relation of the induced SFA. In practice, the implementation of Algorithm 2 can be improved by observing that π_i computed in the i-th iteration of the loop is by construction a subset of π_{i-1}. The symbolic membership oracle $\mathcal{O}_s$ can make use of this observation to limit the search procedure for the construction of the predicate *psi* during the i-th iteration to only symbols that satisfy π_{i-1}, significantly improving its efficiency. Finally, for the same reason, the loop in Algorithm 2 can terminate as soon as $\pi = \bot$, which indicates that no transition exists between the source and destination states.

Example. Referring to the discrimination tree in Figure 5 for the example introduced in Section 3, assume we want to learn transition predicate from State 2 to State 3. Initially, $\pi_0 = \top$. The access string of State 2 is "u^". The suffix of the root node is ϵ. Invoking the symbolic membership oracle, we obtain $\psi = \mathcal{O}_s(\text{"u^"}, \epsilon) = \bot$ (no string of length 3 are accepted by the target language). Because State 3 is in the reject subtree, $\pi_1 = \pi_0 \wedge \neg\bot = \top$ and the execution moves to the internal node labeled with the discriminator suffix "^4_". The corresponding SMQ query returns $\psi = \mathcal{O}_s(\text{"u^"}, \text{"^4_"}) = \{0 \ldots 9, A \ldots Z, \_, a \ldots z\}$. Because State 3 is in the accept subtree of the current node, $\pi_2 = \pi_1 \wedge \psi = \{0 \ldots 9, A \ldots Z, \_, a \ldots z\}$ and the execution moves to the internal node with discriminator prefix "_", where $pi_3 = [0 \ldots 9]$ is finally computed as the transition predicate from State 2 to State 3.

Decorated discrimination tree. For every leaf l and internal node n of a discrimination tree DT, Algorithm 2 issues a SMQ query $(aw(l), d(n))$. The corresponding intermediate value of the transition predicate π is intersected with the result of the SMQ query or its negation depending on whether l is in the accept or the reject subtree of n. Notably, the addition of a newly discovered state to DT does not change the relative positioning of a leaf l with respect to an

18   D. Clun et al.

internal node n, i.e., if l is initially in the accept (respectively, reject) subtree of n, it will remain in that subtree also after a new state is added. This observation implies that the results of the SMQ queries performed through Algorithm 2 remain valid between different executions of the algorithm. Therefore, when a new state is discovered and added to the discrimination tree via the *split* operation defined in Section 3.2, only the membership queries involving the new internal node and the new leaf added by *split* would require an actual execution of the symbolic membership oracle.

To enable the reuse of previous SMQ queries issued through Algorithm 2, we decorate the DT adding to each node a map from the set of leaves L to the value of π computed when traversing the node. We refer to this map as *predicate map*. Every predicate in the root node map is $\top$, as this is the initial value of π in Algorithm 2. The maps in the children nodes are then computed as follows. Let n be a parent node and n_a, n_r its accept and reject children respectively, m be a leaf of DT, and π_n^m, $\pi_{n_a}^m$, $\pi_{n_r}^m$ the predicates for m stored in n, n_a, and n_r, respectively. Then $\pi_{n_a}^m = \mathcal{O}_s(aw(m), d(n)) \wedge \pi_n^m$ and $\pi_{n_r} = \neg \mathcal{O}_s(aw(m), d(n)) \wedge \pi_n^m$. Proceeding recursively a leaf l will be decorated with a predicate map assigning to each leaf l_i in DT the predicate of the transition going from q_{l_i} to q_l.

Figure 7 shows the decorated version of the discrimination tree of Figure 5, constructed for the same example language introduced in Section 3.

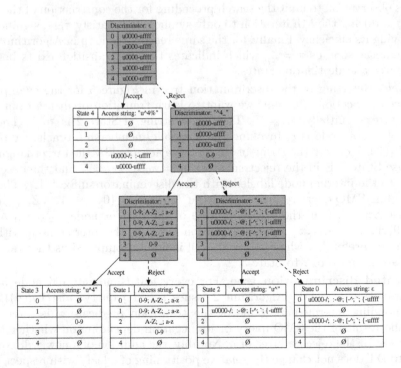

Fig. 7. Decorated version of the discrimination tree in Figure 5.

Induced SFA and number of equivalence queries. Notice that, by construction, for every node n with accept child n_a and reject child n_r, if π_n^l, $\pi_{n_a}^l$, and $\pi_{n_r}^l$ are the predicates the three nodes associate with a leaf l, $\pi_{n_a}^l \vee \pi_{n_r}^l = \pi_n^l$ and $\pi_{n_a}^l \wedge \pi_{n_r}^l = \bot$. As a consequence, after all the maps decorating a node in the discrimination tree are completed, the predicates in the leaves represent the complete transition relation of the induced SFA. Further more, the maps grows monotonically through the learning process, with entries computed in previous iterations remaining valid throughout the entire process. Practically, after each split operation resulting from the counterexample of an equivalence query (see Section 3.2), we traverse the discrimination tree and incrementally update all the predicate maps to include information about transitions to the new leaf, as well as populating the maps of the new internal node and new leaf added by the split.

Differently from the original algorithm MAT^* described in Section 3.2, a counterexample for the induced SFA corresponding to a decorated discrimination tree can only be returned if a new state has been discovered. This bound the number of equivalence query to be at most equal to the minimum number of states needed to represent the target language as an SFA. In our settings, a complete equivalence oracle is not available for the target program $\mathcal{P}$. Equivalence queries are instead solved using a (input bounded) concolic execution that compares the hypothesis SFA (induced by the discrimination tree) with the original program. Because this execution is computationally expensive, reducing the number of necessary equivalence queries has a significant impact on the execution time (at the cost of keeping in memory the node predicate maps).

5   Experimental evaluation

5.1   Experimental Setup

In this section we evaluate a prototype implementation of our contributions, built upon SVPAlib [9] (the symbolic automata and alphabet theory library used by MAT*) and Coastal [12], a concolic execution engine for Java bytecode. in Section 5.2 we consider our approach of using symbolic observations tables from Section 4.1 (referred to as SYMLEARN in the following presentation) and in Section 5.3 we evaluate the use of the symbolic membership queries from Section 4.2 (referred to as MAT*++). All the experiments have been executed on a server equipped with an AMD EPYC 7401P 24-Core CPU and 440Gb of memory. Coastal was configured to use at most 3 threads using its default generational exploration strategy [12] to find counterexamples for equivalence queries.

The experiments in this section are based on regular expressions taken from the AutomatArk [8] benchmark suite. To ensure a uniform difficulty distribution among the experiments, the regular expressions were converted to their automaton representation, sorted by the number of states, and 200 target automata selected by a stratified sampling (maximum number of states in an automaton is 637 and average 33, maximum number of transitions 2,495 and average 96). Each automaton is then translated into a Java program accepting the same language and compiled. The program analysis is performed on the resulting bytecode.

In the first experiment, we demonstrate the increase in query efficiency we achieve, by comparing the number of queries, using a complete oracle that can answer equivalence queries in a negligible amount of time. In this idealised setup the learner halted when the correct automaton was identified, relying on the fact that the oracle can confirm the correctness of the hypothesis. Although this setup does not represent a realistic scenario, it allowed us to reliably evaluate the number of queries of each type that are required to converge to the correct automaton, and to measure the computational requirements of the learning algorithm in isolation.

In the second experiment, we demonstrate the use of a concolic engine as a symbolic oracle, and measure the impact on the execution time of the algorithms. Providing a meaningful evaluation of the cost of the equivalence queries is difficult, as it is essentially a software verification problem over arbitrary Java code, and in principle an equivalence query could never terminate. Instead, a complete concolic analysis of each parser is performed, without using the perfect oracle for any type of query, and enforcing a timeout of ten minutes for each analysis, after which the learner yielded it's latest hypothesis. The correctness of that hypothesis is then confirmed by comparison to the known target automata. Note also that we use an input string length limit of 30 for the words to be parsed during concolic execution.

5.2   Learning with symbolic observation tables

Evaluating the algorithm with a perfect oracle. We learn 78% of the target languages within the ten minute timeout using a perfect oracle for equivalence. We see a 54% reduction in the total number of membership queries, and a 88% reduction in the total number of equivalence queries over MAT* (see Table 1).

Table 1. Number of queries and execution time with perfect oracle.

Algorithm	Membership queries	Equivalence queries	Execution time (s)
MAT*	1,545,255	25,802	38.60
SymLearn	720,658	3,124	1321.70

The SymLearn approach requires the path conditions to be stored in the observation table, even when using a perfect oracle for equivalence. In order to achieve this, concrete counter examples from the perfect oracle are resolved to path conditions via the concolic engine. The slower execution time can be attributed to the infrastructure overhead present in our implementation, and the speed of the concolic engine when performing these resolutions.

Evaluating the algorithm with the concolic oracle. We now replace the perfect equivalence oracle with a concolic execution engine, as described in Section 4.1. We learn 30% of the target automata within the ten minute timeout. The execution time is orders of magnitude slower when compared MAT*, and in our implementation 99% of the learner's execution time is spent running symbolic equivalence queries. While the increase in bandwidth due to the path conditions returned for each query does result in a significant reduction of queries overall, the execution time of the SYMLEARN approach is orders of magnitude slower than MAT*, partly because SYMLEARN requires the actual (concolic) execution of the program implementation, instead of performing queries on an SFA representation of the regular expression. There are however a number of optimizations that can be made to improve the performance (some of which will be discussed in the following section).

5.3   Learning with symbolic membership queries

Under the assumption that the language to be learned is regular, and that the equivalence check will eventually find a counterexample if there exists one, our active learning approach guarantees that eventually the correct hypothesis will be generated. The experimental evaluation was therefore aimed at understanding what is achievable in a realistic setting, with constrained time, and how our methodology improves the outcome.

Table 2. Number of queries and execution time with perfect oracle.

	Membership queries	SMQ	Equivalence queries	Learner execution time
MAT*	3,517,474	–	47,374	137.51 s
MAT*++	42,075	81,401	1,913	1.33 s

Table 2 shows the total number of queries[3] necessary to learn the correct automaton over the 200 test cases, along with the CPU time used by the learner process alone, without considering the time required to answer the queries.

The decrease in the CPU time required by the learner process can be explained by the reduction in the number of counterexamples that the learner has to process (recall that in MAT*++, a counterexample can be caused only by a missing state in the hypothesis, while in MAT* it can be also be due to an incorrect transition predicate). To understand the balance between the benefit due to the sharp reduction in the number of membership and equivalence queries, and the cost due to the introduction of the symbolic queries, the next section will evaluate the cost of answering each type of query without the help of a perfect oracle.

Evaluating the impact of SMQ. First, observe that the impact of membership queries are negligible since it is simply a check to see if an input is accepted. However, measuring the complexity of the symbolic membership queries (SMQs) is crucial to assess the effectiveness of our approach. Answering a SMQ requires the concolic execution of the program under analysis potentially multiple times, and requires processing each resulting path condition to collect the information needed to refine the answer. In this experiment we measured the time and the

---

[3] Note that all 200 automata are included in Table 2 whereas only the results for the subset that finished before the timeout was shown in Table 1.

number of concolic executions required to answer all the SMQs of table 2. The total time required to answer the queries was 4,408s, with an average of 54.15 ms per query. The number of concolic executions per query was between 1 and 31, with an average of 3.45. Since the concolic execution requires the program under analysis to be instrumented and a symbolic state to be maintained, it is orders of magnitude slower than a standard concrete execution.

Evaluating the impact of equivalence queries. Each equivalence query is answered in the same way as in the SYMLEARN approach (see Section 4.1), by doing a concolic execution of the hypothesis and the program being analyzed on the same symbolic input to see if they give a different result; if so, we have a counter-example, otherwise we simply know none could be found before the timeout or within the input string length of 30. As a further optimization, we also maintained two automata *knownAccept* and *knownReject* that were the union of the automata translation of the path conditions of all the previously explored accepted and rejected inputs respectively.

In this experiment 1,207 equivalence queries were issued, and on average it took 56.92s to answer a query. 573 answers were generated in negligible time using the *knownAccept* and *knownReject* automata (demonstrating the usefulness of this optimization), 93 cases Coastal could not find a counter-example (within the input size limit), 107 the timeout occurred and in the rest a counter-example was found by Coastal. In 152 cases the correct automaton was learned (76%), and interestingly in 62 of these cases Coastal timed-out (but the current hypothesis at the time was in fact correct). In 3 of the cases Coastal finished exploring the complete state-space up to the 30 input before the timeout, but the correct automaton was not learned. This happened because a counter-example requiring more than 30 input characters exist.

Discussion of the results.   The benefit of the symbolic membership queries is clear: it reduces the number of equivalence queries by 96%, and the latter is by far the most expensive step in active learning without a perfect oracle. Furthermore, simple engineering optimizations, for example a caching scheme for the accepted and rejected path conditions, can have a significant impact on the execution time.

6 Related work

The problem of learning input grammars has been tackled using a variety of techniques, and with various specific goals in mind.

6.1 Active learning

The active learning algorithms most closely related to our are Λ^* [11] and MAT* [3], which have been extensively discussed in Section 3.

Argyros et al. [4] used Angluin-style active learning of symbolic automata for the analysis of finite state string sanitizers and filters. Being focused on security, their goal was not to learn exactly the filter under analysis, but to verify that it filters every potentially dangerous string. In the proposed approach each equivalence query is approximated with a single membership query, which is a string that is not filtered by the current hypothesis, but belongs to the given language of "dangerous" strings. If no such string exists, the filter is considered successfully validated. If the string exists but is successfully filtered it provides a counterexample with which the hypothesis is refined, otherwise a vulnerability in the filter has been found. This equivalence approximation is incomplete, but greatly simplifies the problem, considering the complexity of equivalence queries.

Multiple other approaches use different active learning techniques not based on L* that, compared to our solution, provide less theoretical guarantees and often rely on a corpus of valid inputs. Glade [6] generates a context free grammar starting from a set of seed inputs that the learner attempts to generalize, using a membership oracle to check whether the generalization is correct. No other information is derived from the execution of the program under analysis, and therefore the set of seed inputs is of crucial importance. Reinam [29] further extends Glade by using symbolic execution to automatically generate the seed inputs, and adding a second probabilistic grammar refinement phase in which reinforcement learning is used to select the generalization rules to be applied.

The approach proposed by Höschele et al. [19] uses a corpus of valid inputs and applies generalizations that are verified with a membership oracle. Dynamic taint analysis is used to track the flow of the various fragments of the input during the execution, extracting additional information that aids in the creation of the hypothesis and generates meaningful non-terminal symbol names. A similar approach is used by Gopinath et al. [16], with the addition of automatic generation of the initial corpus.

6.2 Passive learning

Godefroid et al. [15] use recurrent neural networks and a corpus of sample inputs to create a generative model of the input language. This approach does not learn any information from the system under test, so the sample corpus is important.

A completely different approach is used by Lin et al. [24] to tackle a related problem: reconstructing the syntax tree of arbitrary inputs. The technique is based on the analysis of an execution trace generated by an instrumented version of the program under analysis. This approach relies on the knowledge of the internal mechanisms used by different types of parsers to generate the syntax tree.

Tupni [7] is a tool to reverse engineer input formats and protocols. Starting from one or more seed inputs, it analyzes the parser execution trace together with data flow information generated using taint analysis, identifies the structure of the input format (how the data is segmented in fields of various types, aggregated in records, and some constraints that must be satisfied), and generates a context free grammar.

7 Conclusions

Most established active learning algorithms for (symbolic) finite state automata assume the availability of a minimal adequate teacher, which includes a complete equivalence oracle to produce counterexample disproving an incorrect hypothesis of the learner. This assumption is unrealistic when learning the input grammar of a program from its implementation, as such a complete oracle would need to automatically check the equivalence of the hypothesis with arbitrary software code. In this paper, we explored how the use of a concolic execution engine can improve the information efficiency of membership queries, provide a partial input-bounded oracle to check the equivalence of an hypothesis against a program, and enable the definition of a new class of symbolic membership queries that allow the learner inferring the transition predicates of a symbolic finite state automata representation of the target input language more efficiently.

Preliminary experiments with the Autmatark [8] benchmark showed that our implementations of SYMLEARN and MAT*++ achieve a significant reduction (up to 96%) in the number of queries required to actively learn the input language of a program in the form of a symbolic finite state automaton. Despite bounding the total execution time to 10 minutes, using the concolic execution engine as partial equivalence oracle, MAT*++ managed to learn the correct input language in 76% of the cases.

This results demonstrate the suitability of concolic execution as enabling tool for the definition of active learning algorithms for the input grammar of a program. However, our current solutions learn the input grammar in the form of a symbolic finite state automaton. This implies that only an approximation of non-regular input languages can be constructed. Such approximation can at best match the input language up to a finite length, but would fail in recognizing more sophisticated language features that may require, for example, a context free representation. Investigating how the learning strategies based on concolic execution we explored in this paper can generalize to more expressive language models is envisioned as a future direction for this research, as well as the use of the inferred input languages to support parsers validation and grammar-based fuzzing.

References

1. Angluin, D.: Learning regular sets from queries and counterexamples. Information and Computation **75**(2), 87–106 (1987)
2. Angluin, D.: Queries and Concept Learning. Machine Learning **2**(4), 319–342 (apr 1988)
3. Argyros, G., D'Antoni, L.: The learnability of symbolic automata. In: Chockler, H., Weissenbacher, G. (eds.) Computer Aided Verification. CAV 2018. pp. 427–445. Springer International Publishing, Cham (2018)
4. Argyros, G., Stais, I., Kiayias, A., Keromytis, A.D.: Back in Black: Towards Formal, Black Box Analysis of Sanitizers and Filters. Proceedings - 2016 IEEE Symposium on Security and Privacy, SP 2016 pp. 91–109 (2016). https://doi.org/10.1109/SP.2016.14
5. Aydin, A., Bang, L., Bultan, T.: Automata-Based Model Counting for String Constraints. In: Kroening, D., Păsăreanu, C.S. (eds.) Computer Aided Verification. pp. 255–272. Lecture Notes in Computer Science, Springer International Publishing, Cham (2015)
6. Bastani, O., Sharma, R., Aiken, A., Liang, P.: Synthesizing Program Input Grammars. In: Proceedings of the 38th ACM SIGPLAN Conference on Programming

Language Design and Implementation. pp. 95–110. ACM (2017), http://arxiv.org/abs/1608.01723

7. Cui, W., Peinado, M., Chen, K., Wang, H.J., Irun-Briz, L.: Tupni: Automatic reverse engineering of input formats. Proceedings of the ACM Conference on Computer and Communications Security pp. 391–402 (2008). https://doi.org/10.1145/1455770.1455820

8. D'Antoni, L.: AutomatArk (2018), https://github.com/lorisdanto/automatark

9. D'Antoni, L.: SVPAlib (2018), https://github.com/lorisdanto/symbolicautomata/

10. D'Antoni, L., Veanes, M.: The power of symbolic automata and transducers. Lecture Notes in Computer Science (including subseries Lecture Notes in Artificial Intelligence and Lecture Notes in Bioinformatics) **10426 LNCS**, 47–67 (2017)

11. Drews, S., D'Antoni, L.: Learning symbolic automata. Lecture Notes in Computer Science (including subseries Lecture Notes in Artificial Intelligence and Lecture Notes in Bioinformatics) **10205 LNCS**, 173–189 (2017)

12. Geldenhuys, J., Visser, W.: Coastal (2019), https://github.com/DeepseaPlatform/coastal

13. Godefroid, P., Kiezun, A., Levin, M.Y.: Grammar-based whitebox fuzzing. In: Proceedings of the 29th ACM SIGPLAN Conference on Programming Language Design and Implementation. pp. 206–215 (2008). https://doi.org/10.1145/1379022.1375607

14. Godefroid, P., Klarlund, N., Sen, K.: Dart: Directed automated random testing. In: Proceedings of the 2005 ACM SIGPLAN Conference on Programming Language Design and Implementation. p. 213–223. PLDI '05, Association for Computing Machinery, New York, NY, USA (2005). https://doi.org/10.1145/1065010.1065036, https://doi.org/10.1145/1065010.1065036

15. Godefroid, P., Peleg, H., Singh, R.: Learn&Fuzz: Machine Learning for Input Fuzzing. In: Proceedings of the 32nd IEEE/ACM International Conference on Automated Software Engineering. pp. 50–59. IEEE Press, Urbana-Champaign, IL, USA (2017)

16. Gopinath, R., Mathis, B., Höschele, M., Kampmann, A., Zeller, A.: Sample-Free Learning of Input Grammars for Comprehensive Software Fuzzing (2018). https://doi.org/arXiv:1810.08289v1, http://arxiv.org/abs/1810.08289

17. Heinz, J., Sempere, J.M.: Topics in grammatical inference (2016)

18. de la Higuera, C.: Grammatical Inference: Learning Automata and Grammars. Cambridge University Press, New York, NY, USA (2010)

19. Höschele, M., Kampmann, A., Zeller, A.: Active Learning of Input Grammars (2017), http://arxiv.org/abs/1708.08731

20. Isberner, M.: Foundations of Active Automata Learning: an Algorithmic Perspective. Ph.D. thesis (2015)

21. Isberner, M., Howar, F., Steffen, B.: The TTT Algorithm: A Redundancy-Free Approach to Active Automata Learning. In: Bonakdarpour, B., Smolka, S.A. (eds.) Runtime Verification. pp. 307–322. Springer International Publishing, Cham (2014), http://link.springer.com/10.1007/978-3-319-11164-3{_}26

22. Isberner, M., Steffen, B.: An Abstract Framework for Counterexample Analysis in Active Automata Learning. JMLR: Workshop and Conference Proceedings (1993), 79–93 (2014)

23. Kearns, M.J., Vazirani, U.: Learning Finite Automata by Experimentation. In: An Introduction to Computational Learning Theory, pp. 155–158. The MIT Press (1994)

24. Lin, Z., Zhang, X., Xu, D.: Reverse engineering input syntactic structure from program execution and its applications. IEEE Transactions on Software Engineering **36**(5), 688–703 (2010). https://doi.org/10.1109/TSE.2009.54

25. Maler, O., Mens, I.E.: Learning Regular Languages over Large Alphabets. In: Abraham, E., Havelund, K. (eds.) Tools and Algorithms for the Construction and Analysis of Systems. TACAS 2014. pp. 485–499. Springer Berlin Heidelberg, Berlin, Heidelberg (2014)

26. de Moura, L., Bjørner, N.: Z3: An efficient smt solver. In: Ramakrishnan, C.R., Rehof, J. (eds.) Tools and Algorithms for the Construction and Analysis of Systems. pp. 337–340. Springer Berlin Heidelberg, Berlin, Heidelberg (2008)

27. Sen, K., Marinov, D., Agha, G.: Cute: A concolic unit testing engine for c. SIGSOFT Softw. Eng. Notes **30**(5), 263–272 (Sep 2005). https://doi.org/10.1145/1095430.1081750,   https://doi.org/10.1145/1095430.1081750

28. Veanes, M., De Halleux, P., Tillmann, N.: Rex: Symbolic regular expression explorer. ICST 2010 - 3rd International Conference on Software Testing, Verification and Validation pp. 498–507 (2010). https://doi.org/10.1109/ICST.2010.15

29. Wu, Z., Johnson, E., Bastani, O., Song, D.: REINAM: Reinforcement Learning for Input-Grammar Inference. In: Proceedings of the 2019 27th ACM Joint Meeting on European Software Engineering Conference and Symposium on the Foundations of Software Engineering. pp. 488–498. ACM (2019)

FASE Contributions

Platinum: Reusing Constraint Solutions in Bounded Analysis of Relational Logic

Guolong Zheng[1], Hamid Bagheri[1], Gregg Rothermel[2], and Jianghao Wang[1]

[1] Department of Computer Science and Engineering, University of Nebraska-Lincoln,
Lincoln, NE, USA
[2] Department of Computer Science, North Carolina State University, Raleigh, NC, USA
gzheng@cse.unl.edu, bagheri@unl.edu, gerother@ncsu.edu, jianghaow@cse.unl.edu

Abstract. Alloy is a lightweight specification language based on relational logic, with an analysis engine that relies on SAT solvers to automate bounded verification of specifications. In spite of its strengths, the reliance of the Alloy Analyzer on computationally heavy solvers means that it can take a significant amount of time to verify software properties, even within limited bounds. This challenge is exacerbated by the ever-evolving nature of complex software systems. This paper presents PLATINUM, a technique for efficient analysis of evolving Alloy specifications, that recognizes opportunities for constraint reduction and reuse of previously identified constraint solutions. The insight behind PLATINUM is that formula constraints recur often during the analysis of a single specification and across its revisions, and constraint solutions can be reused over sequences of analyses performed on evolving specifications. Our empirical results show that PLATINUM substantially reduces (by 66.4% on average) the analysis time required on specifications extracted from real-world software systems.

1 Introduction

The growing reliance of society on software and software-intensive systems drives a continued demand for increased software dependability. Software verification provides the highest degree of software assurance, with its strengths residing in the mathematical concepts that can be leveraged to prove correctness with respect to specific properties. Most notably, bounded verification techniques, such as Alloy [28], have recently received a great deal of attention in the software engineering community (e.g., [8, 9, 11, 13, 14, 16, 20, 26, 34, 35, 38, 43, 46, 48, 52, 54, 55, 61, 63, 66]), due to the strength of their automated, yet formally precise, analysis capabilities. The basic idea behind these techniques is to construct a formula that encodes the behavior of a system and examine it up to a user-specified bound. They thus enable analyses of partial models that represent key aspects of a system.

Bounded verification techniques often transform a software specification to be analyzed into a satisfiability problem, and delegate the task of solving this to a constraint solver. In the past decade, constraint solving technologies have made spectacular progress (e.g., [19, 22, 42]). Despite these advances, however, constraint solving continues to be a bottleneck in analyses that rely on it [58]. This is because the magnitude of formulas tends to increase exponentially with the size of the system being analyzed, making it impractical to employ constraint solving on complex systems. Further, despite the many optimizations applied to constraint solvers, they are still unable to detect many instances of subformula recurrence that are generated by Alloy.

H. Wehrheim and J. Cabot (Eds.): FASE 2020, LNCS 12076, pp. 29–52, 2020.
https://doi.org/10.1007/978-3-030-45234-6_2

The foregoing challenges are exacerbated when considering the ever-evolving nature of complex software systems and their corresponding specifications. Formal specifications are developed iteratively, and each iteration involves repeated runs of the analyzer for assessment of their semantics [31, 36]. In online analyses, where specifications are kept in sync with the evolving software and analyses are performed at runtime, the time required to verify the properties of software is of even greater significance. This calls for techniques that assist constraint solvers in dealing with large corpora of formulas, many of which contain tens of thousands of clauses.

In this paper, we introduce PLATINUM, an extension of the Alloy Analyzer that supports efficient analysis of evolving Alloy specifications, by recognizing opportunities for constraint reduction and reuse of previously identified constraint solutions. Unlike the Alloy Analyzer and its other variants, e.g., Aluminum [45], that dispose of prior results in response to changes in the system specification, PLATINUM stores solved constraints incrementally, and retrieves them when they are needed again within the analysis of the revised specification. PLATINUM further improves analysis efficiency by omitting redundant constraints from a specification before translating them into propositional formulas to be solved by expensive constraint solvers, thereby greatly reducing the required computational effort. Although techniques for storing the results of satisfiability checking and reusing them later have been considered in the context of symbolic execution [6, 7, 29, 49, 62], these techniques cannot be directly applied to Alloy due to the specifics of its core logic, which consolidates the quantifiers of first-order logic with the operators of the relational calculus [28]. (Section 5 provides details.)

We evaluate the performance of PLATINUM in several scenarios. First, we apply PLATINUM to several pairs of specifications in which the second contains a small but non-trivial set of changes relative to the first. Second, we apply PLATINUM to several sequences of specifications that model evolution scenarios. Our empirical results show that PLATINUM is able to support reuse of constraint solutions both within a single analysis run and across a sequence of analyses of evolving specifications, while achieving speed-up over the Alloy Analyzer. Third, we show that as the scope of the analysis increases, PLATINUM achieves even greater improvements. Fourth, we show that the overhead associated with PLATINUM is a fraction of that required by the Alloy Analyzer. Finally, we show that PLATINUM substantially reduces (by 66.4% on average) the analysis time required on specifications extracted from real-world software systems.

This paper makes the following contributions:

- *Efficient analysis of evolving relational logic specifications.* We present a novel approach to improve the bounded analysis of relational logic specifications by transforming constraints into more concise forms and enabling substantial reuse of solutions, which in turn substantially reduces analysis costs.
- *Tool implementation.* We implement PLATINUM as an extension to Alloy and its underlying relational logic analyzer, Kodkod [57]. We make PLATINUM available to the research and education community [5].
- *Empirical evaluation.* We evaluate PLATINUM in the context of Alloy specifications found in prior work and specifications automatically extracted from real-world systems, corroborating PLATINUM's ability to substantially outperform the Alloy Analyzer without sacrificing soundness or completeness.

2 Illustrative Example

To motivate this research and illustrate our approach, we provide a simple Alloy specification and describe the analysis process followed by the Alloy Analyzer and PLATINUM.

Consider snippets of the Alloy specification for a simple customer-order class diagram, shown in Listing 1.1 (adapted from [15]). Each Alloy specification consists of data types and formulas that define constraints over those data types. A signature (sig) paragraph introduces a basic data type and a set of its relations, called *fields*, accompanied by the type of each field. The running example defines seven signatures (Lines 2–21). The Customer class (Lines 2–7) has two attributes, customerID and customerName, that are assigned to the attrSet field of the Customer class. The id field specifies that customerID is the identifier of this class. The last two lines of the Customer signature specification indicate that Customer is not an abstract class and that it has no parent. Similarly, the code in Lines 10–15 represents the Order signature specification, and CustOrder (Lines 18–21) specifies an association relationship between Customer and Order.

Facts (fact) are formulas that take no arguments, and define constraints that each instance of a specification must satisfy, restricting the specification's solution space. The formulas can be further structured using predicates (pred) and functions (fun), which are parameterized formulas that can be invoked. The associationMultiplicity fact paragraph (Lines 22–24) states multiplicities of source and destination classes in the CustOrder association relationship.

To analyze such a relational specification, both the Alloy Analyzer and PLATINUM translate it into a corresponding finite relational model in a language called Kodkod [56]. Listing 1.2 shows a partial Kodkod translation of Listing 1.1(a). A specification in Kodkod's relational logic is a triple

```
1   // (a) a simple customer-order class diagram
2   one sig Customer extends Class{}{
3       attrSet = customerID +customerName
4       id=customerID
5       isAbstract = No
6       no parent
7   }
8   one sig customerID extends Integer{}
9   one sig customerName extends string{}
10  one sig Order extends Class{}{
11      attrSet = orderID + orderValue
12      id=orderID
13      isAbstract = No
14      no parent
15  }
16  one sig orderID extends Integer{}
17  one sig orderValue extends Real{}
18  one sig CustOrder extends Association{}{
19      src = Customer
20      dst = Order
21  }
22  fact associationMultiplicity{
23      one CustOrder.src and some CustOrder.dst
24  }
```

```
1   // (b) new constructs added to the revised specification
2   one sig PreferredCustomer extends Class{}{
3       attrSet = discount
4       one parent
5       parent in Customer
6       isAbstract = No
7       id=customerID
8   }
9   one sig discount extends Integer{}
```

Listing 1.1: (a) a specification describing a simple customer order class diagram; (b) new constructs added to a revised version of that specification.

```
1   {C1,O1}
2
3   Customer:  (1,1)::[{<C1>},{<C1>}]
4   Order:     (1,1)::[{<O1>},{<O1>}]
5   parent:    (0,4)::[{},
6                       {<C1,C1>,<C1,O1>,<O1,C1>,<O1,O1>}]
7
8   (no Customer.parent) && (no Order.parent) ...
```

Listing 1.2: Kodkod representation of the Alloy specification of Listing 1.1 (partially elided for space and readability).

consisting of a universe of elements (a.k.a. *atoms*), a set of relation declarations including lower and upper bounds specified over the model's universe, and a relational formula in which the declared relations appear as free variables [56].

The first line of Listing 1.2 declares a universe of two uninterpreted atoms. (Due to space limitations, the listing omits some of the relations and atoms.) While in Kodkod all relations are untyped, in the interest of readability we assume an interpretation of atoms in which C1 represents a Customer element and O1 represents an Order element.

Lines 3–6 of Listing 1.2 declare relational variables. Similar to Alloy, formulas in Kodkod are constraints defined over relational variables. Whereas in Alloy these relational variables are separated into *signatures* that represent *unary* relations establishing a type system, and *fields* that represent non-unary relations, in Kodkod all relations are untyped, with no difference made between unary and non-unary variables.

Kodkod also allows scope to be specified from above and below each relational variable by two *relational constants*; these sets are called *upper* and *lower* bounds, respectively. In principle, a relational constant is a pre-specified set of tuples drawn from a universe of atoms. Each relation in a specification solution must contain all tuples that appear in the lower bound,

```
1    (!(v1|v2))&(!v2||v1)&(!(v3|v4))&(!v4||v3)
2
3    Slices:
4    (!(v1|v2))&(!v2||v1)
5    (!(v3|v4))&(!v4||v3)
6
7    Canonical form:
8    (!(1|2)&(!2|!1))
```

Listing 1.3: Excerpt of the boolean encoding for the Kodkod specification shown in Listing 1.2.

and no tuple that does not appear in the upper bound. That is, the upper bound represents the entire set of tuples that a relational variable may contain, and the lower bound represents a partial solution for a specification.

Consider the Customer declaration (Listing 1.2, Line 3). Both its upper and lower bounds contain just one atom, C1, given that it is defined as a singleton set in Listing 1.1. The upper bound for the variable *parent* $\subseteq Class \times Class$ (Lines 5–6) is a product of the upper bound set for its corresponding domain and co-domain relations, here $(Customer \cup Order) \rightarrow (Customer \cup Order)$, taking every combination of an element from both and concatenating them.

To transform such a finite relational model into a boolean logic formula, Kodkod renders each relation as a boolean matrix, in which any tuple in the upper bound of the given relation that is not in the lower bound maps to a unique boolean variable [56]. Relational constraints are then captured as boolean constraints over the translated boolean variables.

To render this idea concrete, consider the parent relation along with the next constraint defined over it (Listing 1.2, Lines 5–8). Each of the four tuples in the upper bound of the parent relation is allocated a fresh boolean variable (v1 to v4) in the boolean encoding. The relational constraint (no Customer.parent) && (no Order.parent) is then translated as a boolean constraint over those boolean variables, as shown in Listing 1.3, Line 1.

Expressions and constraints in relational specifications typically contain equivalent slices in their boolean representations. PLATINUM detects such semantically redundant slices by refining the specification in its boolean logic form into its essential, independently analyzable slices, and then rendering them in a canonical form. The boolean encoding of the constraints defined over the parent relation, for example, embodies two slices with equivalent but syntactically distinct formulas (Listing 1.3, Lines 4–5). Line 8 represents the result of restructuring the slices into a canonical form, suggesting that the two slices are in fact equivalent. The slicing technique we use to determine the sets of clauses, the satisfiability of which can be analyzed independent of other clauses in the formula, is presented in Section 3.

PLATINUM prevents redundant slices from being propagated to the CNF formula to be solved by the underlying SAT solver, substantially reducing computational effort. In the case of our example specification (Listing 1.1(a)), PLATINUM partitions the original relational specification into 30 slices, with only seven distinct canonical slices. As such, PLATINUM is faster at finding a solution instance, requiring 19 ms to do so compared to the 26 ms that the Alloy Analyzer requires to produce the first solution instance. The time required to compute the entire instance set also improves, from 6481 ms to 246 ms, in this simple example.

PLATINUM also reuses results produced for specification slices to further improve the analysis of evolving specifications. Consider Listing 1.1(b), for example, in which two new signature paragraphs are added, stating that the PreferredCustomer class inherits from the Customer class. Given the updated specification, PLATINUM reuses the results from the prior run and solves a smaller problem. Specifically, after slicing and canonicalizing the formula, the results for 29 slices, out of the total of 30 slices, are already available. As a result, PLATINUM requires only one millisecond to find the first solution for the revised specification, whereas the Alloy Analyzer requires 27 milliseconds to produce the first solution. PLATINUM also produces speed-ups in computing the whole solution space. In the case of this particular example, PLATINUM reduces the time required to produce the entire solution set from 768 milliseconds to two milliseconds.

3 Approach

Fig. 1 provides an architectural overview that shows how PLATINUM fits in with Alloy. As the figure shows (left), the Alloy Analyzer reads in an Alloy specification and translates it into a relational model, then passes that to Kodkod. Kodkod translates the relational model into a boolean formula, then to CNF, and passes the CNF to off-the-shelf SAT solvers to obtain a solution. Last, the Alloy interpreter translates the SAT result into a solution instance.

PLATINUM is inserted between Kodkod and the Alloy interpreter, as shown in the figure. At the highest level, PLATINUM takes in the boolean formula from Kodkod and outputs SAT results to the Alloy interpreter. The box at right shows the steps PLATINUM follows to do this. PLATINUM first decomposes the boolean formula into independent slices. Then, for each slice, PLATINUM canonicalizes it into a normalized format and searches the storage for a previously existing equivalent slice. If such a slice exists, the previous results will be reused. Otherwise, the slice is translated to CNF and assigned to an independent SAT solver for processing. Both the slice and the results of processing it

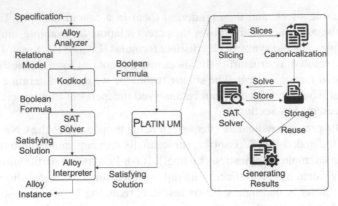

Fig. 1: Overview of Alloy and PLATINUM

are then stored. Finally, PLATINUM combines the results for each slice and passes them to the Alloy interpreter.

Next, we describe each step taken by PLATINUM in detail.

3.1 Slicing

In PLATINUM, the slicing operation takes in the boolean formula generated from Kodkod and decomposes it into a set of independently analyzable subformulas. Formally, given a boolean formula φ, slicing decomposes it into subformulas $\varphi_1, \varphi_2, ..., \varphi_n$, such that the following equations hold:

- $\varphi_1 \wedge \varphi_2 \wedge ... \wedge \varphi_n = \varphi$
- $var(\varphi_1) \cup var(\varphi_2) \cup ... \cup var(\varphi_n) = var(\varphi)$
- $var(\varphi_i) \cap var(\varphi_j) = \emptyset$, for each φ_i and φ_j where $i \neq j$
- $var(\varphi_i) \neq \emptyset, for\ i = 1, 2, ..., n$

where $var(\varphi)$ is the set of boolean variables of φ. Subformulas φ_1 to φ_n can be solved independently. Thus, φ is satisfiable if and only if each slice φ_i is satisfiable individually.

Algorithm 1 Slicing

Require: f: original Boolean Formula root
Ensure: *Slices*: Set of Independent Slices
1: **procedure** SLICE(f)
2: *Slices* ← *null*
3: **for** each variable $v \in f$ **do**
4:   $parent[v] \leftarrow v$
5:   $rank[v] \leftarrow v$
6: **end for**
7: DECOMPOSE(f)
8: **end procedure**

9: **procedure** DECOMPOSE(f)
10: **if** $f.operator = AND$ **then**
11:   **for** each subformula $f_i \in f$ **do**
12:    DECOMPOSE(f_i)
13:   **end for**
14: **else**
15:   UNION-FIND(f)
16: **end if**
17: **end procedure**

A boolean formula can be sliced either logically (based on semantics) or algebraically (based on syntax). In the interest of efficiency, PLATINUM applies a syntactic slicing algorithm. There are two types of boolean formulas in Alloy: a propositional formula that Kodkod translates from the relational model and the conjunctive normal form generated from the propositional formula. PLATINUM applies slicing on the propositional formula level for two reasons. First, translating a propositional formula to CNF introduces many auxiliary variables [21]. For example, when the CustomerOrder specification in Section 2, with 81 variables in its propositional formula, is translated to a CNF formula containing 352 variables, 271 auxiliary variables are introduced. The explosion in the number of variables affects the performance of slicing and canonicalization. Second, in certain cases, auxiliary variables connect two independent formulas together. Given the boolean formula $v_1\&v_2$, its CNF translation is $(v_1|!o)\&(v_2|!o)\&(!v_1|!v_2|o)$, where o is the auxiliary variable. Even if v_1 and v_2 are independent formulas, in the CNF, v_1 and v_2 are dependent on each other.

Slicing can be viewed as identifying connected components in a graph, where the vertices of the graph are boolean variables and the edges of the graph represent two variables that appear within the same clause. Each slice is thus one connected component in the graph. The conventional way to proceed with this is to first build a graph for the entire boolean formula, and then run a depth-first-search (DFS) to identify each connected component [62]. For large specifications this can be both time and memory intensive. To improve performance, our algorithm applies a modified UNION-FIND algorithm [17], that traverses the boolean formula only once to identify connected components.

Algorithm 1 outlines the slicing process. Given boolean formula root, the algorithm first initializes a data structure used by its subroutine (Lines 2–6). Each slice is identified by a representative, which is one variable within the slice. Array Parent is used to find the representative variable. Array Rank is used to construct a balanced parent array. Array Slices maps a representative variable to its corresponding slice; its size equals the number of slices. The algorithm then calls subroutine DECOMPOSE to decompose the root formula.

Algorithm 2 Union-Find

```
 1: procedure UNION-FIND(f)
 2:     represent ← null
 3:     for each variable v ∈ f do
 4:         if v has been visited then
 5:             if UnMeetState then
 6:                 represent ← FINDSLICE(v)
 7:                 add f to Slices[represent]
 8:                 change to MeetState
 9:             else
10:                 if FINDSLICE(v) != FINDSLICE(represent)
    then
11:                     UNIONSLICES(Slices[represent],Slices[v])
12:                 end if
13:             end if
14:         else
15:             UNIONVARS(v, represent)
16:             v.visited ← TRUE
17:         end if
18:     end for
19: end procedure

20: procedure UNIONVARS(v,represent)
21:     if represent is null then
22:         represent ← FINDSLICE(v)
23:     end if
24:     Parent[represent] ← FINDSLICE(v)
25:     Rank[represent] ← Rank[represent] + 1
26: end procedure

27: procedure UNIONSLICES(represent,v)
28:     v ← FindSlice(v)
29:     if Rank[represent] ≤ Rank[v] then
30:         Slices[v].add(Slices[represent])
31:         Parent[represent] ← v
32:         Rank[v] ← Rank[represent] + Rank[v]
33:     else
34:         Slices[represent].add(Slices[v])
35:         Parent[v] ← represent
36:         Rank[represent] ← Rank[represent] + Rank[v]
37:     end if
38: end procedure

39: procedure FINDSLICE(v)
40:     while v != Parent[v] do
41:         v ← Parent[v]
42:         Parent[v] ← Parent[Parent[v]]
43:     end whilereturn v
44: end procedure
```

DECOMPOSE recursively partitions a boolean formula f into subformulas in such a way that the conjunction of all subformulas equals f, and each subformula cannot be decomposed into smaller subformulas.

The UNION-FIND procedure (Algorithm 2) takes a decomposed subformula and finds a slice to which it belongs. The basic idea behind the algorithm is that each slice is represented by one variable. UNION-FIND has two basic operators: *UNION* and *FIND*. If *UNION* operates on two slices, it joins them into one slice (Lines 27–38). If *UNION* operates on two variables, it assigns one variable to be the parent of the other (Lines 20–26). The *FINDSLICE* operation determines the representative variable for the slice – the variable to which the input variable belongs. It does so by traversing the Parent array until it finds one variable v_p whose parent is itself, i.e., parent$[v_p] = v_p$. All variables along this path belong to the same slice and are represented by v_p.

The input boolean formula has two states: UnMeetState, which indicates that f does not belong to any slice yet, and MeetState, which indicates that f belongs to some slice that is represented by *represent*. For each variable v of the input boolean formula f, UnMeetState first obtains the representative variable for v (which could be itself if v does not belong to any slice yet). If v has not been visited, the algorithm unions v and the representative variable of the subformula (Lines 20–26). Otherwise, if v has been visited (i.e., it belongs to some slice), and if f is in UnMeetState, then the algorithm adds f to the slice represented by *represent*. Finally, if f is in MeetState, this means that f belongs to one slice and v belongs to another and these need to be joined together (Lines 27–38).

3.2 Canonicalization

The time complexity of the UNION-FIND algorithm is near linear [17]. Without this improvement and using the conventional DFS-based approach taken by Green [62] among others, in one case in our empirical study, a few minutes were required to produce independently analyzable slices. Using our algorithm, this time was reduced to about 10 milliseconds – an order of magnitude speedup. This speedup occurs for the following reason. A graph is needed to start the DFS. The graph contains information about which variable belongs to which clause and which clause contains which variables, and a map-like data structure is needed to store this information. When the number of variables becomes huge—

Algorithm 3 Canonicalization

Require: f : boolean formulas
Ensure: $f\prime$: canonical boolean formula
1: **procedure** CANONICALIZE(f)
2:      $varSet \leftarrow var\,of\,f$
3:      $varSet \leftarrow sort(varSet)$
4:      **for** i in 0 to varSet.length **do**
5:          $labelMap.add(varSet[i].label,i)$
6:          $varSet[i].label \leftarrow i$
7:      **end for**
8:      $L \leftarrow varSet.length$
9:      **for** each subformula sf $\in$ f **do**
10:          RENAME(sf)
11:      **end for**
12:      $f\prime \leftarrow f$
13: **end procedure**

14: **procedure** RENAME(f)
15:      **for** each subformula sf $\in$ f **do**
16:          $L \leftarrow$ RENAME(sf)
17:      **end for**
18:      $f.label \leftarrow ++L$
19:      return$L$
20: **end procedure**

typically hundreds of thousands in formulas produced for Alloy specifications of real-world systems—it is time and memory consuming to obtain this information and store it. It is also time consuming to retrieve the graph information during the DFS. Our UNION-FIND based algorithm, in contrast, requires information only on the node's parents, and this can be placed in a static array that requires only linear time to store and retrieve.

The slices produced by the prior step are passed to this step, which transforms each slice into a canonical format in order to capture the syntactic equivalence between different slices. For a slice φ, where $\varphi = \varphi_1 \wedge \varphi_2 \wedge \ldots \wedge \varphi_n$, canonicalization generates one boolean formula φ', such that $\varphi' = \varphi'_1 \wedge \varphi'_2 \wedge \ldots \wedge \varphi'_n$, where φ' is the canonical format of φ. The canonical form of the formulas is constructed by renaming variables and formula labels. Algorithm 3 outlines this transformation.

Canonicalization first renames each boolean variable based on its weight (Lines 2–7). For each variable $v \in V$, where $V = var(\varphi_1) \cup var(\varphi_2) \cup \ldots \cup var(\varphi_n)$, the weight of v is calculated as the sum of the number of its occurrences and the number of operators applied on v in all of the subformulas. To improve the performance of this step, the weight for each variable is collected during the slicing phase; then, V is sorted based on variable weight. If two variables have the same weight, their original labels are used to sort them. Each variable is then renamed to their index in the sorted array. The mapping relations from canonical variables to original variables for each slice are stored in *labelMap* for use in assembling the solution for the original boolean formula. Next, the label for each formula is renamed (Lines 8–20). The purpose of this step is to maintain consistency with variables when translating to CNF. The labels of formulas are used as auxiliary variables when they are translated to CNF.

3.3 Storing and Reuse

After slicing and canonicalization have been completed, each boolean formula is decomposed into several independent formulas. For each canonicalized boolean formula, PLATINUM checks its hash code in storage. If there is a hit, this boolean formula is already solved, and the result will then be retrieved. If not, the boolean formula will be translated into CNF and solved by the SAT solver independently. The result will then be stored.

After solving all slices, using the *labelMap* (Algorithm 3) that maps canonical variables to original variables, PLATINUM obtains the solution for the original boolean formula and passes it to Alloy to generate a solution instance.

4 Empirical Study

We empirically evaluated the performance of PLATINUM in relation to the following research questions:

RQ1: How does the performance of PLATINUM compare to the performance of existing approaches on specifications that have undergone relatively small amounts of change?

RQ2: How does the performance of PLATINUM compare to the performance of existing approaches on specifications that have gone through several successive rounds of evolution?

RQ3: How does the performance of PLATINUM compare to the performance of existing approaches on specifications that have run against higher scopes?

RQ4: What is the overhead of PLATINUM in restructuring a relational logic formula into its canonical form?

RQ5: How does the performance of PLATINUM compare to the performance of Alloy Analyzer in practice on specifications automatically extracted from real-world applications?

4.1 Objects of Analysis

Our objects of analysis are specifications drawn from a variety of sources and problem domains. These specifications vary widely in terms of size and complexity. Table 1 lists the specifications that we use, with statistics on their size in terms of the numbers of relations in their underlying logic. Note that this number, in turn, represents the sum of the numbers of signatures and fields, as both are indeed translated into relations in the underlying relational logic.

Table 1: Objects of Analysis

Specification	# Rels
Ecommerce	70
Decider	47
CSOS	64
Wordpress	54
Andr. Bundle 1	665
Andr. Bundle 2	558
Andr. Bundle 3	485
Andr. Bundle 4	569
Andr. Bundle 5	501
Andr. Bundle 6	456

Ecommerce is a model, adopted from Lau and Czarnecki [30], that represents a common architecture for open-source and commercial E-commerce systems. Decider [15] is a model of a system to support design space exploration. CSOS is a model of a cyber-social operating system meant to help coordinate people and tasks. WordPress is an object model obtained by reverse engineering an open-source blog system [3]. Finally, the last six rows of the table correspond to six large specifications intended for the analysis of security properties in the context of the Android platform. Each consists of a bundle of Android applications installed on a mobile device for detecting security vulnerabilities that may arise due to inter-application communication, adopted from [12].

For the first four objects of analysis, we do not have access to actual, modified versions of their Alloy specifications, and even if we did, there would not likely be enough versions to provide data sufficient to support quantitative analyses. Thus, instead, we used a mutation-based approach to create modified versions of the specifications. We used edit operations for Alloy specifications [10] and incorporated into the MuAlloy mutation system [64] to derive a list of mutation operators. Table 2 provides a list of these mutation operators, together with short descriptions.

To investigate RQ1 we wished to apply our mutation operators to create 30 modified versions of each of our objects of study. Because prior work by Li et al. [31] showed that users tend to modify Alloy specifications incrementally by small amounts, we chose to create versions of our object specifications by mutating between one and 10% of the relations in the specifications. Given object specification S, for each modified specification S' of S to be created, we randomly chose a number N in this range;

Table 2: Mutation Operators

	Description
ADS	Add a new signature
DLS	Delete a signature without children
CSM	Change the signature multiplicity,[3] i.e., to set, one, lone or some (one that is different from the multiplicity defined in the original specification)
ABS	Make an abstract signature non-abstract or vice versa
MOV	Move a sub-signature to a new parent signature
ADF	Add a new field to a signature declaration
DLF	Delete a field from a signature declaration
CFM	Change a multiplicity constraint in a field declaration

N denotes the number of mutations to apply to S. We then began randomly choosing relations L in S', then randomly choosing a mutation operator M applicable to L, and applied M to S'. We did not allow a given L to be utilized more than once in this process. Following each operator application, we ran Alloy on the current version of S' to ensure that it is a valid specification. We repeated this process until N mutations had been inserted into S'. Ultimately, this process produced 30 modified versions of each object specification, wherein each version contained a randomly selected number of randomly selected mutations – a number no greater than 10% of the number of relations in the original specification.

To investigate RQ2 we used a similar process; however, in this case our goal was to "evolve" each object specification S iteratively. Given the original version S, we created a successor version S_1 by repeating the process of inserting a randomly selected number of randomly selected mutations (again, a number no greater than 10% of the number of relations in S). However, our next iteration applied this same process to S_1 (which now contains a number of mutations) to produce a version S_2 that potentially contains more mutations. Here, we say "potentially" because we did not place any restrictions on the re-use of mutation operators or mutation locations in subsequent versions S_k of S; thus, conceivably, a mutation could be "undone" in a subsequent version. We repeated this process 30 times on each specification, thereby obtaining a sequence of specifications that have evolved iteratively.

It is common for users of bounded verification techniques such as Alloy to increase the scope of the analysis, in order to obtain greater confidence in the validity of the specification. As the scope of analysis increases, the space of cases that must be examined expands dramatically. To investigate RQ3, we increased the scope of analysis on each of our object specifications. Note that the only change in the specification between two successive runs of the analyzer in this case was the scope of analysis.

To investigate RQ4 we used the dataset created for RQ1. To investigate RQ5, we created six different app bundles, each containing 20 Android apps drawn from public app repositories such as Google Play [2]. We then used the COVERT tool [1] to automatically extract Alloy specifications from the app bundles. Given an original bundle B, we created a successor version B' by adding a new app or removing an existing app (randomly selected) to/from the given bundle. The specifications automatically derived from app bundles tend to evolve as apps are added to, or removed from, the bundles. The resulting app bundles thus provide us with an ideal suite of evolving specifications that can be used for our evaluation. We repeated this process 30 times on each of the app bundles to produce 30 modified versions of each bundle specification.

4.2 Variables and Measures

Independent Variables As independent variables we wished to utilize PLATINUM, as well as baseline techniques representing state of the art approaches capable of performing the same function as PLATINUM.

We consider the Alloy Analyzer (version 4.2) as a baseline technique to compare against PLATINUM. The other potential baseline technique is Green [62], an optimization technique that, during symbolic execution, memoizes and reuses the results of satisfiability checking. The current implementation of Green, however, has two fundamental problems in the context of this study. First, while Green supports the use of Integer and Real variables in expressions, it does not support the use of boolean variables, which are widely used in the context of Alloy's relational logic. We were able to work around this challenge, however, by modeling boolean variables as Green's Integers and limiting their size to zero and one – an approach suggested by Green's developers. A more insidious problem, however, is that the Green framework does not currently support constraints with the disjunction operator. Because Alloy specifications are in relational logic, native support for the disjunction operator is essential to effectively analyze such specifications. This issue has been reported to the Green repository [4], and we have been in contact with the authors about it; however, to date, the issue has not been resolved and there are no workarounds for it. Thus, we were ultimately unable to use Green as a baseline technique.

Additional independent variables used were (b) the size of specifications in terms of relations in the relational logic, (c) the number of mutation operations, (d) the type of mutation operations, and (e) the scope of the analysis.

Dependent Variables We measure several dependent variables. The first variable, analysis time, tracks performance directly. Here, we measure the wall clock time required to run (1) a complete Alloy analysis and (2) a complete PLATINUM analysis on each specification considered. The second variable is the number of unique, independently analyzable slices produced by PLATINUM for each specification under analysis. The third variable is the number of slices for which solutions are already available for each specification under analysis. Finally, the fourth variable is the size of the generated CNF formulas that must be solved by the underlying SAT solver. In the last case, we record the number of CNF variables and clauses produced by each of the two techniques when translating high-level Alloy specifications into SAT formulas.

4.3 Study Operation

For RQ1 and RQ3, for each of our specification pairs, we applied the Alloy Analyzer and PLATINUM, measuring the time required by each approach, and the number of variables and clauses at the SAT level produced by each tool.

For RQ2, for each of our specification sequences, we applied both the Alloy Analyzer and PLATINUM to each pair of successive specifications in the sequence, measuring, for each iteration, the time required by each approach, the size of the SAT formula produced by each tool, and the number of slices reused across sequences.

For RQ4, for each of our specification pairs, we applied PLATINUM, measuring the time required for formula restructuring, including the slicing and canonicalization steps.

Finally, for RQ5, for each of the specification pairs extracted from app bundles, we applied both the Alloy Analyzer and PLATINUM, measuring the time required by each approach.

All of our runs of the Alloy Analyzer and PLATINUM were conducted on an 8-core 2.0 GHz AMD Opteron 6128 system with 40 GB of memory. Both techniques leveraged SAT4J as the SAT solver across the entire study to keep extraneous variables constant.

4.4   Threats to Validity

External validity threats concern the generalization of our findings. We have studied ten sets of Alloy specifications and cannot claim that they are representative of all such specifications. Additionally, our modified specifications for the first four objects of analysis were created via a mutation approach, and while this allows us to obtain large amounts of data, these objects may not directly represent modified specifications that exist in practice. To reduce this threat and help determine whether our results may generalize, we conducted additional studies using real-world software systems, where both the Alloy specifications and their revisions are automatically extracted from evolving bundles of real Android apps. Finally, different versions of the Alloy Analyzer may leverage different translation algorithms to CNF, and this may affect the execution time of the analyzer. To reduce this threat we used the latest stable release of the Alloy Analyzer, Alloy Analyzer 4.2, for all runs collected in the study.

Construct validity threats concern our metrics and measures; we are aware of no such threats in this case.

4.5   Results for RQ1 (Small Changes)

We first assess the effectiveness of PLATINUM with respect to the incremental changes derived from our first four object specifications. The boxplots in Fig. 2 depict the size of the generated CNF formulas, given as the number of variables (Fig. 2a) and clauses (Fig. 2b) across mutations for each object of study. The results show that in comparison to the Alloy Analyzer, PLATINUM's translation of relational logic specifications results in much smaller and simpler SAT formulas, and the numbers of CNF variables and clauses generated by PLATINUM were smaller than the numbers generated by Alloy. Specifically, in the analyses of the CSOS, Decider, Ecommerce, and Wordpress specifications, the numbers of variables

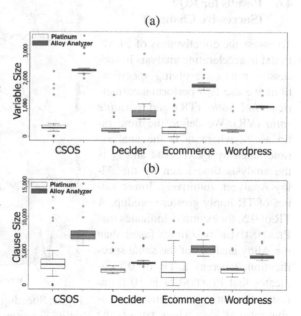

Fig. 2: Sizes of generated CNF formulas in terms of the number of (a) variables and (b) clauses produced by the Alloy Analyzer and PLATINUM across mutations for each object of study.

and the numbers of clauses in the formulas produced by PLATINUM on average were 4.5/2.6/5.1/3.5 and 2.1/1.4/2.0/1.7 times lower, respectively, than the numbers in the formulas produced by the Alloy Analyzer. This is because already analyzed slices do

not need to be translated into SAT formulas, thus reducing the sizes of the generated
CNF formulas.

Table 3 shows the results
of a comparison of the average analysis times required by
the Alloy Analyzer and PLAT-
INUM across the four objects of
study. On average, PLATINUM
exhibited a 67.16% improvement over the Alloy Analyzer,
with the average improvement
across objects of study ranging
from 16.82% to 82.31%.

Table 3: Performance Statistics

	Alloy Analysis Time (S)	PLATINUM Analysis Time (S)	% Improvement
Ecommerce	280.92	49.69	82.31%
CSOS	120.64	56.71	52.99%
Wordpress	57.19	47.57	16.82%
Decider	27.38	5.69	79.21%
Average	121.53	39.91	67.16%

These results demonstrate the potential effectiveness of our optimization technique,
because in every case, the analysis time required by PLATINUM to find solution instances of mutated specifications was less than that required by the state of the art
analysis techniques.

4.6 Results for RQ2 (Successive Changes)

To assess the effectiveness of PLAT-
INUM in accelerating analysis in successive runs on evolving specifications we use two performance metrics: *time ratio* (TR) and *variable
ratio* (VR). We define the time ra-
tio as $\frac{t_P}{t_A}$, where t_P is the analysis
time taken by PLATINUM and t_A is
the analysis time taken by the Alloy Analyzer. Intuitively, lower values of TR imply greater speedup. A
TR of 0.5, for example, indicates that
PLATINUM is two times faster than
the Alloy analysis of the same specification, whereas a TR of 0.1 indicates that PLATINUM is 10 times
faster. Similarly, we define the vari-
able ratio as $\frac{var_P}{var_A}$, where var_P is the
number of variables in a SAT for-
mula produced by PLATINUM and
var_A is the number of variables in
a SAT formula produced by the Alloy Analyzer for the same specification. Again, lower values of VR imply that there are fewer variables in a

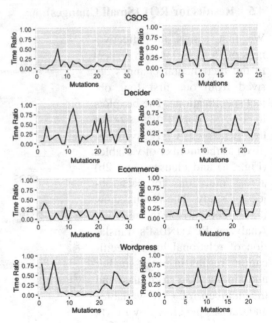

Fig. 3: Speedup and reuse during successive mutation analyses across subject domains. The left
column represents scatter plots of time ratios
(Analysis time taken by PLATINUM / Analysis
time taken by Alloy), and the right column represents scatter plots of reuse ratios (#Variables
in the SAT formula transformed by PLATINUM
/ #Variables in the SAT formula transformed by
the Alloy Analyzer) across systems.

formula generated by PLATINUM than in a formula generated by the Alloy Analyzer. We started PLATINUM with an empty cache, and then analyzed each mutation in turn, continually populating the cache.

Fig. 3 presents a pair of diagrams for each of the four object specifications, demonstrating speedup and reuse during successive mutation analyses. The left column represents scatter plots of time ratios across subject domains, and the right column represents scatter plots of variable ratios. All four sets of experiments exhibit similar behavior: in every case, and for every revision, the analysis time taken by PLATINUM is less than that of using the Alloy Analyzer (values of TR are always less than 1), and the number of variables in formulas generated by PLATINUM is significantly less than those generated by the Alloy Analyzer. The speedup, however, varies for different mutations. Variation across mutations is expected, given that the size and complexity of the mutations produced in successive runs differ greatly. In a few cases, the values for TR jump. Investigation of the data shows that this occurred because the mutations present in those cases contained several new slices not yet observed, which in turn reduced the amount of reuse. Despite these few cases, the empirical results suggest that significant speedup was possible in all cases.

4.7 Results for RQ3 (Scope Changes)

Alloy's analysis is exhaustive, yet bounded, up to a user-specified scope on the size of the domains. In cases in which the analyzer fails to produce a solution that satisfies specification constraints within a given scope, a solution may be found in a larger scope. In practice, Alloy users often conduct consecutive analysis runs of specifications, applying small increases in the analysis scope, in the hopes of gaining further confidence in their results. It has been shown that 17.6% of consecutive Alloy analyses differ only in terms of their analysis scopes [31].

To examine how our optimization approach responds to increases in analysis scope, for each specification, we gradually increased the scope of the analysis. We set the initial scope for the analysis of each specification to the scope that had already been specified by its original modeler, reasoning that whoever had developed and analyzed the specification is most likely the best judge of the scope that is needed. The initial scopes for the CSOS, Decider, Ecommerce, and Wordpress specifications were 51, 27, 50, and 32, respectively. We started PLATINUM with an empty cache for the analysis of each specification, and gradually populated it as the analysis scope increased.

Table 4 shows the time ratios (TRs) measured as the analysis scope increased for each of the objects of study. Recall that lower values for TR indicate that greater acceleration was achieved by our optimization technique. The data shows that overall as scope increased, TR tended to decrease. For example, for the Ecommerce system, the lowest value for TR occurred when the scope increased to five, resulting in a 1 / 0.031 = 32 fold analysis speed acceleration.

Table 4: Analysis Time Improvements Over Increasing Sizes of Analysis Scope

Scope increase	+1	+2	+3	+4	+5
CSOS	0.765	0.122	0.098	0.118	0.035
Decider	0.393	0.036	0.038	0.023	0.034
Ecommerce	0.727	0.234	0.413	0.049	0.031
Wordpress	0.486	0.107	0.079	0.053	0.079

4.8   Results for RQ4 (Overhead)

We next evaluate the performance of PLATINUM's formula restructuring analysis. Table 5 shows the time required to restructure relational logic formulas into their canonical forms. The first column represents the time spent decomposing formulas into independent slices, and the second column represents the time spent canonicalizing them into normalized formats.

Table 5: Analysis Times With Respect to Overhead Incurred Due to Restructuring of Formulas

	Slicing Time(ms)	Canon Time(ms)	%overhead
CSOS	7	268	0.36%
Decider	3	41	0.63%
Ecommerce	10	116	1.01%
Wordpress	5	138	2.44%
Average	6.25	140.75	1.11%

As the data shows, the analysis time overhead incurred by these two steps is 1.11% on average, and no greater than 2.44% in any case. This is negligible, particularly when compared to the analysis time overhead incurred by the Alloy Analyzer (cf. Table 3). While the restructuring steps introduce little overhead, they substantially enable reuse of slice solutions, which in turn greatly reduces analysis costs.

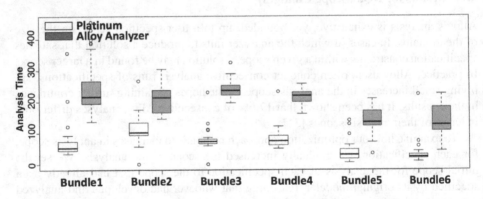

Fig. 4: Analysis times for the Alloy Analyzer and PLATINUM across specifications from real-world Android apps.

4.9   Results for RQ5 (Real-World Specifications)

Finally, to assess the improvements one could expect in practice using PLATINUM, we used Alloy specifications that were automatically extracted from real-world software systems and evolved versions thereof, as described in Section 4.1. Fig. 4 shows the results of a comparison of the analysis time required by each of the two techniques as boxplots across the six bundle specifications. As the results show, PLATINUM exhibited a 66.4% improvement, on average, over the Alloy Analyzer; the average improvement across app bundles ranged from 44.2% to 78.4%, indicating relative stability across bundles. These results further confirm those obtained through our mutation-based experiments, corroborating the effectiveness of PLATINUM in improving the analysis time required by the Alloy Analyzer to find solution instances of revised specifications.

5   Related Work

The literature contains a large body of research related to ours. Here, we provide an overview of the most notable and closely related work and examine it in the light of our research.

The widespread use of Alloy has prompted a number of extensions to the language and its underlying automated analyzer [10, 23, 24, 25, 27, 32, 37, 39, 40, 41, 45, 53, 58, 59]. Among these, Titanium [10] presents an exploration space reduction strategy that narrows the space of values to be explored by an underlying constraint solver. This approach, however, requires an entire solution set to be produced for the original specification, to determine tighter bounds for certain relations in the revised specification. Our work differs primarily in its emphasis on reducing constraints into a more concise form at the level of relational logic abstractions, which in turn allows for substantial reuse of analysis efforts in subsequent analyses. Research efforts on bound adjustment and solution reuse are complementary in that, in spite of the adjustments made to the analysis bounds, the solver still needs to solve for the shared constraints.

Uzuncaova and Khurshid [60] partition a specification into base and derived slices, in which a solution to the base slice can be extended to produce a solution for the entire specification. PLATINUM is fundamentally different from this work in that the problem addressed by Uzuncaova and Khurshid assumes a fixed specification and does not consider specification evolution. Further, their approach does not eliminate the need to solve shared, canonicalized constraints across analyses.

Rosner et al. [51] present a technique, Ranger, that leverages a linear ordering of the solution space to support parallel analysis of first-order logic specifications. While the linear ordering enables partitioning of the solution space into ranges, there is no clear way in which it can be extended with incremental analysis capabilities, which are crucial for effective analysis of evolving specifications.

Several techniques attempt to explore specification instances derived from Alloy's relational logic constraints [18, 33, 44, 45, 56]. Macedo et al. [33] examine scenario explorations in the context of relational logic. Aluminum [45] extends the Alloy Analyzer to generate minimal specification instances. Both of these efforts focus primarily on the order in which solutions are produced, as opposed to facilitating analysis of evolving specifications, which is our goal. Montaghami and Rayside [39] extend the Alloy language to explicitly support partial modeling. Their work, however, does not consider evolving specifications. In fact, it is widely recognized that efficient techniques for analyzing Alloy specifications are needed [58]. To the best of our knowledge, however, no prior research has attempted to reduce the need to call a solver to improve the efficiency of the analysis of evolving Alloy specifications.

The technique most closely related to ours is Green [62]; this technique has been the subject of several more recent papers [6, 7, 29, 47, 49, 50, 65], that improve on its algorithm. As noted in Section 1, Green and its offshoots also rely on back-end constraint solving engines. In contrast to all of this prior work, the problem we address in this paper involves supporting the evolutionary analysis of relational logic. Among other things, this requires the development of both original slicing and canonicalization approaches appropriate for models specified in Alloy's relational logic. Moreover, neither Green's slicer nor its canonicalizer take into account the disjunction operator [4]. While the lack of support for the disjunction operator might be allowable in the context of symbolic execution, that support is essential in the context of first-order logic to allow an approach to effectively recognize opportunities for constraint reduction and reuse. Further, while most of the prior techniques use a classic lexicographic ordering of the variables before transforming each slice into a canonical format, PLATINUM leverages a reverse shortlex order, in which the variables are first sorted by their weight and then sorted lexicographically. This choice improves the identification of syntactic equivalence between different slices. To the best of our knowledge, PLATINUM is the first technique for evolutionary analysis of relational logic specification that operates without requiring an entire solution set for the original specification.

6 Conclusions

We have presented PLATINUM, a novel extension to the Alloy Analyzer that substantially improves the process of analyzing evolving Alloy specifications. Our approach proceeds by storing solved constraints incrementally, and reusing them within subsequent analysis of a revised specification. It also omits redundant constraints from specifications before translating them into formulas that will be sent to constraint solvers. Our evaluation of PLATINUM shows that it is able to support substantial reuse of constraint solutions across analyses of evolving specifications. Our empirical results show significant speedup over the Alloy Analyzer in various scenarios. Our evaluation also shows that as the scope of analysis increases, PLATINUM achieves even further improvements, and that the overhead associated with the approach is negligible. Finally, our evaluation shows that PLATINUM continues to result in savings on specifications extracted from real-world software systems.

Our future work involves extending the optimization ideas presented here to leverage domain-specific knowledge. Specifically, we intend to explore the possibility of driving the automated discovery of domain-specific optimizations, wherein each system of interest can have bounded verification tailored to its specific characteristics. While such optimizations historically have arisen from the insights of a few dozen experts in software verification, we envision a bounded speculative analysis to identify how operations permissible within a certain domain may impact the exploration space of bounded analyses, thereby facilitating efficient analysis of specifications in a given domain.

Acknowledgment

We would like to thank the anonymous reviewers for their valuable comments. This work was supported in part by awards CCF-1755890 and CCF-1618132 from the National Science Foundation.

References

[1] Covert analysis tool. http://www.sdalab.com/projects/covert (2017)

[2] Google play market. http://play.google.com/store/apps/ (2017)

[3] WordPress. http://codex.wordpress.org/Database_Description/3.3 (2017)

[4] Green solver. https://github.com/green-solver/green-solver/tree/master/green/test/za/ac/sun/cs/green/misc (2018)

[5] Platinum repository. https://sites.google.com/view/platinum-repository (2019)

[6] Aquino, A., Bianchi, F.A., Chen, M., Denaro, G., Pezzè, M.: Reusing constraint proofs in program analysis. In: Proceedings of the International Symposium on Software Testing and Analysis. pp. 305–315 (2015)

[7] Aquino, A., Denaro, G., Pezzè, M.: Heuristically Matching Solution Spaces of Arithmetic Formulas to Efficiently Reuse Solutions. In: Proceedings of the 39th International Conference on Software Engineering. pp. 427–437. ICSE '17, IEEE Press, Piscataway, NJ, USA (2017), https://doi.org/10.1109/ICSE.2017.46

[8] Bagheri, H., Kang, E., Malek, S., Jackson, D.: Detection of design flaws in the android permission protocol through bounded verification. In: Bjørner, N., de Boer, F.S. (eds.) FM 2015: Formal Methods - 20th International Symposium, Oslo, Norway, June 24-26, 2015, Proceedings. Lecture Notes in Computer Science, vol. 9109, pp. 73–89. Springer (2015), https://doi.org/10.1007/978-3-319-19249-9_6

[9] Bagheri, H., Kang, E., Malek, S., Jackson, D.: A formal approach for detection of security flaws in the android permission system. Formal Asp. Comput. 30(5), 525–544 (2018), https://doi.org/10.1007/s00165-017-0445-z

[10] Bagheri, H., Malek, S.: Titanium: Efficient analysis of evolving alloy specifications. In: Proceedings of the International Symposium on the Foundations of Software Engineering (2016)

[11] Bagheri, H., Sadeghi, A., Behrouz, R.J., Malek, S.: Practical, formal synthesis and automatic enforcement of security policies for android. In: 46th Annual IEEE/IFIP International Conference on Dependable Systems and Networks, DSN 2016, Toulouse, France, June 28 - July 1, 2016. pp. 514–525. IEEE Computer Society (2016), https://doi.org/10.1109/DSN.2016.53

[12] Bagheri, H., Sadeghi, A., Garcia, J., Malek, S.: Covert: Compositional analysis of android inter-app permission leakage. IEEE Transactions on Software Engineering (2015)

[13] Bagheri, H., Sullivan, K.J.: Model-driven synthesis of formally precise, stylized software architectures. Formal Asp. Comput. 28(3), 441–467 (2016), https://doi.org/10.1007/s00165-016-0360-8

[14] Bagheri, H., Tang, C., Sullivan, K.: Trademaker: Automated dynamic analysis of synthesized tradespaces. In: Proceedings of the 36th International Conference on Software Engineering. pp. 106–116. ICSE 2014, ACM, New York, NY, USA (2014), http://doi.acm.org/10.1145/2568225.2568291

[15] Bagheri, H., Tang, C., Sullivan, K.: Automated synthesis and dynamic analysis of tradeoff spaces for object-relational mapping. IEEE Transactions on Software Engineering 43(2), 145–163 (2017)

[16] Bagheri, H., Wang, J., Aerts, J., Malek, S.: Efficient, evolutionary security analysis of interacting android apps. In: 2018 IEEE International Conference on Software Maintenance and Evolution, ICSME 2018, Madrid, Spain, September 23-29, 2018. pp. 357–368. IEEE Computer Society (2018), https://doi.org/10.1109/ICSME.2018.00044

[17] Cormen, T.H., Leiserson, C.E., Rivest, R.L., Stein, C.: Introduction to Algorithms, Third Edition. The MIT Press, 3rd edn. (2009)

[18] Cunha, A., Macedo, N., Guimaraes, T.: Target oriented relational model finding. In: Proceedings of the International Conference on Fundamental Approaches to Software Engineering. pp. 17–31 (2014)

[19] De Ita Luna, G., Marcial-Romero, J.R., Hernandez, J.: The Incremental Satisfiability Problem for a Two Conjunctive Normal Form. Electronic Notes in Theoretical Computer Science **328**, 31–45 (Dec 2016), http://www.sciencedirect.com/science/article/pii/S1571066116301013

[20] Devdatta Akhawe, Adam Barth, Peifung E. Lamy, John Mitchelly, Dawn Song: Towards a Formal Foundation of Web Security. In: Proceedings of the 23rd International Conference on Computer Security Foundations Symposium (CSF). pp. 290–304 (2010)

[21] Een, N., Sorensson, N.: Translating pseudo-boolean constraints into sat. Journal on Satisfiability, Boolean Modeling and Computation **2**, 1–26 (2006)

[22] Egly, U., Lonsing, F., Oetsch, J.: Automated Benchmarking of Incremental SAT and QBF Solvers. In: Logic for Programming, Artificial Intelligence, and Reasoning. pp. 178–186. Lecture Notes in Computer Science, Springer, Berlin, Heidelberg (Nov 2015)

[23] Galeotti, J.P., Rosner, N., Pombo, C.G.L., Frias, M.F.: Analysis of invariants for efficient bounded verification. In: Proceedings of International Symposium on Software Testing and Analysis. pp. 25–36 (2010)

[24] Galeotti, J.P., Rosner, N., Pombo, C.G.L., Frias, M.F.: TACO: Efficient SAT-based bounded verification using symmetry breaking and tight bounds. IEEE Transactions on Software Engineering **39**(9), 1283–1307 (2013)

[25] Ganov, S., Khurshid, S., Perry, D.E.: Annotations for alloy: Automated incremental analysis using domain specific solvers. In: Proc. of ICFEM. pp. 414–429 (2012)

[26] Hao, J., Kang, E., Sun, J., Jackson, D.: Designing Minimal Effective Normative Systems with the Help of Lightweight Formal Methods. In: Proceedings of the 2016 24th ACM SIGSOFT International Symposium on Foundations of Software Engineering. pp. 50–60. FSE 2016, ACM, New York, NY, USA (2016), http://doi.acm.org/10.1145/2950290.2950307

[27] Heaven, W., Russo, A.: Enhancing the alloy analyzer with patterns of analysis. In: Workshop on Logic-based Methods in Programming Environments (2005)

[28] Jackson, D.: Software Abstractions. MIT Press, 2nd edn. (2012)

[29] Jia, X., Ghezzi, C., Ying, S.: Enhancing reuse of constraint solutions to improve symbolic execution. In: Proceedings of the International Symposium on Software Testing and Analysis. pp. 177–187 (2015)

[30] Lau, S.Q.: Domain Analysis of E-Commerce Systems Using Feature-Based Model Templates. Master's thesis, University of Waterloo, Canada (2006)

[31] Li, X., Shannon, D., Walker, J., Khurshid, S., Marinov, D.: Analyzing the Uses of a Software Modeling Tool. Electronic Notes in Theoretical Computer Science **164**(2), 3–18 (Oct 2006). https://doi.org/10.1016/j.entcs.2006.10.001, http://www.sciencedirect.com/science/article/pii/S1571066106004786

[32] Macedo, N., Brunel, J., Chemouil, D., Cunha, A., Kuperberg, D.: Lightweight Specification and Analysis of Dynamic Systems with Rich Configurations. In: Proceedings of the 2016 24th ACM SIGSOFT International Symposium on Foundations of Software Engineering. pp. 373–383. FSE 2016, ACM, New York, NY, USA (2016), http://doi.acm.org/10.1145/2950290.2950318

[33] Macedo, N., Cunha, A., Guimaraes, T.: Exploring scenario exploration. In: Proceedings of the International Conference on Fundamental Approaches to Software Engineering. pp. 301–315 (2015)

[34] Maldonado-Lopez, F.A., Chavarriaga, J., Donoso, Y.: Detecting Network Policy Conflicts Using Alloy. In: Abstract State Machines, Alloy, B, TLA, VDM, and Z. pp. 314–317. Lecture Notes in Computer Science, Springer, Berlin, Heidelberg (Jun 2014)

[35] Mansoor, N., Saddler, J.A., Silva, B., Bagheri, H., Cohen, M.B., Farritor, S.: Modeling and testing a family of surgical robots: an experience report. In: Leavens, G.T., Garcia, A., Pasareanu, C.S. (eds.) Proceedings of the 2018 ACM Joint Meeting on European Software Engineering Conference and Symposium on the Foundations of Software Engineering, ESEC/SIGSOFT FSE 2018, Lake Buena Vista, FL, USA, November 04-09, 2018. pp. 785–790. ACM (2018), https://doi.org/10.1145/3236024.3275534

[36] Marinov, D., Khurshid, S.: What will the user do (next) in the tool? In: Proceedings of the ACM SIGSOFT First Alloy Workshop. pp. 98–99. ACM (2006)

[37] Milicevic, A., Rayside, D., Yessenov, K., Jackson, D.: Unifying execution of imperative and declarative code. In: Proceedings of the 33rd International Conference on Software Engineering. pp. 511–520. ICSE '11, ACM, New York, NY, USA (2011), http://doi.acm.org/10.1145/1985793.1985863

[38] Mirzaei, N., Garcia, J., Bagheri, H., Sadeghi, A., Malek, S.: Reducing combinatorics in GUI testing of android applications. In: Dillon, L.K., Visser, W., Williams, L. (eds.) Proceedings of the 38th International Conference on Software Engineering, ICSE 2016, Austin, TX, USA, May 14-22, 2016. pp. 559–570. ACM (2016), https://doi.org/10.1145/2884781.2884853

[39] Montaghami, V., Rayside, D.: Extending Alloy with partial instances. In: Proceedings of the International Conferece on Abstract State Machines, Alloy, B, VDM, and Z. pp. 122–135 (2012)

[40] Montaghami, V., Rayside, D.: Staged evaluation of partial instances in a relational model finder. In: Proceedings of the International Conferece on Abstract State Machines, Alloy, B, VDM, and Z. pp. 318–323 (2014)

[41] Montaghami, V., Rayside, D.: Bordeaux: A tool for thinking outside the box. In: Proceedings of the International Conference on Fundamental Approaches to Software Engineering. pp. 22–39 (2017)

[42] Nadel, A., Ryvchin, V., Strichman, O.: Ultimately Incremental SAT. In: Theory and Applications of Satisfiability Testing (SAT 2014). pp. 206–218. Lecture Notes in Computer Science, Springer, Cham (Jul 2014)

[43] Near, J.P., Jackson, D.: Derailer: Interactive security analysis for web applications. In: Proceedings of the 29th ACM/IEEE International Conference on Automated Software Engineering. pp. 587–598. ASE '14, ACM, New York, NY, USA (2014), http://doi.acm.org/10.1145/2642937.2643012

[44] Nelson, T., Danas, N., Dougherty, D.J., Krishnamurthi, S.: The Power of "Why" and "Why Not": Enriching Scenario Exploration with Provenance. In: Proceedings of the 2017 11th Joint Meeting on Foundations of Software Engineering. pp. 106–116. ESEC/FSE 2017, ACM, New York, NY, USA (2017), http://doi.acm.org/10.1145/3106237.3106272

[45] Nelson, T., Saghafi, S., Dougherty, D.J., Fisler, K., Krishnamurthi, S.: Aluminum: Principled scenario exploration through minimality. In: Proceedings of the International Conference on Software Engineering. pp. 232–241 (2013)

[46] Nijjar, J., Bultan, T.: Bounded verification of ruby on rails data models. In: Proceedings of the 2011 International Symposium on Software Testing and Analysis. pp. 67–77. ISSTA '11, ACM, New York, NY, USA (2011), http://doi.acm.org/10.1145/2001420.2001429

[47] Person, S., Yang, G., Rungta, N., Khurshid, S.: Directed incremental symbolic execution. In: Proceedings of the Conference on Programming Language Design and Implementation. pp. 504–515 (2011)

[48] Ponzio, P., Aguirre, N., Frias, M.F., Visser, W.: Field-exhaustive Testing. In: Proceedings of the 2016 24th ACM SIGSOFT International Symposium on Foundations of Software Engineering. pp. 908–919. FSE 2016, ACM, New York, NY, USA (2016), http://doi.acm.org/10.1145/2950290.2950336

[49] Qiu, R., Yang, G., Pasareanu, C.S., Khurshid, S.: Compositional symbolic execution with memoized replay. In: Proceedings of the International Conference on Software Engineering (2015)

[50] Ramos, D.A., Engler, D.R.: Practical, low-effort equivalence verification of real code. In: Gopalakrishnan, G., Qadeer, S. (eds.) Computer Aided Verification, Lecture Notes in Computer Science, vol. 6806, pp. 669–685. Springer Berlin Heidelberg (2011), $http://dx.doi.org/10.1007/978-3-642-22110-1_5$

[51] Rosner, N., Siddiqui, J.H., Aguirre, N., Khurshid, S., Frias, M.F.: Ranger: Parallel analysis of Alloy models by range partitioning. In: Proceeding of the International Conference on Automated Software Engineering. pp. 147–157 (2013)

[52] Ruchansky, N., Proserpio, D.: A (Not) NICE Way to Verify the Openflow Switch Specification: Formal Modelling of the Openflow Switch Using Alloy. In: Proceedings of the ACM SIGCOMM 2013 Conference on SIGCOMM. pp. 527–528. SIGCOMM '13, ACM, New York, NY, USA (2013), http://doi.acm.org/10.1145/2486001.2491711

[53] Semerath, O., Varas, A., Varra, D.: Iterative and Incremental Model Generation by Logic Solvers. In: Fundamental Approaches to Software Engineering. pp. 87–103. Lecture Notes in Computer Science, Springer, Berlin, Heidelberg (Apr 2016), $https://link.springer.com/chapter/10.1007/978-3-662-49665-7_6$

[54] Stevens, C., Bagheri, H.: Reducing run-time adaptation space via analysis of possible utility bounds. In: Proceedings of the 42nd International Conference on Software Engineering. ICSE 2020, ACM (2020)

[55] Taghdiri, M.: Inferring specifications to detect errors in code. In: Proceedings of the 19th IEEE International Conference on Automated Software Engineering. pp. 144–153. ASE '04, IEEE Computer Society, Washington, DC, USA (2004), http://dx.doi.org/10.1109/ASE.2004.42

[56] Torlak, E.: A Constraint Solver for Software Engineering: Finding Models and Cores of Large Relational Specifications. PhD thesis, MIT (Feb 2009), http://alloy.mit.edu/kodkod/

[57] Torlak, E., Jackson, D.: Kodkod: A relational model finder. In: Proceedings of the 13th International Conference on Tools and Algorithms for the Construction and Analysis of Systems. pp. 632–647. TACAS'07, Springer-Verlag, Berlin, Heidelberg (2007), http://dl.acm.org/citation.cfm?id=1763507.1763571

[58] Torlak, E., Taghdiri, M., Dennis, G., Near, J.P.: Applications and extensions of Alloy: Past, present and future. Mathematical Structures in Computer Science **23**(4), 915–933 (2013)

[59] Uzuncaova, E., Khurshid, S.: Kato: A program slicing tool for declarative specifications. In: Proceedings of the International Conference on Software Engineering. pp. 767–770 (2007)

[60] Uzuncaova, E., Khurshid, S.: Constraint prioritization for efficient analysis of declarative models. In: Proceedings of the International Symposium on Formal Methods (2008)

[61] Uzuncaova, E., Khurshid, S., Batory, D.: Incremental test generation for software product lines. IEEE Trans. Software Eng. **36**(3), 309–322 (2010)

[62] Visser, W., Geldenhuys, J., , Dwyer, M.B.: Green: Reducing, reusing and recycling constraints in program analysis. In: Proceedings of the ACM SIGSOFT 20th International Symposium on the Foundations of Software Engineering. pp. 58:1–58:11 (2012)

[63] Wang, J., Bagheri, H., Cohen, M.B.: An evolutionary approach for analyzing alloy specifications. In: Huchard, M., Kästner, C., Fraser, G. (eds.) Proceedings of the 33rd ACM/IEEE International Conference on Automated Software Engineering, ASE 2018, Montpellier, France, September 3-7, 2018. pp. 820–825. ACM (2018), https://doi.org/10.1145/3238147.3240468

[64] Wang, K.: MuAlloy : an automated mutation system for alloy. Thesis (May 2015), https://repositories.lib.utexas.edu/handle/2152/31865

[65] Yang, G., Păsăreanu, C.S., Khurshid, S.: Memoized symbolic execution. In: Proceedings of the International Symposium on Software Testing and Analysis. pp. 144–154 (2012)

[66] Zave, P.: Using Lightweight Modeling to Understand Chord. SIGCOMM Comput. Commun. Rev. **42**(2), 49–57 (Mar 2012), http://doi.acm.org/10.1145/2185376.2185383

Integrating Topological Proofs with Model Checking to Instrument Iterative Design

Claudio Menghi[1], Alessandro Maria Rizzi[2], and Anna Bernasconi[2]

[1] University of Luxembourg, Luxembourg, Luxembourg
claudio.menghi@uni.lu
[2] Politecnico di Milano, Milano, Italy
{alessandromaria.rizzi,anna.bernasconi}@polimi.it

Abstract. System development is not a linear, one-shot process. It proceeds through refinements and revisions. To support assurance that the system satisfies its requirements, it is desirable that continuous verification can be performed after each refinement or revision step. To achieve practical adoption, formal verification must accommodate continuous verification efficiently and effectively. Model checking provides developers with information useful to improve their models only when a property is not satisfied, i.e., when a counterexample is returned. However, it is desirable to have some useful information also when a property is instead satisfied. To address this problem we propose TOrPEDO, an approach that supports verification in two complementary forms: model checking and proofs. While model checking is typically used to pinpoint model behaviors that violate requirements, proofs can instead explain why requirements are satisfied. In our work, we introduce a specific notion of proof, called Topological Proof. A topological proof produces a slice of the original model that justifies the property satisfaction. Because models can be incomplete, TOrPEDO supports reasoning on requirements satisfaction, violation, and possible satisfaction (in the case where satisfaction depends on unknown parts of the model). Evaluation is performed by checking how topological proofs support software development on 12 modeling scenarios and 15 different properties obtained from 3 examples from literature. Results show that: (i) topological proofs are ≈60% smaller than the original models; (ii) after a revision, in ≈78% of cases, the property can be re-verified by relying on a simple syntactic check.

Keywords: Topological Proofs · Iterative Design · Model Checking · Theorem Proving · Unsatisfiable Core.

1 Introduction

One of the goals of software engineering and formal methods is to provide automated verification tools that support designers in producing models of an envisioned system which follows a set of properties of interest. Designers benefit from automated support to understand why their system does not behave as expected (e.g., counterexamples), but they might find it also useful to retrieve

© The Author(s) 2020
H. Wehrheim and J. Cabot (Eds.): FASE 2020, LNCS 12076, pp. 53–74, 2020.
https://doi.org/10.1007/978-3-030-45234-6_3

information when the system already follows the specified requirements. While model checkers provide the former, theorem provers sustain the latter. Theorem provers usually rely on some form of deductive mechanism that, given a set of axioms, iteratively applies a set of rules until a theorem is proved. The proof consists of the specific sequence of deductive rules applied to prove the theorem. In the literature, many approaches have dealt with an integration of model checking and theorem proving at various levels (e.g., [48,60,53,36]). These approaches are oriented to produce *certified model checking* procedures rather than tools that actually help the design process. Even when the idea is to provide a practically useful framework [49,50], the output consists of deductive proofs that are usually difficult to understand and hardly connectable with the designer's modeling choices. Moreover, verification techniques only take into account completely specified designs. This is a remarkable limitation in practical contexts, where the designer may start by providing an initial, high-level version of the model, which is iteratively narrowed down as design progresses and uncertainties are removed [13,42,8,19,65,43]. A recent work [4,5] considered cases in which a partial knowledge of the system model is available. However, the presented approach was mainly theoretical and lacked a practical implementation.

We formulate our problem on models that contain uncertain parts. We choose Partial Kripke Structures (PKSs) as a formalism to represent general models for the following reasons: (i) PKSs have been used in requirement elicitation to reason about system behavior from different points of view [19,8], and are a common theoretical reference language used in the formal method community for the specification of uncertain models (e.g, [26,9,27,10]); (ii) other modeling formalisms commonly used in software development [23,64], such as Modal Transition Systems [37] (MTSs), can be converted into PKSs through a simple transformation [26] making our solution easily applicable to those models.

Kripke Structures (KSs) are particular instances of PKSs that represent complete models. Requirements on the model are expressed in Linear-time Temporal Logic (LTL). As such, the approach presented in the following is generic: it can be applied on models that contain uncertain parts (PKSs) or not (KSs), and can be easily adapted to support MTSs.

Verification techniques that consider PKSs return three alternative values: *true* if the property holds in the partial model, *false* if it does not hold, and *maybe* if the property possibly holds, i.e., its satisfaction depends on the parts of the model that still need to be refined. As models are revised, i.e., they are modified during design iterations, designers need support to understand *why* properties are satisfied, or possibly satisfied.

A comprehensive and integrated design framework able to support software designers in understanding such motivation is still missing. We tackle this problem by presenting TOrPEDO (TOpological Proof drivEn Development framewOrk), a novel automated verification framework, that:

(i) supports a modeling formalism which allows a partial specification of the system design;

(ii) allows performing analysis and verification in the context of systems in which "incompleteness" represents a conceptual uncertainty;

(iii) provides guidance in producing model revisions through complementary outputs: counterexamples and proofs;

(iv) when the system is completely specified, allows understanding which changes impact or not the satisfaction of certain properties.

TOrPEDO is based on the novel notion of *topological proof* (TP), which tries to overcome the complexity of deductive proofs and is designed to make proofs understandable on the original system design. A TP is a *slice* of the original model that specifies which part of it impacts the property satisfaction. If the slice defined by the TP is not preserved during a revision, there is no assurance that the property holds (possibly holds) in the revised model. This paper proposes an algorithm to compute topological proofs—which relies on the notion of *unsatisfiable cores* (UCs) [56]—and proves its correctness on PKSs. It also proposes an algorithm that checks whether a TP is preserved in a model revision. This simple syntactic check avoids (in many cases) the execution of the model checking procedure. While architectural decomposition and composition of components can be considered during the system development [42], in this work we present our solution by assuming that the system is modeled as a single PKS. However, our framework can be extended to consider the composition of components, such as the parallel composition of PKSs or MTSs. This can be done by extracting the portions of the TP that refer to the different components.

TOrPEDO has been implemented on top of NuSMV [14] and PLTL-MUP [58]. The implementation has been exploited to evaluate TOrPEDO by considering a set of examples coming from literature including both completely specified and partially specified models. We considered 3 different example models and 4 variations for each model that was presented in the literature [12,20]. We considered 15 properties, i.e., 5 for each example, leading to a total of 60 (3×4×5) scenarios that require the evaluation of a property on a model. We evaluated how our framework supports model design by comparing the size of the generated topological proofs against the size of the original models. Results show that topological proofs are ≈60% smaller than the original models. Moreover, after a revision, in ≈78% of cases, our syntactic check avoids the re-execution of the model checker.

Organization. Section 2 describes TOrPEDO. Section 3 discusses the background. Sections 4 and 5 present the theoretical results and the algorithms that support TOrPEDO. Section 6 evaluates the achieved results. Section 7 discusses related work. Section 8 concludes.

2   TOrPEDO

TOrPEDO is a proof based development framework which allows verifying PKSs and evaluating their revisions. To illustrate TOrPEDO, we use a simple model describing the states of a vacuum-cleaner robot that has to satisfy the requirements in Fig. 2, specified through LTL formulae and English natural language.

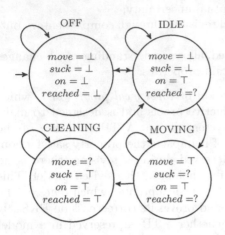

Fig. 1: PKS of a vacuum-cleaner robot.

LTL formulae

$\phi_1 = \mathcal{G}(suck \rightarrow reached)$
$\phi_2 = \mathcal{G}((\neg move)\,\mathcal{W}\,on)$
$\phi_3 = \mathcal{G}(((\neg move) \wedge on) \rightarrow suck)$
$\phi_4 = ((\neg suck)\,\mathcal{W}(move \wedge (\neg suck)))$

Textual requirements

ϕ_1: the robot is drawing dust ($suck$) only if it has $reached$ the cleaning site.
ϕ_2: the robot must be turned on before it can $move$.
ϕ_3: if the robot is on and stationary ($\neg move$), it must be drawing dust ($suck$).
ϕ_4: the robot must $move$ before it is allowed to draw dust ($suck$).

Fig. 2: Natural language and LTL formulation of the requirements of the vacuum-cleaner robot. $\mathcal{G}$ and $\mathcal{W}$ are the "globally" and "weak until" LTL operators.

The TOrPEDO framework is illustrated in Fig. 3 and carries out verification in four phases: INITIAL DESIGN, ANALYSIS, REVISION, and RE-CHECK.

INITIAL DESIGN (1). The model of the system is expressed using a PKS M (1), which can be generated from other languages, along with the property of interest ϕ, in LTL (2).

Running example. The PKS presented in Fig. 1 is defined over two atomic propositions representing actions that a robot can perform: *move*, i.e., the agent travels to the cleaning site; *suck*, i.e., the agent is drawing the dust, and two atomic propositions representing conditions that can trigger actions: *on*, true when the robot is turned on; *reached*, true when the robot has reached the cleaning site. The state *OFF* represents the robot being shut down, *IDLE* the robot being tuned on w.r.t. a cleaning call, *MOVING* the robot reaching the cleaning site, and *CLEANING* the robot performing its duty. Each state is labeled with the actions *move* and *suck* and the conditions *on* and *reached*. Given an action or condition α and a state s, we use the notation: $\alpha = \top$ to indicate that α occurs when the robot is in state s; $\alpha = \bot$ to indicate that α does not occur when the robot is in state s; $\alpha = ?$ to indicate that there is uncertainty on whether α occurs when the robot is in state s.

ANALYSIS (2). TOrPEDO provides automated analysis support, which includes the following elements:

(i) Information about *what is wrong* in the current design. This information includes a definitive-counterexample, which indicates a behavior that depends on already performed design choices and violates the properties of interest. The definitive-counterexample (3 $\bot$-CE) can be used to produce a revised version M' of M that satisfies or possibly satisfies the property of interest.

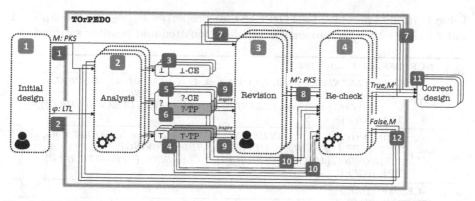

Fig. 3: TOrPEDO structure. Continuous arrows represent inputs and outputs to phases. Numbers are used to reference the image in the text.

(ii) Information about *what is correct* in the current design. This information includes definitive-topological proofs (**4** ⊤-TP) that indicate a portion of the design that ensures satisfaction of the property.

(iii) Information about *what could be wrong/correct* in the current design, depending on how uncertainty is removed. This information includes: a possible-counterexample (**5** ?-CE), indicating a behavior (which depends on uncertain actions and conditions) that violates the properties of interest, and a possible-topological proof (**6** ?-TP), indicating a portion of the design that ensures the possible satisfaction of the property of interest.

In the following we will use the notation x-topological proofs or x-TP to indicate arbitrarily definitive-topological or possible-topological proofs. The results returned by TORPEDO for the different properties in our motivating example are presented in Table 1. Property ϕ_2 is satisfied, ϕ_3 is not. In those cases TOR-PEDO returns respectively a definitive-proof and a definitive-counterexample. Since ϕ_1 and ϕ_4 are possibly satisfied, in both cases a possible-counterexample and a possible-topological proof are returned.

Running example. For ϕ_1 the possible-counterexample shows a run that may violate the property of interest. The possible-topological proof in Table 1 shows that if *OFF* remains the only initial state (**TPI**), *reached* still holds in *CLEANING*, and *suck* does not hold in *OFF* and *IDLE*, while unknown in *MOVING* (**TPP**), property ϕ_1 remains possibly satisfied. In addition, all transitions must be preserved (**TPT**).[3] Note that the proof highlights portions of the model that influence the property satisfaction. For example, by inspecting the proof, the designer understands that she can change the value of the proposition *reached* in all the states of the PKS, with the exception of the state *CLEANING*, without making the property violated.

---

[3] The precise formal descriptions of x-topological proofs, **TPI**, **TPT** and **TPT** are presented in Section 4.

Table 1: Results provided by TOrPEDO for properties ϕ_1, ϕ_2, ϕ_3 and ϕ_4. $\top$, $\bot$ and ? indicate that the property is satisfied, violated and possibly satisfied.

ϕ_1 ?	**?-CE**	*OFF*, *IDLE*, (*MOVING*)$^\omega$.
	?-TP	**TPP:** $\langle CLEANING, reached, \top \rangle$ $\langle OFF, suck, \bot \rangle$, $\langle IDLE, suck, \bot \rangle$, $\langle MOVING, suck, ? \rangle$ **TPT:** $\langle OFF, \{OFF, IDLE\}\rangle$, $\langle IDLE, \{OFF, IDLE, MOVING\}\rangle$, $\langle MOVING, \{MOVING, CLEANING\}\rangle$, $\langle CLEANING, \{CLEANING, IDLE\}\rangle$ **TPI:** $\langle\{OFF\}\rangle$
ϕ_2 $\top$	**$\top$-TP**	**TPP:** $\langle MOVING, on, \top \rangle$, $\langle CLEANING, on, \top \rangle$, $\langle OFF, move, \bot \rangle$, $\langle IDLE, move, \bot \rangle$ **TPT:** $\langle OFF, \{OFF, IDLE\}\rangle$, $\langle IDLE, \{OFF, IDLE, MOVING\}\rangle$, $\langle MOVING, \{MOVING, CLEANING\}\rangle$, $\langle CLEANING, \{CLEANING, IDLE\}\rangle$ **TPI:** $\langle\{OFF\}\rangle$
ϕ_3 $\bot$	**$\bot$-CE**	*OFF*, *IDLE*$^\omega$
ϕ_4 ?	**?-CE**	*OFF*, (*IDLE*, *MOVING*, *CLEANING*, *IDLE*, *OFF*)$^\omega$
	?-TP	**TPP:** $\langle OFF, suck, \bot \rangle$, $\langle IDLE, suck, \bot \rangle$, $\langle MOVING, suck, ? \rangle$, $\langle MOVING, move, \top \rangle$ **TPT:** $\langle OFF, \{OFF, IDLE\}\rangle$, $\langle IDLE, \{OFF, IDLE, MOVING\}\rangle$ **TPI:** $\langle\{OFF\}\rangle$

REVISION (3). Revisions (8) can be obtained by changing some parts of the model: adding/removing states and transitions or by changing propositions labelling inside states, and are defined by considering the TP (9).

Running example. The designer may want to propose a revision that still does not violate properties ϕ_1, ϕ_2, and ϕ_4. Thus, she changes the values of some atomic propositions: *move* becomes $\top$ in state *CLEANING* and *reached* becomes $\bot$ in state *IDLE*. Since ϕ_1, ϕ_2, and ϕ_4 were previously not violated, TOrPEDO performs the RE-CHECK phase for each property.

RE-CHECK (4). The automated verification tool provided by TOrPEDO checks whether all the changes in the current model revision are compliant with the x-TPs (10), i.e., changes applied to the revised model do not include parts that had to be preserved according to the x-topological proof. If a property of interest is (possibly) satisfied in a previous model, and the revision of the model is compliant with the property x-TP, the designer has the guarantee that the property is (possibly) satisfied in the revision. Thus, she can perform another model revision round (7) or approve the current design (11). Otherwise, TOrPEDO re-executes the ANALYSIS (12).

Running example. In the vacuum-cleaner case, the revision passes the RE-CHECK and the designer proceeds to a new revision phase.

3   Background

We present background notions by relying on standard notations for the selected formalisms (see for example [26,9,10,30]).

Partial Kripke Structures (1) are state machines that can be adopted when the value of some propositions is uncertain on selected states.

Definition 1 ([9],[35]). *A* Partial Kripke Structure *(PKS) M is a tuple* $\langle S, R, S_0, AP, L\rangle$*, where: S is a set of states; $R \subseteq S \times S$ is a left-total transition* *relation on S; S_0 is a set of initial states; AP is a set of atomic propositions; $L : S \times AP \rightarrow \{\top, ?, \bot\}$ is a function that, for each state in S, associates a truth value to every atomic proposition in AP. A Kripke Structure (KS) M is a PKS $\langle S, R, S_0, AP, L \rangle$, where $L : S \times AP \rightarrow \{\top, \bot\}$.*

A PKS represents a system as a set of states and transitions between these states. Uncertainty on the AP is represented through the value ?. The model in Fig. 1 is a PKS where propositions in AP are used to model actions and conditions. **LTL properties (②).** For KSs we consider the classical LTL semantics $[M \models \phi]$ over infinite words that associates to a model M and a formula ϕ a truth value in the set $\{\bot, \top\}$. The interested reader may refer, for example, to [3]. Let M be a KS and ϕ be an LTL property. We assume that the function CHECK, such that $\langle res, c \rangle = $ CHECK(M, ϕ), returns a tuple $\langle res, c \rangle$, where res is the model checking result in $\{\top, \bot\}$ and c is the counterexample if $res = \bot$, else an empty set.

The *three-valued LTL semantics* [9] $[M \models \phi]$ associates to a model M and a formula ϕ a truth value in the set $\{\bot, ?, \top\}$ and is defined based on the information ordering $\top > ? > \bot$. The three-valued LTL semantics is defined by considering paths of the model M. A path π is an infinite sequence of states $s_0, s_1, \ldots$ such that, for all $i \geq 0$, $(s_i, s_{i+1}) \in R$. We use the symbol π^i to indicate the infinite sub-sequence of π that starts at position i, and $Path(s)$ to indicate all the paths that start in the state s.

Definition 2 ([9]). *Let $M = \langle S, R, S_0, AP, L \rangle$ be a PKS, $\pi = s_0, s_1, \ldots$ be a path, and ϕ be an LTL formula. Then, the three-valued semantics $[(M, \pi) \models \phi]$ is defined inductively as follows:*

$$[(M, \pi) \models p] \quad = \quad L(s_0, p)$$
$$[(M, \pi) \models \neg\phi] \quad = \quad comp([(M, \pi) \models \phi])$$
$$[(M, \pi) \models \phi_1 \wedge \phi_2] \quad = \quad \min([(M, \pi) \models \phi_1], [(M, \pi) \models \phi_2])$$
$$[(M, \pi) \models \mathcal{X} \phi] \quad = \quad [(M, \pi^1) \models \phi]$$
$$[(M, \pi) \models \phi_1 \, \mathcal{U} \, \phi_2] \quad = \quad \max_{j \geq 0}(\min(\{[(M, \pi^i) \models \phi_1] | i < j\} \cup \{[(M, \pi^j) \models \phi_2]\}))$$

Let $M = \langle S, R, S_0, AP, L \rangle$ be a PKS, and ϕ be an LTL formula. Then $[M \models \phi] = \min(\{[(M, \pi) \models \phi] \mid \pi \in Path(s) \text{ and } s \in S_0\})$.

The conjunction (resp. disjunction) is defined as the minimum (resp. maximum) of its arguments, following the order $\bot < ? < \top$. These functions are extended to sets with $\min(\emptyset)=\top$ and $\max(\emptyset)=\bot$. The *comp* operator maps $\top$ to $\bot$, $\bot$ to $\top$, and ? to ?. The semantics of the $\mathcal{G}$ ("globally") and $\mathcal{W}$ ("weak until") operators is defined as usual [28].

Model Checking. Checking KSs with respect to LTL properties can be done by using classical model checking procedures. For example, the model checking problem of property ϕ on a KS M can be reduced to the satisfiability problem of the LTL formula $\Phi_M \wedge \neg\phi$, where Φ_M represents the behaviors of model M. If $\Phi_M \wedge \neg\phi$ is satisfiable, then $[M \models \phi] = \bot$, otherwise $[M \models \phi] = \top$.

Checking a PKS M with respect to an LTL property ϕ considering the three-valued semantics is done by performing twice the classical model checking procedure for KSs [10], one considering an optimistic approximation M_{opt} and one considering a pessimistic approximation M_{pes}. These two procedures consider the LTL formula $\phi' = \mathbf{F}(\phi)$, where $\mathbf{F}$ transforms ϕ with the following steps: (i) negate ϕ; (ii) convert $\neg\phi$ in negation normal form; (iii) replace every subformula $\neg\alpha$, where α is an atomic proposition, with a new proposition $\overline{\alpha}$.

To create the optimistic and pessimistic approximations M_{opt} and M_{pes}, the PKS $M = \langle S, R, S_0, AP, L \rangle$ is first converted into its *complement-closed* version $M_c = \langle S, R, S_0, AP_c, L_c \rangle$ where the set of atomic propositions $AP_c = AP \cup \overline{AP}$ is such that $\overline{AP} = \{\overline{\alpha} \mid \alpha \in AP\}$. Atomic propositions in $\overline{AP}$ are called complement-closed propositions. Function L_c is such that, for all $s \in S$ and $\alpha \in AP$, $L_c(s, \alpha) = L(s, \alpha)$ and, for all $s \in S$ and $\overline{\alpha} \in \overline{AP}$, $L_c(s, \overline{p}) = comp(L(s, p))$. The complement-closed PKS of the vacuum-cleaner agent in Fig. 1 presents eight propositional assignments in the state $IDLE$: $move = \bot$, $\overline{move} = \top$, $suck = \bot$, $\overline{suck} = \top$, $on = \top$, $\overline{on} = \bot$, $reached = ?$, and $\overline{reached} = ?$.

The two model checking runs for a PKS $M = \langle S, R, S_0, AP, L \rangle$ are based respectively on an optimistic ($M_{opt} = \langle S, R, S_0, AP_c, L_{opt} \rangle$) and a pessimistic ($M_{pes} = \langle S, R, S_0, AP_c, L_{pes} \rangle$) approximation of M's related complement-closed $M_c = \langle S, R, S_0, AP_c, L_c \rangle$. Function L_{pes} (resp. L_{opt}) is such that, for all $s \in S$, $\alpha \in AP_c$, and $L_c(s, \alpha) \in \{\top, \bot\}$, then $L_{pes}(s, \alpha) = L_c(s, \alpha)$ (resp. $L_{opt}(s, \alpha) = L_c(s, \alpha)$), and, for all $s \in S$, $\alpha \in AP_c$, and $L_c(s, \alpha) = ?$, then $L_{pes}(s, \alpha) = \bot$ (resp. $L_{opt}(s, \alpha) = \top$).

Let $\mathcal{A}$ be a KS and ϕ be an LTL formula, $\mathcal{A} \models^* \phi$ is true if no path that satisfies the formula $\mathbf{F}(\phi)$ is present in $\mathcal{A}$.

Theorem 1 ([9]). *Let ϕ be an LTL formula, let $M = \langle S, R, S_0, AP, L \rangle$ be a PKS, and let M_{pes} and M_{opt} be the pessimistic and optimistic approximations of M's relative complement-closed M_c. Then*

$$[M \models \phi] \stackrel{def}{=} \begin{cases} \top & \text{if } M_{pes} \models^* \phi \\ \bot & \text{if } M_{opt} \not\models^* \phi \\ ? & \text{otherwise} \end{cases} \tag{1}$$

We call CHECK* the function that computes the result of operator $\models^*$. It takes as input either M_{pes} or M_{opt} and the property $\mathbf{F}(\phi)$, and returns a tuple $\langle res, c \rangle$, where res is the model checking result in $\{\top, \bot\}$, and c can be an empty set (when M satisfies ϕ), a *definitive*-counterexample (**3**, when M violates ϕ), or a *possible*-counterexample (**5**, when M possibly-satisfies ϕ).

4   Revising models

We define how models can be revised and the notion of *topological proof*, that is used to describe why a property ϕ is (possibly) satisfied in a PKS M.

Initial design and revisions (1, 3). In the initial design a preliminary PKS is manually defined or automatically obtained from other modeling formalisms.

During a revision, a designer can add and remove states and transitions and/or change the labeling of the atomic propositions in the states of the PKS. Let $M = \langle S, R, S_0, AP, L \rangle$ and $M' = \langle S', R', S'_0, AP', L' \rangle$ be two PKSs. Then M' is a *revision* of M if and only if $AP \subseteq AP'$. Informally, the only constraint the designer has to respect during a revision is not to remove propositions from the set of atomic propositions. This condition is necessary to ensure that any property that can be evaluated on M can also be evaluated on M', i.e., every atomic proposition has a value in each of the states of the automaton. The deactivation of a proposition can instead be simulated by associating its value to $\perp$ in all the states of M'.

Topological proofs (4, 6). The pursued proof is made of a set of clauses specifying certain topological properties of M, which ensure that the property is (possibly) satisfied.

Definition 3. *Let $M = \langle S, R, S_0, AP, L \rangle$ be a PKS. A* Topological Proof clause *(TP-clause) γ for M is either:*

- *a* Topological Proof Propositional clause *(TPP-clause), i.e., a triad $\langle s, \alpha, v \rangle$ where $s \in S$, $\alpha \in AP$, and $v \in \{\top, ?, \perp\}$;*
- *a* Topological Proof Transitions-from-state clause *(TPT-clause), i.e., a pair $\langle s, T \rangle$, such that $s \in S, T \subseteq S$;*
- *a* Topological Proof Initial-states clause *(TPI-clause), i.e., an element $\langle S_0 \rangle$.*

These clauses indicate *topological properties* of a PKS M. Informally, TPP-clauses constrain how states are labeled (L), TPT-clauses constrain how states are connected (R), and TPI-clauses constrain from which states the runs on the model begin (S_0). For example, in Table 1, for property ϕ_1, $\langle CLEANING, reached, \top \rangle$ is a TPP-clause that constrains the atomic proposition *reached* to be labeled as true ($\top$) in the state $CLEANING$; $\langle OFF, \{OFF, IDLE\} \rangle$ is a TPT-clause that constrains the transition from OFF to OFF and from OFF to $IDLE$ to not be removed; and $\langle \{OFF\} \rangle$ is a TPI-clause that constrains the state OFF to remain the initial state of the system.

A state s' is constrained: by a TPP-clause $\langle s, \alpha, v \rangle$ if $s = s'$, by a TPT-clause $\langle s, T \rangle$ if $s = s'$ or $s' \in T$, and by a TPI-clause $\langle S_0 \rangle$ if $s' \in S_0$.

Definition 4. *Let $M = \langle S, R, S_0, AP, L \rangle$ be a PKS and let Ω be a set of TP-clauses for M. Then a PKS Ω-related to M is a PKS $M' = \langle S', R', S'_0, AP', L' \rangle$, such that the following conditions hold:*

- *$AP \subseteq AP'$;*
- *for every TPP-clause $\langle s, \alpha, v \rangle \in \Omega$, $s \in S'$, $v = L'(s, \alpha)$;*
- *for every TPT-clause $\langle s, T \rangle \in \Omega$, $s \in S'$, $T \subseteq S'$, $T = \{s' \in S' | (s, s') \in R'\}$;*
- *for every TPI-clause $\langle S_0 \rangle \in \Omega$, $S_0 = S'_0$.*

Intuitively, a PKS Ω-related to M is a PKS obtained from M by changing any topological aspect that does not impact on the set of TP-clauses Ω. Any transition whose source state is not the source state of a transition included in the TPT-clauses can be added or removed from the PKS and any value of a proposition that is not constrained by a TPP-clause can be changed. States can be always added and they can be removed if they are not constrained by any TPT-, TPP-, or TPI-clause. Initial states cannot be changed if Ω contains a TPI-clause.

Definition 5. *Let $M = \langle S, R, S_0, AP, L \rangle$ be a PKS, let ϕ be an LTL property, let Ω be a set of TP-clauses, and let x be a truth value in $\{\top, ?\}$. A set of TP-clauses Ω is an x-topological proof (or x-TP) for ϕ in M if: (i) $[M \models \phi] = x$; and (ii) every PKS M' Ω-related to M is such that $[M' \models \phi] \geq x$.*

Intuitively, an *x-topological proof* is a set of TP-clauses Ω such that every PKS M' that satisfies the conditions specified in Definition 4 is such that $[M' \models \phi] \geq x$. We call $\top$-TP a *definitive-topological proof* and ?-TP a *possible-topological proof*. In Definition 5, the operator $\geq$ assumes that values $\top, ?, \bot$ are ordered considering the classical information ordering $\top > ? > \bot$ among the truth values [9].

Regarding the PKS in Fig. 1, Table 1 shows two ?-TPs for properties ϕ_1 and ϕ_4, and one $\top$-TP for property ϕ_2.

Definition 6. *Let M and M' be two PKSs, let ϕ be an LTL property, and let Ω be an x-TP. Then M' is an Ω_x-revision of M if M' is Ω-related to M.*

Intuitively, since the Ω_x-*revision* M' of M is such that M' is Ω-related to M, it is obtained by changing the model M while preserving the statements that are specified in the x-TP. A revision M' of M is *compliant* with the x-TP for a property ϕ in M if it is an Ω_x-*revision* of M.

Theorem 2. *Let M be a PKS, let ϕ be an LTL property such that $[M \models \phi] = \top$, and let Ω be a $\top$-TP. Then every $\Omega_\top$-revision M' is such that $[M' \models \phi] = \top$. Let M be a PKS, let ϕ be an LTL property such that $[M \models \phi] = ?$, and let Ω be an ?-TP. Then every $\Omega_?$-revision M' is such that $[M' \models \phi] \in \{\top, ?\}$.*

Proof Sketch. We prove the first statement of the Theorem; the proof of the second statement is obtained by following the same steps.

If Ω is a $\top$-TP, it is a $\top$-TP for ϕ in M', since M' is an $\Omega_\top$-revision of M (by Definition 6). Furthermore, since Ω is a $\top$-TP for ϕ in M', then $[M' \models \phi] \geq \top$ (by Definition 5). □

5   TOrPEDO automated support

This section describes the algorithms that support the ANALYSIS and RE-CHECK phases of TOrPEDO.

ANALYSIS (2). To analyze a PKS $M = \langle S, R, S_0, AP, L \rangle$ (1), TOrPEDO uses the three-valued model checking framework based on Theorem 1. The model checking result is provided as output by the ANALYSIS phase of TOrPEDO, whose behavior is described in Algorithm 1.

```
1: function ANALYZE(M, φ)                 1: function CTP_KS(M, A, ψ)
2:   ⟨res, c⟩ = CHECK*(M_opt, φ)          2:   η(C_A ∪ {ψ}) = SYS2LTL(A, ψ)
3:   if res == ⊥ then return ⟨⊥, {c}⟩     3:   η(C'_A ∪ {ψ}) = GETUC(η(C_A ∪ {ψ}))
4:   else                                  4:   TP = GETTP(M, η(C'_A ∪ {ψ}))
5:     ⟨res', c'⟩ = CHECK*(M_pes, φ)       5:   return TP
6:     if res' == ⊤ then return            6: end function
7:       ⟨⊤, {CTP_KS(M, M_pes, F(φ))}⟩    Algorithm 2: Compute Topological Proofs.
8:     else
9:       return
10:      ⟨?, {c', CTP_KS(M, M_opt, F(φ))}⟩
11:    end if
12:  end if
13: end function
```
Algorithm 1: The ANALYSIS algorithm.

The algorithm returns a tuple $\langle x, y \rangle$, where x is the verification result and y is a set containing the counterexample, the topological proof or both of them. The algorithm first checks whether the optimistic approximation M_{opt} of the PKS M satisfies property ϕ (**2**, Line 2). If this is not the case, the property is violated by the PKS and the definitive-counterexample c (**3**, ⊥-CE) is returned (Line 3). Then, it checks whether the pessimistic approximation M_{pes} of the PKS M satisfies property ϕ (Line 5). If this is the case, the property is satisfied and the value ⊤ is returned along with the definitive-topological proof (**4**, ⊤-TP) computed by the CTP_KS procedure applied on the pessimistic approximation M_{pes} and the property $F(\phi)$ (Line 7).

If this is not the case, the property is possibly satisfied and the value ? is returned along with the possible-counterexample c' (**5**, ?-CE) and the possible-topological proof (**6**, ?-TP) computed by the CTP_KS procedure applied to M_{opt} and $F(\phi)$ (Line 10).

The procedure CTP_KS (Compute Topological Proofs) to compute x-TPs is described in Algorithm 2. It takes as input a PKS M, its optimistic/pessimistic approximation, i.e., denoted generically as the KS A, and an LTL formula ψ— satisfied in A— corresponding to the transformed property $F(\phi)$ (see Section 3). The three steps of the algorithm are described in the following.

SYS2LTL. *Encoding of the KS A and the LTL formula ψ into an LTL formula* $\eta(C_A \cup \{\psi\})$. The KS $A = \langle S, R, S_0, AP_c, L_A \rangle$ (where L_A is the optimistic or pessimistic function, L_{opt} or L_{pes}, as defined in Section 3) and the LTL formula ψ are used to generate an LTL formula

$$\eta(C_A \cup \{\psi\}) = \bigwedge_{c \in (C_A \cup \{\psi\})} c$$

Table 2: Rules to transform the KS in LTL formulae.

$c_i = \bigvee\limits_{s \in S_0} p(s)$
The KS is initially in one of its initial states.
$CR = \{\mathcal{G}(\neg p(s) \vee \mathcal{X}(\bigvee\limits_{(s,s') \in R} p(s'))) \mid s \in S\}$
If the KS is in state s in the current instant, in the next instant it is in one of the successors s' of s.
$CL_{\top,\mathcal{A}} = \{\mathcal{G}(\neg p(s) \vee \alpha) \mid s \in S, \alpha \in AP_c, L_\mathcal{A}(s,\alpha) = \top\}$
If the KS is in state s s.t. $L_\mathcal{A}(s,\alpha) = \top$, the atomic proposition α is true.
$CL_{\perp,\mathcal{A}} = \{\mathcal{G}(\neg p(s) \vee \neg\alpha) \mid s \in S, \alpha \in AP_c, L_\mathcal{A}(s,\alpha) = \perp\}$.
If the KS is in state s s.t. $L_\mathcal{A}(s,\alpha) = \perp$, the atomic proposition α is false.
$C_{REG} = \{\mathcal{G}(\neg p(s) \vee \neg p(s')) \mid s, s' \in S \text{ and } s \neq s'\}$
The KS is in at most one state at any time.

where $C_\mathcal{A}$ are sets of LTL clauses obtained from the KS $\mathcal{A}$.[4] The set of clauses that encodes the KS is $C_\mathcal{A} = C_{KS} \cup C_{REG}$, where $C_{KS} = \{c_i\} \cup CR \cup CL_{\top,\mathcal{A}} \cup CL_{\perp,\mathcal{A}}$ and c_i, CR, $CL_{\top,\mathcal{A}}$ and $CL_{\perp,\mathcal{A}}$ are defined as specified in Table 2. Note that the clauses in $C_\mathcal{A}$ are defined on the set of atomic propositions $AP_S = AP_c \cup \{p(s) \mid s \in S\}$, i.e., AP_S includes an additional atomic proposition $p(s)$ for each state s, which is true when the KS is in state s. The size of the encoding depends on the cardinality of $C_\mathcal{A}$ i.e., in the worst case, $1 + |S| + |S| \times |AP_c| + |S| \times |S|$.

GETUC. *Computation of the Unsatisfiable Core (UC)* $\eta(C'_\mathcal{A} \cup \{\psi\})$ *of* $\eta(C_\mathcal{A} \cup \{\psi\})$. Since the property ψ is satisfied on $\mathcal{A}$, $\eta(C_\mathcal{A} \cup \{\psi\})$ is unsatisfiable and the computation of its UC core is performed by using the PLTLMUP approach [58]. Let $C = \{\varphi_1, \varphi_2, \ldots, \varphi_n\}$ be a set of LTL formulae, such that $\eta(C) = \bigwedge\limits_{\varphi \in C} \varphi$ is unsatisfiable, then the function $\eta(C') = \text{GETUC}(\eta(C))$ returns an unsatisfiable core $\eta(C') = \bigwedge\limits_{\varphi \in C'} \varphi$ of $\bigwedge\limits_{\varphi \in C} \varphi$. In our case, since the property holds on the KS $\mathcal{A}$, $\text{GETUC}(\eta(C_\mathcal{A} \cup \{\psi\}))$ returns a subset of clauses $\eta(C'_\mathcal{A} \cup \{\psi\})$, where $C'_\mathcal{A} = C'_{KS} \cup C'_{REG}$ such that $C'_{KS} \subseteq C_{KS}$ and $C'_{REG} \subseteq C_{REG}$.

Lemma 1. *Let $\mathcal{A}$ be a KS and let ψ be an LTL property. Let also $\eta(C_\mathcal{A} \cup \{\psi\})$ be the LTL formula computed in the step SYS2LTL of the algorithm. Then, any unsatisfiable core $\eta(C'_\mathcal{A} \cup \{\psi\})$ of $\eta(C_\mathcal{A} \cup \{\psi\})$ is such that $C'_\mathcal{A} \subseteq C_\mathcal{A}$.*

Proof Sketch. As the property ϕ is satisfied by M, the LTL formula $\eta(C_\mathcal{A} \cup \{\psi\})$, where $\psi = \mathsf{F}(\phi)$ must be unsatisfiable as discussed in the Section 3. Indeed, $\mathsf{F}(\phi)$ simply perform some proposition renaming on the negation of the formula ψ. As $C_\mathcal{A}$ encodes a KS, $\bigwedge\limits_{c \in C_\mathcal{A}} c$ is satisfied. As such, the unsatisfiability is caused by the contradiction of some of the clauses in $C_\mathcal{A}$ and the property ψ, and as a consequence ψ must be a part of the UC.

GETTP. *Analysis of $C'_\mathcal{A}$ and extraction of the topological proof.* The set $C'_\mathcal{A}$, where $C'_\mathcal{A} = C'_{KS} \cup C'_{REG}$, contains clauses regarding the KS (C'_{KS} and C'_{REG})

---

[4] Note that this formula is equivalent to $\phi_M \wedge \neg\phi$ used in Section 3 as ϕ_M is generated by the clauses in $C_\mathcal{A}$ and $\neg\phi$ from ψ.

Table 3: Rules to extract the TP-clauses from the UC LTL formula.

LTL clause	TP clause	Type	LTL clause	TP clause	Type
$c_i = \bigvee\limits_{s \in S_0} p(s)$	$\langle S_0 \rangle$	TPI	$\mathcal{G}(\neg p(s) \vee \neg\alpha)$	$\langle s, \alpha, comp(L(s,\alpha)) \rangle$	TPP
$\mathcal{G}(\neg p(s) \vee$ $\mathcal{X}(\bigvee\limits_{(s,s') \in R} p(s')))$	$\langle s, T \rangle$ where $T = \{s' | (s,s') \in R\}$	TPT	$\mathcal{G}(\neg p(s) \vee \bar{\alpha})$	$\langle s, \alpha, comp(L(s,\alpha)) \rangle$	TPP
$\mathcal{G}(\neg p(s) \vee \alpha)$	$\langle s, \alpha, L(s,\alpha) \rangle$	TPP	$\mathcal{G}(\neg p(s) \vee \neg\bar{\alpha})$	$\langle s, \alpha, L(s,\alpha) \rangle$	TPP

and the property of interest (ψ) that made the formula $\eta(C'_A \cup \{\psi\})$ unsatisfiable. Since we are interested in clauses related to the KS that caused unsatisfiability, we extract the topological proof Ω, whose topological proof clauses are obtained from the clauses in C'_{KS} as specified in Table 3. Since the set of atomic propositions of A is $AP_c = AP \cup \overline{AP}$, in the table we use α for propositions in AP and $\bar{\alpha}$ for propositions in $\overline{AP}$.

The elements in C'_{REG} are not considered in the TP computation as, given an LTL clause $\mathcal{G}(\neg p(s) \vee \neg p(s'))$, either state s or s' is constrained by other TP-clauses that will be preserved in the model revisions.

Lemma 2. *Let A be a KS and let ψ be an LTL property. Let also $\eta(C_A \cup \{\psi\})$ be the LTL formula computed in the step SYS2LTL of the algorithm, where $C_A = C_{REG} \cup C_{KS}$, and let $\eta(C'_A \cup \{\psi\})$ be an unsatisfiable core, where $C'_A = C'_{REG} \cup C'_{KS}$. Then, if $\mathcal{G}(\neg p(s) \vee \neg p(s')) \in C'_{REG}$, either:*

(i) there exists an LTL clause in C'_{KS} that constrains state s (or state s'); or
(ii) $\eta(C''_A \cup \{\psi\})$, s.t. $C''_A = C'_A \setminus \{\mathcal{G}(\neg p(s) \vee \neg p(s'))\}$, is an UC of $\eta(C'_A \cup \{\psi\})$.

Proof Sketch. We indicate $\mathcal{G}(\neg p(s) \vee \neg p(s'))$ as $\tau(s, s')$. Assume per absurdum that conditions (i) and (ii) are violated, i.e., no LTL clause in C'_{KS} constrains state s or s' and $\eta(C''_A \cup \{\psi\})$ is not an unsatisfiable core of $\eta(C'_A \cup \{\psi\})$. Since $\eta(C''_A \cup \{\psi\})$ is not an unsatisfiable core of $\eta(C'_A \cup \{\psi\})$, $\eta(C''_A \cup \{\psi\})$ is satisfiable, as $C''_A \subset C'_A$. Since $\eta(C''_A \cup \{\psi\})$ is satisfiable, $\eta(C'_A \cup \{\psi\})$ s.t. $C'_A = C''_A \cup \{\tau(s, s')\}$ must also be satisfiable. Indeed, it does not exist any LTL clause that constrains state s (or state s') and, in order to generate a contradiction, the added LTL clause must generate it using the LTL clauses obtained from the LTL property ψ. This is a contradiction. Thus, conditions (i) and (ii) must be satisfied. □

The ANALYZE procedure in Algorithm 1 obtains a TP (■, ■) for a PKS by first computing the related optimistic or pessimistic approximation (i.e., a KS) and then exploiting the computation of the TP for such KS.

Theorem 3. *Let $M = \langle S, R, S_0, AP, L \rangle$ be a PKS, let ϕ be an LTL property, and let $x \in \{\top, ?\}$ be an element such that $[M \models \phi] = x$. If the procedure ANALYZE, applied to the PKS M and the LTL property ϕ, returns a TP Ω, this is an x-TP for ϕ in M.*

Proof Sketch. Assume that the ANALYZE procedure returns the value $\top$ and a $\top$-TP. We show that every Ω-related PKS M' is such that $[M' \models \phi] \geq x$

(Definition 5). If ANALYZE returns the value $\top$, it must be that $M_{pes} \models^* \phi$ by Lines 5 and 7 of Algorithm 1. Furthermore, by Line 7, $\psi = \mathbf{F}(\phi)$ and $\mathcal{A} = M_{pes}$.

Let $N = \langle S_N, R_N, S_{0,N}, AP_N, L_N \rangle$ be a PKS Ω-related to M. Let $\eta(C_{\mathcal{A}} \cup \{\psi\})$ be the LTL formula associated with $\mathcal{A}$ and ψ and let $\eta(C_{\mathcal{B}} \cup \{\psi\})$ be the LTL formula associated with $\mathcal{B} = N_{pes}$ and ψ. Let us consider an UC $\eta(C'_{\mathcal{A}} \cup \{\psi\})$ of $\eta(C_{\mathcal{A}} \cup \{\psi\})$, where $C'_{\mathcal{A}} = C'_{KS} \cup C'_{REG}$, $C'_{KS} \subseteq C_{KS}$ and $C'_{REG} \subseteq C_{REG}$. We show that $C'_{\mathcal{A}} \subseteq C_{\mathcal{B}}$, i.e., the UC is also an UC for the LTL formula associated with the approximation $\mathcal{B}$ of the PKS N.

- $C'_{\mathcal{A}} \subseteq C_{\mathcal{B}}$, i.e., $(C'_{KS} \cup C'_{REG}) \subseteq C_{\mathcal{B}}$. By Lemma 2 we can avoid considering C'_{REG}. By construction (see Line 2 of Algorithm 2) any clause $c \in C'_{KS}$ belongs to one rule among CR, $CL_{pes,\top}$, $CL_{pes,\bot}$ or $c = c_i$:
  - if $c = c_i$ then, by the rules in Table 3, there is a TPI-clause $\{S_0\} \in \Omega$. By Definition 4, $S_0 = S'_0$. Thus, $c_i \in C_{\mathcal{B}}$ since N is Ω-related to M.
  - if $c \in CR$ then, by rules in Table 3, there is a TPT-clause $\langle s, T \rangle \in \Omega$ where $s \in S$ and $T \subseteq R$. By Definition 4, $T = \{s' \in S' | (s, s') \in R'\}$. Thus, $c \in C_{\mathcal{B}}$ since N is Ω-related to M.
  - if $c \in CL_{\mathcal{A},\top}$ or $c \in CL_{\mathcal{A},\bot}$, by rules in Table 3, there is a TPP-clause $\langle s, \alpha, L(s, \alpha) \rangle \in \Omega$ where $s \in S$ and $\alpha \in AP$. By Definition 4, $L'(s, \alpha) = L(s, \alpha)$. Thus, $c \in C_{\mathcal{B}}$ since N is Ω-related to M.

Since N is Ω-related to M, it has preserved the elements of Ω. Thus $\eta(C'_{\mathcal{A}} \cup \{\psi\})$ is also an UC of $C_{\mathcal{B}}$. It follows that $[N \models \phi] = \top$.

The proof from the case in which ANALYZE procedure returns the value ? and a ?-TP can be derived from the first case. □

RE-CHECK (4). Let $M = \langle S, R, S_0, AP, L \rangle$ be a PKS. The RE-CHECK algorithm verifies whether a revision M' of M is an Ω-revision. Let Ω be an x-TP (10) for ϕ in M, and let $M' = \langle S', R', S'_0, AP', L' \rangle$ be a revision of M (8). The RE-CHECK algorithm returns $\texttt{true}$ if and only if the following holds:

- $AP \subseteq AP'$;
- for every TPP-clause $\langle s, \alpha, v \rangle \in \Omega$, $s \in S'$, $v = L'(s, \alpha)$;
- for every TPT-clause $\langle s, T \rangle \in \Omega$, $s \in S'$, $T \subseteq S'$, $T = \{s' \in S' | (s, s') \in R'\}$;
- for every TPI-clause $\langle S_0 \rangle \in \Omega$, $S_0 = S'_0$.

These conditions can be verified by a simple syntactic check on the PKS.

Lemma 3. *Let $M = \langle S, R, S_0, AP, L \rangle$ and $M' = \langle S', R', S'_0, AP', L' \rangle$ be two PKSs and let Ω be an x-TP. The RE-CHECK algorithm returns $\texttt{true}$ if and only if M' is Ω-related to M.*

Proof Sketch. Since M' is Ω-related to M, the conditions of Definition 4 hold. Each of these conditions is a condition of the RE-CHECK algorithm. Thus, if M' is Ω-related to M, the RE-CHECK returns $\texttt{true}$. Conversely, if RE-CHECK returns $\texttt{true}$, each condition of the algorithm is satisfied and, since each of these conditions corresponds to a condition of Definition 4, M' is Ω-related to M. □

This Lemma allows us to prove the following Theorem.

Table 4: Properties considered in the evaluation

ϕ_1:	$\mathcal{G}(\neg OFFHOOK) \vee (\neg OFFHOOK \;\mathcal{U}\; CONNECTED)$
ϕ_2:	$\neg OFFHOOK \;\mathcal{W}\; (\neg OFFHOOK \wedge CONNECTED)$
ϕ_3:	$\mathcal{G}(CONNECTED \rightarrow ACTIVE)$
ϕ_4:	$\mathcal{G}(OFFHOOK \wedge ACTIVE \wedge \neg CONNECTED \rightarrow \mathcal{X}(ACTIVE))$
ϕ_5	$\mathcal{G}(CONNECTED \rightarrow \mathcal{X}(ACTIVE))$
ψ_1:	$\mathcal{G}(CONNECTED \rightarrow ACTIVE)$
ψ_2:	$\mathcal{G}(CONNECTED \rightarrow \mathcal{X}(ACTIVE))$
ψ_3:	$\mathcal{G}(CONNECTED) \vee (CONNECTED \;\mathcal{U}\; \neg OFFHOOK)$
ψ_4:	$\neg CONNECTED \;\mathcal{W}\; (\neg CONNECTED \wedge OFFHOOK)$
ψ_5:	$\mathcal{G}(CALLEE\_SEL \rightarrow OFFHOOK)$
η_1:	$\mathcal{G}((OFFHOOK \wedge CONNECTED) \rightarrow \mathcal{X}(OFFHOOK \vee \neg CONNECTED))$
η_2:	$\mathcal{G}(CONNECTED) \vee (CONNECTED \;\mathcal{W}\; \neg OFFHOOK)$
η_3:	$\neg CONNECTED \;\mathcal{W}\; (\neg CONNECTED \wedge OFFHOOK)$
η_4:	$\mathcal{G}(CALLEE\_FREE \vee LINE\_SEL)$
η_5:	$\mathcal{G}(\mathcal{X}(OFFHOOK) \wedge \neg CONNECTED)$

Theorem 4. *Let M be a PKS, let ϕ be a property, let Ω be an x-TP for ϕ in M where $x \in \{\top, ?\}$, and let M' be a revision of M. The RE-CHECK algorithm returns **true** if and only if M' is an Ω-revision of M.*

Proof Sketch. By applying Lemma 3, the RE-CHECK algorithm returns **true** if and only if M' is Ω-related to M. By Definition 6, since Ω is an x-TP, the RE-CHECK algorithm returns **true** if and only if M' is an Ω-revision of M. □

The ANALYSIS and RE-CHECK algorithms assume that the three-valued LTL semantics is considered. While the thorough LTL semantics [10] has been shown to provide an evaluation of formulae that better reflects the natural intuition, the two semantics coincide in the case of self-minimizing LTL formulae. In this case, our results are correct also w.r.t. the thorough semantics. Note that, as shown in [24], most practically useful LTL formulae are self-minimizing. Future work will consider how to extend the ANALYSIS and RE-CHECK to completely support the thorough LTL semantics.

6   Evaluation

We implemented TOrPEDO as a Scala stand alone application and made it available online [62]. We evaluated how the ANALYSIS helps in creating models revisions and how frequently running the RE-CHECK algorithm allows the user to avoid the re-execution of the ANALYSIS algorithm from scratch.

We considered a set of example PKSs proposed in the literature to evaluate the χ*Chek* [20] model checker and defined a set of properties (see Table 4) inspired by the original properties and based on the LTL property patterns [18].[5] **ANALYSIS support (2).** We checked how the size of the proofs compares w.r.t. the size of the original models. Intuitively, since the proofs represent constraints

---

[5] The original properties used in the examples were specified in Computation Tree Logic (CTL), which is currently not supported by TOrPEDO.

Table 5: Cardinalities $|S|$, $|R|$, $|AP|$, $|?|$, and $|M|$ are those of the evaluated model M. $|\Omega_p|_x$ is the size of proof Ω_p for a property p; x indicates if Ω_p is a $\top$-TP or a ?-TP.

Model	$\|S\|$	$\|R\|$	$\|AP\|$	$\|?\|$	$\|M\|$	$\|\Omega_{\phi_1}\|$	$\|\Omega_{\phi_2}\|$	$\|\Omega_{\phi_3}\|$	$\|\Omega_{\phi_4}\|$	$\|\Omega_{\phi_5}\|$	ϕ_1	ϕ_2	ϕ_3	ϕ_4	ϕ_5
					ANALYSIS						RE-CHECK				
callee-1	5	15	3	7	31	$7_?$	$9_?$	$21_?$	$23_?$	$23_?$	-	-	-	-	-
callee-2	5	15	3	4	31	$7_?$	$9_?$	$21_?$	$22_\top$	×	✓	✓	✓	✓	✗
callee-3	5	15	3	2	31	$7_?$	$9_?$	$21_?$	$23_\top$	×	✓	✓	✓	✓	-
callee-4	5	15	3	0	31	×	×	$23_\top$	$21_\top$	×	✗	✗	✓	✓	-

Model	$\|S\|$	$\|R\|$	$\|AP\|$	$\|?\|$	$\|M\|$	$\|\Omega_{\psi_1}\|$	$\|\Omega_{\psi_2}\|$	$\|\Omega_{\psi_3}\|$	$\|\Omega_{\psi_4}\|$	$\|\Omega_{\psi_5}\|$	ψ_1	ψ_2	ψ_3	ψ_4	ψ_5
caller-1	6	21	5	4	52	$28_?$	×	$2_\top$	$9_?$	$28_?$	-	-	-	-	-
caller-2	7	22	5	4	58	$30_?$	×	$2_\top$	$9_?$	$30_?$	✓	-	✓	✓	✓
caller-3	6	19	5	1	50	$26_\top$	$28_\top$	$2_\top$	$11_\top$	$26_\top$	✓	-	✓	✓	✓
caller-4	6	21	5	0	52	$28_\top$	×	$2_\top$	$9_\top$	$28_\top$	✓	✗	✓	✓	✓

Model	$\|S\|$	$\|R\|$	$\|AP\|$	$\|?\|$	$\|M\|$	$\|\Omega_{\eta_1}\|$	$\|\Omega_{\eta_2}\|$	$\|\Omega_{\eta_3}\|$	$\|\Omega_{\eta_4}\|$	$\|\Omega_{\eta_5}\|$	η_1	η_2	η_3	η_4	η_5
caller-callee-1	6	30	6	30	61	$37_?$	$2_\top$	$15_?$	$37_?$	×	-	-	-	-	-
caller-callee-2	7	35	6	36	78	$43_?$	$2_\top$	$18_?$	$43_?$	×	✓	✓	✓	✓	-
caller-callee-3	7	45	6	38	88	$53_?$	$2_\top$	$53_?$	$53_?$	$53_?$	✓	✓	✓	✓	-
caller-callee-4	6	12	4	0	42	×	×	×	$19_\top$	×	✗	✗	✗	✓	✗

that, if satisfied, ensure that the property is not violated (or possible violated), the smaller are the proofs the more flexibility the designer has, as more elements can be changed during the revision. The size of a PKS $M = \langle S, R, S_0, AP, L \rangle$ was defined as $|M| = |AP| * |S| + |R| + |S_0|$. The size of a proof Ω was defined as $|\Omega| = \sum_{c \in \Omega} |c|$ where: $|c| = 1$ if $c = \langle s, \alpha, v \rangle$; $|c| = |T|$ if $c = \langle s, T \rangle$, and $|c| = |S_0|$ if $c = \langle S_0 \rangle$. Table 5 summarizes the obtained results (columns under the label ANALYSIS). We show the cardinalities $|S|$, $|R|$ and $|AP|$ of the sets of states, transitions, and atomic propositions of each considered PKS M, the number $|?|$ of couples of a state s with an atomic proposition α such that $L(s, \alpha) = ?$, the total size $|M|$ of the model, and the size $|\Omega_p|_x$ of the proofs, where p indicates the considered LTL property and x indicates whether p is satisfied ($x = \top$) or possibly satisfied ($x = ?$). Proofs are $\approx 60\%$ smaller than their respective initial models. Thus, we conclude that the proofs are significantly coincise w.r.t. the original model enabling a flexible design.

RE-CHECK support (❸). We checked how the results output by the RE-CHECK algorithm were useful in producing PKSs revisions. To evaluate the usefulness we assumed that, for each category of examples, the designer produced revisions following the order specified in Table 5. The columns under the label RE-CHECK contain the different properties that have been analyzed for each category. A cell contains ✓ if the RE-CHECK was passed by the considered revised model, i.e., a **true** value was returned by the RE-CHECK algorithm, ✗ otherwise. The *dash* symbol - is used when the model of the corresponding line is not a revision (i.e., the first model of each category) or when the observed property was false in the previous model, i.e., an x-TP was not produced. We inspected the results produced by the RE-CHECK algorithm to evaluate their benefit in verifying if revisions were violating the proofs. Table 5 shows that, in $\approx 32\%$ of the cases, the TOrPEDO RE-CHECK notified the designer that the proposed revision violated some of the clauses contained in the Ω-proof, while in $\approx 78\%$ the RE-CHECK allowed designers to avoid re-runnning the ANALYSIS (and thus the model checker).

Scalability. The ANALYSIS phase of TOrPEDO combines three-valued model checking and UCs computation, therefore its scalability improves as the performance of frameworks enhances. Three-valued model checking is as expensive as classical model checking [9], i.e., it is linear in the size of the model and exponential in the size of the property. UCs computation is FPSPACE complete [55]. In our cases running TOrPEDO required on average 8.1s and for the callee examples, 8.2s for the caller examples, and 7.15s for the caller-callee examples.[6] However, while model checking is currently supported by very efficient techniques, UCs computation of LTL formulae is still far from being applicable in complex scenarios. For example, we manually designed an additional PKS with 10 states and 5 atomic propositions and 26 transitions and defined a property satisfied by the PKS and with a T-TP proof that requires every state of the PKS to be constrained by a TPP-clause. We run TOrPEDO and measure the time required to compute this proof. Computing the proof required 1m33s. This results show that TOrPEDO has a limited scalability due to the low efficiency of the procedure that extracts the unsatisfiable core. For an analysis of the scalability of the extraction of the unsatisfiable core the interested reader can refer to [58]. We believe that reporting the current lack of FM techniques to support the proposed framework (that, as just discussed, is effective in our preliminary evaluation), is a further contribution of this paper.

7 Related work

Partial knowledge has been considered in requirement analysis and elicitation [46,45,38,13], in novel robotic planners [40,41,43], software models [66,65,22,1], and testing [15,63,67]. Several researchers analyzed the model checking problem for partially specified systems [44,12], considering both three-valued [37,25,9,10,28] and multi-valued [30,11] semantics. Other works apply model checking to incremental program development [33,6]. However, all these model checking approaches do not provide an *explanation* on why a property is satisfied, by means of a *certificate* or *proof*. Although several works have tackled this problem [4,60,50,49,29,16], differently from this work, they mostly aim to automate proof reproducibility.

Tao and Li [61] propose a theoretical solution to model repair: the problem of finding the minimum set of states in a KS which makes a formula satisfiable. However, the problem is different from the one addressed in this paper. Furthermore, the framework is only theoretical and based on complete systems.

Approaches were proposed in the literature to provide explanations by using different artifacts. For example, some works proposed using witnesses. A witness

---

[6] Processor: 2,7 GHz Quad-Core Intel Core i7, Memory: 16 GB 2133 MHz LPDDR3.

is a path of the model that satisfies a formula of interest [7,34,48]. Other works (e.g., [31,59]) studied how to enrich counterexamples with additional information in a way that allows better understanding the property violation. Work has also been done to generate abstractions of the counterexamples that are easier to understand (e.g., [21]). Alur et al. [2] analyzed the problem of synthesizing a controller that satisfies a given specification. When the specification is not realizable, a counter-strategy is returned as a witness. Pencolé et al. [51] analyzed model consistency, i.e., the problem of checking whether the system run-time behaviour is consistent with a formal specification. Bernasconi et al. [4] proposed an approach that combines model checking and deductive proofs in a multi-valued context. The notion of topological proof proposed in this work is substantially different from the notion of deductive proof.

Some works (e.g., [52,54]) considered how to understand why a property is unsatisfiable. This problem is different from the one considered in this paper.

Approaches that detect unsatisfiable cores of propositional formulae were proposed in the literature [47,39,17,32,57]. Understanding whether these approaches can be re-used to develop more efficient techniques to detect the unsatisfiable cores of LTL formulae is definitely an interesting future work direction, which deserves to be considered in a separate work since it is far from trivial.

8   Conclusions

We have proposed TOrPEDO, an integrated framework that supports the iterative creation of model revisions. The framework provides a guide for the designer who wishes to preserve slices of her model that contribute to satisfy fundamental requirements while other parts of the model are modified. For these purposes, the notion of topological proof has been formally and algorithmically described. This corresponds to a set of constraints that, if kept when changing the proposed model, ensure that the behavior of the model w.r.t. the property of interest is preserved. Our Lemmas and Theorems prove the soundness of our framework, i.e., how it preserves correctness in the case of PKS and LTL. The proposed framework can be used as baseline for other FM frameworks, and can be extended by considering other modeling formalisms that can be mapped onto PKSs.

TOrPEDO was evaluated by showing the effectiveness of the ANALYSIS and RE-CHECK algorithms included in the framework. Results showed that proofs are smaller than the original models, and can be verified in most of the cases using a simple syntactic check, paving the way for an extensive evaluation on real case scenarios. However, the scalability of existing tools, upon which TOrPEDO is based, is not sufficient to efficiently support the proposed framework when bigger models are considered.

Acknowledgments. This work has received funding from the European Research Council under the European Union's Horizon 2020 research and innovation programme (grant agreement No 694277).

References

1. A. Albarghouthi, A. Gurfinkel, and M. Chechik. From under-approximations to over-approximations and back. In *International Conference on Tools and Algorithms for the Construction and Analysis of Systems*. Springer, 2012.
2. R. Alur, S. Moarref, and U. Topcu. Counter-strategy guided refinement of GR(1) temporal logic specifications. In *Formal Methods in Computer-Aided Design*, pages 26–33, Oct 2013.
3. C. Baier and J.-P. Katoen. *Principles of Model Checking*. The MIT Press, 2008.
4. A. Bernasconi, C. Menghi, P. Spoletini, L. D. Zuck, and C. Ghezzi. From model checking to a temporal proof for partial models. In *International Conference on Software Engineering and Formal Methods*. Springer, 2017.
5. A. Bernasconi, C. Menghi, P. Spoletini, L. D. Zuck, and C. Ghezzi. From model checking to a temporal proof for partial models: preliminary example. *arXiv preprint arXiv:1706.02701*, 2017.
6. D. Beyer, T. A. Henzinger, R. Jhala, and R. Majumdar. The software model checker blast. *International Journal on Software Tools for Technology Transfer*, 9(5-6):505–525, 2007.
7. A. Biere, A. Cimatti, E. M. Clarke, M. Fujita, and Y. Zhu. Symbolic model checking using sat procedures instead of bdds. In *Design Automation Conference*. ACM, 1999.
8. G. Brunet, M. Chechik, S. Easterbrook, S. Nejati, N. Niu, and M. Sabetzadeh. A manifesto for model merging. In *International workshop on Global integrated model management*. ACM, 2006.
9. G. Bruns and P. Godefroid. Model checking partial state spaces with 3-valued temporal logics. In *International Conference on Computer Aided Verification*. Springer, 1999.
10. G. Bruns and P. Godefroid. Generalized model checking: Reasoning about partial state spaces. In *International Conference on Concurrency Theory*. Springer, 2000.
11. G. Bruns and P. Godefroid. Model checking with multi-valued logics. In *International Colloquium on Automata, Languages and Programming*. Springer, 2004.
12. M. Chechik, B. Devereux, S. Easterbrook, and A. Gurfinkel. Multi-valued symbolic model-checking. *Transactions on Software Engineering and Methodology*, 12(4):1–38, 2004.
13. M. Chechik, R. Salay, T. Viger, S. Kokaly, and M. Rahimi. Software assurance in an uncertain world. In R. Hähnle and W. van der Aalst, editors, *Fundamental Approaches to Software Engineering*, pages 3–21, Cham, 2019. Springer.
14. A. Cimatti, E. Clarke, E. Giunchiglia, F. Giunchiglia, M. Pistore, M. Roveri, R. Sebastiani, and A. Tacchella. Nusmv 2: An opensource tool for symbolic model checking. In *International Conference on Computer Aided Verification*. Springer, 2002.
15. P. Daca, T. A. Henzinger, W. Krenn, and D. Nickovic. Compositional specifications for ioco testing. In *International Conference on Software Testing, Verification and Validation*, pages 373–382. IEEE, 2014.
16. C. Deng and K. S. Namjoshi. Witnessing network transformations. In *International Conference on Runtime Verification*. Springer, 2017.
17. N. Dershowitz, Z. Hanna, and A. Nadel. A scalable algorithm for minimal unsatisfiable core extraction. In *International Conference on Theory and Applications of Satisfiability Testing*, pages 36–41. Springer, 2006.

18. M. B. Dwyer, G. S. Avrunin, and J. C. Corbett. Patterns in property specifications for finite-state verification. In *International Conference on Software engineering*. ACM, 1999.

19. S. Easterbrook and M. Chechik. A framework for multi-valued reasoning over inconsistent viewpoints. In *International conference on software engineering*. IEEE, 2001.

20. S. Easterbrook, M. Chechik, B. Devereux, A. Gurfinkel, A. Lai, V. Petrovykh, A. Tafliovich, and C. Thompson-Walsh. χChek: A model checker for multi-valued reasoning. In *International Conference on Software Engineering*, pages 804–805, 2003.

21. N. Een, A. Mishchenko, and N. Amla. A single-instance incremental SAT formulation of proof- and counterexample-based abstraction. In *Conference on Formal Methods in Computer-Aided Design*, FMCAD, pages 181–188. FMCAD Inc, 2010.

22. M. Famelis, R. Salay, and M. Chechik. Partial models: Towards modeling and reasoning with uncertainty. In *International Conference on Software Engineering*. IEEE, 2012.

23. H. Foster, S. Uchitel, J. Magee, and J. Kramer. Ltsa-ws: a tool for model-based verification of web service compositions and choreography. In *International conference on Software engineering*. ACM, 2006.

24. P. Godefroid and M. Huth. Model checking vs. generalized model checking: Semantic minimizations for temporal logics. In *Logic in Computer Science*. IEEE, 2005.

25. P. Godefroid, M. Huth, and R. Jagadeesan. Abstraction-based model checking using modal transition systems. In *International Conference on Concurrency Theory*. Springer, 2001.

26. P. Godefroid and R. Jagadeesan. On the expressiveness of 3-valued models. In *International Workshop on Verification, Model Checking, and Abstract Interpretation*. Springer, 2003.

27. P. Godefroid and N. Piterman. LTL generalized model checking revisited. In *Verification, Model Checking, and Abstract Interpretation*, pages 89–104. Springer, 2009.

28. P. Godefroid and N. Piterman. LTL generalized model checking revisited. *International journal on software tools for technology transfer*, 13(6):571–584, 2011.

29. A. Griggio, M. Roveri, and S. Tonetta. Certifying proofs for LTL model checking. In *Formal Methods in Computer Aided Design (FMCAD)*, pages 1–9. IEEE, 2018.

30. A. Gurfinkel and M. Chechik. Multi-valued model checking via classical model checking. In *International Conference on Concurrency Theory*. Springer, 2003.

31. A. Gurfinkel and M. Chechik. Proof-like counter-examples. In *International Conference on Tools and Algorithms for the Construction and Analysis of Systems*, pages 160–175. Springer, 2003.

32. O. Guthmann, O. Strichman, and A. Trostanetski. Minimal unsatisfiable core extraction for SMT. In *Formal Methods in Computer-Aided Design (FMCAD)*, pages 57–64. IEEE, 2016.

33. T. A. Henzinger, R. Jhala, R. Majumdar, and M. A. Sanvido. Extreme model checking. In *Verification: Theory and Practice, Essays Dedicated to Zohar Manna on the Occasion of His 64th Birthday*. Springer, 2003.

34. H. S. Hong, I. Lee, O. Sokolsky, and H. Ural. A temporal logic based theory of test coverage and generation. In *International Conference on Tools and Algorithms for the Construction and Analysis of Systems*. Springer, 2002.

35. S. A. Kripke. Semantical considerations on modal logic. *Acta Philosophica Fennica*, 16(1963):83–94, 1963.

36. O. Kupferman and M. Y. Vardi. From complementation to certification. *Theoretical computer science*, 345(1):83–100, 2005.
37. K. G. Larsen and B. Thomsen. A modal process logic. In *Logic in Computer Science*. IEEE, 1988.
38. E. Letier, J. Kramer, J. Magee, and S. Uchitel. Deriving event-based transition systems from goal-oriented requirements models. *Automated Software Engineering*, 2008.
39. M. H. Liffiton and K. A. Sakallah. Algorithms for computing minimal unsatisfiable subsets of constraints. *Journal of Automated Reasoning*, 40(1):1–33, 2008.
40. C. Menghi, S. Garcia, P. Pelliccione, and J. Tumova. Multi-robot LTL planning under uncertainty. In *Formal Methods*. Springer, 2018.
41. C. Menghi, S. García, P. Pelliccione, and J. Tumova. Towards multi-robot applications planning under uncertainty. In *International Conference on Software Engineering: Companion Proceeedings*. ACM, 2018.
42. C. Menghi, P. Spoletini, M. Chechik, and C. Ghezzi. Supporting verification-driven incremental distributed design of components. In *Fundamental Approaches to Software Engineering*. Springer, 2018.
43. C. Menghi, P. Spoletini, M. Chechik, and C. Ghezzi. A verification-driven framework for iterative design of controllers. *Formal Aspects of Computing*, Jun 2019.
44. C. Menghi, P. Spoletini, and C. Ghezzi. Dealing with incompleteness in automata-based model checking. In *Formal Methods*. Springer, 2016.
45. C. Menghi, P. Spoletini, and C. Ghezzi. COVER: Change-based Goal Verifier and Reasoner. In *International Conference on Requirements Engineering: Foundation for Software Quality: Companion Proceeedings*. Springer, 2017.
46. C. Menghi, P. Spoletini, and C. Ghezzi. Integrating goal model analysis with iterative design. In *International Working Conference on Requirements Engineering: Foundation for Software Quality*. Springer, 2017.
47. A. Nadel. Boosting minimal unsatisfiable core extraction. In *Conference on Formal Methods in Computer-Aided Design*, pages 221–229. FMCAD Inc, 2010.
48. K. S. Namjoshi. Certifying model checkers. In *Computer Aided Verification*. Springer, 2001.
49. D. Peled, A. Pnueli, and L. Zuck. From falsification to verification. In *Foundations of Software Technology and Theoretical Computer Science*. Springer, 2001.
50. D. Peled and L. Zuck. From model checking to a temporal proof. In *International SPIN Workshop on Model Checking of Software*. Springer, 2001.
51. Y. Pencolé, G. Steinbauer, C. Mühlbacher, and L. Travé-Massuyès. Diagnosing discrete event systems using nominal models only. In *DX*, pages 169–183, 2017.
52. I. Pill and T. Quaritsch. Behavioral diagnosis of LTL specifications at operator level. In *Twenty-Third International Joint Conference on Artificial Intelligence*, 2013.
53. S. Rajan, N. Shankar, and M. K. Srivas. An integration of model checking with automated proof checking. In *Computer Aided Verification*. Springer, 1995.
54. V. Raman, C. Lignos, C. Finucane, K. C. Lee, M. P. Marcus, and H. Kress-Gazit. Sorry Dave, I'm Afraid I Can't Do That: Explaining Unachievable Robot Tasks Using Natural Language. In *Robotics: Science and Systems*, volume 2, pages 2–1, 2013.
55. L. Sais, M. Hacid, and F. Hantry. On the complexity of computing minimal unsatisfiable LTL formulas. *Electronic Colloquium on Computational Complexity (ECCC)*, 19:69, 2012.

56. V. Schuppan. Enhancing unsatisfiable cores for LTL with information on temporal relevance. *Theoretical Computer Science*, 655(Part B):155 – 192, 2016. Quantitative Aspects of Programming Languages and Systems (2013-14).

57. V. Schuppan. Enhanced unsatisfiable cores for QBF: Weakening universal to existential quantifiers. In *International Conference on Tools with Artificial Intelligence (ICTAI)*, pages 81–89. IEEE, 2018.

58. T. Sergeant, S. R. Goré, and J. Thomson. Finding minimal unsatisfiable subsets in linear temporal logic using BDDs, 2013.

59. S. Shoham and O. Grumberg. A game-based framework for ctl counterexamples and 3-valued abstraction-refinement. In *International Conference on Computer Aided Verification*, pages 275–287. Springer, 2003.

60. L. Tan and R. Cleaveland. Evidence-based model checking. In *International Conference on Computer Aided Verification*, pages 455–470. Springer, 2002.

61. X. Tao and G. Li. The complexity of linear-time temporal logic model repair. In *International Workshop on Structured Object-Oriented Formal Language and Method*, pages 69–87. Springer, 2017.

62. Torpedo. http://github.com/alessandrorizzi/torpedo, 2020.

63. J. Tretmans. Testing concurrent systems: A formal approach. In *International Conference on Concurrency Theory*, pages 46–65. Springer, 1999.

64. S. Uchitel. Partial behaviour modelling: Foundations for incremental and iterative model-based software engineering. In M. V. M. Oliveira and J. Woodcock, editors, *Formal Methods: Foundations and Applications*. Springer, 2009.

65. S. Uchitel, D. Alrajeh, S. Ben-David, V. Braberman, M. Chechik, G. De Caso, N. D'Ippolito, D. Fischbein, D. Garbervetsky, J. Kramer, et al. Supporting incremental behaviour model elaboration. *Computer Science-Research and Development*, 28(4):279–293, 2013.

66. S. Uchitel, G. Brunet, and M. Chechik. Synthesis of partial behavior models from properties and scenarios. *Transactions on Software Engineering*, 35(3):384–406, 2009.

67. M. van der Bijl, A. Rensink, and J. Tretmans. Compositional testing with ioco. In *Formal Approaches to Software Testing*, pages 86–100. Springer, 2004.

A Generalized Formal Semantic Framework for Smart Contracts

Jiao Jiao[1] (✉), Shang-Wei Lin[1], and Jun Sun[2]

[1] Nanyang Technological University, Singapore
{jiao0023,shang-wei.lin}@ntu.edu.sg
[2] Singapore Management University, Singapore
{junsun}@smu.edu.sg

Abstract. Smart contracts can be regarded as one of the most popular blockchain-based applications. The decentralized nature of the blockchain introduces vulnerabilities absent in other programs. Furthermore, it is very difficult, if not impossible, to patch a smart contract after it has been deployed. Therefore, smart contracts must be formally verified before they are deployed on the blockchain to avoid attacks exploiting these vulnerabilities. There is a recent surge of interest in analyzing and verifying smart contracts. While most of the existing works either focus on EVM bytecode or translate Solidity contracts into programs in intermediate languages for analysis and verification, we believe that a direct executable formal semantics of the high-level programming language of smart contracts is necessary to guarantee the validity of the verification. In this work, we propose a generalized formal semantic framework based on a general semantic model of smart contracts. Furthermore, this framework can directly handle smart contracts written in different high-level programming languages through semantic extensions and facilitates the formal verification of security properties with the generated semantics.

Keywords: Blockchain · Smart contracts · Generalized semantics

1 Introduction

Blockchain [17] technologies have been studied extensively recently. Smart contracts [16] can be regarded as one of the most popular blockchain-based applications. Due to the very nature of the blockchain, credible and traceable transactions are allowed through smart contracts without relying on an external trusted authority to achieve consensus. However, the unique features of the blockchain introduce vulnerabilities [10] absent in other programs.

Smart contracts must be verified for multiple reasons. Firstly, due to the decentralized nature of the blockchain, smart contracts are different from programs written in other programming languages (e.g., C/Java). For instance, the storage of each contract instance is at a permanent address on the blockchain. In this way, each instance is a particular execution context and context switches are possible through external calls. Particularly, in Solidity, `delegatecall` executes

H. Wehrheim and J. Cabot (Eds.): FASE 2020, LNCS 12076, pp. 75–96, 2020.
https://doi.org/10.1007/978-3-030-45234-6_4

programs in the context of the caller rather than the recipient, making it possible to modify the state of the caller. Programmers must be aware of the execution context of each statement to guarantee the programming correctness. Therefore, programming smart contracts is error-prone without a proper understanding of the underlying semantic model. Secondly, a smart contract can be deployed on the blockchain by any user in the network. Vulnerabilities in deployed contracts can be exploited to launch attacks that lead to huge financial loss. Verifying smart contracts against such vulnerabilities is crucial for protecting digital assets. One famous attack on smart contracts is the DAO attack [41] in which the attacker exploited the reentrancy vulnerability and managed to take 60 million dollars under his control. Thirdly, it is very difficult, if not impossible, to patch a smart contract once it is deployed due to the very nature of the blockchain.

Related Works. There is a surge of interest in analyzing and verifying smart contracts [32,12,24,28,26,9,25,31,21,44,20,22,38,36,4,34,43,19,30,35,29,23,46,14]. Some of the existing works focus on EVM [2,47] (Ethereum Virtual Machine). For instance, a symbolic execution engine called Oyente is proposed in [32] to analyze Solidity smart contracts by translating them into EVM bytecode. In addition, a complete formal executable semantics of EVM [24] is developed in the K-framework to facilitate the formal verification of smart contracts at bytecode level. A set of test oracles is defined in [26,45] to detect security vulnerabilities on EVM bytecode. In [21], a semantic framework is proposed to analyze smart contracts at EVM level. Securify [44] translates EVM bytecode into a stackless representation in static-single assignment form for analyzing smart contracts. In other works, Solidity smart contracts are translated into programs in intermediate languages for analysis and verification. Specifically speaking, Solidity programs are formalized with an abstract language and then translated into LLVM bitcode in Zeus [28]. Similarly, Boogie is used to verify smart contracts as an intermediate language in the proposed verifiers in [31,23]. In addition, the formalization in F* [12] is an intermediate-level language for the equivalence checking of Solidity programs and EVM bytecode. In [22], a simple imperative object-based programming language, called SMAC, is used to facilitate the on-line detection of Effectively Callback Free (ECF) objects in smart contracts. To conclude, most of the existing approaches either focus on EVM bytecode, or translate Solidity smart contracts into programs in intermediate languages that are suitable for verifying smart contracts or detecting potential issues in associated verifiers or checkers. Furthermore, none of the existing works can directly handle smart contracts written in different high-level programming languages without translating them into EVM bytecode or intermediate languages.

Motivations. A direct executable formal semantics of the high-level smart contract programming language is a must for both understanding and verifying smart contracts. Firstly, programmers write and reason about smart contracts at the level of source code without the semantics of which they are required to understand how Solidity programs are compiled into EVM bytecode in order to understand these contracts, which is far from trivial. In addition, there may be semantic gaps between high-level smart contract programming languages and low-level bytecode. Therefore, both high-level [27,48,49,15,11] and low-level [24,21] semantics definitions are necessary to conduct equivalence checking to guarantee that security properties are preserved at both levels and reason about compiler bugs. Secondly, even though smart contracts can be transformed into programs in intermediate languages to be analyzed and verified in existing model checkers and verifiers, the equivalence checking of the high-level smart contract programming language and the intermediate language considered is crucial to the validity of the verification. For instance, most of the false positives reported in Zeus [28] are caused by the semantic inconsistency of the abstract language and Solidity.

As domain-specific languages, high-level smart contract programming languages, such as Solidity, Vyper, Bamboo, etc, intend to implement the correct or desired semantics of smart contracts although they may not actually achieve this. This means that these languages are semantically similar in order to interpret the same high-level semantics of smart contracts. For instance, Vyper is quite similar to Solidity in spite of syntax differences and the semantics interpreted by Bamboo is consistent with that of Solidity (cf. Section 2.1 for details). Considering this fact, we propose a generalized formal semantic framework based on a general semantic model of smart contracts. Different from previous works which either analyze and verify smart contracts on EVM semantics or interpret Solidity semantics with the semantics of intermediate languages, the proposed framework aims to generate a direct executable formal semantics of a particular high-level smart contract programming language to facilitate the high-level verification of contracts and reason about compiler bugs. Furthermore, this framework provides a uniform formal specification of smart contracts, making it possible to apply verification techniques to contracts written in different languages.

Challenges. The challenges of developing a generalized formal semantic framework mainly lie in the construction of a general semantic model of smart contracts. Firstly, different high-level smart contract programming languages differ in syntax which limits state transitions. Compared with Solidity, Vyper [8] and Bamboo [1] have more syntax limits to exclude some vulnerabilities reported in Solidity. For instance, Vyper eliminates `gasless send` by blocking recursive calls and infinite loops, and `reentrancy attacks` by excluding the possibility of state changes after external calls [40]. In addition, there are no state variables in Bamboo and each contract represents a particular execution state, making it possible to limit operations to certain states to prevent attacks. Therefore, we need to take into account the syntax differences when constructing a general semantic model for smart contracts. Secondly, semantics developed with the general semantic model must be direct to guarantee the validity of the verification. For instance, as discussed above, even though intermediate languages may be a good solution to construct a general semantic model, they introduce semantic-level equivalence checking issues due to pure syntax translations.

Contributions. In this work, we develop a generalized formal semantic framework for smart contracts. The contributions of this work lie in three aspects. Firstly, our work is the first approach, to our knowledge, to a generalized formal semantic framework for smart contracts which can directly handle contracts written in different high-level programming languages. Secondly, a general semantic model of smart contracts is constructed with rewriting logic in the K-framework. With the general semantic model, a direct executable formal semantics of a particular high-level smart contract programming language can be constructed as long as its core features fall into the ones defined in this model. The general semantic model is validated with its interpretation in Solidity using the Solidity compiler test set [6] and evaluation results show that it is complete and correct. Lastly, the generated semantics facilitates the formal verification of smart contracts written in a particular high-level programming language as a formal specification of the corresponding language. Together with low-level specifications [24,21], it allows us to conduct equivalence checking on high-level programs and low-level bytecode to reason about compiler bugs and guarantee that security properties are preserved at both levels.

Outline. The remaining part of this paper is organized as follows. In Section 2, we introduce smart contracts and the K-framework. The general semantic model of smart contracts is introduced in Section 3. In Section 4, we take Solidity as an example to illustrate how to generate a direct executable formal semantics of a particular high-level smart contract programming language based on the general semantic model. Section 5 shows the evaluation results of the proposed framework. Section 6 concludes this work.

2   Preliminaries

In this section, we briefly introduce smart contracts and the K-framework.

2.1   Smart Contracts

Solidity Smart Contracts. Ethereum [2,47], proposed in late 2013 by Vitalik Buterin, is a blockchain-based distributed computing platform supporting the functionality of smart contracts. It provides a decentralized international network where each participant node equipped with EVM can execute smart contracts. It also provides a cryptocurrency called "ether" (ETH) which can be transferred between different accounts and used to compensate participant nodes for their computations on smart contracts.

Solidity is one of the high-level programming languages to implement smart contracts on Ethereum. A smart contract written in Solidity can be compiled into EVM bytecode and executed by any participant node equipped with EVM. A Solidity smart contract is a collection of code (its functions) and data (its state) that resides at a specific address on the Ethereum blockchain [7]. Fig. 1 shows an example of Solidity smart contracts, named `Coin`, implementing a very simple cryptocurrency. In line 2, the public state variable `minter` of type `address` is declared to store the address of the minter of the cryptocurrency, i.e., the owner of the smart contract. The constructor, denoted by `constructor()`, is defined in lines 5–7. Once the smart contract is created and deployed[3], its

---

[3] How to create and deploy a smart contract is out of scope and can be found in:
https://solidity.readthedocs.io

```
1   contract Coin {
2      address public minter;
3      mapping (address => uint) public balances;
4
5      constructor() public {
6         minter = msg.sender;
7      }
8
9      function mint(address receiver, uint amount) public {
10         if (msg.sender != minter) return;
11         balances[receiver] += amount;
12      }
13
14      function send(address receiver, uint amount) public {
15         if (balances[msg.sender] < amount) return;
16         balances[msg.sender] -= amount;
17         balances[receiver] += amount;
18      }
19   }
```

Fig. 1. Solidity Smart Contract Example

constructor is invoked automatically, and `minter` is set to be the address of its creator (owner), represented by the built-in keyword `msg.sender`. In line 3, the public state variable `balances` is declared to store the balances of users. It is of type `mapping`, which can be considered as a hash-table mapping from keys to values. In this example, `balances` maps from a user (represented as an address) to his/her balance (represented as an unsigned integer value). The `mint` function, defined in lines 9–12, is supposed to be invoked only by its owner to mint coins, the number of which is specified by `amount`, for the user located at the `receiver` address. If `mint` is called by anyone except the owner of the contract, nothing will happen because of the guarding `if` statement in line 10. The `send` function, defined in lines 14–18, can be invoked by any user to transfer coins, the number of which is specified by `amount`, to another user located at the `receiver` address. If the balance is not sufficient, nothing will happen because of the guarding `if` statement in line 15; otherwise, the balances of both sides will be updated accordingly.

A blockchain is actually a globally-shared transactional database or ledger. If one wants to make any state change on the blockchain, he or she has to create a so-called *transaction* which has to be accepted and validated by all other participant nodes. Furthermore, once a transaction is applied to the blockchain, no other transactions can alter it. For example, deploying the `Coin` smart contract generates a transaction because the state of the blockchain is going to be changed, i.e., one more smart contract instance will be included. Similarly, any invocation of the function `mint` or `send` also generates a transaction because the state of the contract instance, which is a part of the whole blockchain, is going to be changed. Transactions have to be selected and added into blocks to be appended to the blockchain. This procedure is the so-called *mining*, and the participant nodes are called *miners*.

Vyper Smart Contracts. Vyper is a high-level programming language for smart contracts running on EVM. As an alternative to Solidity, Vyper is con-

```
1   minter: public(address)
2   balances: map(address, wei_value)
3
4   @public
5   def __init__():
6       self.minter = msg.sender
7
8   @public
9   def mint(receiver: address, amount: wei_value):
10      if (msg.sender != self.minter): return
11      self.balances[receiver] += amount
12
13  @public
14  def send(receiver: address, amount: wei_value):
15      if (self.balances[msg.sender] < amount): return
16      self.balances[msg.sender] -= amount
17      self.balances[receiver] += amount
```

Fig. 2. Vyper Smart Contract Example

sidered to be more secure by blocking recursive calls and infinite loops to avoid gasless send, and excluding the possibility of state changes after external calls to prevent reentrancy attacks [40]. Thus, it is more difficult to write vulnerable code in Vyper. In addition, it supports bounds and overflow checking, and strong typing. Particularly, timing features such as block timestamps are supported as types, making it possible to detect the vulnerability of timestamp dependence [32] on Vyper semantics. This is not possible on Solidity semantics since Solidity does not support timing features. Apart from security, simplicity is another goal of Vyper. It aims to provide a more human-readable language, and a simpler compiler implementation. An example Vyper smart contract corresponding to the Solidity smart contract illustrated in Fig. 1 is shown in Fig. 2.

Bamboo Smart Contracts. Bamboo is another high-level programming language for Ethereum smart contracts. In Bamboo, state variables are eliminated and each contract represents a particular execution state, making state transitions explicit to avoid reentrancy attacks by default. This is because operations in functions are limited to certain states. An example Bamboo smart contract which is equivalent to the Solidity smart contract illustrated in Fig. 1 is shown in Fig. 3. In this example, explicit state transitions are applied to strictly limit operations in the constructor to a certain state. To be specific, the default part in the contract PreCoin which is equivalent to the constructor in Fig. 1 can only be invoked once, after which the state is always Coin. This is consistent with the fact that the constructor of a Solidity smart contract is only invoked once when a new contract instance is created.

Comparison. As introduced above, Vyper smart contracts are similar to Solidity smart contracts regardless of the differences in syntax formats. Compared with Solidity, Vyper simply excludes the vulnerabilities reported in Solidity at syntax level. Apart from the syntax differences, explicit state transitions are applied in Bamboo to prevent potential attacks. Despite the limits in syntax and state transitions, high-level smart contract programming languages have a lot in common in semantics due to the fact that they have to be functionally the same.

```
1   contract PreCoin(address => uint balances){
2       default{
3           return then become Coin(sender(msg), balances);
4       }
5   }
6
7   contract Coin(address minter, address => uint balances){
8       case(void mint(address receiver, uint amount)){
9           if (sender(msg) != minter)
10              return then become Coin(minter, balances);
11          balances[receiver] = balances[receiver] + amount;
12          return then become Coin(minter, balances);
13      }
14      case(void send(address receiver, uint amount)){
15          if (balances[sender(msg)] < amount)
16              return then become Coin(minter, balances);
17          balances[sender(msg)] = balances[sender(msg)] - amount;
18          balances[receiver] = balances[receiver] + amount;
19          return then become Coin(minter, balances);
20      }
21  }
```

Fig. 3. Bamboo Smart Contract Example

2.2 The K-framework

The K-framework ($\mathbb{K}$) [39] is a rewriting logic [33] based formal *executable* semantics definition framework. The semantics definitions of various programming languages have been developed using $\mathbb{K}$, such as Java [13], C [18], etc. Particularly, an executable semantics of EVM [24], the bytecode language of smart contracts, has been constructed in the K-framework. $\mathbb{K}$ backends, like the Isabelle theory generator, the model checker, and the deductive verifier, can be utilized to prove properties on the semantics and construct verification tools [42].

A language semantics definition in the K-framework consists of three main parts, namely the language syntax, the configuration specified by the developer and a set of rules constructed based on the syntax and the configuration. Given a semantics definition and some source programs, the K-framework executes the source programs based on the semantics definition. In addition, specified properties can be verified by the formal analysis tools in $\mathbb{K}$ backends. We take IMP [37], a simple imperative language, as an example to show how to define a language semantics in the K-framework.

The configuration of the IMP language is shown in Fig. 4. There are only two cells, namely k and state, in the whole configuration cell T. The cells in the configuration are used to store some information related to the program execution. For instance, the cell k stores the program for execution Pgm, and in the cell state a map is used to store the variable state.

$$\left\langle \ \langle \ \text{\$PGM:Pgm} \ \rangle_k \quad \langle \ \text{.Map} \ \rangle_{state} \ \right\rangle_T$$

Fig. 4. IMP Configuration

Here, we introduce some basic rules in the K-IMP semantics. These rules are allocate, read and write. The syntax of IMP is also given in Fig. 5.

```
Pgm  ::= "int" Ids ";" Stmt   Ids ::= List{Id, ","}
AExp ::= Int | Id | "-" Int | AExp "/" AExp  > AExp "+" AExp | "(" AExp ")"
BExp ::= Bool | AExp "<=" AExp | "!" BExp  > BExp "&&" BExp | "(" BExp ")"
Block ::= "{" "}" | "{" Stmt "}"
Stmt ::= Block | Id "=" AExp ";" | "if" "(" BExp ")" Block "else" Block |
"while" "(" BExp ")" Block > Stmt Stmt
```

Fig. 5. Syntax of IMP

RULE ALLOCATE

$$\left\langle \frac{\texttt{int X,Xs;S}}{\texttt{int Xs;S}} \cdots \right\rangle_k \quad \left\langle \frac{\texttt{Rho:Map}}{\texttt{Rho (X |-> 0)}} \right\rangle_{state}$$

requires notBool (X in keys(Rho))

RULE FINISH-ALLOCATE

$$\left\langle \frac{\texttt{int .Ids;S}}{\texttt{S}} \cdots \right\rangle_k$$

RULE READ

$$\left\langle \frac{\texttt{X:Id}}{\texttt{I}} \cdots \right\rangle_k \quad \left\langle \cdots \texttt{X |-> I} \cdots \right\rangle_{state}$$

RULE WRITE

$$\left\langle \frac{\texttt{X = I:Int;}}{.} \cdots \right\rangle_k \quad \left\langle \cdots \frac{\texttt{X |-> \_}}{\texttt{X |-> I}} \cdots \right\rangle_{state}$$

Let us start with the rule of memory allocations in IMP shown in ALLOCATE. When Pgm, interpreted as int X,Xs;S, is encountered, we need to store a list of variables (X,Xs) starting from X in the cell state with a list of mappings. Here state can be regarded as a physical memory or storage, and Xs is also a list of variables which can be empty. X is popped out of the cell k and a new mapping from X to 0 is created in the cell state, which means that a memory slot has been allocated for X to store its initial value 0. No duplicate names are allowed in state, which is guaranteed by the require condition. Then we go like this until Xs becomes empty, which means that all the variables have already been stored in state. At this point, the execution of the first part of Pgm has been finished and we proceed to the execution of the statement S. This can be summarized in FINISH-ALLOCATE where .Ids is an empty list of identifiers, which means that the variable list is empty. Please note that . means an empty set in the K-framework. If a rule ends with ., it means that nothing will be executed.

Then we come to the rules of read and write for variables. As shown in READ, if we want to look up the value of the variable X, we need to search it in the cell state by mapping the variable name X to its value I. So the evaluation of this expression X is its value I. If we cannot find a mapping for X, the program execution will stop at this point. Particularly, ... means there can be something in the corresponding position. For instance, the mapping of X can be in any position in the cell state. However, for rules in the cell k, ... can only be at the end since the program which is stored in k is executed sequentially. As illustrated in WRITE, if we want to assign the integer I to the variable X, similarly we need to search it in state by mapping the variable name. We also need to rewrite the value of X, denoted by "_" which is a placeholder, to I.

Rewriting logic facilitates the construction of a general semantic model for smart contracts. This is because a rewriting logic style semantics consists of a set of rewriting steps from the language syntax to its evaluations. In spite of syntax differences, different smart contract languages have a lot in common in logical

RULE ALLOCATE-GENERAL

$$\left\langle \frac{\text{\#allocate(X, I)}}{\cdot} \cdots \right\rangle_k \quad \left\langle \frac{\text{Rho:Map}}{\text{Rho (X |-> I)}} \right\rangle_{state}$$

requires notBool (X in keys(Rho))

RULE READ-GENERAL

$$\left\langle \frac{\text{\#read(X)}}{\text{I}} \cdots \right\rangle_k$$

$$\left\langle \text{... X |-> I ...} \right\rangle_{state}$$

RULE WRITE-GENERAL

$$\left\langle \frac{\text{\#write(X, I)}}{\cdot} \cdots \right\rangle_k \quad \left\langle \text{...} \frac{\text{X |-> \_}}{\text{X |-> I}} \cdots \right\rangle_{state}$$

RULE ALLOCATE-IMP

$$\left\langle \frac{\text{int X,Xs;S}}{\text{\#allocate(X, 0) ...}} \right\rangle_k \\ \curvearrowright \text{int Xs;S}$$

RULE READ-IMP

$$\left\langle \frac{\text{X:Id}}{\text{\#read(X)}} \cdots \right\rangle_k$$

RULE WRITE-IMP

$$\left\langle \frac{\text{X = I:Int;}}{\text{\#write(X, I)}} \cdots \right\rangle_k$$

MemoryOperations ::= #read(Id) | #write(Id, Int) | #allocate(Id, Int)

Fig. 6. Syntax of General Memory Operations

aspects to achieve the equivalent functionality. Rewriting logic makes it possible to separate the language syntax from the common logical aspects based on which the general semantic model is constructed. The semantics rules introduced above can be general and not specific to IMP. We show the general rules for **read**, **write** and **allocate** in READ-GENERAL, WRITE-GENERAL and ALLOCATE-GENERAL, respectively. In these rules, **#read**, **#write** and **#allocate** represent the functions to read, write and allocate memory slots for variables with specified parameters and their syntax is shown in Fig. 6. The semantics rules for memory operations in IMP can be obtained by rewriting the corresponding IMP syntax to the general memory operations defined above, namely **#read**, **#write** and **#allocate**, which form a general semantic model. The semantics rules for **read**, **write** and **allocate** in IMP based on the general semantic model are shown in READ-IMP, WRITE-IMP and ALLOCATE-IMP, respectively. Particularly, the symbol $\curvearrowright$ means "followed by". The semantics rules interpreted with the internal semantics of the general memory operations defined in Fig. 6 are equivalent to those developed from scratch, namely READ, WRITE and ALLOCATE. Rather than pure syntax translations to intermediate languages, a general semantic model enables semantic-level mappings to commonly shared high-level features.

3   A General Semantic Model

Different high-level smart contract programming languages vary in syntax but have a lot in common semantically to achieve the equivalent functionality. Considering this fact, we construct a general semantic model for smart contracts based on the commonly shared high-level semantic features that are independent of any specific language or platform. The semantics of a high-level smart contract programming language can be summarized into three aspects in terms of its functionality, namely memory operations, new contract instance creations

and function calls. Particularly, new contract instance creations and function
calls are the two kinds of transactions on the blockchain. In this section, we
present an overview of the desired semantics of these three core features.

3.1 Syntax

The syntax of the general semantic model is defined in the K-framework and
shown in Fig. 7. Due to limit of space, we only present the syntax of rewriting
steps related to memory operations, new contract instance creations and function
calls with `MemOp`, `NewInstanceCreation` and `InstanceStateUpdate`, respectively. Particularly, `ExpressionList` is a list of `Expressions`. `TypeName` consists
of `ElementaryTypeName` which takes one memory slot, `ComplexTypeName` which
is composed of a set of `ElementaryTypeNames`, and `ReferenceTypeName` which
refers to a pre-defined instance. For Solidity, `ElementaryTypeName` consists of
all the elementary types defined in the official documentation [7] except `Byte`.
`ComplexTypeName` refers to mappings, arrays and `Byte`. `ReferenceTypeName` involves user-defined types and function types. `Id` stands for identifiers. `Int` and
`Bool` represent integers and Boolean values, respectively. `Values`, a subset of
`ExpressionList`, is a list of `Value` types which can be integers (`Int`) or Boolean
types (`Bool`). `Msg` is the type of transaction information. `VarInfo` stores variable
information. `MemberAccess` deals with expressions in member access formats.

```
RewritingSteps ::= MemOp | NewInstanceCreation | InstanceStateUpdate

MemOp ::= read(Expression) | readAddress(Int, Id) | write(Expression, Value)
        | writeAddress(Int, Id, Value) | allocate(Int, VarInfo)
        | allocateAddress(Int, Int, Id, Value)

NewInstanceCreation ::= createNewInstance(Id, ExpressionList)
        | updateState(Id) | allocateStorage(Id)
        | initInstance(Id, ExpressionList)

InstanceStateUpdate ::= functionCall(Expression; Expression; Id;
        ExpressionList; Msg) | functionCall(Id; ExpressionList)
        | switchContext(Int, Int, Id, Msg) | returnContext(Int)
        | exception() | updateExceptionState() | revertState()

Expression ::= Id | Value | Msg | VarInfo | MemberAccess
ExpressionList ::= List{Expression, ","} | Values
Value ::= Int | Bool   Values ::= List{Value, ","}
Msg ::= #msgInfo(Int, Int, Int, Int)
VarInfo ::= #varInfo(Id, TypeName, Id, Value)
MemberAccess ::= #memberAccess(Expression, Id)
TypeName ::= ElementaryTypeName | ComplexTypeName | ReferenceTypeName
```

Fig. 7. Syntax of the General Semantic Model

3.2 Configuration

The runtime configuration indicates program states at each execution step, making detailed runtime features available. The runtime configuration of the general
semantic model is illustrated in Fig. 8. Due to limit of space, only a part of the

cells is presented here. In this configuration, there are six main cells in the whole configuration cell T and they are k, controlStacks, contracts, functions, contractInstances and transactions. The value of each cell is initialized in the configuration with its type specified. A dot followed by any type represents an empty set of this type. For instance, .List is an empty list. Particularly, K is the most general type which can be any specific type defined in the K-framework.

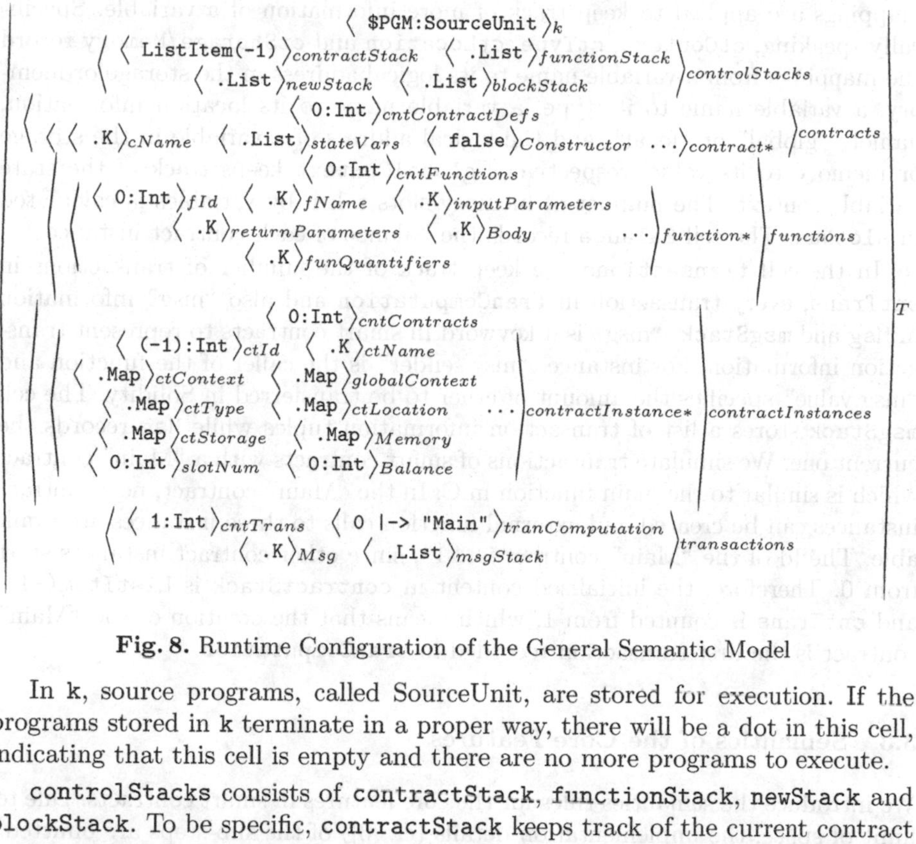

$$
\left|
\begin{array}{l}
\langle\, \texttt{\$PGM:SourceUnit}\,\rangle_k \\[4pt]
\left\langle\begin{array}{l}
\langle\ \texttt{ListItem(-1)}\ \rangle_{contractStack}\quad \langle\ \texttt{.List}\ \rangle_{functionStack} \\
\quad\langle\ \texttt{.List}\ \rangle_{newStack}\quad \langle\ \texttt{.List}\ \rangle_{blockStack}
\end{array}\right\rangle_{controlStacks} \\[12pt]
\left\langle\begin{array}{l}
\langle\ \texttt{0:Int}\ \rangle_{cntContractDefs} \\
\left\langle\langle\ \texttt{.K}\ \rangle_{cName}\quad \langle\ \texttt{.List}\ \rangle_{stateVars}\quad \langle\ \texttt{false}\ \rangle_{Constructor}\ \cdots\right\rangle_{contract*}
\end{array}\right\rangle_{contracts} \\[12pt]
\left\langle\begin{array}{l}
\langle\ \texttt{0:Int}\ \rangle_{cntFunctions} \\
\left\langle\begin{array}{l}
\langle\ \texttt{0:Int}\ \rangle_{fId}\quad \langle\ \texttt{.K}\ \rangle_{fName}\quad \langle\ \texttt{.K}\ \rangle_{inputParameters} \\
\quad\langle\ \texttt{.K}\ \rangle_{returnParameters}\quad \langle\ \texttt{.K}\ \rangle_{Body} \\
\qquad\langle\ \texttt{.K}\ \rangle_{funQuantifiers}
\end{array}\ \cdots\right\rangle_{function*}
\end{array}\right\rangle_{functions} \\[16pt]
\left\langle\begin{array}{l}
\langle\ \texttt{0:Int}\ \rangle_{cntContracts} \\
\left\langle\begin{array}{l}
\langle\ \texttt{(-1):Int}\ \rangle_{ctId}\quad \langle\ \texttt{.K}\ \rangle_{ctName} \\
\langle\ \texttt{.Map}\ \rangle_{ctContext}\quad \langle\ \texttt{.Map}\ \rangle_{globalContext} \\
\langle\ \texttt{.Map}\ \rangle_{ctType}\quad \langle\ \texttt{.Map}\ \rangle_{ctLocation} \\
\langle\ \texttt{.Map}\ \rangle_{ctStorage}\quad \langle\ \texttt{.Map}\ \rangle_{Memory} \\
\langle\ \texttt{0:Int}\ \rangle_{slotNum}\quad \langle\ \texttt{0:Int}\ \rangle_{Balance}
\end{array}\ \cdots\right\rangle_{contractInstance*}
\end{array}\right\rangle_{contractInstances} \\[16pt]
\left\langle\begin{array}{l}
\langle\ \texttt{1:Int}\ \rangle_{cntTrans}\quad \langle\ \texttt{0 |-> "Main"}\ \rangle_{tranComputation} \\
\quad\langle\ \texttt{.K}\ \rangle_{Msg}\quad \langle\ \texttt{.List}\ \rangle_{msgStack}
\end{array}\right\rangle_{transactions}
\end{array}
\right|_{T}
$$

Fig. 8. Runtime Configuration of the General Semantic Model

In k, source programs, called SourceUnit, are stored for execution. If the programs stored in k terminate in a proper way, there will be a dot in this cell, indicating that this cell is empty and there are no more programs to execute.

controlStacks consists of contractStack, functionStack, newStack and blockStack. To be specific, contractStack keeps track of the current contract instance. functionStack stores a list of function calls. newStack records a list of new contract instance creations. blockStack stores a list of variable contexts to look up and assign values to variables in different scopes.

In contracts, a set of contract definitions is stored. Each cell contract represents a contract definition. The number of distinct contracts is counted in cntContractDefs. In contract, the contract name is stored in cName. State variable information is stored in stateVars. In addition, Constructor indicates whether the contract has a constructor or not and its initial value is false.

Similarly, functions stores a set of function definitions. Each cell function represents a function definition. The total number of function definitions is stored in cntFunctions. For each function definition, the function Id and the function name are stored in fId and fName, respectively. In addtion, function parameters, including input parameters and return parameters, are recorded in the corresponding cells. We also store the function body in the cell `Body` and the function quantifiers which can be modifiers or specifiers in the cell `funQuantifiers`.

In `contractInstances`, there is a set of contract instances. Each cell `contract-Instance` represents a contract instance. The number of contract instances is counted in `cntContracts`. We store the contract instance Id and the name of its associated contract in the cells `ctId` and `ctName`, respectively. Four different mappings are applied to keep track of more information of a variable. Specifically speaking, `ctContext`, `ctType`, `ctLocation` and `ctStorage/Memory` record the mappings from a variable name to its logical address in the storage or memory, a variable name to its type, a variable name to its location information, namely "global" or "local", and the logical address of a variable in the storage or memory to its value, respectively. `globalContext` keeps track of the state variable context. The number of memory slots taken by variables is calculated in `slotNum`. The cell `Balance` records the balance of each contract instance.

In the cell `transactions`, we keep track of the number of transactions in `cntTrans`, every transaction in `tranComputation` and also "msg" information in `Msg` and `msgStack`. "msg" is a keyword in smart contracts to represent transaction information. For instance, "msg.sender" is the caller of the function and "msg.value" specifies the amount of ether to be transferred in Solidity. The cell `msgStack` stores a list of transaction information tuples while `Msg` records the current one. We simulate transactions of smart contracts with a "Main" contract which is similar to the main function in C. In the "Main" contract, new contract instances can be created and external function calls to these instances are available. The Id of the "Main" contract is "-1", since other contract instances start from 0. Therefore, the initialized content in `contractStack` is `ListItem(-1)`, and `cntTrans` is counted from 1, which means that the creation of the "Main" contract is the first transaction recorded in `tranComputation`.

3.3 Semantics of the Core Features

We introduce the semantics rules for the core features in smart contracts. Due to limit of space, the implementation details (cf. [3]) of the sub-steps are omitted.

Memory Operations. We present an overview of the semantics rules for memory operations on elementary types, such as `int`, `uint` and `address` in Solidity, each of which takes only one memory slot. Complex types, such as arrays, mappings, etc, are compositions of elementary types. A memory operation on a complex type can be regarded as a set of recursive memory operations on elementary types. For instance, the memory allocation for a one-dimensional fixed-size array is equivalent to allocating an elementary type for each index of this array. Reading and writing a particular index involve recursive steps to retrieve the logical address of this index from the base address of the array. Mappings are similar to dynamic arrays. For a mapping from `address` to `uint`, the memory allocation for this mapping is equivalent to allocating an unsigned integer type at each address involved. Reference types which refer to pre-defined instances can be simply implemented as mappings in the K-framework.

RULE READ

$$\left\langle \frac{\texttt{read(X:Id)}}{\texttt{readAddress(Addr, L)}} \cdots \right\rangle_k \quad \left\langle \texttt{ListItem(N:Int)} \cdots \right\rangle_{contractStack}$$

$$\left\langle \begin{array}{l} \left\langle \texttt{N} \right\rangle_{ctId} \quad \left\langle \texttt{... X |-> Addr ...} \right\rangle_{ctContext} \\ \qquad \left\langle \texttt{... X |-> L ...} \right\rangle_{ctLocation} \qquad \cdots \\ \left\langle \texttt{... X |-> T:ElementaryTypeName ...} \right\rangle_{ctType} \end{array} \right\rangle_{contractInstance}$$

RULE WRITE

$$\left\langle \frac{\texttt{write(X:Id, V:Value)}}{\texttt{writeAddress(Addr, L, V)}} \cdots \right\rangle_k \quad \left\langle \texttt{ListItem(N:Int)} \cdots \right\rangle_{contractStack}$$

$$\left\langle \begin{array}{l} \left\langle \texttt{N} \right\rangle_{ctId} \quad \left\langle \texttt{... X |-> Addr ...} \right\rangle_{ctContext} \\ \qquad \left\langle \texttt{... X |-> L ...} \right\rangle_{ctLocation} \qquad \cdots \\ \left\langle \texttt{... X |-> T:ElementaryTypeName ...} \right\rangle_{ctType} \end{array} \right\rangle_{contractInstance}$$

RULE ALLOCATE

$$\left\langle \frac{\texttt{allocate(N:Int, \#varInfo(X:Id, T:ElementaryTypeName, L:Id, V:Value))}}{\texttt{allocateAddress(N, Addr, L, V)}} \cdots \right\rangle_k$$

$$\left\langle \left\langle \texttt{N} \right\rangle_{ctId} \quad \left\langle \frac{\texttt{Addr}}{\texttt{Addr +Int 1}} \right\rangle_{slotNum} \quad \left\langle \frac{\texttt{TYPE:Map}}{\texttt{TYPE (X |-> T)}} \right\rangle_{ctType} \right.$$
$$\left. \left\langle \frac{\texttt{CON:Map}}{\texttt{CON (X |-> Addr)}} \right\rangle_{ctContext} \quad \left\langle \frac{\texttt{LOC:Map}}{\texttt{LOC (X |-> L)}} \right\rangle_{ctLocation} \qquad \cdots \right\rangle_{contractInstance}$$

RULE NEW-CONTRACT-INSTANCE-CREATION

$$\left\langle \frac{\texttt{createNewInstance(X:Id, E:ExpressionList)}}{\texttt{updateState(X)} \curvearrowright \texttt{allocateStorage(X)} \curvearrowright \texttt{initInstance(X, E)}} \cdots \right\rangle_k$$

RULE FUNCTION-CALL

$$\left\langle \frac{\texttt{functionCall(C:Int; R:Int; F:Id; Es:Values; M:Msg)}}{\texttt{switchContext(C, R, F, M)} \curvearrowright \texttt{functionCall(F; Es)} \curvearrowright \texttt{returnContext(R)}} \cdots \right\rangle_k$$

Let us start with the **read** operation on elementary types shown in READ. Here, we consider the object X as a variable which is an Id type. The first thing to do is to get the current execution context. This is achieved by retrieving the current contract instance Id N in **contractStack** and mapping the corresponding contract instance with N in the cell **ctId**. After that, we retrieve the logical address of X, denoted by Addr, in **ctContext** and the location information of X, denoted by L, in **ctLocation**. With these two parameters, we can obtain the evaluation of X through **readAddress** which retrieves the value located at Addr in the associated cell specified by L. To be specific, if L specifies this variable as a global one, the search space is **ctStorage**. Otherwise, the value is retrieved in **Memory**. **write** is similar to **read**. After retrieving the logical address of X, denoted by Addr, and the location information of X, denoted by L, we rewrite the value at Addr to the value V in the cell specified by L through **writeAddress**.

Then we come to the allocation for elementary types shown in ALLOCATE. The first input parameter N indicates the object contract instance Id. The variable information including the name X, the type T, the location information L and the initial value V, is stored in **#varInfo**. First, we retrieve the corresponding instance by mapping the Id N in **ctId**. Then the number of memory slots is increased by 1 in **slotNum**. After that, the variable information is recorded in the associated cells. To be specific, we record the logical address Addr, the type T, and the location information L in ctContext, ctType and ctLocation, respectively. Finally, a memory slot is allocated for this variable through allocateAddress.

New Contract Instance Creations. As illustrated in NEW-CONTRACT-INSTANCE-CREATION, the contract name X and the arguments in the constructor E are taken as input parameters to create a new instance of X. There are altogether three sub-steps for this transaction and they are updateState, allocateStorage and initInstance. To be specific, updateState updates the blockchain states, including the states of contract instances and transactions, and the stack information to indicate the new contract instance creation. In addition, allocateStorage allocates state variables and initInstance deals with initialization issues, such as calling the constructor, in the new instance.

Function Calls. In order to make the semantics of function calls general for all kinds of calls and extensible for different smart contract languages, a uniform format is applied to generalize the semantics. The uniform format is functionCall(Id_of_Caller; Id_of_Recipient; Function_Name; Arguments; Msg_Info). Particularly, Msg_Info represents the transaction information, including the Ids of the caller and the recipient instances, the value of digital assets to be transferred and the transaction fees to be consumed. The semantics rule for function calls based on this format is shown in FUNCTION-CALL.

In the rule FUNCTION-CALL, the caller of this function is C and the recipient is R. F is the function name and Es specifies the function call arguments. M is the "msg" information to keep track of transactions. In particular, the types of these parameters have been specified. The semantics of function calls is designed from a general point of view. Each external function call is regarded as an extension of an internal function call. Whenever there is an external function call, we first switch to the recipient instance and then call the function in this instance as an internal call. Finally, we switch back to the caller instance. In this way, external function calls can be achieved through internal function calls and switches of contract instances. This mechanism also applies to internal function calls where the caller is the same as the recipient. There are three sub-steps in FUNCTION-CALL. The first one is to switch to the recipient instance from the caller through switchContext. The second is an internal function call functionCall. The last one is to return to the caller instance through returnContext.

Particularly, the semantics of function calls is equipped with exception handling features. If an exception is encountered, it will be propagated to the transactional function call to revert the whole transaction. The propagation of exceptions is a sub-step in returnContext. The exception handling mechanism is also general, making it possible to deal with all kinds of exception handling features in smart contracts, such as revert and assert in Solidity, in a similar way.

RULE EXCEPTION-PROPAGATION
$$\left\langle \frac{\text{exception()}}{\text{updateExceptionState()}} \cdots \right\rangle_k$$
$$\langle \text{ListItem(R)ListItem(C)} \cdots \rangle_{contractStack}$$
requires C >=Int 0

RULE TRANSACTION-REVERSION
$$\left\langle \frac{\text{exception()}}{\text{updateExceptionState()} \cdots} \right\rangle_k$$
$$\curvearrowright \text{revertState()}$$
$$\langle \text{ListItem(R)ListItem(-1)} \rangle_{contractStack}$$

There are two stages in handling exceptions. The first one is the propagation of exceptions to the transactional function call as shown in EXCEPTION-PROPAGATION, and the second is the reversion of the transaction as shown in TRANSACTION-REVERSION. The first stage is present in nested calls to propagate exceptions to the transactional function call, while the second stage is only present in the transactional function call stemming from the "Main" contract. In the stage of propagating exceptions, the exception state is updated through `updateExceptionState()` to indicate that an exception has been encountered. Particularly, the Id of the caller instance should be larger than or equal to 0 since the caller cannot be the "Main" contract. And in the stage of reverting transactions, the caller is the "Main" contract whose Id is "-1". In addition to updating the exception state, the whole transaction is reverted through `revertState()`.

4 Direct Semantics Generation

A direct semantics of a high-level smart contract programming language can be developed based on the general semantic model introduced above. From the perspective of rewriting logic, a language semantics is a set of rewriting steps from the language syntax to its evaluations. Each of these rewriting steps implements a function to move the syntax a step further to its final evaluations. The general semantic model which consists of a set of internal rewriting steps and defines the desired semantics of smart contracts can be regarded as a logical intermediate language. A direct semantics of a high-level smart contract programming language can be constructed by rewriting its syntax to the features in the general semantic model with several functional steps. This also indicates the process of smart contract language design. We take Solidity as an example to illustrate how to generate the semantics based on the general semantic model. The semantics rules presented below are based on the Solidity syntax defined in [7].

Let us start with the `look-up` operation in Solidity. As shown in LOOK-UP, the object is considered to be a variable X. X is evaluated with `read` in the general semantic model. We simply rewrite the corresponding Solidity syntax to `read`. `assignment` is similar to `look-up`. As shown in ASSIGNMENT, we simply rewrite the assignment syntax in Solidity to `write` in the general semantic model.

RULE LOOK-UP RULE ASSIGNMENT   RULE NEW-INSTANCE-SOLIDITY

$$\left\langle \frac{\texttt{X:Id}}{\texttt{read(X)}} \cdots \right\rangle_k \quad \left\langle \frac{\texttt{X:Id = V:Value}}{\texttt{write(X, V)}} \cdots \right\rangle_k \quad \left\langle \frac{\texttt{new X:Id (E:ExpressionList)}}{\texttt{createNewInstance(X, E)}} \cdots \right\rangle_k$$

Both state and local variable allocations are achieved through `allocate` in the general semantic model. State variables are allocated when new contract instances are created, while local variables are allocated right after declarations.

In NEW-INSTANCE-SOLIDITY, the syntax of new contract instance creations in Solidity is rewritten to `createNewInstance` in the general semantic model.

Function calls in Solidity are written in a format similar to member access. For instance, `target.deposit.value(2)()` is a typical function call in Solidity. To be specific, `target` specifies the recipient instance and `deposit` is the function

RULE FUNCTION-CALL-SOLIDITY

$$\left\langle \frac{\texttt{\#memberAccess(R:Int, F:Id)} \curvearrowright \texttt{Es:Values} \curvearrowright \texttt{MsgValue:Int} \curvearrowright \texttt{MsgGas:Int}}{\texttt{functionCall(C; R; F; Es; \#msgInfo(C, R, MsgValue, MsgGas))}} \cdots \right\rangle_k$$
$$\left\langle \texttt{ListItem(C:Int)} \cdots \right\rangle_{contractStack}$$

RULE REVERT   RULE ASSERT

$$\left\langle \frac{\texttt{revert(.ExpressionList);}}{\texttt{exception()}} \cdots \right\rangle_k \quad \left\langle \frac{\texttt{assert(true);}}{\texttt{.}} \cdots \right\rangle_k \quad \left\langle \frac{\texttt{assert(false);}}{\texttt{exception()}} \cdots \right\rangle_k$$

RULE REQUIRE

$$\left\langle \frac{\texttt{require(true);}}{\texttt{.}} \cdots \right\rangle_k \quad \left\langle \frac{\texttt{require(false);}}{\texttt{exception()}} \cdots \right\rangle_k$$

to be called in that instance. value specifies msg.value as 2. In addition, we can specify other parameters, such as msg.gas, function arguments, etc. When it comes to the semantics of function calls in Solidity, the first thing to do is to decompose the member access like format and transform it into the one in the general semantic model. As shown in FUNCTION-CALL-SOLIDITY, each decomposed part in Solidity calls is reorganized in functionCall. Specifically speaking, #memberAccess(R:Int, F:Id) specifies the recipient instance R and the function to be called in this instance F. Es specifies the function arguments. MsgValue and MsgGas represent msg.value and msg.gas, respectively.

The semantics rules for function calls apply to all kinds of function calls in Solidity, including high-level and low-level calls, constructors and fallback functions. For instance, if there is no function name specified in a function call or the specified function name does not match any existing function in the recipient instance, the first decomposed part in FUNCTION-CALL-SOLIDITY will be #memberAccess(R:Int, String2Id("fallback")) where R is the Id of the recipient instance and "fallback" refers to the fallback function in that instance. In this case, the fallback function in R will be invoked. In addition, in the case of delegatecall, the recipient instance R is the same as the caller instance C since the execution takes place in the caller's context.

Exception handling features in Solidity can be interpreted with the semantics of exception() in the general semantic model. The semantics rules for revert, assert and require are shown in REVERT, ASSERT and REQUIRE, respectively.

5   Evaluation

We evaluate the proposed generalized formal semantic framework for smart contracts by showing that the generated semantics, an interpretation of the general semantic model with a particular language, is consistent with the semantics interpreted by the corresponding official compiler on benchmarks. The testing language makes no difference to the evaluation since it aims to validate the semantics of the commonly shared high-level features defined in the general semantic model. We take Solidity as an object for the evaluation since there are sufficient Solidity smart contracts available for testing the generated Solidity

Table 1. Coverage of the Generated Solidity Semantics

Features	Coverage	Features	Coverage
Types(Core)		**Statements(Core)**	
Elementary Types		If Statement	FC
address	FC	While Statement	FC
bool	FC	For Statement	FC
string	FC	Block	FC
Int	FC	Inline Assembly	N
Uint	FC	Statement	
Byte	FC	Do While Statement	FC
Fixed	N	Place Holder Statement	FC
Ufixed	N	Continue	FC
User-defined Types	FC	Break	FC
Mappings	FC	Return	FC
Array Types	FC	Throw,Revert,Assert,Require	FC
Function Types	FC	Simple Statement	FC
address payable	FC	Emit Statement	FC
Functions(Core)		**Expressions(Core)**	
Function Definitions		Bitwise Operations	FC
Constructors	FC	Arithmetic Operations	FC
Normal Functions	FC	Logical Operations	FC
Fallback Functions	FC	Comparison Operations	FC
Modifiers	FC	Assignment	FC
Function Calls		Look Up	FC
Internal Function Calls	FC	New Expression	FC
External Function Calls	FC	Other Expressions	FC
Using For	FC	**Inheritance**	FC
Event	FC		

FC: Fully Covered and Consistent with Solidity IDE   N: Not Covered

semantics. The Solidity semantics developed with the proposed framework is publicly available at https://github.com/kframework/solidity-semantics.

The generated Solidity semantics is evaluated from two perspectives: the first one is its coverage (i.e., completeness), and the second is its correctness (i.e., consistency with Solidity compilers). Evaluation results show that the Solidity semantics developed with the proposed framework completely covers the supported high-level core language features specified by the official Solidity documentation [7] and is consistent with the official Solidity compiler Remix [5].

We evaluate and test the Solidity semantics developed with the proposed framework with the Solidity compiler test set [6]. This test set is regarded as a standard test set or benchmarks for evaluating Solidity semantics since the test programs are written in a standard or correct way defined by the language developers and cover all the features in Solidity. There are altogether 482 tests in the Solidity compiler test set. The evaluation is done by manually comparing the execution behaviours of the generated Solidity semantics with the ones of the Remix compiler on the test programs. We consider the generated Solidity semantics is correct if the execution behaviours indicated in the configuration are consistent with the ones of the Remix compiler. A feature is considered to be fully covered if all the compiler tests involving this feature are passed. We list the coverage of the generated Solidity semantics in Table 1 from the perspective of each feature specified by the official documentation.

From Table 1, we can observe that the generated Solidity semantics completely covers the supported high-level core features of Solidity. As for types, the generated Solidity semantics covers the following elementary types: `address`, `bool`, `string`, `Int`, `Uint` and `Byte`. `Fixed` and `Ufixed` are not covered because they are not fully supported by Solidity yet [7]. User-defined types, including `struct`, contract types and `enum`, are covered. Mappings, arrays, function types and `address payable` are also covered. In addition, the semantics associated with functions, such as function definitions and function calls, is fully covered. The semantics of statements is completely covered except that of `inline assembly statements` which are considered to be low-level features accessing EVM (i.e., this part of semantics can be integrated with KEVM [24]). All kinds of expressions in Solidity are covered. Lastly, the semantics of `event` is also covered and the parts of semantics for `using for` and `inheritance` are covered with rewriting. For all the parts of covered semantics, they are considered to be correct since the execution behaviours involved are consistent with the ones of Remix. Therefore, the generated Solidity semantics can be considered to be complete and correct in terms of the supported high-level core features of Solidity, indicating the completeness and correctness of the general semantic model.

Threats to Validity. We validate the general semantic model with its interpretation in Solidity. The validity of the proposed framework holds for any particular high-level smart contract programming language as long as its core features fall into or can be properly rewritten to the ones defined in the general semantic model. The proposed framework may not work if the core features cannot be interpreted with the ones defined in the general semantic model. However, this is unlikely due to the nature of smart contract executions. For instance, transactions in existing instances are implemented with or can be transformed into function calls regardless of the platforms of smart contract programs.

6   Conclusion

In this paper, we propose a generalized formal semantic framework for smart contracts. This framework can directly handle smart contracts written in different high-level programming languages, such as Solidity, Vyper, Bamboo, etc, without translating them into EVM bytecode or intermediate languages. In this framework, a direct executable formal semantics of a particular high-level smart contract programming language is constructed based on a general semantic model with rewriting logic. The general semantic model is validated with its interpretation in Solidity and evaluation results show that it is complete and correct. Furthermore, the proposed framework provides a formal specification of smart contracts written in different languages.

Acknowledgements. This work is supported by the Ministry of Education, Singapore under its Tier-2 Project (Award Number: MOE2018-T2-1-068) and partially supported by the National Research Foundation, Singapore under its NSoE Programme (Award Number: NSOE-TSS2019-03).

References

1. Bamboo (2018), https://github.com/pirapira/bamboo
2. Ethereum (2020), https://www.ethereum.org
3. Implementation Details (2020), https://github.com/SmartContractSemantics/SemanticFrameworkforSmartContracts
4. Mythril (2020), https://github.com/ConsenSys/mythril
5. Remix - Solidity IDE (2020), https://remix.ethereum.org
6. Solidity Compiler Test Set (2020), https://github.com/ethereum/solidity
7. Solidity Documentation (2020), https://solidity.readthedocs.io/en/latest
8. Vyper Documentation (2020), https://vyper.readthedocs.io/en/latest
9. Amani, S., Bégel, M., Bortin, M., Staples, M.: Towards Verifying Ethereum Smart Contract Bytecode in Isabelle/HOL. In: Proceedings of the 7th ACM SIGPLAN International Conference on Certified Programs and Proofs. pp. 66–77. CPP 2018, ACM, New York, NY, USA (2018)
10. Atzei, N., Bartoletti, M., Cimoli, T.: A Survey of Attacks on Ethereum Smart Contracts (SoK). In: Maffei, M., Ryan, M. (eds.) Principles of Security and Trust - 6th International Conference, POST 2017, Held as Part of the European Joint Conferences on Theory and Practice of Software, ETAPS 2017, Uppsala, Sweden, April 22-29, 2017, Proceedings. Lecture Notes in Computer Science, vol. 10204, pp. 164–186. Springer (2017). https://doi.org/10.1007/978-3-662-54455-6_8
11. Bartoletti, M., Galletta, L., Murgia, M.: A Minimal Core Calculus for Solidity Contracts. In: DPM/CBT@ESORICS (2019)
12. Bhargavan, K., Delignat-Lavaud, A., Fournet, C., Gollamudi, A., Gonthier, G., Kobeissi, N., Kulatova, N., Rastogi, A., Sibut-Pinote, T., Swamy, N., Béguelin, S.Z.: Formal Verification of Smart Contracts: Short Paper. In: Murray, T.C., Stefan, D. (eds.) Proceedings of the 2016 ACM Workshop on Programming Languages and Analysis for Security, PLAS@CCS 2016, Vienna, Austria, October 24, 2016. pp. 91–96. ACM (2016)
13. Bogdanas, D., Rosu, G.: K-Java: A Complete Semantics of Java. In: Rajamani, S.K., Walker, D. (eds.) Proceedings of the 42nd Annual ACM SIGPLAN-SIGACT Symposium on Principles of Programming Languages, POPL 2015, Mumbai, India, January 15-17, 2015. pp. 445–456. ACM (2015)
14. Chen, T., Zhang, Y., Li, Z., Luo, X., Wang, T., Cao, R., Xiao, X., Zhang, X.: TokenScope: Automatically Detecting Inconsistent Behaviors of Cryptocurrency Tokens in Ethereum. In: Cavallaro, L., Kinder, J., Wang, X., Katz, J. (eds.) Proceedings of the 2019 ACM SIGSAC Conference on Computer and Communications Security, CCS 2019, London, UK, November 11-15, 2019. pp. 1503–1520. ACM (2019)
15. Crafa, S., Pirro, M., Zucca, E.: Is Solidity Solid Enough? In: Financial Cryptography Workshops (2019)
16. Delmolino, K., Arnett, M., Kosba, A.E., Miller, A., Shi, E.: Step by Step Towards Creating a Safe Smart Contract: Lessons and Insights from a Cryptocurrency Lab. In: Clark, J., Meiklejohn, S., Ryan, P.Y.A., Wallach, D.S., Brenner, M., Rohloff, K. (eds.) Financial Cryptography and Data Security - FC 2016 International Workshops, BITCOIN, VOTING, and WAHC, Christ Church, Barbados, February 26, 2016, Revised Selected Papers. Lecture Notes in Computer Science, vol. 9604, pp. 79–94. Springer (2016). https://doi.org/10.1007/978-3-662-53357-4_6
17. Drescher, D.: Blockchain Basics (2017)
18. Ellison, C., Rosu, G.: An Executable Formal Semantics of C with Applications. In: Field, J., Hicks, M. (eds.) Proceedings of the 39th ACM SIGPLAN-SIGACT

Symposium on Principles of Programming Languages, POPL 2012, Philadelphia, Pennsylvania, USA, January 22-28, 2012. pp. 533–544. ACM (2012)

19. Feist, J., Grieco, G., Groce, A.: Slither: A Static Analysis Framework for Smart Contracts. In: Proceedings of the 2nd International Workshop on Emerging Trends in Software Engineering for Blockchain, WETSEB@ICSE 2019, Montreal, QC, Canada, May 27, 2019. pp. 8–15. IEEE / ACM (2019)

20. Grech, N., Kong, M., Jurisevic, A., Brent, L., Scholz, B., Smaragdakis, Y.: Mad-Max: Surviving Out-of-gas Conditions in Ethereum Smart Contracts. PACMPL 2(OOPSLA), 116:1–116:27 (2018)

21. Grishchenko, I., Maffei, M., Schneidewind, C.: A Semantic Framework for the Security Analysis of Ethereum Smart Contracts. In: Bauer, L., Küsters, R. (eds.) Principles of Security and Trust - 7th International Conference, POST 2018, Held as Part of the European Joint Conferences on Theory and Practice of Software, ETAPS 2018, Thessaloniki, Greece, April 14-20, 2018, Proceedings. Lecture Notes in Computer Science, vol. 10804, pp. 243–269. Springer (2018). https://doi.org/10.1007/978-3-319-89722-6_10

22. Grossman, S., Abraham, I., Golan-Gueta, G., Michalevsky, Y., Rinetzky, N., Sagiv, M., Zohar, Y.: Online Detection of Effectively Callback Free Objects with Applications to Smart Contracts. PACMPL 2(POPL), 48:1–48:28 (2018)

23. Hajdu, Á., Jovanovic, D.: solc-verify: A Modular Verifier for Solidity Smart Contracts. arXiv preprint abs/1907.04262 (2019)

24. Hildenbrandt, E., Saxena, M., Rodrigues, N., Zhu, X., Daian, P., Guth, D., Moore, B.M., Park, D., Zhang, Y., Stefanescu, A., Roşu, G.: KEVM: A Complete Formal Semantics of the Ethereum Virtual Machine. In: 31st IEEE Computer Security Foundations Symposium, CSF 2018, Oxford, United Kingdom, July 9-12, 2018. pp. 204–217. IEEE Computer Society (2018)

25. Hirai, Y.: Defining the Ethereum Virtual Machine for Interactive Theorem Provers. In: Brenner, M., Rohloff, K., Bonneau, J., Miller, A., Ryan, P.Y.A., Teague, V., Bracciali, A., Sala, M., Pintore, F., Jakobsson, M. (eds.) Financial Cryptography and Data Security - FC 2017 International Workshops, WAHC, BITCOIN, VOTING, WTSC, and TA, Sliema, Malta, April 7, 2017, Revised Selected Papers. Lecture Notes in Computer Science, vol. 10323, pp. 520–535. Springer (2017). https://doi.org/10.1007/978-3-319-70278-0_33

26. Jiang, B., Liu, Y., Chan, W.K.: ContractFuzzer: Fuzzing Smart Contracts for Vulnerability Detection. In: Huchard, M., Kästner, C., Fraser, G. (eds.) Proceedings of the 33rd ACM/IEEE International Conference on Automated Software Engineering, ASE 2018, Montpellier, France, September 3-7, 2018. pp. 259–269. ACM (2018)

27. Jiao, J., Kan, S., Lin, S., Sanán, D., Liu, Y., Sun, J.: Executable Operational Semantics of Solidity. arXiv preprint abs/1804.01295 (2018)

28. Kalra, S., Goel, S., Dhawan, M., Sharma, S.: ZEUS: Analyzing Safety of Smart Contracts. In: 25th Annual Network and Distributed System Security Symposium, NDSS 2018, San Diego, California, USA, February 18-21, 2018. The Internet Society (2018)

29. Kolluri, A., Nikolic, I., Sergey, I., Hobor, A., Saxena, P.: Exploiting the Laws of Order in Smart Contracts. In: Zhang, D., Møller, A. (eds.) Proceedings of the 28th ACM SIGSOFT International Symposium on Software Testing and Analysis, ISSTA 2019, Beijing, China, July 15-19, 2019. pp. 363–373. ACM (2019)

30. Krupp, J., Rossow, C.: teEther: Gnawing at Ethereum to Automatically Exploit Smart Contracts. In: Enck, W., Felt, A.P. (eds.) 27th USENIX Security Sym-

posium, USENIX Security 2018, Baltimore, MD, USA, August 15-17, 2018. pp. 1317–1333. USENIX Association (2018)

31. Lahiri, S.K., Chen, S., Wang, Y., Dillig, I.: Formal Specification and Verification of Smart Contracts for Azure Blockchain. arXiv preprint **abs/1812.08829** (2018)

32. Luu, L., Chu, D., Olickel, H., Saxena, P., Hobor, A.: Making Smart Contracts Smarter. In: Weippl, E.R., Katzenbeisser, S., Kruegel, C., Myers, A.C., Halevi, S. (eds.) Proceedings of the 2016 ACM SIGSAC Conference on Computer and Communications Security, Vienna, Austria, October 24-28, 2016. pp. 254–269. ACM (2016)

33. Martí-Oliet, N., Meseguer, J.: Rewriting Logic: Roadmap and Bibliography. Theor. Comput. Sci. **285**, 121–154 (2002)

34. Mossberg, M., Manzano, F., Hennenfent, E., Groce, A., Grieco, G., Feist, J., Brunson, T., Dinaburg, A.: Manticore: A User-Friendly Symbolic Execution Framework for Binaries and Smart Contracts. In: 34th IEEE/ACM International Conference on Automated Software Engineering, ASE 2019, San Diego, CA, USA, November 11-15, 2019. pp. 1186–1189. IEEE (2019)

35. Nehai, Z., Bobot, F.: Deductive Proof of Ethereum Smart Contracts Using Why3. arXiv preprint **abs/1904.11281** (2019)

36. Nikolic, I., Kolluri, A., Sergey, I., Saxena, P., Hobor, A.: Finding the Greedy, Prodigal, and Suicidal Contracts at Scale. In: Proceedings of the 34th Annual Computer Security Applications Conference, ACSAC 2018, San Juan, PR, USA, December 03-07, 2018. pp. 653–663. ACM (2018)

37. Nipkow, T., Klein, G.: IMP: A Simple Imperative Language. Concrete Semantics. Springer, Cham (2014)

38. Rodler, M., Li, W., Karame, G.O., Davi, L.: Sereum: Protecting Existing Smart Contracts Against Re-Entrancy Attacks. In: 26th Annual Network and Distributed System Security Symposium, NDSS 2019, San Diego, California, USA, February 24-27, 2019. The Internet Society (2019)

39. Roşu, G., Şerbănuţă, T.F.: An Overview of the K Semantic Framework. Journal of Logic and Algebraic Programming **79**(6), 397–434 (2010)

40. Sergey, I., Kumar, A., Hobor, A.: Scilla: A Smart Contract Intermediate-level Language. arXiv preprint **abs/1801.00687** (2018)

41. Siegel, D.: Understanding the DAO Attack (2016), https://www.coindesk.com/understanding-dao-hack-journalists

42. Stefanescu, A., Park, D., Yuwen, S., Li, Y., Roşu, G.: Semantics-based Program Verifiers for All Languages. In: Visser, E., Smaragdakis, Y. (eds.) Proceedings of the 2016 ACM SIGPLAN International Conference on Object-Oriented Programming, Systems, Languages, and Applications, OOPSLA 2016, part of SPLASH 2016, Amsterdam, The Netherlands, October 30 - November 4, 2016. pp. 74–91. ACM (2016)

43. Tikhomirov, S., Voskresenskaya, E., Ivanitskiy, I., Takhaviev, R., Marchenko, E., Alexandrov, Y.: SmartCheck: Static Analysis of Ethereum Smart Contracts. In: 1st IEEE/ACM International Workshop on Emerging Trends in Software Engineering for Blockchain, WETSEB@ICSE 2018, Gothenburg, Sweden, May 27 - June 3, 2018. pp. 9–16. ACM (2018)

44. Tsankov, P., Dan, A.M., Drachsler-Cohen, D., Gervais, A., Bünzli, F., Vechev, M.T.: Securify: Practical Security Analysis of Smart Contracts. In: Lie, D., Mannan, M., Backes, M., Wang, X. (eds.) Proceedings of the 2018 ACM SIGSAC Conference on Computer and Communications Security, CCS 2018, Toronto, ON, Canada, October 15-19, 2018. pp. 67–82. ACM (2018)

45. Wang, H., Li, Y., Lin, S., Ma, L., Liu, Y.: VULTRON: Catching Vulnerable Smart Contracts Once and for All. In: Sarma, A., Murta, L. (eds.) Proceedings of the 41st International Conference on Software Engineering: New Ideas and Emerging Results, ICSE (NIER) 2019, Montreal, QC, Canada, May 29-31, 2019. pp. 1–4. IEEE / ACM (2019)
46. Wang, S., Zhang, C., Su, Z.: Detecting Nondeterministic Payment Bugs in Ethereum Smart Contracts. PACMPL 3(OOPSLA), 189:1–189:29 (2019)
47. Wood, G.: Ethereum: A Secure Decentralised Generalised Transaction Ledger. Ethereum project yellow paper **151**, 1–32 (2014)
48. Yang, Z., Lei, H.: Lolisa: Formal Syntax and Semantics for a Subset of the Solidity Programming Language. arXiv preprint **abs/1803.09885** (2018)
49. Zakrzewski, J.: Towards Verification of Ethereum Smart Contracts: A Formalization of Core of Solidity. In: Piskac, R., Rümmer, P. (eds.) Verified Software. Theories, Tools, and Experiments - 10th International Conference, VSTTE 2018, Oxford, UK, July 18-19, 2018, Revised Selected Papers. Lecture Notes in Computer Science, vol. 11294, pp. 229–247. Springer (2018). https://doi.org/10.1007/978-3-030-03592-1_13

An Empirical Study on the Use and Misuse of Java 8 Streams

Raffi Khatchadourian[1,2], Yiming Tang[2], Mehdi Bagherzadeh[3], and Baishakhi Ray[4]

[1] CUNY Hunter College, New York, NY USA
[2] CUNY Graduate Center, New York, NY USA
{raffi.khatchadourian,ytang3}@{hunter,gradcenter}.cuny.edu
[3] Oakland University, Rochester, MI USA
mbagherzadeh@oakland.edu
[4] Columbia University, New York, NY USA
rayb@cs.columbia.edu

Abstract. Streaming APIs allow for big data processing of native data structures by providing MapReduce-like operations over these structures. However, unlike traditional big data systems, these data structures typically reside in shared memory accessed by multiple cores. Although popular, this emerging hybrid paradigm opens the door to possibly detrimental behavior, such as thread contention and bugs related to non-execution and non-determinism. This study explores the use and misuse of a popular streaming API, namely, Java 8 Streams. The focus is on how developers decide whether or not to run these operations sequentially or in parallel and bugs both specific and tangential to this paradigm. Our study involved analyzing 34 Java projects and 5.53 million lines of code, along with 719 manually examined code patches. Various automated, including interprocedural static analysis, and manual methodologies were employed. The results indicate that streams are pervasive, parallelization is not widely used, and performance is a crosscutting concern that accounted for the majority of fixes. We also present coincidences that both confirm and contradict the results of related studies. The study advances our understanding of streams, as well as benefits practitioners, programming language and API designers, tool developers, and educators alike.

Keywords: empirical studies · functional programming · Java 8 · streams · multi-paradigm programming · static analysis.

1 Introduction

Streaming APIs are widely-available in today's mainstream Object-Oriented programming (MOOP) languages and platforms [5], including Scala [14], JavaScript [44], C# [33], F# [47], Java [39], and Android [27]. These APIs allow for "big data"-style processing of *native* data structures by incorporating MapReduce-like [10] operations. A "sum of even squares" example in Java, where a `stream` of numbers is derived from a `list`, `filtered` for evens, `mapped` to its squared, and summed [5] is: `list.stream().filter(x -> x % 2 == 0).map(x -> x * x).sum()`.

H. Wehrheim and J. Cabot (Eds.): FASE 2020, LNCS 12076, pp. 97–118, 2020.
https://doi.org/10.1007/978-3-030-45234-6_5

Traditional big data systems, for which MapReduce is a popular backbone [3], minimize the complexity of writing massively distributed programs by facilitating processing on multiple nodes using succinct functional-like constructs. This makes writing parallel code easier, as writing such code can be difficult due to possible data races, thread interference, and contention [1,4,28]. The code above, e.g., can execute in parallel simply by replacing `stream()` with `parallelStream()`.

However, unlike traditional big data systems, data structures processed by streaming APIs like Java 8 Streams typically reside in shared memory accessed by multiple cores. Therefore, issues may arise from the close intimacy between shared memory and the operations being performed, especially for developers not previously familiar with functional programming. Streams are not just an API but rather an emerging, hybrid paradigm. To obtain the expressiveness, speed, and parallelism that streams have to offer, developers must adopt the paradigm as well as the API [6, Ch. 7]. This requires determining whether running stream code in parallel yields an efficient yet interference-free program [24] and ensuring that no operations on different threads interleave [42].

Despite the benefits [53, Ch. 1], misusing streams may result in detrimental behavior, and the ~4K questions related to streams on Stack Overflow [48], of which ~5% remain unanswered, suggest that there is ample confusion surrounding the topic. Bugs related to thread contention (due to λ-expressions, i.e., units of computation, side-effects, buffering), non-execution (due to deferred execution), non-determinism (due to non-deterministic operations), operation sequencing (ordering of stream operations), and data ordering (ordering of stream data) can lead to programs that undermine concurrency, underperform, are incorrect, and are inefficient. Worse yet, these problems may increase over time as streams rise in popularity, with Mazinanian et al. [32] finding a two-fold increasing trend in the adoption of λ-expressions, an essential part of streams.

This study explores the use and misuse of a popular and representative streaming API, namely, Java 8 Streams. We set out to understand the *usage* and *bug* patterns involving streams in real software. Particularly, we are interested in discovering (i) how developers decide whether to run streams *sequentially* or in *parallel,* (ii) common stream *operations,* (iii) common stream *attributes* and whether they are amenable to safe and efficient parallelization, (iv) *bugs* both specific and tangential to streams, (v) how often *incorrect* stream APIs were used, and (vi) how often stream APIs were *misused* and in which ways?

Knowing the kinds of bugs typically associated with streams can, e.g., help improve (automated) bug detection. Being aware of the typical usage patterns of streams can, e.g., improve code completion in IDEs. In general, the results (i) advance our understanding of this emerging hybrid paradigm, (ii) provide feedback to language and API designers for future API versions, (iii) help tool designers comprehend the struggles developers have with streams, (iv) propose preliminary *best practices* and *anti-patterns* for practitioners to use streaming APIs effectively, (v) and assist educators in teaching streaming APIs.

We analyzed 34 Java projects and 5.53 million lines of source code (SLOC), along with 140,446 code patches (git commits), of which 719 were manually

---

Listing 1 Snippet of `Widget` collection processing using Java 8 streams [24,39].

```
1   Collection<Widget> unorderedWidgets = new HashSet<>(); // populate ...
2   Collection<Widget> orderedWidgets = new ArrayList<>(); // populate ...
3   List<Widget> sortedWidgets = unorderedWidgets.stream()
4       .sorted(Comparator.comparing(Widget::getWeight)).collect(Collectors.toList());
5   // collect weights over 43.2 into a set in parallel.
6   Set<Double> heavyWidgetWeightSet = orderedWidgets.parallelStream().map(Widget::getWeight)
7       .filter(w -> w > 43.2).collect(Collectors.toSet());
8   // sequentially collect into a list, skipping first 1000.
9   List<Widget> skippedWidgetList = orderedWidgets.stream().skip(1000)
10      .collect(Collectors.toList());
```

---

examined. The methodologies varied depending on the research questions and encompassed both automated, including interprocedural static analysis, and manual processes aided by automated software repository mining. Our study indicates that (i) streams have become widely used since their inception in 2014, (ii) developers tend to reduce streams back to iterative-style collections, favor simplistic, linear reductions, and prefer deterministic operations, (iii) stream parallelization is not widely used, yet streams tend not to have side-effects, (iv) performance is the largest category of stream bugs and is crosscutting.

This work makes the following contributions:

Stream usages patterns A large-scale analysis of stream and collector method calls and an interprocedural static analysis on 1.65 million lines source code is performed, reporting on attributes essential to efficient parallel execution.

Stream bug hierarchical taxonomy From the 719 git patches from 22 projects manually examined using 140 identifying keywords, we build a rich hierarchical, crosscutting taxonomy of common stream bugs and fixes.

Best practices and anti-patterns We propose preliminary best practices and anti-patterns of using streams in particular contexts from our statistical results as well as an in-depth analysis of first-hand conversations with developers.

2 Motivating Example and Conceptual Background

Lst. 1 portrays code that uses the Java 8 Stream API to process collections of `Widgets` (class not shown) with `colors` and `weights`. A `Collection` of `Widgets` is declared (line 1) that does not maintain element ordering as `HashSet` does not support it [38]. Note that ordering is dependent on the run time type.

A `stream` (a view representing element sequences supporting MapReduce-style operations) of `unorderedWidgets` is created on line 3. It is sequential, i.e., its operations will execute serially. Streams may also have an *encounter order* that may depend on its source. Here, it is unordered since `HashSets` are unordered.

On line 4, the stream is `sorted` by the corresponding *intermediate* operation, the result of which is a stream with the encounter order rearranged. `Widget::getWeight` is a method *reference* denoting the comparison scheme. Intermediate operations are deferred until a *terminal* operation is executed like `collect()` (line 4). The `collect()` operation is a (mutable) reduction that aggregates results of prior intermediate operations into a given `Collector`. In this case, it is one that yields a `List`. The result is a `Widget List` sorted by `weight`.

To potentially improve performance, this stream's "pipeline" (sequence of operations) may be executed in parallel. Note, however, that had the stream been *ordered*, running the pipeline in parallel may result in worse performance due to the multiple passes or data buffering required by *stateful* intermediate operations (SIOs) like `sorted()`. Because the stream is *unordered*, the reduction can be done more efficiently as the run time can use divide-and-conquer [39].

In contrast, line 2 instantiates an `ArrayList`, which maintains element ordering. Furthermore, a parallel stream is derived from this collection (line 6), with each `Widget` mapped to its weight, each weighted filtered (line 7), and the results `collected` into a `Set`. Unlike the previous example, however, no optimizations are available here as an SIO is not included in the pipeline and, as such, the parallel computation does not incur possible performance degradation.

Lines 9–10 create a list of `Widgets` gathered by (sequentially) skipping the first thousand from `orderedWidgets`. Like `sorted()`, `skip()` is also an SIO. Unlike the previous example, executing this pipeline in parallel could be counterproductive because the stream is ordered. It may be possible to unorder the stream (via `unordered()`) so that its pipeline would be more amenable to parallelization. In this situation, however, unordering could alter semantics as the data is assembled into a structure maintaining ordering. As such, the stream *correctly* executes sequentially as element ordering must be preserved.

This simplified example demonstrates that using streams effectively is not always straight-forward and can require complex (and interprocedural due to aliasing) analysis. It necessitates a thorough understanding of API intricacies, a problem that can be compounded in more extensive programs. As streaming APIs become more pervasive, it would be extremely valuable to MOOP developers not familiar with functional programming if statistical insight can be given on how best to use streams efficiently and how to avoid common bugs.

3   Study Subjects

At the core of our study is 34 open source Java projects that use streams. They vary widely in their domain and application, as well as size and popularity. All the subjects have their sources publicly available on GitHub and include popular libraries, frameworks, and applications. Many subjects were selected from previous studies [20,21,22,24], others because they contained relatively diverse stream operations and exhibited non-trivial metrics, including stars, forks, and number of collaborators. It was necessary to use different subjects for different parts of the study due to the computationally intensive nature of some of the experiments. For such experiments, subjects were chosen so that the analysis could be completed in a reasonable time period with reasonable resources.

4   Stream Characteristics

We explore the typical usage patterns of streams, including the frequency of parallel vs. sequential streams and amenability to safe and efficient parallelism, by examining stream characteristics. This has important implications for understanding the use of this incredibly expressive and powerful language feature. It also offers insight into developers' perceived risks concerning parallel streams.

Table 1. Stream characteristics.

subject	KLOC	age	eps	k	str	seq	para	ord	unord	se	SIO
bootique	4.91	4.18	362	4	14	14	0	11	3	4	0
cryptomator	7.99	6.05	148	3	12	12	0	11	1	2	0
dari	64.86	5.43	3	2	18	18	0	15	3	0	0
elasticsearch	585.71	10.03	78	6	210	210	0	165	45	10	0
htm.java	41.14	4.53	21	4	190	188	2	189	1	22	5
JabRef	138.83	16.36	3,064	2	301	290	11	239	62	9	0
JacpFX	23.79	4.71	195	4	12	12	0	9	3	1	0
jdp*	19.96	5.53	25	4	38	38	0	35	3	11	1
jdk8-exp*	3.43	6.35	34	4	49	49	0	47	2	5	0
jetty	354.48	10.93	106	4	57	57	0	47	10	8	0
JetUML	20.95	5.09	660	2	7	7	0	4	3	0	0
jOOQ	154.01	8.58	43	4	23	23	0	22	1	2	0
koral	7.13	3.47	51	3	8	8	0	8	0	0	0
monads	1.01	0.01	47	2	3	3	0	3	0	0	0
retrolambda	5.14	6.52	1	4	11	11	0	8	3	0	0
spring*	188.46	11.62	5,981	4	61	61	0	60	1	21	0
streamql	4.01	0.01	92	2	22	22	0	22	0	2	18
threeten*	27.53	7.01	36	2	2	2	0	2	0	0	0
Total	1,653.35	116.40	11,047	6	1,038	1,025	13	897	141	97	24

* jdp is java-design-patterns, jdk8-exp is jdk8-experiments, spring is a portion of spring-framework, and threeten is threeten-extra.

4.1 Methodology

For this part of the study, we examined 18 projects that use streams,[5] spanning ~1.65 million lines of Java source code. The subjects are depicted in tab. 1. Column **KLOC** corresponds to thousands of source lines of code, which ranges from ~1K for monads to ~586K for elasticsearch. Column **age** is the age of the subject project in years, averaging 6.47 years per subject. Column **str** is the total number of streams analyzed. The remaining columns are discussed in § 4.2.

Stream Pipeline Tracking Several factors contribute to determining stream attributes. First, streams are typically derived from a source (e.g., a collection) and take on its characteristics (e.g., ordering), as seen in lst. 1. There are several ways to create streams, including being derived from Collections, being created from arrays (e.g., Arrays.stream()), and via static factory methods (e.g., IntStream.range()). Second, stream attributes can change by the invocation of various intermediate operations in the building of the stream pipeline. Such attributes must be tracked, as it is possible to have arbitrary assignments of stream references to variables, as well as be data-dependent.

Our study involved tracking streams and their attributes (i.e., state) using a series of labeled transition systems (LTSs). The LTSs are fed into the static analysis portion of a refactoring tool [23] based on typestate analysis [16,49]. Stream pipelines are tracked and stream state when a terminal operation is issued is determined by the tool. Typestate analysis is a program analysis that augments the type system with "state" information and has been traditionally used for prevention of program errors such as those related to resource usage. It works by assigning each variable an initial ($\perp$) state. Then, method calls transition the object's state. States are represented by a lattice and possible transitions

---

[5] Recall from § 3 that it was necessary to use different subjects for different parts of the study due to the computationally intensive nature of some of the experiments.

are represented by LTSs. If each method call sequence on the receiver does not eventually transition the object back to the $\perp$ state, the object may be left in a nonsensical state, indicating the potential presence of a bug.

The LTSs for execution mode and ordering work as follows. The state $\perp$ is a phantom initial state immediately before stream creation. Different stream creation methods may transition the newly created stream to one that is either sequential or parallel or ordered or unordered. The transition continues for each invoked intermediate operation and ends with a terminal operation.

Since the analysis is focused on client-side analysis of stream APIs, the call graph is constructed using a k-CFA, where k is the call string length. It is an analysis parameter, with $k = 2$ being the default, as it is the minimum k needed to consider client-code, for methods returning streams and $k = 1$ elsewhere. The refactoring tool includes heuristics for determining sufficient and tractable k.

Counting Streams Since stream attributes are control flow sensitive, the streams studied must be in the control flow of entry points. For non-library subjects, all main methods were chosen, otherwise, all unit tests were chosen.

Streams are counted as follows. First, every *syntactic* stream is counted, i.e., every allocation site. Streams in the control flow of the program starting from an entry point transition according to the LTSs. If a stream is not in the control flow, it is still counted but it remains at the state following $\perp$. This way, more information about various stream attributes is available for the study as we do not need control flow to determine the state following $\perp$.

Side-effects and Stateful Intermediate Operations Stream side-effects are determined using a ModRef analysis on stream operation parameters (λ-expressions) using WALA [52]. SIOs are obtained from the documentation [39].

4.2   Results

Tab. 1 illustrates our findings on stream characteristics. Column **eps** is the number of entry points. Column **k** is the maximum k value used (see § 4.1). Columns **seq** and **para** correspond to the number of *sequential* and *parallel* streams, respectively. Column **ord** is the number of streams that are *ordered*, i.e., those whose operations must maintain an encounter order, which can be detrimental to efficient parallel performance, while column **unord** is the number *unordered* streams. Column **se** is the number of stream pipelines that include *side-effects*, which may induce race conditions. Finally, column **SIO** is the number of pipelines that include *stateful intermediate operations*, which may also be detrimental to efficient parallel performance.

4.3   Discussion

Parallel streams are not popular (1.25%) despite their ease-of-use. Although Nielebock et al. [36] did not consider λ-expressions in stream contexts, this confirms that their findings extend into stream contexts. It may also coincide with the finding of Lu et al. [28], i.e., that developers tend to "think" sequentially.

Finding 1: Stream parallelization is not widely used.

When considering using parallel streams, it may also be important to consider the *context*. For example, many server applications deal with thread pools that span the JVM, and developers may be leery of the interactions of such pools with the underlying stream parallelization run time system. We found this to be the case with several pull requests [15,45] that were issued by Khatchadourian et al. [24] as part of their refactoring evaluation to introduce parallel streams into existing projects. It may also be the case that the locations where streams operate are already fast enough or do not process significant amounts of data [7,30]. In fact, Naftalin [35, Ch. 6] found that there is a particular threshold in data size that must be reached to compensate for overhead incurred by parallel stream processing. Lastly, developers pointed us to several blog articles [54,59] expressing that parallel streams could be problematic under certain conditions.

There were, however, two projects that use parallel streams. Particularly, JabRef used the most parallel streams at 11. We conjecture that JabRef's use of parallel streams may stem from its status as a desktop application. Such applications typically are not managed by application containers and thus may not utilize global thread pools as in more traditional server applications.

Many streams are ordered (86.42%), which can prevent optimal performance of parallel streams under certain conditions [24,35,40]. Thus, even if streams were run in parallel, they may not reap all of the benefits. This extends the findings of Nielebock et al. [36] that λ-expressions do not appear in contexts amenable to parallelization to streams for the case of ordering. Streams may still be amenable to parallelization, as § 5.2 shows that many streams are traversed using API that *ignores* ordering (e.g., `forEach()` vs. `forEachOrdered()`).

Finding 2: Streams are largely *ordered*, possibly hindering parallelism.

That only $\sim$10% of streams have side-effects and only 2.31% have SIOs contradict the findings of Nielebock et al. [36] in the context of streams. This suggests that streams may run efficiently in parallel as, although they are largely ordered, they include minimal side-effects and SIOs. streamql had the most streams with SIOs ($18/22$), which may be due to its querying features using aggregate operations that are manifested as SIOs in the Java 8 Streaming API (e.g., `distinct()`).

Finding 3: Streams tend *not* to have side-effects.

---

5 Stream Usage

We discover the common operations on streams and the underlying reasons by examining stream method calls. This has important implications in understanding how streams are used, and studying language feature usage has been shown to be beneficial [11,43]. It provides valuable insight to programming language API designers and tool-support engineers on where to focus their evaluation efforts. We may also comprehend contexts where developers struggle with using streams.

5.1 Methodology

We examined 34 projects that use streams, spanning $\sim$5.53 million lines of source code. To find method calls, we parsed ASTs with source-symbol bindings using the Eclipse Java Developer Tools (JDT) [12]. Then, method invocation nodes were extracted whose compile-time targets are declared in types residing in the `java.util.stream` package. This includes types such as `Streams` and `Collectors`.

While stream creation is interesting and a topic for future work, our focus is on operations *on* streams as our scope is stream *usage*. We also combined methods with similar functionalities, e.g., `mapToLong()` with `map()` but not `forEach()` and `forEachOrdered()`. Additionally, only the method name is presented, resulting in a comparison of methods from both streams and collectors. The type is clear from the method name (e.g., `map()` is for `Streams`, while `groupingBy()` is for `Collectors`). We then proceeded to count the number of method calls in each project.

5.2   Results

Fig. 1 depicts the result of our analysis.[6] A full table is available in our dataset [25]. The horizontal axis lists the method name, and the legend depicts projects analyzed. The chart is sorted by the total number of calls in descending order. Calls per project range from 4 for threeten-extra to 4,635 for cyclops. Calls per method range from 2 for `characteristics()`, which returns stream attributes such as whether it is ordered or parallel, and 3,161 for `toList()`.

5.3   Discussion

The number of method calls in fig. 1 is substantial. There are 14,536 calls to methods operating on streams in 34 projects. This is impressive considering that Android, which uses the Java syntax, did not adopt streams immediately.

It is not surprising that the four most used stream methods are `toList()`, `collect()`, `map()`, and `filter()`, as these are the core MapReduce data transformation operations. `collect()` is a specialized reduction that reduces to a non-scalar type (e.g., a map) as opposed to the traditional scalar type. The `toList()` method is a static method of `Collectors`, which are pre-made reductions, in this case, to an `ArrayList`. This informs the `collect()` operation of the non-scalar type to use. It is peculiar that there are more calls to `toList()` than `collect()`. This is due to cyclops. We conjecture that it has some unorthodox usages of `Collectors` as it is a platform for writing functional-style programs in Java ≥ 8 [2].

That `collect()` and `toList()`, along with other terminal operations such as `forEach()`, `iterator()`, `toSet()`, and `toArray()`, appear towards the top to the list suggest that, although developers are writing functional-style code to process data in a "big data" processing style, they are not staying there. Instead, they are "bridging" back to imperative-style code, either by collecting data into imperative-style collections or processing the data further iteratively.

There can be various reasons for this, such as unfamiliarity with functional programming, the need to introduce side-effects, or the need to interoperate with legacy code. Further investigation is necessary, yet, Nielebock et al. [36] mention that developers tend to introduce side-effects into λ-expressions, which is related.

> *Finding 4*: Although stream usage is high, developers tend to reduce streams back to iterative-style collections.

We infer that developers tend to favor more simplistic (linear) rather than more specialized (higher-dimensionality) non-scalar reductions. It is surprising that more of the advanced reductions, such as those that return maps (e.g., `toMap()`,

---

[6] Similar conclusions hold when normalizing with subject KLOC.

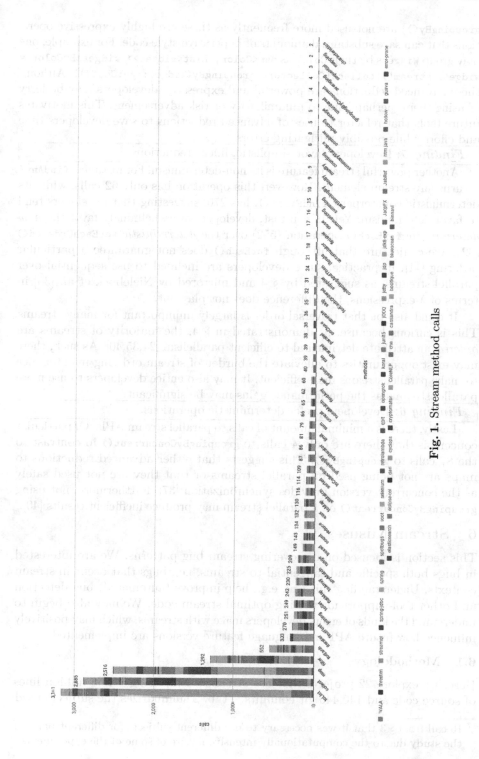

Fig. 1. Stream method calls

`groupingBy()`) are not used more frequently as these are highly expressive operations that can save substantial amounts of imperative-style code. For example, one may group `Widgets` by their `Color` as `Map<Color, List<Widget>> widgetsByColor = widgets.stream().collect(Collectors.groupingBy(Widget::getColor))`. Although these advanced reductions are powerful and expressive, developers may be leery of using them, perhaps due to unfamiliarity or risk adversement. This motivates future tools that refactor to uses of advanced reductions to save developers time and effort while possibly mitigating errors.

Finding 5: Developers favor simplistic, linear reductions.

Another powerful stream feature is its non-determinism. For instance, `findAny()` returns any stream element. However, this operation has only 62 calls, while its deterministic counterpart, `findFirst()`, has 270, suggesting that developers tend to favor determinism. Yet, in contrast, developers overwhelmingly favor the *non-deterministic* `forEach()` operation (552) over the *deterministic* `forEachOrdered()` (32). We conjecture that although `forEach()` does not guarantee a particular ordering [41], in practice, since developers are inclined to use sequential over parallel streams, as suggested by § 4 and mirrored by Nielebock et al. [36] in terms of λ-expressions, the difference does not play out.

It could also be that traversal order is largely unimportant for many streams. This is curious because, as demonstrated in § 4, the majority of streams are *ordered*, an attribute detrimental to efficient parallelism [24,35,40]. As such, there may exist opportunities to alleviate the burden of stream ordering maintenance to make parallel streams more efficient. It may also entice developers to use more parallel streams as the performance gains may be significant.

Finding 6: Developers prefer deterministic operations.

Lastly, there is a minimal amount of calls to parallel stream APIs. Of particular concern is that there are only 4 calls to `groupingByConcurrent()` in contrast to the 87 calls to `groupingBy()`. This suggests that either advanced reductions to maps are not being used on parallel streams or that they are not used safely as the concurrent version provides synchronization [37]. Furthermore, not using `groupingByConcurrent()` on a parallel stream may produce inefficient results [40].

6 Stream Misuses

This section is focused on discovering stream bug patterns. We are interested in bugs both specific and tangential to streams, i.e., bugs that occur in stream contexts. Understanding this can, e.g., help improve (automated) bug detection and other tool-support for writing optimal stream code. We may also begin to understand the kinds of errors developers make with streams, which may positively influence how future API and language feature versions are implemented.

6.1 Methodology

Here, we explore 22 projects that use streams, comprising ~4.68 million lines of source code and 140,446 git commits.[7] Tab. 2 summarizes the subjects used.

---

[7] Recall from § 3 that it was necessary to use different subjects for different parts of the study due to the computationally intensive nature of some of the experiments.

An Empirical Study on the Use and Misuse of Java 8 Streams 107

Table 2. Studied subjects.

subject	KLOC	studied periods	cmts	kws	exe
binnavi	328.28	2015-08-19 to 2019-07-17	286	4	4
blueocean-plugin	49.70	2016-01-23 to 2019-07-24	4,043	118	25
bootique	15.47	2015-12-10 to 2019-08-08	1,106	5	5
che	189.24	2016-02-11 to 2019-08-19	8,093	75	75
cryptomator	9.83	2014-02-01 to 2019-08-08	1,443	50	10
dari	72.46	2012-09-26 to 2018-03-02	2,466	18	6
eclipse.jdt.core	1,527.89	2001-06-05 to 2019-08-07	24,085	234	106
eclipse.jdt.ui	712.91	2001-05-02 to 2019-08-09	28,136	149	32
error-prone	165.85	2011-09-14 to 2019-08-15	3,893	71	71
guava	393.47	2009-06-18 to 2019-08-15	5,031	36	36
htm.java	41.63	2014-08-09 to 2019-02-19	1,507	40	1
JacpFX	24.06	2013-08-12 to 2018-04-27	365	37	14
jdk8-experiments	3.47	2013-08-03 to 2018-03-10	8	1	1
java-design-patterns	33.52	2014-08-09 to 2019-07-31	2,192	37	12
jetty	400.26	2009-03-16 to 2019-08-02	17,051	835	219
jOOQ	184.25	2011-07-24 to 2019-07-31	7,508	94	4
qbit	52.27	2014-08-25 to 2018-01-18	1,717	65	9
retrolambda	5.10	2013-07-20 to 2018-11-30	522	17	4
selenium	234.12	2004-11-03 to 2019-08-09	24,145	114	57
streamql	4.26	2014-04-27 to 2014-04-29	27	2	2
threeten-extra	31.26	2012-11-17 to 2019-07-14	559	28	2
WALA	203.84	2006-11-22 to 2019-07-24	6,263	52	24
Total	4,683.12		140,446	2,082	719

To find changesets (patches) corresponding to stream fixes, we compiled 140 keywords from the API documentation [39] that match stream operations and related method names from the `java.util.stream` package. We then randomly selected a subset of these commits whose changesets included these keywords and were likely to be bug fixes to manually examine.

Commit Mining To discover commits that had changesets including stream API keywords, we used `gitproc` [9], a tool for processing and classifying git commits, which has been used in previous work [17,50]. Due to the keyword-based search used, not all of the examined commits pertained to streams (e.g., "map" has a broad range of applications outside of streams). To mitigate this, we focused more on keywords that were specific to stream contexts, e.g., "Collector." Also to reduce false positives, we only considered commits after the Java 8 release date of March 18, 2014, which is when streams were introduced.

Finding Bug Fixes We used a feature of `gitproc` that uses heuristics based on commit log messages to identify commits that are bug fixes. Natural language processing (NLP) is used to determine which commits fall in this category. This helps us to focus on the likely bug-fix commits for further manual examination.

Next, the authors manually examine these commits to determine if the commits were indeed related to stream-related bugs. Three of the authors are software engineering and programming language professors with extensive expertise in streaming and parallel systems, concurrent systems, and empirical software engineering. The authors also have several years of industrial experience working as software engineers. As the authors did not always have expertise in the subject domains, only changes where a bug fix was extremely likely were marked as such. The authors also used commit comments and referenced bug databases to ascertain whether a change was a bug fix. This is a common practice [8,26,28].

Table 3. Stream bug/patch category legend.

name	description	acronym
Bounds	Incorrect/Missing Bounds Check	BC
Exceptions	Incorrect/Missing Exception Handling	EH
Other	Other change (e.g., syntax, refactoring)	Other
Perf	Poor Performance	PP
Concur	Concurrency Issue	CI
Stream Source	Incorrect/Missing Stream Source	SS
Intermediate Operations	Incorrect/Missing Intermediate Operations	IO
Data Ordering	Incorrect Data Ordering	DO
Operation Sequencing	Incorrect Operation Sequencing	OS
Filter Operations	Incorrect/Missing Filter Operations	FO
Map Operations	Incorrect/Missing Map Operations	MO
Terminal Operations	Incorrect/Missing Terminal Operations	TO
Reduction Operations	Incorrect Reduction Operations	RO
Collector Operations	Incorrect/Missing Collector Operations	CO
Incorrect Action	Incorrect Action (e.g., λ-expression)	IA

Classifying Bug Fixes Once bug fixes were identified, the authors studied the code changes to determine the category of bug fixes and whether the category relates to streams. Fortunately, we found that many commits reference bug reports or provide more details about the fix. Such information proved highly valuable in understanding the fixes. When in doubt, we also sent emails to developers for clarification purposes as git commits include email addresses.

6.2   Results

Quantitative Column **kws** of tab. 2 is the number of commits where occurrences of keywords were found and correspond to possible stream bug fixes. Column **exe** depicts the number of commits manually examined. From these 719 commits, we found 61 stream client code bug fixes. This is depicted in column **total** of tab. 4. Finding these bugs and understanding their relevance required a significant amount of manual labor that may not be feasible in more larger-scale, automated studies. Nevertheless, as streams become more popular (they were only introduced in 2014), we expect the usage and number of bugs related to streams to grow.

From the manual changes, we devised a set of common problem categories. Fixes were then grouped into these categories as shown in fig. 2 and tab. 4. A category legend appears in tab. 3, where column **name** is the "short" name of the bug category and is used in fig. 2. Column **description** is the categories extended name and column **acronym** is used in tab. 4.

Fig. 2 presents a hierarchical categorization of the 61 stream-related bug fixes. Bugs are represented by their category name (column **name** in tab. 3) and their bug counts. Categories with no count are *abstract*, i.e., those grouping categories.

Bugs are separated into two top-level categories, namely, bugs specifically related to stream API usage (stream-specific) and those tangentially related, i.e., bugs appearing in stream contexts but not specifically having to do with streams (generic). Generic bugs were further categorized into related to exception handling (EH), bounds checking (BC), poor performance (PP), and "other." Generic exception handling bugs (6) include those where, e.g., λ-expressions passed to stream operations threw exceptions that were not handled properly. Generic bounds checking bugs (2) included those where λ-expressions missed traversal boundary checks, and generic performance bugs (2) were those involving,

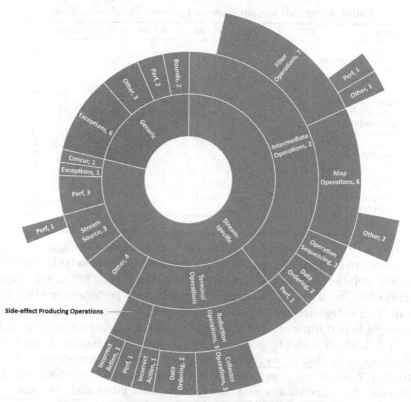

Fig. 2. Studied stream bugs and patches (hierarchical).

e.g., local variables holding stream computation results. The "other" category (3) is aligned with a similar one used by Tian and Ray [50] and involved syntactic corrections, e.g., incorrect types, and refactorings. Generally, "other" bugs can either be stream-specific or generic.

Stream-specific bugs are further divided into several categories corresponding to whether they involved intermediate operations (IO), terminal operations (TO), the stream source (SS), concurrency (CI), and performance and exception handling bugs specific to streams. IO-specific bugs (2) are related to intermediate operations other than filter operations (FO, 7) and map operations (MO, 6), e.g., distinct(). IO bugs are additionally partitioned into those involving incorrect operation sequencing (OS, 2), e.g., map() before filter(), data ordering (DO, 2), e.g., operating on a stream that should have been sorted, and performance bugs appearing in intermediate operations other than map() and filter() (1).

Terminal operations are split into two categories, namely, reduction operations (RO), e.g., collect(), reduce(), and side-effect producing operations, e.g., forEach(), iterator(). RO-specific bugs (3) were those related to scalar reductions, e.g., anyMatch(), allMatch(). RO-specific bugs related to collector operations (CO, 3), on the other hand, involve non-scalar reductions, e.g., a collector malfunction. RO-specific data ordering bugs (DO, 2) correspond to ordering of data related to scalar reductions, e.g., using findAny() instead of

Table 4. Studied stream bugs and patches (nonhierarchical).

subject	BC	CI	CO	DO	EH	FO	IA	IO	MO	OS	PP	RO	SS	Other	Total
binnavi														1	1
blueocean-plugin														1	1
bootique									1						1
che					1	1		1		1					4
cryptomator	1				2				1					2	6
dari														2	2
eclipse.jdt.core														1	1
eclipse.jdt.ui													1		1
error-prone					2	1	1	3		1	1	2		1	12
guava													1		1
JacpFX		1		1					2						4
jdp										1					1
jetty			1	2				1	3						7
jOOQ								1							1
selenium		2	1	2	5	1	2		2			1		1	17
threeten-extra	1														1
Total	2	1	3	4	7	7	2	2	6	2	9	3	3	10	61

findFirst(). RO-specific incorrect actions (IA, 1) is where there is a problematic λ in a scalar reduction, e.g., an incorrect predicate in noneMatch(). Side-effect producing operation bugs also include incorrect actions (IA, 1), e.g., a problematic λ in forEach(). Such operations can also exhibit poor performance (PO, 1).

Some bug categories are crosscutting, appearing under *multiple* categories. An example is performance. For this reason, tab. 4 portrays a nonhierarchical view of fig. 2, which is also broken down by **subject**, including a column for each bug category regardless of its parent category (acronyms correspond to tab. 3).

Finding 7: Bugs, e.g., performance, *crosscut* concerns, affecting multiple categories, both specifically and tangentially, associated with streams.

Performance issues dominate the functional (excluding "other") bugs depicted in tab. 4, making up the categories "Performance/API misuse" and "Performance," accounting for 14.75% (9/61) of the bugs found. While some of these fixes were more cleaning-based (e.g., superfluous operations), others affected central parts of the system and were found during performance regression testing [56].

Finding 8: Although streams feature performance improving parallelism, developers tend to struggle with using streams efficiently.

Despite widespread performance issues, concurrency issues (CI), on the other hand, were not prevalent (1.64%). The one concurrency bug was where a stream operation involved non-atomic variable access, which resulted in improper initialization [34]. Given that such a variable is accessed in a stream operation, however, it does indicate a possible side-effect and a need to consider refactoring such accesses to remove side-effects. This would make streams more amenable to efficient parallelization and perhaps promote more usage of parallel streams.

Finding 9: Concurrency issues were the *least* common streams bugs. However, concurrent variable access can cause thread contention, motivating future refactoring approaches that may promote more parallel streams.

The subjects selenium and error-prone had the most stream bugs with 27.87% and 19.67%, respectively. We hypothesize that this is due to the relatively large size of these projects, as well as their high usage of streams. Specifically, they fell into the top ten in terms of KLOC and stream method calls in tab. 2 and fig. 1, respectively, with ~400 combined KLOC and 1,414 combined calls. Naturally, projects that use streams more are likely to have more bugs involving streams.

Qualitative We highlight several of the most common bug categories with examples, summarize common fixes, and propose preliminary best practices (**BP**) and anti-patterns (**AP**). Due to space limitations, only a single example of each BP/AP is shown; a complete set is available in our dataset [25]. Although some APs may seem applicable beyond streams, e.g., avoiding superfluous operations, we conjecture that streams are more prone to such patterns, e.g., due to the ease in which operations can be chained and the deferred execution they offer.

SS→PP Performance issues dominated the number of stream bugs found and also crosscut multiple categories. Consider the following performance regression [56]:

```
      Project: jetty
  Commit ID: 70311fe98787ffb8a74ad296c9dd2ba9ac431c9c
       Log: Issue #3681
1 -  List<HttpField> cookies = preserveCookies ? _fields.stream().filter(f ->
2 -      f.getHeader() == HttpHeader.SET_COOKIE).collect(Collectors.toList()) : null;
3 +  List<HttpField> cookies = preserveCookies?_fields.getFields(HttpHeader.SET_COOKIE):null;
```

The stream field is replaced with `getFields()`, which performs an iterative traversal, effectively replacing streams with iteration. The developer found that using iteration was faster than using streams [57] and wanted more "JIT-friendly" code. The developer further admitted that using streams can make code more easy to read but can also be associated with "allocation/complexity cost [55]."

> **BP1**: Use performance regression testing to verify that streams in *critical* code paths perform efficiently.

In the following, a pair of superfluous operations are removed:

```
       Project: JacpFX
   Commit ID: 4f0d62d3a0987e47a4cbdf8e056bdf89713e6aac
        Log: fixed class scanning
1     final Stream<String> componentIds = CommonUtil
2         .getStringStreamFromArray(annotation.perspectives());
3     final Stream<Injectable> perspectiveHandlerList =
4 -        componentIds.parallel().sequential().map(this::mapToInjectable);
5 +        componentIds.map(this::mapToInjectable);
```

`getStringStreaFromArray()` returns a sequential stream, which is then converted to `parallel` and then to `sequential`. The superfluous operations are then removed.

> **AP1**: Avoid superfluous intermediate operations.

Fix: Generally, fixes for performance problems varied widely. They ranged from replacing stream code with iterative code, as seen above, to removing operations, to changing the stream source representations. Depending on context, the bugs' effect can be either innocuous and cause server performance degradation.

SS→TO→RO→CO The stream API provides several ready-made `Collectors` for convenience. However, the API does not guarantee a *specific* non-scalar used during the reduction. On one hand, this is convenient as developers may not need a specific collection type; on the other hand, however, developers must be careful to ensure that the specific subclass returned by the API meets their needs.

In the following, the developer does not realize, until an incorrect program output, that the `Map` returned by `Collectors.toMap()` does not support nulls:

```
     Project: selenium
  Commit ID: 91eb004d230d8d78ec97180e66bcc7055b16130f
       Log: Fix wrapping of maps with null values. Fixes #3380
1 if (result instanceof Map) {
2 -   return ((Map<String, Object>) result).entrySet().stream().collect(Collectors.toMap(
3 -     e -> e.getKey(), e -> wrapResult(e.getValue())));
4 +   return ((Map<String, Object>) result).entrySet().stream().collect(HashMap::new,
5 +     (m, e) -> m.put(e.getKey(), e.getValue()), Map::putAll);
```

The ready-made collector (line 2) is replaced with a direct call to `collect()` with a particular `Map` implementation specified (line 4), i.e., `HashMap`.

BP2: Use collectors *only* if client code is *agnostic* to particular container implementations. Otherwise, use the *direct* form of `collect()`.

Fix: Collector-related bugs are typically corrected by not using a `Collector` (as above), changing the `Collector` used, or altering the `Collector` arguments. They often adversely affect program behavior but are also caught by unit tests.

SS→IO In the ensuing commit, `distinct()` is called on a concatenated stream to ensure that no duplicates are created as a result of the concatenation:

```
     Project: selenium
  Commit ID: eb7d9bf9cea19b8bc1759c4de1eb495829489cbe
       Log: Fix tests failing because of ProtocolHandshake
1 -     return Stream.concat(fromOss, fromW3c);
2 +     return Stream.concat(fromOss, fromW3c).distinct();
```

BP3: Ensure concatenated streams have distinct elements.

Fix: SS→IO bugs tend to be fixed by adding *additional* operations.

SS→IO→Other Developers "bridged" back to an imperative-style performed an operation, then switched back to streams to continue a more functional-style:

```
     Project: jetty
  Commit ID: 91e9e7b76a08b776be21560d7ba20f9bfd943f04
       Log: Issue #984 Improve module listing
1 -   List<String> ordered = _modules.stream()
2 -     .map(m->{return m.getName();}).collect(Collectors.toList());
3 -   Collections.sort(ordered);
4 -   ordered.stream().map(n->{return get(n);}).forEach(module->
5 +   _modules.stream().filter(m->...).sorted().forEach(module->
```

Each module is mapped to its name and collected into a list. Then, `ordered` is sorted via a non-stream `Collections` API. Another stream is then derived from `ordered` to perform further operations. However, on line 5, the bridge to a collection and subsequent sort operation is removed, and the computation remains within the stream API. It is now more amenable to parallelization.

AP2: Avoid "bridging" between stream API and legacy collection APIs.

Using a long λ-expression in a single `map()` operation may make stream code less "functional," more difficult to read [29], and less amenable to parallelism. Consider the abbreviated commit below that returns the occupied drive letters on Windows systems by `collect`ing the first uppercase character of the path:

```
     Project: cryptomator
  Commit ID: b691e374eb2dad0284e13927e7c3fc1fdccae9bf
       Log: fixes #74
1 - return rootDirs.stream().map(path -> path.toString().toUpperCase()
2 -   .charAt(0)).collect(toSet());
3 + return rootDirs.stream().map(Path::toString).map(CharUtils::toChar)
4 +   .map(Character::toUpperCase).collect(toSet());
```

The λ-expression has been replaced with method references, however, there are more subtle yet import changes. Firstly, as `CharUtils.toChar()` returns the first character of a `String`, there is a small performance improvement as the entire string is no longer turned to uppercase but rather only the first character. Also, the new version is written in more of a functional-style by replacing the single λ-expression passed to `map()` with multiple `map()` operations. How data is transformed in the pipeline is easily visible, and future data transformations can be easily integrated by simply adding operations.

AP3: Avoid too many operations within a single `map()` operation.

Fix: "Other" non-type correcting fixes, e.g., refactorings, included introducing streams, sometimes from formerly iterative code (3), replacing `map()` with `mapToInt()` [20], and dividing "larger" operations into smaller ones.

7   Threats to Validity

Subjects may not be representative. To mitigate this, subjects were chosen from diverse domains and sizes. They have also been used in previous studies (e.g., [20,22]). Although java-design-patterns is artificial, it is a reference implementation similar to that of JHotDraw, which has been studied extensively (e.g., [31]). Also, as streams are relatively new, we expect a larger selection of subjects as they grow in popularity.

Entry points may not be correct, which could affect how stream attributes are calculated. Since standard entry points were chosen, these represent a superset of practically true entry points. Furthermore, there may be custom streams or collectors outside the standard API that we are not considered. As we aim to understand stream usage and misuse in the large, we hypothesize that the vast majority of projects using streams use ones from the standard libraries.

Our study involved many hours of manual validation, which can be subject to bias. However, we investigated referenced bug reports and other comments from developers to help us understand changes more fully. We also reached out to several developers via email correspondence when in doubt. All but one returned the correspondence. The NLP features of `gitcproc` may have missed changesets that were indeed bug fixes. Nevertheless, we were still able to find 61 bugs that contributed to a rich bug categorization, best practices, and anti-patterns. Furthermore, `gitcproc` has been used previously in other studies.

8   Related Work

Previous studies [29,32,36,46,51] have focused specifically on λ-expressions. While λ-expressions are used as arguments to stream operations, our focus is on stream *operations* themselves. Such operations transition streams to different states, which can be detrimental to parallel performance [24,35]. Also, since streams can be aliased, we use a tool [24] based on typestate analysis to obtain stream attributes more reliably than AST-based approaches. We also study bugs related to stream usage and present developer feedback—fixing bugs related to streams may not involve changing λ-expressions; bugs can be caused by, e.g., an incorrect sequence of stream operations. Lastly, although Nielebock et al. [36] consider λ-expressions in "concurrency contexts," such contexts do not include streams, where λ-expressions can easily execute in parallel with minimal syntactical effort.

Khatchadourian et al. [24] report on some stream characteristics as part of their refactoring evaluation but do so on a much smaller-scale, as their focus was on the refactoring algorithm. The work presented here goes significantly above in beyond by reporting on a richer set of stream characteristics (e.g., execution mode, ordering), with a noteworthy larger and updated corpus. We also include a comprehensive categorization of stream-related bug fixes, with 719 commits *manually* analyzed. Preliminary best practices and anti-patterns are also proposed.

Zhou et al. [60] conduct an empirical study on 210 service quality issues of a big data platform at Microsoft to understand their common symptoms, causes, and mitigations. They identify hardware faults, systems, and customer side effects as major causes of quality issues. There are also empirical studies on data-parallel programs. Kavulya et al. [19] study failures in MapReduce programs. Jin et al. [18] study performance slowdowns caused by system side inefficiencies. Xiao et al. [58] conduct a study on commutativity, nondeterminism, and correctness of data-parallel programs, revealing that non-commutative reductions lead to bugs. Though related, our work specifically focuses on stream APIs as a language feature and programming paradigm, which pose special considerations due to its shared memory model, i.e., interactions between the operations and local memory. Bloch [6, Ch. 7] also puts-forth stream best practices and anti-patterns. However, ours are based on a statistical analysis of real-world software and first-hand interactions with real-world developers.

Others also study language features. Parnin et al. [43] study the adoption of Java generics. Dyer et al. [11] build an expansive infrastructure for studying the use of language features over time. Khatchadourian and Masuhara [22] employ a proactive approach in empirically assessing new language features and present a case study on default methods. There are also many studies regarding bug analysis. For example, Engler et al. [13] present a general approach to inferring errors in systems code, and Tian and Ray [50] study error handling bugs in C.

9   Conclusion & Future Work

This study advances our understanding of stream usage and bug patterns. We have surveyed common stream operations, attributes, and bugs specific and tangentially related to streams. A hierarchical taxonomy of stream bugs was devised, preliminary best practices and anti-patterns were proposed, and first-hand developer interactions were detailed. In the future, we will explore stream creation, use our findings to devise automated error checkers, and explore topics that interest stream developers. Lastly, we will investigate applicability to other streaming frameworks and languages.

Acknowledgments We would like to thank Krishna Desai and Robert Dyer for work on data summarization and discussions, respectively. Support for this project was provided by PSC-CUNY Award #617930049, jointly funded by The Professional Staff Congress and The City University of New York. This material is based upon work supported by the National Science Foundation under Grant No. CCF 1845893, CNS 1842456, and CCF 1822965.

References

1. Ahmed, S., and Bagherzadeh, M.: What Do Concurrency Developers Ask About?: A Large-scale Study Using Stack Overflow. In: International Symposium on Empirical Software Engineering and Measurement, 30:1–30:10 (2018). DOI: 10.1145/3239235. 3239524
2. AOL: AOL/cyclops: An advanced, but easy to use, platform for writing functional applications in Java 8. (2019). http://git.io/fjxzF (visited on 08/29/2019)
3. Bagherzadeh, M., and Khatchadourian, R.: Going Big: A Large-scale Study on What Big Data Developers Ask. In: Joint Meeting on European Software Engineering Conference and Symposium on the Foundations of Software Engineering. ESEC/FSE 2019, pp. 432–442. ACM, Tallinn, Estonia (2019). DOI: 10.1145/3338906.3338939
4. Bagherzadeh, M., and Rajan, H.: Order Types: Static Reasoning About Message Races in Asynchronous Message Passing Concurrency. In: International Workshop on Programming Based on Actors, Agents, and Decentralized Control, pp. 21–30 (2017). DOI: 10.1145/3141834.3141837
5. Biboudis, A., Palladinos, N., Fourtounis, G., and Smaragdakis, Y.: Streams a la carte: Extensible Pipelines with Object Algebras. In: European Conference on Object-Oriented Programming, pp. 591–613 (2015). DOI: 10.4230/LIPIcs.ECOOP.2015.591
6. Bloch, J.: Effective Java. Prentice Hall, Upper Saddle River, NJ, USA (2018)
7. Bordet, S.: Pull Request #2837 • eclipse/jetty.project, Webtide. (2018). http://git.io/JeBAF (visited on 10/20/2019)
8. Casalnuovo, C., Devanbu, P., Oliveira, A., Filkov, V., and Ray, B.: Assert Use in GitHub Projects. In: International Conference on Software Engineering. ICSE '15, pp. 755–766. IEEE Press, Florence, Italy (2015). http://dl.acm.org/citation.cfm?id=2818754.2818846
9. Casalnuovo, C., Suchak, Y., Ray, B., and Rubio-González, C.: GitcProc: A Tool for Processing and Classifying GitHub Commits. In: International Symposium on Software Testing and Analysis. ISSTA 2017, pp. 396–399. ACM, Santa Barbara, CA, USA (2017). DOI: 10.1145/3092703.3098230
10. Dean, J., and Ghemawat, S.: MapReduce: Simplified Data Processing on Large Clusters. Commun. ACM 51(1), 107–113 (2008). DOI: 10.1145/1327452.1327492
11. Dyer, R., Rajan, H., Nguyen, H.A., and Nguyen, T.N.: Mining Billions of AST Nodes to Study Actual and Potential Usage of Java Language Features. In: International Conference on Software Engineering. ICSE 2014, pp. 779–790. ACM, Hyderabad, India (2014)
12. Eclipse Foundation: Eclipse Java development tools (JDT), Eclipse Foundation. (2019). http://eclipse.org/jdt (visited on 10/19/2019)
13. Engler, D., Chen, D.Y., Hallem, S., Chou, A., and Chelf, B.: Bugs As Deviant Behavior: A General Approach to Inferring Errors in Systems Code. In: Symposium on Operating Systems Principles. SOSP '01, pp. 57–72. ACM, Banff, Alberta, Canada (2001). DOI: 10.1145/502034.502041
14. EPFL: Collections–Mutable and Immutable Collections–Scala Documentation, (2017). http://scala-lang.org/api/2.12.3/scala/collection/index.html (visited on 08/24/2018)
15. Erdfelt, J.: Pull Request #2837 • eclipse/jetty.project, Eclipse Foundation. (2018). http://git.io/JeBAM (visited on 10/20/2019)
16. Fink, S.J., Yahav, E., Dor, N., Ramalingam, G., and Geay, E.: Effective Typestate Verification in the Presence of Aliasing. ACM Transactions on Software Engineering and Methodology 17(2), 91–934 (2008). DOI: 10.1145/1348250.1348255

17. Gharbi, S., Mkaouer, M.W., Jenhani, I., and Messaoud, M.B.: On the Classification of Software Change Messages Using Multi-label Active Learning. In: Symposium on Applied Computing. SAC '19, pp. 1760–1767. ACM, Limassol, Cyprus (2019). DOI: 10.1145/3297280.3297452

18. Jin, H., Qiao, K., Sun, X.-H., and Li, Y.: Performance Under Failures of MapReduce Applications. In: International Symposium on Cluster, Cloud and Grid Computing. CCGRID '11, pp. 608–609. IEEE Computer Society, Washington, DC, USA (2011). DOI: 10.1109/ccgrid.2011.84

19. Kavulya, S., Tan, J., Gandhi, R., and Narasimhan, P.: An Analysis of Traces from a Production MapReduce Cluster. In: International Conference on Cluster, Cloud and Grid Computing. CCGrid 2010, pp. 94–103. IEEE, Melbourne, Australia (2010). DOI: 10.1109/CCGRID.2010.112

20. Ketkar, A., Mesbah, A., Mazinanian, D., Dig, D., and Aftandilian, E.: Type Migration in Ultra-large-scale Codebases. In: International Conference on Software Engineering. ICSE '19, pp. 1142–1153. IEEE Press, Montreal, Quebec, Canada (2019). DOI: 10.1109/ICSE.2019.00117

21. Khatchadourian, R., and Masuhara, H.: Automated Refactoring of Legacy Java Software to Default Methods. In: International Conference on Software Engineering, pp. 82–93 (2017). DOI: 10.1109/ICSE.2017.16

22. Khatchadourian, R., and Masuhara, H.: Proactive Empirical Assessment of New Language Feature Adoption via Automated Refactoring: The Case of Java 8 Default Methods. In: International Conference on the Art, Science, and Engineering of Programming, 6:1–6:30 (2018). DOI: 10.22152/programming-journal.org/2018/2/6

23. Khatchadourian, R., Tang, Y., Bagherzadeh, M., and Ahmed, S.: A Tool for Optimizing Java 8 Stream Software via Automated Refactoring. In: International Working Conference on Source Code Analysis and Manipulation, pp. 34–39 (2018). DOI: 10.1109/SCAM.2018.00011

24. Khatchadourian, R., Tang, Y., Bagherzadeh, M., and Ahmed, S.: Safe Automated Refactoring for Intelligent Parallelization of Java 8 Streams. In: International Conference on Software Engineering. ICSE '19, pp. 619–630. IEEE Press (2019). DOI: 10.1109/ICSE.2019.00072

25. Khatchadourian, R., Tang, Y., Bagherzadeh, M., and Ray, B.: *An Empirical Study on the Use and Misuse of Java 8 Streams*, (2020). DOI: 10.5281/zenodo.3677449. Feb. 2020.

26. Kochhar, P.S., and Lo, D.: Revisiting Assert Use in GitHub Projects. In: International Conference on Evaluation and Assessment in Software Engineering. EASE'17, pp. 298–307. ACM, Karlskrona, Sweden (2017). DOI: 10.1145/3084226.3084259

27. Lau, J.: Future of Java 8 Language Feature Support on Android. Android Developers Blog (2017). http://android-developers.googleblog.com/2017/03/future-of-java-8-language-feature.html (visited on 08/24/2018)

28. Lu, S., Park, S., Seo, E., and Zhou, Y.: Learning from Mistakes: A Comprehensive Study on Real World Concurrency Bug Characteristics. In: International Conference on Architectural Support for Programming Languages and Operating Systems, pp. 329–339. ACM (2008). DOI: 10.1145/1346281.1346323

29. Lucas, W., Bonifácio, R., Canedo, E.D., Marcílio, D., and Lima, F.: Does the Introduction of Lambda Expressions Improve the Comprehension of Java Programs? In: Brazilian Symposium on Software Engineering. SBES 2019, pp. 187–196. ACM, Salvador, Brazil (2019). DOI: 10.1145/3350768.3350791

30. Luontola, E.: Pull Request #140 • orfjackal/retrolambda, Nitor Creations. (2018). http://git.io/JeBAQ (visited on 10/20/2019)

31. Marin, M., Moonen, L., and Deursen, A. van: An Integrated Crosscutting Concern Migration Strategy and its Application to JHotDraw. In: International Working Conference on Source Code Analysis and Manipulation (2007)

32. Mazinanian, D., Ketkar, A., Tsantalis, N., and Dig, D.: Understanding the Use of Lambda Expressions in Java. Proc. ACM Program. Lang. 1(OOPSLA), 85:1–85:31 (2017). DOI: 10.1145/3133909

33. Microsoft: LINQ: .NET Language Integrated Query, (2018). http://msdn.microsoft.com/en-us/library/bb308959.aspx (visited on 08/24/2018)

34. Moncsek, A.: allow OnShow when Perspective is initialized, fixed issues with OnShow/OnHide in perspective • JacpFX/JacpFX@f2d92f7, JacpFX. (2015). http://git.io/Je0X8 (visited on 10/24/2019)

35. Naftalin, M.: Mastering Lambdas: Java Programming in a Multicore World. McGraw-Hill (2014)

36. Nielebock, S., Heumüller, R., and Ortmeier, F.: Programmers Do Not Favor Lambda Expressions for Concurrent Object-oriented Code. Empirical Softw. Engg. 24(1), 103–138 (2019). DOI: 10.1007/s10664-018-9622-9

37. Oracle: Collectors (Java Platform SE 10 & JDK 10)–groupingByConcurrent, (2018). http://docs.oracle.com/javase/10/docs/api/java/util/stream/Collectors.html#groupingByConcurrent(java.util.function.Function) (visited on 08/29/2019)

38. Oracle: HashSet (Java SE 9) & JDK 9, (2017). http://docs.oracle.com/javase/9/docs/api/java/util/HashSet.html (visited on 04/07/2018)

39. Oracle: java.util.stream (Java SE 9 & JDK 9), (2017). http://docs.oracle.com/javase/9/docs/api/java/util/stream/package-summary.html (visited on 02/22/2020)

40. Oracle: java.util.stream (Java SE 9 & JDK 9)–Parallelism, (2017). http://docs.oracle.com/javase/9/docs/api/java/util/stream/package-summary.html#Parallelism (visited on 02/22/2020)

41. Oracle: Stream (Java Platform SE 10 & JDK 10)–forEach, (2018). http://docs.oracle.com/javase/10/docs/api/java/util/stream/Stream.html#forEach(java.util.function.Consumer) (visited on 08/29/2019)

42. Oracle: Thread Interference, (2017). http://docs.oracle.com/javase/tutorial/essential/concurrency/interfere.html (visited on 04/16/2018)

43. Parnin, C., Bird, C., and Murphy-Hill, E.: Adoption and Use of Java Generics. Empirical Softw. Engg. 18(6), 1047–1089 (2013). DOI: 10.1007/s10664-012-9236-6

44. Refsnes Data: JavaScript Array map() Method, (2015). http://w3schools.com/jsref/jsref_map.asp (visited on 02/22/2020)

45. Rutledge, P.: Pull Request #1 • RutledgePaulV/monads, Vodori. (2018). http://git.io/JeBAZ (visited on 10/20/2019)

46. Sangle, S., and Muvva, S.: On the Use of Lambda Expressions in 760 Open Source Python Projects. In: Joint Meeting on European Software Engineering Conference and Symposium on the Foundations of Software Engineering. ESEC/FSE 2019, pp. 1232–1234. ACM, Tallinn, Estonia (2019). DOI: 10.1145/3338906.3342499

47. Shilkov, M.: Introducing Stream Processing in F#, (2016). http://mikhail.io/2016/11/introducing-stream-processing-in-fsharp (visited on 07/18/2018)

48. Stack Overflow: Newest 'java-stream' Questions, (2018). http://stackoverflow.com/questions/tagged/java-stream (visited on 03/06/2018)

49. Strom, R.E., and Yemini, S.: Typestate: A programming language concept for enhancing software reliability. IEEE Transactions on Software Engineering SE-12(1), 157–171 (1986). DOI: 10.1109/tse.1986.6312929

50. Tian, Y., and Ray, B.: Automatically Diagnosing and Repairing Error Handling Bugs in C. In: Joint Meeting on European Software Engineering Conference and

Symposium on the Foundations of Software Engineering. ESEC/FSE 2017, pp. 752–762. ACM, Paderborn, Germany (2017). DOI: 10.1145/3106237.3106300

51. Uesbeck, P.M., Stefik, A., Hanenberg, S., Pedersen, J., and Daleiden, P.: An empirical study on the impact of C++ lambdas and programmer experience. In: International Conference on Software Engineering. ICSE '16, pp. 760–771. ACM, Austin, Texas (2016). DOI: 10.1145/2884781.2884849

52. WALA Team: T.J. Watson Libraries for Analysis, (2015). http://wala.sf.net (visited on 01/18/2017)

53. Warburton, R.: Java 8 Lambdas: Pragmatic Functional Programming (2014)

54. Weiss, T.: Java 8: Behind The Glitz and Glamour of The New Parallelism APIs. OverOps Blog (2014). http://blog.overops.com/new-parallelism-apis-in-java-8-behind-the-glitz-and-glamour (visited on 10/20/2019)

55. Wilkins, G.: Issue #3681 • eclipse/jetty.project@70311fe, Webtide, LLC. (2019)

56. Wilkins, G.: Jetty 9.4.x 3681 http fields optimize by gregw • Pull Request #3682 • eclipse/jetty.project, Webtide, LLC. (2019). http://git.io/JeBAq (visited on 09/18/2019)

57. Wilkins, G.: Jetty 9.4.x 3681 http fields optimize by gregw • Pull Request #3682 • eclipse/jetty.project. Comment, Webtide, LLC. (2019). http://git.io/JeOMS (visited on 10/24/2019)

58. Xiao, T., Zhang, J., Zhou, H., Guo, Z., McDirmid, S., Lin, W., Chen, W., and Zhou, L.: Nondeterminism in MapReduce Considered Harmful? An Empirical Study on Non-commutative Aggregators in MapReduce Programs. In: ICSE Companion, pp. 44–53 (2014). DOI: 10.1145/2591062.2591177

59. Zhitnitsky, A.: How Java 8 Lambdas and Streams Can Make Your Code 5 Times Slower. OverOps Blog (2015). http://blog.overops.com/benchmark-how-java-8-lambdas-and-streams-can-make-your-code-5-times-slower (visited on 10/20/2019)

60. Zhou, H., Lou, J.-G., Zhang, H., Lin, H., Lin, H., and Qin, T.: An Empirical Study on Quality Issues of Production Big Data Platform. In: International Conference on Software Engineering. ICSE 2015, pp. 17–26. ACM, Florence, Italy (2015)

Extracting Semantics from Question-Answering Services for Snippet Reuse

Themistoklis Diamantopoulos(iD), Nikolaos Oikonomou(iD), and Andreas Symeonidis(iD)

Electrical and Computer Engineering Dept., Aristotle University of Thessaloniki
Thessaloniki, Greece
thdiaman@issel.auth.gr, nikooiko@ece.auth.gr, asymeon@eng.auth.gr

Abstract. Nowadays, software developers typically search online for reusable solutions to common programming problems. However, forming the question appropriately, and locating and integrating the best solution back to the code can be tricky and time consuming. As a result, several mining systems have been proposed to aid developers in the task of locating reusable snippets and integrating them into their source code. Most of these systems, however, do not model the semantics of the snippets in the context of source code provided. In this work, we propose a snippet mining system, named StackSearch, that extracts semantic information from Stack Overflow posts and recommends useful and in-context snippets to the developer. Using a hybrid language model that combines Tf-Idf and fastText, our system effectively understands the meaning of the given query and retrieves semantically similar posts. Moreover, the results are accompanied with useful metadata using a named entity recognition technique. Upon evaluating our system in a set of common programming queries, in a dataset based on post links, and against a similar tool, we argue that our approach can be useful for recommending ready-to-use snippets to the developer.

Keywords: Code Search · Snippet Mining · Code Semantic Analysis · Question-Answering Systems.

1 Introduction

Lately, the widespread use of the Internet and the introduction of the open-source development initiative have given rise to a new way of developing software. Developers nowadays rely more than ever on online services in order to solve common problems arising during development, including e.g. developing a component, integrating an API, or even fixing a bug. This new reuse paradigm has been greatly supported by search engines, code hosting facilities, programming forums, and question-answering communities, such as Stack Overflow[1]. One could even argue that software today is built using reusable components, which are found in software libraries and are exposed via APIs.

---

[1] https://stackoverflow.com/

© The Author(s) 2020
H. Wehrheim and J. Cabot (Eds.): FASE 2020, LNCS 12076, pp. 119–139, 2020.
https://doi.org/10.1007/978-3-030-45234-6_6

As a result, the challenge lies in properly integrating these APIs/components in order to support the required functionality. This process is typically performed via *snippets*, i.e. small code fragments that usually perform clearly defined tasks (e.g. reading a CSV file, connecting to a database, etc.). Given the vastness of data in the services outlined in the previous paragraph (e.g. Stack Oveflow alone has more than 18 million question posts[2]), locating the most suitable snippet to perform a task and integrating it to one's own source code can be hard. In this context, developers often have to leave the IDE, form a query in an online tool and navigate through several solutions before finding the most suitable one.

To this end, several systems have been proposed. Some of these systems focus on the *API usage mining* problem [5,9,13,14,17,18,27,30] and extract examples for specific library APIs, while others offer more generic *snippet mining* solutions [3,6,28,29] and further allow queries for common programming problems (e.g. how to read a file in Java). Both types of systems usually employ an indexing mechanism that allows developers to form a query and retrieve relevant snippets.

These systems, however, have important limitations. First of all, several of them do not allow queries in natural language and may require the developer to spend time in order to form a query in some specialized format. Secondly, most systems index only information extracted from source code, without accounting for the semantics that can be extracted from comments or even from the surrounding text in the context (web location) that each snippet is found. Furthermore, most tools employ some type of lexical (term frequency) indexing, thus not exploiting the benefits of embeddings that can lead to semantic-aware retrieval. Finally, the format and the presentation of the results is most of the time far from optimal. There are systems that return call sequences as opposed to ready-to-use snippets, while, even when snippets are retrieved, they are sometimes provided as-is without any additional information concerning their APIs.

In this paper, we design and develop StackSearch, a system that receives queries in natural language and employs an indexing mechanism on Stack Overflow data in order to retrieve useful snippets. The indexing mechanism takes advantage of all possible information about a snippet by extracting semantics from both the textual (title, tags, body) and the source code part of Stack Overflow posts. The information is extracted using lexical matching as well as embeddings in order to produce a hybrid model and retrieve the most useful results, even when taking into account the possible ambiguities of natural language. Finally, the snippets retrieved by StackSearch are accompanied by relevant labels that provide an interpretation of the semantics of the posts and the employed APIs.

2   Related Work

As already mentioned, we focus on snippet mining systems that recommend solutions to typical programming problems. Some of the first systems proposed in this area were Prospector [16] and PARSEWeb [25]. These systems focus on

---

[2] Source: https://data.stackexchange.com/

recommending snippets that form a path between a source object to a target object. For Prospector, these paths are called jungloids and the program flow is a jungloid graph. Though interesting, the system has a local database, which limits its applicability. PARSEWeb, on the other hand, uses the Google search engine and produces better results in most scenarios [25]). However, both systems have important limitations; they require the developer to know which API calls to use and further receive queries in a specialized format, and not in natural language.

Another popular category of systems in current research involves those focusing on the challenge of API usage mining, such as MAPO [30], UP-Miner [27] or PAM [9]. The problem is typically defined as extracting common usage patterns from client source code, i.e. source code that uses the relevant API. To do so, MAPO employs frequent sequence mining, while UP-Miner uses graphs and mines frequent closed API call paths. PAM, on the other hand, employs probabilistic machine learning to extract sequences that exhibit higher coverage of the API under analysis and are more diverse [9]. Though quite effective, these systems are actually limited to the API under analysis and cannot support more generic queries. Furthermore, they too do not accept queries in natural language, while their output is in the form of sequences, instead of ready-to-use snippets.

Similar conclusions can be drawn for API mining systems that output snippets. For example, APIMiner [17] performs code slicing in order to generate common API usage examples, while eXoaDocs [14] further performs semantic clustering (using the DECKARD code clone detection algorithm [11]) to group them according to their functionality. CLAMS [13] also clusters the snippets and further generates the most representative (medoid) snippet of each cluster using slicing and code summarization techniques. Another interesting approach is MUSE [18], which employs a novel ranking scheme for the recommended snippets based on metrics such as the ease of reuse, a metric computed by determining whether a snippet has custom object types, and thus requires external dependencies. As with the previous approaches, these systems are effective for mining API usage examples, however they do not generalize to the problem of receiving natural language queries and retrieving API-agnostic reusable solutions.

This more generic snippet mining scenario is supported by several contemporary systems. One such system is SnipMatch [29], which employs pattern-based code search to retrieve useful snippets. SnipMatch, however, relies on a local index that has to be updated from the developer. More advanced systems in this aspect usually connect to online search engines and process their results to extract and recommend snippets. For example, Blueprint [3] and CodeCatch [6] employ the Google search engine, while Bing Code Search [28] employs Bing. Due to the integration with strong engines, these systems tend to offer effective natural language understanding features and their results are adequate even in less common queries. However, the text surrounding the code is not parsed for semantic information, so the quality of the retrieved snippets is bound only to the semantics introduced by the search engines. Moreover, the agnostic web search that these systems perform may often be suboptimal compared to issuing the queries to a better focused question-answering service.

These limitations have led to more specialized tools that employ Stack Overflow in order to recommend snippets that are proposed by the community and are accompanied by useful metadata. One of the first such systems is Example Overflow [35], an online code search engine that uses Tf-Idf as a scoring mechanism and retrieves snippets relevant to the jQuery framework. Two other systems in this area, which are built as plugins of the Eclipse IDE, are Prompter [22] and Seahawk [21]. Prompter employs a sophisticated ranking mechanism based not only on the code of each snippet, but also on metadata, such as the score of the post or reputation of the user that posted it on Stack Overflow. Seahawk also uses similar metadata upon building a local index using Apache Solr[3]. The main limitation of the systems in this category is their reliance on term occurrence; the lack of more powerful semantics restricts the retrieved results to cases where the query terms appear as-is within the Stack Overflow posts.

Finally, there are certain research efforts towards semantic-aware snippet retrieval. SWIM [23], for instance, which is proposed by the research team behind Bing Code Search [28], uses a natural language to API mapper that computes the probability $Pr(t|Q)$ that an API t appears as a result to a query Q. The system retrieves the most probable snippets and synthesizes them to produce valid and human-readable snippets. A limitation of SWIM, which was highlighted by Gu et al. [10], is that it follows the bag-of-words assumption, therefore it cannot distinguish among certain queries (e.g. "convert number to string" and "convert string to number). The authors instead propose DeepAPI [10], a system that defines snippet recommendation as a machine translation problem, where natural language is the source language and source code is the target language. DeepAPI employs a model with three recurrent neural networks (one for the text of the query as-is, one for the same text reversed, and one to combine them) that retrieves the most relevant API call sequence given a query. The system, however, is largely based on code comments, so its performance depends on whether there is sufficient documentation in the snippets of its index. A similar approach is followed by T2API [20], another Ecliple plugin that uses a graph-based translation approach to translate query text into API usages. This system, however, is also largely based on synthesizing API calls and does not focus on semantic retrieval. Finally, an even more recent system is CROKAGE [24], which employs embeddings and further expands the query with relevant API classes from Stack Overflow. The final results are ranked according to multiple factors, including their lexical and semantic similarity with the query and their similar API usage.

In conclusion, the systems analyzed in the above paragraphs have the limitations that were discussed also in the introduction of this work. Several of them are focused only on APIs without generalizing to common programming problems. And while there are certain systems that allow queries in natural language, most of them rely on term frequency indexing and do not incorporate semantics extracted by the context of the snippets. In this work, we design a hybrid system that employs both a lexical (term frequency) and a word embeddings model on Stack Overflow posts' data. Note that, compared to source code comments that

---

[3] https://lucene.apache.org/solr/

may be incomplete or sometimes even non-existent, the text of Stack Overflow posts is a more complete source of information as it is the outcome of the explanation efforts of different members of the community [7]. As a result, our system can extract the semantic meaning of natural language queries and retrieve useful snippets, which are accompanied by semantic-aware labels.

3 StackSearch: A Semantic-aware Snippet Recommender

3.1 Overview

The architecture of StackSearch is shown in Figure 1. The left part of the figure refers to building the index while the right one refers to answering user queries.

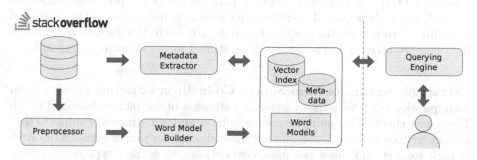

Fig. 1. Architecture of StackSearch

At first, our system retrieves information from Stack Overflow[4] and builds an SQLite[5] database of all Java posts. Note that our methodology is mostly language agnostic, however we use Java here as a proof of concept[6]. We created four tables in order to store question posts, answer posts, comments, and post links (to be used for evaluation, see subsection 4.2). For each of these tables we kept all information, i.e. title, tags, body, score, etc., as well as all connections of the data dump as foreign keys (e.g. any answer has a foreign key towards the corresponding question), so that we fully take into account the post context.

Upon storing the data in a suitable format, the Preprocessor receives as input all question posts, answer posts, and comments and extracts a corpus of texts. The corpus is then given to the Word Model Builder, which trains different models to transform the text to vector form. Finally, the system includes a vector index, where each set of vectors corresponds to to the title, tags, and body of one question post, the produced word models, and certain metadata for each question, which are extracted by the Metadata Extractor.

---

[4] We used the latest official data dump provided by Stack Overflow, which is available at https://archive.org/details/stackexchange

[5] https://www.sqlite.org/

[6] Applying our methodology to a different language requires only providing a preprocessor in order to extract the relevant source code elements from the post snippets.

When the developer issues a query, the Querying Engine initially extracts a vector for the query given the stored vector models, and then computes the similarity between the query vector and each vector in the vector index. The engine then ranks the results and presents them to the user along with their metadata. The steps required to build the index as well as the issuing of queries are discussed in detail in the following subsections.

3.2   Preprocessor

Upon creating our database, the next step is to preprocess the data in order to build the corpus that will be used to train our models. We extract the text and the code of each post by parsing the <pre> and <code> tags. We further remove all html tags from text and then perform a series of preprocessing steps. At first, the code is parsed to extract its semantic information. The posts are then filtered to remove the ones that introduce noise to the dataset and, finally, the texts are tokenized. These steps are outlined in the following paragraphs.

Extracting Semantics from Source Code Upon extracting the code from each question post, we parse it using an extension of the parser described in [8]. The parser checks if the snippets are compilable and also drops any snippets that are not written in Java. Upon making these checks, our parser extracts the AST of each snippet and takes two passes over it, one to extract type declarations, and one to extract method invocations (i.e. API calls). For example, in the snippet of Figure 2, the parser initially extracts the declarations is: InputStream, br: BufferedReader, and sb: StringBuilder (strings and exceptions are excluded). After that, it extracts the relevant API calls, which are highlighted in Figure 2.

```
// initialize an InputStream
InputStream is = new ByteArrayInputStream ("sample" .getBytes());
// convert InputStream to String
BufferedReader br = null;
StringBuilder sb = new StringBuilder ();
String line;
try {
    br = new BufferedReader (new InputStreamReader (is));
    while ((line = br. readLine ()) != null) { sb. append (line); }
} catch (IOException e) {
    e.printStackTrace();
} finally {
    if (br != null) {
        try { br. close (); } catch (IOException e) { e.printStackTrace(); }
    }
}
```

Fig. 2. Example snippet for "How to read a file line by line" (API calls highlighted)

Finally, the calling object of each API call is replaced by its type and the text of comments is also retrieved to produce the sequence shown in Figure 3.

---

initialize an InputStream, InputStream, ByteArrayInputStream, convert InputStream to String, BufferedReader, StringBuilder, StringBuilder, BufferedReader, InputStreamReader, BufferedReader.readLine, StringBuilder.append, BufferedReader.close

---

Fig. 3. Extracted sequence for the snippet of Figure 2

Filtering the Posts Filtering is performed using a classifier that rules out any posts that are considered by our system as noise. We used the regional CNN-LSTM model of Wang et al. [26], a model shown in Figure 4 that combines the CNN and LSTM architectures and achieves in capturing the characteristics of text considering also its order. Our classifier is binary; it receives as input the data of each post and its output determines whether a post is *useful* or *noisy*.

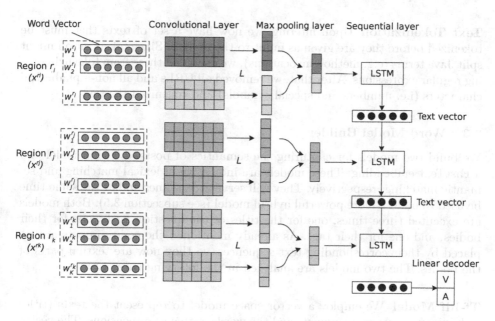

Fig. 4. Architecture of Regional CNN-LSTM model by Wang et al. [26]

The input embedding layer receives a one-hot encoding that corresponds to the concatenation of the title, body and tags of each post. Tokenization and one-hot encoding are performed before the text is given as input so no rules are given other than splitting on spaces and punctuation (this tokenization process is only used here on-the-fly to filter the posts, while we fully tokenize the text afterwards as described in the next paragraph). Punctuation marks are also kept as each of them is actually a token. After that, the classifier includes a CNN layer, which extracts and amplifies the terms (including punctuation) that cause noise. The CNN layer is followed by a max pooling layer that is used to reduce the number of parameters that have to be optimized by the model. Finally, the next layer is the LSTM that captures semantic information from nearby terms, which is finally given to the output to provide the binary decision.

To train our classifier, we have annotated a set of 2500 posts. For each post, we consider it noisy if it has error logs, debug logs or stack traces. Though useful in other contexts, in our case these posts would skew our models, as they contain a lot of generic data. Furthermore we deem noisy any posts with large amounts of numeric data (usually in tables) and any posts with code snippets in languages other than Java. The training was performed with accuracy as the metric to optimize, while we also used dropout to avoid overfitting. Upon experimenting with different parameter values, we ended up using the Adagrad optimizer, while the dropout and recurrent dropout parameters were set to 0.6 and 0.05 respectively. Setting the embedding length to 35 and the number of epochs to 5 proved adequate, as our classifier achieved accuracy equal to 0.94.

Text Tokenization Upon filtering, we now have a set of texts that must be tokenized before they are given as input to the models. Since tokenization might split Java terms (e.g. method invocations), we excluded these from tokenizing using regular expressions. After that, we removed all URLs and all non-alphabetical characters (i.e. numbers and special symbols) and tokenized the text.

3.3 Word Model Builder

We build two models for capturing the semantics of posts, a Tf-Idf model and a FastText embedding. These models are indicative of lexical matching and semantic matching, respectively. They will serve as baselines and at the same time be used to build a more powerful hybrid model (see subsection 3.5). Both models are executed three times, one for the titles of the question posts, one for their bodies, and one for their tags. As already mentioned the code snippets are replaced by their corresponding text sequences, so they now are textual parts of the bodies. The two models are analyzed in the following paragraphs.

Tf-Idf Model We employ a vector space model to represent the texts (titles or bodies or tags) as documents and the words/terms as dimensions. The vector representation for each document is extracted using Tf-Idf vectorizer. According to Tf-Idf, the weight (vector value) of each term t in a document d is defined as:

$$tfidf(t, d, D) = tf(t, d) \cdot idf(t, D) \tag{1}$$

where $tf(t, d)$ is the term frequency of term t in document d and refers to the number of occurrences of the term t in the document (title, body or tag). Also,

$idf(t, D)$ is the inverse document frequency of term t in the set of all documents D, and is used as a normalizing factor to indicate how common the term is in the corpus. In our implementation (we used scikit-learn), $idf(t, D)$ is equal to $1 + log((1 + |D|)/(1 + d_t))$, where $|d_t|$ is the number of documents containing the term t, i.e. the number of titles, bodies or tags that include the relevant term. Intuitively, very common terms (e.g. "Java" or "Exception") may act as noise for our dataset, as they could appear to semantically different posts.

FastText Model FastText is a neural language model proposed by Facebook's AI Research (FAIR) lab [2,12]. Practically, fastText is a shallow neural network that is trained in order to reconstruct linguistic contexts of words. In our case, we transform the terms of the documents in one-hot encoding format and give the documents as input to the network during the training step. The result, i.e. the output of the hidden layer, is actually a set of word vectors. So, in this case, the resulting model is one where terms are represented as vectors. Given proper parameters, these vectors should incorporate semantic information, so that our model will have learned from the context.

We used the official implementation of fastText[7], selected the skip-gram variation of the model and we also set it up to use n-grams of size 3, 4, 5, 6, and 7. Upon experimenting with the parameters of the model, we ended up building a model with 300 dimensions and training it for 25 epochs. We used the negative sampling cost function (with number of negative samples equal to 10) and set the learning rate to 0.025 and the window size (i.e. number of terms that are within the context of a word) to 10. Also, the sampling threshold was set to 10^{-6}, while we also dropped any words with fewer than 5 occurrences. Upon extracting all word vectors, we create the vector of each document level (title, body or tags) by averaging over its word vectors.

Finally, the output of either of our two models is a set of vectors, one for the title, one for the body and one for the tags of each post. In the case of Tf-Idf the dimensions of the vector are equal to the total number of words, while in the case of fastText there are 300 dimensions. In both cases, the vectors are stored in a vector index, which also contains ids that point to the original posts.

3.4 Metadata Extractor

As metadata, we extract the named entities of each post, i.e. useful terms that may help the developer understand the semantics behind each post. To do so, we build a Conditional Random Fields (CRF) classifier [15], which performs named entity recognition based on features extracted from the terms themselves and from their context (neighboring terms). The goal is to estimate the probability that a term belongs to one of the available categories. To create a feature set for each term, we initially use two models.

At first, we employ the Brown hierarchical clustering algorithm [4] to generate a binary representation of all terms in the corpus. The algorithm clusters all

---

terms in a binary tree structure. An example fragment of such a tree is shown in Figure 5. The leaf nodes of the tree are all the terms, so by traversing the tree from the root to a leaf we are given a binary representation known as *bitstring* for the corresponding term. Semantically similar terms are expected to share more similar tree paths. For instance, in the fragment of Figure 5, the terms 'array' and 'table' have binary representations 00100000 and 00100001 respectively, which are quite similar, as is their semantic meaning. The terms 'collection' and 'list' are also similar, yet somewhat less, as their representations (001000010 and 001001 respectively) differ more.

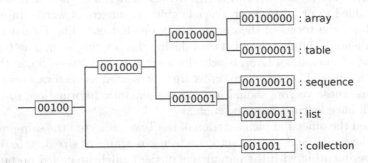

Fig. 5. Example Fragment of Binary Tree generated by the Brown Algorithm

Secondly, we use the fastText model of subsection 3.3. As already mentioned, our model extracts vector representations of terms so that semantically similar terms have vectors that are closer to each other (where proximity is computed using cosine similarity, see section 3.5). To reduce the size of these vectors (and thus avoid the curse of dimensionality), we further employ K-Means to cluster them into 5 configurations with different number of clusters (500, 1000, 1500, 2000, and 3000), an idea originating from similar natural language approaches [33,34]. Thus, instead of using the term vector, we use 5 features for each term, each one corresponding to the id of the cluster that the feature is assigned.

Upon applying the two models, we finally build the feature set for the CRF classifier. Given each term t_i, its preceding term t_{i-1} its following term t_{i+1}, we define their Brown bitstrings as b_i, b_{i-1}, and b_{i+1} respectively, and we also define their K-Means cluster assignments as k_i, k_{i-1}, and k_{i+1} respectively. Note that the k_i includes all 5 cluster configurations used, thus producing on its own five features. Using these definitions, we build the following feature set:

- the term itself (t_i), and its combination with the preceding term ($t_{i-1}t_i$), and the following term ($t_i t_{i+1}$);
- the ids of the cluster assigned by K-Means to the term (k_i), the preceding term (k_{i-1}), and the following term (k_{i+1});
- the bigram of the ids of K-Means clusters for the three terms ($k_{i-1}k_i k_{i+1}$);
- the bitstrings of the term (b_i), the preceding term (b_{i-1}), and the following term (b_{i+1});

- the bigram of the three bitstrings $(b_{i-1}b_ib_{i+1})$;
- the prefixes with length 2, 4, 6, 8, 10, 12 of each one of the three bitstrings (e.g. for a bitstring 100100 the prefixes are 10, 1001, and 100100).

Finally, our features are augmented by employing the dataset proposed by Ye et al. [31,32]. The dataset comprises annotated entities extracted from Stack Overflow that lie in five categories: API calls, programming languages, platforms (e.g. Android), tools-frameworks (e.g. Maven), and standards (e.g. TCP). For each of these categories, we check whether the term is found in the corresponding dataset file and produce a true/false decision that is added as one more feature in our feature set. After that, we apply the CRF classifier for all terms and build a metadata index. Using this index we can produce a list of semantically rich named entities for each post in the dataset.

3.5   Querying Engine

As already mentioned in subsection 3.3, the vector index comprises a set of vectors, three for each question post, corresponding to the title, the body and the tags of the post. When a developer issues a new query, it is initially preprocessed and tokenized, and then it is vectorized using either of our models. After that, we now have to produce a similarity score between each question post p and the query q of the developer. To do so, we use the following equation:

$$sim_{model}(q,p) = \frac{csim(v_q, v_{title(p)}) + csim(v_q, v_{body(p)}) + csim(v_q, v_{tags(p)})}{3} \quad (2)$$

where v_q is the vector of the query and $v_{title(p)}$, $v_{body(p)}$, and $v_{tags(p)}$ are the vectors of the title, the body, and the tags of the question post respectively. Finally, $csim$ is the cosine similarity, which is computed for two vectors v_1 and v_2 as follows:

$$csim(v_1, v_2) = \frac{v_1 \cdot v_2}{|v_1| \cdot |v_2|} \quad (3)$$

Apart from the two models described so far, we also created a hybrid model by taking the average between the two scores computed by our models:

$$sim_{hybrid}(q,p) = \frac{sim_{Tf-Idf}(q,p) + sim_{fastText}(q,p)}{2} \quad (4)$$

This hybrid model incorporates the advantages of fastText, while giving more weight than only fastText to well-formed queries (i.e. with expected terms).

Finally, the user is presented with a list of possible results to the query, ranked according to their score. Each result contains information extracted by a question post and the corresponding answer posts. In specific, we include the title of the question post, the snippets extracted by the answer posts, the links to the question and answer posts (should the developer want to examine them), the Stack Overflow score of the answer posts, and the 8 most frequent named entities among all answer posts of the relevant question post. For example, assuming our system receives the query "How to read from text file?", an example result is shown in Table 1. The developer can obviously select to check the second most relevant snippet of this question post, or even check another question post.

Table 1. Example StackSearch Response to Query "How to read from text file?"

Type	Data
Post title	Reading a plain text file in Java
Question post link	https://stackoverflow.com/questions/4716503
Top 8 labels	FileReader, BufferedReader, FileInputStream, InputStreamReader, Scanner.hasNext, Files.readAllBytes, FileUtils.readLines, Scanner

Snippet 1	`Scanner in = new Scanner(new FileReader("file.txt"));`
	`StringBuilder sb = new StringBuilder();`
	`while(in.hasNext()) {`
	`    sb.append(in.next());`
	`}`
	`in.close();`
	`outString = sb.toString();`

Answer post link	https://stackoverflow.com/questions/4716556
Answer post score	117

4 Evaluation

To fully evaluate StackSearch, we perform three experiments. The first experiment involved annotating the results of common programming problems and is expected to illustrate the usefulness of our system. The second experiment relies on post links and is used to provide proof that our system is effective (and minimize possible threats to validity). Finally, for our third experiment, we compare StackSearch to the tool CROKAGE [24], which is quite similar to our system. Comparing StackSearch with other approaches was not possible, since several systems are not maintained and/or they are not publicly available (to facilitate researchers with similar challenges, we uploaded our code at https://github.com/AuthEceSoftEng/StackSearch).

4.1 Evaluation using Programming Queries

We initially evaluate StackSearch using a set of common programming queries shown in Table 2. The dataset includes certain queries that are semantically very similar, which are marked as belonging to the same group, to determine whether our method captures the semantic features of the dataset. Queries in the same group call for the same solutions, i.e. their only difference is in the phrasing.

We evaluate all three implementations of our system, the Tf-Idf model, the fastText model, and the hybrid model. For each implementation, upon giving the queries as input, we retrieve the first 20 results and annotate them as relevant or non-relevant. A result is marked as relevant if its snippet covers the functionality that is described by the query. We gathered the results of all three algorithms together and randomly permuted them, so the annotation was performed without any prior knowledge about which result corresponds to each model, in order to be as objective as possible.

Table 2. Dataset used for Semantically Evaluating StackSearch

ID	Query	Group
1	How to read a comma separated file?	1
2	How to read a CSV file?	1
3	How to read a delimited file?	1
4	How to read input from console?	2
5	How to read input from terminal?	2
6	How to read input from command prompt?	2
7	How to play an mp3 file?	3
8	How to play an audio file?	3
9	How to compare dates?	4
10	How to compare time strings?	4
11	How to dynamically load a class?	5
12	How to load a jar/class at runtime?	5
13	How to calculate checksums for files?	6
14	How to calculate MD5 checksum for files?	6
15	How to iterate through a hashmap?	7
16	How to loop over a hashmap?	7
17	How to split a string?	8
18	How to handle an exception?	9

For each query, we evaluate each implementation by computing the average precision of the results. Given a ranked list of results, the average precision is computed by the following equation:

$$AveP = \frac{\sum_{k=1}^{n} (P(k) \cdot rel(k))}{number \ of \ relevant \ results} \tag{5}$$

where $P(k)$ is the precision at k and corresponds to the percentage of relevant results in the first k, and $rel(k)$ denotes if the result in the position k is relevant. We also use the mean average precision, defined us the mean of the average precision values of all queries.

We calculated the average precision at 10 and 20 results. The values for each query are shown in Figure 6. As shown in these graphs, the fastText and the hybrid models clearly outperform the Tf-Idf model, which is expected as they incorporate semantic information. We also note that the hybrid implementation is even more effective than fastText for most queries. Interestingly, there are certain queries in which Tf-Idf outperforms one or both of the other implementations. Consider, for example, query 17; this is a very specific query with clear terms (i.e. developers would rarely form such a query without using the term 'string') so there is not really any use for semantics. For most queries, however, better results are proposed by fastText or by our hybrid model.

We note, especially, what is the case with queries in the same group (divided by gray lines in the graphs of Figure 6). Given, for instance, the second group, query 4, which refers to input from the console, returns multiple useful results using any of the three models. The results, however are quite different for queries

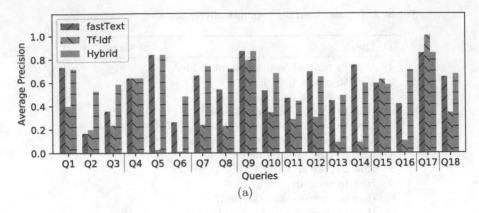

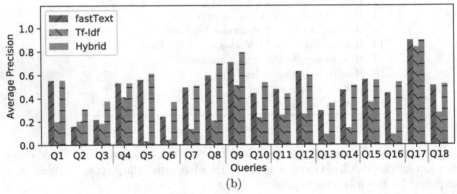

Fig. 6. Average Precision for the three Implementations (a) at 10, and (b) at 20 Results

5 and 6, which are similar albeit for the replacement of the term 'console' with 'terminal' and with 'command prompt' respectively. This indicates that our word embedding successfully captures the semantics of the text and considers the aforementioned terms as synonyms. This advantage of our system is also clear in group 1 (comma-separated vs CSV vs delimited file), group 4 (dates vs time strings), etc., and even in more difficult semantic relationships, such as the one of group 5 (i.e. loading dynamically vs at runtime).

Finally, we calculated the mean average precision for the same configurations as before. The values for the three implementations are shown in Figure 7a, where it is clear once again that the word embeddings outperform the Tf-Idf model, while our hybrid model is the most effective of the three models.

To further outline the differences among the models we also computed the mean search length. The search length is a very useful metric since it intuitively simulates the process used when searching for relevant results. The metric is defined as the number of non-relevant results that one must examine in order to find a number of relevant results. We computed the search length for all queries for finding from 1 up to 10 relevant results.

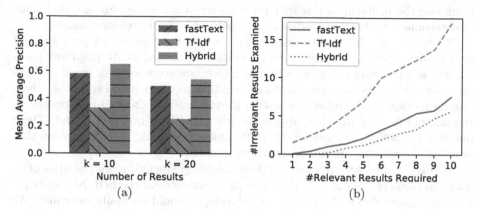

Fig. 7. Results depicting (a) the Mean Average Precision, and (b) the Mean Search Length, for the three Implementations

Averaging over all queries provides the mean search length, of which the results are shown in Figure 7b. The results are again encouraging for our proposed models. Indicatively, to find the first useful result, the developer has to examine less than 0.1 irrelevant results on average for fastText and for the hybrid model, whereas using Tf-Idf requires examining 1.5 irrelevant results. Furthermore, when the developer skims over the results of fastText, he/she will only need to view 2.11 irrelevant snippets on average, before finding the first 5 relevant. Using the hybrid model, he/she will only need to see 1.22. Tf-Idf is clearly outperformed in this case, providing on average almost 7 irrelevant results, along with the first 5 relevant. Similar conclusions can be drawn for the first 10 relevant results. In this case, the developer would need to examine around 17.5, 7.5, and 5.5 results on average, for Tf-Idf, fastText, and our hybrid model, respectively.

4.2   Evaluation using Post Links

The main goal of the previous subsection was to illustrate the potential of our word embedding models. The results, especially for the groups of queries, have shown that our models indeed capture the semantics of text. As already mentioned, the annotation process was performed in such a way to limit any threats to validity. Nevertheless, to further strengthen the objectivity of the results, we perform one more experiment, which is described in this subsection.

In the lack of a third-party annotated Stack Overflow dataset, what we decided to do is evaluate our models using the post links provided by Stack Overflow, an idea found in [8]. In Stack Overflow, the presence of a link between two questions is an indicator that the two questions are similar. Note, of course, that the opposite assumption, i.e. that any two questions that are not linked are not similar to each other, is not necessarily correct. There are many questions that are asked and perhaps not linked to similar ones. In our evaluation, however, we formulate the problem as a search/retrieval scenario, so we only use post links to determine whether our models can retrieve objectively relevant results.

To create our link evaluation dataset, we first extracted all post links of Java question posts. After that, for performance reasons, we dropped any posts without snippets and any posts with Stack Overflow score lower or equal to -3, as these are not within the scenario of a system that retrieves useful snippets. These criteria reduced the number of question posts to roughly 200000 (as opposed to the original dataset that had approximately 1.3 million question posts). These question posts have approximately 37000 links, reinforcing our assumption that non-linked questions are not necessarily dissimilar.

We execute StackSearch with all three models giving as queries the titles of all question posts of the dataset. For each query, we retrieve the first 20 results (as we may assume this is the maximum a developer would normally examine). We determine how many of these 20 results are linked to the specific question post, and compute the percentage of relevant results compared to the total number of relevant post links of the question post. By averaging over all queries (i.e. titles of question posts of the dataset), we compute the percentage of relevant links retrieved on average for each model. The results are shown in Figure 8.

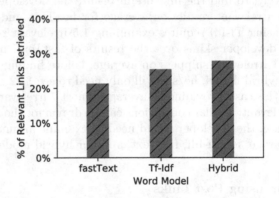

Fig. 8. Percentage of Relevant Results (compared to the number of Links of each Question Post) in the first 20 Results for the three Implementations

At first, one may note that the results for all models are below 30%, a rather low number, which is however expected, given the shortcomings of our dataset. Many retrieved results are actually relevant, however they are not linked to the question posts of the queries. In any case, we are given an objective relative comparison of the three models. And this comparison provides some interesting insights. An interesting observation is that Tf-Idf outperforms fastText. This is not totally unexpected, if we consider that the post links of Stack Overflow are created by the community, therefore it is possible that posts with similar meanings but different key terms are not linked. As a result, fastText may discover several posts that should be linked, yet they are not. On the other hand, Tf-Idf focuses on identical terms which are rather easier to discover using the Stack Overflow service. In any case, however, our hybrid model outperforms Tf-Idf and fastText, as it combines the advantages of Tf-Idf and fastText.

4.3   Comparative Evaluation

Upon demonstrating the effectiveness of StackSearch in the previous subsections, we now proceed to compare it with a similar system, the tool CROKAGE. To do so, we have employed the dataset proposed by CROKAGE [24]. The dataset involves 48 programming queries, similar to those introduced in subsection 4.1. The queries include diverse tasks, such as comparing dates, resizing images, pausing the current thread, etc.

Given that our dataset comprises Stack Overflow posts, it can be used to assess both tools. Thus, we issued the queries at both StackSearch and CROK-AGE. The results of the queries had been originally annotated by two annotators (of which the results were merged) in Stack Overflow posts, marking any post as relevant if it addresses the query with a feasible amount of changes [24]. So we have used these annotations and only had to update a small part of them in order to make sure that they are on par with our dataset, which includes the latest data dump of Stack Overflow. As before, for each query we have calculated the average precision at 5 and 10 results as well as the search length for finding 1 up to 10 relevant results. The mean average precision and the mean search length results for the two tools are shown in Figures 9a and 9b, respectively (results per query are omitted due to space limitations).

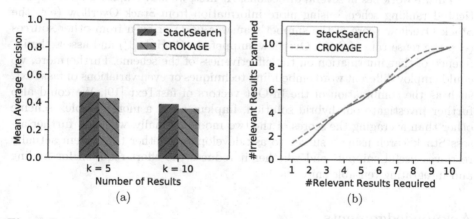

Fig. 9. Results depicting (a) the Mean Average Precision, and (b) the Mean Search Length, for StackSearch and CROKAGE

Both tools seem to be effective on the provided dataset. Concerning mean average precision, StackSearch outperforms CROKAGE both at 5 and at 10 results, indicating that it retrieves more useful results on average. Moreover, it seems that their difference is more noticeable when a fewer number of results is required, indicating that StackSearch provides a better ranking.

This difference is also illustrated by the mean search length for the two approaches. Indicatively, using StackSearch, the developer will need to examine only 0.66 irrelevant snippets on average, before finding the first relevant one (the corresponding value for CROKAGE is 1.42). Our tool also performs better for finding the second and third relevant results, while the two tools perform equally well for finding five or more results.

5   Conclusion

Although several API usage and snippet mining solutions have been proposed, most of them do not account for the semantics of the source code and the surrounding text. Furthermore, most contemporary systems do not employ word embeddings to enable semantic-aware retrieval of snippets, and are limited either by the format of their input, which is not natural language, or by their output, which is not ready-to-use snippets. In this work, we have created a novel snippet mining system that extracts snippets from Stack Overflow and employs word embeddings to model code and as well as contextual information. Given our evaluation, we conclude that the hybrid model of StackSearch effectively extracts the semantics of the data and outperforms both our baselines (Tf-Idf and fastText) as well as the snippet mining tool CROKAGE. Finally, our system accompanies the retrieved snippets with useful metadata that convey the meaning of each post.

Future work lies in several directions. At first, we may employ a more sophisticated ranking scheme using more information from Stack Overflow (e.g. the Stack Overflow score of the snippet's answer post) or even from other sources (e.g. the reuse rate of Stack Overflow snippets in GitHub [1]) and assess the influence of that information on the effectiveness of the scheme. Furthermore, we could employ different word embedding techniques or even variations of fastText, such as the combination of the In-Out vectors of fastText [19]. We could also further investigate our hybrid solution, implementing a more complex scheme other than averaging the scores of the two models. Finally, we could further assess StackSearch using a survey to ask developers whether the system actually retrieves useful snippets and whether it reduces the effort required for finding and integrating reusable snippets.

Acknowledgements

This research has been co-financed by the European Regional Development Fund of the European Union and Greek national funds through the Operational Program Competitiveness, Entrepreneurship and Innovation, under the call RESEARCH - CREATE - INNOVATE (project code: T1EDK-02347).

References

1. Baltes, S., Treude, C., Diehl, S.: SOTorrent: Studying the Origin, Evolution, and Usage of Stack Overflow Code Snippets. In: Proceedings of the 16th International Conference on Mining Software Repositories. pp. 191–194. MSR '19, IEEE Press, Piscataway, NJ, USA (2019)
2. Bojanowski, P., Grave, E., Joulin, A., Mikolov, T.: Enriching Word Vectors with Subword Information. Transactions of the Association for Computational Linguistics 5, 135–146 (2017)
3. Brandt, J., Dontcheva, M., Weskamp, M., Klemmer, S.R.: Example-centric Programming: Integrating Web Search into the Development Environment. In: Proceedings of the SIGCHI Conference on Human Factors in Computing Systems. pp. 513–522. CHI '10, ACM, New York, NY, USA (2010)
4. Brown, P.F., deSouza, P.V., Mercer, R.L., Pietra, V.J.D., Lai, J.C.: Class-based N-gram Models of Natural Language. Computational Linguistics 18(4), 467–479 (1992)
5. Buse, R.P.L., Weimer, W.: Synthesizing API Usage Examples. In: Proceedings of the 34th International Conference on Software Engineering. pp. 782–792. ICSE '12, IEEE Press, Piscataway, NJ, USA (2012)
6. Diamantopoulos, T., Karagiannopoulos, G., Symeonidis, A.L.: CodeCatch: Extracting Source Code Snippets from Online Sources. In: Proceedings of the 6th International Workshop on Realizing Artificial Intelligence Synergies in Software Engineering. pp. 21–27. RAISE '18, ACM, New York, NY, USA (2018)
7. Diamantopoulos, T., Sifaki, M.I., Symeonidis, A.L.: Towards Mining Answer Edits to Extract Evolution Patterns in Stack Overflow. In: Proceedings of the 16th International Conference on Mining Software Repositories. p. 215–219. MSR '19, IEEE Press (2019)
8. Diamantopoulos, T., Symeonidis, A.L.: Employing Source Code Information to Improve Question-answering in Stack Overflow. In: Proceedings of the 12th Working Conference on Mining Software Repositories. pp. 454–457. MSR '15, IEEE Press, Piscataway, NJ, USA (2015)
9. Fowkes, J., Sutton, C.: Parameter-free Probabilistic API Mining across GitHub. In: Proceedings of the 2016 24th ACM SIGSOFT International Symposium on Foundations of Software Engineering. pp. 254–265. FSE 2016, ACM, New York, NY, USA (2016)
10. Gu, X., Zhang, H., Zhang, D., Kim, S.: Deep API Learning. In: Proceedings of the 2016 24th ACM SIGSOFT International Symposium on Foundations of Software Engineering. pp. 631–642. FSE 2016, ACM, New York, NY, USA (2016)
11. Jiang, L., Misherghi, G., Su, Z., Glondu, S.: DECKARD: Scalable and Accurate Tree-Based Detection of Code Clones. In: Proceedings of the 29th International Conference on Software Engineering. pp. 96–105. ICSE '07, IEEE Computer Society, Washington, DC, USA (2007)
12. Joulin, A., Grave, E., Bojanowski, P., Mikolov, T.: Bag of Tricks for Efficient Text Classification. In: Proceedings of the 15th Conference of the European Chapter of the Association for Computational Linguistics: Volume 2, Short Papers. pp. 427–431. Association for Computational Linguistics, Valencia, Spain (2017)
13. Katirtzis, N., Diamantopoulos, T., Sutton, C.: Learning a Metric for Code Readability. In: 21th International Conference on Fundamental Approaches to Software Engineering. pp. 189–206. FASE 2018, Springer International Publishing, Boston, MA, USA (2018)

14. Kim, J., Lee, S., Hwang, S.w., Kim, S.: Towards an Intelligent Code Search Engine. In: Proceedings of the 24th AAAI Conference on Artificial Intelligence. pp. 1358–1363. AAAI '10, AAAI Press, Palo Alto, CA, USA (2010)
15. Lafferty, J.D., McCallum, A., Pereira, F.C.N.: Conditional Random Fields: Probabilistic Models for Segmenting and Labeling Sequence Data. In: Proceedings of the Eighteenth International Conference on Machine Learning. pp. 282–289. ICML '01, Morgan Kaufmann Publishers Inc., San Francisco, CA, USA (2001)
16. Mandelin, D., Xu, L., Bodík, R., Kimelman, D.: Jungloid Mining: Helping to Navigate the API Jungle. SIGPLAN Not. **40**(6), 48–61 (2005)
17. Montandon, J.E., Borges, H., Felix, D., Valente, M.T.: Documenting APIs with Examples: Lessons Learned with the APIMiner Platform. In: Proceedings of the 20th Working Conference on Reverse Engineering. pp. 401–408. WCRE 2013, IEEE Computer Society, Piscataway, NJ, USA (2013)
18. Moreno, L., Bavota, G., Di Penta, M., Oliveto, R., Marcus, A.: How Can I Use This Method? In: Proceedings of the 37th International Conference on Software Engineering - Volume 1. pp. 880–890. ICSE '15, IEEE Press, Piscataway, NJ, USA (2015)
19. Nalisnick, E., Mitra, B., Craswell, N., Caruana, R.: Improving Document Ranking with Dual Word Embeddings. In: Proceedings of the 25th International Conference Companion on World Wide Web. pp. 83–84. WWW '16 Companion, International World Wide Web Conferences Steering Committee, Republic and Canton of Geneva, Switzerland (2016)
20. Nguyen, T., Rigby, P.C., Nguyen, A.T., Karanfil, M., Nguyen, T.N.: T2API: Synthesizing API Code Usage Templates from English Texts with Statistical Translation. In: Proceedings of the 2016 24th ACM SIGSOFT International Symposium on Foundations of Software Engineering. pp. 1013–1017. FSE 2016, ACM, New York, NY, USA (2016)
21. Ponzanelli, L., Bacchelli, A., Lanza, M.: Seahawk: Stack Overflow in the IDE. In: Proceedings of the 2013 International Conference on Software Engineering. pp. 1295–1298. ICSE '13, IEEE Press, Piscataway, NJ, USA (2013)
22. Ponzanelli, L., Bavota, G., Di Penta, M., Oliveto, R., Lanza, M.l.: Mining Stack-Overflow to Turn the IDE into a Self-confident Programming Prompter. In: Proceedings of the 11th Working Conference on Mining Software Repositories. pp. 102–111. MSR 2014, ACM, New York, NY, USA (2014)
23. Raghothaman, M., Wei, Y., Hamadi, Y.: SWIM: Synthesizing What I Mean: Code Search and Idiomatic Snippet Synthesis. In: Proceedings of the 38th International Conference on Software Engineering. pp. 357–367. ICSE '16, ACM, New York, NY, USA (2016)
24. Silva, R.F.G., Roy, C.K., Rahman, M.M., Schneider, K.A., Paixao, K., de Almeida Maia, M.: Recommending Comprehensive Solutions for Programming Tasks by Mining Crowd Knowledge. In: Proceedings of the 27th International Conference on Program Comprehension. p. 358–368. ICPC '19, IEEE Press (2019)
25. Thummalapenta, S., Xie, T.: PARSEWeb: A Programmer Assistant for Reusing Open Source Code on the Web. In: Proceedings of the 22nd IEEE/ACM International Conference on Automated Software Engineering. pp. 204–213. ASE '07, ACM, New York, NY, USA (2007)
26. Wang, J., Yu, L.C., Lai, K.R., Zhang, X.: Dimensional sentiment analysis using a regional CNN-LSTM model. In: Proceedings of the 54th Annual Meeting of the Association for Computational Linguistics (Volume 2: Short Papers). pp. 225–230. Association for Computational Linguistics, Berlin, Germany (2016)

27. Wang, J., Dang, Y., Zhang, H., Chen, K., Xie, T., Zhang, D.: Mining Succinct and High-Coverage API Usage Patterns from Source Code. In: Proceedings of the 10th Working Conference on Mining Software Repositories. pp. 319–328. MSR '13, IEEE Press, Piscataway, NJ, USA (2013)
28. Wei, Y., Chandrasekaran, N., Gulwani, S., Hamadi, Y.: Building Bing Developer Assistant. Tech. Rep. MSR-TR-2015-36, Microsoft Research (2015)
29. Wightman, D., Ye, Z., Brandt, J., Vertegaal, R.: SnipMatch: Using Source Code Context to Enhance Snippet Retrieval and Parameterization. In: Proceedings of the 25th Annual ACM Symposium on User Interface Software and Technology. pp. 219–228. UIST '12, ACM, New York, NY, USA (2012)
30. Xie, T., Pei, J.: MAPO: Mining API Usages from Open Source Repositories. In: Proceedings of the 2006 International Workshop on Mining Software Repositories. pp. 54–57. MSR '06, ACM, New York, NY, USA (2006)
31. Ye, D., Xing, Z., Foo, C.Y., Ang, Z.Q., Li, J., Kapre, N.: Software-Specific Named Entity Recognition in Software Engineering Social Content. In: 2016 IEEE 23rd International Conference on Software Analysis, Evolution, and Reengineering (SANER). vol. 1, pp. 90–101. IEEE Press (2016)
32. Ye, D., Xing, Z., Foo, C.Y., Li, J., Kapre, N.: Learning to Extract API Mentions from Informal Natural Language Discussions. In: 2016 IEEE International Conference on Software Maintenance and Evolution (ICSME). pp. 389–399. IEEE Press (2016)
33. Yin, W., Kann, K., Yu, M., Schütze, H.: Comparative Study of CNN and RNN for Natural Language Processing. arXiv:1702.01923 (2017)
34. Yu, M., Zhao, T., Dong, D., Tian, H., Yu, D.: Compound Embedding Features for Semi-supervised Learning. In: Proceedings of the 2013 Conference of the North American Chapter of the Association for Computational Linguistics: Human Language Technologies. pp. 563–568. Association for Computational Linguistics, Atlanta, Georgia (2013)
35. Zagalsky, A., Barzilay, O., Yehudai, A.: Example Overflow: Using Social Media for Code Recommendation. In: Proceedings of the Third International Workshop on Recommendation Systems for Software Engineering. pp. 38–42. RSSE '12, IEEE Press, Piscataway, NJ, USA (2012)

Global Reproducibility through Local Control for Distributed Active Objects

Lars Tveito, Einar Broch Johnsen(i), and Rudolf Schlatte

Department of Informatics, University of Oslo, Oslo, Norway
{larstvei,einarj,rudi}@ifi.uio.no

Abstract. Non-determinism in a concurrent or distributed setting may lead to many different runs or executions of a program. This paper presents a method to reproduce a specific run for non-deterministic actor or active object systems. The method is based on recording traces of events reflecting local transitions at so-called stable states during execution; i.e., states in which local execution depends on interaction with the environment. The paper formalizes trace recording and replay for a basic active object language, to show that such local traces suffice to obtain global reproducibility of runs; during replay different objects may operate fairly independently of each other and in parallel, yet a program under replay has guaranteed deterministic outcome. We then show that the method extends to the other forms of non-determinism as found in richer active object languages. Following the proposed method, we have implemented a tool to record and replay runs, and to visualize the communication and scheduling decisions of a recorded run, for Real-Time ABS, a formally defined, rich active object language for modeling timed, resource-aware behavior in distributed systems.

1 Introduction

Non-determinism in a concurrent or distributed setting leads to many different possible runs or executions of a given program. The ability to reproduce and visualize a particular run can be very useful for the developer of such programs. For example, reproducing a specific run representing negative (or unexpected) behavior can be beneficial to eliminate bugs which occur only in a few out of many possible runs (so-called Heisenbugs). Conversely, reproducing a run representing positive (and expected) behavior can be useful for regression testing for new versions of a system.

Deterministic replay is an emerging technique to provide deterministic executions of programs in the presence of different non-deterministic factors [1]. In a first phase, the technique consists of *recording* sufficient information in a trace during a run to reproduce the same run during a *replay* in a second phase. Approaches to reproduce runs of non-deterministic systems can be classified as either *content-based* or *ordering-based* replay. Content-based replay records the results of all non-deterministic operations whereas ordering-based replay records the ordering of non-deterministic events.

© The Author(s) 2020
H. Wehrheim and J. Cabot (Eds.): FASE 2020, LNCS 12076, pp. 140–160, 2020.
https://doi.org/10.1007/978-3-030-45234-6_7

This paper considers deterministic replay for non-deterministic runs of Active Object languages [2], which combine the asynchronous message passing of Actors with object-oriented abstractions. Compared to standard OO languages, these languages decouple communication and synchronization by communicating through asynchronous method calls without transfer of control and by synchronizing via futures. We develop a method to reproduce the runs of active objects. The method is ordering-based, as we represent the parallel execution of active objects as traces of events. We show that locally recording events at so-called *stable states* suffice to obtain deterministic replay. In these states, local execution needs to interact with the environment, e.g., to make a scheduling decision or to send or receive a message. We formalize execution with record and replay for a basic active object language, and show that its executions enjoy confluence properties which can be described using such traces. These confluence properties justify the recording and replay of local traces to reproduce global behavior.

Active object languages may also contain more advanced features [2], such as *cooperative scheduling* [3, 4], *concurrent object groups* [3, 5] and *timed, resource-aware behavior* [6]. With cooperative scheduling, an object may suspend its current task while waiting for the result of a method call and instead schedule a different task. With concurrent object groups, several objects share an actor's lock abstraction. With timed, resource-aware behavior, local execution requires resources from resource-centers (e.g., virtual machines) to progress. These features introduce additional non-determinism in the active object systems, in addition to the non-determinism caused by asynchronous calls. We show that the proposed method extends to handle these additional sources of non-determinism.

The proposed method to deterministically replay runs has been realized for Real-Time ABS [6], a modeling language with these advanced features, which has been used to analyze, e.g., industrial scale cloud-deployed software [7], railway networks [8], and complex low-level multicore systems [9, 10]. Whereas the language supports various formal analysis techniques, most validation of complex models (at least in an early stage of model development) is based on simulation. The tracing capabilities have a small enough performance impact to be enabled by default in the simulator. The simulator itself is implemented as a distributed system in Erlang [11]. The low performance overhead comes from only recording local events in each actor, which does not impose any additional communication or synchronization, which are typically bottlenecks in a distributed system.

Contributions. Our main contributions can be summarized as follows:

- we propose a method to reproduce runs for active object systems based on recording events reflecting local transitions from stable object states;
- we provide a formal justification for the method in terms of confluence and progress properties for ordering-based record & replay for a basic actor language with asynchronous communication and synchronization via futures;
- we show that the method extends to address additional sources of non-determinism as found in richer active object languages; and
- we provide an implementation of the proposed method to record, replay and visualize runs for the active object modeling language Real-Time ABS.

```
class C {
  Int n = 1;
  Unit m1() { n = n - 1; }
  Unit m2() { n = n * 3; }
}

// Main block
{
  C o = new C();
  o!m1();
  o!m2();
}
```

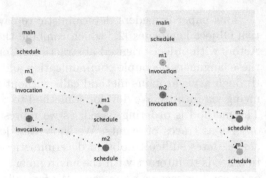

Fig. 1: A simple program, with two possible results

Fig. 2: The executions leading to the two different results for the simple program.

Paper overview Section 2 provides a motivating example, Section 3 considers the problem of reproducibility for a formalization of a basic active object language and Section 4 formalizes record and replay over the operational semantics of the basic language. Section 5 considers reproducibility for extensions to the basic language. Section 6 presents our implementation of the method for Real-Time ABS. Section 7 discusses related work and Section 8 concludes the paper.

2 Motivating Example

Consider the program in Fig. 1. It consists of a class C, with a single integer field, initialized to 1 and two methods m1 and m2. The main block of the program creates an active object o as an instance of the class, and performs two asynchronous calls on o, o!m1() and o!m2() respectively. Since the calls are asynchronous, the caller can proceed to make the second call immediately, without waiting for the first call to complete. The two calls are placed in the queue of o and scheduled in some order for execution by o. (We here assume method execution is atomic, but this assumption will be relaxed in Section 5.)

Thus, even the execution of this very simple program can lead to two different results, depending on whether o!m1() is scheduled before o!m2(), and conversely, o!m2() is scheduled before o!m1(). In the first case, the field n (which is initially 1) will first be decremented by 1 and then be multiplied with 3, resulting in a final state in which the field n has the value 0. In the second case, the field n is first multiplied by 3, then decremented by 1, resulting in a final state in which the field n has the value 2. Fig. 2 depicts the two cases (using the visualization support in our tool, described in Section 6.3). Note that this problem still occurs for languages with ordered message passing between two actors (e.g., Erlang [11]) when the two calls are made by different callers.

The selection of run to execute is decided by the runtime system and is thus non-deterministic for the given source program. In general, there can be much more than two possible runs for a parallel active object system. If only a few of the possible runs exhibit a particular behavior (e.g., a bug), it can be very interesting to be able to reproduce a particular run of the given program. We propose a method to instrument active objects systems which allows global reproducibility of runs through local control for each active object.

3 A Formal Model of Reproducibility

To formalize the problem of global reproducibility through local control for active object systems, we consider a basic active object language in which non-determinism stems from the order in which method calls are selected from the queue of the active objects.

3.1 A Basic Active Object Language

Consider a basic active object language with asynchronous method calls and synchronization via futures. The language has a Java-like syntax, given in Fig. 3. Let T, C and m range over type, class and method names, respectively, and let e range over side-effect free expressions. Overlined terms denote possibly empty lists over the corresponding syntactic categories (e.g., $\bar{e}$ and $\bar{x}$).

$$
\begin{aligned}
P &::= \overline{CL} \ \{\overline{T\ x};\ s\} \\
CL &::= \mathtt{class}\, C\, \{\overline{T\ x};\ \overline{M}\} \\
M &::= T\ m\ (\overline{T\ x})\, \{\overline{T\ x};\ s\} \\
s &::= s; s \mid \mathtt{skip} \mid x = rhs \\
  &\quad \mid \mathtt{if}\ e\ \{s\}\, \mathtt{else}\, \{s\} \\
  &\quad \mid \mathtt{while}\ e\, \{s\} \mid \mathtt{return}\ e \\
rhs &::= e \mid \mathtt{new}\ C\, (\bar{e}) \mid e!m(e) \mid x.\mathtt{get}
\end{aligned}
$$

Fig. 3: BNF for the basic active object language.

A program P consists of a list $\overline{CL}$ of class declarations and a main block $\{\overline{T\ x}; s\}$, with variables x of type T and a statement s. A class C declares fields (both with types T) and contains a list $\overline{M}$ of methods. A method m has a return type, a list of typed formal parameters and a method body which contains local variable declarations and a statement s. Statements are standard; assignments $x = rhs$ allow expressions with side-effects on the right-hand side rhs.

Asynchronous method calls decouple invocation from synchronization. The execution of a call $\mathtt{f} = \mathtt{o!m(args)}$ corresponds to sending a message $\mathtt{m(args)}$ asynchronously to the callee object o and initializes a future, referenced by $\mathtt{f}$, where the return value will be stored. The statement $\mathtt{x} = \mathtt{f.get}$ retrieves the value stored in the future $\mathtt{f}$. This operation synchronizes with the method return; i.e., the execution of this statement *blocks* the active object until the future $\mathtt{f}$ has received a value. Messages are *not* assumed to arrive in the same order as they are sent. The selection of messages in an object gives rise to non-determinism in the execution. An example of a program in this language was given in Section 2.

3.2 An Operational Semantics for the Basic Language

We present the semantics of the basic active object language as a transition relation between configurations cn. In the runtime syntax (Fig. 4), a configuration cn can be empty (ϵ), or a set of objects, futures, and invocation messages. We let o and f be dynamically created names from a set of object and future

$$
\begin{aligned}
cn &::= \epsilon \mid object \mid future \mid invoc \mid cn\ cn & q &::= \epsilon \mid process \mid q\ q \\
future &::= fut(f, val) & val &::= v \mid \bot \\
object &::= ob(o, a, p, q) & a &::= x \mapsto v \mid a, a \\
process &::= \{a \mid s\} & p &::= process \mid \texttt{idle} \\
invoc &::= inv(o, f, m, \overline{v}) & v &::= o \mid f \mid \texttt{true} \mid \texttt{false} \mid t
\end{aligned}
$$

Fig. 4: Runtime syntax; here, o and f are object and future identifiers.

identifiers, denoted *Identifiers*. An active object $ob(o, a, p, q)$ has an identifier o, attributes a, an active process p (that may be $\texttt{idle}$) and an unordered process pool q. A future $fut(f, val)$ has an identifier f and a value val (which is $\bot$ if the future is not resolved). An invocation $inv(o, f, m, \overline{v})$ is a message to object o to activate method m with actual parameters $\overline{v}$ and send the return value to the future f. Attributes bind program variables x to values v. A process $\{a \mid s\}$ has local variables a and a statement list s to execute. Values are object identifiers o, future identifiers f, Boolean values $\texttt{true}$ and $\texttt{false}$, and other literal values t (e.g., natural numbers). The initial state of a program consists of a single active objects $ob(o_{\texttt{main}}, a, p, \varnothing)$, where the active process p corresponds to the main block of the program. Let $names(cn)$ denote the set of object and future identifiers occurring in a configuration cn.

Figure 5 presents the main rules of the transition relation $cn \rightarrow cn'$. A *run* is a finite sequence of configurations $cn_0, cn_1, \ldots, cn_n$ such that $cn_i \rightarrow cn_{i+1}$ for $0 \leqslant i < n$. We assume configurations to be associative and commutative (so we can reorder configurations to match rules), where $\xrightarrow{*}$ denotes the reflexive and transitive closure of $\rightarrow$. Let $bind(m, \overline{v}, f, C)$ denote method lookup in the class table, returning the process corresponding to method m in class C with actual parameters $\overline{v}$ and with future f as the return address of the call. Thus, every process has a local variable *destiny* which denotes the return address of the process (i.e., the future that the process will resolve upon completion), similar to the self-reference *this* for objects. We omit explanations for the standard rules for assignment to fields and local variables, conditionals, while and skip.

Rule ACTIVATE formalizes the scheduling of a process p from the unordered queue q when an active object is idle. In ASYNC-CALL, an asynchronous method call creates a message to a target object o' and an unresolved future with a fresh name f. Object creation in NEW-ACTOR creates a new active object with a fresh identifier o', and initializes its attributes with initAttributes(C, o'), including reference to itself ($\texttt{this}$). These are the only rules that introduce new names for identifiers; let a predicate fresh(o) denote that o is a fresh name in the global configuration (abstracting from how this is implemented). Rule LOAD puts the process corresponding to an invocation message in called object's queue. Rule RETURN resolves the future associated with a process with return value v, and READ-FUT fetches the value v of a future f into a variable. With rule CONTEXT, parallel execution in different active objects has an interleaving semantics.

Definition 1 (Stable configurations). *A configuration cn is stable if, for all objects in cn, the execution is blocked or the object needs to make a scheduling*

(ACTIVATE)
$$\frac{p \in q}{\begin{array}{l} ob(o, a, \texttt{idle}, q) \\ \to ob(o, a, p, q \backslash \{p\}) \end{array}}$$

(ASSIGN1)
$$\frac{v = [\![e]\!]_{(a \circ l)} \quad x \in \text{dom}(l)}{\begin{array}{l} ob(o, a, \{l \mid x = e; s\}, q) \\ \to ob(o, a, \{l[x \mapsto v] \mid s\}, q) \end{array}}$$

(ASSIGN2)
$$\frac{v = [\![e]\!]_{(a \circ l)} \quad x \notin \text{dom}(l)}{\begin{array}{l} ob(o, a, \{l \mid x = e; s\}, q) \\ \to ob(o, a[x \mapsto v], \{l \mid s\}, q) \end{array}}$$

(COND1)
$$\frac{\texttt{true} = [\![e]\!]_{(a \circ l)}}{\begin{array}{l} ob(o, a, \{l \mid \texttt{if } e \ \{s_1\} \texttt{ else } \{s_2\}; s\}, q) \\ \to ob(o, a, \{l \mid s_1; s\}, q) \end{array}}$$

(COND2)
$$\frac{\texttt{false} = [\![e]\!]_{(a \circ l)}}{\begin{array}{l} ob(o, a, \{l \mid \texttt{if } e \ \{s_1\} \texttt{ else } \{s_2\}; s\}, q) \\ \to ob(o, a, \{l \mid s_2; s\}, q) \end{array}}$$

(WHILE)
$$\frac{s_1' = s_1; \texttt{while } e \ \{s_1\}}{\begin{array}{l} ob(o, a, \{l \mid \texttt{while } e \ \{s_1\}; s_2\}, q) \\ \to ob(o, a, \{l \mid \texttt{if } e \ \{s_1'\} \texttt{ else } \{\texttt{skip}\}; s_2\}, q) \end{array}}$$

(SKIP1)
$$\begin{array}{l} ob(o, a, \{l \mid \texttt{skip}; s\}, q) \\ \to ob(o, a, \{l \mid s\}, q) \end{array}$$

(SKIP2)
$$\begin{array}{l} ob(o, a, \{l \mid \texttt{skip}\}, q) \\ \to ob(o, a, \texttt{idle}, q) \end{array}$$

(NEW-ACTOR)
$$\frac{a' = \text{initAttributes}(C, o') \quad \text{fresh}(o')}{\begin{array}{l} ob(o, a, \{l \mid x = \texttt{new } C(); s\}, q) \\ \to ob(o, a, \{l \mid x = o'; s\}, q) \ ob(o', a', \texttt{idle}, \varnothing) \end{array}}$$

(CONTEXT)
$$\frac{cn_1 \to cn_1'}{cn_1 \ cn_2 \to cn_1' \ cn_2}$$

(ASYNC-CALL)
$$\frac{o' = [\![e]\!]_{(a \circ l)} \quad \overline{v} = [\![\overline{e}]\!]_{(a \circ l)} \quad \text{fresh}(f)}{\begin{array}{l} ob(o, a, \{l \mid x = e!m(\overline{e}); s\}, q) \\ \to ob(o, a, \{l \mid x = f; s\}, q) \ inv(o', f, m, \overline{v}) \ fut(f, \bot) \end{array}}$$

(LOAD)
$$\frac{p' = \text{bind}(m, \overline{v}, f, \text{classOf}(o))}{\begin{array}{l} inv(o, f, m, \overline{v}) \ ob(o, a, p, q) \\ \to ob(o, a, p, q \cup \{p'\}) \end{array}}$$

(RETURN)
$$\frac{v = [\![e]\!]_{(a \circ l)} \quad l(\text{destiny}) = f}{\begin{array}{l} ob(o, a, \{l \mid \texttt{return } e\}, q) \ fut(f, \bot) \\ \to ob(o, a, \texttt{idle}, q) \ fut(f, v) \end{array}}$$

(READ-FUT)
$$\frac{v \neq \bot \quad f = [\![e]\!]_{(a \circ l)}}{\begin{array}{l} ob(o, a, \{l \mid x = e.\texttt{get}; s\}, q) \ fut(f, v) \\ \to ob(o, a, \{l \mid x = v; s\}, q) \ fut(f, v) \end{array}}$$

Fig. 5: Semantics of the basic active object language.

decision. An object is blocked if it needs to execute a get-statement. An object needs to make a scheduling decision if its active process is idle.

Let G denote a stable configuration. We say that two stable configurations G_1 and G_2 are *consecutive* in a run $G_1 \xrightarrow{*} G_2$ if, for all cn such that $G_1 \xrightarrow{*} cn$ and $cn \xrightarrow{*} G_2$, if $cn \neq G_1$ and $cn \neq G_2$ then cn is not a stable configuration.

Lemma 1 (Reordering of atomic sections). *Let G_1 and G_2 be stable configurations. If $G_1 \xrightarrow{*} G_2$, then there exists a run between G_1 and G_2 in which only a single object executes between any two consecutive stable configurations.*

Proof (sketch). Observe that the notion of stability captures any state of an object in which it needs input from its environment. The proof then follows from the fact that the state spaces of different objects are disjoint and that message passing is unordered. This allows consecutive independent execution steps from different objects to be reordered. □

$$(\textsc{Local-Assign1})$$
$$\frac{v = [\![e]\!]_{(a \circ l)} \quad x \in \mathrm{dom}(l)}{a, \{l \mid x = e; s\} \rightsquigarrow a, \{l[x \mapsto v] \mid s\}}$$

$$(\textsc{Local-Assign2})$$
$$\frac{v = [\![e]\!]_{(a \circ l)} \quad x \notin \mathrm{dom}(l)}{a, \{l \mid x = e; s\} \rightsquigarrow a[x \mapsto v], \{l \mid s\}}$$

$$(\textsc{Local-While})$$
$$\frac{s_1' = s_1; \mathtt{while}\ e\ \{s_1\}}{a, \{l \mid \mathtt{while}\ e\ \{s_1\}; s_2\} \rightsquigarrow a, \{l \mid \mathtt{if}\ e\ \{s_1'\}\ \mathtt{else}\ \{\mathtt{skip}\}; s_2\}}$$

$$(\textsc{Local-Skip1})$$
$$a, \{l \mid \mathtt{skip}; s\} \rightsquigarrow a, \{l \mid s\}$$

$$(\textsc{Local-Cond1})$$
$$\frac{\mathtt{true} = [\![e]\!]_{(a \circ l)}}{\substack{a, \{l \mid \mathtt{if}\ e\ \{s_1\}\ \mathtt{else}\ \{s_2\}; s\} \\ \rightsquigarrow a, \{l \mid s_1; s\}}}$$

$$(\textsc{Local-Cond2})$$
$$\frac{\mathtt{false} = [\![e]\!]_{(a \circ l)}}{\substack{a, \{l \mid \mathtt{if}\ e\ \{s_1\}\ \mathtt{else}\ \{s_2\}; s\} \\ \rightsquigarrow a, \{l \mid s_2; s\}}}$$

$$(\textsc{Local-Skip2})$$
$$a, \{l \mid \mathtt{skip}\} \rightsquigarrow a, \mathtt{idle}$$

$$(\textsc{Global-Activate})$$
$$\frac{p \in q \quad a, p \overset{!}{\rightsquigarrow} a', p' \quad p = \{l \mid s\} \\ l(\mathtt{destiny}) = f \quad q' = q \backslash \{p\}}{ob(o, a, \mathtt{idle}, q) \xrightarrow{sched\langle o, f\rangle} ob(o, a', p', q')}$$

$$(\textsc{Global-Return})$$
$$\frac{v = [\![e]\!]_{(a \circ l)} \quad l(\mathtt{destiny}) = f}{ob(o, a, \{l \mid \mathtt{return}\ e\}, q)\ fut(f, \bot) \\ \xrightarrow{futWr\langle o, f\rangle} ob(o, a, \mathtt{idle}, q)\ fut(f, v)}$$

$$(\textsc{Global-Context})$$
$$\frac{cn_1 \xrightarrow{ev?} cn_1'}{cn_1\ cn_2 \xrightarrow{ev?} cn_1'\ cn_2}$$

$$(\textsc{Global-New-Actor})$$
$$\frac{a'' = \mathrm{initAttributes}(C, o') \\ \mathrm{fresh}(o') \quad a, \{l \mid x = o'; s\} \rightsquigarrow a', p'}{ob(o, a, \{l \mid x = \mathtt{new}\ C(); s\}, q) \\ \xrightarrow{new\langle o, o'\rangle} ob(o, a', p', q)\ ob(o', a'', \mathtt{idle}, \varnothing)}$$

$$(\textsc{Global-Read-Fut})$$
$$\frac{v \neq \bot \quad f = [\![e]\!]_{(a \circ l)} \\ a, \{l \mid x = v; s\} \overset{!}{\rightsquigarrow} a', p}{ob(o, a, \{l \mid x = e.\mathtt{get}; s\}, q)\ fut(f, v) \\ \xrightarrow{futRe\langle o, f\rangle} ob(o, a', p, q)\ fut(f, v)}$$

$$(\textsc{Global-Async-Call})$$
$$\frac{o' = [\![e]\!]_{(a \circ l)} \quad \overline{v} = [\![\overline{e}]\!]_{(a \circ l)} \\ \mathrm{fresh}(f) \quad a, \{l \mid x = f; s\} \overset{!}{\rightsquigarrow} a', p}{ob(o, a, \{l \mid x = e!m(\overline{e}); s\}, q) \\ \xrightarrow{inv\langle o, f\rangle} ob(o, a', p, q)\ inv(o', f, m, \overline{v})\ fut(f, \bot)}$$

$$(\textsc{Global-Load})$$
$$\frac{p' = \mathrm{bind}(m, \overline{v}, f, \mathrm{classOf}(o))}{inv(o, f, m, \overline{v})\ ob(o, a, p, q) \\ \rightarrow ob(o, a, p, q \cup \{p'\})}$$

Fig. 6: Coarse-grained, labelled semantics of the basic active object language.

3.3   A Labelled Operational Semantics for the Basic Language

Based on Lemma 1, we can define a semantics of the basic active object language with a more coarse-grained model of interleaving which is equivalent to the semantics presented in Fig. 5. We let this coarse-grained semantics be labeled by events to record the interaction between an active object and its environment. The events are defined as follows:

Definition 2 (Events). *Let $o, f \in Identifiers$. The set $\mathcal{E}$ of events ev is given by*

$$ev ::= new\langle o, o\rangle \mid inv\langle o, f\rangle \mid sched\langle o, f\rangle \mid futWr\langle o, f\rangle \mid futRe\langle o, f\rangle.$$

In the coarse-grained semantics, a transition relation $a, p \rightsquigarrow a', p'$ captures *local execution* in an active object with attributes a. These rules are given in

Fig. 6 (top) and correspond to the rules ASSIGN1, ASSIGN2, WHILE, COND1, COND2, SKIP1 and SKIP2 of Fig. 5. These rules are deterministic as there is at most one possible reduction for any given pair a, p. Let $\overset{*}{\leadsto}$ denote the reflexive, transitive closure of $\leadsto$, let the unary relation $\not\leadsto$ denote that there is no transition from a given pair a, p, and let the relation $\overset{!}{\leadsto}$ denote the reduction to normal form according to $\leadsto$; i.e.,

$$a, p \overset{!}{\leadsto} a', p' \iff a, p \overset{*}{\leadsto} a', p' \wedge a', p' \not\leadsto$$

In the remaining rules, given in Fig. 6 (bottom), a labelled transition relation $cn \overset{ev}{\longrightarrow} cn'$ captures transitions in which the local execution of an active object interacts with its environment through scheduling, object creation, method invocation, or interaction with futures. These rules also correspond to the similar rules in Fig. 5, with two differences:

1. The rules are labelled with an event reflecting the particular action taken in the transition, and
2. the rules perform a local deterministic reduction to normal form according to the $\leadsto$ relation in each step.

Remark that rule GLOBAL-LOAD is identical to LOAD of Fig. 5; although we do not need to add an explicit label the rule is kept at the global level since it involves both an object and a message. Rule GLOBAL-CONTEXT is labeled by ev? to capture that the label is optional (i.e., the rule also combines with GLOBAL-LOAD). We henceforth consider runs for the basic active object language based on this labelled semantics.

3.4   Execution Traces and their Reordering

This section looks at traces reflecting the runs of programs in the basic active object language according to the semantics of Section 3.3, and their reordering. We consider traces over events in $\mathcal{E}$. Let ϵ denote the empty trace, and $\tau_1 \cdot \tau_2$ the concatenation of traces τ_1 and τ_2. For an event ev and a trace τ, we denote by $ev \in \tau$ that ev occurs somewhere in τ and by $\tau \textbf{ ew } ev$ that τ ends with ev (i.e., $\exists \tau'. \tau = \tau' \cdot ev$). Define τ/o and τ/f as the projection of a trace τ to the alphabet of an object o and a future f, by their first or second argument respectively (where an alphabet is the set of events involving that name). Finally, let $names(\tau)$ denote the inductively defined function returning the set of identifiers that occur in a trace τ (e.g., $names(inv\langle o, f \rangle) = \{o, f\}$). We assume that every initial configuration has a main object and process, and let $names(\epsilon) = \{o_{\text{main}}, f_{\text{main}}\}$.

Given a run $cn_0 \overset{ev_0}{\longrightarrow} \cdots \overset{ev_n}{\longrightarrow} cn_{n+1}$, we denote $cn_0 \overset{\tau}{\Rightarrow} cn_{n+1}$ that a trace τ is the trace of the run if $\tau = ev_0 \cdots ev_n$ (where τ ignores the unlabeled transition steps of the run). Well-formed traces can be defined as follows, based on [12]:

Definition 3 (Well-formed Traces). *Given $o, o', f \in$ Identifiers. Let $wf(\tau)$ denote that τ is* well-formed, *defined inductively:*

$$wf(\epsilon) \iff True$$
$$wf(\tau \cdot new\langle o, o' \rangle) \iff wf(\tau) \wedge o \in names(\tau) \wedge o' \notin names(\tau)$$
$$wf(\tau \cdot inv\langle o, f \rangle) \iff wf(\tau) \wedge o \in names(\tau) \wedge f \notin names(\tau)$$
$$wf(\tau \cdot sched\langle o, f \rangle) \iff wf(\tau) \wedge o \in names(\tau) \wedge \tau/f = inv\langle o', f \rangle$$
$$wf(\tau \cdot futWr\langle o, f \rangle) \iff wf(\tau) \wedge \tau/f \text{ ew } sched\langle o, f \rangle$$
$$wf(\tau \cdot futRe\langle o, f \rangle) \iff wf(\tau) \wedge futWr\langle o', f \rangle \in \tau$$

Wellformedness thus captures a happens-before relation over events while ensuring that certain identifiers are new at given points in the trace. Din and Owe have shown that the trace of any run of the semantics of an active object language similar to ours is well-formed [12]. For example, no process can be scheduled unless it has been invoked (which again requires the GLOBAL-LOAD rule to apply in between GLOBAL-ASYNC-CALL and GLOBAL-ACTIVATE). Given a trace τ, we can now define the equivalence class $[\tau]$ of traces which preserve the local ordering and the wellformedness of τ, as follows:

Definition 4 (Global trace set). *Let τ be a trace and define*

$$[\tau] = \{\tau' \mid \tau'/o = \tau/o \text{ for all object identifiers } o \in names(\tau) \wedge wf(\tau')\}.$$

Remark that this construction is closely related to equivalence classes in Mazurkiewics trace theory [13], with wellformedness as the dependency relation of the equivalence classes.

Example 1. The program from Fig. 1 (Section 2) has the following traces:

$$\tau_1 = new\langle o_{\text{main}}, o \rangle \cdot inv\langle o_{\text{main}}, f_{\text{m1}} \rangle \cdot inv\langle o_{\text{main}}, f_{\text{m2}} \rangle \cdot sched\langle o, f_{\text{m1}} \rangle \cdot sched\langle o, f_{\text{m2}} \rangle$$
$$\tau_2 = new\langle o_{\text{main}}, o \rangle \cdot inv\langle o_{\text{main}}, f_{\text{m1}} \rangle \cdot sched\langle o, f_{\text{m1}} \rangle \cdot inv\langle o_{\text{main}}, f_{\text{m2}} \rangle \cdot sched\langle o, f_{\text{m2}} \rangle$$
$$\tau_3 = new\langle o_{\text{main}}, o \rangle \cdot inv\langle o_{\text{main}}, f_{\text{m1}} \rangle \cdot inv\langle o_{\text{main}}, f_{\text{m2}} \rangle \cdot sched\langle o, f_{\text{m2}} \rangle \cdot sched\langle o, f_{\text{m1}} \rangle$$

Observe that traces τ_1 and τ_2 belong to the same global trace set (i.e. $[\tau_1] = [\tau_2]$), and will produce the same final state.

Let $G \xRightarrow{o:f} G'$ denote a run between consecutive stable configurations which executes the process identified by f on object o in the stable configuration G until the next stable configuration G'. If $sched\langle o, f \rangle \cdot \tau$ is the trace of $G \xRightarrow{o:f} G'$, then τ is a trace over the event set $\{inv\langle o, f' \rangle, new\langle o, o' \rangle, futWr\langle o, f \rangle \mid o', f' \in$ Identifiers$\}$. This observation provides an intuition for the following lemma:

Lemma 2 (Local confluence). *Let G_1, G_2, G_3 be stable configurations, o, o' object and f, f' future identifiers, with $o \neq o'$, $f \neq f'$. If $G_1 \xRightarrow{o:f} G_2$ and $G_1 \xRightarrow{o':f'} G_3$, then there is a stable configuration G_4 such that $G_2 \xRightarrow{o':f'} G_4$ and $G_3 \xRightarrow{o:f} G_4$.*

Proof (sketch). The proof follows from the fact that execution in an object does not inhibit a process to run in another object. □

The following theorem shows that local confluence implies global confluence for executions in the *same global trace set* (which means that the two executions agree on the local trace projections).

Theorem 1 (Global confluence). *Let G_1, G_2, G_3 be stable configurations and τ_1, τ_2 traces such that $G_1 \overset{\tau_1}{\Rightarrow} G_2$ and $G_1 \overset{\tau_2}{\Rightarrow} G_3$. If $\tau_2 \in [\tau_1]$ then $G_2 = G_3$.*

Proof (sketch). Observe that runs with traces in the same global trace set must agree on the naming of objects and futures. The result then follows by induction over the length of $G_1 \overset{\tau_1}{\Rightarrow} G_2$ from local confluence (Lemma 2).   □

4   Global Reproducibility with Local Traces

The global confluence of executions with traces in the same global trace set provides a formal justification for a method to obtain global reproducibility for distributed active object systems which exhibit non-deterministic behavior. The method is based on enforcing the local trace projection from the global trace set on each active object. For the basic active object language, the method is based on recording the events from the set $\mathcal{E}$ during an execution. This set of events, which includes events capturing the scheduling decisions of the runtime system as well as the choice of dynamically created names during a particular execution, is sufficient to establish the wellformedness of the recorded trace and identify the global trace set of the recorded run. Furthermore, if we record local traces for each active object, these will correspond to the local trace projections of the global trace set. In fact, any composition of local traces recorded during a run will result in the same global trace set. Similarly, any composition of local trace projections enforced during a replay will result in a trace in the same global trace set. Thus, Theorem 1 guarantees that local recording and replay of different traces from the same global trace set will result in the same final state. It remains to show that for any such trace in the global trace set corresponding to a recorded run, the execution during replay will not get stuck. For this purpose, we now formalize record and replay as extensions to the semantics of the basic active object language.

We extend the operational semantics of Fig. 6 to record and replay traces. Let $\tau \rhd cn$ denote an extended runtime configuration, where τ is a witness for cn, playing dual roles for recording and replaying. A *recorded run* starts from an initial configuration $\epsilon \rhd cn$, where cn is the initial configuration of the run to be recorded. The reduction system for recording a trace is given as a relation $\overset{\bullet}{\longrightarrow}$ by the rules in Fig. 7; the two rules correspond to the unlabeled (just GLOBAL-LOAD) and labeled transitions of the semantics, respectively. A replay starts from an initial configuration $\tau \rhd cn$, where τ is a trace and cn the initial configuration of the run to be replayed. The reduction system for replaying a trace is given as a relation $\overset{\blacktriangleright}{\longrightarrow}$ by the rules in Fig. 8, the two rules are symmetric to those for recording a run. The rules in Fig. 7 and Fig. 8 formalize the obvious relation between the recording and replaying of a trace and a run in the semantics of the

(Unlabeled-Record)
$$\frac{cn \rightarrow cn'}{\tau \rhd cn \xrightarrow{\bullet} \tau \rhd cn'}$$

(Unlabeled-Replay)
$$\frac{cn \rightarrow cn'}{\tau \rhd cn \xrightarrow{\blacktriangleright} \tau \rhd cn'}$$

(Labeled-Record)
$$\frac{cn \xrightarrow{ev} cn'}{\tau \rhd cn \xrightarrow{\bullet} \tau \cdot ev \rhd cn'}$$

(Labeled-Replay)
$$\frac{cn \xrightarrow{ev} cn'}{ev \cdot \tau \rhd cn \xrightarrow{\blacktriangleright} \tau \rhd cn'}$$

Fig. 7: Semantics of Record   Fig. 8: Semantics of Replay

basic active object language. Let $\xRightarrow{\bullet}$ and $\xRightarrow{\blacktriangleright}$ denote the reflexive, transitive closures of $\xrightarrow{\bullet}$ and $\xrightarrow{\blacktriangleright}$, respectively.

Lemma 3 (Freshness of names). *For any recording $\epsilon \rhd cn \xRightarrow{\bullet} \tau \rhd cn'$ or replay $\tau \cdot \tau' \rhd cn \xRightarrow{\blacktriangleright} \tau' \rhd cn'$, we have that $names(\tau) = names(cn')$.*

Proof (sketch). Follows by induction over the length of $\epsilon \rhd cn \xRightarrow{\bullet} \tau \rhd cn'$ and $\tau \cdot \tau' \rhd cn \xRightarrow{\blacktriangleright} \tau' \rhd cn'$, respectively.   □

It follows from Lemma 3 that given an identifier $x \in Identifiers$ and a run $\epsilon \rhd cn \xRightarrow{\bullet} \tau \rhd cn'$, if $x \notin names(\tau)$, then $x \notin names(cn')$ and consequently, the predicate $fresh(x)$ will hold as a premise for any rule in the semantics that one may want to apply to cn'. Consequently, fresh-predicates in the premises of the transition rules of the basic active language will accept the identifier names chosen from the recorded trace when replaying a run.

Lemma 4 (Progress for replay by global trace). *Let G, G' be stable configurations. If $\epsilon \rhd G \xRightarrow{\blacktriangleright} \tau \rhd G'$ then $\tau \rhd G \xRightarrow{\blacktriangleright} \epsilon \rhd G'$.*

Proof. The proof is by induction over the length of the run $\epsilon \rhd G \xRightarrow{\bullet} \tau \rhd G'$. The base case is obvious. We assume (IH) that if $\epsilon \rhd G \xRightarrow{\bullet} \tau \rhd cn$ then $\tau \rhd G \xRightarrow{\blacktriangleright} \epsilon \rhd cn$ and show that if $\epsilon \rhd G \xrightarrow{\bullet} \tau \cdot ev \rhd cn'$ then $\tau \cdot ev \rhd G \xrightarrow{\blacktriangleright} \tau \rhd cn'$. By the IH, this amounts to showing that if $\epsilon \rhd cn \xrightarrow{\bullet} \epsilon \cdot ev \rhd cn'$ then $ev \cdot \epsilon \rhd cn \xrightarrow{\blacktriangleright} \epsilon \rhd cn'$. The proof proceeds by cases over the transition rules of the basic active object language (cf. Fig. 5). The interesting cases are the rules which need new names. Lemma 3 ensures that the predicate $fresh(o)$ will hold for a new name o in ev (and similarly for f), and the corresponding rules can be applied.   □

It follows from Theorem 1 that if we can replay a run which is equivalent to a recorded run τ, the final state of the replayed run will be the same as for the recorded run. It remains to show that any run in the equivalence class $[\tau]$ can in fact be replayed.

Theorem 2 (Progress for replay by local control). *Let G, G' be stable configurations, τ, τ' traces. If $\epsilon \rhd G \xRightarrow{\bullet} \tau \rhd G'$ and $\tau' \in [\tau]$, then $\tau' \rhd G \xRightarrow{\blacktriangleright} \epsilon \rhd G'$.*

Proof (sketch). We show by induction over the length of trace τ that if $\epsilon \rhd G \xRightarrow{\bullet} \tau \rhd cn$ and $\tau' \in [\tau]$, then $\tau' \rhd G \xRightarrow{\blacktriangleright} \epsilon \rhd cn'$. It then follows from Theorem 1 that $cn = cn'$.   □

5 Extensions for Richer Active Object Languages

The method for global reproducibility of executions for a basic active object language based on record & replay of local traces, may be extended to include features introducing other sources of non-determinism in richer active object languages [2]. We here briefly review some such features and how the method may be extended to cover them.

Cooperative scheduling. In cooperatively scheduled languages (e.g., [3–5, 14]), methods may explicitly *release control*, allowing other pending method invocations be scheduled. The criteria for being rescheduled may be that some boolean condition is met, or a future being resolved. Note that methods still execute until it cooperatively releases control; i.e., a method will not be interrupted because the condition of another method is satisfied. With cooperative scheduling, the same task may be scheduled several times, which means that the same scheduling event may occur multiple times in a trace. In the method for reproducibility, this extension can be covered by an additional suspension-event reflecting the processor release and an adjustment of the wellformedness condition to reflect that a scheduling event either comes after a invocation event (as for the basic language) or after a suspension event on the same future.

Concurrent object groups. In language with concurrent object groups (e.g., [3,5]), a group of concurrent objects (or cog) share a common scheduler, which becomes the unit of distribution; this gives an interleaved semantics between objects within the same cog, while separate cogs are truly concurrent. For record & replay, the events of a trace need to capture the cog, rather than the object, in which an event originated. Recording the names of cogs is sufficient for reproducibility without controlling the naming of objects. For the reproducibility method, the proofs in Section 4 would use an equivalence relation between configurations that only differ in the choice of object names inside the cogs and the global trace set (Def. 4) would project on cogs rather than objects.

Resource-aware behavior. Active objects may reside in a resource center with limited resources, e.g. CPU or memory restrictions, with regards to time (e.g., [6, 15]). Statements may have some associated cost which requires available resources in order to execute. If there are insufficient resources, then execution is blocked in that object until time advances. Here, object compete for resources, in the same sense that tasks compete for processing time. Following our method for deterministic replay, the traces can be extended with events for resource request in a similar manner as method invocations in the basic active objects language, and resource provision with events similar to the task scheduling events.

External non-determinism and random numbers. Active object languages may also feature external factors that may influence an execution, such as input from a user, fetching data from a database or receiving input from a socket, or random number generation. Here, a purely *ordering-based* method is insufficient. Our replay method needs to be extended with events which include the data received from the external source and the replay would need to fetch data from the trace rather than from the external source, similar to the reuse of object and future identifiers from the trace in the previous section. Random number generation can be seen as a special case of external non-determinism; for pseudo-random number generators it would be sufficient to only record the initial seed for reuse during replay.

6   Implementing Record & Replay for Real-Time ABS

We report on our implementation[1] of *record & replay*, based on the formalization in Section 4. The implementation was done for Real-Time ABS [6, 16], an active object modeling language which includes the following features discussed in Section 5: cooperative scheduling, concurrent object groups, and timed, resource-aware behavior, all of which are handled by our implementation. The simulator for Real-Time ABS models, written in Erlang, supports interaction with a model during execution via the Model API [17] in order to, e.g. fetch the current state of an object, advance the simulated clock or visualize the resource consumption of a running model. In addition, we have implemented a *visualizer* for recorded traces. In this section, we discuss the following aspects of the implementation: the recording of traces in a distributed setting, the handling of names, the visualization of traces, and performance characteristics for the implementation of record & replay.

6.1   Recording Traces in a Distributed Setting

For simulation, ABS models are transpiled to Erlang code by representing most entities as Erlang actors, e.g., concurrent object groups (or cogs), resource centers, futures and ABS-level processes. Thus, execution is concurrent and may be distributed over multiple machines. This leads to two important differences from the formalization in Section 4:

- *True concurrency:* The formalization is based on an interleaved concurrency model, which yields a total order of events. In the simulator, cogs are implemented as Erlang actors and may operate in true parallel, where two events may happen *simultaneously*, which corresponds to a partial order of events.
- *Distributed state:* Because the state of the model is distributed over many independent actors, we cannot easily synchronize over the state of different actors. In the implementation, such synchronization in the formalization must be realized by asynchronous message passing protocols.

---

[1] The Real-Time ABS simulator is available at
https://github.com/abstools/abstools
The accompanying visualization tool is available at
https://github.com/larstvei/ABS-traces

These differences pose challenges for recording and replaying global traces in the implementation. When recording a run, it is not trivial to obtain a global trace. If all cogs and resource centers were to report their recorded events to a single actor maintaining the global trace, races could occur between different asynchronous messages. For example, if an object o invokes a method on another object o', then the corresponding invocation and scheduling events could arrive in any order. Such races could be resolved by, e.g., introducing additional synchronization or using Lamport timestamps [18, 19]. Similarly, precisely replaying a global trace would require some synchronization protocol with the actor holding the global trace, severely increasing the level of synchronization during execution.

We address these challenges by only considering the local projections of the global trace for each cog and resource center. The information needed to construct local traces does not require any additional synchronization. During replay, only the local execution of an actor is controlled, which is sufficient to obtain a run with a trace in the same global trace set.

6.2   Names in the Erlang Simulator

The formalization allows recorded names to be reused when replaying a run. In contrast, in the Erlang system cogs, resource centers and futures are implemented as actors (i.e. Erlang actors) and identified by a process identifier (pid) determined by Erlang. To ensure that names in the events of the recorded trace are easily identifiable in a replay without modifying the naming scheme of Erlang, we construct additional names that are associated with the given pid. The constructed names follow a deterministic naming scheme, which guarantees that names are globally unique without depending on knowledge of names generated in other actors (in contrast to the fresh-predicate in the semantics).

Cogs, resource centers and futures can be named locally following a naming scheme based on existing actors already having such unique, associated names. The name $\langle A_{id}, i + 1 \rangle$ of a new actor can be determined by the actor A_{id} in which it is created, together with a local counter denoting the number i of actors previously created in A_{id}. Thus, the name of the actor corresponds to its place in the topology and is guaranteed to be fresh.

6.3   Visualization of Recorded Traces

The trace recorded during a simulation can give the user insight into that execution of a model, since it captures the model's communication structure. The recorded trace may be extracted from a running simulation via the Model API or written to file on termination. However, the terse format of the traces makes it hard for users to quickly get an intuitive idea of what is happening in the model. Complementing the replay facility, we have developed a tool to visualize recorded traces, which conveys information from traces in a more intuitive format. To facilitate visualization, the events in our implementation are slightly richer than those in Definition 2; e.g., they include the name of the method corresponding to the future in the event.

The visualization reconstructs a global trace τ from its local projections. Since the local ordering of events is already preserved by the recorded traces, we only need to compose local traces in a way that preserves wellformedness. We derive a happens-before relation $\prec$ from wellformedness (Definition 3), and denote its transitive closure by $\lll$.

The happens-before relation $\lll$ gives a partial order of events. In the visualization of the trace τ, all events are depicted by a colored dot. For any two events e_1, e_2, e_1 is drawn above e_2 if $e_1 \lll e_2$; the events are drawn in the same column only if they reside in the same cog or resource center. An arrow is drawn between any two events e_1, e_2 if $e_1 \prec e_2$. Events that are independent (i.e., neither $e_1 \lll e_2$ nor $e_2 \lll e_1$) may be drawn in the same row. Events with the same future as argument are drawn with the same color. The tool additionally supports simple navigation in the trace, gives visual indicators of simulated time steps, and supports time advancement in a running model through the model API, making it easy to step forward in time. Fig. 2 illustrates the visualization for two runs of the motivating example.

6.4   Example

Consider a Real-Time ABS model of an image rendering service which can process either still photos or video. The service is modeled as a class `Service` with two methods `photo_request` and `video_request`. The model captures *resource-sensitive behavior* in terms of cost annotations associated with the execution of `skip`-statements inside the two methods and in terms of deadlines provided to each method call. The processing cost for rendering an image is constant (here, the cost is given by the field `image_cost`), but the processing cost of rendering a video depends on the number of frames (captured by a parameter `n` to the method `video_request`). The success of each method call depends on whether it succeeded in processing its job, as specified by the cost annotation, before its deadline passes; this is captured by the expression in the return statement `return (Duration(0) < deadline())`. Remark that `deadline()` is a predefined read-only variable in Real-Time ABS processes. Its value is given by the caller.

In the main block, a server is created on which the service can run. This server is a resource-center with limited processing capacity (called a deployment component in Real-Time ABS [6]), restricting the amount of computation that can happen on the server per time interval in the execution of the model. The service is then deployed on the server (by an annotation [DC: `server`] to `new`-statement. We let a class `Client` (omitted here) model a given number of processing requests to the image rendering service in terms of asynchronously calling the two methods a given number of times (e.g., the call to `video_request` takes the form `[Deadline: Duration(10)] f = s!video_request(n)`, pushing the associated futures `f` to a list, and then counting the number of successful requests when the corresponding futures have been resolved. It is easy to see that the success of calls to the `video_request` method which requires more resources, may depend on whether it is scheduled before or after calls to `photo_request`,

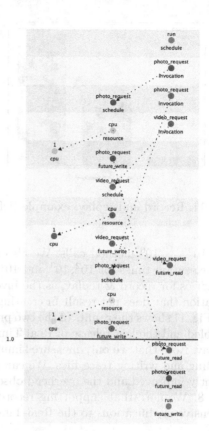

```
class Service {
  Int image_cost = 1;

  Bool photo_request() {
    [Cost: image_cost] skip;
    return (Duration(0)
            < deadline());
  }

  Bool video_request(Int n) {
    [Cost: n*image_cost] skip;
    return (Duration(0)
            < deadline());
  }
}

// Main block
{
  DC server
    = new DC("Server", 2);
  [DC: server] Service s1
    = new Service();
  new Client(s1, 1, 100);
}
```

Fig. 9: Real-Time ABS code for the photo rendering service.

Fig. 10: Visualization of a run of the photo rendering service.

depending on the provided deadlines. Thus, the model exhibits both scheduling non-determinism for asynchronous calls and resource-aware behavior. The image in Fig. 10 depicts a trace from a simulation of the model, showing interactions between a deployment component (left), the service (middle) and the client (right).

6.5 Performance Characteristics of the Implementation

We give a brief evaluation of the performance characteristics of record & replay for Real Time ABS. The size of the traces is proportional to the number of objects, method invocations and resource provisions. Because we do not impose additional synchronization, we are able to achieve a constant-time overhead. To investigate how record & replay scales, we created a micro-benchmark performing method invocations on an active object, and recorded execution times for

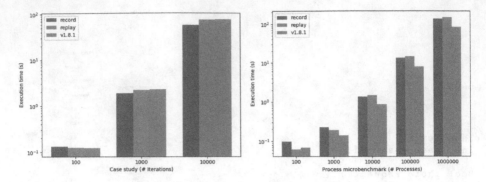

Fig. 11: Record and replay: example (left) and process microbenchmark (right)

$10^2, 10^3, \ldots, 10^6$ method calls. We also ran the example of Section 6.4, recording execution times for $10^2, 10^3$ and 10^4 Client iterations. These are worst-case scenarios for record & replay, as the invoked methods do not perform any computation that does not result in creating an event.

Fig. 11 shows the results of the two programs with replay enabled, with record enabled and the last release of Real-Time ABS which does not feature record & replay. Note that we only measure simulation time and do not include the time reading and writing trace files. We can see that the results of Fig. 11 (left) are slightly improved and the overhead observed in Fig. 11 (right) is about a factor of 1.8. We note that supporting record & replay in Real-Time ABS required extensive modifications to the Real-Time ABS simulators implementation.

7   Related Work

This work complements other analysis techniques for Real-Time ABS models, such as simulation [17], deductive verification [9], and parallel cost analysis [20] and testing [21]. We here discuss related work on deterministic replay. Deterministic replay is an emerging technique to reproduce executions of computer programs in the presence of different non-deterministic factors [1]. It enables cyclic debugging [22] in non-deterministic execution environments. Our focus is on software-level reproducibility in the context of actor-systems. Approaches to reproduce specific runs of non-deterministic systems can be either *content-based* or *ordering based* [23].

Content-based methods trace the values read from a shared memory location. These are particularly suitable when there is a lot of external non-determinism (typically I/O operations, like user input). Content-based replay for actor systems typically record messages, including the sender, receiver and message content, (see, e.g., [24–26]). This technique is typically used for rich debuggers like Actoverse [24] for Scala's Akka library, which provides visualization support similar to ours. However, content-based approaches do not scale well [27], because the traces can become very large for message-intensive applications.

Ordering-based (or control-based) methods trace a system's *control-flow*. Our work fits within this category. Without external non-determinism, replaying the control-flow will reproduce the data of the recorded run. Ordering-based methods exist for asynchronous message passing using the message passing interface (MPI) [19,28]. MPI assumes that messages from the same source are received in order, this does not generally hold for actor systems. Aumayr *et al.* in [27] study ordering-based replay for actor systems with a memory-efficient representation of the generated traces. Netzer *et al.* [29] propose an interesting method to only trace events directly related to races, rather than all events (removing up to 99% of the events). This line of work is complementary to our focus on formal correctness and low runtime-overhead during record and replay. We believe we could benefit from their work to obtain more efficient trace representations. Lanese *et al.* recently proposed a notion of causal-consistent replay based on reversible debugging [30], which enables replay to a state by only replaying its causal dependencies. Similar to our work, they also formalize record & replay for an actor language. In contrast to our work, their approach is based on a centralized actor for tracing, and can only be used in combination with a debugger [31].

8 Conclusion and Future Work

This paper has introduced a method for global reproducibility for runs of distributed Active Object systems, based on local control. The proposed method is order-based and decentralized in that local traces are recorded and replayed without incurring any additional synchronization at the global level. The method is formalized as an operational semantics for a basic active object language, with trace recording and replay. This system exhibits non-determinism through the scheduling of asynchronous method calls and synchronization using first-class futures. Based on this formalization, we justify in terms of properties of trace equivalence classes that local control suffices to reproduce runs with a final state which is equivalent to the final state of a recorded run. We then discuss how other features of active object languages which introduce additional non-determinism can be supported by our method, including cooperative concurrency, concurrent object groups and resource-aware behavior.

The proposed method has been implemented for Real-Time ABS, an Active Object modeling language which includes most of the above-mentioned features and which has a simulator written in Erlang. The implementation only records local ordering information, which allows the overhead of both the record and replay phases to be kept low compared to deterministic replay systems which reproduce an exact global run.

In future work, we plan to build on the proposed record & replay tool for systematic model exploration, by modifying traces between the record and replay phase to explore different runs. This can be done by means of DPOR-algorithms for actor-based systems [32–34]. Combining DPOR with our proposed tool for record & replay would result in a stateless model checker [35] for Active Object systems.

References

1. Chen, Y., Zhang, S., Guo, Q., Li, L., Wu, R., Chen, T.: Deterministic replay: A survey. ACM Comput. Surv. **48**(2) (September 2015) 17:1–17:47
2. de Boer, F., Serbanescu, V., Hähnle, R., Henrio, L., Rochas, J., Din, C.C., Johnsen, E.B., Sirjani, M., Khamespanah, E., Fernandez-Reyes, K., Yang, A.M.: A survey of active object languages. ACM Comput. Surv. **50**(5) (October 2017) 76:1–76:39
3. Johnsen, E.B., Hähnle, R., Schäfer, J., Schlatte, R., Steffen, M.: ABS: A core language for abstract behavioral specification. In Aichernig, B., de Boer, F.S., Bonsangue, M.M., eds.: Proc. 9th Intl. Symp. on Formal Methods for Components and Objects (FMCO 2010). Volume 6957 of Lecture Notes in Computer Science., Springer (2011) 142–164
4. Brandauer, S., Castegren, E., Clarke, D., Fernandez-Reyes, K., Johnsen, E.B., Pun, K.I., Tapia Tarifa, S.L., Wrigstad, T., Yang, A.M.: Parallel objects for multicores: A glimpse at the parallel language encore. In: Formal Methods for Multicore Programming (SFM 2015). Volume 9104 of Lecture Notes in Computer Science., Springer (2015) 1–56
5. Schäfer, J., Poetzsch-Heffter, A.: JCoBox: Generalizing active objects to concurrent components. In D'Hondt, T., ed.: Proc. 24th European Conference on Object-Oriented Programming (ECOOP 2010). Volume 6183 of Lecture Notes in Computer Science., Springer (2010) 275–299
6. Johnsen, E.B., Schlatte, R., Tapia Tarifa, S.L.: Integrating deployment architectures and resource consumption in timed object-oriented models. J. Log. Algebr. Meth. Program. **84**(1) (2015) 67–91
7. Albert, E., de Boer, F.S., Hähnle, R., Johnsen, E.B., Schlatte, R., Tapia Tarifa, S.L., Wong, P.Y.H.: Formal modeling and analysis of resource management for cloud architectures: an industrial case study using real-time ABS. Service Oriented Computing and Applications **8**(4) (2014) 323–339
8. Kamburjan, E., Hähnle, R., Schön, S.: Formal modeling and analysis of railway operations with active objects. Sci. Comput. Program. **166** (2018) 167–193
9. Din, C.C., Tapia Tarifa, S.L., Hähnle, R., Johnsen, E.B.: History-based specification and verification of scalable concurrent and distributed systems. In: Proc. 17th Intl. Conf. on Formal Engineering Methods (ICFEM 2015). Volume 9407 of Lecture Notes in Computer Science., Springer (2015) 217–233
10. Bezirgiannis, N., de Boer, F.S., Johnsen, E.B., Pun, K.I., Tapia Tarifa, S.L.: Implementing SOS with active objects: A case study of a multicore memory system. In: Proc. 22nd Intl. Conf. on Fundamental Approaches to Software Engineering (FASE 2019). Volume 11424 of Lecture Notes in Computer Science., Springer (2019) 332–350
11. Armstrong, J.: Programming Erlang: Software for a Concurrent World. Pragmatic Bookshelf Series. Pragmatic Bookshelf (2007)
12. Din, C.C., Owe, O.: A sound and complete reasoning system for asynchronous communication with shared futures. J. Log. Algebr. Meth. Program. **83**(5-6) (2014) 360–383
13. Mazurkiewicz, A.W.: Trace theory. In Brauer, W., Reisig, W., Rozenberg, G., eds.: Advances in Petri Nets 1986. Volume 255 of Lecture Notes in Computer Science., Springer (1987) 279–324
14. Johnsen, E.B., Owe, O.: An asynchronous communication model for distributed concurrent objects. Software and Systems Modeling **6**(1) (2007) 39–58

15. Albert, E., Genaim, S., Gómez-Zamalloa, M., Johnsen, E.B., Schlatte, R., Tapia Tarifa, S.L.: Simulating concurrent behaviors with worst-case cost bounds. In Butler, M.J., Schulte, W., eds.: Proc. 17th International Symposium on Formal Methods (FM 2011). Volume 6664 of Lecture Notes in Computer Science., Springer (2011) 353–368

16. Bjørk, J., de Boer, F.S., Johnsen, E.B., Schlatte, R., Tapia Tarifa, S.L.: User-defined schedulers for real-time concurrent objects. Innovations in Systems and Software Engineering 9(1) (2013) 29–43

17. Schlatte, R., Johnsen, E.B., Mauro, J., Tapia Tarifa, S.L., Yu, I.C.: Release the beasts: When formal methods meet real world data. In: It's All About Coordination - Essays to Celebrate the Lifelong Scientific Achievements of Farhad Arbab. Volume 10865 of Lecture Notes in Computer Science., Springer (2018) 107–121

18. Lamport, L.: Time, clocks, and the ordering of events in a distributed system. Commun. ACM 21(7) (1978) 558–565

19. Ronsse, M., Kranzlmüller, D.: Rolt^{mp}-replay of Lamport timestamps for message passing systems. In: Proc. 6th Euromicro Workshop on Parallel and Distributed Processing (PDP'98), IEEE (1998) 87–93

20. Albert, E., Correas, J., Johnsen, E.B., Pun, V.K.I., Román-Díez, G.: Parallel cost analysis. ACM Trans. Comput. Log. 19(4) (2018) 31:1–31:37

21. Albert, E., Gómez-Zamalloa, M., Isabel, M.: SYCO: a systematic testing tool for concurrent objects. In Zaks, A., Hermenegildo, M.V., eds.: Proc. 25th Intl. Conf. on Compiler Construction (CC 2016), ACM (2016) 269–270

22. LeBlanc, T.J., Mellor-Crummey, J.M.: Debugging parallel programs with instant replay. IEEE Trans. Computers 36(4) (1987) 471–482

23. Ronsse, M., Bosschere, K.D., de Kergommeaux, J.C.: Execution replay and debugging. In: AADEBUG. (2000)

24. Shibanai, K., Watanabe, T.: Actoverse: a reversible debugger for actors. In Koster, J.D., Bergenti, F., eds.: Proc. 7th Intl. Workshop on Programming Based on Actors, Agents, and Decentralized Control (AGERE 2017), ACM (2017) 50–57

25. Barr, E.T., Marron, M., Maurer, E., Moseley, D., Seth, G.: Time-travel debugging for javascript/node.js. In Zimmermann, T., Cleland-Huang, J., Su, Z., eds.: Proc. 24th Intl. Symp. on Foundations of Software Engineering (FSE 2016), ACM (2016) 1003–1007

26. Burg, B., Bailey, R., Ko, A.J., Ernst, M.D.: Interactive record/replay for web application debugging. In Izadi, S., Quigley, A.J., Poupyrev, I., Igarashi, T., eds.: Proc. 26th Symp. on User Interface Software and Technology (UIST'13), ACM (2013) 473–484

27. Aumayr, D., Marr, S., Béra, C., Boix, E.G., Mössenböck, H.: Efficient and deterministic record & replay for actor languages. In Tilevich, E., Mössenböck, H., eds.: Proc. 15th Intl. Conf. on Managed Languages & Runtimes (ManLang'18), ACM (2018) 15:1–15:14

28. de Kergommeaux, J.C., Ronsse, M., Bosschere, K.D.: MPL*: Efficient record/play of nondeterministic features of message passing libraries. In Dongarra, J.J., Luque, E., Margalef, T., eds.: Recent Advances in Parallel Virtual Machine and Message Passing Interface, proc. 6th European PVM/MPI Users' Group Meeting. Volume 1697 of Lecture Notes in Computer Science., Springer (1999) 141–148

29. Netzer, R.H.B., Miller, B.P.: Optimal tracing and replay for debugging message-passing parallel programs. The Journal of Supercomputing 8(4) (1995) 371–388

30. Lanese, I., Palacios, A., Vidal, G.: Causal-consistent replay debugging for message passing programs. In Pérez, J.A., Yoshida, N., eds.: Proc. 39th Intl. Conf. on

Formal Techniques for Distributed Objects, Components, and Systems (FORTE 2019). Volume 11535 of Lecture Notes in Computer Science., Springer (2019) 167–184

31. Lanese, I., Nishida, N., Palacios, A., Vidal, G.: Cauder: A causal-consistent reversible debugger for erlang. In Gallagher, J.P., Sulzmann, M., eds.: Proc. 14th Intl. Symp. on Functional and Logic Programming (FLOPS 2018). Volume 10818 of Lecture Notes in Computer Science., Springer (2018) 247–263

32. Flanagan, C., Godefroid, P.: Dynamic partial-order reduction for model checking software. In Palsberg, J., Abadi, M., eds.: Proc. 32nd Symp. on Principles of Programming Languages (POPL 2005), ACM (2005) 110–121

33. Abdulla, P.A., Aronis, S., Jonsson, B., Sagonas, K.: Optimal dynamic partial order reduction. In Jagannathan, S., Sewell, P., eds.: Proc. 41st Symposium on Principles of Programming Languages (POPL'14), ACM (2014) 373–384

34. Albert, E., Arenas, P., de la Banda, M.G., Gómez-Zamalloa, M., Stuckey, P.J.: Context-sensitive dynamic partial order reduction. In Majumdar, R., Kuncak, V., eds.: Proc. 29th Intl. Conf. on Computer Aided Verification (CAV 2017). Volume 10426 of Lecture Notes in Computer Science., Springer (2017) 526–543

35. Godefroid, P.: Model checking for programming languages using Verisoft. In Lee, P., Henglein, F., Jones, N.D., eds.: Proc. 24th Symp. on Principles of Programming Languages (POPL 1997), ACM (1997) 174–186

Multi-level Model Product Lines

Open and closed variability for modelling language families

Juan de Lara and Esther Guerra

Universidad Autónoma de Madrid (Spain)
{Juan.deLara, Esther.Guerra}@uam.es

Abstract. Modelling is an essential activity in software engineering processes. It typically involves two meta-levels: one includes meta-models that describe modelling languages, and the other contains models built by instantiating those meta-models. *Multi-level modelling* generalizes this approach by allowing models to span an arbitrary number of meta-levels.

A scenario that profits from multi-level modelling is the definition of language families that become specialized by successive refinements at subsequent meta-levels, hence promoting language reuse. This enables an *open* set of variability options for the possible specializations of a given language. However, multi-level modelling lacks the ability to express *closed* variability regarding the supported language primitives and their realizations. This limits the reuse opportunities of a language family. To improve this situation, we propose a novel combination of product lines with multi-level modelling to cover both open and closed variability. Our proposal is backed by a formal theory that guarantees correctness, and is implemented atop the METADEPTH multi-level modelling tool.

Keywords: Meta-modelling, Multi-level modelling, Product lines, Domain-specific languages, METADEPTH

1 Introduction

Modelling is intrinsic to most engineering disciplines. Within software engineering, it plays a pivotal role in model-driven engineering (MDE) [43]. This is a software construction paradigm where models are actively used to describe, analyse, validate, verify, generate code and maintain the application to be built, among other activities.

Models are built using modelling languages, which can be either general-purpose, like the UML [46], or domain-specific languages (DSLs) tailored to a specific concern [25]. In MDE, the abstract syntax of modelling languages is defined through a meta-model that describes the primitives that models can use one meta-level below. This modelling approach, which is the standard nowadays, constrains engineers to confine their models within one meta-level (the "model" level).

Some researchers have observed that domain modelling can benefit from the use of more than one meta-level [6, 14, 17, 19, 29]. This way of modelling – called multi-level modelling [4] or deep meta-modelling [12] – results in simpler models in scenarios that involve the type-object pattern [6, 14, 30]. Moreover, it permits defining language families (e.g., for process modelling), which can be specialized to specific domains (e.g., software process modelling, industrial process modelling) via instantiation

© The Author(s) 2020
H. Wehrheim and J. Cabot (Eds.): FASE 2020, LNCS 12076, pp. 161–181, 2020.
https://doi.org/10.1007/978-3-030-45234-6_8

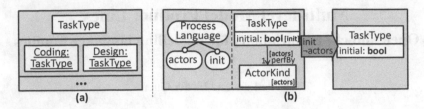

Fig. 1. (a) Open variability through instantiation. (b) Closed variability through product lines.

at lower meta-levels [15]. Instantiation is an *open* variability mechanism that permits the language customization by specializing the language primitives for a domain, or adding new ones via linguistic extensions [12]. Fig. 1(a) shows a tiny process modelling language that defines the primitive TaskType, which is customized by instantiation in the lower meta-level for the software process modelling domain (Coding and Design). However, multi-level modelling lacks support for expressing optionality of language primitives or alternative primitive realizations. This prevents wider language reuse and customization possibilities.

Software product lines (SPLs) encompass methods, tools and techniques to engineer collections of similar software systems using a common means of production [32, 35]. SPLs support *closed* variability, where a concrete software product is obtained by selecting among a finite set of available features (i.e., by setting a *configuration*). SPL techniques have been applied to language engineering to define product lines of languages representing a close set of predefined language variants [20, 34, 47]. As an example, Fig. 1(b) shows a process modelling language product line with two configurable features: actors and initial tasks. Selecting a configuration of features (in the figure, initial tasks but no actors) yields a language variant. Languages so defined can be configured with respect to the primitives they offer and their realization, but cannot be specialized for specific domains as this requires from open variability mechanisms.

To improve current language reuse techniques, we propose combining multi-level modelling and product lines. This allows the definition of highly configurable language families that profit from both open variability (as given by instantiation) and closed variability (as given by configuration). This way, this paper makes the following contributions: (i) a novel notion of multi-level model product line; (ii) a theory that guarantees the correctness of (certain) interleavings of instantiation and configuration steps; and (iii) an implementation of these ideas on top of the METADEPTH tool [12].

Paper organization. Section 2 introduces multi-level modelling and identifies the challenges tackled in this paper. Section 3 provides a light formalization of multi-level modelling, which is extended with product line techniques in Section 4. Section 5 describes tool support. Section 6 discusses related research, and Section 7 ends with the conclusions and future work. An appendix includes the proofs of the theorems in the paper.

2   Multi-level modelling: intuition and challenges

In this section, we introduce the main concepts of multi-level modelling by example (Section 2.1), and then discuss the challenges that we aim to tackle (Section 2.2).

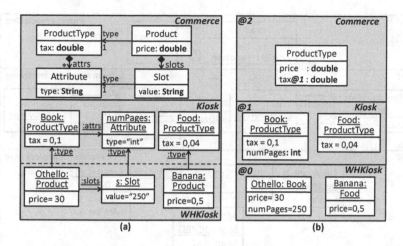

Fig. 2. Commerce example using (a) standard modelling and (b) multi-level modelling.

2.1 Multi-level modelling, by example

Multi-level modelling permits the definition of models using multiple meta-levels [6, 14]. To understand its rationale, assume we would like to create a language to define commerce information systems (a standard example often used in the multi-level modelling literature [6, 14]). This language should allow defining *product types* (like *books* or *food*) which have a *tax*, as well as *products* of the defined types (like *Othello* or *banana*) which have a *price*. Moreover, some product types may need to define specific properties, like the number of *pages* in books.

Fig. 2(a) shows a solution using two meta-levels. In this solution, the meta-model of the language uses the *type-object* pattern [30] to emulate the typing relation between Product and ProductType. In addition, classes Attribute and Slot permit defining properties in ProductTypes and assigning them a value in Products (called *dynamic features* pattern in [14]). The model in the bottom meta-level represents an information system for Kiosks, and defines the product types Book and Food. The model also defines the products sold by a particular kiosk: the Othello book and Bananas.

On reflection, one can realize that this solution emulates two meta-levels within one, as we convey with the dashed line in Fig. 2(a). Therefore, Fig. 2(b) shows an alternative multi-level solution using three meta-levels. The top level defines just ProductType, which is instantiated at the next level to create Book and Food product types, which in turn are instantiated at the bottom level to create specific products. Hence, elements in this approach are called *clabjects* [2] (from the contraction of the words *cla*ss and *object*), as they are types for the elements in the level below, and instances of the elements in the level above (see for instance Book).

The multi-level solution leads to a simpler model (with fewer elements) as it requires just a clabject to represent both ProductType and Product. However, one needs to control the properties of instances beyond the next meta-level. In the example, we need to control that the direct instances of ProductType have a tax, and the instances of

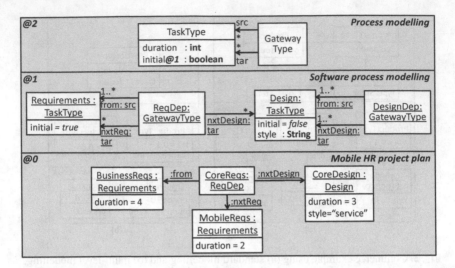

Fig. 3. Multi-level model for process modelling, and application to software process modelling.

its instances have a price. For this purpose, we use a *deep characterization* mechanism called potency [2, 4]. This is a natural number, or zero, which governs the instantiation depth of elements. Fig. 2(b) depicts the potency after the "@" symbol, and the elements that do not declare potency take the potency from their container (e.g., attribute price takes its potency from ProductType, and this from the Commerce model). When an element is instantiated, the instance gets the potency of the element minus 1. Elements with potency 0 are pure instances and cannot be instantiated. This way, attribute ProductType.tax is instantiated into Book.tax and Food.tax, which therefore have potency 0 and can receive values. As model Commerce has potency 2, it can be instantiated at the two subsequent meta-levels. The potency of a model is often called its *level* [6].

Sometimes, it is not possible to foresee every possible property required by clabject instances several meta-levels below, like the number of pages in books. To handle those cases, multi-level modelling supports *linguistic extensions*. These are clabjects or features with no ontological type, but with a linguistic type which corresponds to the meta-modelling primitive used to create it (see Orthogonal Classification Architecture in [5] for more details). As an example, Book.numPages is a linguistic extension modelling a property specific to Book but not to other product types. Instead, in the two-level solution in Fig. 2(a), the properties of specific ProductTypes need to be explicitly modelled by classes Attribute and Slot, leading to more complexity.

2.2   Improving reuse in multi-level modelling: some challenges

Multi-level modelling enables language reuse by supporting the definition of language families. For example, Fig. 3 shows at the top a generic process modelling language that can be used to define process modelling languages for different domains, like education, software engineering, or production engineering. The language is designed to consider three levels. Level 2 contains the language definition, consisting of primitives

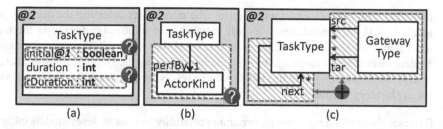

Fig. 4. Examples of variability needs: (a) optional attributes, (b) optional primitives, (c) alternative primitive realizations.

to define task and gateway types. Level 1 contains language specializations for specific domains. The figure shows the case for the software engineering domain, which defines the task types Requirements and Design, and two gateway types: ReqDep to transition from requirement tasks to either design or requirement tasks, and DesignDep to declare dependencies between design tasks. Finally, level 0 contains domain-specific processes. The one in the figure declares three tasks and one gateway.

This example shows how instantiation permits customizing the language primitives offered at the top level for particular domains, and how linguistic extensions (e.g., attribute Design.style at level 1 in Fig. 3) allow adding domain-specific primitives to language specializations. However, the following scenarios require further facilities that enable a better fit for particular domains and increase language reuse.

- **Alternative realizations**. A language primitive may be realised in different ways, each more adequate than the others depending on the domain. For example, in Fig. 3, dependencies between task types are modelled by GatewayType. However, in domains that do not require distinguishing gateway types, a simpler representation of dependencies as a reference between TaskTypes is enough (see Fig. 4(c)). Unfortunately, multi-level modelling does not support this kind of variability.
- **Primitive excess**. Some offered language primitives may be unnecessary in simple domains. This can be controlled by not instantiating the primitive, but still, withdrawing the needless primitives to simplify the language usage may be a better option. Moreover, there are problematic situations. First, if the primitive is an attribute (like initial in Fig. 4(a)), then it becomes instantiated by force, polluting the model with unnecessary information. Second, some mandatory primitives may not be needed in certain domains. For example, in Fig. 4(b), the language designer assumes that any TaskType (e.g., Requirements) will be performed by one ActorKind (e.g., Analyst or DomainExpert). However, there may be domains that do not involve actors (e.g., if tasks are automated), but the mandatory relation perfBy forces having instances of ActorKind associated to instances of TaskType.
- **Deferred variability resolution and exploratory modelling**. The decision about the inclusion or not of a primitive may not be clear when the language is instantiated for a domain, but this is determined later at lower meta-levels. For example, in Fig. 4(a), an engineer might hesitate whether, in addition to the expected task duration (attribute duration), s/he may want to store the real task duration (attribute

rDuration with potency 2), in which case, s/he may prefer deferring the decision to levels 1 or 0. In general, resolving all variability in a language family at the top level may be hasty in some cases, as the suitability of a primitive may become evident only when a language has reached certain specificity (i.e., at lower meta-levels). Moreover, enabling modelling before resolving the variability may be good for exploratory purposes.

To tackle these challenges, we incorporate variability into multi-level models taking ideas from SPLs. As a first step, next we formalize multi-level models.

3   A formal foundation for multi-level modelling

We start defining the structure of models equipped with deep characterization, which we call *deep* models. We represent models at different meta-levels in a uniform way, in order to cope with an arbitrary number of meta-levels. For simplicity of presentation, we omit inheritance, cardinalities and integrity constraints in our formalization.

Def. 1 (Deep model) *A deep model is a tuple* $M = \langle p, C, S, R, src, tar, pot \rangle$, *where:*

- $p \in \mathbb{N}_0$ *is called the model potency, or level.*
- C, S *and* R *are disjoint sets of clabjects, slots and references, respectively.*
- $src \colon S \cup R \to C$ *is a function assigning slots and references to clabjects.*
- $tar \colon R \to C$ *is a function assigning the target clabject to references.*
- $pot \colon C \cup S \cup R \to \mathbb{N}_0$ *is a function assigning a potency to each element, s.t.:*
  1. $\forall e \in C \cup S \cup R \bullet pot(e) \leq p$
  2. $\forall s \in S \cup R \bullet pot(s) \leq pot(src(s))$
  3. $\forall r \in R \bullet pot(r) \leq pot(tar(r))$

In the previous definition, we assign a level p to deep models. Elements in a deep model have a potency via function *pot*, which must satisfy three conditions: (1) the potency of an element should not be larger than the model level, (2) the potency of slots and references should not be larger than the one of their container clabject, and (3) the potency of references should not be larger than the one of the clabjects they point to.

Next, we define a general notion of mapping (a *morphism*) between deep models as a tuple of three (total) functions between the sets of clabjects, slots and references. Each morphism has a *depth* (an integer or 0) controlling the distance between the levels of the involved models. We use two particular types of mappings to represent the *type* relation between deep models at adjacent meta-levels (when the morphism depth is 1), and *extensions* of a deep model to add linguistic extensions (when the depth is 0).

Def. 2 (D-morphism, type and extension) *Given two deep models* $M_i = \langle p_i, C_i, S_i, R_i, src_i, tar_i, pot_i \rangle$ *for* $i = \{0, 1\}$, *a deep model morphism (D-morphism in short)* $m = \langle d, m_C, m_S, m_R \rangle \colon M_0 \to M_1$ *is a tuple made of a number* $d \in \mathbb{N}_0$ *called depth, and three functions* $m_C \colon C_0 \to C_1$, $m_S \colon S_0 \to S_1$ *and* $m_R \colon R_0 \to R_1$ *s.t.:*

1. $p_0 + d = p_1$
2. $\forall e \in X_0 \bullet pot_0(e) + d = pot_1(m_X(e))$ *(for* $X = \{C, S, R\}$)

$$S_1 \xrightarrow{src_1} C_1 \qquad\qquad C_1 \xleftarrow{src_1} R_1 \xrightarrow{tar_1} C_1$$

$$m_S^{\uparrow} \;=\; m_C^{\uparrow} \qquad\qquad m_C^{\uparrow} \;=\; m_R^{\uparrow} \;=\; m_C^{\uparrow}$$

$$S_0 \xrightarrow{src_0} C_0 \qquad\qquad C_0 \xleftarrow{src_0} R_0 \xrightarrow{tar_0} C_0$$

Fig. 5. Commutativity conditions for D-morphisms.

3. *Each function m_C, m_S, m_R commutes with functions src_i and tar_i (see Fig. 5)*

D-morphism $tp = \langle d, tp_C, tp_S, tp_R \rangle \colon M_0 \to M_1$ is called type *if $d = 1$, and is called* indirect type *if $d > 1$. M_1 is called the (indirect) model type of M_0.*
D-morphism $ex = \langle d, ex_C, ex_S, ex_R \rangle \colon M_0 \to M_1$ is called level-preserving *if $d = 0$. A level-preserving D-morphism ex is called* extension *if each ex_X (for $X = \{C, S, R\}$) is an inclusion. An extension is called* identity *if each ex_X is surjective.*

In the previous definition, condition 1 ensures that the D-morphism connects models of suitable levels, condition 2 checks that the potency decreases according to the depth of the D-morphism, and condition 3 ensures that the D-morphism is coherent with the source and target of slots and references (just like in standard graph morphisms [16]). We use total functions to represent the type, which ensures that each element in a deep model has a type. Linguistic extensions are not typed, but they are modelled as an extension D-morphism of a (typed) deep model into a larger model. This avoids resorting to partial functions to represent the type, which would complicate the formalization [38]. Identity extensions map isomorphic deep models. D-morphisms can be composed by composing the three mappings and adding their depths.

A multi-level model is made of a root deep model, and a sequence of instantiations and extensions. The length of this sequence is equal to the root model level. The extensions are allowed to be identity extensions.

Def. 3 (Multi-level model) *A multi-level model $MLM = \langle M_0', ML = \langle (M_i' \xleftarrow{tp_{i+1}}$ $M_{i+1}' \xrightarrow{ex_{i+1}} M_{i+1}') \rangle_{i=0..p_0'-1} \rangle$ is made of a deep model M_0' called the root and a sequence ML (of length p_0', the level of M_0') of spans of D-morphisms, where the left D-morphism is a* type *and the right D-morphism a (possibly identity)* extension.

Example. Fig. 6 shows a multi-level model (an excerpt of the one in Fig. 3) according to Def. 3. Slots are represented as rounded nodes, instead of inside the owner clabject box. In Fig. 3, we do not show slots with potency bigger than 0 that are typed, like Design.duration at level 1, which is omitted. However, such instances do exist, and are explicitly shown in Fig. 6 (see slot duration'@1 in models M_1 and M_1'). If a model does not include linguistic extensions (like M_2), then we use the identity extension D-morphism. Finally, it would be possible to derive the (indirect) type of M_2 w.r.t. M_0' by defining a construction akin to a pullback that yields the part of M_2 typed by M_1 [28].

4 Multi-level model product lines

In order to solve the challenges identified in Section 2.2, we extend deep models with closed variability options by borrowing concepts from product lines. We use feature models [24] to represent the allowed variability.

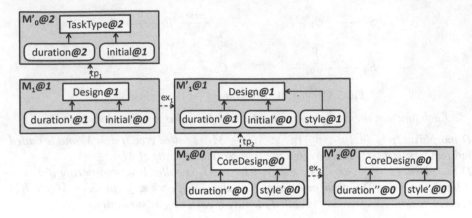

Fig. 6. Multi-level model example, according to Def. 3.

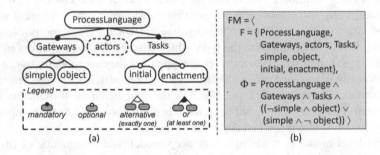

Fig. 7. Feature model for the example. (a) Feature diagram notation. (b) Using Def. 4.

Def. 4 (Feature model) *A feature model $FM = \langle F, \Phi \rangle$ is a tuple made of a set F of features and a propositional formula Φ specifying the valid feature configurations.*

Example. Fig. 7 shows the feature model for the running example using both the feature diagram notation (a), and our definition (b). The feature model permits choosing if the process modelling language will have primitives to define actors (feature actors, cf. Fig. 4(b)), initial tasks and their enactment at level 0 (features initial and enactment, cf. Fig. 4(a)), as well as selecting whether gateways are to be represented either as references or objects (features simple and object, cf. Fig. 4(c)). The feature model includes the mandatory features ProcessLanguage, Gateways and Tasks as syntactic sugar to obtain a tree representation, but they are not needed in our formalization.

The selection of one option within the variability space offered by a feature model is done through a configuration. This assigns *true* to the selected features, and *false* to the discarded ones. To enhance flexibility of use, we also support partial configurations, where some features are not given any value. This will be used to allow deferring the resolution of some variability options to lower meta-levels.

Def. 5 (Configuration) *Given a feature model* $FM = \langle F, \Phi \rangle$, *a* configuration *of* FM *is a tuple* $C = \langle F^+, F^- \rangle$ *made of two disjoint sets* $F^+ \subseteq F$ *and* $F^- \subseteq F$, *s.t.* $\Phi[F^+/true, F^-/false] \not\cong false$. *C is* total *if* $F = F^+ \cup F^-$, *otherwise it is* partial.

In the previous definition, F^+ contains the selected features (i.e., given the value *true*), F^- the discarded features (i.e., given the value *false*), and $F \setminus (F^+ \cup F^-)$ is the set of features whose value has not been set. A configuration must be compatible with the feature model formula, so the definition demands that the formula Φ once we substitute F^+ by *true* and F^- by *false* is not false. If the configuration is total, then the condition entails that Φ must evaluate to true.

Next, we assign a level to feature models, and potencies to features, in order to restrict the level at which features can be assigned a value.

Def. 6 (Deep feature model) *A* deep feature model $DFM = \langle l, FM = \langle F, \Phi \rangle, pot \rangle$ *is made of a level* $l \in \mathbb{N}_0$, *a feature model* FM, *and a function* $pot \colon F \to \mathbb{N}_0$ *assigning a potency to each feature, s.t.* $\forall f \in F \bullet pot(f) \leq l$.

Next, we define a mapping between deep feature models, called F-morphism. Similar to D-morphisms (cf. Def. 2), F-morphisms have a depth which can be positive or 0. In addition, they include a configuration, and a mapping for the features excluded from the configuration. There are two special kinds of F-morphisms: one representing a type relationship between feature models (where the morphism depth is 1 and the configuration empty), and the other expressing a specialization relationship between two feature models via a total or partial configuration (where the morphism depth is 0).

Def. 7 (F-morphism, type and specialization) *Given two deep feature models* $DFM_i = \langle l_i, FM_i, pot_i \rangle$ *(for* $i = \{0, 1\}$*), a* deep feature model morphism *(F-morphism in short)* $m = \langle d, m_F, C \rangle \colon DFM_0 \to DFM_1$ *is made of:*

- *a depth* $d \in \mathbb{N}_0$ *s.t.* $l_0 + d = l_1$
- *an injective set morphism* $m_F \colon F_0 \to F_1$ *s.t.* $\forall f \in F_0 \bullet pot_0(f) + d = pot_1(m_F(f))$
- *a configuration* $C = \langle F_1^+, F_1^- \rangle$ *of* FM_1 *s.t.:*
    1. $m_F(F_0) = F_1 \setminus (F_1^+ \cup F_1^-)$
    2. $\Phi_1[F_1^+/true, F_1^-/false] \cong \Phi_0[F_0/m_F(F_0)]$

F-morphism tp *is a* type *morphism if* $d = 1$ *and* $C = \langle \emptyset, \emptyset \rangle$, *and it is an* indirect type *morphism if* $d > 1$ *and* $C = \langle \emptyset, \emptyset \rangle$. *F-morphism* sp *is a* specialization *if* $d = 0$.

The definition requires that the F-morphism depth fills the gap between the feature model levels, and between the potencies of the mapped features. FM_0 may have fewer features than FM_1, in case the configuration C assigns a value to features of FM_1. In particular, the injectivity condition of m_F and requiring $m_F(F_0) = F_1 \setminus (F_1^+ \cup F_1^-)$ ensures that only the features left undefined by C are mapped from FM_0. Moreover, when the configuration C assigns a value to some feature, we require that the formula Φ_1, once we substitute the features in C by their value *true* or *false*, be equivalent to Φ_0, once we substitute the features in F_0 by their mapping in F_1. This corresponds to a (partial) evaluation of the formula Φ_1 as a result of a feature model specialization.

As a remark, F-morphisms so defined are composable by adding their depths and making the union of the positive (resp. negative) features in the configurations.

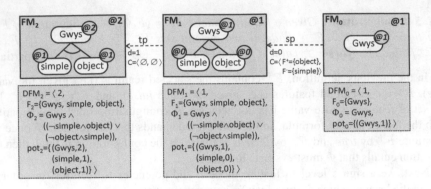

Fig. 8. Examples of F-morphisms.

Example. Fig. 8 shows two F-morphisms, with tp a type and sp a specialization. F-morphism $tp: FM_1 \to FM_2$ relates two deep feature models FM_1 and FM_2, where the level and potencies of FM_1 are one less than those in FM_2, and the formulae are the same modulo feature renaming. Specialization $sp: FM_0 \to FM_1$ has depth 0 and partial configuration $C = \langle F^+ = \{\text{object}\}, F^- = \{\text{simple}\}\rangle$. Hence, the levels and potencies are maintained, but the feature set F_0 is decreased by removing from F_1 the features that appear in C. According to condition 1 in Def. 7, $\{\text{Gwys}\} = \{\text{Gwys, simple, object}\} \setminus (\{\text{simple}\} \cup \{\text{object}\})$. According to condition 2 in the definition, the formula Φ_0 is equivalent to replacing object by *true* and simple by *false* in Φ_1. If we compose sp with tp, the resulting F-morphism $tp \circ sp$ has depth 1 and configuration $C = \langle F^+ = \{\text{object}\}, F^- = \{\text{simple}\}\rangle$, which is neither a type nor a specialization.

Finally, we are ready to characterize deep model product lines (PLs) as a deep model, a deep feature model with the same level as the deep model, and a mapping of presence conditions (PCs) to deep model elements.

Def. 8 (Deep model PL) *A deep model PL* $DM = \langle M, DFM, \phi \rangle$ *is made of:*

- *A deep model M and a deep feature model DFM with the same level ($p = l$).*
- *A function $\phi: C \cup S \cup R \to \mathbb{B}(F)$ mapping each element in M to a (non-false) propositional formula over the features in F, called presence condition (PC), s.t.:*
  1. *$\forall s \in S \cup R \bullet \phi(s) \implies \phi(src(s))$*
  2. *$\forall r \in R \bullet \phi(r) \implies \phi(tar(r))$*
  3. *$\forall e \in C \cup S \cup R, \forall v \in Var(\phi(e)) \bullet pot(v) \leq pot(e)$*

Intuitively, given a configuration, we can derive a *product* (a deep model) of the PL by deleting the model elements whose PC evaluates to false. To avoid dangling references and slots, Def. 8 requires their PC not to be weaker than that of their owning clabject (condition 1), and the PC of references not to be weaker than the one of their target clabject (condition 2). In addition, the variability of an element must be resolved in a level that contains the element. To this aim, condition 3 ensures that the potency of the variables in the PC of an element is not higher than the element's potency (we use function Var to return all variables within a propositional formula).

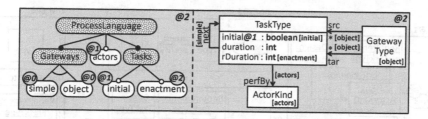

Fig. 9. Deep model PL example.

Example. Fig. 9 shows a deep model PL for process modelling languages. The left compartment shows the deep feature model, and the one to the right the deep model with its elements annotated with their PC between square brackets. If an element does not show a PC (like TaskType), then its PC is true. The deep model PL permits selecting between two alternative realizations for gateways, either as the reference next or the clabject GatewayType. This variability needs to be resolved before instantiating the language for a specific domain, as features simple and object have potency 0. The PL also offers the choice to add or not the primitive ActorKind to the language, but this decision can be taken before specializing the language or at level 1 to enable exploratory modelling. Finally, the PL allows selecting whether tasks can be initial and whether they hold enactment information. Feature initial in the feature model cannot have potency 2 because the feature is used in the PC of attribute TaskType.initial, which has potency 1. The feature model shows features ProcessLanguage, Gateways and Tasks in colour and without a potency; this is so as these features are mandatory (i.e., their value is *true* in any valid configuration), and while they enable a hierarchical representation of the feature model, the formalization of the example does not include them.

Next, we introduce mappings between deep model PLs (called PL-morphisms) as a tuple of morphisms between their constituent deep models and deep feature models. As in the previous cases, we are interested in type morphisms, linguistic extensions, and specializations of deep model PLs via a (partial) configuration.

Def. 9 (PL-morphism, type, extension, specialization) *Given two deep model PLs*
$DM_i = \langle M_i, DFM_i, \phi_i \rangle$ *(for $i = \{0, 1\}$), a PL-morphism $m = \langle m^D, m^F \rangle$ is made of a D-morphism $m^D \colon M_0 \to M_1$ and an F-morphism $m^F \colon DFM_0 \to DFM_1$ with configuration $C = \langle F^+, F^- \rangle$, s.t. $\forall e \in C_0 \cup S_0 \cup R_0 \bullet \phi_1(e)[F_1^+/true, F_1^-/false]$*
$\cong \phi_0(e)[F_0/m_F^F(F_0)]$.
PL-morphism $tp = \langle tp^D, tp^F \rangle$ is a type if both tp^D and tp^F are types.
PL-morphism $ex = \langle ex^D, id^F \rangle$ is an extension if ex^D is an extension and id^F is an identity.
PL-morphism $sp = \langle m^D, sp^F \rangle$ is a specialization if sp^F is a specialization and m^D is injective, level-preserving, and the elements $e \in C_1 \cup S_1 \cup R_1$ s.t. $\phi_1(e)[F_1^+/true, F_1^-/false] \not\cong false$ are in its co-domain.

Remark. No condition on the equality of depths of m^D and m^F is required, since the levels of M_0 and DFM_0 are the same (and similar for the levels of M_1 and DFM_1).

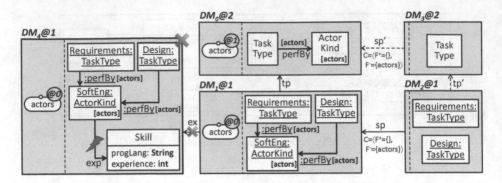

Fig. 10. Examples of PL-morphisms and deferred configuration.

The condition for PL-morphisms demands that the PCs in the deep model M_0 are modified according to the selection of features in configuration C of m^F. In addition, in specialization PL-morphisms, M_0 should contain just the elements whose PC is not false after substituting the features in F^+ by *true*, and the ones in F^- by *false*. Therefore, in case of a specialization, the definition requires that, when the configuration C is considered, exactly the elements in M_1 whose PC is not false receive a mapping from M_0, while the mapping needs to be injective. Moreover, by Def. 8 of deep model PL, no element in M_0 can have a PC that is false.

Other kinds of PL-morphisms are possible, for example, adding features to a feature model in lower meta-levels to increase its variability. While this is an interesting possibility to increase language reuse, we leave its formalization to future work.

Example. Fig. 10 shows four valid PL-morphisms (tp, tp', sp, sp') and an invalid one (ex). Both tp and tp' are types: they relate models at adjacent levels, where one is an instance of the other. Types always use the empty configuration $C = \langle \emptyset, \emptyset \rangle$ (cf. Def. 7), and therefore, a model element and its instances have the same PC (see, e.g., ActorKind and its instance SoftEng). Both sp and sp' are specialization PL-morphisms. This is so as they preserve level and potencies, and the deep models only contain elements with non-false PC. As the configuration C of both PL-morphisms is total, the PC of the elements in DM_3 and DM_2 evaluates to true, and hence, these models do not have more closed variability options to configure (i.e., they are final products of the PL). The figure also shows an attempt to extend DM_1 by a linguistic extension made of the clabject Skill connected to SoftEng through reference exp. However, the result is not a valid deep model PL as the PC of SoftEng (*actors*) is stronger than the PC of exp (true). This could be solved by adding *actors* as PC of exp (and Skill).

When the configuration C of a specialization PL-morphism sp is total, DM_0 is a *product* of DM_1 with no variability, being equivalent to a deep model (cf. Def. 1). However, the question remains whether for any valid configuration C of a deep model PL DM, we can find a deep model PL DM' and a specialization PL-morphism $sp: DM' \rightarrow DM$ that uses C. This requires showing that any choice of F^+ and F^- results in a valid deep model PL DM' as given by Def. 8. Theorem 1 captures this result.

Theorem 1 (Derivation through specialization morphisms). *Given a deep model PL*
$DM = \langle M, DFM, \phi \rangle$ *and any configuration C of DFM, there is one deep model PL*
DM' *and a specialization morphism $sp\colon DM' \to DM$ with configuration C.*

Proof. In appendix.

Next, we look into the soundness of deferring the configuration of an element after
it is instantiated. The question is whether, in any situation that allows configuring an
element after its instantiation, we obtain the same result by resolving the element variability first and then instantiating. This result is important as, regardless of the order
in which configurations and instantiation are performed, we can calculate the language
that results of applying the configurations as the first step, by advancing the configuration steps over the instantiations.

The next theorem captures the fact that if we can instantiate and then configure, then
we obtain the same result if we configure and then instantiate.

Theorem 2 (Specialization can be advanced to instantiation). *Given three deep model
PLs $DM_i = \langle M_i, DFM_i, \phi_i \rangle$ (for $i = \{0, 1, 2\}$), a type PL-morphism $tp\colon DM_1 \to
DM_0$ and a specialization PL-morphism $sp\colon DM_2 \to DM_1$, there is a unique deep
model PL DM_3, a unique type PL-morphism $tp'\colon DM_2 \to DM_3$ and a unique specialization PL-morphism $sp'\colon DM_3 \to DM_0$ s.t. the diagram in Fig. 11 commutes.*

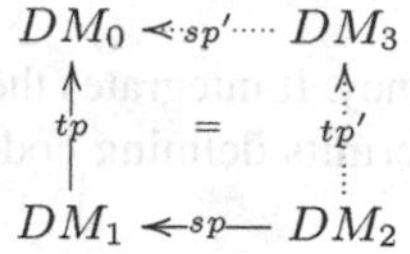

$$DM_0 \xleftarrow{\quad sp' \quad} DM_3$$
$$\uparrow tp \qquad = \qquad \uparrow tp'$$
$$DM_1 \xleftarrow{\quad sp \quad} DM_2$$

Fig. 11. Deferred configuration: specialization can be advanced to instantiation.

Proof. In appendix.

Remark. Note that the converse is not true in general, that is, instantiation cannot be
advanced to specialization. The reason is that a type morphism is not allowed from
features with potency 0, meaning that they must be configured first.

Example. Fig. 10 shows a deferred configuration. Deep model PL DM_0 is instantiated
into DM_1, and then configured using $C = \langle F^+ = \{\}, F^- = \{actors\} \rangle$ to yield DM_2.
Instead, we obtain the same result by first configuring DM_0 to yield DM_3, and then
instantiating DM_3 into DM_2. Deep model PL DM_3 is relevant as it corresponds to the
fully-configured language (i.e., with no variability) employed to build DM_2.

5 Tool support

We have implemented the notions presented so far atop METADEPTH [12]. This is a textual multi-level modelling tool which supports an arbitrary number of meta-levels and

```
1  @Variability(model="ProcessOptions")
2  Model ProcessModel@2 {
3    Node TaskType {
4      @Presence(condition="initial")
5      initial@1 : boolean = false;
6      duration : int;
7      @Presence(condition="enactment")
8      rDuration : int;
9      @Presence(condition="simple")
10     next : TaskType;
11     @Presence(condition="actors")
12     perfBy : ActorKind;
13   }
14
15   @Presence(condition="actors")
16   Node ActorKind;
17
18   @Presence(condition="object")
19   Node GatewayType {
20     src : TaskType[*];
21     tar : TaskType[*];
22   }
23 }
```

Listing 1. Deep model with PCs.

```
1  FeatureModel ProcessOptions@2 {
2    ProcessLanguage : Gateways Tasks actors?@1;
3    alt Gateways : simple@0 object@0;
4    Tasks : initial?@1 enactment?@2;
5  }
```

Listing 2. Deep feature model.

```
1  config ProcessModel with { !simple }
```

Listing 3. Feature configuration.

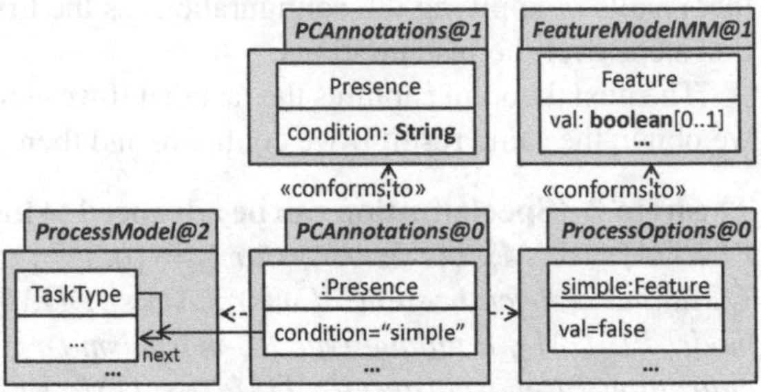

Fig. 12. Internal representation of deep model PL.

deep characterization through potency. It integrates the Epsilon family of languages for model management [33], which permits defining code generators and model transformations for multi-level models.

METADEPTH was used to define language families via multi-level modelling in [15], but it did not support the definition of closed sets of variability options by means of PLs. For this work, we have extended the tool to allow creating deep feature models and multi-level models with PCs, and specializing deep model PLs via configurations. The extended tool is available at http://metadepth.org/pls.

Listing 1 specifies the deep model in the right part of Fig. 9, using METADEPTH's syntax. First, line 1 states the name of the deep feature model (defined in Listing 2) associated to the deep model. Then, line 2 declares the deep model, named ProcessModel, with level 2. This contains three clabjects: TaskType (lines 3–13), ActorKind (lines 15–16) and GatewayType (lines 18–22). PCs are specified as annotations. This is possible as, similar to Java [10], METADEPTH permits defining annotation types by providing their syntax, parameters, and kind of elements they can annotate (i.e., models, clabjects or fields) [40]. This definition is a meta-model, and so, when annotations are parsed, they are transformed into an annotation model that refers to the annotated model. Regarding the PC of fields, for usability reasons, our implementation internally conjoins the PC of fields with the PC of their owner clabject. For example, the PC of reference GatewayType.src is *object* because the PC of GatewayType is *object*.

Listing 2 shows the METADEPTH definition of the deep feature model in Fig. 9. This conforms to a meta-model that we have created to represent deep feature models, and to which we have assigned a concrete syntax similar to the FAMILIAR tool [1]. Line 1 declares a feature model called ProcessOptions with level 2. Line 2 declares the root feature ProcessLanguage, and its children features Gateways, Tasks and actors. Children features can specify a potency after the "@" symbol, and be declared optional using the "?" symbol. Line 3 declares the children of Gateways, which are alternative as specified by the keyword alt. Line 4 declares the children of Tasks, which are optional.

Fig. 12 shows the internal representation of a deep model PL in METADEPTH. The PC annotations are automatically converted into an annotation model, which is also linked to the deep feature model (ProcessOptions).

Annotations in METADEPTH can attach actions to be triggered upon certain modelling events, like instantiation or value assignment. These actions are defined via a meta-object protocol (MOP) [26, 40]. This way, we have defined a MOP with actions for the PC annotations, to help instantiating deep model PLs. Specifically, when an element of a model with variability is instantiated (like ProcessModel in Listing 1), its PC is copied to the instance. Moreover, a constraint forbids instantiating a deep model PL if the associated deep feature model has features with potency 0.

Finally, we have created a command called config to specialize a deep model PL via a configuration (see Listing 3). When the command is applied, the PCs attached to model elements are evaluated (partially if the configuration is partial), and then removed if their value is *false*. The applied configuration (i.e., the boolean values assigned to the features) is stored in the deep feature model itself (cf. model ProcessOptions in Fig. 12). Overall, this simple example language already admits 16 total configurations, which can be succinctly represented as a PL, increasing its reuse possibilities.

6   Related work

Next, we review related research coming from language PLs; variability in multi-level modelling; and SPLs.

Language PLs. Some researchers have proposed increasing the reusability of modelling languages by incorporating SPL techniques. For example, in [47], DSL meta-models can be configured using a feature model. In [34], the authors propose featured model types: meta-models whose elements have PCs, and with operations that are offered depending of the chosen variant. In [20], meta-models can have variability, and their instantiability is analysed at the PL level. However, all these works only consider closed variability, while our work also supports open variability through instantiation.

Variability in multi-level modelling. A plethora of multi-level modelling approaches and tools have emerged recently, like DeepTelos [22], FMMLx [18], Melanee [3], MultEcore [29], MLT [17] and OMLM [21]. Some of them are based on deep characterization through potency [3, 18, 21, 29], while others rely on powertypes [17] or most-general instances [22]. None of them support variability based on feature models as we describe here. However, there have been some attempts to improve multi-level modelling with SPL techniques, which we describe next.

Reinhartz-Berger and collaborators [37] present a preliminary proposal to support the configuration of classes with optional attributes. It is based on a *kernel language* which supports multiple meta-levels but not deep characterization. The proposal is incipient as it is neither formalized nor implemented. In [9], the authors analyse the limitations of feature models alone to describe a set of assets, and propose using multi-level models instead. As multi-level models have limitations to express variability – as described in Section 2.2 – we propose to combine feature models and multi-level models.

Nesic and collaborators [31] explore the use of MLT [17] to reverse engineer sets of related legacy assets into PLs. MLT is a multi-level modelling approach based on powertypes and first order logic. In their work, the authors represent variability concepts like PCs and product groups within MLT models. This embedding may result in complex models where elements can represent either variability concepts or domain concepts. Instead, we separate PCs and feature models to avoid cluttering the multi-level model. Our goal is to define highly reusable language families, for which we provide feature models to describe variability options, and offer the possibility to defer configurations; instead, the approach in [31] lacks an explicit representation of feature models. Finally, we provide both a theory and a working implementation.

Other formalizations of potency-based multi-level modelling exist, like [38]. That theory does not account for variability, but it could be extended with feature models, in a similar way as we do.

SPLs. Our deferred configurations can be seen as a particular case of *staged configurations* [11]. These permit selecting a member of the PL in stages, where each stage removes some choices. In our approach, the *potency* controls the level where the variability can be resolved. Staged configurations are also useful in software design reuse. In this setting, Kienzle and collaborators [27] propose Concern-Oriented Reuse, a paradigm where reusable modules (called *concerns*) define variability interfaces as feature models. The variability of a reused concern can be resolved partially, in which case, the undefined features are re-exposed in the interface of the resulting concern. We also support deferring the variability resolution, but composing deep model PLs is future work.

Taentzer and collaborators [45] formalized model-based SPLs using category theory. Different from ours, their formalization does not capture typing (it is within a single meta-level), while their morphisms can expand the feature model but cannot be used to model partial configurations. Borba and collaborators [8] have studied PL refinements to add new products maintaining the behaviour of existing ones. In our case, we do not increase variability, but it would be interesting to consider mechanisms to do so combined with instantiation.

To cope with large variability spaces, partitioning techniques can be applied to feature models to yield so-called multi-level feature models [11, 36]. However, the term multi-level does not refer to multiple levels of classification (as in our case), but to multiple partitions of a feature model.

Other modelling notations support variability. For example, Clafer [23] is an approach that unifies feature and class modelling. It supports both class and (partial) object models, feature models, (partial) configurations and logic constraints. However, it does not support multi-level modelling or deep characterization. Similar to delta-oriented programming [42], Δ-modelling [41] permits defining a set of products as a core model plus a set of modification deltas to the core model according to given application conditions. The approach has been combined with MDE, showing that model configuration and refinement (e.g., a component being refined by a set of classes) commute. This is in line with our Theorem 2, but we are interested in instantiation (instead of refinement), and need to incorporate potency for deep characterization. Hence, in our case, instantiation and specialization (configuration) do not commute, but the latter can be advanced to former.

In the programming world, Batory [7,44] proposes mixin layers, a composition mechanism to add features to sets of base classes (so called two-level designs). Higher-level designs can be obtained by applying the same techniques. In [7], these higher-level designs are called multi-level models. Again, the use of the term multi-level is different from ours, which refers to models related by classification relations.

Overall, our proposal is the first one adding variability to multi-level models with support for deep characterization.

7 Conclusions and future work

In this paper, we have proposed a new notion of multi-level model PL to improve current reuse techniques for modelling languages. This is so as it permits both *open* variability (by successive instantiations leading to language refinements for specific domains), and *closed* variability (by selecting among a set of variants). We have presented a theory, with results ensuring the proper interleave of instantiation and configuration steps. The ideas have implemented on top of the multi-level modelling tool METADEPTH.

In the future, we plan to provide a categorical formalization of the theory which brings operations like intersection via common parts (pullbacks) and merging (pushouts) of deep model PLs. We also want to offer the possibility of extending a deep model PL with new features (i.e., extra variability) and move this variability to the top model whenever possible. We would like to develop analysis techniques for multi-level model PLs, e.g., to check instantiability properties in the line of [20]. Finally, our goal is to make multi-level model PLs ready for MDE. This would entail the ability to define MDE services like transformations and code generators on multi-level model PLs. Technically, our plan is to use the Epsilon languages supported by METADEPTH, and follow ideas from existing works on PLs of transformations [13], and transformation of PLs [39].

Acknowledgments. Work funded by the Spanish Ministry of Science (project MASSIVE, RTI2018-095255-B-I00) and the R&D programme of Madrid (project FORTE, P2018/TCS-4314). We thank the anonymous referees for their useful comments.

Appendix

Proof of Theorem 1: Given a deep model PL DM and a configuration $C = \langle F^+, F^- \rangle$, we build $DM' = \langle M', DFM', \phi' \rangle$ as follows:

- M' has the same level as M, and contains the elements e of M s.t. $\phi(e)[F^+/true, F^-/false] \not\cong false$. Functions src', tar' and pot' are restrictions of src, tar and pot to the elements in M'.

- $DFM' = \langle l, FM' = \langle F', \Phi' \rangle, pot' \rangle$, where $F' = F \backslash (F^+ \cup F^-)$, $\Phi' = \Phi[F^+/true,$ $F^-/false]$, and pot' is the restriction of pot to F'.
- $\forall e \in C' \cup S' \cup R' \bullet \phi'(e) = \phi(e)[F^+/true, F^-/false]$.

Now we show that M' is a valid deep model according to Def. 1:

- To check that src' is well formed, we show that $\forall s \in S' \cup R'$, $src(s')$ is defined. By condition 1 in Def. 8, $\phi(s) \implies \phi(src'(s))$. This precludes the source of any $s \in S' \cup R'$ to be absent from C', since if $\phi(src'(s))[F^+/true, F^-/false] = false$, then $\phi'(s)[F^+/true, F^-/false] = false$.
- The well-formedness of tar' is shown like in the previous case.
- Function pot' satisfies conditions 1–3 of Def. 1, since pot satisfies them, and pot' is just a restriction of pot.

Now we show that DM' is a valid deep model PL according to Def. 8:

- M' and DFM' have the same level (l).
- The three conditions over ϕ' and pot' hold, since they hold for ϕ and pot.

Finally, we build a specialization PL-morphism $sp = \langle m^M, sp^F \rangle \colon DM' \to DM$ as follows:

- $m^M = \langle 0, inc_C^M, inc_S^M, inc_R^M \rangle$, where $X' \xrightarrow{inc_X^M} X$ (for $X = \{C, S, R\}$) are inclusion set morphisms,
- $sp^M = \langle 0, inc^F, C \rangle$, where $F' \xrightarrow{inc^F} F$ is an inclusion morphism.

We need to show that: (i) $m_F(F') = F' = F \backslash (F^+ \cup F^-)$, which holds since F' was defined above as $F \backslash (F^+ \cup F^-)$; and (ii) $\Phi[F^+/true, F^-/false] \equiv \Phi'[F'/inc_F(F')]$, which holds since Φ' was defined above as $\Phi[F^+/true, F^-/false]$. $\square$

Proof of Theorem 2: Let $C = \langle F^+, F^- \rangle$ be the configuration of the specialization PL-morphism $sp \colon DM_2 \to DM_1$. From DM_0 and C, we construct a deep model DM_3 and a specialization PL-morphism $sp' \colon DM_3 \to DM_0$ as described in the proof of Theorem 1. Then, we build a type PL-morphism $tp' = \langle tp'^D, tp'^F \rangle \colon DM_2 \to DM_3$ as follows:

- $tp'^D = \langle 1, tp_C^D|_{C_2}, tp_S^D|_{S_2}, tp_R^D|_{R_2} \rangle$, with $tp_X^D|_{X_2}$ the restriction of tp_X^D to set X_2 in DM_2 (for $X = \{C, S, R\}$).
- $tp'^F = \langle 1, tp_F^F|_{F_2}, C \rangle$ with $tp_F^F|_{F_2}$ the restriction of tp_F^F to set F_2.

D-morphism tp'^D is well defined because $\forall c \in C_2$, $\exists c' \in C_3$ s.t. $tp_C^D(sp_C^D(c)) = sp_C'^D(c')$. This is so as $\phi_1(sp_C^D(e))[F^+/true, F^-/false] \not\equiv false$ due to Def. 9 of specialization PL-morphism. And now, since the configuration of tp is empty, we have $\phi_0(tp_C^D(sp_C^D(e))[F^+/true, F^-/false] \not\equiv false$. This means that, according to Def. 9, this element is in the co-domain of $sp_C'^D$, and is assigned to c by $tp_C'^D$. The same reasoning applies to sets S_2 and F_2. Function $tp_F^F|_{F_2}$ is also well formed, since the same configuration C was used to derive DM_2 and DM_3.

This reasoning also shows that $tp \circ sp = sp' \circ tp'$, as Theorem 2 demands. $\square$

References

1. M. Acher, P. Collet, P. Lahire, and R. B. France. FAMILIAR: A domain-specific language for large scale management of feature models. *Sci. Comput. Program.*, 78(6):657–681, 2013.
2. C. Atkinson. Meta-modeling for distributed object environments. In *EDOC*, pages 90–101. IEEE Computer Society, 1997.
3. C. Atkinson and R. Gerbig. Flexible deep modeling with melanee. In *Modellierung 2016, 2.-4. März 2016, Karlsruhe - Workshopband*, pages 117–122, 2016.
4. C. Atkinson and T. Kühne. The essence of multilevel metamodeling. In *UML*, volume 2185 of *LNCS*, pages 19–33. Springer, 2001.
5. C. Atkinson and T. Kühne. Rearchitecting the UML infrastructure. *ACM Trans. Model. Comput. Simul.*, 12(4):290–321, 2002.
6. C. Atkinson and T. Kühne. Reducing accidental complexity in domain models. *Software and Systems Modeling*, 7(3):345–359, 2008.
7. D. S. Batory. Multilevel models in model-driven engineering, product lines, and metaprogramming. *IBM Systems Journal*, 45(3):527–540, 2006.
8. P. Borba, L. Teixeira, and R. Gheyi. A theory of software product line refinement. *Theor. Comput. Sci.*, 455:2–30, 2012.
9. T. Clark, U. Frank, I. Reinhartz-Berger, and A. Sturm. A multi-level approach for supporting configurations: A new perspective on software product line engineering. In *ER Forum Demo Track*, volume 1979 of *CEUR Workshop Proceedings*, pages 156–164. CEUR-WS.org, 2017.
10. I. Córdoba-Sánchez and J. de Lara. Ann: A domain-specific language for the effective design and validation of java annotations. *Computer Languages, Systems & Structures*, 45:164–190, 2016.
11. K. Czarnecki, S. Helsen, and U. W. Eisenecker. Staged configuration through specialization and multilevel configuration of feature models. *Software Process: Improvement and Practice*, 10(2):143–169, 2005.
12. J. de Lara and E. Guerra. Deep meta-modelling with MetaDepth. In *TOOLS*, volume 6141 of *LNCS*, pages 1–20. Springer, 2010.
13. J. de Lara, E. Guerra, M. Chechik, and R. Salay. Model transformation product lines. In *MoDELS*, pages 67–77. ACM, 2018.
14. J. de Lara, E. Guerra, and J. Sánchez Cuadrado. When and how to use multilevel modelling. *ACM Trans. Softw. Eng. Methodol.*, 24(2):12:1–12:46, 2014.
15. J. de Lara, E. Guerra, and J. Sánchez Cuadrado. Model-driven engineering with domain-specific meta-modelling languages. *Software and Systems Modeling*, 14(1):429–459, 2015.
16. H. Ehrig, K. Ehrig, U. Prange, and G. Taentzer. *Fundamentals of Algebraic Graph Transformation*. Monographs in Theoretical Computer Science. An EATCS Series. Springer, 2006.
17. C. M. Fonseca, J. P. A. Almeida, G. Guizzardi, and V. A. de Carvalho. Multi-level conceptual modeling: From a formal theory to a well-founded language. In *ER*, volume 11157 of *LNCS*, pages 409–423. Springer, 2018.
18. U. Frank. Multilevel modeling - toward a new paradigm of conceptual modeling and information systems design. *Business & Information Systems Engineering*, 6(6):319–337, 2014.
19. C. González-Pérez and B. Henderson-Sellers. A powertype-based metamodelling framework. *Software and Systems Modeling*, 5(1):72–90, 2006.
20. E. Guerra, J. de Lara, M. Chechik, and R. Salay. Analysing meta-model product lines. In *SLE*, pages 160–173. ACM, 2018.
21. M. Igamberdiev, G. Grossmann, M. Selway, and M. Stumptner. An integrated multi-level modeling approach for industrial-scale data interoperability. *Software and Systems Modeling*, 17(1):269–294, 2018.

22. M. A. Jeusfeld and B. Neumayr. Deeptelos: Multi-level modeling with most general instances. In *ER*, volume 9974 of *LNCS*, pages 198–211, 2016.

23. P. Juodisius, A. Sarkar, R. R. Mukkamala, M. Antkiewicz, K. Czarnecki, and A. Wasowski. Clafer: Lightweight modeling of structure, behaviour, and variability. *Programming Journal*, 3(1):2, 2019.

24. K. Kang, S. Cohen, J. Hess, W. Novak, and A. Peterson. Feature-oriented domain analysis (foda) feasibility study. Technical Report CMU/SEI-90-TR-021, Software Engineering Institute, Carnegie Mellon University, Pittsburgh, PA, 1990.

25. S. Kelly and J. Tolvanen. *Domain-Specific Modeling - Enabling Full Code Generation*. Wiley, 2008.

26. G. Kiczales and J. D. Rivieres. *The Art of the Metaobject Protocol*. MIT Press, Cambridge, MA, USA, 1991.

27. J. Kienzle, G. Mussbacher, P. Collet, and O. Alam. Delaying decisions in variable concern hierarchies. In *GPCE*, pages 93–103. ACM, 2016.

28. S. M. Lane. *Categories for the Working Mathematician*. Springer, 1971.

29. F. Macías, A. Rutle, V. Stolz, R. Rodríguez-Echeverría, and U. Wolter. An approach to flexible multilevel modelling. *EMISA*, 13:10:1–10:35, 2018.

30. R. C. Martin, D. Riehle, and F. Buschmann. *Pattern Languages of Program Design 3*. Addison-Wesley, 1997.

31. D. Nesic, M. Nyberg, and B. Gallina. Modeling product-line legacy assets using multi-level theory. In *SPLC*, pages 89–96. ACM, 2017.

32. L. Northrop and P. Clements. *Software Product Lines: Practices and Patterns*. Addison-Wesley Longman Publishing Co., Inc., 2002.

33. R. F. Paige, D. S. Kolovos, L. M. Rose, N. Drivalos, and F. A. C. Polack. The design of a conceptual framework and technical infrastructure for model management language engineering. In *ICECCS*, pages 162–171. IEEE Computer Society, 2009.

34. G. Perrouin, M. Amrani, M. Acher, B. Combemale, A. Legay, and P. Schobbens. Featured model types: Towards systematic reuse in modelling language engineering. In *MiSE@ICSE*, pages 1–7. ACM, 2016.

35. K. Pohl, G. Böckle, and F. J. v. d. Linden. *Software Product Line Engineering: Foundations, Principles and Techniques*. Springer-Verlag, Berlin, Heidelberg, 2005.

36. D. Rabiser, H. Prähofer, P. Grünbacher, M. Petruzelka, K. Eder, F. Angerer, M. Kromoser, and A. Grimmer. Multi-purpose, multi-level feature modeling of large-scale industrial software systems. *Software and Systems Modeling*, 17(3):913–938, 2018.

37. I. Reinhartz-Berger, A. Sturm, and T. Clark. Exploring multi-level modeling relations using variability mechanisms. In *MULTI@MoDELS*, volume 1505 of *CEUR Workshop Proceedings*, pages 23–32. CEUR-WS.org, 2015.

38. A. Rossini, J. de Lara, E. Guerra, A. Rutle, and U. Wolter. A formalisation of deep metamodelling. *Formal Asp. Comput.*, 26(6):1115–1152, 2014.

39. R. Salay, M. Famelis, J. Rubin, A. D. Sandro, and M. Chechik. Lifting model transformations to product lines. In *ICSE*, pages 117–128. ACM, 2014.

40. J. Sánchez Cuadrado and J. de Lara. Open meta-modelling frameworks via meta-object protocols. *Journal of Systems and Software*, 145:1–24, 2018.

41. I. Schaefer. Variability modelling for model-driven development of software product lines. In *Variability Modelling of Software-Intensive Systems (VaMoS)*, pages 85–92, 2010.

42. I. Schaefer, L. Bettini, V. Bono, F. Damiani, and N. Tanzarella. Delta-oriented programming of software product lines. In *SPLC*, volume 6287 of *LNCS*, pages 77–91. Springer, 2010.

43. D. C. Schmidt. Guest editor's introduction: Model-driven engineering. *Computer*, 39(2):25–31, Feb. 2006.

44. Y. Smaragdakis and D. S. Batory. Mixin layers: an object-oriented implementation technique for refinements and collaboration-based designs. *ACM Trans. Softw. Eng. Methodol.*, 11(2):215–255, 2002.
45. G. Taentzer, R. Salay, D. Strüber, and M. Chechik. Transformations of software product lines: A generalizing framework based on category theory. In *MODELS*, pages 101–111. IEEE Computer Society, 2017.
46. UML 2.5.1 OMG specification. http://www.omg.org/spec/UML/2.5.1/, 2017.
47. J. White, J. H. Hill, J. Gray, S. Tambe, A. S. Gokhale, and D. C. Schmidt. Improving domain-specific language reuse with software product line techniques. *IEEE Software*, 26(4):47–53, 2009.

Computing Program Reliability using Forward-Backward Precondition Analysis and Model Counting

Aleksandar S. Dimovski[1] and Axel Legay[2]

[1] Mother Teresa University, 12 Udarna Brigada 2a, 1000 Skopje, N. Macedonia
aleksandar.dimovski@unt.edu.mk
[2] Université catholique de Louvain, 1348 Ottignies-Louvain-la-Neuve, Belgium
axel.legay@uclouvain.be

Abstract. The goal of probabilistic static analysis is to quantify the probability that a given program satisfies/violates a required property (assertion). In this work, we use a static analysis by abstract interpretation and model counting to construct probabilistic analysis of deterministic programs with uncertain input data, which can be used for estimating the probabilities of assertions (*program reliability*).

In particular, we automatically infer necessary preconditions in order a given assertion to be satisfied/violated at run-time using a combination of forward and backward static analyses. The focus is on numeric properties of variables and numeric abstract domains, such as polyhedra. The obtained preconditions in the form of linear constraints are then analyzed to quantify how likely is an input to satisfy them. Model counting techniques are employed to count the number of solutions that satisfy given linear constraints. These counts are then used to assess the probability that the target assertion is satisfied/violated. We also present how to extend our approach to analyze non-deterministic programs by inferring sufficient preconditions. We built a prototype implementation and evaluate it on several interesting examples.

1 Introduction

Program verification is often concerned by only determining whether one assertion always holds at a given program point. However, there are many applications where we need to know a more fine-grained information about how likely a target assertion (event) is to be satisfied/violated. Examples of other target events include the invocation of a certain method, the access to confidential information, etc. In those cases, we want to distinguish between what is possible event (even with extremely low probability) and what is likely event (possible with higher probability). In this work, we show how to calculate the reliability of programs by using combination of static analysis by abstract interpretation and model counting. In particular, we are interested to learn how the presence of uncertainty in the inputs can affect the probability of assertions at the exit of the program.

© The Author(s) 2020
H. Wehrheim and J. Cabot (Eds.): FASE 2020, LNCS 12076, pp. 182–202, 2020.
https://doi.org/10.1007/978-3-030-45234-6_9

This is an important problem to consider, since uncertainty is a common aspect of many real-world software systems today (e.g., medicine and aerospatial domains).

Abstract interpretation [6,7,8] is a general theory for approximating the semantics of programs. It provides safe (all answers are correct) and efficient (with a good trade-off between precision and cost) static analyses of run-time properties of real programs. It is based on the idea of *approximations* between concrete and abstract domains of program properties. Its practical success is mainly enabled by the design of numerical abstract domains, which reason on numerical properties of variables. For example, the interval domain [6], which is non-relational, infers the information about the possible values of individual variables; the octagon domain [25], which is weakly relational, infers unit binary linear constraints between program variables; and the polyhedra domain [10], which is fully relational, infers the linear constraints between all program variables. Abstract interpretation is a powerful technique for deriving approximate, albeit computable analyses, by using fully automatic algorithms. These abstract analyses pay the price for finite computability (always terminate) by an inevitable loss of precision. We use abstract analyses for automatic inference of (over-approximated) *invariants* by *forward analysis*, and (over-approximated) *necessary preconditions* by *backward analysis*. These two abstract analyses can be combined such that the results of the first analysis refine the results of the second one. In this work, we use a combination of forward and backward analyses to automatically generate the necessary preconditions on input variables that lead to the satisfaction/violation of a given assertion. If obtained preconditions are satisfied by some concrete values for input variables, then they represent input values that will allow the given assertion to be definitely satisfied/violated by all program executions branching from them. In fact, we run two backward analyses: the first one determines necessary preconditions for the given assertion to be satisfied, while the second one determines necessary preconditions for the given assertion to be violated.

Model counting is the problem of determining the number of solutions of a given constraint (formula). The LATTE tool [1] implements state-of-the-art algorithms for computing volumes, both real and integral, of convex polytopes as well as integrating functions over those polytopes. More specifically, we use the LATTE tool to estimate algorithmically the exact number of points of a bounded (possibly very large) discrete domain that satisfy given linear constraints.

In this paper, we describe a method which uses abstract interpretation-based static analysis and model counting to perform a specific type of quantitative analysis of deterministic programs, that is the calculation of *program reliability*. Calculating the program reliability involves counting the number of solutions to preconditions, which are given in the form of linear constraints between variables, i.e. elements from the polyhedra domain, that ensure satisfaction/violation of a given assertion by using model counting, and dividing it by the total space of values of the inputs. We assume that the input values are *uniformly distributed* within their finite discrete domain. Since the set of generated preconditions represents an over-approximation, we compute the reliability of programs as upper and lower bounds of exact probabilities that a given assertion is satisfied or violated. The reported uncertainty is due to the approximation inherent in abstract interpretation, which is introduced in order to obtain a scalable and fully automatic analysis.

The focus here is on programs whose input values range over finite discrete domains. Thus, we obtain a finite input domain and so we can use model counting algorithms to compute the required probabilities. We also restrict ourselves to the domain of linear integer arithmetic, since this is supported by LATTE and the polyhedra numeric domain we use.

We also consider an extension of our approach to non-deterministic programs. For non-deterministic programs, sufficient and necessary preconditions no more coincide [26]. Sufficient preconditions ensure that the target invariant holds for all sequences of non-deterministic choices made at each execution step, whereas necessary preconditions ensure that the target invariant holds for at least one sequence of non-deterministic choices made at each execution step. In effect, increasing the non-determinism will reduce the set of sufficient preconditions and enlarge the set of necessary preconditions. Hence, for non-deterministic programs we construct backward analyses for inferring (under-approximated) sufficient preconditions that lead to the satisfaction/violation of a given assertion. The calculation of reliability is then similar to the one for deterministic programs.

We have developed a prototype probabilistic static analyzer which uses the APRON library [21] to implement numeric property domains and the LATTE tool [1] to implement model counting algorithms. APRON provides a common high-level API to the most common numerical property domains, such as intervals, octagons, and polyhedra. We have implemented a combination of forward and backward analyses of deterministic (resp., non-deterministic) C programs for the automatic inference of *invariants* and *necessary* (resp. *sufficient*) *preconditions* in all program points. Our static analyzer has two components: (1) it computes the required preconditions in the input program point for a given assertion to be satisfied/violated, and (2) it then calls LATTE to count the number of solutions of those preconditions and calculates the program reliability.

The main contributions of this work are:

- We demonstrate how to calculate the program reliability of deterministic and non-deterministic programs using static analysis by abstract interpretation and model counting.
- We develop a probabilistic static analyzer, which uses numerical property domains from the APRON library and the LATTE model counting tool.
- Finally, we evaluate our method for probabilistic static analysis of C programs and show how to handle a set of small but compelling benchmarks.

2 Motivating Examples

Consider the program P_1 in Fig. 1. Suppose that the initial value of i ranges over the integer domain $[0, 19]$, and the initial value is independently and uniformly distributed across this range. When $(i \geq 10)$ the variable k is assigned to 12, otherwise k is assigned to 50. A forward invariant analysis will find the invariant

```
                                          void   main() {
                                          ①:       int j:=[0,9]; l_input :
  void   main() {                         ②:       int i:=0;
  ①:       int i:=[0,19]; l_input :       ③:       while (i < 100) {
  ②:       int k:=0;                      ④:            i:=i+1;
  ③:       if (i ≥ 10) k:=12; else k:=50; ⑤:            j:=j+1; }
  l_final : assert (k ≤ 30);              l_final : assert (j ≤ 105);
          }                                       }
```

Fig. 1: The program P_1 Fig. 2: The program P_2

$k = 12 \lor k = 50$ at point l_{final}. Therefore, the assertion ($k \le 30$) can be satisfied (when $k = 12$) and can be violated (when $k = 50$). We are interested in inferring necessary preconditions on the input state at control point l_{input}, when the assertion is satisfied and when the assertion is violated. We back-propagate necessary conditions of satisfaction and violation of the assertion from point l_{final} to l_{input}. A backward necessary condition analysis will infer the precondition $i \ge 10$ at point l_{input} assuming that the assertion is satisfied, and the precondition $i < 10$ at point l_{input} assuming that the assertion is violated. The size of the input domain is 20, since $i \in [0, 19]$. By calling LATTE to count the number of solutions to the above preconditions, we can calculate that the probability for the assertion to be satisfied (*success probability*) is: $\frac{10}{20} = 50\%$, and the probability for the assertion to be violated (*failure probability*) is: $\frac{10}{20} = 50\%$.

Consider the program P_2 in Fig. 2. A forward invariant analysis will find the invariant $100 \le j \le 109$ at point l_{final}, so the corresponding assertion can be satisfied (when $100 \le j \le 105$) and can be violated (when $105 < j \le 109$). A backward necessary condition analysis will infer the precondition $0 \le j \le 5$ at point l_{input} for the assertion to be satisfied, and the precondition $5 < j \le 9$ at point l_{input} for the assertion to be violated. Therefore, we can calculate that the *success probability* is: $\frac{6}{10} = 60\%$, and the *failure probability* is: $\frac{4}{10} = 40\%$.

3   Forward-Backward Precondition Analyses

We describe the combination of forward and backward analyses in the framework of abstract interpretation for inferring necessary preconditions that a given assertion is satisfied/violated. The principle of the combination is to use the result of the forward invariant analysis in the subsequent backward necessary condition analysis in order to get more precise results which are still sound.

Syntax. We consider a simple deterministic programming language that is a subset of C, which will be used to exemplify our work. The control point (location) before each statement and at the end of each block is associated to a unique label $l \in \mathbb{L}$. The syntax of the language is given by:

$$s ::= \mathtt{skip} \mid \mathtt{x:=}e \mid \mathtt{x:=}[n, n'] \mid s; s \mid \mathtt{if}\ (e)\ \mathtt{then}\ s\ \mathtt{else}\ s \mid \mathtt{while}\ (e)\ \mathtt{do}\ s \mid \mathtt{assert}(e)$$

$$e ::= n \mid \mathtt{x} \mid e \oplus e$$

where n ranges over integers, $[n, n']$ ranges over integer intervals, x ranges over variable names *Var*, and $\oplus$ over arithmetic-logic operators. Non-deterministic interval assignment $\mathtt{x} := [n, n']$ represents an input statement which assigns to the input variable x a uniformly distributed random value from the interval $[n, n']$. This interval assignment can occur only in the *input section* of the program, and is used to model input uncertainties. The set of all generated statements s is denoted by *Stm*, whereas the set of all expressions e is denoted by *Exp*. We assume $l_{\mathtt{input}}$ is the location after the input statements (i.e. it denotes the end of the input section) and $l_{\mathtt{final}}$ is the location at the end of the program, where an assertion $\mathtt{assert}(e_{\mathtt{f}})$ is posed. Without loss of generality, a program is a sequence of statements followed by a single assertion.

Concrete semantics. A *program state* is given by a control location in $\mathbb{L}$ and an environment in $\mathcal{E} : Var \to \mathbb{Z}$ mapping each variable to its value (integer number). We write $\Sigma = \mathbb{L} \times \mathcal{E}$ to denote the set of all possible program states. Programs are modelled as transition systems $(\Sigma, \longrightarrow)$, where Σ is a set of states and $\longrightarrow \subseteq \Sigma \times \Sigma$ is a transition relation modelling atomic execution steps. The relation $\longrightarrow$ is defined by local rules, such as the following:

assignment $l_0 : \mathtt{x} := e; l_1 ::\ (l_0, \rho) \longrightarrow (l_1, \rho[\mathtt{x} \mapsto \llbracket e \rrbracket(\rho)])$, where $\llbracket e \rrbracket(\rho) \in \mathbb{Z}$ is the result of the evaluation of e in the environment ρ, and $\rho[\mathtt{x} \mapsto n]$ denotes the environment that updates ρ at variable x with the value n.

input $l_0 : \mathtt{x} := [n, n']; l_1 ::\ (l_0, \rho) \longrightarrow (l_1, \rho[\mathtt{x} \mapsto n''])$, where $n'' \in [n, n']$.

conditional $l_0 :$ if (e) then $\{l_0^t : s; l_1^t\}$ else $\{l_0^f : s'; l_1^f\}; l_1 ::\ (l_0, \rho) \longrightarrow (l_0^t, \rho)$ if $\llbracket e \rrbracket(\rho) \neq 0$ [3], $(l_0, \rho) \longrightarrow (l_0^f, \rho)$ if $\llbracket e \rrbracket(\rho) = 0$, $(l_1^t, \rho) \longrightarrow (l_1, \rho)$, and $(l_1^f, \rho) \longrightarrow (l_1, \rho)$.

loop $l_0 :$ while (e) do $\{l_0^t : s; l_1^t\}; l_1 ::\ (l_0, \rho) \longrightarrow (l_0^t, \rho)$ if $\llbracket e \rrbracket(\rho) \neq 0$, $(l_0, \rho) \longrightarrow (l_1, \rho)$ if $\llbracket e \rrbracket(\rho) = 0$, and $(l_1^t, \rho) \longrightarrow (l_0, \rho)$. [4]

Let $\mathbb{E} \subseteq \mathcal{E}$ be the set of input environments obtained after executing the input statements. The set of input states is $\mathcal{I} = \{(l_{\mathtt{input}}, \rho) \mid \rho \in \mathbb{E}\}$. The invariant inference (reachability) problem consists of finding out the possible environments (values of all variables) that may arise at each control location. The concrete semantic domain is the complete lattice of the powerset of states $(\mathcal{P}(\Sigma), \subseteq, \cup, \cap, \emptyset, \Sigma)$, and the concrete semantics in the form of invariant states encountered branching from $\mathcal{I}$, denoted $\mathtt{inv}(\mathcal{I})$, is:

$$\mathtt{inv}(\mathcal{I}) = \mathtt{lfp}_{\mathcal{I}} \lambda X. X \cup \mathtt{post}(X)$$

where $\mathtt{post}(X) = \{\sigma \in \Sigma \mid \exists \sigma' \in X. \sigma' \longrightarrow \sigma\}$ and $\mathtt{lfp}_{\mathcal{I}} f$ is the least fixed point of the function f greater than $\mathcal{I}$.

In this work, we consider the problem of inferring necessary preconditions. Assume that a program exits with $l_{\mathtt{final}} : \mathtt{assert}(e_{\mathtt{f}})$. We want to distinguish

---

[3] Following the convention popularized by C, we model Boolean values as integers, with zero interpreted as false and everything else as true.

[4] Note that control moves from the final label l_1^t of s to the initial label l_0 of while.

between program termination that leads to the satisfaction of the final assertion at $l_{\texttt{final}}$ from the one that leads to the violation of the final assertion at $l_{\texttt{final}}$. Let $\mathcal{F}_{sat} = \{(l, \rho) \in \texttt{inv}(\mathcal{I}) \mid l = l_{\texttt{final}} \implies [\![e_{\texttt{f}}]\!](\rho) \neq 0\}$ and $\mathcal{F}_{viol} = \{(l, \rho) \in \texttt{inv}(\mathcal{I}) \mid l = l_{\texttt{final}} \implies [\![e_{\texttt{f}}]\!](\rho) = 0\}$ be the invariant sets which enforce the assertion at the point $l_{\texttt{final}}$ to be satisfied and violated, respectively, and coincide with $\texttt{inv}(\mathcal{I})$ everywhere else. In the following, $\mathcal{F}$ may represent either $\mathcal{F}_{sat}$ or $\mathcal{F}_{viol}$. Given an invariant set $\mathcal{F}$ to obey, we want to infer the set of input states $\texttt{cond}(\mathcal{F})$ that guarantee that all program executions stay in $\mathcal{F}$:

$$\texttt{cond}(\mathcal{F}) = \texttt{gfp}_{\mathcal{F}} \lambda X. X \cap \texttt{pre}(X)$$

where $\texttt{pre}(X) = \{\sigma \in \Sigma \mid \exists \sigma' \in X. \sigma \longrightarrow \sigma'\}$ is the set of predecessors of X, and $\texttt{gfp}_{\mathcal{F}} f$ is the greatest fixed point of the function f smaller than $\mathcal{F}$. The above two fixed points ($\texttt{lfp}$ and $\texttt{gfp}$) exist according to Tarski, as the corresponding functions are monotone and continuous in the complete lattice of state sets.

Given a set of input environments $\mathbb{E} \subseteq \mathcal{E}$, we can compute the subsets $\mathbb{E}_{sat}$ and $\mathbb{E}_{viol}$ of input environments that lead to satisfaction and violation of the final assertion as:

$$\mathbb{E}_{sat} = \mathbb{E} \cap \{\rho \mid (l_{\texttt{input}}, \rho) \in \texttt{cond}(\mathcal{F}_{sat})\}, \mathbb{E}_{viol} = \mathbb{E} \cap \{\rho \mid (l_{\texttt{input}}, \rho) \in \texttt{cond}(\mathcal{F}_{viol})\}$$

Abstract semantics. Transition systems can become large or infinite for real programs, so that neither $\texttt{inv}(\mathcal{I})$ nor $\texttt{cond}(\mathcal{F})$ can be computed at all. Therefore, we seek for sound approximations. The actual computable abstract analyses can be defined as over-approximations of the concrete semantics. A static analyzer will infer over-approximated necessary preconditions so that all program executions that lead to satisfaction (resp., violation) of the final assertion are taken into account, thus computing an over-approximation of $\mathbb{E}_{sat}$ (resp., $\mathbb{E}_{viol}$).

We consider an abstract domain $(\mathbb{D}, \sqsubseteq_{\mathbb{D}})$, such that there exist a Galois connection [5] $\langle \mathcal{P}(\mathcal{E}), \subseteq \rangle \xrightarrow[\alpha_{\mathbb{D}}]{\gamma_{\mathbb{D}}} \langle \mathbb{D}, \sqsubseteq_{\mathbb{D}} \rangle$. We assume that the abstract domain $\mathbb{D}$ is equipped with sound operators for ordering $\sqsubseteq_{\mathbb{D}}$, least upper bound (join) $\sqcup_{\mathbb{D}}$, greatest lower bound (meet) $\sqcap_{\mathbb{D}}$, bottom $\bot_{\mathbb{D}}$, top $\top_{\mathbb{D}}$, widening $\triangledown_{\mathbb{D}}$, and narrowing $\triangle_{\mathbb{D}}$, as well as sound transfer functions for assignments $\overrightarrow{\texttt{assign}_{\mathbb{D}}}$: $Var \times Exp \times \mathbb{D} \to \mathbb{D}$, tests $\texttt{filter}_{\mathbb{D}} : Exp \times \mathbb{D} \to \mathbb{D}$, and backward assignments $\overleftarrow{\texttt{b-assign}_{\mathbb{D}}} : Var \times Exp \times \mathbb{D} \times \mathbb{D} \to \mathbb{D}$. We let $\texttt{lfp}^{\#}$ (resp., $\texttt{gfp}^{\#}$) denote an abstract post-fixpoint (resp., pre-fixpoint) operator, derived using widening $\triangledown_{\mathbb{D}}$ and narrowing $\triangle_{\mathbb{D}}$, that over-approximates the concrete $\texttt{lfp}$ (resp., $\texttt{gfp}$) [8]. Finally, the concrete domain on which concrete semantics is defined $(\mathcal{P}(\Sigma), \subseteq)$ is abstracted using a Galois connection $\langle \mathcal{P}(\Sigma), \subseteq \rangle \xrightarrow[\alpha]{\gamma} \langle \mathbb{L} \to \mathbb{D}, \dot{\sqsubseteq} \rangle$ where $\alpha(R) = \lambda l \in \mathbb{L}. \sqcup_{\mathbb{D}} \{d \in \mathbb{D} \mid (l, \rho) \in R, \alpha_{\mathbb{D}}(\rho) = d\}$. Hence, each control point $l \in \mathbb{L}$ is associated with an element $d \in \mathbb{D}$ in the abstract semantics.

---

[5] $\langle L, \leq_L \rangle \xrightarrow[\alpha]{\gamma} \langle M, \leq_M \rangle$ is a *Galois connection* between complete lattices L and M iff α and γ are total functions that satisfy: $\alpha(l) \leq_M m \iff l \leq_L \gamma(m)$ for all $l \in L, m \in M$. Here $\leq_L$ and $\leq_M$ are the pre-order relations for L and M, respectively.

We define a family of forward transfer functions $\overrightarrow{\delta}_{l,l'} : \mathbb{D} \to \mathbb{D}$ that compute the effect of any concrete transition at the abstract level. The definition of $\overrightarrow{\delta}_{l,l'}$ for some statements is:

assignment $l_0 : \mathbf{x} := e; l_1 :: \overrightarrow{\delta}_{l_0,l_1}(d) = \overrightarrow{\mathtt{assign}}_{\mathbb{D}}(\mathbf{x}, e, d)$.

conditional l_0 : if (e) then $\{l_0^t : s; l_1^t\}$ else $\{l_0^f : s'; l_1^f\}; l_1 :: \overrightarrow{\delta}_{l_0,l_0^t}(d) = \overrightarrow{\mathtt{filter}}_{\mathbb{D}}(e, d), \overrightarrow{\delta}_{l_0,l_0^f}(d) = \overrightarrow{\mathtt{filter}}_{\mathbb{D}}(\neg e, d), \overrightarrow{\delta}_{l_1^t,l_1}(d) = d, \overrightarrow{\delta}_{l_1^f,l_1}(d) = d$.

loop l_0 : while (e) do $\{l_0^t : s; l_1^t\}; l_1 :: \overrightarrow{\delta}_{l_0,l_0^t}(d) = \overrightarrow{\mathtt{filter}}_{\mathbb{D}}(e, d), \overrightarrow{\delta}_{l_0,l_1}(d) = \overrightarrow{\mathtt{filter}}_{\mathbb{D}}(\neg e, d)$, and $\overrightarrow{\delta}_{l_1^t,l_0}(d) = d$.

The soundness of $\{\overrightarrow{\delta}_{l,l'} \mid l, l' \in \mathbb{L}\}$ is written as: $\forall d \in \mathbb{D}, \forall \rho \in \gamma_{\mathbb{D}}(d), (l, \rho) \longrightarrow (l', \rho') \implies \rho' \in \gamma_{\mathbb{D}}(\overrightarrow{\delta}_{l,l'}(d))$.

Suppose that the abstract element $\alpha_{\mathbb{D}}(\mathbb{E}) = d_{\mathtt{input}} \in \mathbb{D}$ is at the input control point $l_{\mathtt{input}}$. We can collect the abstractions of possible environments at each program control point using the following forward interpreter:

$$\overrightarrow{F}^{\#} = \lambda I. \lambda(l \in \mathbb{L}). \sqcup_{\mathbb{D}} \{\overrightarrow{\delta}_{l',l}(I(l')) \mid l' \in \mathbb{L}\}$$

such that the result of the forward analyzer is $\overrightarrow{\mathcal{I}}^{\#} = \mathtt{lfp}_{I_0}^{\#} \overrightarrow{F}^{\#}$, where $I_0(l_{\mathtt{input}}) = d_{\mathtt{input}}$. Assume that $\mathtt{lfp}_{I_0}^{\#} \overrightarrow{F}^{\#}(l_{\mathtt{final}}) = d_{\mathtt{final}}$. Let $d_{\mathtt{final}}^{sat} = \overrightarrow{\mathtt{filter}}_{\mathbb{D}}(e, d_{\mathtt{final}})$ and $d_{\mathtt{final}}^{viol} = \overrightarrow{\mathtt{filter}}_{\mathbb{D}}(\neg e, d_{\mathtt{final}})$. We want to design two backward abstract interpreters that propagate backwards the invariants ensuring that the final assertion is satisfied $d_{\mathtt{final}}^{sat}$ and violated $d_{\mathtt{final}}^{viol}$, respectively. The backward interpreters refine the invariants found by $\overrightarrow{F}^{\#}$. Thus, they take two elements of $\mathbb{D}$ as inputs: an invariant to refine and an invariant to propagate backwards. They are based on a family of backward transfer functions $\overleftarrow{\delta}_{l,l'} : \mathbb{D} \times \mathbb{D} \to \mathbb{D}$, which map a precondition to refine and a postcondition into a refined precondition. The definition of $\overleftarrow{\delta}_{l,l'}$ for some statements is:

assignment $l_0 : \mathbf{x} := e; l_1 :: \overleftarrow{\delta}_{l_0,l_1}(d, d') = \overleftarrow{\mathtt{b\text{-}assign}}_{\mathbb{D}}(\mathbf{x}, e, d, d')$.

conditional l_0 : if (e) then $\{l_0^t : s; l_1^t\}$ else $\{l_0^f : s'; l_1^f\}; l_1 :: \overleftarrow{\delta}_{l_0,l_0^t}(d, d') = d \sqcap d', \overleftarrow{\delta}_{l_0,l_0^f}(d, d') = d \sqcap d', \overleftarrow{\delta}_{l_1^t,l_1}(d, d') = d \sqcap d', \overleftarrow{\delta}_{l_1^f,l_1}(d, d') = d \sqcap d'$.

loop l_0 : while (e) do $\{l_0^t : s; l_1^t\}; l_1 :: \overleftarrow{\delta}_{l_0,l_0^t}(d, d') = d \sqcap d', \overleftarrow{\delta}_{l_0,l_1}(d, d') = d \sqcap d'$, and $\overleftarrow{\delta}_{l_1^t,l_0}(d, d') = d \sqcap d'$.

The soundness of $\{\overleftarrow{\delta}_{l,l'} \mid l, l' \in \mathbb{L}\}$ is written as: $\forall d, d' \in \mathbb{D}, \forall \rho \in \gamma_{\mathbb{D}}(d), \rho' \in \gamma_{\mathbb{D}}(d'), (l, \rho) \longrightarrow (l', \rho') \implies \rho \in \gamma_{\mathbb{D}}(\overleftarrow{\delta}_{l,l'}(d, d'))$. That is, d is refined into a stronger precondition by taking into account the postcondition d'.

Suppose that $F_{\mathbb{D}}^{sat}(l_{\mathtt{final}}) = d_{\mathtt{final}}^{sat}$, $F_{\mathbb{D}}^{viol}(l_{\mathtt{final}}) = d_{\mathtt{final}}^{viol}$, and $F_{\mathbb{D}}^{sat}(l) = F_{\mathbb{D}}^{viol}(l) = \overrightarrow{\mathcal{I}}^{\#}(l)$ for $l \neq l_{\mathtt{final}}$. The backward interpreters are defined as:

$$\overleftarrow{F}^{\#} = \lambda(I, F). \lambda(l \in \mathbb{L}). \sqcap_{\mathbb{D}} \{\overleftarrow{\delta}_{l,l'}(I(l), F(l')) \mid l' \in \mathbb{L}\}$$

such that the results of the two backward analyzers are: $\overleftarrow{C}^{\#}_{sat} = \mathtt{gfp}^{\#}_{(\overrightarrow{\mathcal{I}}^{\#}, F^{sat}_{\mathbb{D}})} \overleftarrow{F}^{\#}$ and $\overleftarrow{C}^{\#}_{viol} = \mathtt{gfp}^{\#}_{(\overrightarrow{\mathcal{I}}^{\#}, F^{viol}_{\mathbb{D}})} \overleftarrow{F}^{\#}$. The necessary preconditions that the final assertion is satisfied and violated are $d^{sat}_{\mathtt{input}} = \overleftarrow{C}^{\#}_{sat}(l_{\mathtt{input}})$ and $d^{viol}_{\mathtt{input}} = \overleftarrow{C}^{\#}_{viol}(l_{\mathtt{input}})$, respectively. We can now compute the over-approximated sets $\mathbb{E}^{\#}_{sat}$ and $\mathbb{E}^{\#}_{viol}$ of input environments $\mathbb{E}_{sat}$ and $\mathbb{E}_{viol}$ that lead to satisfaction and violation of the final assertion as:

$$\mathbb{E}^{\#}_{sat} = \mathbb{E} \cap \gamma_{\mathbb{D}}(d^{sat}_{\mathtt{input}}), \quad \mathbb{E}^{\#}_{viol} = \mathbb{E} \cap \gamma_{\mathbb{D}}(d^{viol}_{\mathtt{input}})$$

such that $\mathbb{E}^{\#}_{sat} \supseteq \mathbb{E}_{sat}$ and $\mathbb{E}^{\#}_{viol} \supseteq \mathbb{E}_{viol}$.

Polyhedra numeric abstract domain. Although, the abstract domain $\mathbb{D}$ can be instantiated with different property domains, in the following, we will use the polyhedra numerical abstract domain for $\mathbb{D}$. This is due to the fact that only for the polyhedra domain all necessary abstract operations and transfer functions, such as $\overrightarrow{\mathtt{assign}_{\mathbb{D}}}$, $\overleftarrow{\mathtt{b\text{-}assign}_{\mathbb{D}}}$, $\overleftarrow{\mathtt{b\text{-}assign\text{-}under}_{\mathbb{D}}}$ (see Section 5), are implemented in the APRON library. The *Polyhedra domain* [10], denoted as $\langle P, \sqsubseteq_P \rangle$, is a fully relational numerical property domain, which allows manipulating conjunctions of linear inequalities of the form $\alpha_1 x_1 + \ldots + \alpha_n x_n \geq \beta$, where $x_1, \ldots, x_n$ are program variables and $\alpha_i, \beta \in \mathbb{R}$ (reals). The abstract operations of the *Polyhedra domain* are defined in [10]. Polyhedra analysis is expensive but also very precise.

A property element is represented as a conjunction of linear constraints given in the matrix form $\langle \mathbf{A}, \mathbf{b} \rangle$ that consists of a matrix $\mathbf{A} \in \mathbb{R}^{m \times n}$ and a vector $\mathbf{b} \in \mathbb{R}^m$, where n is the number of variables and m is the number of constraints. This is called the constraint representation of polyhedra elements, and there is another so-called generator representation. One representation can be converted to the other one using the Chernikova's algorithm [5]. Some domain operations can be performed more efficiently using the generator representation only, others based on the constraint representation, and some making use of both. We now present some operations that can be defined using the constraint representation.

The concretization function is: $\gamma_P(\langle \mathbf{A}, \mathbf{b} \rangle) = \{\mathbf{v} \in \mathbb{R}^n \mid \mathbf{A} \cdot \mathbf{v} \geq \mathbf{b}\}$. The meet $\sqcap_P$ is defined as: $\langle \mathbf{A_1}, \mathbf{b_1} \rangle \sqcap_P \langle \mathbf{A_2}, \mathbf{b_2} \rangle = \langle \binom{\mathbf{A_1}}{\mathbf{A_2}}, \binom{\mathbf{b_1}}{\mathbf{b_2}} \rangle$. We also need widening since the polyhedra domain has infinite strictly increasing chains.

$$\langle \mathbf{A_1}, \mathbf{b_1} \rangle \nabla_P \langle \mathbf{A_2}, \mathbf{b_2} \rangle = \{c \in \langle \mathbf{A_1}, \mathbf{b_1} \rangle \mid \langle \mathbf{A_2}, \mathbf{b_2} \rangle \sqsubseteq_P \{c\}\}$$

where c represents one constraint from $\langle \mathbf{A_1}, \mathbf{b_1} \rangle$. The transfer function $\overrightarrow{\mathtt{filter}_P}$ abstracts affine inequality expressions by adding them to the input polyhedra.

$$\overrightarrow{\mathtt{filter}_P}(\sum_i \alpha_i x_i \geq \beta, \langle \mathbf{A}, \mathbf{b} \rangle) = \langle \begin{pmatrix} \mathbf{A} \\ \alpha_1 \ldots \alpha_n \end{pmatrix}, \begin{pmatrix} \mathbf{b} \\ \beta \end{pmatrix} \rangle$$

Example 1. Consider the program P_1 from Fig. 1. Assume that $\mathbb{D}$ is the polyhedra domain. The input abstract element is $d_{\mathtt{input}} = (0 \leq i \leq 19)$. Using the forward analyzer $\overrightarrow{F}^{\#}$, we obtain $d_{\mathtt{final}} = (k = 12 \vee k = 50)$, and so $d^{sat}_{\mathtt{final}} = (k = 12)$ and $d^{viol}_{\mathtt{final}} = (k = 50)$. Using backward analyzers $\overleftarrow{F}^{\#}$, we obtain $d^{sat}_{\mathtt{input}} = (i \geq 10)$ and $d^{viol}_{\mathtt{input}} = (i < 10)$. $\qquad\square$

4   Computing Success and Failure Probabilities

The overall goal of our approach is to answer questions about the probability of assertions at the exit of a deterministic program P. We define the *success probability* as the probability that a program terminates successfully with the target assertion being satisfied. The *failure probability* is the probability that a program hits a failure caused by the target assertion being violated.

The combination of forward and two backward analyses infers the necessary preconditions, denoted $d_{\text{input}}^{sat} = \overleftarrow{C}_{sat}^{\#}(l_{\text{input}})$ and $d_{\text{input}}^{viol} = \overleftarrow{C}_{viol}^{\#}(l_{\text{input}})$, that the target assertion is satisfied and violated, respectively. Calculating the likelihood of satisfying/violating the given assertion involves counting the number of solutions to $d_{\text{input}}^{sat}/d_{\text{input}}^{viol}$ and dividing it by the total space of possible values in its input domain $\mathbb{E}$. In particular, we use model counting techniques and LATTE tool [1] to estimate algorithmically the exact number of points of a bounded (possibly very large) discrete domain $\mathbb{E}$ that satisfy the (linear) constraints d_{input}^{sat} and d_{input}^{viol}. We restrict our attention on programs that have *finite input domains* $\mathbb{E}$ and on numeric abstract elements from the polyhedra domain expressed as *linear integer arithmetic* (LIA) constraints over program variables whose values are *uniformly distributed* over their input domain.

We use the LATTE tool to compute the number of elements of $\mathbb{E}$ that satisfy d_{input}^{sat} and d_{input}^{viol}, denoted $\#(d_{\text{input}}^{sat})$ and $\#(d_{\text{input}}^{viol})$. The size of $\mathbb{E}$, denoted $\#(\mathbb{E})$, is the product of domain's sizes of all input variables in program P. Thus, we have: $\#(\mathbb{E}) = \prod_{\mathbf{x}:=[n,n'] \in P} |n'-n+1|$. Note that the exact sets of input states that lead to satisfaction and violation of the given assertion are $\mathbb{E}_{sat}$ and $\mathbb{E}_{viol}$, and their sizes are denoted $\#(\mathbb{E}_{sat})$ and $\#(\mathbb{E}_{viol})$. Since the found necessary preconditions d_{input}^{sat} and d_{input}^{viol} are over-approximations of $\mathbb{E}_{sat}$ and $\mathbb{E}_{viol}$ respectively, we have $\#(\mathbb{E}_{sat}) \leq \#(d_{\text{input}}^{sat})$ and $\#(\mathbb{E}_{viol}) \leq \#(d_{\text{input}}^{viol})$. Moreover, the input environments which are not in $\gamma_{\mathbb{D}}(d_{\text{input}}^{sat})$, that is they are in $\mathbb{E} \backslash \gamma_{\mathbb{D}}(d_{\text{input}}^{sat})$, definitely lead to the violation of the assertion. Therefore, we have $\#(\mathbb{E}) - \#(d_{\text{input}}^{sat}) \leq \#(\mathbb{E}_{viol}) \leq \#(d_{\text{input}}^{viol})$. By similar reasoning as above, we can also establish that: $\#(\mathbb{E}) - \#(d_{\text{input}}^{viol}) \leq \#(\mathbb{E}_{sat}) \leq \#(d_{\text{input}}^{sat})$. Finally, we calculate the *success* and *failure probability* of a program P as follows:

$$
\begin{aligned}
\frac{\#(\mathbb{E})-\#(d_{\text{input}}^{viol})}{\#(\mathbb{E})} \leq \mathbf{Pr^s(P)} = \frac{\#(\mathbb{E}_{sat})}{\#(\mathbb{E})} \leq \frac{\#(d_{\text{input}}^{sat})}{\#(\mathbb{E})} \\
\frac{\#(\mathbb{E})-\#(d_{\text{input}}^{sat})}{\#(\mathbb{E})} \leq \mathbf{Pr^f(P)} = \frac{\#(\mathbb{E}_{viol})}{\#(\mathbb{E})} \leq \frac{\#(d_{\text{input}}^{viol})}{\#(\mathbb{E})}
\end{aligned}
\tag{1}
$$

Note that $Pr^s(P) + Pr^f(P) = 1$.

Example 2. Consider the program P_1 from Fig. 1. We have $\mathbb{E} = \{[\mathbf{i} \mapsto n] \mid n \in [0, 19]\}$, and so $\#(\mathbb{E}) = 20$. Using forward and two backward analyses, we obtain $d_{\text{input}}^{sat} = (\mathbf{i} \geq 10)$ and $d_{\text{input}}^{viol} = (\mathbf{i} < 10)$, and so $\#(d_{\text{input}}^{sat}) = 10$ and $\#(d_{\text{input}}^{viol}) = 10$. Thus, the success and failure probabilities are:

$$
Pr^s(P_1) = \frac{10}{20} \, (50\%), \quad \text{and} \quad Pr^f(P_1) = \frac{10}{20} \, (50\%) \qquad \square
$$

We use model counting and the LATTE tool [1] to determine the number of solutions of a given constraint. LATTE accepts LIA constraints expressed as a system of linear inequalities each of which defines a hyperplane encoded as the matrix inequality: $Ax \leq B$, where A is an $m \times n$ matrix of coefficients and B is an $m \times 1$ column vector of constants. Most LIA constraints can easily be converted into the form: $a_1 x_1 + \ldots + a_n x_n \leq b$. For example, $\geq$ and $>$ can be flipped by multiplying both sides by -1, and strict inequalities $<$ can be converted by decrementing the constant b. In LATTE, equalities $=$ can be expressed directly. If we have disequalities $\neq$, they can be handled by counting a set of constraints that encode all possible solutions. For example, the constraint $\alpha \wedge (x_1 \neq x_2)$ is handled by finding the sum of solutions for $\alpha \wedge (x_1 \leq x_2 - 1)$ and $\alpha \wedge (x_1 \geq x_2 + 1)$. For a system $Ax \leq B$, where A is an $m \times n$ matrix and B is an $m \times 1$ column vector, the input LATTE file is:

$$\begin{matrix} m & n+1 \\ B & -A \end{matrix}$$

where the first line indicates the matrix size: the number of inequalities m by the number of variables n plus one. The following lines encode all inequalities.

5 Extension to non-deterministic programs

Let us reconsider the program P_2 from Fig. 2, where the assignment in point ⑤ is now replaced with: j:=j+[0,1]. That is, the variable j is incremented by a uniformly distributed random integer between 0 and 1 at each iteration. We denote this non-deterministic program as P_3 (taken from [26]), given below:

```
void  main() {
 ① :      int j:=[0,9]; l_input :
 ② :      int i:=0;
 ③ :      while (i < 100) {
 ④ :          i:=i+1;
 ⑤ :          j:=j+[0,1]; }
 l_final : assert (j ≤ 105); }
```

A forward invariant analysis will find that at l_{final} holds: $0 \leq j \leq 109$, and so the assertion ($j \leq 105$) can be both satisfied and violated. A backward necessary condition analysis for assertion satisfaction will infer the precondition $0 \leq j \leq 9$ at l_{input}, since for any value $j \in [0, 9]$ there exists an program execution satisfying the assertion (e.g., consider the executions where the random integer from $[0, 1]$ always evaluates to 0 in the body of while). However, a *backward sufficient condition analysis* for assertion satisfaction computes the set of input states such that all program executions branching from them satisfy the assertion. In this case, the sufficient condition analysis will infer the precondition $0 \leq j \leq 5$ at l_{input}, since even if the random integer from $[0, 1]$ always evaluates to 1 in the body of while, the assertion will always hold. As a result of this, we can conclude that the success probability is greater or equal to: $\frac{6}{10} = 60\%$.

We can see that necessary and sufficient preconditions are different in the presence of non-determinism [26]. Note that, if the non-determinism is increased in a program, then the set of sufficient preconditions will be reduced, while the set of necessary preconditions will be enlarged. For non-deterministic programs, $\mathbb{E}_{sat}$ and $\mathbb{E}_{viol}$ are subsets of input environments $\mathbb{E}$ that definitely lead to satisfaction and violation of the final assertion for all possible non-deterministic choices, respectively. We define the *success probability* $Pr^s(P)$ as the probability that a program terminates successfully with the target assertion being satisfied for all possible non-deterministic choices taken at each step. The *failure probability* $Pr^f(P)$ is the probability that a program hits a failure caused by the target assertion being violated for all possible non-deterministic choices taken at each step. We now show how to compute the success and failure probabilities for non-deterministic programs using sufficient conditions.

Remark. Note that in case of deterministic programs, $\mathbb{E}_{sat}$ and $\mathbb{E}_{viol}$ form a partition of the set of input environments $\mathbb{E}$ ($\mathbb{E}_{sat} \cup \mathbb{E}_{viol} = \mathbb{E}$), thus we have $Pr^s(P) + Pr^f(P) = 1$ for any deterministic program P. However, for non-deterministic programs this is not true anymore. That is, $\mathbb{E}_{sat} \cup \mathbb{E}_{viol} \subseteq \mathbb{E}$ and $Pr^s(P) + Pr^f(P) \leq 1$ for any non-deterministic program P. This means that there exist input environments for which it is possible the target assertion to be both satisfied and violated depending on non-deterministic choices made at each step of the given execution. For example, in the above program P_3, for input environments that satisfy $6 \leq \mathtt{j} \leq 9$, the target assertion is satisfied (when $[0,1]$ in the body of `while` always evaluates to 0) and violated (when $[0,1]$ in the body of `while` always evaluates to 1), so those input environments are neither in $\mathbb{E}_{sat}$ nor in $\mathbb{E}_{viol}$. We have, $\mathbb{E}_{sat} = \{\rho \mid 0 \leq [\![\mathtt{j}]\!]\rho \leq 5\}$ and $\mathbb{E}_{viol} = \emptyset$, thus $Pr^s(P_3) = 60\%$ and $Pr^f(P_3) = 0\%$.

Syntax. The extended non-deterministic programming language includes the same expression and statement productions as previously (see Section 3), but we add a support for non-deterministic expressions by using integer intervals $[n, n']$:

$$e ::= \ldots \mid [n, n']$$

The integer interval $[n, n']$ denotes a uniformly distributed random integer from the interval $[n, n']$ (non-deterministic choice of an integer). Note that the interval assignment $\mathtt{x}\!:=\![n, n']$ can now be freely used everywhere in programs, not only in the input section as in deterministic programs.

Concrete semantics. We now consider the problem of backward sufficient condition inference. Given an invariant set $\mathcal{F}$ to obey, we want to infer the set of input states $\mathrm{cond}(\mathcal{F})$ that guarantee that all program executions branching from them for all possible non-deterministic choices taken at each step stay in $\mathcal{F}$:

$$\mathrm{cond}(\mathcal{F}) = \mathrm{gfp}_{\mathcal{F}} \lambda X. X \cap \widetilde{\mathrm{pre}}(X)$$

where $\widetilde{\mathrm{pre}}(X) = \{\sigma \in \Sigma \mid \forall \sigma' \in \Sigma . \sigma \longrightarrow \sigma' \implies \sigma' \in X\}$ is the set of states which represent predecessors only of states in X. Note that the function $\widetilde{\mathrm{pre}}(X)$

differs from the function $\text{pre}(X)$ used in Section 3, that is $\widetilde{\text{pre}}(X) \neq \text{pre}(X)$, if the transition system is non-deterministic (i.e. some states have several successors or none). Using $\widetilde{\text{pre}}(X)$ ensures that the invariant set $\mathcal{F}$ holds for all sequences of non-deterministic choices made at each execution step, while $\text{pre}(X)$ ensures that the invariant set $\mathcal{F}$ holds for at least one sequence of non-deterministic choices. Note that $\widetilde{\text{pre}}(X) = \text{pre}(X)$ for deterministic programs, since $|\text{post}(\{\sigma\})| = 1$ for every state $\sigma \in \Sigma$ in this case.

Abstract semantics. In order to compute an *under-approximating set of sufficient preconditions*, we require an abstract domain $\mathbb{D}$ with the following backward abstract operators: meet $\sqcap_{\mathbb{D}}^{\text{under}}$, backward assignment $\overleftarrow{\text{b-assign-under}}_{\mathbb{D}} : \text{Var} \times \text{Exp} \times \mathbb{D} \times \mathbb{D} \to \mathbb{D}$, backward tests $\overleftarrow{\text{b-filter-under}}_{\mathbb{D}} : \text{Exp} \times \mathbb{D} \times \mathbb{D} \to \mathbb{D}$, and a lower widening $\underline{\triangledown}_{\mathbb{D}}$ [26]. The above abstract operators represent a sound under-approximation of the corresponding concrete operators. We let $\text{gfp}^{\#\text{under}}$ denote an abstract pre-fixpoint operator, derived using lower widening $\underline{\triangledown}_{\mathbb{D}}$, that under-approximates the concrete gfp.

We design two backward sufficient condition abstract interpreters that propagate backwards the invariants ensuring that the final assertion is satisfied d_{final}^{sat} and violated d_{final}^{viol}, respectively. They are based on a family of backward transfer functions $\overleftarrow{\delta}_{l,l'}^{\text{under}} : \mathbb{D} \times \mathbb{D} \to \mathbb{D}$, which for some statements are defined as:

- assignment $l_0 : \text{x:=}e; l_1 :$ $\overleftarrow{\delta}_{l_0,l_1}^{\text{under}}(d, d') = \overleftarrow{\text{b-assign-under}}_{\mathbb{D}}(\text{x}, e, d, d')$
- if statement $l_0 : \text{if } (e) \text{ then } \{l_0^t : s; l_1^t\} \text{ else } \{l_0^f : s'; l_1^f\}; l_1 :$ $\overleftarrow{\delta}_{l_0,l_0^t}(d, d') =$ $\overleftarrow{\text{b-filter-under}}_{\mathbb{D}}(e, d, d'), \overleftarrow{\delta}_{l_0,l_0^f}(d, d') = \overleftarrow{\text{b-filter-under}}_{\mathbb{D}}(\neg e, d, d')$, and $\overleftarrow{\delta}_{l_1^t,l_1}(d, d') = d \sqcap d', \overleftarrow{\delta}_{l_1^f,l_1}(d, d') = d \sqcap d'$
- $l_0 : \text{while } (e) \text{ do } \{l_0^t : s; l_1^t\}; l_1 :$ $\overleftarrow{\delta}_{l_0,l_0^t}(d, d') = \overleftarrow{\text{b-filter-under}}_{\mathbb{D}}(e, d, d'),$ $\overleftarrow{\delta}_{l_0,l_1}(d, d') = \overleftarrow{\text{b-filter-under}}_{\mathbb{D}}(\neg e, d, d')$, and $\overleftarrow{\delta}_{l_1^t,l_0}(d, d') = d \sqcap d'$.

The soundness of $\{\overleftarrow{\delta}_{l,l'}^{\text{under}} \mid l, l' \in \mathbb{L}\}$ is written as: $\forall d, d' \in \mathbb{D}, \forall \rho \in \gamma_{\mathbb{D}}(d), \rho' \in \gamma_{\mathbb{D}}(d'), \rho \in \gamma_{\mathbb{D}}(\overleftarrow{\delta}_{l,l'}(d, d')) \implies (l, \rho) \longrightarrow (l', \rho')$.

The backward sufficient condition interpreters are defined as:

$$\overleftarrow{F}^{\#\text{under}} = \lambda(I, F).\lambda(l \in \mathbb{L}). \sqcap_{\mathbb{D}}^{\text{under}} \{\overleftarrow{\delta}_{l,l'}^{\text{under}}(I(l), F(l')) \mid l' \in \mathbb{L}\}$$

such that results of backward analyzers are: $\overleftarrow{C}_{sat}^{\#\text{under}} = \text{gfp}_{(\vec{\mathcal{I}}^\#, F_{\mathbb{D}}^{sat})}^{\#\text{under}} \overleftarrow{F}^{\#\text{under}}$ and $\overleftarrow{C}_{viol}^{\#\text{under}} = \text{gfp}_{(\vec{\mathcal{I}}^\#, F_{\mathbb{D}}^{viol})}^{\#\text{under}} \overleftarrow{F}^{\#\text{under}}$. The sufficient preconditions that the final assertion is satisfied and violated are $d_{\text{input}}^{sat,\text{under}} = \overleftarrow{C}_{sat}^{\#\text{under}}(l_{\text{input}})$ and $d_{\text{input}}^{viol,\text{under}} = \overleftarrow{C}_{viol}^{\#\text{under}}(l_{\text{input}})$, respectively. We can now compute the under-approximated sets $\mathbb{E}_{sat}^{\#\text{under}}$ and $\mathbb{E}_{viol}^{\#\text{under}}$ of input environments $\mathbb{E}_{sat}$ and $\mathbb{E}_{viol}$ that definitely lead to satisfaction and violation of the final assertion as:

$$\mathbb{E}_{sat}^{\#\text{under}} = \mathbb{E} \cap \gamma_{\mathbb{D}}(d_{\text{input}}^{sat,\text{under}}), \quad \mathbb{E}_{viol}^{\#\text{under}} = \mathbb{E} \cap \gamma_{\mathbb{D}}(d_{\text{input}}^{viol,\text{under}})$$

such that $\mathbb{E}_{sat}^{\#\text{under}} \subseteq \mathbb{E}_{sat}$ and $\mathbb{E}_{viol}^{\#\text{under}} \subseteq \mathbb{E}_{viol}$.

Computing success and failure probabilities. As before, we instantiate $\mathbb{D}$ with the polyhedra numeric abstract domain, since all under-approximating sound backward operators for it have been implemented in the APRON library [26]. The sufficient preconditions $d_{\text{input}}^{sat,\text{under}}$ and $d_{\text{input}}^{viol,\text{under}}$ are under-approximations of $\mathbb{E}_{sat}$ and $\mathbb{E}_{viol}$ respectively, so $\#(d_{\text{input}}^{sat,\text{under}}) \leq \#(\mathbb{E}_{sat})$ and $\#(d_{\text{input}}^{viol,\text{under}}) \leq \#(\mathbb{E}_{viol})$. Moreover, the input environments which are not in $\gamma_{\mathbb{D}}(d_{\text{input}}^{sat,\text{under}})$, that is they are in $\mathbb{E}\backslash\gamma_{\mathbb{D}}(d_{\text{input}}^{sat,\text{under}})$, may lead to the violation of the assertion. Therefore, we have $\#(d_{\text{input}}^{viol,\text{under}}) \leq \#(\mathbb{E}_{viol}) \leq \#(\mathbb{E}) - \#(d_{\text{input}}^{sat,\text{under}})$. By similar reasoning, we can also establish that: $\#(d_{\text{input}}^{sat,\text{under}}) \leq \#(\mathbb{E}_{sat}) \leq \#(\mathbb{E}) - \#(d_{\text{input}}^{viol,\text{under}})$. We calculate the *success* and *failure probability* of a program P as follows:

$$
\begin{aligned}
\frac{\#(d_{\text{input}}^{sat,\text{under}})}{\#(\mathbb{E})} &\leq \mathbf{Pr^s(P)} = \frac{\#(\mathbb{E}_{sat})}{\#(\mathbb{E})} \leq \frac{\#(\mathbb{E}) - \#(d_{\text{input}}^{viol,\text{under}})}{\#(\mathbb{E})} \\
\frac{\#(d_{\text{input}}^{viol,\text{under}})}{\#(\mathbb{E})} &\leq \mathbf{Pr^f(P)} = \frac{\#(\mathbb{E}_{viol})}{\#(\mathbb{E})} \leq \frac{\#(\mathbb{E}) - \#(d_{\text{input}}^{sat,\text{under}})}{\#(\mathbb{E})}
\end{aligned}
\tag{2}
$$

Example 3. Consider the program P_3 from the beginning of this section. Using two backward sufficient condition analyses, we obtain $d_{\text{input}}^{sat,\text{under}} = (0 \leq \text{j} \leq 5)$ and $d_{\text{input}}^{viol,\text{under}} = (\bot_{\mathbb{D}})$, and so $\#(d_{\text{input}}^{sat,\text{under}}) = 6$ and $\#(d_{\text{input}}^{viol,\text{under}}) = 0$. Thus, the success and failure probabilities are:

$$
(60\%)\frac{6}{10} \leq Pr^s(P_3) \leq 1\,(100\%) \quad \text{and} \quad (0\%)\,0 \leq Pr^f(P_1) \leq \frac{4}{10}(40\%) \qquad \square
$$

6   Implementation

We now describe the implementation and evaluation of the ideas presented so far. The evaluation aims to show the following objectives:

O1: The probabilistic analysis can be used to analyze the behaviour of various interesting programs;

O2: The probabilistic analysis gives exact results (with no precision loss) in many cases, especially for deterministic programs;

O3: The performance time of probabilistic analysis is largely insensitive to domain sizes of input variables;

O4: We can find practical application scenarios of using our probabilistic analysis to efficiently analyze C programs.

Implementation. We have implemented a prototype probabilistic static analyzer that accepts programs written in a subset of C. It does not support **struct** and **union** types, and provides only a limited support of arrays and pointers. The only basic data types considered are integers. As output, the tool reports the upper and lower bounds of probabilities that the target assertion is satisfied or violated. The prototype tool is written in OCAML. As the abstract analysis domain $\mathbb{D}$ for encoding program properties, we use the polyhedra numeric abstract domain [10]. All abstract operators and sound transfer functions for the polyhedra domain are provided by the APRON library [21,26]. The tool performs one forward reachability analysis and two backward necessary/sufficient condition analyses (one for satisfaction and one for violation of the assertion). The tool calls a model counter, LATTE [1], to determine the number of solutions to discovered preconditions for satisfaction or violation of the assertion. Note that if an input state satisfies the discovered precondition for satisfaction (resp., violation) of the assertion, then all program executions branching from that state will satisfy (resp., violate) the given assertion. The analysis proceeds by structural induction on the program syntax, iterating while-s until a fixed point is reached. They compute the unique solution which to every program point assigns an element from the abstract domain $\mathbb{D}$.

Experimental setup and benchmarks. All experiments are executed on a 64-bit Intel®Core^{TM} i5 CPU, Lubuntu VM, with 8 GB memory. The reported times represent the average runtime of five independent executions. We report TIME_{an} to perform all static analyses tasks (one forward plus two backward static analyses), TIME_{pr} to compute the needed probability bounds (call to LATTE plus additional calculations), and TIME to complete the overall probabilistic analysis task. The implementation, benchmarks, and all results obtained are available from: https://aleksdimovski.github.io/probab-analysis.html (or, https://github.com/aleksdimovski/probab_analyzer).

For our experiment, we use a dozen of C programs taken from several folders (categories) of the 8th International Competition on Software Verification (SV-COMP 2019) [6], as well as from the abstract interpretation community [26,30]. The folders from SV-COMP 2019 we consider are: loops, loop-lit, termination-crafted (which is denoted ter-crafted for short), as well as termination-restricted-15 (which is denoted ter-restricted for short). We have selected some numeric programs with integers that our tool can handle. We have manually added input sections, and in some of the programs we have also defined target assertions. Then, we have analyzed those programs using our prototype static analyzer. Table 1 summarizes relevant characteristics for each benchmark: the folder (source) where it is taken from, the number of lines of code (LOC), and the number of integer variables (#var). There are two classes of benchmarks in Table 1 separated by a double horizontal line. The first (upper) class of benchmarks consists of deterministic programs for which backward necessary condition analysis is performed, while the second (lower) class of benchmarks are non-deterministic programs for which backward sufficient condition analysis is performed.

Performances Table 1 shows the performance of our technique on a set of small and compelling examples (addresses Objective (**O1**)). We can note that for most of our deterministic benchmarks, the technique gives exact results without any approximation (which are marked with ✓ in the EXACT column of Table 1). This means that the lower and upper bounds for success and failure probabilities

---

[6] https://sv-comp.sosy-lab.org/2019/

coincide. This is due to the fact that we use the expressive and very precise polyhedra abstract domain (addresses Objective (**O2**)). For the remaining cases, the technique gives approximate results (which are marked with $\approx$ in the EXACT column of Table 1), since the abstraction was too coarse to calculate exact results. We can also see that the time for static analysis TIME_{an} dominates in the overall probabilistic analysis time TIME, whereas the probability computation time TIME_{pr} is a smaller fraction of the total time. The small probability computation times indicate that preconditions obtained from our analyses are relatively simple, and so LATTE can handle them very efficiently. We have also experimented with different domain sizes n of input variables (for $n = 10$ and $n = 1000$). Thus, n denotes the number of possible values per input variable. We observe that we obtain similar time performance results for $n = 10$ and $n = 1000$, which means that the performance is not affected by the fact that inputs come from a bigger pool of possible values. This is mostly due to the fact that LATTE and APRON are largely insensitive to those values in terms of time (addresses Objective (**O3**)). In general, the obtained probability bounds provide non-trivial information about the behaviour of these programs and are quite hard to estimate by hand even if the programs in question are small.

Application scenarios. Consider the following program (called `Waldkirch.c` from `termination-crafted` folder of SV-COMP 2019):

$$① : \text{int } \mathtt{x} := [-5, 4]; \; l_{\text{input}} :$$
$$② : \text{while} \,(\mathtt{x} \geq 0) \, \{$$
$$③ : \qquad \mathtt{x} := \mathtt{x} - 1; \, \}$$
$$l_{\text{final}} : \text{assert} \,(\mathtt{x} \geq -1);$$

We want to prove this assertion, since, for example, later on in the program there are references to an array using the index `x+1` (e.g. `a[x+1]:=0`). In this way, we want to verify that there are no array-out-of-bounds references. The tool will find that the necessary precondition for assertion satisfaction is: $-1 \leq \mathtt{x} \leq 4$, thus computing the success probability of 60%. The found necessary precondition for assertion violation is: $-5 \leq \mathtt{x} \leq -2$, so the failure probability is 40% (addresses Objective (**O4**)).

Approximate results We now give an example where we obtain a precision loss in practice due to the approximation inherent in abstract analyses. Consider the following program (taken from [30]):

$$① : \text{int } \mathtt{x} := [0, 9], \; \mathtt{y} := [0, 9]; \; l_{\text{input}} :$$
$$② : \text{int } \mathtt{s} := \mathtt{x} - \mathtt{y};$$
$$③ : \text{if} \,(\mathtt{s} \geq 2) \, \mathtt{y} := \mathtt{y} + 2;$$
$$l_{\text{final}} : \text{assert} \,(\mathtt{y} > 3);$$

The forward analysis will infer that the program can both satisfy and violate the assertion. The backward necessary condition analysis for assertion satisfaction will discover the constraint: $\mathtt{x} + 2\mathtt{y} \geq 8 \wedge 0 \leq \mathtt{x} \leq 9 \wedge 2 \leq \mathtt{y} \leq 9$, thus we

Table 1: Experimental evaluation for probabilistic static analyses of C programs. This table contains the following columns: (1) *benchmark* - the name of the analyzed program; (2) *source* - the source (folder) where the benchmark is taken from; (3) *LOC* - the number of lines of code; (4) *#var* - the number of integer variables; (5) TIME_{an}^{10} - the static analysis time in seconds for input domains of size 10; (6) TIME_{pr}^{10} - the probability computation time in seconds for input domains of size 10; (7-8) TIME^{10} and TIME^{1000} - the overall times in seconds required to completely analyze a benchmark which has input domain of size 10 and size 1000, respectively; (9) *Exact* - the preciseness of the reported result (✓ - result is exact, ≈ - result is approximate). Benchmarks above the double horizontal line are deterministic programs, while those below are non-deterministic programs.

Bench.	source	LOC	#var	TIME_{an}^{10}	TIME_{pr}^{10}	TIME^{10}	TIME^{1000}	EXACT
count_up_down*.c	loops	20	3	0.043	0.001	0.004	0.049	✓
hhk2008.c	loop-lit	20	4	0.103	0.001	0.104	0.113	✓
gsv2008.c	loop-lit	20	2	0.027	0.001	0.028	0.030	✓
Log.c	ter-restricted	30	4	0.194	0.001	0.195	0.197	≈
Mono3-1.c	loops-crafted-1	15	2	0.044	0.001	0.045	0.046	≈
Waldkirch.c	ter-crafted	20	1	0.010	0.001	0.011	0.012	✓
bwd-loop1a.c	[26]	15	1	0.008	0.001	0.009	0.010	✓
bwd-loop2.c	[26]	15	2	0.020	0.002	0.022	0.022	✓
example1a.c	[30]	10	1	0.008	0.001	0.009	0.008	✓
example7a.c	[30]	15	2	0.023	0.001	0.024	0.026	✓
for-bounded*.c	loops	30	4	0.049	0.002	0.051	0.053	≈
bwd-loop7.c	[26]	15	2	0.027	0.001	0.029	0.030	≈
bwd-loop10.c	[26]	20	2	0.046	0.001	0.047	0.048	≈
example7b.c	[30]	15	2	0.039	0.001	0.040	0.048	≈

find that the upper bound probability for assertion satisfaction is 74%. The backward necessary condition analysis for assertion violation will discover the constraint: $x + 5y \leq 23 \land 0 \leq x \leq 9 \land 0 \leq y \leq 3$, thus we find that the upper bound probability for assertion violation is 32%. In this way, we conclude that the success probability is between 68% and 74%, while the failure probability is between 26% and 32%. On the other hand, we can calculate by hand that the success probability is exactly 71%, while the failure probability is exactly 29%.

7   Related work

Probabilistic analysis of imperative programs based on symbolic execution has been introduced before [18,17,3,29]. They calculate path probabilities by counting the number of solutions to a path condition, which represents a constraint on inputs. The analyses in [18,17] address programs with integer domains and linear constraints, whereas the analyses in [3] address programs with linear and complex floating-point computations. While the previous analyses are restricted to discrete, uniform random variables that take on a finite set of values, the probabilistic analysis in [29] can also handle non-uniform distributions over the reals and integers using a branch-and-bound technique over polyhedra. However, in presence of loops all above analyses based on symbolic execution lose precision, since they cannot enumerate all program paths. The solution is to consider bounded exploration of loops and only a finite number of feasible program paths. Thus, they also define a measure of *confidence* on the obtained probabilistic estimations in order to take into account the contribution from the unexplored feasible paths. For example, if we set the exploration bound of the loop of program P_2 in Fig. 2 to any number less than 100, both success and failure probabilities will be 0% and the confidence will be also 0. This is due to the fact that the while loop in Fig. 2 has to be unrolled at least 100 times in order to obtain a feasible path on which it can be decided whether the assertion at point l_{final} is satisfied or violated. In this work, instead of symbolic execution we use abstract interpretation to analyze programs and infer preconditions for success and failure. Thus, our approach for computing program reliability represents one of the pioneering works that provides a complete and fast treatment of while loops. In particular, the strength of our approach is being an abstract interpretation of a complete semantics for computing program reliability. This is stronger than fixing a priori an incomplete reasoning approach that can miss some feasible program paths (executions). The work [13] performs a probabilistic analysis of open programs using symbolic game semantics [12] and model counting. It uses game semantics to model open programs with undefined identifiers (e.g. calls to library functions), such that the model takes into account all possible contexts in which those programs can be placed. In the presence of loops and undefined functions, bounded exploration in the model is also used to obtain a feasible analysis. Probabilistic model checking [2] is yet another approach to perform probabilistic analysis on a high-level design of software. However, such high-level models are difficult to maintain and may abstract important details that impact the chance of property satisfaction. So the goal is to do probabilistic analysis directly on source code as here, not on high-level models.

Backward precondition analyses by abstract interpretation have also been used in practice for a long time [4,9,26,28]. Sufficient preconditions have been first introduced by Bourdoncle [4] in his work on abstract debugging of deterministic programs. He uses a combination of forward-backward analyses to find preconditions for invariant and intermittent assertions to always hold. Cousot et. al. [9] propose a method for automatically inferring contract preconditions for intermittent assertions. The preconditions extracted by their method are necessary preconditions, i.e. they do not exclude unsafe executions. Mine [26] presents a method for automatically inferring sufficient preconditions of non-deterministic programs by using a polyhedral backward analysis. The under-approximating sound abstract operators for this backward analysis are implemented as part of the APRON library. Rival [28] uses forward-backward analysis to inspect more closely reported alarms by ASTREE, which are then classified as true errors (bugs) or false alarms. Urban and Mine [30] use forward-backward analysis for the automatic inference of sufficient preconditions for program termination. The elements of the analysis domain are decision trees, where decision nodes are labeled with linear numerical constraints and leaf nodes are affine ranking functions for proving program termination. Forward-backward analysis schemes have been used in [20] for the inference of safety properties of declarative synchronous programs. In this work, for the first time we employ forward-backward precondition analysis for estimating program reliability.

Static analysis of probabilistic programs by abstract interpretation has also been a topic of research [27,11]. Monniaux [27] proposes a probabilistic analysis that annotates abstract domains with upper bounds on the probability measure associated with abstract objects. However, the measure bound is associated with the entire abstract object, without tracking how it is distributed amongst the individual states present in the concretization. This restriction makes the analysis quite conservative. Cousot and Monerau [11] provide a general framework that encompasses a variety of probabilistic interpretation schemes. However, no concrete implementation of the above probabilistic abstract interpretations is provided yet. A backward abstract interpretation for probabilistic programs [23] uses expectations that are real-valued functions of the program state and quantitative loop invariants. The automatic inference of such quantitative loop invariants was proposed in the recent work of Katoen et al [22].

8   Conclusion

We have presented a new static, abstract interpretation-based approach for computing program reliability, which allows to calculate upper and lower bounds of probabilities that a given assertion is satisfied or violated. We construct a combination of forward-backward abstract analyses, in order to find an approximation of a set of input states which lead to definite satisfaction (resp., violation) of the given assertion. Our approach to calculating program reliability is semantics-based and approximate in a provably sound way. Still, it often yields very precise results, especially for deterministic programs.

We currently support only uniform distribution of input values within their finite discrete domains. In future, we plan to model imprecision in the input by different non-uniform distributions, such as Binomial, Poisson, etc [29]. The current implementation of LATTE is limited in handling non-uniform distributions, so we will explore the use of statistical sampling techniques in those cases. Our focus here is on estimating probability for safety properties. We also plan to consider liveness properties (such as termination) and expectation queries [30]. An interesting direction for future work would also be to consider general probabilistic programs [19], as well as program families implemented with #ifdef-s from the C-preprocessor where we can use lifted static analyses to efficiently analyze all variants of the family simultaneously at once [14,24,15,16].

References

1. Latte integrale. UC Davis, Mathematics.
2. Christel Baier and Joost-Pieter Katoen. *Principles of model checking*. MIT Press, 2008.
3. Mateus Borges, Antonio Filieri, Marcelo d'Amorim, Corina S. Pasareanu, and Willem Visser. Compositional solution space quantification for probabilistic software analysis. In *ACM SIGPLAN Conference on Programming Language Design and Implementation, PLDI'14*, page 15. ACM, 2014.
4. François Bourdoncle. Abstract debugging of higher-order imperative languages. In *Proceedings of the ACM SIGPLAN'93 Conference on Programming Language Design and Implementation (PLDI)*, pages 46–55. ACM, 1993.
5. N. V. Chernikova. Algorithm for finding a general formula for the non-negative solutions of a system of linear inequalities. *USSR Computational Mathematics and Mathematical Physics*, 5(2):228—233, 1965.
6. Patrick Cousot and Radhia Cousot. Abstract interpretation: A unified lattice model for static analysis of programs by construction or approximation of fixpoints. In *Conference Record of the Fourth ACM Symposium on Principles of Programming Languages (POPL'77)*, pages 238–252. ACM, 1977.
7. Patrick Cousot and Radhia Cousot. Systematic design of program analysis frameworks. In *6th Annual ACM Symposium on Principles of Programming Languages, POPL '79*, pages 269–282, 1979.
8. Patrick Cousot and Radhia Cousot. Abstract interpretation and application to logic programs. *J. Log. Program.*, 13(2–3):103–179, 1992.
9. Patrick Cousot, Radhia Cousot, and Francesco Logozzo. Precondition inference from intermittent assertions and application to contracts on collections. In *Verification, Model Checking, and Abstract Interpretation - 12th International Conference, VMCAI 2011. Proceedings*, volume 6538 of *LNCS*, pages 150–168. Springer, 2011.
10. Patrick Cousot and Nicolas Halbwachs. Automatic discovery of linear restraints among variables of a program. In *Conference Record of the Fifth Annual ACM Symposium on Principles of Programming Languages (POPL'78)*, pages 84–96. ACM Press, 1978.
11. Patrick Cousot and Michael Monerau. Probabilistic abstract interpretation. In *Programming Languages and Systems - 21st European Symposium on Programming, ESOP 2012, Held as Part of the European Joint Conferences on Theory and Practice of Software, ETAPS 2012. Proceedings*, volume 7211 of *LNCS*, pages 169–193. Springer, 2012.
12. Aleksandar S. Dimovski. Program verification using symbolic game semantics. *Theor. Comput. Sci.*, 560:364–379, 2014.
13. Aleksandar S. Dimovski. Probabilistic analysis based on symbolic game semantics and model counting. In *Proceedings Eighth International Symposium on Games, Automata, Logics and Formal Verification, GandALF 2017, Roma, Italy, 20-22 September 2017.*, volume 256 of *EPTCS*, pages 1–15, 2017.
14. Aleksandar S. Dimovski. Lifted static analysis using a binary decision diagram abstract domain. In *Proceedings of the 18th ACM SIGPLAN International Conference on Generative Programming: Concepts and Experiences, GPCE 2019*, pages 102–114. ACM, 2019.
15. Aleksandar S. Dimovski, Claus Brabrand, and Andrzej Wasowski. Variability abstractions: Trading precision for speed in family-based analyses. In *29th European Conf. on Object-Oriented Programming, ECOOP 2015*, volume 37 of *LIPIcs*, pages 247–270. Schloss Dagstuhl - Leibniz-Zentrum fuer Informatik, 2015.

16. Aleksandar S. Dimovski, Claus Brabrand, and Andrzej Wasowski. Finding suitable variability abstractions for lifted analysis. *Formal Asp. Comput.*, 31(2):231–259, 2019.

17. Antonio Filieri, Corina S. Pasareanu, and Willem Visser. Reliability analysis in symbolic pathfinder. In *35th International Conference on Software Engineering, ICSE'13*, pages 622–631. IEEE / ACM, 2013.

18. Jaco Geldenhuys, Matthew B. Dwyer, and Willem Visser. Probabilistic symbolic execution. In *International Symposium on Software Testing and Analysis, ISSTA 2012*, pages 166–176. ACM, 2012.

19. Andrew D. Gordon, Thomas A. Henzinger, Aditya V. Nori, and Sriram K. Rajamani. Probabilistic programming. In *Proceedings of the on Future of Software Engineering, FOSE 2014*, pages 167–181. ACM, 2014.

20. Bertrand Jeannet. Dynamic partitioning in linear relation analysis: Application to the verification of reactive systems. *Formal Methods in System Design*, 23(1):5–37, 2003.

21. Bertrand Jeannet and Antoine Miné. Apron: A library of numerical abstract domains for static analysis. In *Computer Aided Verification, 21st International Conference, CAV 2009. Proceedings*, volume 5643 of *LNCS*, pages 661–667. Springer, 2009.

22. Joost-Pieter Katoen, Annabelle McIver, Larissa Meinicke, and Carroll C. Morgan. Linear-invariant generation for probabilistic programs: - automated support for proof-based methods. In *Static Analysis - 17th International Symposium, SAS 2010. Proceedings*, volume 6337 of *LNCS*, pages 390–406. Springer, 2010.

23. Annabelle McIver and Carroll Morgan. *Abstraction, Refinement and Proof for Probabilistic Systems*. Monographs in Computer Science. Springer, 2005.

24. Jan Midtgaard, Aleksandar S. Dimovski, Claus Brabrand, and Andrzej Wasowski. Systematic derivation of correct variability-aware program analyses. *Sci. Comput. Program.*, 105:145–170, 2015.

25. Antoine Miné. The octagon abstract domain. *Higher-Order and Symbolic Computation*, 19(1):31–100, 2006.

26. Antoine Miné. Backward under-approximations in numeric abstract domains to automatically infer sufficient program conditions. *Sci. Comput. Program.*, 93:154–182, 2014.

27. David Monniaux. An abstract monte-carlo method for the analysis of probabilistic programs. In *Conference Record of POPL 2001: The 28th ACM SIGPLAN-SIGACT Symposium on Principles of Programming Languages*, pages 93–101. ACM, 2001.

28. Xavier Rival. Understanding the origin of alarms in astrée. In *Static Analysis, 12th International Symposium, SAS 2005, Proceedings*, volume 3672 of *LNCS*, pages 303–319. Springer, 2005.

29. Sriram Sankaranarayanan, Aleksandar Chakarov, and Sumit Gulwani. Static analysis for probabilistic programs: inferring whole program properties from finitely many paths. In *ACM SIGPLAN Conference on Programming Language Design and Implementation, PLDI '13*, pages 447–458. ACM, 2013.

30. Caterina Urban and Antoine Miné. A decision tree abstract domain for proving conditional termination. In *Static Analysis - 21st International Symposium, SAS 2014. Proceedings*, volume 8723 of *LNCS*, pages 302–318. Springer, 2014.

Skill-Based Verification of Cyber-Physical Systems

Alexander Knüppel[1] , Inga Jatzkowski[1] , Marcus Nolte[1] , Thomas Thüm[1,2],
Tobias Runge[1], and Ina Schaefer[1]

[1] TU Braunschweig, Braunschweig, Germany
{a.knueppel, tobias.runge, i.schaefer}@tu-bs.de
{jatzkowski, nolte}@ifr.ing.tu-bs.de
[2] University of Ulm, Ulm, Germany
thomas.thuem@uni-ulm.de

Abstract. Cyber-physical systems are ubiquitous nowadays. However, as automation increases, modeling and verifying them becomes increasingly difficult due to the inherently complex physical environment. *Skill graphs* are a means to model complex cyber-physical systems (e.g., vehicle automation systems) by distributing complex behaviors among skills with interfaces between them. We identified that skill graphs have a high potential to be amenable to scalable verification approaches in the early software development process. In this work, we suggest combining skill graphs with hybrid programs. Hybrid programs constitute a program notation for hybrid systems enabling the verification of cyber-physical systems. We provide the first formalization of skill graphs including a notion of compositionality and propose SKEDITOR, an integrated framework for modeling and verifying them. SKEDITOR is coupled with the theorem prover KEYMAERA X, which is specialized in the verification of hybrid programs. In an experiment exhibiting the *follow mode* of a vehicle, we evaluate our skill-based methodology with respect to savings in verification effort and potential to find modeling defects at design time. Compared to non-compositional verification, the initial verification effort needed is reduced by more than 53%.

Keywords: Deductive verification, design by contract, formal methods, theorem proving, KEYMAERA X, hybrid systems, automated reasoning, cyber-physical systems

1 Introduction

Cyber-physical systems combine digital computations and physical processes by tightly integrating discrete and continuous dynamics [6]. The last decade has witnessed an increase in the degree of automation in *safety-critical* cyber-physical systems (e.g., such as self-driving cars and transportation in general). Furthermore, the complexity of formally modeling and verifying such systems (e.g., by means of hybrid systems models [11, 19, 30]) to reason about safety increased simultaneously. Although there is a clear desire for an early identification and

© The Author(s) 2020
H. Wehrheim and J. Cabot (Eds.): FASE 2020, LNCS 12076, pp. 203–223, 2020.
https://doi.org/10.1007/978-3-030-45234-6_10

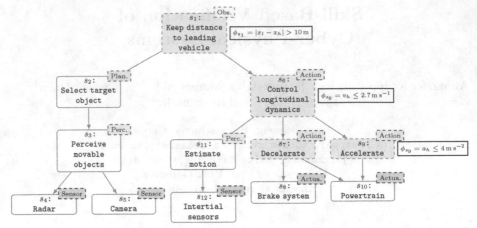

Fig. 1: Excerpt of a skill graph representing an operation to keep distance to a leading vehicle. We illustrate informal safety guarantees for the three skills s_1, s_6, and s_9.

elimination of severe mistakes [9], there is still a remarkable lack of formal methods integrated in the software development cycle [16, 17]. The challenge is to derive modeling and verification approaches that are applicable in the early development stages (e.g., requirements analysis and design time). To address this challenge, we present a model-based verification framework unifying the decomposition and modeling of cyber-physical systems by means of skill graphs [33] and a formal verifcation of these models by means of hybrid systems [2, 3, 5, 25].

A skill is a simple capability (e.g., acceleration in the context of a vehicle) *explicitly* provided by a cyber-physical system. Skills exhibit specific behaviors (i.e., control algorithms) by a mapping to some implementation unit (e.g., *source code* or interacting *software components*). Skills are assigned to a specific category (e.g., *actuator*, *sensor*, or *observable behavior*) with a defined hierarchy to prevent modeling mistakes. This categorization follows the design principle of *separation of concerns* [27], which ensures that skills only have single well-defined responsibilities. Separation of concerns is known to have a positive effect on modeling complexity, comprehensibility, functional reusability, fault localization, and artifact traceability [15, 36]. Skills can be annotated with safety guarantees obtained from a preceding requirements analysis, which enables the application of verification techniques.

Skill graphs, informally introduced by Reschka et al. [32, 33], are a promising means to model complex actions of cyber-physical systems from an architectural point of view. A skill graph [26, 32, 33, 37] is a directed acyclic graph comprising a set of *skills* (i.e., nodes) and dependencies between them (i.e., edges). To describe the properties we want to verify in a skill graph, we illustrate a skill graph representing a driving task in Figure 1. The task exhibits that a vehicle autonomously tries to keep a distance of at least 10 m to a leading vehicle. On the top level, skill **Keep distance to leading vehicle** (s_1) depends on two other skills, namely (1) the planning skill **Select target object** (s_2) and (2) the action skill *Control the longitudinal dynamics* (s_6). Whereas sensor-dependent skills are typically realized by software algorithms only (e.g., deep learning for detecting an obstacle), actuator-dependent skills (highlighted with a dashed border) also need to incorporate control theory, as the physical environment has to be taken into account. Skills are annotated with safety requirements (e.g., maximum acceleration or minimum distance to other vehicles). Together with the skill's realization and its dependencies to other skills, this requirement expresses the property we want to verify at design time. Successfully verifying all skills in the context of a skill graph ensures that the represented task complies to the complete set of safety requirements.

Conceptually, skill graphs as applied in this work are used for designing and organizing the architecture of a cyber-physical system. First, they facilitate the modeling of complex maneuvers built from simpler skills, which interact through explicit *interfaces*. Second, they advocate the systematic reuse of ready-to-integrate skills for multiple skill graphs, which reduces maintenance costs and increases software quality in general. Third, skill graphs are intuitive and therefore accommodate good potential for communicating with stakeholders and non-experts. Typically, skill graphs are supplied with performance measurements with the goal to enforce safety requirements at run-time. We are the first to exploit skill graphs to formally reason about the satisfiability of safety requirements at design time. Both areas of application complement each other, as they cover the full range from static analysis in the design phase to run-time verification and monitoring during operation.

As the foundation for our model-based verification approach, we propose to realize skills that interact with the physical environment by means of hybrid systems based on the *differential dynamic logic d$\mathcal{L}$* [28, 29, 31]. Hybrid systems represent complex physical systems, typically modeled as automata, where states are defined by continuous variables based on differential equations and transitions between states are discrete. Differential dynamic logic enables the deductive verification of hybrid systems, and as such is suitable for reasoning automatically about the correctness of hybrid systems. The key step of our approach is to decompose complex tasks of a cyber-physical system into skills connected by means of a skill graph and to provide a translation of skills to hybrid systems. The combination of skill graphs and hybrid systems allows the identification of severe mistakes during early design phases and also – in case of success – to generate correctness proofs, which increases trust that the system under design behaves as intended. Moreover, we propose a notion of compositionality for skill graphs, which is crucial to manage scalability during the verification phase. While skill graphs may only model simple functional aspects, they can be assembled to exhibit more complex behaviors, and verification results of skills can be reused.

We have implemented a prototype for modeling and verifying skill graphs called SKEDITOR. SKEDITOR supports the graphical modeling of skill graphs, allows to specify safety guarantees, and enables formal verification through a mapping to hybrid programs [30] (i.e., a program notation for hybrid systems as required by the theorem prover KEYMAERA X [14]). In a case study exhibiting

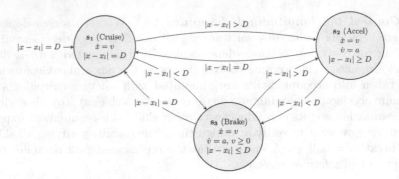

Fig. 2: Simplified hybrid system of a vehicle with automatic headway control.

the *follow mode* of an automated vehicle, we evaluate SKEDITOR with respect to its potential to find modeling defects. In particular, SKEDITOR allowed us to find conceptual defects of control algorithms early on in the design phase of our case study. To summarize, the contribution of this work is threefold.

- **Framework:** We are the first to formalize skill graphs and propose *skill-based verification*, a model-based verification technique allowing us to identify poorly defined safety requirements in early design phases by combining skill graphs with hybrid programs.
- **Tool support:** We implemented skill-based verification in a prototypical open-source tool called SKEDITOR, which paves the way for users to model and verify cyber-physical systems based on skill graphs.
- **Evaluation:** We demonstrate our approach on a realistic case study examining the *follow mode* of an automated vehicle. We show that skill-based verification decreases effort compared to monolithic modeling.

2   Background on Hybrid-System Modeling

A prominent mathematical foundation for cyber-physical systems is constituted by *hybrid systems* [2, 11, 19, 30], which enable a mixed modeling of continuous dynamics (expressed by differential equations) and discrete dynamics (expressed by automata). The states change on the basis of flow conditions.

Example 1 *Consider the example of an automatic headway control of a vehicle depicted in Figure 2. Four variables exist: the host's current position (x), the current position of the leading vehicle (x_l), the current velocity (v), and the current acceleration (a). The headway control exhibits three states: (s_1) the vehicle is in cruise mode when the current distance to the leading vehicle is equal to a defined constant D, (s_2) the vehicle accelerates when the distance is greater than D, and (s_3) the vehicle decelerates when the distance is less than D, but only until the vehicle comes to a full stop. The headway control ensures that the distance to the leading vehicle is approximately equal to D.*

Hybrid programs define an imperative-like program notation for hybrid systems [28], which support the definition of variables that evolve along a differential equation and are interpreted by tools such as KEYMAERA X [14]. The syntax of hybrid programs is as follows.

$$\alpha ::= \alpha; \beta \,|\, \alpha \cup \beta \,|\, \alpha^* \,|\, x := \Theta \,|\, x := * \,|\, x' = \Theta \,\&\, H \,|\, ?H \qquad (1)$$

$\alpha; \beta$ represents the sequential composition of two hybrid programs. $\alpha \cup \beta$ expresses the non-deterministic choice between two hybrid programs. α^* expresses that the execution of α may be repeated zero or more times. The discrete assignment to x is either a term Θ (possibly over x) or an arbitrary value represented by the wildcard $*$. The continuous evolution of a variable x along a differential equation is described by $x' = \Theta \,\&\, H$, where H is an optional evolution domain. Finally, $?H$ describes a testable condition that aborts the evolution if H is false. For instance, the program $\alpha \dot{=} (v := *; a := *; \,?(-a_b \le a \le 0); \{v' = a \,\&\, v \ge 0\})$ sets velocity v to an arbitrary value and acceleration a to a value between $-a_b$ (i.e., maximum braking force) and zero. The execution stops nondeterministically at any time but at the latest before velocity v reaches a negative value.

Semantics of hybrid programs are based on differential dynamic logic $d\mathcal{L}$ [28, 29, 31] to specify and verify properties of hybrid programs associated with a skill in a skill graph. Models specified in $d\mathcal{L}$ can be verified with KEYMAERA X, a matured open-source theorem prover for hybrid programs. The following grammar describes all valid formulas of $d\mathcal{L}$. Symbol $\sim$ is a placeholder for a comparison operator (i.e., $\sim \in \{<, \le, >, \ge, =, \neq\}$) between two terms Θ_1 and Θ_2. Terms are polynomials with rational coefficients over the set of continuous variables.

$$\Phi ::= \Theta_1 \sim \Theta_2 \,|\, \neg\Phi \,|\, \Phi \wedge \Psi \,|\, \Phi \vee \Psi \,|\, \Phi \to \Psi \,|\, \forall x\, \Phi \,|\, \exists x\, \Phi \,|\, [\alpha]\Phi \qquad (2)$$

The semantics of the logical connectives is defined as in first-order logic. Additionally, the modal formula $[\alpha]\Phi$ holds if all runs of the hybrid program α end in a state that satisfies the given condition Φ. Following the idea of Hoare-style specification in classical deductive reasoning [1, 7, 10, 18, 34], we are particularly interested to prove validity of the condition $\Psi \to [\alpha]\Phi$ with Ψ expressing assumptions we have and Φ expressing guarantees to meet by the hybrid program α.

3   A Formalization for Skill-Based Modeling

In this section, we propose the first formalization of modeling cyber-physical systems based on skill graphs. First, we define the essence of a skill. Second, we continue with the definition of a skill graph and what makes it well-formed. Third, we define how to compose skill graphs to exhibit more complex behaviors.

3.1   Formalizing Skills

In the context of cyber-physical systems, *skills* describe fine-grained executable activities inspired by human behaviors [32, 33]. For instance, a skill may represent longitudinal driving (i.e., driving with constant velocity) or even a more complex combination of longitudinal and lateral maneuvers (i.e., following the lane). To ensure that such maneuvers are executed safely, skills are associated with so-called *safety guarantees*, which they must fulfill to be considered *safe*. For example, a skill exhibiting the following of a leading vehicle should keep a minimum distance of a specified constant D (cf. Fig. 2). Informal safety guarantees are typically formulated by experts who identify numerous hazardous scenarios with respect to a maneuver and resolutions to prevent them.

The implementation of skills was only vaguely specified before. Typically, skills are implemented by software components [33]. However, our goal of early verification at design time requires to also consider a model of the physical environment. Therefore, we propose to implement skills by hybrid programs [28], which already incorporate assumptions about the physical environment and enable the verification of implementation against safety guarantees *at design time*.

To separate concerns, a skill has an associated type. We define the set $\texttt{Type}$ = {observable behavior, action, perception, planning, sensor, actuator}, which categorizes the purpose of a skill. Moreover, a skill has dependency-relationships with other skills. Informally, the idea is that a hybrid program of a skill may introduce a set of continuous state variables, their computation, and their valid domains (e.g., velocity $v \in [0, 60]$ with $v' = a$), but may also require the presence of variables and their domains defined by other skills (e.g., acceleration $a \in [0, 4]$). In the following, we formally define a skill. Let $\mathcal{X}$ denote the universe of continuous variables. The syntactic domain of a skill is defined as follows.

Definition 1 (Skill). *A skill is a 5-tuple* $\langle X_{\texttt{def}}, X_{\texttt{req}}, \alpha, \tau, \Phi \rangle$*, where*

- $X_{\texttt{def}} \subseteq \mathcal{X}$ *is a finite set of variables defined in the hybrid program* α,
- $X_{\texttt{req}} \subseteq \mathcal{X}$ *is a finite set of variables required by the hybrid program* α,
- α *is the (possibly empty) hybrid program (cf. Eq. 1) over variables in* $X_{\texttt{def}} \cup X_{\texttt{req}}$,
- $\tau \in \texttt{Type}$ *is the associated type,*
- $\Phi = \{\phi_1, \dots, \phi_m\}$ *is a finite set of safety guarantees in first-order logic over variables in* $X_{\texttt{def}} \cup X_{\texttt{req}}$ *(cf. Eq. 2).*

To be well-formed, we require that the sets of defined and required variables of a skill are disjoint (i.e., $X_{\texttt{def}} \cap X_{\texttt{req}} = \emptyset$*). To access a skill's attribute, we use the '.' (dot) operator (e.g.,* $s.\tau$ *expresses the type of skill* s*).*

3.2 Formalizing Skill Graphs

We formalize skill graphs as directed acyclic graphs comprising a set of skills (i.e., nodes), which are connected through directed edges representing their dependencies. We denote by $\mathcal{S}$ the universe of all skills and define the syntactic domain of skill graphs as follows.

Definition 2 (Skill Graph). *A skill graph is given by* $G \triangleq \langle S, r, E \rangle$*, where*

- $S \subset \mathcal{S}$ *is a finite set of skills,*
- $r \in S$ *is the root skill,*
- $E \subseteq S \times S$ *is set of directed edges between skills. We denote* $(s_c, s_p) \in E$ *as* $s_c \prec s_p$ *meaning that* s_c *is a child of* s_p*.*

$\tau_s \setminus \tau_t$	observable	action	actuator	planning	perception	sensor
observable	✓	✓	-	✓	✓	-
action	-	✓	✓	✓	✓	-
planning	-	-	-	✓	✓	-
perception	-	-	-	-	✓	✓

Table 1: Valid types of a child skill t for a skill s (i.e., $t \prec s$).

A skill graph is an acyclic directed graph with exactly one root skill r. To guarantee that skill graphs are *well-formed*, we impose specific constraints. We formally introduce the *path* between two skills as follows.

Definition 3 (Path). *Let E be a set of edges and $s_1, \ldots, s_l \in S$ skills of a skill graph. A path of length $l - 1$ is a (possibly empty) sequence of $l - 1$ edges (s_1, s_2), $(s_2, s_3), \ldots, (s_{l-1}, s_l) \in E$ denoted by $\pi_{s_1 \to s_l} = [(s_1, s_2), (s_2, s_3), \ldots, (s_{l-1}, s_l)]$. We say that a path between skills $s, s' \in S$ exists if $\pi_{s \to s'}$ is non-empty, and does not exists otherwise.*

As mentioned before, each skill has an assigned type. Based on our definition of a well-formed graph, we enforce that only skills with particular types can form valid parent-child relationships (cf. Table 1). For instance, for two skills $s, s' \in S$, if $s \prec s'$ holds and skill s' is of type perception, then skill s is only allowed to have type sensor or perception.

Definition 4 (Well-Formed Skill Graph). *Let $G = \langle S, r, E \rangle$ be a skill graph. G is* well-formed *if and only if*

- *each skill $s \in S \setminus \{r\}$ in a skill graph has at least one parent skill $s' \in S$ (i.e., $\{s' \in S \mid s \prec s'\} \neq \emptyset$) and there exists at least one path from skill s to root skill r,*
- *for each edge $(s, s') \in E$, skills s, s' satisfy the typing restriction depicted in Table 1,*
- *for each skill $s \in S$ and variable $x \in s.X_{\text{req}}$ there exists a path $\pi_{s' \to s'}$ from a skill $s' \in S$ that introduces variable x (i.e., $x \in s'.X_{\text{def}}$),*
- *for each pair of skills $s, s' \in S$, the sets of defined variables are disjoint (i.e., $s.X_{\text{def}} \cap s'.X_{\text{def}} = \emptyset$).*
- *for each skill s in G, formula $\bigwedge_{\phi \in s'.\Phi \wedge s' \prec s} \phi$ must be satisfiable.*

Remark. Unlike behavioral models, skill graphs as defined here do not suggest an execution order of skills on the same level (i.e., child skills). The reason is twofold. First, the information needed for the scheduling may be incomplete at design time (i.e., concrete hardware and scheduling parameters). Second, the intent of skill graphs is to abstract away from implementation details, while providing guarantees about the correctness of defined safety requirements. In Section 4.2, we illustrate how to assemble the decomposed hybrid programs of a skill graph to a complete hybrid program, while being safe with respect to our chosen level of abstraction.

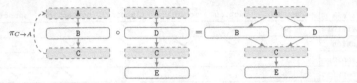

Fig. 3: Example of a composition of two skill graphs.

3.3 Composition of Skill Graphs

From the perspective of software engineering practices, an advantage of skill graphs is their modular nature. Multiple skill graphs can be designed in isolation, but may also share the same skills. To model and verify more complex skill graphs and to prevent unnecessary redundancy, the idea is to adequately *reuse* previously designed skill graphs and subsequently compose them together. This method further supports the identification and location of design mistakes, maintenance of skill graphs in general, and also enables the distribution of modeling tasks in multi-team software development.

Our composition technique of skill graphs is inspired by *superimposition* [8], a simple process that composes two graphs recursively together by merging their substructures. Starting from the root skill of one of the skill graphs, skills at the same level fulfilling defined criteria can then be composed to form a new resulting skill. Starting from a joint root skill of two different skill graphs $G_1 = \langle S_1, r, E_1 \rangle$ and $G_2 = \langle S_2, r, E_2 \rangle$, two skills $s_1 \in S_1$ and $s_2 \in S_2$ are composed to a new skill s if:

- both paths, $\pi_{s_1 \to s_1'}$ and $\pi_{s_2 \to s_2'}$, exist and s_1', s_2' are already composed,
- s_1 and s_2 have an equal type and equal sets of defined and required variables,
- and either any of the two hybrid programs is empty or both are identical.

For illustration, Fig. 3 depicts an abstraction of the composition of two skill graphs. Both skill graphs share the identical skills A and C. First, the root skill A of both skill graphs is superimposed, and second, skill C is superimposed after identifying that in both skill graphs there exists a path to a skill already subject to composition (i.e., A). In the following, we call two skills from different skill graphs *composable* if they are subject to the composition as explained here. The resulting skill s receives all the properties (i.e., variables, type, and hybrid program) from the composable skills and additionally the union of their safety guarantees:

Definition 5 (Composition of Skills). *Let $s_1 \in S_1$ and $s_2 \in S_2$ be two composable skills. The binary composition of s_1 and s_2 then produces the skill*

$$s_1 \oplus s_2 = \langle s_1.X_{\mathtt{def}}, s_1.X_{\mathtt{req}}, s_1.\alpha, s_1.\tau, s_1.\Phi \cup s_2.\Phi \rangle. \tag{3}$$

The binary composition of two skill graphs is then formally defined as follows, where $M = \{(s_1, s_2) \in S_1 \times S_2 \mid s_1$ and s_2 are composable$\}$ is the set of composable skills and f is a function that maps every skill in $(S_1 \cup S_2) \setminus \{s_1, s_2 \in S_1 \cup S_2 \mid (s_1, s_2) \in M\}$ to itself and maps all skills s_1, s_2 with $(s_1, s_2) \in M$ to a new skill $s = s_1 \oplus s_2$.

Definition 6 (Composition of Skill Graphs). *Let $G_1 = \langle S_1, r_1, E_1 \rangle$ and $G_2 = \langle S_2, r_2, E_2 \rangle$ be two well-formed skill graphs with $r_2 \in S_1$. The composition of G_1 and G_2 then produces the skill graph*

$$G_1 \circ G_2 = \langle S, f(r_1), E \rangle \tag{4}$$

where
- $S = \{f(s) \mid s \in S_1 \cup S_2\}$,
- *for every $s, s' \in (S_1 \cup S_2)$, there exists an edge $(f(s), f(s')) \in E$ if and only if there exists an edge $(s, s') \in (E_1 \cup E_2)$.*

A mathematical convenience of our definition of composition is that it requires the root skill of one skill graph to be present in the second skill graph. This is not a severe limitation, as it is always possible to add an artificial root to one skill graph (or both) with respect to well-formedness.

4 Compositional Verification of Skill Graphs

In this section, we formalize the generation of verification conditions to check correctness of skills in the context of a skill graph, show how correctness results transfer to the composition of skill graphs, and discuss how this methodology can be integrated into the development process for cyber-physical systems.

4.1 Verification Condition Generation

Our verification procedure relies on assume-guarantee reasoning. Thus, to verify whether a skill s in the context of a skill graph adheres to its safety guarantees $s.\Phi$, we have to construct two logical conditions: (1) necessary assumptions on a skill's behavior denoted by assume_s and (2) the overall safety condition in the context of the skill graph denoted by safe_s. For instance, assume_s for leaf skills valuates trivially to true, but child skills impose constraints on their parent skills through their safety guarantees. Both conditions can be computed automatically based on the skill's dependencies and by the manually defined safety guarantees $s.\Phi$. The overall verification condition then becomes $\text{assume}_s \rightarrow [s.\alpha]\text{safe}_s$ (cf. Sec. 2). In the following, we describe how both conditions are constructed.

In the context of a skill graph, a particularity to deal with is that a skill may *require* variables introduced in a *distant* skill (i.e., path length greater than one), possibly with numerous updates along the path. These variables may be unknown in direct children, so it is not possible to only define the assumption (i.e., assume_s) of a skill s as the conjunction of the safety guarantees of all children (i.e., $\bigwedge \text{safe}_{s'}$ with $s' \prec s$). In Fig. 4, we illustrate this problem and its solution on a simple skill graph comprising three skills.

Skill #1 introduces variables A and B including safety guarantees on them in ϕ_1. Typical for assume-guarantee reasoning, ϕ_1 becomes the assumption for all parent skills (i.e., Skill #2 in this case). However, the safety guarantee of Skill #2 (i.e., ϕ_2) states only a modification of variable A and not B, but Skill

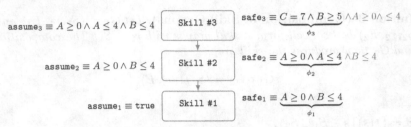

Fig. 4: Computation of $\mathtt{assume}_t$ and $\mathtt{safe}_t$.

#3 may indeed need the information of the current domain of variable B to be verifiable. To keep assume-guarantee propagation intact, we resolve this issue by additionally encoding all safety guarantees that *remain valid* for a skill in its safety guarantee $\mathtt{safe}_s$ (highlighted in blue). In the following, we introduce our formalization.

The definitions of both formulas, $\mathtt{assume}_s$ and $\mathtt{safe}_s$, are mutually recursive. The logical formula $\mathtt{assume}_s$ for a skill s results from the conjunction of the overall safety guarantees $\mathtt{safe}_{s'}$ of all children $s' \prec s$. The assumption for skills with no children valuates trivially to **true**.

$$\mathtt{assume}_s \equiv \bigwedge_{s' \prec s} \mathtt{safe}_{s'} \qquad (5)$$

To compute the overall safety guarantee $\mathtt{safe}_s$, we exploit that $\mathtt{assume}_s$ exhibits an overapproximation on the current state of the required variables for a skill s prior to executing the hybrid program $s.\alpha$. As the behavior of a skill may change the initial state, we discard all clauses in $\mathtt{assume}_s$ sharing a variable with one of the user provided safety guarantees in $s.\Phi$. The remaining clauses become part of $\mathtt{safe}_s$. For instance, in Fig. 4, Skill #3 guarantees a change of variable B in ϕ_1. Thus, only clauses of $\mathtt{assume}_3$ without mentioning B transfer to $\mathtt{safe}_3$. For mathematical convenience, we denote the conjunction of all safety guarantees of a skill by the logical formula $\phi_s \equiv \bigwedge_{\phi \in s.\Phi} \phi$ and the set of assumptions of a skill in a skill graph by the set $\mathcal{A}_s = \{\psi_1, \ldots, \psi_n \mid \mathtt{assume}_s \equiv \psi_1 \wedge \cdots \wedge \psi_n\}$. Furthermore, set $\mathtt{var}(\cdot)$ denotes the set of variables of a logical formula. The overall safety guarantee of a skill is then computed as follows.

$$\mathtt{safe}_s \equiv \phi_s \wedge \left(\bigwedge_{\substack{\psi \in \mathcal{A}_s \wedge \\ \mathtt{var}(\phi_s) \cap \mathtt{var}(\psi) = \emptyset}} \psi \right) \qquad (6)$$

We can now define the *validity* of a skill graph as follows.

Definition 7 (Valid Skill Graph). *Let $G = \langle S, r, E \rangle$ be a well-formed skill graph. We say that skill graph G is valid if and only if $\forall s \in S$ formula $\mathtt{assume}_s$ is satisfiable and formula $\mathtt{assume}_s \to [s.\alpha]\mathtt{safe}_s$ is valid. We denote by $s \models_G s.\Phi$ the validity of a skill s in a skill graph G with respect to its safety guarantees and by $\models G$ the validity of the entire skill graph (i.e., $\models G \equiv \forall s \in S, s \models_G s.\Phi$).*

The upcoming important theorem states that the individual validity of two skill graphs also transfers to the validity of their composition. However, based on

Def. 6, composition may also lead to an invalid skill graph if the assumption of a skill in the new skill graph is not satisfiable (e.g., possible in case of diamond structures). Therefore, we require satisfiability checks for the computed assumptions and define the *compatibility* between two skill graphs as follows.

Definition 8 (Compatible Skill Graphs). *Let G_1 and G_2 be two well-formed skill graphs. We say that G_1 and G_2 are* compatible *if the following holds.*

- $G_1 \circ G_2$ *is a well-formed skill graph,*
- *for each skill s in $G_1 \circ G_2$, formula* assume$_s$ *is satisfiable.*

Theorem 1 (Composition of Skill Graphs Retains Validity). *Let G_1 and G_2 be two compatible skill graphs and $G = G_1 \circ G_2$ their composition. Then, G is valid if G_1 and G_2 are valid (i.e., $\models G$ if $\models G_1$ and $\models G_2$).*

Proof. Let s_1 and s_2 be two composed skills and $s = s_1 \oplus s_2$ their composition. Following Def. 6, the verification condition for s becomes

$$(\text{assume}_{s_1} \wedge \text{assume}_{s_2}) \rightarrow [s.\alpha](\text{safe}_{s_1} \wedge \text{safe}_{s_2}).$$

Based on the semantics of $d\mathcal{L}$ [31], condition $\Psi \rightarrow [\alpha]\Phi_1 \wedge \Psi \rightarrow [\alpha]\Phi_2 \leftrightarrow \Psi \rightarrow [\alpha](\Phi_1 \wedge \Phi_2)$ holds. As the hybrid programs of s_1 and s_2 are identical (or at least one of them is empty), the resulting two conditions to check are the following:

(1) $(\text{assume}_{s_1} \wedge \text{assume}_{s_2}) \rightarrow [s_1.\alpha](\text{safe}_{s_1})$

(2) $(\text{assume}_{s_1} \wedge \text{assume}_{s_2}) \rightarrow [s_2.\alpha](\text{safe}_{s_2})$

Satisfiability of $(\text{assume}_{s_1} \wedge \text{assume}_{s_2})$ follows from Def. 8. Then, validity of both conditions follow from Def. 7 and, consequently, $\models G$ holds.   □

4.2   Assembling Hybrid Programs in a Skill graph

Skill graphs decompose the system into smaller parts. Likewise, the hybrid program that represents the complete behavior is also distributed over the skill graph. Now that we have defined the structure and behavior of single skills in the context of a skill graph, we define how we can construct the complete behavior of a skill as a single monolithic hybrid program. The resulting hybrid program is then a complete representation of the skill's behavior while also retaining all safety guarantees without the need of re-verifying skills or even entire skill graphs. We start by giving a definition on *how* hybrid programs of skills are assembled together.

Definition 9 (Hybrid Program Assembly). *Let $G = \langle S, r, E \rangle$ be a skill graph, HP the set of all hybrid programs, and let $s \in S$ denote an arbitrary skill of G. A hybrid program assembly of s is a function $\rho : S \rightarrow HP$, which is recursively defined as follows.*

$$\rho(s) = \begin{cases} s.\alpha & \text{if } s \text{ has no children (i.e., } \neg \exists s' \in S : s' \prec s) \\ (\bigcup_{s' \prec s} \rho(s')); s.\alpha & \text{otherwise} \end{cases}$$

The motivation is that such assemblies are safe to be used in other contexts, such as code generation for the validation of prototypes or monitor generation. Assuming a valid skill graph G, the following theorem guarantees that any hybrid program assembly over skills in G retains the respective safety guarantees.

Theorem 2 (Safety Compliance of Hybrid Program Assemblies). *Let $G = \langle S, r, E \rangle$ be a valid skill graph and let $s \in S$ denote an arbitrary skill of G. Then, formula $[\rho(s)]\mathsf{safe}_s$ is valid.*

Proof. We proceed by induction on the skills of skill graph G. For the basis step, we assume that s has no children (i.e., $\neg \exists s' \in S : s' \prec s$). Because $[\rho(s)]\mathsf{safe}_s \equiv [s.\alpha]\mathsf{safe}_s$ and G is a valid skill graph, it follows from Def. 7 that formula $[\rho(s)]\mathsf{safe}_s$ is valid. From now on, we assume that s has children. Our induction hypothesis is that if for each skill $s' \prec s$ program assembly $\rho(s')$ satisfies $\mathsf{safe}_{s'}$, then hybrid program assembly $\rho(s)$ satisfies safe_s:

$$
\textbf{(IH)} \qquad (\bigwedge_{s' \prec s} [\rho(s')]\mathsf{safe}_{s'}) \rightarrow [\rho(s)]\mathsf{safe}_s
$$

$$
(1) \qquad \leftrightarrow \quad (\bigwedge_{s' \prec s} [\rho(s')]\mathsf{safe}_{s'}) \rightarrow [\bigcup_{s' \prec s} \rho(s'); s.\alpha]\mathsf{safe}_s
$$

$$
(2) \qquad \leftrightarrow \quad (\bigwedge_{s' \prec s} [\rho(s')]\mathsf{safe}_{s'}) \rightarrow [\bigcup_{s' \prec s} \rho(s')][s.\alpha]\mathsf{safe}_s
$$

$$
(3) \qquad \leftrightarrow \quad (\bigwedge_{s' \prec s} [\rho(s')]\mathsf{safe}_{s'}) \rightarrow \bigwedge_{s' \prec s} [\rho(s')][s.\alpha]\mathsf{safe}_s
$$

$$
(4) \qquad \leftrightarrow \quad (\bigwedge_{s' \prec s} \mathsf{safe}_{s'}) \rightarrow [s.\alpha]\mathsf{safe}_s
$$

$$
(5) \qquad \leftrightarrow \quad \mathsf{assume}_s \rightarrow [s.\alpha]\mathsf{safe}_s
$$

Transformation step (1) follows from substituting $\rho(s)$ with its definition given in Def. 9. Steps (2)–(4) are again based on the semantics of $d\mathcal{L}$ [31]. Step (2) follows from the *sequential composition axiom* $[a; b]P \leftrightarrow [a][b]P$, step (3) from the *nondeterministic choice axiom* $[a \cup b]P \leftrightarrow [a]P \wedge [b]P$, and step (4) from *monotonicity*. Because G is a valid skill graph, validity of $\mathsf{assume}_s \rightarrow [s.\alpha]\mathsf{safe}_s$ follows again from Def. 7. Consequently, $[\rho(s)]\mathsf{safe}_s$ is valid. □

4.3 Integration into the Software Development Process

In Figure 5, we summarize the methodology for modeling and verifying skill graphs. The main idea is that the safety verification of skill graphs modeled in isolation transfers to the composition of compatible skill graphs. This (a) eases the modeling process, as smaller models tend to be less complex and easier to repair, (b) fosters reusability, which is known to be cost-effective and less error-prone, and (c) is promising for scaling the verification to large skill graphs.

In particular, the methodology consists of five major parts. In the first part (*1*), practitioners define and model skills together with their hybrid programs and relevant safety guarantees in isolation and subsequently connect them to form well-formed skill graphs (if possible). In the second part (*2*), for each

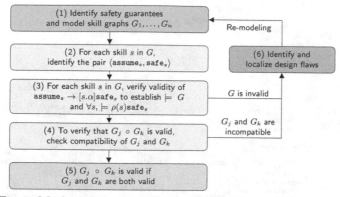

Fig. 5: Methodology of modeling and verifying skill graphs.

skill s in a skill graph, the assumption $\texttt{assume}_s$ and safety guarantee $\texttt{safe}_s$ are computed by evaluating the context of the skill in the skill graph. The third part (*3*) uses the identified assumptions and the safety guarantee to validate each skill in a skill graph individually. If each skill is proven valid (cf. Theorem 1), the complete skill graph is proven valid and can be put into a repository to be reused. Following Theorem 2, all program assemblies over skills in this skill graph retain the respective safety guarantees. The fourth part (*4*) becomes relevant, if two skill graphs are composed together to represent a more complex task of a cyber-physical system. In this case, compatibility of the skill graphs is checked and, if successful, the validity of the composed skill graph is established (*5*). The final part (*6*) is relevant in the presence of unsuccessful proof attempts. If validity of a skill graph or the composition of multiple skill graphs cannot be established, practitioners need to identify and fix mistakes in their models. Typically, the complexity of localizing design mistakes is reduced with our methodology, as it is explicitly known which exact skills in a skill graph with respect to their safety guarantees could not be verified.

5   Evaluation and Discussion

We evaluate our skill-based verification approach on a case study to answer the following two research questions.

RQ-1 *How does the skill-based methodology compare to monolithic modeling and verification?*

RQ-2 *To what extent can skill-based compositional verification reduce the verification effort?*

5.1   Open-Source Implementation

We implemented skill-based verification in a tool with the name SKEDITOR. The implementation is written in JAVA as an Eclipse plug-in based on Graphiti [13],

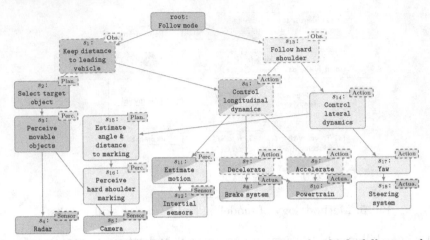

Fig. 6: Complete skill graph expressing an automated vehicle follow mode.

a framework for developing diagram editors in the context of model-driven development. The prototype allows practitioners to model and annotate well-formed skill graphs with safety guarantees as described in Section 3.

Thereupon, we implemented our compositional verification approach as described in Section 4. SKEDITOR allows to synthesize hybrid programs of specific skills with respect to their dependencies in the skill graph. Compliance checks of the provided safety guarantees are performed by employing the deductive theorem prover KEYMAERA X [14] in version 4.7.3. SKEDITOR and all experimental results can be found online.[3] We use the SKEDITOR to answer research questions *RQ-1* and *RQ-2*.

5.2   Case Study: Vehicle Follow Mode

To illustrate the practicality of our approach, we model and verify the *vehicle follow mode* of an automated protective vehicle as adopted from Nolte et al. [26] and depicted in Figure 6. The aim of was to develop an unmanned protective vehicle which is able to drive on the hard shoulder autonomously (i.e., without any human interaction). On the lowest level, the skill graph consists of three sensors (i.e., **Radar**, **Camera**, and **Inertial sensor**) to perceive information from the environment. Additionally, three actuators (i.e., **Brake system**, **Powertrain**, and **Steering system**) represent concrete technical aspects. These skills propagate information about typical properties of a concrete model of a vehicle (e.g., the *maximal deceleration*). As highlighted with two shades of gray, this skill graph is dividable into two separate skill graphs, which we refer to as G_1 and G_2. G_1 has **Keep distance to leading vehicle** as the root skill, which is responsible for ensuring a minimum distance to a leading vehicle. G_2 has **Follow hard shoulder** as root skill, which is responsible for ensuring the vehicle's position inside the lane markings on a road. Skills shared by both skill graphs are highlighted with both shades.

---

[3] https://github.com/TUBS-ISF/Skeditor

Skill	Requirement
Follow hard shoulder	Vehicle deviates from the center of the lane by at most half the lane width
Control lateral dynamics	Lateral controller must guarantee overshoot of less than 25 cm
Yaw	Vehicle yaw rate must not exceed $0.3 \, \mathrm{rad \, s^{-1}}$
Control longitudinal dynamics	Vehicle speed must not exceed $2.7 \, \mathrm{m \, s^{-1}}$
Accelerate	Acceleration must not exceed $4 \, \mathrm{m \, s^{-2}}$
Decelerate	Vehicle must at least provide a deceleration of $5 \, \mathrm{m \, s^{-2}}$
Keep distance to leading vehicle	Vehicle must keep a minimum distance of 10 m to leading vehicle
Select target object	Object recognition must always select an object of lateral position of $x > 10 \, \mathrm{m}$
Perceive movable objects	Object recognition must track vehicles of relative speeds between 0 and $60 \, \mathrm{m \, s^{-1}}$
Estimate angle and distance to marking	Angle to lanemarking must be extracted with maximum error of ± 0.5 degrees and distance to lanemarking must be extracted with maximum error of $\pm 3 \, \mathrm{cm}$
Perceive hard shoulder	Image processing must extract right edge of shoulder marking with a maximum error of 20 cm
Estimate motion	Vehicle velocity must be estimated with a maximal error of $\pm 0.03 \, \mathrm{m \, s^{-1}}$

Table 2: Specified safety requirements for the vehicle follow mode as adopted from Nolte et al. [26].

The overall procedure **Follow mode** (i.e., the composition $G_1 \circ G_2$) requires a combination of autonomously following a leading vehicle (i.e., skill s_1) and following the lane marking (i.e., skill s_{13}). The informal safety guarantees for the skill graph of our case study are adopted from Nolte et al. [26] and illustrated in Table 2. Requirements are typically given informally, which is why we translated them to their formal counterpart. For our case study, we focus on four particular skills, as these are the only non-trivial skills in our case study that comprise both, the vehicle's dynamics and a control algorithm. Namely, these skills are *Control longitudinal dynamics* (s_6), *Control lateral dynamics* (s_{14}), *Follow hard shoulder* (s_{13}), and *Keep distance to leading vehicle* (s_1).

Example 2 *Consider skill* **Control longitudinal dynamics** *(s_6) in the context of the overall skill graph. Skill s_6 comprises the dynamic system for the longitudinal motion of the vehicle while depending on skills* **Accelerate** *and* **Decelerate** *as well as the perception skill* **Estimate motion**. *The control algorithm of this skill as part of the hybrid program complies with the safety requirements as given in Table 2 (e.g., velocity (v_s) must not exceed $2.7 \, \mathrm{m \, s^{-1}}$). Preconditions for this skill are propagated from skills* **Estimate motion**, **Accelerate**, *and* **Decelerate**, *and guarantee that the vehicle provides a maximal deceleration of $5 \, \mathrm{m \, s^{-2}}$ (B) and a maximal acceleration of $4 \, \mathrm{m \, s^{-2}}$ (A). Table 3 summarizes all attributes of skill s_6.*

$X_{\texttt{def}} = \{x, v, v_{\max}\}$
$X_{\texttt{req}} = \{a, A, B, ep, t\}$
$\alpha ::= \begin{cases} \texttt{init} \rightarrow [(ctrl; dyn)*](\texttt{guar}) \\ \quad \texttt{init} \equiv v \geq 0 \wedge v \leq v_{\max} \wedge A > 0 \wedge A \leq 4 \wedge B \geq 5 \wedge v_{\max} = 2.7 \\ \quad ctrl \equiv (?v_{\max} - v \leq \texttt{margin}); a = *; -B \leq a \leq 0; \\ \qquad \cup ?v_{\max} - v \geq \texttt{margin}); a = *; -B \leq a \leq A;) \\ \texttt{margin} \equiv ep * A \\ dyn \equiv t := 0; x' = v, v' = a, t' = 1 \& v \geq 0 \wedge t \leq ep \\ \texttt{guar} \equiv v \leq v_{\max} \end{cases}$
$\tau = \texttt{action}$
$\Phi = \{v_s \leq v_{\max} \ (2.7\,\mathrm{m\,s^{-1}})\}$

Table 3: Attributes for skill *Control longitudinal dynamics* (s_6).

5.3 Results

All measurements were conducted on an Intel i7-6600U CPU @ 2.60GHz with 12 GB RAM and Z3 [12] in version 4.6.0 was used as the underlying solver for KEYMAERA X in version 4.7.3.

RQ-1: How does the skill-based methodology compare to monolithic modeling and verification? We modeled the overall behavior of $G_1 \circ G_2$ as a monolithic model (i.e., following the hard shoulder and following a leading vehicle in concert) as described in Section 4.2. As mentioned before, the skill-based approach has a high reuse potential. Each skill needs to be verified only once, and the verification results can be reused in other skill graphs (cf. Theorem 1). While in case of a change of parameters or an update of control algorithms the monolithic model has to be re-modeled and re-verified completely, a change impact analysis identifying only affected skills may reduce the re-verification effort even further for the compositional approach. Importantly, skill s_{13} and the monolithic model could only be verified interactively, whereas skills s_1, s_{14}, and s_6 were verified fully automatically with the automatic proof search of KEYMAERA X. Chances of an automatic re-verification are thus higher with the skill-based methodology.

An important hypothesis of ours is that skill-based verification is more effective in discovering modeling defects compared to a monolithic model. To get some insights into this hypothesis, we developed three initial experiments to render the verification attempt invalid. We (1) changed the safety guarantee of skills, (2) changed the control algorithm of skills, and (3) did a combination of both and compared these results to the same changes performed in the monolithic model. Following our methodology helped to trace and resolve defects effectively with respect to this case study, whereas identifying multiple modeling defects in the monolithic model became quickly intractable. During the resolution of Scenario 3, re-verification had to be performed several times for the monolithic model (i.e., resolving one conflict at a time), which emphasizes the advantage of our compositional approach over the monolithic modeling. However, we do not want to overclaim the importance of our insights, as more complex experiments

	Verified Skill				Proof steps					
	s_1	s_6	s_{13}	s_{14}	s_1	s_6	s_{13}	s_{14}	Σ	Σ_{reuse}
G_1	✓	✓			4,746	3,769			8,515	8,515
G_2		✓	✓	✓		3,769	16,924	7,223	27,916	24,147
$G_1 \circ G_2$	✓	✓	✓	✓	4,746	3,769	16,924	7,223	32,662	0*
Σ_{total}									**69,093**	**32,662**

*No re-verification of skills with Theorem 1

Table 4: Comparison of the verification effort for skill-based compositional verification.

and a larger evaluation have to be conducted to adequately test whether our hypothesis is significant.

RQ-2: To what extent can skill-based compositional verification reduce the verification effort? To answer RQ-2, we measured the verification effort in proof steps for each of the three skills mentioned before per skill graph. In Table 4, we summarize the results. Column *Verified Skill* describes which skill is part of which skill graph and column *Proof steps* compares the number of proof steps needed for each skill individually. A common scenario is to model and verify each maneuver individually (i.e., each skill graph). The total verification effort Σ_{total} would then cumulate to 69,093 proof steps. Instead, our skill-based approach allows to reuse verification results for skill s_6 in skill graph G_2 and per Theorem 1 even the verification results for all skills in skill graph $G_1 \circ G_2$. Entries highlighted in gray indicate that the respective skill could be reused instead of re-verification. The compositional approach needs approximately 53% less proof steps in our case study.

6   Related Work

Skill Graphs. Maurer [23] pioneered the concept of skills by introducing so-called *abilities* in vehicle guidance systems. Abilities are similar to skills, as they concisely describe the capabilites of a vehicle, and are intended to be permanently monitored at run-time to enforce safety mechanics. Reschka et al. [32, 33] introduced skill graphs informally in their work giving definitions for skills and abilities in relation to autonomous vehicles. Nolte et al. [26] built upon this approach by employing the informal concept of skill graphs for the development of self-aware automated road vehicles. We adopted their case study to evaluate our skill-based verification approach.

Hybrid Systems and Verification of Cyber-Physical Systems. Hybrid systems [3] are a generalization of timed automata [4] and well-suited for modeling and verifying cyber-physical systems. Krishna et al. [20] show that using hybrid automata to model and verify cyber-physical systems is, in principle, feasible. Typically, hybrid systems are verified employing reachability analyses and model checking [2, 21, 22, 35]. However, these technqiues are not compositional in general (i.e., modular verification of individual parts to establish correctness of the entire systems is not possible). It is also not intended to generate and reuse proofs to increase trust in the system's correctness, as, for instance, possible with theorem proving. To address this issue, we built our methodology upon the notion of *hybrid programs* [30] and the theorem prover KEYMAERA X [14], which helped us to also satisfy the important property of compositionality in the modeling and formal verification of hybrid systems. We further extend this concept with skill graphs by modularizing the verification of complex driving tasks, such that the verification of the entire behavior is reduced to simpler sub-tasks and compatibility checks.

Finally, there exists a seamless connection to the work conducted by Müller et al. [24], who present a compositional component-based approach for the verification of hybrid systems based on hybrid programs. Skill graphs provide an abstract and organized view of the system and are applied (1) in the verification and validation phase of the *requirements analysis* and (2) the early stages of the *design phase*. Subsequently, a skill may be implemented by a set of multiple interacting components to take more necessary specifics into account, such as communication protocols and resource consumption. To conclude, the process of refining skill graphs including their safety requirements to formally specified component-based systems exhibits a high level of quality assurance at the level of both, requirement engineers and software architects.

7 Conclusion and Future Work

In this work, we proposed skill-based verification of cyber-physical systems with the notion of skill graphs that (1) encourages the modular development of small and reusable actions in isolation, and (2) enables the identification of poorly defined requirements in early software development processes by considering formal verification of hybrid systems. We provide the first formalization of skill graphs, showed how skill graphs and hybrid programs can be combined, and also introduced a proved notion of compositionality for skills. The investigated case study on a *vehicle follow mode* showcases that the compositionality property of skill graphs is important for scaling, as the verification effort is reduced by more than 53%. Compositionality is particularly important for model and software evolution, as costly re-verification of a skill's requirement can be minimized.

For the future, we want to enable the composition of skills with dissimilar hybrid programs, for which the theoretical groundwork partially exists. Moreover, our current focus is on the integration of skill graphs into software engineering practices for cyber-physical systems to amplify the utilization of formal methods from the start of new software projects.

Acknowledgements. We are grateful to Enis Belli and Arne Windeler for their help with the implementation of SKEDITOR. This work was supported by the DFG (German Research Foundation) under the Researcher Unit FOR1800: Controlling Concurrent Change (CCC).

References

1. Ahrendt, W., Beckert, B., Bubel, R., Hähnle, R., Schmitt, P.H., Ulbrich, M.: Deductive Software Verification–The KeY Book: From Theory to Practice. Springer (2016)
2. Alur, R.: Formal Verification of Hybrid Systems. In: Embedded Software (EMSOFT), 2011 Proceedings of the International Conference on. pp. 273–278. IEEE (2011)
3. Alur, R., Courcoubetis, C., Henzinger, T.A., Ho, P.H.: Hybrid Automata: An Algorithmic Approach to the Specification and Verification of Hybrid Systems. In: Hybrid systems, pp. 209–229. Springer (1993)
4. Alur, R., Dill, D.L.: A Theory of Timed Automata. Theoretical computer science 126(2), 183–235 (1994)
5. Alur, R., Henzinger, T.A., Sontag, E.D.: Hybrid Systems III: Verification and Control, vol. 3. Springer Science & Business Media (1996)
6. Baheti, R., Gill, H.: Cyber-physical Systems. The impact of control technology 12(1), 161–166 (2011)
7. Barnett, M., Fähndrich, M., Leino, K.R.M., Müller, P., Schulte, W., Venter, H.: Specification and Verification: The Spec# Experience. Communications of the ACM 54, 81–91 (Jun 2011)
8. Batory, D., Sarvela, J.N., Rauschmayer, A.: Scaling Step-Wise Refinement. IEEE Transactions on Software Engineering (TSE) 30(6), 355–371 (2004)
9. Broy, M.: Yesterday, Today, and Tomorrow: 50 Years of Software Engineering. IEEE Software 35(5), 38–43 (2018)
10. Burdy, L., Cheon, Y., Cok, D.R., Ernst, M.D., Kiniry, J., Leavens, G.T., Leino, K.R.M., Poll, E.: An Overview of JML Tools and Applications 7(3), 212–232 (Jun 2005)
11. Cuijpers, P.J.L., Reniers, M.A.: Hybrid Process Algebra. The Journal of Logic and Algebraic Programming 62(2), 191–245 (2005)
12. De Moura, L., Bjørner, N.: Z3: An Efficient SMT Solver. In: Proceedings of the International Conference on Tools and Algorithms for the Construction and Analysis of Systems. pp. 337–340. Springer (2008)
13. Foundation, T.E.: Graphiti - a Graphical Tooling Infrastructure, [Available at https://www.eclipse.org/graphiti/; accessed 22-January-2018
14. Fulton, N., Mitsch, S., Quesel, J.D., Völp, M., Platzer, A.: KeYmaera X: An Axiomatic Tactical Theorem Prover for Hybrid Systems. In: International Conference on Automated Deduction. pp. 527–538. Springer (2015)
15. Garcia, A., Sant'Anna, C., Chavez, C., da Silva, V.T., de Lucena, C.J., von Staa, A.: Separation of Concerns in Multi-agent Systems: An Empirical Study. In: International Workshop on Software Engineering for Large-Scale Multi-agent Systems. pp. 49–72. Springer (2003)
16. Gleirscher, M., Foster, S., Woodcock, J.: Opportunities for Integrated Formal Methods. CoRR abs/1812.10103 (2018), http://arxiv.org/abs/1812.10103
17. Gleirscher, M., Marmsoler, D.: Formal Methods: Oversold? Underused? A Survey. arXiv preprint arXiv:1812.08815 (2018)
18. Hatcliff, J., Leavens, G.T., Leino, K.R.M., Müller, P., Parkinson, M.: Behavioral Interface Specification Languages 44(3), 16:1–16:58 (Jun 2012)
19. Henzinger, T.A.: The Theory of Hybrid Automata. In: Verification of Digital and Hybrid Systems, pp. 265–292. Springer (2000)

20. Krishna, S.N., Trivedi, A.: Hybrid Automata for Formal Modeling and Verification of Cyber-Physical Systems (Mar 2015)
21. Lunze, J., Lamnabhi-Lagarrigue, F.: Handbook of Hybrid Systems Control: Theory, Tools, Applications. Cambridge University Press (2009)
22. Maler, O.: Algorithmic Verification of Continuous and Hybrid Systems. arXiv preprint arXiv:1403.0952 (2014)
23. Maurer, M.: Flexible Automatisierung von Straßenfahrzeugen mit Rechnersehen (2000)
24. Müller, A., Mitsch, S., Retschitzegger, W., Schwinger, W., Platzer, A.: Tactical Contract Composition for Hybrid System Component Verification. International Journal on Software Tools for Technology Transfer **20**(6), 615–643 (2018)
25. Nerode, A., Kohn, W.: Models for Hybrid Systems: Automata, Topologies, Controllability, Observability. In: Hybrid systems, pp. 317–356. Springer (1993)
26. Nolte, M., Bagschik, G., Jatzkowski, I., Stolte, T., Reschka, A., Maurer, M.: Towards a Skill-and Ability-based Development Process for Self-aware Automated Road Vehicles. In: Intelligent Transportation Systems (ITSC), 2017 IEEE 20th International Conference on. pp. 1–6. IEEE (2017)
27. Parnas, D.L.: On the Criteria to be used in Decomposing Systems into Modules. Communications of the ACM **15**(12), 1053–1058 (Dec 1972). https://doi.org/10.1145/361598.361623
28. Platzer, A.: Differential Dynamic Logic for Hybrid Systems. Journal of Automated Reasoning **41**(2), 143–189 (2008)
29. Platzer, A.: Logics of Dynamical Systems. In: Proceedings of the 2012 27th Annual IEEE/ACM Symposium on Logic in Computer Science. pp. 13–24. IEEE Computer Society (2012)
30. Platzer, A.: The Complete Proof Theory of Hybrid Systems. In: Proceedings of the 2012 27th Annual IEEE/ACM Symposium on Logic in Computer Science. pp. 541–550. IEEE Computer Society (2012)
31. Platzer, A.: A Complete Uniform Substitution Calculus for Differential Dynamic Logic. Journal of Automated Reasoning **59**(2), 219–265 (2017)
32. Reschka, A.: Fertigkeiten- und Fähigkeitengraphen als Grundlage des sicheren Betriebs von automatisierten Fahrzeugen im öffentlichen Straßenverkehr in städtischer Umgebung. Ph.D. thesis (Jul 2017)
33. Reschka, A., Bagschik, G., Ulbrich, S., Nolte, M., Maurer, M.: Ability and Skill Graphs for System Modeling, Online Monitoring, and Decision Support for Vehicle Guidance Systems. In: Intelligent Vehicles Symposium (IV), 2015 IEEE. pp. 933–939. IEEE (2015)
34. Schumann, J.M.: Automated Theorem Proving in Software Engineering. Springer Science & Business Media (2001)
35. Tabuada, P.: Verification and Control of Hybrid Systems: A Symbolic Approach. Springer Science & Business Media (2009)
36. Tarr, P., Ossher, H., Harrison, W., Sutton, Jr., S.M.: N Degrees of Separation: Multi-Dimensional Separation of Concerns. In: Proceedings of the International Conference on Software Engineering (ICSE). pp. 107–119. ACM (1999)
37. Ulbrich, S., Reschka, A., Rieken, J., Ernst, S., Bagschik, G., Dierkes, F., Nolte, M., Maurer, M.: Towards a Functional System Architecture for Automated Vehicles. arXiv preprint arXiv:1703.08557 (2017)

Generating Large EMF Models Efficiently
A Rule-Based, Configurable Approach[*]

Nebras Nassar[1]([⊠])[iD], Jens Kosiol[1][iD], Timo Kehrer[2][iD], and Gabriele Taentzer[1][iD]

[1] Philipps-Universität Marburg, Marburg, Germany
{nassarn,kosiolje,taentzer}@informatik.uni-marburg.de
[2] Humboldt-Universität zu Berlin, Berlin, Germany
timo.kehrer@informatik.hu-berlin.de

Abstract. There is a growing need for the automated generation of instance models to evaluate model-driven engineering techniques. Depending on a chosen application scenario, a model generator has to fulfill different requirements: As a modeling language is usually defined by a meta-model, all generated models are expected to *conform to their meta-models*. For performance tests of model-driven engineering techniques, the efficient generation of *large* models should be supported. When generating several models, the resulting set of models should show some *diversity*. *Interactive model generation* may help in producing relevant models. In this paper, we present a rule-based, configurable approach to automate model generation which addresses the stated requirements. Our model generator produces valid instance models of meta-models with multiplicities conforming to the Eclipse Modeling Framework (EMF). An evaluation of the model generator shows that large EMF models (with up to half a million elements) can be produced. Since the model generation is rule-based, it can be configured beforehand or during the generation process to produce sets of models that are diverse to a certain extent.

Keywords: Model generation · Model transformation · Eclipse Modeling Framework (EMF)

1 Introduction

The need for the automated generation of instance models grows with the steady increase of domains and topics to which model-driven engineering (MDE) is applied. In particular, there is a growing need for large instances of a given meta-model [14,26]. As most of the available MDE tools are based on the Eclipse Modeling Framework (EMF) [34], instances should be conformant to EMF.

Depending on the chosen application scenario, a model generator has to fulfill different requirements: As a modeling language is usually defined by a meta-model, all generated models are expected to *conform to their meta-models*. For

---

[*] This work was partially funded by the German Research Foundation (DFG), projects *Generating Development Environments for Modeling Languages (TA294/13-2)* and *Triple Graph Grammars (TGG) 2.0 (TA294/17-1)*.

H. Wehrheim and J. Cabot (Eds.): FASE 2020, LNCS 12076, pp. 224–244, 2020.
https://doi.org/10.1007/978-3-030-45234-6_11

performance tests of model-driven engineering techniques, the efficient generation of *large* models should be supported. When several models are generated,
they should show some diversity. *Interactive model generation* may help in producing relevant models. While there are several tools and approaches to instance
model generation in the literature, e.g. [15,16,30,32,36], we are not aware of any
tool satisfying all the requirements stated above. Two extreme approaches are
the following: The approach in [16] is very fast but does not address any modeling framework and provides very few guarantees concerning the properties of
the generated output models. As EMF has developed to the de-facto standard
for modeling in MDE, respecting the EMF constraints is crucial to guarantee
the usability of the resulting models in practice for processing them by other
tools, e.g., for opening them in standard editors. On the contrary, solver-based
approaches such as [15,32,36] provide high guarantees by generating instance
models that even conform to additional well-formedness constraints (expressed
in, e.g., OCL [20]), but they suffer from severe scalability issues.

We suggest finding a good trade-off between having a scalable generation
process for models and generating well-formed models. In this paper, we propose a rule-based approach to the generation of models which has the following
distinguishing features: (i) To guarantee interchangeability, generated models
conform to the standards of EMF. In particular, this means that the containment structure of a generated model forms a tree. (ii) Generated models exhibit
a basic consistency in the sense that they conform to the structure and the multiplicities specified by the meta-model. (iii) The generation of models can be
configured to obtain models that are diverse to a certain extent. (iv) The implementation is efficient in the sense that instance models with several hundred
thousand elements can be generated. (v) The approach is meta-model agnostic
and customizable to a given domain-specific modeling language (DSML) in a
fully automated way. (vi) It is possible to generate models in a batch mode or
interactively to somewhat guide the generation process towards relevant models. User interaction includes the setting of seed models as well as interactively
choosing between alternative generation strategies.

Our rule-based approach to model generation consists of two main tasks:
(1) The meta-model of a given modeling language is translated into a rule-
based model transformation system (MTS) containing rules for model generation. (2) These rules are consecutively applied to generate instance models. This
generation process may be further configured by the user. Especially, a potentially inconsistent model may be used as a seed for generating valid models.

Our approach is implemented in two Eclipse plug-ins: A meta-tool, called
Meta2GR, automatically derives the MTS from a given meta-model. A second
plug-in, called *EMF Model Generator*, is automatically configured with the resulting MTS. A modeler uses the configured model generator, which takes additional user specifications and an optional seed EMF model as inputs and generates a valid EMF model. We argue for the soundness of our approach and
evaluate its scalability by generating large, valid EMF models (up to half a mil-

lion elements). Furthermore, we show how to generate a set of models that are diverse to some extent.

2 Related Work

In our discussion of related work, we focus on generic approaches and discern between *solver-based*, *tableaux-based* and *rule-based* generic approaches. We omit *language-* and *application-specific approaches* (like, e.g. [7,10]).

2.1 Solver-Based Approaches

Solver-based approaches generate models by (i) translating a meta-model into a logical formula, (ii) using an off-the-shelf solver to find possible solutions, and (iii) translating back the found solutions into instances of the meta-model. In most cases, solver-based approaches are capable of generating models that respect well-formedness constraints such as OCL constraints since these can be translated into the logical formula as well. The approaches presented in [15,32,36] use Alloy [12] for this purpose. Although we do not see any general limitation for them to be applied to arbitrary meta-models, the translations to Alloy presented in [15,36] target dedicated domain-specific languages. The language-independent translation presented by Sen et al. [32] is not fully automated. Performed evaluations show that the scalability of using an off-the-shelf solver is limited to pretty small models.

2.2 A Tableaux-Based Approach

Schneider et al. [27] present an automated approach for the generation of symbolic attributed typed graphs fulfilling a given set of first-order constraints. The approach is based on a tableaux calculus for graph constraints. It produces minimal symbolic models encoding (infinitely) many instances that fulfill the set of constraints. While this is highly desirable to get an overview of possible instance structures, retrieving large graphs from symbolic instances is not directly supported. Moreover, the work does not aim at EMF; it is also not possible to add the EMF constraints as not all of them are first-order. The authors extend their work in [28] to be able to also repair given instances. This model repair can be used to support the generation of instances from a given seed model. The applied repair strategy does not incorporate any deletions of model elements.

2.3 Rule-Based Approaches

Ehrig et al. [9] present an approach for converting type graphs with restricted multiplicity constraints into instance-generating graph grammars. Taentzer generalizes that approach in [37] to arbitrary multiplicity constraints. Both approaches are presented for typed graphs, which means that containment edge types and other EMF constraints are not considered. Moreover, there is no implementation of these approaches.

Radke et al. [24] present a translation of OCL constraints to graph constraints which can be integrated as application conditions into a given set of transformation rules [17]. The resulting rules guarantee validity w.r.t. these constraints but might be rendered inapplicable. The work is motivated by instance generation; however, no dedicated algorithm is presented.

Another grammar-based approach is presented by Mougenot et al. [16]. By reducing models to their containment structure, a tree grammar is derived from that meta-model projection. For a given size (representing the number of nodes), the method is capable of uniformly generating all tree structures of that size. Similarly, the tool *EMF random instantiator* [11] considers containment edges only. While both approaches are highly efficient, reducing models to their containment structure is a severe oversimplification in practice.

The frameworks *RandomEMF* presented by Scheidgen [26] and *EMG* presented by Popoola et al. [23] aid users to manually specify a generator that automatically generates models. These frameworks do not offer any help, however, to ensure that the generated models conform to the meta-model and that the generated models satisfy the required constraints.

The SiDiff model generator (SMG) has been proposed by Pietsch et al. [22]. It takes an existing model as input and manipulates it by applying model editing operations, configured by a stochastic controller. On the meta-level, the SMG was integrated into the approach and tool presented by Kehrer et al. [13,25], which generates a complete set of consistency-preserving edit operations for a given meta-model. It supports meta-models with somewhat restricted multiplicities, however. Generated edit operations can be applied to valid models only. Its stochastic controller has been designed to generate sequences of models that mimic realistic model histories [38]. The generated models are, on purpose, very similar to each other, i.e. they lack diversity.

2.4   A Hybrid Approach

A hybrid approach is implemented within the VIATRA Solver [29,30]: Rules are used to generate an instance model from scratch or a seed model. A solver is used to guarantee validity concerning additional well-formedness constraints. During the generation process, a partial model is extended using rules. This partial model is continuously evaluated w.r.t. the validity of these constraints using a 3-valued logic [31]. By under-approximation, the search space is pruned as soon as the partial model cannot be refined into a valid model. The evaluation of constraints is performed with a specifically developed solver or an off-the-shelf one. All resulting instance models fulfill the additional constraints and conform to EMF. Moreover, the VIATRA Solver has been investigated successfully for generating diverse and realistic models. While experimental results indicate that the approach is 1–2 orders of magnitude better than existing approaches using Alloy, the authors also mention that the scalability of their approach is not yet sufficient [30,29].

Table 1. Summary of selected generic approaches to model generation w.r.t. important characteristics we aim at in this paper.

Category	Approach	Input		Output		Algorithm		
		impl.	ex. seed	EMF	wf	config.	interact.	scal.
Solver	Sen et al. [32]	+	−	o	+++	−	−	−
Tableaux	Schneider et al. [27,28]	+	o	−	+++	−	−	?
Rule-based	Taentzer [37]	−	−	−	++	o	+	?
	Mougenot et al. [16]	o	−	o	+	o	−	+
	Pietsch et al. [22]	+	o	+	+	+	+	o
Hybrid	Semeráth et al. [30]	+	o	+	+++	+	−	o
Rule-based	Our approach	+	+	+	++	+	+	+

2.5 Need for Further Research

We summarize the related work through selected approaches from all categories in Table 1 w.r.t. important characteristics. First, we indicate whether the approach is implemented in a tool (column 1). Second, we are interested in manipulating an existing seed model (column 2), e.g., for the sake of generating model evolution scenarios. Here, o indicates that only special kinds of seeds are possible. Third, concerning the consistency level of generated output models, we are interested in the conformance with EMF (column 3) and additional well-formedness constraints, including multiplicities (column 4). Here, + indicates partly and ++ full support of multiplicity constraints, whereas + + + means support of more general well-formedness constraints. Fourth, we are interested in the properties of the generation algorithm itself, which should be configurable (column 5), offer interaction possibilities (column 6), and be scalable (column 7) in order to support the generation of diverse and large instances, respectively.

None of the generic approaches to model generation fully meets all criteria. Given a meta-model with multiplicities as the only well-formedness constraints, we are heading towards a model generator that supports all quality attributes.

3   Running Example and Preliminaries

This section presents our running example and preliminaries. After introducing the running example, we recall the Eclipse Modeling Framework (EMF), rule-based model transformation and a rule-based approach to model repair that we utilize for our approach to instance generation.

3.1   Running Example

As running example we use an excerpt of the GraphML meta-model [3] as shown in Fig. 1. GraphML [6] is a file format for different kinds of graphs; it separates

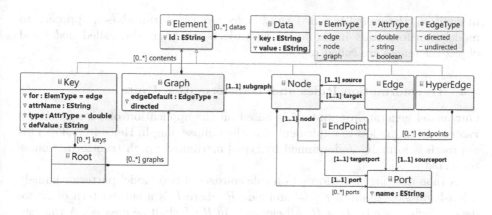

Fig. 1. Excerpt of the GraphML meta-model

the graph structure from additional data. We use this example to illustrate how
our rule-based approach generates instances from a given meta-model.

3.2 The Eclipse Modeling Framework

The Eclipse Modeling Framework (EMF) [34] has evolved into a de-facto standard technology for defining models and modeling languages. In EMF, meta-
models are defined using Ecore, an implementation of the OMG's EMOF standard [21]. Meta-models in Ecore prescribe the structures that instance models of
the modeled domain should exhibit. Concepts known from UML class diagrams
are used, namely the classification of objects and their attributes, references to
objects, and constraints on object structures. References may be *opposite* to each
other and constrained by *multiplicities*. A specific kind of references are *containments*. The conformance of an instance model to a meta-model can formally be
expressed using typed attributed graphs with inheritance [4]. EMF models have
to fulfill the following constraints:

- At-most-one-container: Each object must not have more than one container.
- No-containment-cycles: Cycles of containments must not occur.
- No-parallel-edges: There are no two references of the same type from the same
  source to the same target object.
- All-opposite-edges: If reference types $t1$ and $t2$ are opposite to each other: For
  each reference of type $t1$, there has to be a reference of type $t2$ linking the
  same objects in the opposite direction.
- Rootedness (optional): There is an object, called *root object*, that contains all
  other objects of a model directly or transitively.

In the sequel, we use the terms *EMF model* and *instance model* interchangeably.
Each model conforming to its meta-model and fulfilling the EMF constraints
listed above is called *EMF model*. If the meta-model's multiplicities are fulfilled

in addition, the model is called *valid*. Since we use a graph-based approach to model transformation in the following, objects are often also called *nodes* and object references are called *edges*.

3.3 Transformation Rules and Transformation Units

Our model generation approach is based on the application of *transformation rules* to EMF models as implemented in the Eclipse plug-in Henshin [1,35]. This approach is formally underpinned by typed attributed graph transformation as presented in [4].

A (non-deleting) transformation rule consists of two model patterns, namely a left-hand side L and a right-hand side R where L is a sub-pattern of R; we denote such a rule by $L \Rightarrow R$. All elements in $R \setminus L$ shall be created. A rule can be equipped with *negative application conditions* (NACs) [8]. Each NAC N is an additional pattern that includes L. All elements in $N \setminus L$ are forbidden to exist. An application of a transformation rule to a model M amounts to finding the pattern L in M and, if such a *match* is found, creating a copy of $R \setminus L$ there. A rule is applicable at a match only if this match cannot be extended to a match for any of the NACs.

In Henshin, rules are specified in an integrated form where elements are annotated and colored according to their roles. While a created element is depicted in green, a forbidden element is shown in blue. Besides, it may be equipped with the name of the NAC it belongs to for distinguishing several NACs. For example, the rule *insert_additionalEdge_targetport* in Fig. 7 matches nodes of types Edge and Port and inserts an edge of type targetport between them but only if such an edge does not already exist and the selected Edge does not already refer to another Port.

To construct more complex transformations in Henshin, rules may be composed in *(transformation) units*. Units may have parameters that can be passed to contained units or rules. A '?' indicates that the parameter may be randomly chosen. We sketch the semantics of those units which we use in the following. Note that each rule is already considered as a unit.

- An independent unit comprises an arbitrary number of sub-units that are checked for applicability in a non-deterministic order. One applicable unit is executed.
- A loop unit comprises one sub-unit and executes it as often as possible.
- A conditional unit comprises either two or three sub-units specifying the if-unit, the then-unit, and optionally, the else-unit. If the if-unit is executed successfully, the then-unit is executed. Otherwise, if defined, the else-unit is executed.
- A sequential unit comprises an arbitrary number of sub-units that are executed in the given order. If a sub-unit is not applicable, it is skipped and the execution continues with the next sub-unit.
- A priority unit comprises an arbitrary number of sub-units that are checked for applicability in the defined order. If a sub-unit is executed successfully, the check and execution of the following sub-units are skipped.

3.4   EMF Repair

Our generation process of instance models uses the repair process for EMF instance models presented in [19]. The basic approach is to derive repair rules from a given meta-model. The derived rules allow to first *trim* the model such that no upper bound is violated any longer. Subsequently, it *completes* the model by adding nodes and edges until no lower bound is violated. The rules are designed such that, during the completion phase, no upper bound violation is introduced and that both phases terminate only if no violation of multiplicities occurs any longer. We formally proved these properties in [18]. While this process does not necessarily terminate, its termination has been proven for instance models of *fully finitely instantiable* meta-models. A meta-model is called *fully finitely instantiable* (f.f.i.) if, for every given finite EMF-model M that instantiates it and respects upper bounds but may violate lower bounds, there exists a finite and valid EMF-model M' such that M is a submodel of M'.

4   Rule-Based Instance Generation

We start this section with an overview of our approach to the generation of valid EMF models. Thereafter, we present the kinds of generation rules that are derived from a given meta-model, introduce four parametrization strategies for generation processes, and show possibilities of user-interaction. Finally, we discuss the limitations of our generation approach and the formal guarantees that have been shown.

4.1   Overall Approach

Our overall approach to instance generation is depicted in Fig. 2. The fundamental idea behind our approach is to base model generation as far as possible on rule-based model repair using the tool EMF Repair [19]. All rules needed to perform model generation steps are automatically derived from the given meta-model by the meta-tool *Meta2GR*. If a non-empty seed model is given, the model generation process starts with checking it for upper bound violations and potentially trimming it using EMF Repair (*model trimming*). Thereafter, the EMF model is extended with object nodes and references without violating upper bounds using the rules derived by Meta2GR (*model increase*). The resulting model shall meet user specifications w.r.t. its size which will be discussed in more detail in Sect. 4.3 below. In the next step, the EMF model is completed to a valid EMF model, again using EMF Repair (*model completion*). As this repair process adds elements only, the user specifications are still met by the resulting model. Moreover, the result is guaranteed to be a valid EMF model [18]. EMF Repair is also used to set attribute values, either randomly or using user input which is provided in a JSON-file.

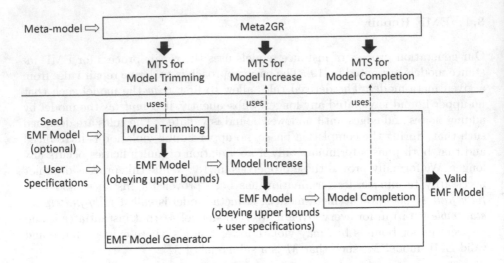

Fig. 2. Rule-based EMF Model Generator

4.2 Generated Rules for Model Generation

Given a meta-model, different kinds of rules are derived for generating EMF models. They are listed in Table 2. The derived rules are needed to perform the following tasks: (i) creation of nodes, (ii) insertion of non-containment edges, and (iii) checking for the existence of source or target nodes for an edge of a certain type. All rules that create model elements (i.e., the rules of kinds (i) and (ii)) are generated with NACs to not introduce upper bound violations during generation. Moreover, they all are *consistent transformation rules* in the sense of [4]. This means that they preserve consistency w.r.t. the EMF constraints including rootedness (compare [4, Theorems 1 and 2]). For example, our rules cannot introduce containment cycles or parallel edges by design.

Table 2. Overview of rule kinds used for model generation

Role	Kind	Semantics
Create node	Additional-node-creation rules	Create a node of a certain type and insert it into one of its direct containers
	Transitive-node-creation rules	Create a node of a certain type and insert it into one of its transitive containers
Create edge	Additional-edge-creation rules	Create an edge of non-containment type between two nodes
Check edge	Additional-edge-checking rules	Check if possible source and target nodes exist for an edge of a certain type

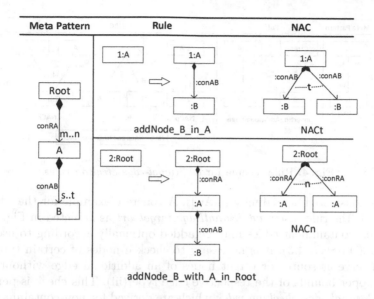

Fig. 3. Rule schema for *transitive-node-creation rules* (of length 2)

Node creation (i) is performed by two sets of rules, *additional-node-creation rules* and *transitive-node-creation rules*. The latter ones are described as follows: For every concrete node type in the meta-model, every possible incoming path over containment edges is computed such that each containment type occurs maximally once. For each such path, a rule is derived that matches the node where this path starts and creates the rest of this path. Each rule is equipped with a NAC ensuring that no upper bound violation can be introduced. An example schema of length 2 for this kind of rule is depicted in Fig. 3. The lower part of Fig. 6 depicts all *transitive-node-creation rules* that are derived for the type port. Only one rule is equipped with a NAC as the edge type subgraph is the only one with an upper bound (of 1). In EMF, if a containment edge has an opposite edge, the upper bound of the opposite edge must be 1. If a containment edge is created, the opposite edge is created automatically. Therefore, we do not represent it here. *Additional-node-creation rules* are *transitive-node-creation rules* of length 1. We derive both kinds of rules for different parametrizations of our generation algorithm which are introduced in Sect. 4.3. The rule *add_in_Node_a_Port* in Fig. 6 is an example derived for the containment edge type ports. It does not have a NAC since the upper bound of ports is unlimited.

To create non-containment edges (ii), *additional-edge-creation rules* are generated. The general schema for these kinds of rules is depicted in Fig. 4. For each non-containment edge type, a rule is derived that matches the source and the target nodes suitable to this edge type and creates an edge of the corresponding type. Again, a NAC prevents that an upper bound is violated (NACn). A second NAC prevents that parallel edges are introduced (NACp). If the given edge type has an opposite edge type, the opposite edge is created as well and its upper

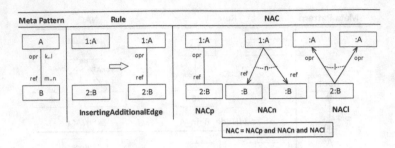

Fig. 4. Rule schema for *additional-edge-creation rules*

bound is considered accordingly (NACl). A concrete example for the edge type targetport is the rule *insert_additionalEdge_targetport* as depicted in Fig. 7.

As non-containment edges may be added optionally according to user specifications (in Sect. 4.3), it is necessary to check if nodes of certain types exist and can serve as source or target nodes of an additional edge without violating the upper bounds of the respective edge type (iii). This check is performed with *additional-edge-checking rules* which are derived for non-containment edge types. The general schema is depicted in Fig. 5. Such a rule is applicable if and only if there exists a source node where the upper bound of the edge type is not yet reached. The same kind of rule is derived for the target node type as well. The rule *check_proper_sourceNode_for_targetport* in Fig. 7 is a concrete example for the edge type targetport.

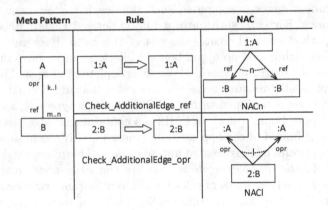

Fig. 5. Rule schema for *additional-edge-checking rules*

4.3   Generation Strategies: Parameterization

Since we use a rule-based approach, the model generator can be parameterized w.r.t. a given user specification. In the following, we present four strategies for generating models w.r.t. user specifications; they serve to specify the model increase phase of the generation process. The models resulting from this phase conform to EMF and meet the user specification but may violate lower bounds.

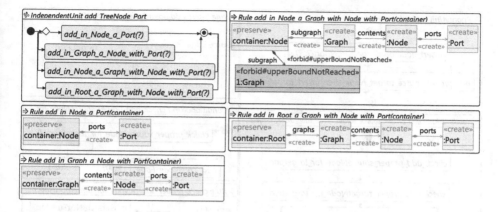

Fig. 6. Independent unit for randomly creating a containment tree containing a fixed number of nodes of type Port

They are used as input for the model repair algorithm of EMF repair to obtain a valid EMF model. The user may (1) specify the number of elements that is to be created *minimally*, (2) specify a node type and the number of nodes of this type that is to be created *minimally*, (3) specify an edge type and the number of edges of this type that is to be created *minimally*, or (4) combine the above-mentioned strategies sequentially in arbitrary order. If the user has not specified any model as a seed, the generation is initialized by creating a root node.

Adding elements of arbitrary types. In this strategy, the user specifies the minimum of model elements (i.e., nodes and edges) to be created. The idea behind this strategy is to randomly execute a set of rules for adding nodes and edges of arbitrary types without violating the corresponding upper bounds and the EMF constraints. Hence, all rules of kinds *additional-node-creation* and *additional-edge-insertion* are collected into an independent unit which is applied as often as the user specification requires. While the independent unit is implemented in Henshin using a uniform distribution, this strategy may also be performed using other distributions by, e.g., leveraging a stochastic controller [38].

Adding nodes of a specific type. In this strategy, the user specifies a node type and the minimum number of nodes of this type that shall be created. This strategy is implemented as an independent unit containing all *transitive-node-creation rules* for the specified node type being applied as often as the user has specified. An example unit for the node type Port is given in Fig. 6.

Adding edges of a specific type. In this strategy, the user specifies a (non-containment) edge type and the minimum number of edges that shall be created of this type. This strategy is similar to the previous one, thus its basis is a unit that contains the *additional-edge creation rule* for the specified type. If this rule is not applicable, however, a source or a target node (or both) for an additional edge of that type is missing. The *additional-edge-checking rules* for this edge type are used to detect such situations. Then, corresponding *transitive-node-creation rules* for the type of the missing node are used to create the missing source

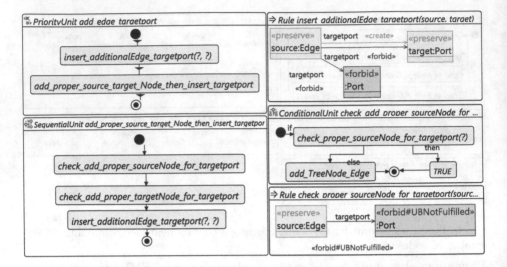

Fig. 7. Units for inserting a fixed number of edges of type targetport

and/or target node(s). This strategy is implemented as a priority unit where the first contained unit is the *additional-edge-insertion rule*. Its second contained unit is a sequential one with two conditional units checking for missing source or target nodes, respectively, and creating corresponding nodes if needed.

Figure 7 presents a priority unit using this strategy at the example of the targetport-edge. The first level contains the rule *insert_additionalEdge....* The second level is the sequential unit *add_proper_source_target_Node...*: The conditional unit *check_add_proper_sourceNode...* uses the rule *check_proper_sourceNode...* in the if-statement. The then-statement is set to true whereas the else-statement is configured with a priority unit *add_treeNode_Edge* which adds an Edge-node respecting upper bounds and the EMF constraints. The conditional unit adding a missing target node is defined analogously.

Sequential combination of strategies. As our approach allows for an arbitrary seed model as input, the result of applying one strategy can be used as input for applying the second one. This allows for arbitrary sequential combinations of strategies.

4.4   User Interaction

Since our approach is rule-based, it is also possible to allow for user interaction. Instead of random rule applications at random matches, the available rules and matches can be presented to the user for selecting at which match a rule has to be applied and how many times. That is promising for generating different tree structures of various weights. While it may not desirable to completely generate large models in such a way, a hybrid strategy can be applied to utilize the selection process, e.g., by employing heuristic data. EMF Repair already supports this kind of user interaction.

4.5   Limitations and Formal Guarantees

Limitations. A user may only specify the *minimum* number of desired elements; the specification of a maximum number is not yet supported within our approach. Although the generation process applies the respective rules exactly as often as specified during the model increase phase, some of the rules create more than one element and additional model elements may be created to repair violations of lower bounds during the consecutive model repair. Moreover, we cannot guarantee that the user specification is fully met since necessary rules may not be applicable as often as specified and backtracking is not used. Even if the specification could be met in principle, it may happen that the specific selection, order, and matches of rules do not succeed as they are randomly chosen in the current version of the approach. By counting created elements, it can always be decided whether a user specification has been met, and thus, the user can be informed. In our experiments (in Sect. 6), every generated output meets the selected specifications. Thus, while more research is needed to precisely evaluate the severity of our limitations, the performed experiments are positive evidence that these limitations are rather small even for reasonably complex meta-models.

Formal guarantees. In case of termination, our approach guarantees a valid EMF model as output: All generation rules conform to a design that is proven to preserve EMF constraints in [4]. Moreover, applications of these rules cannot introduce violations of upper bounds as they are equipped with corresponding NACs. So each strategy mentioned above is guaranteed to result in an instance model that conforms to EMF and does not violate any upper bounds. Moreover, it is ensured by the finite number of rule calls specified in each strategy that the increase phase terminates. Thus, suitable input for the model completion process of EMF Repair [19] is ensured after finitely many steps. For model completion, termination was proven in the case of f.f.i. meta-models while correctness was proven in all cases in [18]. If the user specification is met after a model has been increased, it is met after model completion as well since no deletion takes place during model completion. Even an increased model that does not meet the user specification is an EMF model and hence a suitable input for EMF Repair. Thus, it can be completed and returned to the user as a valid EMF model. The given user specification, however, is only partly satisfied in this case.

5   Tooling

We have developed two Eclipse plug-ins that are available for download.[3] The first plug-in is a meta-tool, called *Meta2GR*. It takes a domain meta-model as input and derives an MTS in Henshin. This is achieved by applying the meta-patterns that are depicted in Figs. 3 to 5 to the given domain meta-model. These meta-patterns are specified as rules typed over the Ecore meta-metamodel. Based on their matches, domain-specific model generation rules of different kinds are

---

[3] https://github.com/RuleBasedApproach/EMFModelGenerator/wiki

created. For a given meta-model, the MTS has to be generated only once. The second Eclipse plug-in, called *EMF Model Generator*, is a modeling tool that uses the derived MTS to generate instance models. Given a user specification and, optionally, one or more seed EMF models, this model generator creates valid EMF models in batch mode or incrementally.

6   Evaluation

Next to the formal guarantees which are provided by construction, we empirically evaluate our approach w.r.t. the following research questions:

RQ 1: *How fast can instance models of varying sizes be generated?*

RQ 2: *Does the use of parametrization help to increase the diversity?*

All experiments were performed on a desktop PC, Intel Core i7, 16 GB RAM, Windows 7 x64 using Eclipse Oxygen. Our Eclipse-based tool was configured to use the default settings, e.g., the heap size was limited to 1 GB. All the evaluation artifacts are available for download.[3]

6.1   Scalability Experiments

To answer RQ 1, we conducted two scalability experiments. We used 8 meta-models taken from the literature and projects, namely the Statechart meta-model of Magicdraw [13], Web model [5], Car Rental and Class model [2], Bugzilla, Latex, Warehouse, and GraphML (GML) [3]. The average size of the meta-models is 44 elements (16 nodes, 17 edges, 11 attributes) and the number of multiplicity bounds is 24 on average. The overhead for generating the needed transformation rules and units was, on average, less than 5 seconds, and we will thus focus on the run-time of the model generation in the sequel.

Experiment 1. In the first experiment, we randomly generated valid EMF models of varying sizes up to 10 000 elements (counting nodes and edges) for each meta-model using Strategy (1) (in Sect. 4.3). For each size category, we generated 10 valid EMF models and calculated the average run-time. Table 3 presents the results of this experiment. Considering all the meta-models and generated models of varying sizes, our tool always generates a valid EMF model with at least 10 000 elements. Generation times were fastest for the Bugzilla meta-model and slowest for the GraphML one. To assess how robust the times are, we measured the time for generating a seed and for the subsequent repair separately. For each one, we also computed the corrected standard deviation (which is presented for model size 10 000 only). Generating the seed is generally faster than the subsequent repair, except for the StateChart and Warehouse meta-models. If the standard deviation is rather high, this tends to be the case for both, the seed generation and the repair (as for GraphML, Web Model, and Class Model). A closer inspection of the meta-models shows that higher run-times, as well as higher deviations of run-times, are caused by larger meta-model sizes (and hence larger sizes of derived MTSs) and higher numbers of interrelated multiplicity constraints.

Table 3. Average run-time (in seconds) for generating valid EMF models of varying sizes for 8 meta-models (MM) using Strategy (1); for size 10 000, run-time is split into the generation of seed and subsequent repair where the corrected standard deviation is added in brackets, respectively.

MM\Model Size	1 000	3 000	5 000	8 000	10 000
Bugzilla	0.05	0.1	0.1	0.1	0.08 (0.006) + 0.04 (0.01)
Car Rental	0.27	5	17.9	72.3	65.5 (7.2) + 78.1 (4)
Class Model	0.16	1.7	9.4	61.5	13.2 (14.2) + 85 (113.8)
CoreWarehouse	0.81	4.5	18.9	67.9	0.4 (0.02) + 131 (10.9)
GraphML	0.4	2.6	16.7	79.2	39.3 (56) + 168.1 (119.6)
Latex	1.27	1.3	1.3	1.5	0.7 (0.01) + 0.8 (0.03)
StateChart	0.55	1.7	5.5	18.7	35.8 (3.9) + 1 (0.3)
Web Model	0.16	1.4	5.1	14.6	18.7 (18.8) + 6.2 (2.6)

Table 4. Average run-time and standard deviation (in minutes) for generating valid EMF models of varying huge sizes for the GraphML meta-model using Strategy (3). The standard deviations are presented in brackets.

Model Size	200 000	300 000	400 000	half a million
Average Time (Min.)	6 (1.4)	11.4 (2.6)	23.3 (5.7)	32.5 (6.5)

Experiment 2. The second experiment is dedicated to generating huge models for a complex meta-model which would lead to complex model repair processes. The meta-model GraphML is right for this purpose as its number of lower bounds being non-zero is above the average. Fulfilling these bounds renders model repair into a complex process. We expect the generation of models to become faster when using Strategy (3), i.e., when specifying a minimal number of edge occurrences of a certain type. In this case, nodes are introduced together with incident edges; this generation behavior should reduce the number of repairs needed to take place for fixing lower bound violations. Models of an average size of between 200 000 and 500 000 elements are generated in 6 to 32.5 minutes on average. Each generation process was repeated five times. The standard deviation was between 1.4 to 6.5 minutes, i.e., the run-times for the generation of these huge models are pretty stable. Table 4 presents the experiment results. Moreover, to give an impression of the tool performance for simple meta-models, we applied it to the Bugzilla meta-model. It is considered as simple since it consists of unrestricted containment edges only. The tool needed 1.2 minutes only to generate a valid EMF model with a minimum of 500 000 elements.

6.2 Diversity Experiment

To test if the parametrization of our algorithm has some effect on the diversity of generated models, we conducted the following experiment. We took the GraphML meta-model and chose Strategy (1) to randomly create 10 instance

Table 5. Diversity of randomly generated instance models parametrized by node types of the GraphML meta-model (EL = Element, K = Key, etc.; compare Fig. 1)

Specified Type	Str. 1) All	Str. 2) EL.	K.	G.	E.	H.E.	N.	P.	E.P.	D.
Shannon Index	3	2.12	0.82	0.76	0.94	0.92	0.99	1.57	1.48	2.06

models containing about 2 000 elements. For each node type as parameter, we created 10 instance models containing about 2 000 elements according to Strategy (2) which specifies that this node type has to occur at least 500 times. For each of the resulting sets of model instances we calculated the Shannon index [33], $\sum_{i=1}^{9} \frac{n_i}{N} \cdot \lg \frac{n_i}{N}$, an established diversity measure. Here, N is the total number of nodes in the given set, i ranges over the 9 non-abstract node types in the GraphML meta-model, and n_i is the number of nodes of that type in the given set. The resulting indices are presented in Table 5. Considering Strategy (1), the types of occurring elements show nearly uniform distribution as the maximal possible Shannon index is $\lg 9 \approx 3.17$. The indices for Strategy (2) show that the distribution of elements significantly differs, depending on the selected node type.

To assess that even the sets with similar Shannon indexes differ from one another, we checked for the types actually occurring in each set and compared them. The results are depicted in Fig. 8. For example, 66 % of the nodes are of type HyperEdge if HyperEdge (H.E.) is chosen as type parameter, and 68 % of the nodes are of type Edge if Edge (E.) is chosen as parameter, even though both sets of models exhibit almost the same Shannon index.

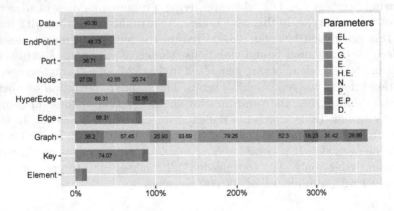

Fig. 8. Relative number of occurrences (x-axis) of node types (y-axis) in all the instance models generated using Strategy (2); results obtained for different parameter settings are encoded in colors and each color indicates one instance model. For example, 79.26% nodes of type Graph and 20.74% nodes of type Node are created in an instance model for parameter Graph (G.).

To answer RQ 2, choosing different node types as parameter leads to significantly different distributions of the node types of occurring elements. Hence, Strategy (2) can be used to introduce a certain diversity.

6.3   Threats to Validity

In our evaluation, we selected 8 meta-models. Evaluation results might differ when choosing others. We are confident, however, that our results are representative as we selected meta-models from diverse backgrounds, with reasonable sizes, and with varying numbers and forms of multiplicities. The used metric to measure diversity completely abstracts from details of the underlying graph structures of generated instance models. On the one hand, abstracting from such details typically underrates diversity rather than overrating it. On the other hand, we have to acknowledge that the form of diversity we show in our experiments is limited to the distribution of types.

7   Conclusion and Future Work

We developed a rule-based approach for generating valid models w.r.t. arbitrary multiplicities and EMF constraints. Since we use a rule-based approach, our generator is configurable to support user specifications and to allow user interaction. Several parameterization strategies are presented to generate different sets of valid EMF models. Two Eclipse plug-ins have been developed: *Meta2GR* automatically translates the meta-model of a given DSML to an MTS and the *EMF Model Generator* uses the derived MTS to generate valid EMF models. We evaluated the scalability of our approach by generating large instances of several meta-models of different domains and showed that models with 10 000 elements can be generated in about a minute on average. Furthermore, our tool can generate valid EMF models of 500 000 elements in less than 2 minutes for a meta-model with largely unrelated multiplicity constraints and in about 30 minutes for a meta-model with closely interrelated ones. Moreover, we showed that a certain form of diversity between the generated models can be achieved by configuration. As future work, we intend to support meta-models with OCL constraints, at least partly: Integrating the constraints as application conditions into rules [17,24] is a promising basis to extend our approach in this direction. Besides, we want to support further configuration facilities which allow us to generate realistic models by leveraging a stochastic controller [38].

References

1. Arendt, T., Biermann, E., Jurack, S., Krause, C., Taentzer, G.: Henshin: Advanced Concepts and Tools for In-Place EMF Model Transformations. In: Proc. MODELS. pp. 121–135. Springer (2010)
2. Arendt, T., Taentzer, G.: A tool environment for quality assurance based on the eclipse modeling framework. Automated Software Engineering **20**(2), 141–184 (2013)

3. Atlantic Zoo. http://web.imt-atlantique.fr/x-info/atlanmod/index.php?title=Zoos (2019)
4. Biermann, E., Ermel, C., Taentzer, G.: Formal Foundation of Consistent EMF Model Transformations by Algebraic Graph Transformation. SoSyM **11**(2), 227–250 (2012)
5. Brambilla, M., Cabot, J., Wimmer, M.: Model-Driven Software Engineering in Practice. Morgan & Claypool Publishers (2012)
6. Brandes, U., Eiglsperger, M., Herman, I., Himsolt, M., Marshall, M.S.: GraphML Progress Report: Structural Layer Proposal. In: Graph Drawing. pp. 501–512. Springer (2002)
7. Brottier, E., Fleurey, F., Steel, J., Baudry, B., Le Traon, Y.: Metamodel-based test generation for model transformations: an algorithm and a tool. In: Symp. on Software Reliability Engineering. pp. 85–94 (2006)
8. Ehrig, H., Ehrig, K., Prange, U., Taentzer, G.: Fundamentals of Algebraic Graph Transformation. Springer (2006)
9. Ehrig, K., Küster, J.M., Taentzer, G.: Generating instance models from meta models. SoSyM **8**(4), 479–500 (2009)
10. Fleurey, F., Steel, J., Baudry, B.: Validation in model-driven engineering: testing model transformations. In: Proc. Intl. Workshop on Model, Design and Validation. pp. 29–40. IEEE (2004)
11. Gómez, A., AtlanMod Team: EMF random instantiator (2015), https://github.com/atlanmod/mondo-atlzoo-benchmark/tree/master/fr.inria.atlanmod.instantiator, (visited on 2020-02-18)
12. Jackson, D.: Alloy: A lightweight object modelling notation. ACM Trans. Softw. Eng. Methodol. **11**(2), 256–290 (2002)
13. Kehrer, T., Taentzer, G., Rindt, M., Kelter, U.: Automatically Deriving the Specification of Model Editing Operations from Meta-Models. In: Proc. ICMT. pp. 173–188 (2016)
14. Kolovos, D.S., Rose, L.M., Matragkas, N., Paige, R.F., Guerra, E., Cuadrado, J.S., De Lara, J., Ráth, I., Varró, D., Tisi, M., et al.: A research roadmap towards achieving scalability in model driven engineering. In: Workshop on Scalability in Model Driven Engineering. ACM (2013)
15. McGill, M.J., Stirewalt, R.K., Dillon, L.K.: Automated test input generation for software that consumes ORM models. In: OTM Confederated Intl. Conferences. pp. 704–713. Springer (2009)
16. Mougenot, A., Darrasse, A., Blanc, X., Soria, M.: Uniform random generation of huge metamodel instances. In: European Conf. on Model Driven Architecture-Foundations and Applications. pp. 130–145. Springer (2009)
17. Nassar, N., Kosiol, J., Arendt, T., Taentzer, G.: OCL2AC. Automatic Translation of OCL Constraints to Graph Constraints and Application Conditions for Transformation Rules. In: Proc. ICGT 2018. pp. 171–177. Springer (2018)
18. Nassar, N., Kosiol, J., Radke, H.: Rule-based Repair of EMF Models: Formalization and Correctness Proof. In: Electronic Pre-Proc. Intl. Workshop on Graph Computation Models (2017)
19. Nassar, N., Radke, H., Arendt, T.: Rule-based repair of EMF models: An automated interactive approach. In: Proc. ICMT. pp. 171–181 (2017)
20. OMG: Object Constraint Language. (2014), http://www.omg.org/spec/OCL/
21. OMG: OMG Meta Object Facility (MOF). Version 2.5.1 (11 2016), http://www.omg.org/spec/MOF/
22. Pietsch, Pit and Yazdi, Hamed Shariat and Kelter, Udo: Generating realistic test models for model processing tools. In: Proc. ASE. pp. 620–623. IEEE CS (2011)

23. Popoola, S., Kolovos, D.S., Rodriguez, H.H.: EMG: A domain-specific transformation language for synthetic model generation. In: Proc. ICMT. vol. 9765, pp. 36–51. Springer (2016)
24. Radke, H., Arendt, T., Becker, J.S., Habel, A., Taentzer, G.: Translating Essential OCL Invariants to Nested Graph Constraints for Generating Instances of Metamodels. Science of Computer Programming **152**, 38–62 (2018)
25. Rindt, M., Kehrer, T., Kelter, U.: Automatic generation of consistency-preserving edit operations for mde tools. Demos @ MoDELS **14** (2014)
26. Scheidgen, M.: Generation of large random models for benchmarking. In: Big-MDE@ STAF. pp. 1–10 (2015)
27. Schneider, S., Lambers, L., Orejas, F.: Automated reasoning for attributed graph properties. Intl. Journal on Software Tools for Technology Transfer **20**(6), 705–737 (2018)
28. Schneider, S., Lambers, L., Orejas, F.: A logic-based incremental approach to graph repair. In: Fundamental Approaches to Software Engineering. pp. 151–167. Springer (2019)
29. Semeráth, O., Babikian, A.A., Pilarski, S., Varró, D.: Viatra solver: a framework for the automated generation of consistent domain-specific models. In: Proc. ICSE. pp. 43–46. IEEE/ACM (2019)
30. Semeráth, O., Nagy, A.S., Varró, D.: A Graph Solver for the Automated Generation of Consistent Domain-specific Models. In: Proc. ICSE. pp. 969–980. ACM (2018)
31. Semeráth, O., Varró, D.: Graph constraint evaluation over partial models by constraint rewriting. In: Proc. ICMT. pp. 138–154 (2017)
32. Sen, S., Baudry, B., Mottu, J.M.: Automatic model generation strategies for model transformation testing. In: Proc. ICMT. pp. 148–164 (2009)
33. Shannon, C.E.: A Mathematical Theory of Communication. SIGMOBILE Mob. Comput. Commun. Rev. **5**(1), 3–55 (2001), reprint
34. Steinberg, D., Budinsky, F., Paternostro, M., Merks, E.: EMF: Eclipse Modeling Framework. Addison Wesley, Upper Saddle River, NJ, 2 edn. (2008)
35. Strüber, D., Born, K., Gill, K.D., Groner, R., Kehrer, T., Ohrndorf, M., Tichy, M.: Henshin: A Usability-Focused Framework for EMF Model Transformation Development. In: Proc. ICGT. pp. 196–208 (2017)
36. Svendsen, A., Haugen, Ø., Møller-Pedersen, B.: Synthesizing software models: generating train station models automatically. In: Intl. SDL Forum. pp. 38–53. Springer (2011)
37. Taentzer, G.: Instance generation from type graphs with arbitrary multiplicities. ECEASST **47** (2012)
38. Yazdi, H.S., Angelis, L., Kehrer, T., Kelter, U.: A framework for capturing, statistically modeling and analyzing the evolution of software models. Journal of Systems and Software **118**, 176–207 (2016)

Family-Based SPL Model Checking
Using Parity Games with Variability

Maurice H. ter Beek[1], Sjef van Loo[2], Erik P. de Vink[2], and
Tim A. C. Willemse[2]

[1] ISTI–CNR, Pisa, Italy
[2] TU Eindhoven, Eindhoven, The Netherlands

Abstract. Family-based SPL model checking concerns the simultaneous
verification of multiple product models, aiming to improve on enumerative product-based verification, by capitalising on the common features
and behaviour of products in a software product line (SPL), typically
modelled as a featured transition system (FTS). We propose efficient
family-based SPL model checking of modal μ-calculus formulae on FTSs
based on variability parity games, which extend parity games with conditional edges labelled with feature configurations, by reducing the SPL
model checking problem for the modal μ-calculus on FTSs to the variability parity game solving problem, based on an encoding of FTSs as
variability parity games. We validate our contribution by experiments on
SPL benchmark models, which demonstrate that a novel family-based
algorithm to collectively solve variability parity games, using symbolic
representations of the configuration sets, outperforms the product-based
method of solving the standard parity games obtained by projection with
classical algorithms.

1 Introduction

Software product line engineering (SPLE) is a software engineering method for
cost-effective and time-efficient development of a family of software-intensive
configurable systems, according to which individual products (system variants)
can be distinguished by the features they provide, where a feature is typically
understood as some user-aware (difference in) functionality [1,2]. The intrinsic
variability of SPLs challenges formal methods and analysis tools, because the
number of possible products may be exponential in the number of features and
each product may moreover exhibit a large behavioural state space.

The SPL model checking problem, first recognised in the seminal paper [3],
generalises the classical model checking problem in the following way: given a
formula, determine for each product whether it satisfies the formula (and, ideally,
provide a counterexample for each product that does not satisfy the formula). A
straightforward way to solve this problem is to provide a model for each product
and apply classical model checking. This enumerative, product-based method has
several drawbacks. Most importantly, the state-space explosion problem –typical
of model checking– is amplified with the number of products, while products of a
product line usually have a large amount of features and behaviour in common.

H. Wehrheim and J. Cabot (Eds.): FASE 2020, LNCS 12076, pp. 245–265, 2020.
https://doi.org/10.1007/978-3-030-45234-6_12

Therefore, Classen et al. have extended labelled transition systems (LTSs) with features to concisely describe and analyse the combined behaviour of a family of models [3–5]. Concretely, transitions in the resulting featured transition systems (FTSs) are labelled with actions and feature expressions. Given a product, a transition can be executed if the product fulfills the feature expression. Hence, an FTS incorporates all eligible product behaviour, and each individual product's behaviour can be obtained as an LTS. Moreover, FTSs cater for the simultaneous verification of multiple products, known as family-based analysis [6].

Properties of behavioural models for SPLs such as FTSs can be verified with dedicated SPL model checkers like SNIP [7], ProVeLines [8], VMC [9], ProFeat [10,11], or QFLan [12,13], or with classical model checkers like NuSMV [14, 15], SPIN [16], Maude [17], or mCRL2 [18, 19]. The advantage of using established off-the-shelf model checkers for SPL analysis is obvious: it lifts the burden of maintaining dedicated model checkers in favour of highly optimised tools with a broad user base. In [19], it was shown how to perform family-based SPL model checking with mCRL2 [20, 21] of properties of FTSs expressed in a feature-oriented variant of the modal μ-calculus to deal with transitions labelled with feature expressions [22]. However, this approach is based on a decision procedure for the binary partitioning of the product space into products that do and those that do not satisfy a given formula, and it is underlined that computing suitable partitionings for the conducted experiments is a largely manual activity.

In this paper, we present efficient family-based SPL model checking of modal μ-calculus formulae on FTSs based on parity games with variability. Years after its introduction [3, 14], family-based model checking of SPLs or program families is still a popular topic [10, 16, 19, 23–26], including a few game-theoretic approaches based on solving (3-valued) model checking games on featured symbolic automata and on modal transition systems. A parity game is a 2-player turn-based graph game. It is well known that the model checking problem for modal μ-calculus formulae on LTSs is equivalent to parity game solving, for which Zielonka defined a recursive algorithm that performs well in practice [27–29].

Here we introduce variability parity games as a generalisation of parity games with conditional edges labelled with feature configurations. We then show how the SPL model checking problem for modal μ-calculus formulae on FTSs can be reduced to the variability parity game solving problem based on an encoding of FTSs as variability parity games. Finally, we show the results of implementing two different methods, product-based and family-based, to solve variability parity games and of experimenting with them on two well-known SPL case studies, the minepump and the elevator. The product-based method simply projects a variability parity game to the different configurations and independently solves all resulting parity games with existing algorithms. The family-based method, instead, is based on a novel algorithm to collectively solve variability parity games, using symbolic representations of sets of configurations. The experiments clearly show that the family-based method outperforms the product-based method.

Outline. After defining some preliminary notions in Section 2, we introduce SPL model checking in Section 3. In Section 4, we introduce variability parity games and show how they can be used to solve the SPL model checking problem.

In Section 5, we present a family-based, collective strategy for recursively solving variability parity games, which we experiment with on two SPL case studies in Section 6. Section 7 concludes the paper and provides directions for future work. Relevant related work other than the above is mentioned throughout the paper.

2   Preliminaries

We give a brief overview of *labelled transition systems* and the *modal μ-calculus*.

Definition 1. *A labelled transition system or LTS L over a non-empty set of actions $\mathcal{Act}$ is a triple $L = (S, \rightarrow, s_0)$, where S is the set of states with $s_0 \in S$ and $\rightarrow \subseteq S \times \mathcal{Act} \times S$ is the transition relation.*

The modal μ-calculus is an expressive logic, subsuming LTL and CTL, for reasoning about the behaviours of LTSs, among others.

Definition 2. *Formulae in the modal μ-calculus are given by the following (minimal) grammar.*

$$\phi ::= \mathsf{true} \mid \mathsf{false} \mid X \mid \phi \wedge \phi \mid \phi \vee \phi \mid \langle a \rangle \phi \mid [a]\phi \mid \mu X.\phi \mid \nu X.\phi$$

where $a \in \mathcal{Act}$ is an action and $X \in \mathcal{X}$ is some propositional variable taken from a sufficiently large set of variables $\mathcal{X}$.

Next to the Boolean constants and the propositional connectives, the modal μ-calculus contains the existential diamond operator $\langle\,\rangle$ and its dual universal box operator $[\,]$ of modal logic as well as the least and greatest fixed point operators μ and ν that provide recursion used for 'finite' and 'infinite' looping, respectively.

Given a formula ϕ, an occurrence of a variable X in ϕ is said to be *bound* iff this occurrence is within a formula ψ, where $\mu X.\psi$ or $\nu X.\psi$ is a subformula of ϕ; an occurrence of a variable is *free* otherwise. A formula ϕ is *closed* iff all variables occurring in ϕ are bound; here we only consider closed formulae. For simplicity, we assume that the formulae that we consider are *well-named, i.e.,* formulae do not contain two fixed point subformulae binding the same variable.

Given an LTS, the semantics of a μ-calculus formula is the set of states of the LTS that satisfy the formula. Since we focus on games in this paper, we introduce two auxiliary concepts, *viz.* the *Fischer-Ladner closure* of a formula and the *alternation depth* of a formula. The Fischer-Ladner closure $FL(\phi)$ of a formula ϕ is the smallest set of formulae satisfying

- $\phi \in FL(\phi)$;
- if $\phi_1 \wedge \phi_2 \in FL(\phi)$ or $\phi_1 \vee \phi_2 \in FL(\phi)$ then $\phi_1, \phi_2 \in FL(\phi)$;
- if $\langle a \rangle \phi_1 \in FL(\phi)$ or $[a]\phi_1 \in FL(\phi)$ then $\phi_1 \in FL(\phi)$;
- if $\sigma X.\phi_1 \in FL(\phi)$ then $\phi_1[X := \sigma X.\phi_1] \in FL(\phi)$.

Note that for a closed formula ϕ, the set $FL(\phi)$ contains no variables.

The complexity of a μ-calculus formula is given by its *alternation depth*; the larger the alternation depth, the harder the formula is to solve (and, incidentally, also to understand). The alternation depth of a formula ϕ is defined as the largest alternation depth of the bound propositional variables in ϕ, defined as follows.

Definition 3. *The* dependency order *on bound variables of a formula ϕ is the smallest partial order $\leq_\phi$ satisfying $X \leq_\phi Y$ if X occurs free in $\sigma Y.\psi$. The alternation depth of a μ-variable X in ϕ, denoted $AD_\phi(X)$, is the maximal length of a chain $X_1 \leq_\phi \cdots \leq_\phi X_n$, where $X_1 = X$, variables $X_1, X_3, \ldots$ are μ-variables and $X_2, X_4, \ldots$ are ν-variables. Analogously for the alternation depth of a ν-variable.*

Definition 4. *A* parity game *is a tuple $G = (V, E, p, (V_0, V_1))$ where*

- *V is a finite set of vertices, partitioned into a set V_0 of vertices owned by player 0 and a set V_1 of vertices owned by player 1;*
- *$E \subseteq V \times V$ is the edge relation;*
- *$p : V \to \mathbb{N}$ is the priority function.*

We depict parity games as graphs in which diamond-shaped vertices represent vertices owned by player 0 and box-shaped vertices represent vertices owned by player 1. Edges are annotated with configurations while priorities are typically written inside vertices.

We write $v \to w$ instead of $(v, w) \in E$ and let α range over the set of players, *i.e.* $\alpha \in \{0, 1\}$. For a given vertex v, we write vE to denote the set $\{w \in V \mid v \to w\}$ of successors of v. Likewise, Ev denotes the set $\{w \in V \mid w \to v\}$ of predecessors of v. A sequence of vertices $v_1 \cdots v_n$ is a *path* if for all $1 \leqslant m < n$ we have $v_{m+1} \in v_m E$. Infinite paths are defined in a similar way. We write π_n to denote the n-th vertex in a path π and $\pi^{\leqslant n}$ to indicate the prefix $\pi_1 \cdots \pi_n$ of π.

A play, starting in a vertex $v \in V$, starts by placing a token on that vertex. Players then move the token according to a single simple rule: if a token is on a vertex $u \in V_\alpha$ and $uE \neq \emptyset$, player α pushes it to some successor vertex $w \in uE$. The finite and infinite paths thus constructed are referred to as *plays*. For an infinite play, and the infinite sequence of priorities it induces, the *parity* of the highest priority that occurs infinitely often on that play defines its *winner*: player 0 wins if this priority is even; player 1 wins otherwise. A finite play is won by the player that does *not* own the vertex on which the token is stuck.

The moves of players 0 and 1 are determined by their respective *strategies*. Informally, a strategy for a player α determines, for a vertex $\pi_i \in V_\alpha$ the next vertex π_{i+1} that will be visited if a token is on π_i, provided π_i has successors. In general, a strategy is a partial function $\sigma : V^* V_\alpha \to V$ which, for a given history of vertices of the locations of the token and a vertex on which the token currently resides, determines the next vertex by selecting an edge to that vertex. A finite or infinite path π *conforms to* a given strategy σ if for all prefixes $\pi^{\leqslant i}$ for which σ is defined, we have $\pi_{i+1} = \sigma(\pi^{\leqslant i})$.

A strategy σ for player α is *winning* from a vertex v iff α is the winner of every play starting in v that conforms to σ. Parity games are known to be *positionally determined* [30]. This means that a vertex is won by player α iff α has a winning strategy that does not depend on the history of vertices visited by the token. Such strategies can be represented by partial functions $\sigma : V_\alpha \to V$. Note that every vertex in a parity game is won by one of the two players.

Closed modal μ-calculus formulae can be interpreted by associating a game semantics to these formulae. The definition we provide below is adopted from [30].

Table 1. The game semantics for a closed modal μ-calculus formula ϕ: vertex v (1st column), its owner α (2nd column), its successors (if any) $w \in vE$ (3rd column), and priority $p(v)$ (4th column). Vertices of the form $(s, \langle a \rangle \psi)$ and $(s, [a]\psi)$ have no successors when s has no a-successors.

Vertex	Owner	Successor(s)	Priority
(s, true)	1		0
(s, false)	0		0
$(s, \psi_1 \wedge \psi_2)$	1	(s, ψ_1) and (s, ψ_2)	0
$(s, \psi_1 \vee \psi_2)$	0	(s, ψ_1) and (s, ψ_2)	0
$(s, [a]\psi)$	1	(t, ψ) for every $s \xrightarrow{a} t$	0
$(s, \langle a \rangle \psi)$	0	(t, ψ) for every $s \xrightarrow{a} t$	0
$(s, \nu X.\psi)$	1	$(s, \psi[X := \nu X.\psi])$	$2\lfloor AD_\phi(X)/2 \rfloor$
$(s, \mu X.\psi)$	1	$(s, \psi[X := \mu X.\psi])$	$2\lfloor AD_\phi(X)/2 \rfloor + 1$

Definition 5. *Let $L = (S, \rightarrow, s_0)$ be an LTS and ϕ be a closed modal μ-calculus formula. A state $s \in S$ satisfies formula ϕ, denoted by $L, s \models \phi$, iff vertex (s, ϕ) is won by player 0 in the game $G_{L,\phi} = (V, E, p, (V_0, V_1))$, where $V = S \times FL(\phi)$, and the sets E, V_0, and V_1 and priority function p are given by Table 1.*

If the context is such that no confusion can arise, we write $s \models \phi$ for $L, s \models \phi$.

For a more in-depth treatment of the modal μ-calculus, we refer to [30]. Here, we finish by illustrating the game semantics on a small example, drawing inspiration from an example in [19].

Example 1. Consider the LTS L depicted in the bottom-left corner of Fig. 1, modelling a coffee machine that after inserting one or two units of some currency (indicated by action *ins*) can dispense a standard regular coffee (indicated by action *std*) or an extra large coffee (indicted by action *xxl*), respectively.

The LTL-type formula ϕ, depicted in the top-left corner of Fig. 1, asserts that on all infinite runs of the coffee machine, it infinitely often dispenses a regular coffee. (Note, nothing is required to hold on finite runs.) The parity game that can answer whether $s_0 \models \phi$ holds is depicted on the right in Fig. 1. Each node is annotated with a pair consisting of a state of the LTS and a (sub)formula of ϕ. Note that the references to ϕ_1, ϕ_2, and ϕ_3 are meant as an indication and not to be interpreted exactly, since they lack the substitution that needs to be carried out. We remark that the parity game is *solitair*: only one player can make decisions. Vertex (s_0, ϕ) is won by player 1 by enforcing a 1-dominated infinite play, bypassing the vertex with priority 2 on the loop. Consequently, $s_0 \not\models \phi$. □

3 Software Product Lines Model Checking

Software products with variability can be modelled effectively using so-called *featured transition systems* or FTSs [3]. Fix a finite non-empty set $\mathcal{F}$ of features, with f as typical element. Let $\mathbb{B}[\mathcal{F}]$ denote the set of Boolean expressions over $\mathcal{F}$. Elements χ and γ of $\mathbb{B}[\mathcal{F}]$ are referred to as feature expressions. A product P is a set of features, $\mathcal{P}$ denotes the set of products, thus $\mathcal{P} \subseteq 2^{\mathcal{F}}$.

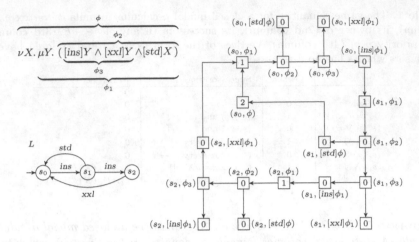

Fig. 1. Parity game encoding the model checking problem $s_0 \models \phi$

A feature expression γ, as Boolean expression over $\mathcal{F}$, can be interpreted as a set of products P_γ, *viz.* all products P for which the induced truth assignment (true for $f \in P$, false for $f \notin P$) validates γ. Reversely, for each family $P \subseteq \mathcal{P}$ we fix a feature expression γ_P to represent it. The constant $\top$ denotes the feature expression that is always true. We now recall FTSs from [4] as a model for software product lines, using the notation of [19, 22].

Definition 6. *An FTS F over Act and $\mathcal{F}$ is a triple $F = (S, \theta, s_0)$, where S is the set of states with $s_0 \in S$ and $\theta : S \times Act \times S \to \mathbb{B}[\mathcal{F}]$ is the transition constraint function.*

For states $s, t \in S$, we write $s \xrightarrow{a|\gamma}_F t$ if $\theta(s, a, t) = \gamma$ and $\gamma \neq \bot$. The projection of F onto a product $P \in \mathcal{P}$ is the LTS $F|P = (S, \to_{F|P}, s_0)$ over Act with $s \xrightarrow{a}_{F|P} t$ iff $P \in P_\gamma$ for a transition $s \xrightarrow{a|\gamma}_F t$ of F.

Example 2. Assume that the coffee machine from Example 1 is to model a family of coffee machines for different countries, depending on whether a coffee machine accepts the insertion of dollars or euros, or both. Let P be a product line of coffee machines, with the independent features \$ and €, representing the presence of a coin slot accepting dollars or euros, respectively, leading to a set of four products: $\{\varnothing, \{\$\}, \{€\}, \{\$, €\}\}$. The FTS F below models the family behaviour of P.

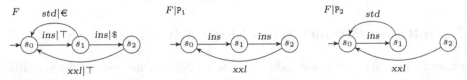

The idea is that extra large coffee is exclusively available for 2 dollars, whereas 1 euro or dollar suffices for a standard regular coffee. The behaviour of products $P_1 = \{\$\}$ and $P_2 = \{€\}$ is modelled by the LTSs $F|P_1$ and $F|P_2$ depicted above.

Note that coffee machine $F|P_1$ accepting only dollars lacks the transition from s_1 to s_0 requiring feature €, while coffee machine $F|P_2$ accepting only euros lacks the one from s_1 to s_2 requiring feature \$. The behaviour of product $P_3 = \{\$, €\}$ is modelled by the LTS $L = F|\{\$, €\}$ depicted in Fig. 1. Finally, the product without any features is not depicted, but it deadlocks at state s_1.   □

Definition 7. *The* SPL *model checking problem is to compute, for a given* FTS $F = (S, \theta, s_0)$ *and closed modal μ-calculus formula ϕ, the largest subsets P^+ and P^- of $\mathcal{P}$ such that $F|P, s_0 \models \phi$ for all $P \in P^+$ and $F|P, s_0 \not\models \phi$ for all $P \in P^-$.*

Sets P^+ and P^- partition $\mathcal{P}$: a formula either does or does not hold in a state.

Example 3. It is not difficult to see that the formula ϕ from Example 1 does not hold for all products. In fact, $P^+ = \{\varnothing, \{€\}\}$ and $P^- = \{\{\$\}, \{\$, €\}\}$. For products with feature \$, there is an infinite run that avoids action *std* altogether, whereas for products not containing feature \$, either all runs are finite, or all infinite runs contain an infinite number of *std* actions.   □

4 Variability Parity Games and SPL Model Checking

In practice, the model checking problem for LTSs, yielding a *yes/no* answer, can efficiently be decided using parity game solving algorithms [27,30]. The SPL model checking problem can be solved in a similar fashion by constructing parity games associated with the formula and with each individual product separately. Such an approach, however, does not take full advantage of the efficient, compact representation of the variation points in the individual product LTSs represented by an FTS. The *variability parity games* we introduce in Section 4.1, exploit constructs similar to those in FTSs to compactly encode variation points in the parity games they represent. We show in Section 4.2 that the SPL model checking problem can be solved by solving such variability parity games.

4.1 Variability Parity Games

A variability parity game is a generalisation of a parity game. It is a two-player game, again played by players *odd*, denoted by 1, and *even*, denoted by 0, on a finite directed graph. Contrary to parity games, an edge in a variability parity game is associated with a set of *configurations*.

Definition 8 (Variability Parity Game). *A variability parity game $\mathcal{G}$ is a sextuple $\mathcal{G} = (V, E, \mathfrak{C}, p, \theta, (V_0, V_1))$, where*

- *V is a finite set of vertices, partitioned into sets V_0 and V_1 of vertices owned by player 0 and player 1, respectively;*
- *$E \subseteq V \times V$ is the edge relation;*
- *$\mathfrak{C}$ is a finite set of configurations;*
- *$p : V \to \mathbb{N}$ is the priority function that assigns priorities to vertices;*
- *$\theta : E \to 2^{\mathfrak{C}} \setminus \{\emptyset\}$ is the configuration mapping.*

In line with our depiction of parity games, we visualise variability parity games as graphs with diamond-shaped and box-shaped vertices, and directed edges connecting vertices. Moreover, edges are annotated with configurations. A variability parity game $\mathcal{G} = (V, E, \mathfrak{C}, p, \theta, (V_0, V_1))$ is called *total* if, for all $u \in V$, it holds that $\bigcup\{\,\theta(u, v) \mid v \in V, (u, v) \in E\,\} = \mathfrak{C}$.

As before, we write $v \rightarrow w$ for $(v, w) \in E$, and we use α to range over $\{0, 1\}$. We use $v \xrightarrow{c} w$ to denote $v \rightarrow w$ and $c \in \theta(v, w)$ and say that the edge between v and w is *compatible* with c. The notions of a finite and infinite path from parity games carry over to variability parity games, and we use similar notation to denote the prefixes of a path and the vertices along a path. A finite path $v_1 \cdots v_n$ is *admitted* for a configuration $c \in \mathfrak{C}$ iff for all $m < n$, $c \in \theta(v_m, v_{m+1})$. In a similar vein, an infinite path can be said to be admitted for a given configuration.

A play starts by placing a *configured* token $c \in \mathfrak{C}$ on vertex $v \in V$. The players move configured token c in the game according to the following rule: if token $c \in \mathfrak{C}$ is on some vertex $v \in V_\alpha$, player α pushes c, if possible, to some adjacent vertex w along an edge compatible with c, *i.e.* $c \in \theta(v, w)$. The finite and infinite paths thus constructed are admitted by c, and are again referred to as *plays*; the conditions for players 0 and 1 for winning such plays are identical to those for parity games.

For a configuration $c \in \mathfrak{C}$, a strategy is a partial function $\sigma_c : V^* V_\alpha \rightarrow V$ which, when defined for $\pi^{\leqslant i}$, yields a vertex π_{i+1} that is reachable from π_i via an edge that is compatible with c. A path π, admitted by configuration c, *conforms to* a given strategy σ_c iff for all prefixes $\pi^{\leqslant i}$ for which σ is defined, we have $\pi_{i+1} = \sigma_c(\pi^{\leqslant i})$. Strategy σ_c for player α and configuration c is *winning* from a vertex v iff α is the winner of every play starting in v that conforms to σ_c.

Definition 9. *The* variability parity game solving problem *for a vertex v is the problem of computing the largest set of configurations $C_0, C_1 \subseteq \mathfrak{C}$ such that:*

- *player 0 has a winning strategy for v for each $c \in C_0$;*
- *player 1 has a winning strategy for v for each $c \in C_1$.*

For a given variability parity game $\mathcal{G}$ and a configuration $c \in \mathfrak{C}$, we define the projection of $\mathcal{G}$ onto c, denoted $\mathcal{G}|c$ as the parity game obtained by retaining only those edges from $\mathcal{G}$ that are compatible with c. We note that it follows rather immediately that variability parity games are also *positionally determined*: player 0 (player 1, respectively) has a winning strategy σ_c for vertex v for configuration c iff she has a winning strategy for v in the projection of the variability parity game onto configuration c. Since parity games are positionally determined, so are variability parity games. Consequently, the variability parity game solving problem asks for the computation of a partition of the set of configurations $\mathfrak{C}$.

4.2   Solving SPL Model Checking Using Variability Parity Games

If we ignore the representation of the sets of configurations decorating the edges, a variability parity game is a compact representation of a set of parity games. The

Table 2. Transformation of the SPL model checking problem to the variability parity game solving problem. For a given vertex v (1st column), its owner α (2nd column), successors $w \in vE$ (3rd column) and configuration mapping $\theta(v, w)$ (3rd column), and priority $p(v)$ (4th column) are given.

Vertex	Owner	Successor(s) | Configurations	Priority
(s, true)	1		0
(s, false)	0		0
$(s, \psi_1 \wedge \psi_2)$	1	$(s, \psi_1) \mid \mathcal{P}$ and $(s, \psi_2) \mid \mathcal{P}$	0
$(s, \psi_1 \vee \psi_2)$	0	$(s, \psi_1) \mid \mathcal{P}$ and $(s, \psi_2) \mid \mathcal{P}$	0
$(s, [a]\psi)$	1	$(t, \psi) \mid P_\gamma$ for every $s \xrightarrow{a\mid\gamma}_F t$	0
$(s, \langle a \rangle \psi)$	0	$(t, \psi) \mid P_\gamma$ for every $s \xrightarrow{a\mid\gamma}_F t$	0
$(s, \nu X.\psi)$	1	$(s, \psi[X := \nu X.\psi]) \mid \mathcal{P}$	$2\lfloor AD_\phi(X)/2 \rfloor$
$(s, \mu X.\psi)$	1	$(s, \psi[X := \mu X.\psi]) \mid \mathcal{P}$	$2\lfloor AD_\phi(X)/2 \rfloor + 1$

next definition shows how to exploit these configurations to efficiently encode the SPL model checking problem as a variability parity game solving problem, based on the game-based semantics of the modal μ-calculus we presented in Section 2.

Definition 10. *Let $F = (S, \theta_F, s_0)$ be an FTS, let $\mathcal{P}$ be the set of all products, and let ϕ be a closed modal μ-calculus formula. The variability parity game $F_\phi = (V, E, \mathfrak{C}, p, \theta, (V_0, V_1))$ associated with F and ϕ, with $V = S \times FL(\phi)$ and $\mathfrak{C} = \mathcal{P}$, is defined by the rules given in Table 2.*

Note that the size of the graph underlying variability parity game F_ϕ, measured in terms of $|V| + |E|$, is linear in the size of formula ϕ and the FTS F, measured in terms of $|S| + |\{(s, a, t) \in S \times Act \times S \mid \theta(s, a, t) \neq \bot\}|$. Hence, the structural information in an FTS is compactly reflected in the variability parity game which encodes the SPL model checking problem for the FTS. The correctness of the encoding is expressed by the Theorem 1.

Theorem 1. *For a given FTS F, a closed modal μ-calculus formula ϕ, and a product P, we have $F|P, s \models \phi$ iff player 0 wins the vertex (s, ϕ) for configuration P in the variability parity game F_ϕ associated to F and ϕ.*

Proof (sketch). Fix an FTS F and a closed modal μ-calculus formula ϕ. Let P be a product. It is not hard to show that the parity game we obtain by encoding the model checking problem $F|P, s \models \phi$ (cf. Definition 5) is isomorphic to the projection of F_ϕ onto P, viz. $F_\phi|P$. □

We revisit the SPL model checking problem of Example 3, illustrating the encoding of Definition 10. By abuse of notation, we write feature expressions instead of sets of configurations in variability parity games associated to SPL model checking problems.

Example 4. Consider the FTS F of Example 2 and the modal μ-calculus formula ϕ of Example 1, both for convenience repeated in Fig. 2. The variability parity game F_ϕ encoding the SPL model checking problem for F and ψ is depicted on the right in Fig. 2 (ignoring all dashed self loops for now). We omitted most state annotations to yield a more readable figure.

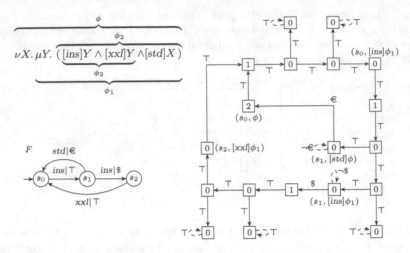

Fig. 2. Variability parity game encoding the SPL model checking problem for F and ϕ.

Observe that the graph structure of the variability parity game F_ϕ is the same as that of the parity game of Example 1 in Fig. 1. The construction leading to the variability parity game only differs in the construction of the parity game with respect to the edge annotations. Furthermore, note that vertex (s_0, ϕ) is won by player 0 for the set of configurations ¬\$, whereas player 1 wins the set of configurations \$: for configurations containing the feature \$, player 1 can essentially reuse the strategy of Example 1, avoiding the vertex with priority 2. For configurations not containing the feature \$, this option is not available, since the vertex $(s_1, [ins]\phi_1)$ is a sink. For products with feature € but not \$, the only infinite play infinitely often visits vertex (s_0, ϕ). For products without features € and \$ all plays starting in (s_0, ϕ) are finite. Hence, by Theorem 1, the solution to the SPL model checking problem is the pair $(\neg\$, \$)$, as expected.   □

5   Recursively Solving Variability Parity Games

Given a variability parity game $\mathcal{G}$ and a vertex v of $\mathcal{G}$, a straightforward way of solving the variability parity game problem for v is by simply solving the standard parity game problem $\mathcal{G}|c$ for every $c \in \mathfrak{C}$. In doing so, however, we ignore that players can potentially use (parts of) a single strategy for possibly many different configurations. As opposed to the above solving strategy, to which we refer as the *individual solving strategy*, we investigate an alternative for variability parity games, called the *collective solving strategy*.

We provide an algorithm, Algorithm 1, for solving variability parity games inspired by the classical *recursive* algorithm for solving parity games [27]. The recursive algorithm is, despite its unappealing theoretical worst-case complexity, in practice one of the most effective algorithms for solving parity games [28,29]. It is a divide-and-conquer algorithm that relies on two building blocks, *viz.* the concept of a *subgame computation* and of an *attractor computation*. We generalise and adapt these concepts to the setting of variability parity games.

Fix a variability parity game $\mathcal{G} = (V, E, \mathfrak{C}, p, \theta, (V_0, V_1))$. For simplicity we assume that $\mathcal{G}$ is total. This is not a limitation; any variability parity game can be turned into a total one. The auxiliary notion of a *restriction* is a mapping $\varrho : V \to 2^{\mathfrak{C}}$ which, for a variability parity game $\mathcal{G}$, indicates which configurations are under consideration for a vertex. Given such a restriction ϱ, we say that a vertex v for configuration $c \in \mathfrak{C}$ is won by player α in the game $\mathcal{G}$ restricted to ϱ iff $c \in \varrho(v)$ and the winning strategy for α only passes through vertices v' for which $c \in \varrho(v')$. We say that $\mathcal{G}$ is *total* with respect to ϱ iff for all $v \in V$ and all $c \in \varrho(v)$, there is a vertex w such that $w \in vE$ and $c \in \theta(v, w) \cap \varrho(w)$.

Let $U, U' : V \to 2^{\mathfrak{C}}$ be arbitrary mappings. The union of U and U', denoted $U \cup U'$, is defined point-wise, *i.e.* $(U \cup U')(v) = U(v) \cup U(v')$. We say that mapping U is a *sub-mapping* of ϱ iff for all $v \in V$ we have $U(v) \subseteq \varrho(v)$. The reduction of ϱ with respect to a sub-mapping U, denoted $\varrho \backslash U$, is a new restriction defined as $(\varrho \backslash U)(v) = \varrho(v) \backslash U(v)$.

For a given sub-mapping $U : V \to 2^{\mathfrak{C}}$ of a restriction ϱ, the α-*attractor* towards U is a sub-mapping of ϱ which assigns those configurations to a vertex for which player α can force the play to reach some vertex v for which that configuration belongs to $U(v)$. Formally, we define $Attr_\alpha(U)$, in the context of ϱ and $\mathcal{G}$, as $Attr_\alpha(U)(v) = \bigcup_{i \geq 0} Attr_\alpha^i(U)(v)$, where

$$
\begin{aligned}
Attr_\alpha^0(U)(v) \;\;&= U(v) \\
Attr_\alpha^{i+1}(U)(v) &= Attr_\alpha^i(U)(v) \cup \\
&\quad \{\, c \in \varrho(v) \mid v \in V_\alpha \wedge \exists w \in vE \colon c \in \theta(v, w) \cap \varrho(w) \cap Attr_\alpha^i(U)(w) \,\} \;\cup \\
&\quad \{\, c \in \varrho(v) \mid v \in V_{\bar{\alpha}} \wedge \forall w \in vE \colon c \in (\mathfrak{C} \backslash (\theta(v, w) \cap \varrho(w))) \cup Attr_\alpha^i(U)(w) \,\}
\end{aligned}
$$

Thus, in case $v \in V_\alpha$ and $c \in \varrho(v)$, configuration c is in $Attr_\alpha^{i+1}(U)(v)$ if for a move by player α to some vertex w allowed for configuration c, the sub-attractor $Attr_\alpha^i(U)(w)$ can be reached. In case $v \in V_{\bar{\alpha}}$ and $c \in \varrho(v)$, configuration c is in $Attr_\alpha^{i+1}(U)(v)$ if all moves for player $\bar{\alpha}$ are not allowed for configuration c or lead to a vertex w in the sub-attractor $Attr_\alpha^i(U)(w)$ for player α for A.

Example 5. Reconsider the variability parity game of Example 4. First, observe that it is not total. In this case, the variability parity game can be made total without changing the solution by taking into account also the dashed self loops.

Let $\varrho(v) = \mathfrak{C}$ and define $U(s_0, \phi) = \mathfrak{C}$ and $U(v) = \varnothing$ for all $v \neq (s_0, \phi)$. For vertex (s_0, ϕ) we have $Attr_0(U)(s_0, \phi) = \{\varnothing, \{\$\}, \{\math{€}\}, \{\$, \math{€}\}\}$. All vertices v on the (single) path starting in $(s_0, [ins]\phi_1)$ and ending in $(s_1, [std]\phi)$ satisfy $Attr_0(U)(v') = \{\{\$, \math{€}\}\}$. The remaining vertices v' satisfy $Attr_0(U)(v') = \varnothing$. Note that for no configuration the immediate predecessor of $(s_0, [ins]\phi_1)$ is attracted to U because of the escape to the sink that player 1 can use. $\square$

We have the following result, which can be proven by induction on i following the definition of $Attr_\alpha(U)(v) = \bigcup_{i \geq 0} Attr_\alpha^i(U)(v)$.

Algorithm 1 Recursive Algorithm for a fixed variability parity game $\mathcal{G} = (V, E, \mathfrak{C}, p, \theta, (V_0, V_1))$. Given a restriction $\varrho : V \to 2^{\mathfrak{C}}$, the algorithm returns a pair of functions (W_0, W_1) where $W_0, W_1 : V \to 2^{\mathfrak{C}}$ denote, for each vertex, which set of configurations is won by player 0 (player 1, respectively).

```
 1: function SOLVE(ϱ)
 2:     if ϱ = λv ∈ V.∅ then
 3:         (W₀, W₁) ← (λv ∈ V.∅, λv ∈ V.∅)
 4:     else
 5:         m ← max{ p(v) | v ∈ V ∧ ϱ(v) ≠ ∅ }
 6:         α ← m mod 2
 7:         U ← λv ∈ V. {ϱ(v) | p(v) = m}
 8:         A ← Attrα(U)
 9:         (W₀′, W₁′) = SOLVE(ϱ\A)
10:         if Wᾱ′ = λv ∈ V.∅ then
11:             Wα ← Wα′ ∪ A
12:             Wᾱ ← Wᾱ′
13:         else
14:             B ← Attrᾱ(Wᾱ′)
15:             (W₀″, W₁″) = SOLVE(ϱ\B)
16:             Wα ← Wα″
17:             Wᾱ ← Wᾱ″ ∪ B
18:         end if
19:     end if
20:     return (W₀, W₁)
21: end function
```

Lemma 1. *Let $\mathcal{G} = (V, E, \mathfrak{C}, p, \theta, (V_0, V_1))$ be a variability parity game, let $\varrho : V \to 2^{\mathfrak{C}}$ a restriction, and let α be an arbitrary player. Then for all sub-mappings U of ϱ, also $Attr_{\alpha}(U)$ is a sub-mapping of ϱ.*   □

Totality of a game is preserved for the complements of attractors of sub-mappings.

Lemma 2. *Let $\mathcal{G} = (V, E, \mathfrak{C}, p, \theta, (V_0, V_1))$ be a variability parity game and let $\varrho : V \to 2^{\mathfrak{C}}$ be a restriction such that $\mathcal{G}$ is total with respect to ϱ. Then $\mathcal{G}$ is total with respect to $\varrho \backslash Attr_{\alpha}(U)$ for all sub-mappings U of ϱ and each player α.*

Proof. Let $\mathcal{G}$ and ϱ be as stated. Consider an arbitrary mapping $U : V \to 2^{\mathfrak{C}}$, and let $A = Attr_{\alpha}(U)$ be the α-attractor towards U. By Lemma 1, A is a sub-mapping of ϱ. Towards a contradiction, assume that $\mathcal{G}$ is not total with respect to $\varrho \backslash A$. Then there is some vertex $v \in V$ and some configuration $c \in (\varrho \backslash A)(v)$ such that for all $w \in vE$, if $c \in \theta(v, w)$ then $c \notin (\varrho \backslash A)(w)$. Pick such a vertex v and configuration c. Since $\mathcal{G}$ is total with respect to ϱ, we know that there is at least one $w \in vE$ with $c \in \theta(v, w)$ and $c \in \varrho(w)$. Let $w \in vE$ be such that $c \in \theta(v, w)$ and $c \in \varrho(w)$. It then follows that $c \notin (\varrho \backslash A)(w)$, and, hence, $c \in A(w)$. So, for all $w \in vE$ for which $c \in \theta(v, w)$ and $c \in \varrho(w)$ we have $c \in A(w)$. But then, by definition of α-attractor, also $c \in A(v)$. Contradiction, since $c \in (\varrho \backslash A)(v)$.   □

We proceed with the following result regarding the propagation of winning with respect to a sub-mapping along an attractor.

Lemma 3. *Let $\mathcal{G} = (V, E, \mathfrak{C}, p, \theta, (V_0, V_1))$ be a variability parity game and let $\varrho : V \to 2^{\mathfrak{C}}$ be a restriction. Let α be an arbitrary player and suppose U is a sub-mapping of ϱ. If for all $v \in V$, player α wins vertex v for all configurations $c \in U(v)$, then α wins vertex v for all configurations $c \in Attr_\alpha(U)(v)$.*

Proof. Let ϱ, α and U be as stated. We proceed by induction on i with respect to the definition of $Attr_\alpha^i(U)$.

Base case ($i = 0$): Follows by assumption. Induction step ($i > 0$): Suppose player α wins vertex v for all configurations $c \in Attr_\alpha^i(U)(v)$. Pick an arbitrary vertex v' and configuration $c' \in Attr_\alpha^{i+1}(U)(v')$. Since $c' \in Attr_\alpha^{i+1}(U)(v')$, we have $c' \in \varrho(v)$. If $c' \in Attr_\alpha^i(U)(v')$, the result follows instantly by induction. If $c' \notin Attr_\alpha^i(U)(v')$, then we distinguish two cases.

Case $v' \in V_\alpha$: Then there must be some $w \in v'E$ such that $c' \in \theta(v', w)$ and $c' \in Attr_\alpha^i(U)(w)$. Let w be such. Then player α can play a c'-configured token from v' to w and, by induction, win vertex w for configuration c'. But then she also wins vertex v' for configuration c'.

Case $v' \in V_{\bar{\alpha}}$. Then, for all $w \in v'E$ such that $c' \in \theta(v', w)$, also $c' \in Attr_\alpha^i(U)(w)$. Since regardless of how player $\bar{\alpha}$ moves the c'-configured token from v' along an edge admitting c', she will end up in a vertex that, by induction, is won by α for configuration c'. $\qquad\square$

The next theorem captures the correctness of Algorithm 1.

Theorem 2. *Let $\mathcal{G} = (V, E, \mathfrak{C}, p, \theta, (V_0, V_1))$ be a variability parity game and let $\varrho : V \to 2^{\mathfrak{C}}$ be a restriction such that $\mathcal{G}$ is total with respect to ϱ. Then $\textsc{Solve}(\varrho)$ returns the mappings $W_0, W_1 : V \to 2^{\mathfrak{C}}$ such that for all $v \in V$, $W_0(v) \cup W_1(v) = \mathfrak{C}$ and both for player 0 and 1, for each $c \in W_\alpha(v)$, player α wins vertex v for configuration c.*

Proof. Fix a total variability parity game $\mathcal{G} = (V, E, \mathfrak{C}, p, \theta, (V_0, V_1))$. We prove a slightly stronger property, *viz.* for all restrictions $\varrho : V \to 2^{\mathfrak{C}}$ such that $\mathcal{G}$ is total with respect to ϱ, procedure $\textsc{Solve}(\varrho)$ returns mappings $W_0, W_1 : V \to 2^{\mathfrak{C}}$ that are sub-mappings of ϱ such that for all $v \in V$ it holds that $W_0(v) \cup W_1(v) = \varrho(v)$ and player α wins vertex v for each configuration $c \in W_\alpha(v)$. Let us define $|\varrho| = \sum_{v \in V} |\varrho(v)|$. The proof will proceed by induction on $|\varrho|$ and closely follows the standard proofs of correctness for parity games.

Base case: We have $\varrho(v) = \emptyset$ for all $v \in V$. Consequently, the algorithm returns the functions W_0 and W_1 satisfying $W_0(v) = W_1(v) = \emptyset$ for all $v \in V$. Trivially W_0 and W_1 satisfy the statement.

Induction step: Let ϱ be a restriction such that $\mathcal{G}$ is total with respect to ϱ. As our induction hypothesis, assume that the statement holds for all ϱ' such that $|\varrho'| < |\varrho|$. Let m be the maximal priority among those vertices in $\mathcal{G}$ for which ϱ yields a non-empty set of configurations, and let α be $m \bmod 2$. Let U be the sub mapping of ϱ for which $U(v) = \varrho(v)$ if $p(v) = m$, and $U(v) = \emptyset$ otherwise, and let A be the sub-mapping $Attr_\alpha(U)$. By Lemma 2, $\mathcal{G}$ is total with respect to $\varrho \backslash A$, and hence, by induction, the functions W_0', W_1' returned by $\textsc{Solve}(\varrho \backslash A)$ satisfy the statement. Next, we distinguish two cases.

Case $W'_{\bar{\alpha}}(v) = \emptyset$ for all v. Then, by our induction hypothesis, player α wins all vertices v for configurations $c \in W'_{\alpha}(v)$ in the game restricted to $\varrho \backslash A$. Regarding the remaining vertices, note that for vertices $v \in V_{\bar{\alpha}}$ and configurations $c \in W'_{\alpha}(v)$ with an edge to a vertex w with $c \in A(w)$, player $\bar{\alpha}$ may escape to such vertices. However, then α can force the play to visit a vertex with priority m. Remaining in vertices with priority m means losing for $\bar{\alpha}$. Playing to any vertex other than those in U leads to a play that remains either in W_{α} or infinitely often revisits U. In either case, α wins such plays. For vertices $v \in V_{\alpha}$ and configurations $c \in \varrho(v)$, player α either follows the winning strategy in W'_{α} or the attractor strategy for A towards a vertex in U. Consequently, α wins all vertices v for all configurations $c \in \varrho(v)$, which is consistent with W_{α} and $W_{\bar{\alpha}}$ as returned by SOLVE.

Case $W'_{\bar{\alpha}}(v) \neq \emptyset$ for some v. Since player $\bar{\alpha}$ wins any vertex v for configuration $c \in W'_{\bar{\alpha}}(v)$ in the game restricted to $\varrho \backslash A$, and player α cannot force the play to a vertex w for which $c \in A(w)$, player $\bar{\alpha}$ also wins all such vertices and configurations in $\mathcal{G}$ restricted to ϱ. By Lemma 3, $\bar{\alpha}$ thus also wins all vertices v for configurations $c \in B = Attr_{\bar{\alpha}}(W'_{\bar{\alpha}})(v)$. By Lemma 2, $\mathcal{G}$ is total with respect to $\varrho \backslash B$, and hence, by induction, the functions W''_0, W''_1 returned by the call SOLVE$(\varrho \backslash B)$ satisfy the statement. It then follows that player α wins all vertices v for configurations $c \in W''_{\alpha}(v)$ and player $\bar{\alpha}$ wins all vertices v for configurations $c \in (W_{\bar{\alpha}} \cup B)(v)$ as set by SOLVE. $\square$

Algorithm 1 requires that the attractor $Attr_{\alpha}(U)$ for a sub-mapping U can be computed (cf. line 8 of the algorithm). To cater for this, the attractor computation for sub-mappings can be implemented following the pseudo-code of Algorithm 2, the correctness of which is claimed by Lemma 4.

Lemma 4. *For a restriction $\varrho : V \to 2^{\mathfrak{C}}$, a sub-mapping $U : V \to 2^{\mathfrak{C}}$ of ϱ and a player α, ATTR(α, U) terminates and returns a sub-mapping A of ϱ satisfying $A = Attr_{\alpha}(U)$.* $\square$

Algorithm 2 is actually a straightforward implementation of the definition of the attractor set computation following the high-level structure of the attractor computation for standard parity games. We forego a detailed proof of Lemma 4, which, for soundness, uses an invariant stating that the computed sub-mapping A under-approximates $Attr_{\alpha}(U)$ and for completeness uses an invariant that asserts for all configurations $c \in Attr_{\alpha}(U)(v)$ either $c \in A(v)$ or there is a vertex $v' \in Q$ and attractor strategy underlying $Attr_{\alpha}(U)(v)$ inducing a play for c, starting in v, visiting v' and not visiting vertices v'' with $c \in A(v'')$ in between.

Instead, we briefly explain the underlying intuition. It conducts a typical backwards reachability analysis, maintaining a queue Q of vertices that are at the frontier of the search for at least some configurations. For each vertex w in this frontier, its predecessors $v \in Ew$ are inspected in a for-loop. Either such a predecessor is owned by player α, in which case all configurations that can reach w in one step are added to the attractor set for v, or such a predecessor is owned by player $\bar{\alpha}$, in which case *all* v's successors must be inspected, and only those configurations c of v for which all their successor options are to move to some vertex w' already satisfying $c \in A(w')$ are added to its attractor.

Algorithm 2 Attractor computation. Given a variability parity game $\mathcal{G} = (V, E, \mathfrak{C}, p, \theta, (V_0, V_1))$, a restriction $\varrho : V \to 2^{\mathfrak{C}}$ and a sub-mapping U of ϱ, the algorithm computes the α-attractor towards U.

```
1: function ATTR(α, U)
2:     Queue Q ← {v ∈ V | U(v) ≠ ∅}
3:     A ← U
4:     while Q is not empty do
5:         w ← Q.pop()
6:         for every v ∈ Ew such that ϱ(v) ∩ θ(v, w) ∩ A(w) ≠ ∅ do
7:             if v ∈ Vα then
8:                 a ← ϱ(v) ∩ θ(v, w) ∩ A(w)
9:             else
10:                a ← ϱ(v)
11:                for w' ∈ vE such that ϱ(v) ∩ θ(v, w') ∩ ϱ(w') ≠ ∅ do
12:                    a ← a ∩ (𝔠 \ (θ(v, w') ∩ ϱ(w')) ∪ A(w'))
13:                end for
14:            end if
15:            if a \ A(v) ≠ ∅ then
16:                A(v) ← A(v) ∪ a
17:                if v ∉ Q then Q.push(v)
18:            end if
19:        end for
20:    end while
21:    return A
22: end function
```

---

6   Implementation and Experiments

As an initial validation of our approach we experimented with two SPL examples, *viz.* the well-known minepump and elevator case studies first recognised as SPLs in [3, 14], modelled for the mCRL2 toolset [20, 21].

A prototype for solving variability parity games connecting to the mCRL2 toolset was implemented in C++ using the BuDDy package [31, 32] for BDD operations. The prototype uses BDDs to represent product families; parity games are represented as graphs with adjacency lists for incoming and outgoing edges. For the recursive algorithm, bit vectors are used to represent sets of vertices sorted by parity then by priority. All experiments were run on a standard Linux desktop with Intel i5-4570 3.20Hz processor and 8GB DDR3 internal memory.[3]

6.1   Minepump Case Study

The minepump example of [33], in the SPL variant of [4], describes a configurable software system coordinating the sensors and actuators of a pump for mine drainage. The purpose of the system is to keep a mine shaft free from water.

---

[3] Solvers and experiments: https://github.com/SjefvanLoo/VariabilityParityGames

A controller operates a pump that may not start nor continue running in the presence of dangerously high levels of methane gas. To this end, it needs to communicate with sensors that measure the water and methane levels. The SPL model has 11 features and 128 products; the resulting FTS consists of 582 states and 1376 transitions. The mCRL2 code of this model, developed for [19], closely follows the fPROMELA code of [4] (also used in [16]) that is distributed with [8].

We verified nine properties, φ_1 to φ_9, for the minepump case study, examined also elsewhere in the SPL literature (cf., *e.g.* [3, 4, 7, 16, 19, 24, 34–36]). These induce variability parity games consisting of approximately 3000 to 9200 vertices and 2 to 4 different priorities. Specifically, for properties φ_1, φ_4, and φ_7, we used the following formulae, expressed in the mCRL2 variant of the modal μ-calculus, which allows to mix fixed points, regular expressions, and first-order constructs.

Property φ_1. Absence of deadlock: `[true*] <true> true`

Property φ_4. The pump cannot be switched on infinitely often:

```
( mu X. nu Y. ([pumpStart] [!pumpStop*] [pumpStop] X &&
    [!pumpStart] Y )) && ( [true*] [pumpStart] mu Z. [!pumpStop] Z )
```

Property φ_7. The controller can always eventually receive/read a message, *i.e.* return to its initial state from any state: `[true*] <true*> <receiveMsg> true`

While φ_4 is a common LTL-type formula, φ_7 is typical for CTL. Table 3 provides the running times for verification of properties φ_1 to φ_9 via variability parity games, and the sizes of classes (P^+, P^-) partitioning $\mathcal{P}$. The results show that the collective solving strategy for family-based SPL model checking outperforms the individual solving strategy for product-based SPL model checking.

While a full baseline comparison with other SPL model checking algorithms was not performed, our approach promises to be at least as efficient as related approaches. This conjecture is based on the running times reported for properties φ_1, φ_4, and φ_6 in [4,16,19] (all verified with standard computers of that time).

Table 3. Running times (**in ms**) for experiments for the product-based and family-based SPL model checking of the minepump and elevator case studies using recursive algorithm for variability parity games.

Minepump SPL				Elevator SPL			
Property	product	family	$|P^+|/|P^-|$	Property	product	family	$|P^+|/|P^-|$
φ_1	28.88	3.92	128/0	ψ_1	14335	5409	2/30
φ_2	54.79	6.76	0/128	ψ_2	14988	5744	4/28
φ_3	184.7	24.70	0/128	ψ_3	16045	5020	4/28
φ_4	145.0	37.46	96/32	ψ_4	16865	5272	4/28
φ_5	144.5	12.19	96/32	ψ_5	8954	3013	16/16
φ_6	242.9	42.79	112/16	ψ_6	4252	772	32/0
φ_7	134.3	11.71	128/0	ψ_7	4171	765	32/0
φ_8	17.44	1.058	128/0				
φ_9	110.0	6.853	0/128				

6.2   Elevator Case Study

The other configurable system we considered is the elevator example of [37] of a lift travelling between five floors. A product in the elevator system may or may not provide the features of parking, load and overload detection, cancelling on emptiness, and priority for specific floors. Absence or presence of specific features in a system configuration generally leads to different behaviour. The behaviour of the lift itself is governed by the so-called single button collective control strategy, deciding which floor is visited next. Roughly speaking, and dependent on the specific feature setting, the lift operates in sweeps, only changing direction if there are no outstanding calls in the current direction. The FTS implementation in mCRL2 underlying the experiments is derived from the 120 lines of SMV code presented in [37]. Although the number of features in this SPL example is small, *viz.* only 5 independent features resulting in 32 different configurations, the FTS consists of 95591 states and 622265 transitions.

The seven properties, ψ_1 to ψ_7 for the elevator case study, also examined elsewhere in the literature (cf., *e.g.* [10–12, 14, 15, 25, 26, 35, 38]), which we experimented with were adapted from [37]. These induce variability parity games consisting of approximately 440000 to 18500000 vertices with 2 to 3 different priorities. The properties cover a proper handling of requests, correct behaviour with respect to the control strategy, proper behaviour when idling, and the possibility to stop at floors while passing. By way of illustration, properties ψ_2, ψ_3, and ψ_5 are expressed as follows in the mCRL2 variant of the modal μ-calculus.

Property ψ_2. Invariantly, if a lift button is pressed for a floor, the lift will eventually open its doors on this floor:

```
[true*] forall i:Floor. [liftButton(i)]
         ( mu X. ( [!open(i)] X && <true> true ) )
```

Property ψ_3. Invariantly, if the lift is travelling up while there are calls above the lift will not change direction:

```
[true*] ( ([ direction(up).
      (!(direction(down) || exists k:Floor. open(k)))* ]
       forall i:Floor. val(1 <= i && i <= 5) =>
         [ open(i) ] forall j:Floor. val(i < j && j <= 5) =>
           [ liftButton(j) ] mu Y. ( [!open(j)] Y &&
             [direction(down)] false && < true > true ) ) )
```

Property ψ_5. Invariantly, if the lift is idling, it does not change floors:

```
( forall i:Floor. val(1 <= i && i <= 5) =>
    <true*.idling(i)> true ) &&
  ( [true*] forall i:Floor. val(1 <= i && i <= 5) =>
     [ idling(i) ] nu Y. <idling(i)> Y )
```

It is noted, in particular with regard to property ψ_5, that unlike the original SMV elevator system, our lift idles with its doors open, to prevent the situation where someone in the lift infinitely often presses the landing button for the current floor, keeping the process busy without the lift making any movement.

Also in the case of the elevator system we notice a significant difference in performance when doing product-based model checking calling the individual solving strategy or family-based model checking calling the collective solving strategy. The difference is, however, not that striking compared to the minepump case study, which, we believe, is due to the small number of different features.

As said, a full baseline comparison with other SPL model checking algorithms was not performed. For one, the efficiency of our approach with respect to related approaches is not easily measured with the elevator case study. While properties ψ_2 and ψ_5 were verified also in [14, 15, 25, 26, 35, 38], not much can be concluded from the reported running times. First, our model's mCRL2 code was developed from scratch, following the SMV code from [37], and not the fPROMELA code of [14, 15, 25, 26, 35, 38]. Moreover, the number of floors in these models ranges from 4 to 6. In [10–12], finally, the models are probabilistic, the number of floors ranges from 2 to 40, and different (probabilistic) properties were verified.

7   Conclusions

We have introduced variability parity games as a generalisation of parity games, reflecting the generalisation by FTSs of LTSs, and have defined the SPL model checking problem of modal μ-calculus formulae on FTSs as a variability parity game solving problem, for which we have provided a recursive algorithm based on a collective, family-based solving strategy. To illustrate the efficiency of the approach, we have applied it to two classical examples from the SPL literature, *viz.* the minepump and the elevator case studies. The experiments show that the collective, family-based strategy of solving variability parity games typically outperforms the individual, product-based strategy of solving the standard parity games obtained by projection from the variability parity games

Further experiments are needed to measure and pinpoint the differences in efficiency. One direction for future work is to generate a sufficient number of random variability parity games to this aim. In particular, the configuration sets that label the edges of the variability parity games for the minepump and elevator case studies obey a very specific distribution, typically admitting either 100% or 50% of the configurations. It would be interesting to see how our approach behaves in case of SPLs with more complexly structured feature diagrams.

There is a wealth of different algorithms available for parity games, of which the recursive algorithm that we have here lifted to variability parity games is one of the most competitive ones in practice. Nevertheless, we think it pays to study other algorithms and lift these to variability parity games, too. Finally, we believe that variability parity games have applications beyond SPL model checking; *e.g.* in (parameter) synthesis problems. We leave these topics for future research.

Acknowledgements Work partially supported by the MIUR PRIN 2017FTXR7S project IT MaTTerS (Methods and Tools for Trustworthy Smart Systems).

References

1. A. Classen, P. Heymans, and P.-Y. Schobbens. What's in a Feature: A Requirements Engineering Perspective. In J.L. Fiadeiro and P. Inverardi, editors, *FASE'08*, volume 4961 of *LNCS*, pages 16–30. Springer, 2008.
2. S. Apel, D. Batory, C. Kästner, and G. Saake. *Feature-Oriented Software Product Lines: Concepts and Implementation*. Springer, 2013.
3. A. Classen, P. Heymans, P.-Y. Schobbens, A. Legay, and J.-F. Raskin. Model Checking Lots of Systems: Efficient Verification of Temporal Properties in Software Product Lines. In *Proc. ICSE'10*, pages 335–344. ACM, 2010.
4. A. Classen, M. Cordy, P.-Y. Schobbens, P. Heymans, A. Legay, and J.-F. Raskin. Featured Transition Systems: Foundations for Verifying Variability-Intensive Systems and their Application to LTL Model Checking. *IEEE Trans. Softw. Eng.*, 39(8):1069–1089, 2013.
5. M. Cordy, X. Devroey, A. Legay, G. Perrouin, A. Classen, P. Heymans, P.-Y. Schobbens, and J.-F. Raskin. A Decade of Featured Transition Systems. In M.H. ter Beek, A. Fantechi, and L. Semini, editors, *From Software Engineering to Formal Methods and Tools, and Back*, volume 11865 of *LNCS*, pages 285–312. Springer, 2019.
6. T. Thüm, S. Apel, C. Kästner, I. Schaefer, and G. Saake. A Classification and Survey of Analysis Strategies for Software Product Lines. *ACM Comput. Surv.*, 47(1):6:1–6:45, 2014.
7. A. Classen, M. Cordy, P. Heymans, A. Legay, and P.-Y. Schobbens. Model checking software product lines with SNIP. *Int. J. Softw. Tools Technol. Transf.*, 14(5):589–612, 2012.
8. M. Cordy, A. Classen, P. Heymans, P.-Y. Schobbens, and A. Legay. ProVeLines: a product line of verifiers for software product lines. In *Proc. SPLC'13*, volume 2, pages 141–146. ACM, 2013.
9. M.H. ter Beek, F. Mazzanti, and A. Sulova. VMC: A Tool for Product Variability Analysis. In D. Giannakopoulou and D. Méry, editors, *Proc. FM'12*, volume 7436 of *LNCS*, pages 450–454. Springer, 2012.
10. P. Chrszon, C. Dubslaff, S. Klüppelholz, and C. Baier. Family-Based Modeling and Analysis for Probabilistic Systems – Featuring PROFEAT. In P. Stevens and A. Wąsowski, editors, *Proc. FASE'16*, volume 9633 of *LNCS*, pages 287–304, 2016.
11. P. Chrszon, C. Dubslaff, S. Klüppelholz, and C. Baier. ProFeat: feature-oriented engineering for family-based probabilistic model checking. *Form. Asp. Comp.*, 30(1):45–75, 2018.
12. M.H. ter Beek, A. Legay, A. Lluch Lafuente, and A. Vandin. A framework for quantitative modeling and analysis of highly (re)configurable systems. *IEEE Trans. Softw. Eng.*, 2018.
13. A. Vandin, M.H. ter Beek, A. Legay, and A. Lluch Lafuente. QFLan: A Tool for the Quantitative Analysis of Highly Reconfigurable Systems. In K. Havelund, J. Peleska, B. Roscoe, and E. de Vink, editors, *Proc. FM'18*, volume 10951 of *LNCS*, pages 329–337. Springer, 2018.
14. A. Classen, P. Heymans, P.-Y. Schobbens, and A. Legay. Symbolic Model Checking of Software Product Lines. In *Proc. ICSE'11*, pages 321–330. ACM, 2011.
15. A. Classen, M. Cordy, P. Heymans, A. Legay, and P.-Y. Schobbens. Formal semantics, modular specification, and symbolic verification of product-line behaviour. *Sci. Comput. Program.*, 80(B):416–439, 2014.

16. A.S. Dimovski, A.S. Al-Sibahi, C. Brabrand, and A. Wąsowski. Family-Based Model Checking Without a Family-Based Model Checker. In B. Fischer and J. Geldenhuys, editors, *Proc. SPIN'15*, volume 9232 of *LNCS*, pages 282–299. Springer, 2015.
17. M. Lochau, S. Mennicke, H. Baller, and L. Ribbeck. Incremental model checking of delta-oriented software product lines. *J. Log. Algebr. Meth. Program.*, 85(1):245–267, 2016.
18. M.H. ter Beek and E.P. de Vink. Using mCRL2 for the Analysis of Software Product Lines. In *Proc. FormaliSE'14*, pages 31–37. IEEE, 2014.
19. M.H. ter Beek, E.P. de Vink, and T.A.C. Willemse. Family-Based Model Checking with mCRL2. In M. Huisman and J. Rubin, editors, *Proc. FASE'17*, volume 10202 of *LNCS*, pages 387–405. Springer, 2017.
20. S. Cranen, J.F. Groote, J.J.A. Keiren, F.P.M. Stappers, E.P. de Vink, W. Wesselink, and T.A.C. Willemse. An Overview of the mCRL2 Toolset and Its Recent Advances. In N. Piterman and S.A. Smolka, editors, *Proc. TACAS'13*, volume 7795 of *LNCS*, pages 199–213. Springer, 2013.
21. O. Bunte, J.F. Groote, J.J.A. Keiren, M. Laveaux, T. Neele, E.P. de Vink, W. Wesselink, A. Wijs, and T.A.C. Willemse. The mCRL2 Toolset for Analysing Concurrent Systems: Improvements in Expressivity and Usability. In T. Vojnar and L. Zhang, editors, *Proc. TACAS'19*, volume 11428 of *LNCS*, pages 21–39. Springer, 2019.
22. M.H. ter Beek, E.P. de Vink, and T.A.C. Willemse. Towards a Feature mu-Calculus Targeting SPL Verification. *Electr. Proc. Theor. Comput. Sci.*, 206:61–75, 2016.
23. A.S. Dimovski. Symbolic Game Semantics for Model Checking Program Families. In D. Bošnački and A. Wijs, editors, *Proc. SPIN'16*, volume 9641 of *LNCS*, pages 19–37. Springer, 2016.
24. A.S. Dimovski and A. Wąsowski. Variability-Specific Abstraction Refinement for Family-Based Model Checking. In M. Huisman and J. Rubin, editors, *Proc. FASE'17*, volume 10202 of *LNCS*, pages 406–423. Springer, 2017.
25. A.S. Dimovski. Abstract Family-Based Model Checking Using Modal Featured Transition Systems: Preservation of CTL*. In A. Russo and A. Schürr, editors, *Proc. FASE'18*, volume 10802 of *LNCS*, pages 301–318. Springer, 2018.
26. A.S. Dimovski, A. Legay, and A. Wąsowski. Variability Abstraction and Refinement for Game-Based Lifted Model Checking of Full CTL. In R. Hähnle and W. van der Aalst, editors, *Proc. FASE'19*, volume 11424 of *LNCS*, pages 192–209. Springer, 2019.
27. W. Zielonka. Infinite games on finitely coloured graphs with applications to automata on infinite trees. *Theor. Comput. Sci.*, 200(1-2):135–183, 1998.
28. O. Friedmann and M. Lange. Solving Parity Games in Practice. In Z. Liu and A.P. Ravn, editors, *Proc. ATVA'09*, volume 5799 of *LNCS*, pages 182–196. Springer, 2009.
29. T. van Dijk. Oink: An Implementation and Evaluation of Modern Parity Game Solvers. In D. Beyer and M. Huisman, editors, *Proc. TACAS'18*, volume 10805 of *LNCS*, pages 291–308. Springer, 2018.
30. J.C. Bradfield and I. Walukiewicz. The mu-calculus and model checking. In E.M. Clarke, T.A. Henzinger, H. Veith, and R. Bloem, editors, *Handbook of Model Checking*, chapter 26, pages 871–919. Springer, 2018.
31. J. Lind-Nielsen. BuDDy: A Binary Decision Diagram package. Technical Report IT-TR 1999–028, IT University of Copenhagen, 1999.
32. H. Cohen, J. Whaley, J. Wildt, and N. Gorogiannis. BuDDy: A Binary Decision Diagram library. http://sourceforge.net/p/buddy/. Last visited October 18, 2019.

33. J. Kramer, J. Magee, M. Sloman, and A. Lister. CONIC: an integrated approach to distributed computer control systems. *IEE Proc. E*, 130(1):1–10, 1983.

34. X. Devroey, G. Perrouin, M. Papadakis, A. Legay, P.-Y. Schobbens, and P. Heymans. Featured Model-based Mutation Analysis. In *Proc. ICSE'16*, pages 655–666. ACM, 2016.

35. A.S. Dimovski, A.S. Al-Sibahi, C. Brabrand, and A. Wąsowski. Efficient family-based model checking via variability abstractions. *Int. J. Softw. Tools Technol. Transf.*, 19(5):585–603, 2017.

36. M.H. ter Beek, F. Damiani, M. Lienhardt, F. Mazzanti, and L. Paolini. Static Analysis of Featured Transition Systems. In *Proc. SPLC'19*, pages 39–51. ACM, 2019.

37. M. Plath and M. Ryan. Feature integration using a feature construct. *Sci. Comput. Program.*, 41(1):53–84, 2001.

38. A.S. Dimovski. CTL* family-based model checking using variability abstractions and modal transition systems. *Int. J. Softw. Tools Technol. Transf.*, 22(1):35–55, 2020.

Model-based tool support for Service Design

Francisco J. Pérez-Blanco, Juan M. Vara,
Cristian Gómez, Valeria De Castro, Esperanza Marcos

Kybele Research Group, Universidad Rey Juan Carlos, Madrid, Spain
{francisco.perez,juanmanuel.vara,cristian.gomez,valeria.decastro
,esperanza.marcos}@urjc.es

Abstract. This paper introduces a modelling environment for service design that currently supports 5 different notations (Business Model Canvas, e³value, Service Blueprint, Process Chain Network and BPMN). Besides, the tool supports the generation of partial views of models based on a particular notation from models made with another one, along with the corresponding relations model.

Keywords. Service Design, Business Modelling, Model Driven Engineering.

1   Motivation

Born in the context of research on services marketing, service design evolved and gained impact thanks to the promotion of IDEO and it has been eventually established as the entry point to service development for any organization seriously concerned with user experience and digital transformation. For example, take a look at the British government's efforts in this regard, which have been materialized through the Government's Digital Service initiative.

Business modeling is essential in order to achieve a successful service design, since companies need to constantly redesign their business model [3] in their strive towards a successful servitization process. To that end it is key that all the departments of the organization share a clear vision and a common understanding of such models, even when the working languages are different, which, in the case of business models, implies using different notations [4]. Literature reveals indeed that there is a huge number of definitions of what a business model is since the concept has been historically considered from three different perspectives: technology-oriented, strategy-oriented and organization-oriented [2]. Some authors even distinct four categories of business modelling, namely: business process models, business motivation models, business organization models and business rules models [1].

Two of these business modeling disciplines, namely business organization and business process models, are at the core of service design. It implies indeed the use of business models more oriented towards providing a quick and strategic overview of the organization, such as the Business Model Canvas or the e³value model, and business models that are more oriented to show the details of a particular service offering, like Service Blueprints, Process Chain Networks or BPMN models.

© The Author(s) 2020
H. Wehrheim and J. Cabot (Eds.): FASE 2020, LNCS 12076, pp. 266–272, 2020.
https://doi.org/10.1007/978-3-030-45234-6_13

Even though tool support is currently available for some of these techniques, there is no comprehensive solution that allows working with all of them. Therefore, different stand-alone tools must be used for each notation, like generic diagramming tools or web-based apps, such as MS-Visio or Lucidchart. Although these can be good options for quick sketching, such tools were not devised to enable later processing of the information gathered in such models [5].

So, provided that the only option to support some notations was to develop a new tool due to the lack of previous tool support (PCN) and the lack of model-based tool support for other notations (Canvas and e³value), a comprehensive toolkit was developed in order to facilitate the building of technological bridges among notations as well as the implementation of post processing tasks, such as validation, autocorrection or model transformations.

To address these problems this report introduces the last version of INNoVaServ[1]: a modelling toolkit that comprises a set of visual DSLs implementing different business modeling notations. Regarding previous versions, this one provides tool support for new notations (PCN and BPMN) in the shape of DSLs and it also bundles the tooling needed to register and manage the relationships among business models defined through such DSLs. To that end, the toolkit supports the generation of partial models from models expressed with another notation, along with traces or relations models collecting the relationships between the elements of the models involved in such transformation. In addition to that, INNoVaServ supports the formal validation of Service Blueprint and PCN models by means of formal techniques [6, 7] and puts together syntax and semantic checkers for each of the notations supported by the framework.

2   Technological Solution

This section first discusses the conceptual architecture of the modelling toolkit introduced in this work to later summarize its development process.

2.1   Conceptual Architecture

The conceptual architecture of *INNoVaServ*, which results in a high level of modularization, is illustrated in Figure 1 and can be described according to two orthogonal dimensions.

On the one hand, INNoVaServ can be thought of as a set of five integrated DSLs, one for each business modelling notation supported by the tool. This way, in the horizontal dimension of Figure 1 five different modules corresponding to five different DSLs can be distinguished: Business Model Canvas, e³value, Service Blueprint, PCN and BPMN.

On the other hand, the conceptual architecture of INNoVaServ leans on the functionality provided by EMF to follow the *separation of concerns* principle [9] by distinguishing the presentation of each model from the model itself. This way, the *presentation* tier includes the components needed to support the edition and representation of models whereas the models are managed by the *logic* tier. As right-hand side of Figure

---

[1] http://kybele.es/innovaserv/finalthesis/

1 shows, this distinction corresponds to the usual distinction between the concrete and the abstract syntax of any modelling language.

Besides, a layer connecting the five DSLs is depicted at lower part of Figure 1. Following the idea suggested in [10] to refer to all the tasks related with model management, this layer is called *model processor* and serves as container for different components supporting different model management tasks to be bundled in the tool (validation, weaving, transformation, etc.).

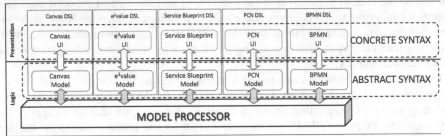

Figure 1. INNoVaServ conceptual architecture.

2.2   Development Process

Initially, each of the DSLs bundled in INNoVaServ were built atop of Eclipse EMF/GMF according to the guidelines sketched in [5] for the development of model-based tools that take the shape of DSL toolkits.

However, due to the recent lack of GMF support, it was necessary the migration of the DSLs from GMF to Sirius. Sirius is also based on Eclipse EMF, and the development process of editors for graphical DSLs with Sirius is still similar to that of GMF: specification of the metamodel; definition of the concrete syntax (Sirius allows to see real time results, besides easily creating different *viewpoints* for the same abstract syntax); identification of the relationships between the models collecting the definition of the abstract and the concrete syntax; creation of the tool palette and finally, manual refinement (if needed) of the generated code.

A series of additional functionalities have been also added to the graphical editors developed, such as the automatic validation and fixing of models using the *Acceleo* language. In addition, to materialize the relationships among the notations supported by the tool, a generic relations (or traces) metamodel (Figure 2) has been defined to support the creation of simplistic relations models and the Epsilon family of languages has been then used to implement a set of model transformations. This way, when any of these transformations runs, a relations model is generated along with the corresponding target model. Specifically, ETL has been used since it supports many-to-many model transformations and it eases the combination of declarative rules with imperative constructions and lazy and greedy rules. This is an essential feature, since many of the model transformations developed are not direct, but require certain level of interaction with the user in order to collect some design decisions that should guide the transformation. In this sense, EOL has been used to improve user interaction by means of dialog boxes and to handle the transformations accordingly.

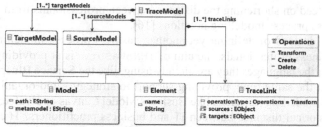

Figure 2. Generic relations metamodel for *INNoVaServ*.

We are conscious of the variety of traces metamodels existing in the literature. Indeed, some of them have been co-authored by us [11]. Nevertheless, a generic simplistic metamodel seemed enough to provide a proof of concept for the proposal. In the meantime, a more complete metamodel, enabling the identification of more sophisticated relationships could be used.

To handle and visualize the information collected in the relationships models, Modelink, a simple yet useful multi-panel editor provided by Epsilon is used. It consists of 2-3 side-by-side EMF tree-based editors, which allows visualizing the source and target models, along with the relations model. Note that relationships collected in the latter can be directly edited in the editor.

Again, it is worth noting that the visualizations provided by Modelink are planned to be improved by developing ad-hoc multi-panel editors like those presented in [11]. For instance, integrated overviews of all the models involved in a given project and their relationships could be supported this way.

Finally, since the toolkit is still basically an EMF/GMF tool, it is consequently interoperable with any other EMF/GMF existing tool. Note that there exists plenty of them since EMF/GMF has turned to be the de-facto standard for the development of model-based tools for the last 10 years. For instance, leaning on Papyrus, UML models could be almost immediately combined with those supported by INNoVaServ for Service Design tasks.

3   Related Works

This section reviews existing works in the area from both the methodological and technical point of view. However, it is worth noting from the beginning that none of the existing works or tools deal with all the notations supported by INNoVaServ, neither provide tool support to enable the processing of the information generated during a service design project.

A quick look at the plenty of systematic literature reviews on business process modelling and the topics covered by them shows that this is somehow the most mature business modelling discipline. Recent reviews are indeed not focused on characterizing existing proposals, since that has been largely done in the past, but on available mechanisms to assess their quality [12] or complexity [13].

However, despite the number of works in the area, still new approaches for business process modelling [15] and BPMN dialects [14] appear every so often. Many of them are focused indeed on shortening the distance between professionals from business areas and business process modelling notations [16].

By contrast, instead of defining yet-another business process modelling language tailored to business professionals, the aim of INNoVaServ is at providing them with tool support for the languages they are already using, like the Service Blueprint, BPMN or the PCN. At the same time, providing support to strategy - and organization - oriented business modelling notations like Business Model Canvas or e³value, will help to shorten the historical distance between IT and business practitioners. The models defined and handled by management areas become directly connected (or even mapped) to the models used by IT practitioners, more frequently expressed in terms of BPMN or UML.

On the other hand, despite the recent interest attracted by the field due to the rise of product-service-systems [8], business intelligence modelling [17] and some other disciplines, research on strategic- and organization-oriented business modelling, is still at an early stage, probably because the business process model hype preceded the business model one [4].

Regarding tool-support, provided that no tool has been found supporting the five notations integrated in INNoVaServ, some of the existing tools supporting at least two of them are briefly discussed in the following.

*Canvanaizer*² and *Real Time Board*³ are web-based applications that supports collaborative edition of Business Model Canvas and Service Blueprint diagrams. They own a simple and intuitive graphical interface (specially the latter) but they are not based on models, so the represented information is merely graphical. They do not offer export capabilities in a format suitable for post-processing (such as XML), so the output format is reduced to a simple image. Both are commercial solutions, offering free limited editions.

Tool support for e³value was so far limited to the *e³editor*, a desktop application that allows representing graphically and accurately e³value diagrams. Models can be persisted in RDF format, which simplifies export/import tasks.

Regarding PCN, no tool has been found supporting this notation. The only way of defining PCN diagrams to date was using generic diagramming apps or even image editors, like MS Visio or Lucidchart.

Finally, as already mentioned, there are plenty of BPMN tools, such as Bonita Studio, Signavio, BizAgi or IBM WebSphere, each one providing different capabilities.

All this given, to the best of our knowledge this is the first proposal to consider the business modelling notations discussed here and providing tool support to use them in the context of an integrated environment which ease the transition between each of the notations considered.

Acknowledgements. This work has been partially funded by the Regional Government of Madrid, through the FORTE-CM project (S2018/TCS-4314) and the Spanish MINECO, through the MADRID project (TIN2017-88557-R).

---

² https://canvanizer.com/
³ https://realtimeboard.com/

References

1. Bridgeland, D. M., & Zahavi, R. (2009). Business modelling: a practical guide to realizing business value. Morgan Kaufmann/Elsevier.
2. Wirtz, B. W., Pistoia, A., Ullrich, S., & Göttel, V. (2015). Business models: origin, development and future research perspectives. Long Range Planning.
3. Holmlid, S., & Evenson, S. (2008). Bringing service design to service sciences, management and engineering. In Service science, management and engineering education for the 21st century (pp. 341-345). Springer, Boston, MA.
4. DaSilva, C. M., & Trkman, P. (2014). Business model: What it is and what it is not. Long range planning, 47(6), 379-389.
5. Vara, J. M., & Marcos, E. (2012). A framework for model-driven development of information systems: Technical decisions and lessons learned. Journal of Systems and Software, 85(10), 2368-2384.
6. Estañol M., Marcos E., Oriol X., Pérez F.J., Teniente E., Vara J.M. (2017) Validation of Service Blueprint Models by Means of Formal Simulation Techniques. ICSOC 2017.
7. Gómez-Martínez, E., Pérez-Blanco, F.J., De Lara, J., Vara, J.M., Marcos, E. (2019) Formal Support of Process Chain Networks using Model-driven Engineering and Petri nets. The 34th ACM/SIGAPP Symposium on Applied Computing (SAC 2019). Limassol, Cyprus. April 8-12, 2019.
8. Cavalieri, S., & Pezzotta, G. (2012). Product–Service Systems Engineering: State of the art and research challenges. Computers in industry, 63(4), 278-288.
9. Parnas, D.L. On the criteria to be used in decomposing systems into modules. Communications of the ACM, 15 (12) (1972), pp. 1053–1058.
10. Völter, M. (2009). Best practices for DSLs and model-driven development. Journal of Object Technology, 8(6), 79-102.
11. Vara, J. M., Bollati, V. A., Jiménez, Á., & Marcos, E. (2014). Dealing with traceability in the MDD of model transformations. IEEE Trans. on Software Engineering, 40(6), 555-583.
12. de Oca, I. M. M., Snoeck, M., Reijers, H. A., & Rodríguez-Morffi, A. (2015). A systematic literature review of studies on business process modelling quality. Information and Software Technology, 58, 187-205.
13. Polančič, G., & Cegnar, B. (2017). Complexity metrics for process models – A systematic literature review. Computer Standards & Interfaces, 51, 104–117.
14. Solís-Martínez, J., Espada, J. P., Pelayo, C., -Bustelo, G., & Cueva Lovelle, J. M. (2014). BPMN MUSIM: Approach to improve the domain expert's efficiency in business processes modelling for the generation of specific software applications. Expert Systems with Applications, 41(4), 1864–1874.
15. Estanol, M., Queralt, A., Sancho, M. R., & Teniente, E. (2012, September). Artifact-centric business process models in UML. In International Conference on Business Process Management (pp. 292-303). Springer, Berlin, Heidelberg.
16. Umuhoza, E., Brambilla, M., Ripamonti, D., & Cabot, J. (2015). An empirical study on simplification of business process modelling languages. Proceedings of SLE 2015, 13–24. ACM.
17. Horkoff, J., Barone, D., Jiang, L., Yu, E., Amyot, D., Borgida, A., Borgida, A. (2014). Strategic business modelling: representation and reasoning. Software & Systems Modelling, 13(3), 1015–1041.

272   F. J. Pérez-Blanco et al.

Incremental Concurrent Model Synchronization using Triple Graph Grammars*

Fernando Orejas[1] , Elvira Pino[1] , and Marisa Navarro[2]

[1] Universitat Politècnica de Catalunya Barcelona, Spain
{orejas,pino@cs.upc.edu}
[2] Universidad del País Vasco, San Sebastián, Spain
marisa.navarro@ehu.es

Abstract. In the context of software model-driven development, artifacts are specified by several models describing different aspects, e.g., different views, dynamic behavior, structure, distributed information, etc. Then, maintaining and repairing consistency of the whole specification are crucial issues if the models can be separately developed and updated. *Model Synchronization* is the process of restoring consistency after the update of one or several of the models. In the present work, we approach the case when conflicts may arise due to concurrently updating different models. Specifically, based on the *Triple Graph Grammar* approach, we propose an incremental algorithm CSynch for solving conflicts and repairing consistency. In addition, we identify and formalize when a synchronizing solution can be considered adequate and show that our procedure CSynch is sound and complete.

1 Introduction

In the context of model-driven development, artifacts are specified by several models describing different aspects, e.g., different views, dynamic behaviour, structure, interactions, etc. Moreover, a given set of models is said to be *consistent* if they describe some software artifact. Along the process of designing and implementing an artifact, and also after the artifact is implemented, it is common to modify or update some aspects of a given model, or of several models. These changes may cause inconsistencies between the given set of models. To restore consistency, we have to *propagate* these modifications to the rest of the models. This process is called *model synchronization*. If at each time, we just propagate the updates on one model, synchronization is said *sequential*, but if we propagate simultaneously updates on several models, synchronization is called *concurrent*. Most existing work on model synchronization deals with the sequential case, which is simpler than the concurrent one, since in the latter case we have to deal with possible inconsistencies between the modifications applied to different models, implying that in the synchronization process we may need to backtrack some updates. Moreover, the existing approaches to concurrent synchronization [37,38,14,11,34,35]

---

* This work has been partially supported by funds from the Spanish Research Agency (AEI) and the European Union (FEDER funds) under grant GRAMM (ref. TIN2017-86727-C2-1-R and TIN2017-86727-C2-2-R)

H. Wehrheim and J. Cabot (Eds.): FASE 2020, LNCS 12076, pp. 273–293, 2020.
https://doi.org/10.1007/978-3-030-45234-6_14

are based on sequentializing the process, i.e., on combining in some way propagation procedures defined in sequential synchronization. For this reason, these approaches are called propagation-based in [24], where it is shown that they have important limitations.

When the given concurrent updates are inconsistent among themselves, the synchronization procedure must backtrack some of these updates to restore consistency. However, in this case, not all synchronizing solutions are adequate. For instance, a possible inadequate solution could be backtracking all updates. None of the approaches considering conflict resolution [14,11,34,35] define any form of adequacy, other than consistency of the given result. Moreover, these approaches return only one possible solution, which may not coincide with the user wishes.

A simple but powerful way of describing a class of consistent (synchronized) models is by using a *Triple Graph Grammar* (TGG) [27,28], since this approach provides techniques and tools that allow the general formulation and resolution of problems associated with synchronization. In these years these techniques have had considerable success, producing a large number of contributions of proven utility.

In [10], it is claimed that synchronization procedures should be incremental, meaning that their execution cost should not depend on the size of the models, but on the size of the update, so that the final consistent models must not be rebuilt from scratch. Other approaches that propose incremental sequential synchronization procedures are [22,12,25]. In contrast, none of the existing approaches to concurrent synchronization is incremental.

The main contributions of this paper are:

- The definition of properties, other than consistency, to ensure the adequacy of concurrent synchronization solutions.
- The definition of a non-deterministic incremental algorithm for concurrent synchronization, that is not propagation-based, whose solutions satisfy our adequacy properties. The algorithm is nondeterministic to consider the possible choices of conflict resolution. In particular, the algorithm is shown to be complete, in the sense that it finds all adequate solutions to the synchronization problem.

The rest of the paper is organized as follows. In Sect. 2, we summarize the basic and preliminary notions and terminology required in the rest of the paper, and we introduce a running example. In Sect. 3 we introduce and formalize the properties that should be satisfied by the synchronizing solutions in order to be considered adequate. In Sect. 4, we propose our synchronizing algorithm which is proven to find all solutions that satisfy the properties mentioned above. Finally, in Sections 5 and 6 we present related work, conclude and describe future work.

2   Preliminaries

In this section, we describe some basic notions and terminology concerning model transformation and model synchronization by Triple Graph Grammars (TGGs). Moreover, we introduce the example that we will use in the paper.

2.1 Triple Graph Grammars

TGGs are a formalism developed by Schürr ([27]) to specify and implement model transformations. They are based on three main ideas:

- Models can be represented by some kind of graphs.
- Instead of representing a consistent pair of models by two graphs, it is better to do it by a *triple graph* ([27]) which, in addition, includes the correspondence between the elements of the two models.
- To specify the class of consistent triple graphs we use a (triple graph) grammar, i.e., a triple graph is *consistent* if it can be generated from a given start graph (typically, the empty graph) using the production rules of the grammar.

More precisely, a triple graph $\overline{G} = (G^S \xleftarrow{s_G} G^C \xrightarrow{t_G} G^T)$ consists of a *source graph* G^S and a *target graph* G^T, which are related via the *correspondence graph* G^C and two mappings (graph morphisms) $s_G : G^C \to G^S$ and $t_G : G^C \to G^T$ specifying how source elements correspond to target elements[3]. For simplicity, we use the notation $\langle G^S, G^T \rangle$ whenever the explicit correspondence graph can be omitted.

Then, a TGG $\mathcal{G}$ consists of a start triple graph[4], $\overline{SG}$, and a set of production rules of the form $r : \overline{L} \to \overline{R}$, where $\overline{L}$ and $\overline{R}$ are triple graphs and $\overline{L} \subseteq \overline{R}$. Then, $\mathcal{L}(\mathcal{G}) = \{\overline{G} \mid \overline{SG} \overset{*}{\Rightarrow} \overline{G}\}$ is called the class of *consistent models* and $\mathcal{D}(\mathcal{G}) = \{\overline{SG} \overset{*}{\Rightarrow} \overline{G}\}$ is the set of derivations defined by $\mathcal{G}$, where $\overset{*}{\Rightarrow}$ is the reflexive and transitive closure

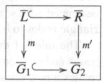

of the one step transformation relation $\Rightarrow$ defined as follows: $\overline{G}_1 \Rightarrow \overline{G}_2$ if there is a production rule $r : \overline{L} \to \overline{R}$ in $\mathcal{G}$ and a matching monomorphism $m : \overline{L} \to \overline{G}_1$ such that $\overline{G}_2$ can be obtained by replacing (the image of) $\overline{L}$ in $\overline{G}_1$ by (a corresponding image of) $\overline{R}$. Formally, this means that the diagram above on the right is a pushout in the category of triple graphs. In this case, we write $\overline{G}_1 \overset{r,m}{\Rightarrow} \overline{G}_2$, or just $\overline{G}_1 \Rightarrow \overline{G}_2$ if r and m are implicit.

For instance, in Fig.1 we depict the graph grammar that we use as a running example to illustrate our techniques. It is a simplified, and slightly modified, version of the well-known transformation between class diagrams and relational schemas.

The graphs considered in this example are typed, which means that a *type graph* describes the different classes of nodes and edges of our triple graphs, in a similar way as a metamodel describes the kinds of elements that we have in a model. In particular, the type graph of our example is depicted on the left of Fig.1. Source models, whose type graph is depicted on the left, consist of three kinds of nodes: classes, attributes and sub-attributes[5], and three kinds of edges: A (thick) edge between two classes represents a subclass relationship between them; attributes are bound to their associated classes and sub-attributes to their associated attribute, respectively, by the second and third kind of (thin) edges. Similarly, the type graph of target models is depicted on the right of the

---

[3] In the context of this paper, it does not make too much sense to speak about source and target models. Nevertheless, we have kept this terminology to simplify the notation for referring to each of the two models involved.

[4] As said above, without loss of generality, we consider that $\overline{SG}$ is always the empty triple graph.

[5] It is not necessary to associate any semantics to sub-attributes and sub-columns since we just use them to introduce a bit more complexity to the example.

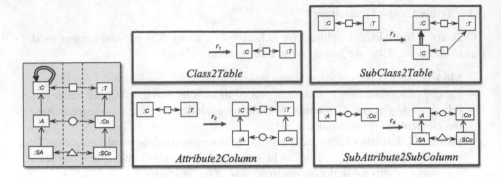

Fig. 1. Type graph, four rules for class-to-table transformations

type triple graph, consisting of tables, columns and sub-columns, together with edges between them. Finally, in the middle, there is the type graph of the correspondence models, consisting of three kinds of nodes: square nodes to bind classes with their associated tables, round nodes to bind attributes with their associated columns, and triangle nodes to bind sub-attributes with their associated sub-columns.

The rules of the TGG defining the consistent transformations between class diagrams and relational schemas are depicted on the right of Fig. 1. Rule r_1, *Class2Table*, creates a new class and its corresponding table, together with the correspondence element that relates the class and the table. Rule r_2, *Attribute2Column*, given a class and a corresponding table, creates an attribute of that class, a related column of the table, and their associated correspondence element. Rule r_3, *Subclass2Table*, given a class and a corresponding table, creates a new subclass. In this case, the subclass is related to the table through a new correspondence element. Finally, rule r_4, *SubAttribute2SubColumn*, creates a new sub-attribute together with its corresponding sub-column.

On the left of Fig. 2 we depict a triple graph generated by this grammar. For instance, it could have been created from the empty graph, firstly, applying twice rule *Class2Table* to create classes c_1 and c_2 together with their associated tables t_1 and t_2 and correspondence elements; next, applying rule *Subclass2Table*, to create c_3 as a subclass of c_2, together with a correspondence element that specifies that t_2 is the table associated to c_3; finally, applying three times the rule *Attribute2Column*, to create attributes a_1, a_2 and a_3, together with their associated columns, the associated edges binding attributes and columns to their classes and tables, and their correspondence elements.

2.2 Model Update and Model Synchronization

For different reasons, given a consistent model $\overline{G}$, we may perform some modifications or updates in it producing a model $\overline{G}'$ that is not consistent anymore. Then the synchronization problem consists of repairing that model, so that it becomes consistent.

For instance, in our running example, we assume given the consistent model on the left of Fig. 2, and that two updates are defined on that consistent model: removing the subclass relation between c_2 and c_3 in the source model, and adding a new sub-column

sco_3 to the column co_3 in the target model. In the middle of the figure some elements of the triple graph have been marked. These marks ($\{+, \mathrm{x}, !, ?\}$) represent possible actions to be taken on the elements (adding, deleting or keeping them) as the result of the analysis performed in our algorithm, which we describe in the paper. Some elements have several marks that are contradictory. This tells us that some conflicting situations may arise when defining a repair. Finally, on the right of the figure, there is one possible repair of the marked triple graph that avoids conflicts and restores consistency. As we will see, this repair can be made incrementally, acting only on some elements (grey area) without having to rebuild the whole triple graph.

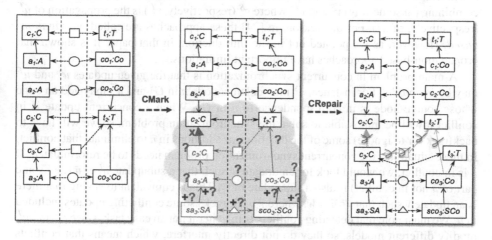

Fig. 2. Concurrent update, marked affected area with conflict and possible repair

Formally, an *update* or *modification* [8] u on a graph G is a span of inclusions $u : G \leftarrow K \to G'$ for some graph K. Intuitively, the elements in G that are not in K are the elements deleted by u, and the elements in G' that are not in K are the elements added by u. So, K consists of all the elements in G that remain invariant after the modification. When K may remain implicit we will denote the update $u : G \leftarrow K \to G'$ by $u : G \Longrightarrow G'$.

Updates can be composed and decomposed [24]. Given two updates $v :$ $G \leftarrow K_1 \to X$ and $w : X \leftarrow K_2 \to H$, the *composition* of v and w is the update $u = w \circ v : G \leftarrow K \to H$ such that, roughly, K

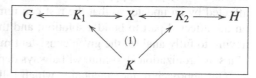

is the intersection of K_1 and K_2, i.e. K includes all the elements of G that are neither deleted by v nor by w. In addition, we say that u *decomposes* into v and w if $u = w \circ v$ and moreover no element added by v is deleted by w. Roughly this means that X is the union of K_1 and K_2 with respect to the common part K. If u decomposes into v and w, we also say that v is a *subupdate* of u, which we denote by $v \preceq u$, since in this case, v adds and deletes less elements than u.

In the non-concurrent case, given a triple graph $\overline{G}$ and an update $w^S : G^S \Longrightarrow H^S$ on the source graph, the *synchronization problem* [16] is to find an update $w^T : G^T \Longrightarrow H^T$, such that $\overline{H}$ is consistent. In this case, we say that w^T is the propagation of w^S.

In contrast, in the concurrent case, given updates $u^S : G^S \Longrightarrow H_0^S$ and $u^T : G^T \Longrightarrow H_0^T$, or equivalently the triple graph update $\langle u^S, id, u^T \rangle : \overline{G} \Longrightarrow \overline{H}_0$, also called a *concurrent update*, the *concurrent synchronization problem* is to find a concurrent update $\overline{w} : \overline{G} \Longrightarrow \overline{H}$, such that $\overline{u} = \langle u^S, id, u^T \rangle$ is a subupdate of $\overline{w}$ and $\overline{H}$ is

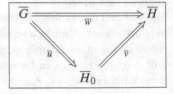

consistent. Previous work on this problem is based on building concurrent solutions by combining (in some way) v^S and v^T, where v^S (respectively, v^T) is the propagation of u^T (respectively, of u^S). For this reason, in [24] these approaches are called *propagation-based*. However, as we pointed out in the introduction, in that paper it is shown that propagation-based approaches have important limitations.

A main problem in concurrent synchronization is that the given updates u^S and u^T may be *in conflict*. For instance, u^S may delete a node n in G^S and u^T may add an edge whose source-node is in correspondence to n in G^S. When a concurrent update is in conflict it will be impossible to solve the synchronization problem, so we will have to backtrack (or to ignore) some of the deletions or additions in $\overline{u}$ to eliminate that conflict. In these situations, the concurrent synchronization problem needs to be reformulated. If $\overline{u}$ is in conflict, we would look for an update $\overline{w}$ such that a subupdate $\overline{u}'$ of $\overline{u}$ (i.e., some part of $\overline{u}$ not in conflict) is also a subupdate of $\overline{w}$. This is equivalent to saying that there is an update $\overline{v}$ such that $\overline{v} \circ \overline{u} = \overline{w}$, where $\overline{v}$ backtracks some conflicting updates included in $\overline{u}$. We must note that detecting conflicts is in general not an easy task, since u^S and u^T modify different models, so they do not directly interfere, which means that conflicts are never explicit. We may also note that, according to this definition, $\overline{id} : \overline{G} \Longrightarrow \overline{G}$, i.e., the identity modification that changes nothing, would always be a solution to the concurrent synchronization problem (in this case $\overline{v}$ would be the inverse of $\overline{u}$, so we would completely backtrack $\overline{u}$). Obviously, this is not the kind of solution that we want.

2.3 Dependency Relations

Incrementality of (sequential or concurrent) model synchronization requires two conditions for any given approach: to be able to identify what part of the given model is affected by an update, so that the rest can remain unchanged and we can concentrate on the affected part to build a solution; and that we can do this identification without having to fully analyze the given consistent model. Otherwise, the computational cost of a synchronization algorithm will always depend on the size of the given models.

Our approach to incrementality, which follows the ideas introduced in [25] for sequential synchronization, is based on the idea that the structure of a given consistent model depends essentially on the derivation that was used to create it. We mean that if we perform any update on the model, we just have to care about the parts of that derivation that are affected by the update. For instance, if the update consists of the deletion of some element, then the application of the rule that created that element in the original derivation and the further application of other rules that depend on that creation, will be considered the affected part of the derivation. It must be clear that this does not mean that, if $\overline{SG} \Rightarrow \overline{G}_1 \Rightarrow \cdots \Rightarrow \overline{G}_k \Rightarrow \cdots \Rightarrow \overline{G}$ is the derivation used to create $\overline{G}$, the deletion of an element in $\overline{G}_k$ will affect all the rule applications in the derivation $\overline{G}_k \Rightarrow \cdots \Rightarrow \overline{G}$, because some of these rule applications may be independent of that deletion. For instance, in our example, if the deleted element is a class, the creation of other classes, attributes or subattributes that are not related to that class would be independent of that deletion. Technically, the reason would be that the application of these rules is *sequentially independent* ([6]) of the application of the rule that created the class. In what follows we will denote by $d_{\overline{G}}$ the derivation[6] used to create $\overline{G}$.

Since in the synchronization algorithm we need to know which is the derivation used to create the given consistent model and storing and analyzing that derivation may be costly, the second idea of our approach is to define some dependency relations between the elements of $\overline{G}$ that allow us to know if the application of some rule depends on the application of another rule. We assume that these relations are stored together with $\overline{G}$. The first relation, called *strict dependency*, denoted $e_1 \lhd^{\overline{G}} e_2$, holds if e_1 is matched by the left-hand side of the rule that created e_2. For instance, in the triple graph on the left of Fig. 2, we have $c_2 \lhd^{\overline{G}} c_3$ and $t_2 \lhd^{\overline{G}} c_3$, since the application of rule *Subclass2Table* that creates c_3 has to match its left hand side to c_2 and t_2. The second relation, called *interdependency*, denoted $e_1 \bowtie^{\overline{G}} e_2$, holds if e_1 and e_2 are created by the same rule. For instance, in Fig. 2, $c_2 \bowtie^{\overline{G}} t_2$, since they are both created by the same application of the *Class2Table* rule in $d_{\overline{G}}$. Finally, *dependency*, denoted $\trianglelefteq^{\overline{G}}$, is the reflexive and transitive closure of the union of $\lhd^{\overline{G}}$ and $\bowtie^{\overline{G}}$.

Definition 1 (Dependency Relations [25]). *Given a TGG $\mathcal{G}$ and a derivation $d_{\overline{G}}$: $\overline{SG} \overset{*}{\Rightarrow} \overline{G}$, we define the following relations on elements of $\overline{G}$:*

1. *Strict dependency: $\lhd^{\overline{G}}$ is the smallest relation satisfying that if $d_{\overline{G}}$ includes the transformation step depicted on the right, then for every e in $\overline{L}$ and e' in $\overline{R} \setminus \overline{L}$, $m(e) \lhd^{\overline{G}} m'(e')$.*
2. *Strict interdependency: $\bowtie^{\overline{G}}$ is the smallest relation satisfying that if $d_{\overline{G}}$ includes the transformation step depicted on the right, then for every e, e' in $\overline{R} \setminus \overline{L}$, $m'(e) \bowtie^{\overline{G}} m'(e')$.*
3. *Dependency: $\trianglelefteq^{\overline{G}} = (\lhd^{\overline{G}} \cup \bowtie^{\overline{G}})^*$.*

$$\begin{array}{ccc} \overline{L} & \hookrightarrow & \overline{R} \\ {\scriptstyle m}\downarrow & & \downarrow{\scriptstyle m'} \\ \overline{G}_{i-1} & \hookrightarrow & \overline{G}_i \end{array}$$

It may be noticed that there is a bijective correspondence between derivations (up to permutation equivalence) and their associated relations. This means that storing these relations together with a model is equivalent to storing the derivation used to create it.

3 Synchronizing Solutions for Concurrent Updates

According to what we discussed in the previous section, we consider the general problem of concurrent synchronization when there may be conflicts in the given concurrent update. Moreover, we assume that we are only interested in incremental solutions,

---

[6] It may be noted that there may be many derivations that lead to $\overline{G}$, here we assume that $d_{\overline{G}}$ is the one chosen to generate it.

which means that our solutions are assumed to preserve a certain triple subgraph of the given consistent model[7]. Finally, to avoid having to mention explicitly the TGG of the given synchronization problem, we will consider that we are working with a fixed TGG, $\mathcal{G}$, which has been given a priori.

Definition 2 (Incremental Synchronizing Solutions). *Given a concurrent update $\overline{u}$: $\overline{G} \Longrightarrow \overline{H}_0$, such that $\overline{G}$ is a consistent model, and given a submodel $\overline{G}_0 \subseteq \overline{G}$, a concurrent incremental solution of $\overline{u}$ with respect to $\overline{G}_0$ is an update $\overline{w}: \overline{G} \Longrightarrow \overline{H}$ such that $\overline{H}$ is consistent and $d_{\overline{H}}$ includes the derivation $d_{\overline{G}_0}$. Then, $SynchSol(\overline{G}, \overline{G}_0, \overline{u})$ is the set of all concurrent incremental solutions of $\overline{u}$ with respect to $\overline{G}_0$.*

In general, a concurrent synchronization problem may have several possible solutions especially if it has some conflicts, because in this case there may be different options of backtracking to eliminate the conflicts. To decide which solutions are "better", we may use different criteria but, unfortunately, these criteria may be contradictory. For this reason, we believe that it should be the user who decides which is the preferred solution. Nevertheless, there are solutions which may be considered inadequate or not fully adequate. For instance, backtracking all updates, so that the final outcome is the original consistent model, would technically be a correct solution, but we can not consider that it is adequate. The adequacy criteria that we consider are the following:

- *Maximal covering:* When $\overline{u}$ has conflicts, we would like that our solution backtracks as few as possible additions and deletions in $\overline{u}$, because users decided these additions and deletions. In this sense, the solution $\overline{w}$ has a maximal covering if $\overline{H}$ contains as many as possible elements that are added by $\overline{u}$ and as few as possible elements that are deleted by $\overline{u}$. In this case, a solution would be optimal if $\overline{H}$ includes all the elements added by $\overline{u}$ and no elements deleted by $\overline{u}$.
- *Minimal information loss:* The addition or deletion of an element in $\overline{u}$ may force the deletion of other elements from $\overline{G}$. Since these elements may include some information, their deletion will cause an information loss in the model, which we would like to minimize. In this sense, the solution $\overline{w}$ has minimal information loss if $\overline{H}$ cannot be extended to a solution that contains more elements from $\overline{G}$ without having more additions than $\overline{H}$.
- *Minimal unrelated additions:* The addition or deletion of an element in $\overline{u}$ may cause the addition of other elements in $\overline{w}$. For instance, if in our example we add a table the synchronization procedure will need to add its associated class. However, a solution may include other added elements that are not required by the given update. We consider that we should minimize this kind of additions.

Definition 3 (Properties of Synchronizing Solutions). *Given a derivation $d = \overline{SG} \overset{*}{\Rightarrow} \overline{G} \in \mathcal{D}(\mathcal{G})$ and a concurrent update $\overline{u}: \overline{G} \leftarrow \overline{K}_0 \rightarrow \overline{H}_0$, we say that a consistent incremental solution $\overline{w}: \overline{G} \leftarrow \overline{K} \rightarrow \overline{H} \in SynchSol(\overline{G}, G_0, \overline{u})$ has:*

1. *Maximal covering: if there does not exist any other solution $\overline{v} \in SynchSol(\overline{G}, G_0, \overline{u})$, such that $\overline{w}' \preceq \overline{v}'$, where $\overline{v}'$ is the largest common subupdate of $\overline{v}$ and $\overline{u}$, and $\overline{w}'$ is the*

---

[7] We may notice that if that subgraph is the empty graph then we would be looking for all possible solutions.

largest common subupdate of $\overline{w}$ and $\overline{u}$, i.e., $\overline{v}'$ (resp. $\overline{w}'$) consists of all the additions and deletions that are both in $\overline{u}$ and $\overline{v}$ (resp. $\overline{w}$).

2. Minimal information loss: *if there is no other update $\overline{v} \in SynchSol(\overline{G}, G_0, \overline{u})$, with $\overline{v} = \overline{G} \leftarrow \overline{K}' \rightarrow \overline{H}'$, such that $\overline{H} \overset{*}{\Rightarrow} \overline{H}'$, $\overline{K} \subset \overline{K}'$ and $(\overline{H}' \backslash \overline{K}') = (\overline{H} \backslash \overline{K})$.*

3. Minimal unrelated additions: *if for any element $x \in \overline{H}$ added by $\overline{w}$, there is an element $y \in \overline{H} \cap \overline{G}$, such that $x \trianglelefteq^H y$.*

For instance, on the right of Fig. 2 we can see an example of a consistent solution which has maximal covering, minimal information loss and no unrelated additions. In contrast, in Fig. 3 neither the solution on the left nor the one in the middle have maximal covering, even though both of them are consistent. The solution on the right of Fig. 3 has maximal covering, minimal information loss, and no unrelated additions, but it is not comparable with the one in Fig. 2.

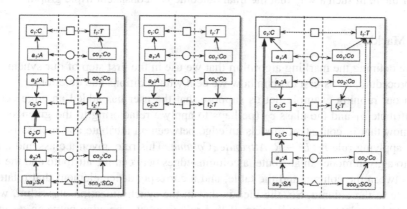

Fig. 3. Other three consistent solutions for example in Fig. 2.

4   An Incremental Procedure CSynch

In this section we propose a two-step nondeterministic incremental algorithm CSynch that allow us to find all solutions to the concurrent synchronization problem that are minimal, in the sense that they do not have unrelated additions, and that, moreover, have maximal covering and minimal information loss. More precisely, depending on the choices made we will get a different solution.

The algorithm is not based on propagation, but on using rules derived from the given TGG which allow us to identify which elements are affected by the update, to identify and solve possible conflicts, and to restore consistency. This identification is done by a marking algorithm CMark that simulates the addition and deletion of elements by applying these derived rules on the model such that some of its elements have being decorated with some marks from the set $\{+, \times, !, ?\}$. If an element e is marked with any of these marks, it means that e has been added or deleted by a user ($+$ or $\times$, respectively), it is required for an addition ($!$), or it is affected by a deletion ($?$). Technically, this means that every element of the model has an attribute called marks $\subseteq \{+, \times, !, ?\}$ that denotes the set of marks that an element has at a given moment. Initially, before starting the synchronization process, it is assumed that marks $= \emptyset$ for every element of the model. If it happens that, at certain point, an element is marked with different marks, it may denote an apparent conflict[8], which may need to be solved.

Since we need to know the dependencies between the marked elements, we will build extensions of the dependency relations of the given model $\overline{G}$. This extended relations are denoted $\trianglelefteq'$, $\triangleleft'$, and $\bowtie'$, i.e., $\trianglelefteq^{\overline{G}} \subseteq \trianglelefteq'$, $\triangleleft^{\overline{G}} \subseteq \triangleleft'$, and $\bowtie^{\overline{G}} \subseteq \bowtie'$. In addition, using these relations, CMark computes $\overline{G}_0$, the submodel of $\overline{G}$ not affected by the update.

Once the model is marked, an algorithm CRepair detects and solves conflicts and repairs the model. This process removes the marks of some elements and deletes the rest of them, in such a way that the final outcome is a consistent triple graph.

4.1 Marking

Before defining the marking algorithm that we use in the first step of our synchronization procedure, let us first explain how we deal with additions and deletions.

In our running example, let us suppose that the user has added an edge between the attribute a_1 and the class c_2 (perhaps to apply a refactoring to the given system). We know that in consistent models an edge between an attribute and a class is added when applying rule $r_2 : \overline{L} \to \overline{R}$, *Attribute2Column*. This rule, given a class and a table, adds to a given model an attribute, a column, edges between the attribute and the class, and between the column and the table, and a correspondence element that relates the attribute to the column. So, the idea is that in the synchronization algorithm, we are going to "simulate" the application of that rule to create the edge between a_1 and c_2, and to do this, we are going to apply a rule $r_2' : \overline{L}' \to \overline{R}'$, derived from r_2, but before describing this rule, we have to take into account two questions:

1. Some of the elements that are created by r_2 may be already in the model. So, instead of creating them again, we include them in the left-hand side $\overline{L}'$ of the derived rule. Similarly, some other elements created by r_2 may coincide with other elements added by $\overline{u}$, then we will consider that r_2' creates also these elements. For instance, if $\overline{u}$ would create an attribute a and an edge associating a to a class c, in this case, the associated marking rule would create simultaneously the attribute and the edge. But this is not enough to ensure that the final outcome is consistent, we need to be sure that all the elements in $\overline{L}'$ are in the final result. Otherwise, these elements could be deleted as a consequence of some other addition or deletion in the given update $\overline{u}$. For this reason, r_2' will mark the elements in $\overline{L}' \setminus \overline{L}$ with $!$, expressing that they are required for the correctness of the result. In addition, the rule will also mark the elements created by the rule, i.e. in $\overline{R}' \setminus \overline{L}'$, with the mark $+$. This includes the elements added by $\overline{u}$, but also some other elements created by the rule. For

---

[8] As we will see, not all apparent conflicts are real conflicts.

instance, if we want to add the edge from a_1 to c_2 to the model, we must also add the edge from co_1 to t_2. Following these ideas, rule r_2' is depicted on the left of Fig. 4. Moreover, on the right of that figure we also show which would be the associated marking rule, when we add an attribute to a class in a given model.

2. Since in the resulting model, $\overline{H}$, we assume that this edge from a_1 to c_2 is created using r_2, this means that we assume that in $\overline{H}$, the edge was created together with the attribute a_1, the corresponding column co_1, the edge between a_1 and c_2, the edge between co_1 and t_2, and the correspondence element between a_1 and co_1. However, in the original model $\overline{G}$ these elements were created using a different application of r_2, and together with them, some other elements were also created (in this case, the edges between a_1 and c_1 and between co_1 and t_1), that are still part of the model. So if we want $\overline{H}$ to be consistent, we will need to delete these elements from the model. As a consequence, we will mark them with ?, denoting that in principle, we have to delete them, and we will say that they have been *revoked*. Finally, if some elements are revoked, we may need to delete all the elements in the model that depend on them. So we will mark all these other elements with ?, expressing that they may need to be deleted too.

The case of marking the deletions in the update $\overline{u}$ is simpler. If an element x in $\overline{G}$ is deleted by $\overline{u}$, we will just mark it with x, denoting that x has to be deleted and, as before, we will mark all the elements that depend on x with ?.

Finally, if we call $\overline{G}_0$ the graph consisting of all elements that have not been marked with +, x, or ? then, as a consequence of the way that the marking algorithm works, we can be sure that $\overline{G}_0$ is consistent (as shown in Thm. 1), since all elements in $\overline{G}_0$ were already in $\overline{G}$ and they are not dependent of any element that is not in $\overline{G}_0$. Hence, building our solution by adding to $\overline{G}_0$ some of the marked elements, using rules from the given TGG, ensures that the final result is consistent. Moreover, the algorithm would be incremental with respect to $\overline{G}_0$, since its elements will not be processed by CRepair (except for deleting some ! marks).

Definition 4 (Derived Marking Rules). *We say that a triple graph $\overline{G}$ is decorated with marks if each of its elements has a marking attribute* marks $\subseteq \{+, x, !, ?\}$. *Let us denote as RemAttr($\overline{G}$) the triple graph resulting from removing from $\overline{G}$ the attribute* marks.

Given the rule $r : \overline{L} \to \overline{R}$, we say that $r' : \overline{L}' \to \overline{R}'$ is a derived marking rule from r for adding a set of elements X, if $\overline{L}'$ and $\overline{R}'$ are two decorated triple graphs such that:

1. $\overline{L} \subseteq RemAttr(\overline{L}') \subseteq \overline{R}$, $RemAttr(\overline{R}') = \overline{R}$, *and* $X \subseteq \overline{R}' \setminus \overline{L}'$.
2. *All elements in $RemAttr(\overline{L}') \setminus \overline{L}$ are included in $\overline{R}'$ with the mark* !.
3. *All elements in $\overline{R}' \setminus \overline{L}'$ are included in $\overline{R}'$ with the mark* +.

For instance, the rule on the left of Fig. 4 is derived from the rule r_2 *Attribute2Column* to add a new arrow from an already existing attribute to an already existing class in the model. Notice that the elements that are really new, i.e., produced by the application of r_2, are marked with +, while the ones produced by r_2 but reused from the model by the derived rule, are marked with !. The rule on the right is also derived from *Attribute2Column* but now to add a new attribute to an existing class. As a consequence, there are not reused elements that should be marked with !.

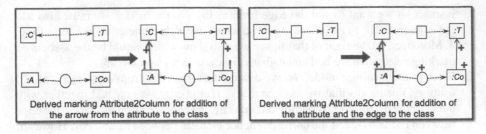

Fig. 4. Examples of derived marking rules

Now we can introduce the marking algorithm CMark following the explanations given above. A and D will be the set of elements that have to be added or deleted, respectively. Initially, we assume that A and D consist of the elements added and deleted by $\bar{u}$, and that the sets of marks are empty for all the elements in the model. Then:

Algorithm 1 (CMark **Algorithm**)
Initialize relations $\trianglelefteq' = \trianglelefteq$, $\triangleleft' = \triangleleft$, and $\bowtie' = \bowtie$.

1. **Addition and revocation:** *For every element $x \in A$, select a marking rule $r' : \overline{L}' \to \overline{R}'$ derived from $r : \overline{L} \to \overline{R}$ that may be used to create x, and let $X \subseteq A$ be a set of elements that can also be created by r':*
   - *Eliminate from A the elements in $\{x\} \cup X$.*
   - *Apply $r' : \overline{L}' \to \overline{R}'$.*
   - *Add ? to the attribute* marks *of every element which is not in $RemAttr(\overline{L}') \setminus \overline{L}$ but it is strictly interdependent with an element matched to $RemAttr(\overline{L}') \setminus \overline{L}$.*
   - *Add ? to the attribute* marks *of every element which is dependent on a ?-marked element.*
2. *Update the dependency relations adding the new dependencies and interdependencies defined by the application of the original rules used in 1. to relations $\trianglelefteq'$, $\triangleleft'$, and $\bowtie'$; and computing the new transitive closure.*
3. **Deletion:**
   - *Add x to the attribute* marks *of every element intended to be deleted.*
   - *Add ? to the attribute* marks *of every element that is dependent of an x-marked element.*
4. **Computing $\overline{G}_0$:** *Delete from $\trianglelefteq$, $\triangleleft$, and $\bowtie$ all elements marked with +, ?, or x. Then $\overline{G}_0$ would be the model generated by the derivation associated to the dependency relations.*

For instance, in the middle of Fig. 2 and Fig. 5 we can see examples of a marked model following the above algorithm. In the case of the example in Fig. 5, the concurrent update would consist of adding a subclass relation between classes c_1 and c_2, in the source; and, adding a new sub-column sco_3 to the column co_2 in the target. Again, in the model of the middle, some elements are marked with contradictory marks. Notice that now, possible conflicts arise because of trying to integrate concurrent additions. In fact, this example serves to illustrate that some additions may imply the deletion of elements created by the original derivation, for instance, it is the case of the table t_2. That is, some additions may imply revocation of original derivation steps.

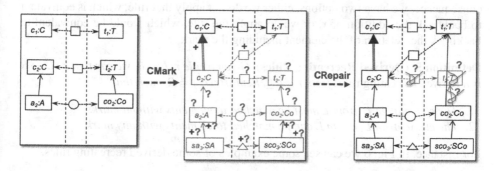

Fig. 5. Other example of concurrent updated, marked and possible repair

We must note that this algorithm is nondeterministic since, when we want to add an element x to the model there may be more than one rule that can be used to create x. Then, choosing different rules will lead to different results of our synchronizing procedure.

4.2 Repairing and Conflict-Solving

The first idea underlying our repair algorithm, used as a second step of our synchronization procedure, is to extend the model $\overline{G}_0$, represented by the dependency relations $\lhd$, $\vartriangleleft$, and $\bowtie$, using rules from the given TGG, to include the elements that the user asked to add to the model (i.e. added by the given update $\overline{u}$) and to reduce the information loss. In particular, if in the marking process we decided to use a rule $r : \overline{L} \to \overline{R}$ to create an element x required by $\overline{u}$ (i.e., to create x we used a marking rule r'' associated to r), we will use another rule also derived from r, $r' : \overline{L}' \to \overline{R}$, where $\overline{L} \subseteq RemAttr(\overline{L}') = \overline{R}$ that unmarks all the elements that we marked with + or !, i.e., if we remove all marks in $\overline{L}'$ we get $\overline{R}$. We call these rules *derived recreating rules*, because they create again (by reusing them) some elements that were originally in $\overline{G}$. We must note that, using the information in the dependence relations $\lhd'$, $\vartriangleleft'$, and $\bowtie'$, we may know which is the rule r. In particular, $\overline{L}$ would consist of x and all the elements y such that $x \bowtie' y$, and $\overline{R}$ would consist of all the elements z such that $x \vartriangleleft' z$.

This idea for reusing elements from the original model has already been used in [12,25]. Notice that these rules eliminate the marks from the recreated elements, and as a consequence, the recreated elements will be now part of the solution.

The second idea for our repair algorithm is that we can also use derived recreation rules for reducing the information loss, including in the solution elements that were removed from the given model because they depended on elements that could have been deleted.

Finally, the third idea in which our algorithm is based is that, if we try to create an added element x using the derived rule $r' : \overline{L'} \to \overline{R}$, if an element of $\overline{L'}$ is matched to an element y of the model having the mark $\mathbf{x}$, this means that we have discovered a conflict, because we have a conflict between the deletion of y and the addition of x. As a consequence, we have two options, either we do not apply that rule, which is equivalent to backtrack the addition of x, or we do apply the rule, which would be equivalent to backtrack the deletion of the element including the mark $\mathbf{x}$.

Definition 5 (Derived Recreating Rules). *Given a rule* $r : \overline{L} \to \overline{R}$*, we say that* $r' : \overline{L'} \to \overline{R}$ *is a* derived recreating rule[9] *from* r *if* $\overline{L} \subseteq RemAttr(\overline{L'}) = \overline{R}$*, such that*

1. *The elements in* $\overline{L'}$ *from* $\overline{L}$ *must be matched to elements without marks.*
2. *The elements in* $\overline{L'}$ *not in* $\overline{L}$ *can be matched to elements with any mark.*

For instance, in Fig. 6 we can see some examples of some derived recreating rules.

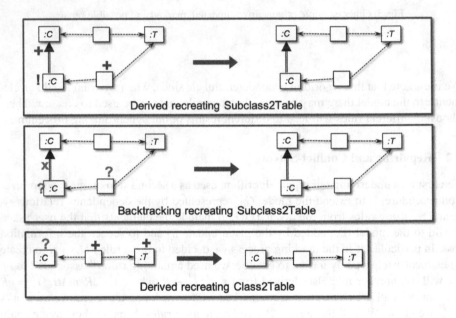

Derived recreating Subclass2Table

Backtracking recreating Subclass2Table

Derived recreating Class2Table

Fig. 6. Examples of derived recreating rules

---

[9] To be precise, recreating rules are like standard DPO rules, i.e. of the form $\overline{L'} \leftarrow \overline{R} \to \overline{R}$, which means that the rule does not add anything, since it just deletes the marks from the given elements. We may note that an unmarking rule is always applicable, since the gluing conditions always hold. For details, we may look at [17,15].

Algorithm 2 (CRepair)

1. **Recreating and conflict solving**: *While there is a recreation rule that can be applied:*
   - *If there is an element marked + by a marking rule associated to a rule $r : \overline{L} \to \overline{R}$ and when trying to apply the associated recreating rule $r' : \overline{L}' \to \overline{R}$, no element in $\overline{L}'$ is matched to an element including the x mark, then apply r' and modify accordingly the dependency relations of the solution, adding to $\lhd$ and $\bowtie$ the dependency and interdependency relations between the elements matched by elements in $\overline{L}$ and $\overline{R}$; and computing the new transitive closure for $\trianglelefteq$.*
   - *In the same situation as in the previous case, but where there is an element in $\overline{L}'$ that is matched to an element marked x, choose between applying r' modifying accordingly the dependency relations of the solution, or replacing the mark + by the mark x for all elements matched by $\overline{L}'$ that include the mark +.*
   - *Otherwise, apply a recreating rule $r' : \overline{L}' \to \overline{R}$ such that no element in $\overline{L}'$ is matched to an element marked x and modify accordingly the dependency relations of the solution.*
2. **Removing**: *Delete every marked element.*

That is, in step 1. of CRepair, we first try to recreate every + or ! element and to reduce information loss as much as possible. However, when we detect a conflict when trying to recreate an element marked +, it is nondeterministically chosen between applying the addition or the deletion. And in step 2 all elements still marked are removed from the model, because they needed to be deleted or because it was not possible to recreate them.

Algorithm 3 (CSynch)

1. *Apply* CMark.
2. *Apply* CRepair

The resulting update is $\overline{w} : \overline{G} \Longrightarrow \overline{H}$, where $\overline{H}$ is the result obtained by CSynch.

4.3 Properties of CSynch

In this subsection we prove the properties that our algorithm satisfies. Firstly, we will prove that all solutions obtained by CSynch are consistent, incremental and they have no unrelated additions. We will also prove that CSynch can compute all incremental solutions that, in addition, have maximal covering and minimal information loss, provided that the right choices are made.

Theorem 1. *Given a consistent model $\overline{G}$ and an update $\overline{u} : \overline{G} \Longrightarrow \overline{H}'$ if the update $\overline{w} : \overline{G} \Longrightarrow \overline{H}$ is a solution obtained by CSynch, then:*

1. *$\overline{H}$ is consistent.*
2. *$\overline{w}$ is incremental with respect to the triple graph $\overline{G}_0$ computed by CMark.*
3. *$\overline{w}$ has no unrelated additions*
4. *$\overline{w}$ has minimal information loss.*

Proof. The last three properties are just a consequence of how CSynch is defined. Let us prove that $\overline{H}$ is consistent, but before we will prove that $\overline{G}_0$ is consistent.

Let $\overline{SG} \Rightarrow \overline{G}_1 \Rightarrow \cdots \Rightarrow \overline{G}_k \Rightarrow \cdots \Rightarrow \overline{G}$ be the derivation used to create $\overline{G}$ and let $\overline{SG} \Rightarrow \overline{G}_1 \Rightarrow \cdots \Rightarrow \overline{G}_i$ be its longest subderivation such that $\overline{G}_i \subseteq \overline{G}_0$, let us show that $\overline{G}_i = \overline{G}_0$, which implies the consistency of $\overline{G}_0$.

Suppose that there is an element $x \in \overline{G}_0$, which means that x is not marked with $+$, ?, or x and it does not depend on any marked element, such that $x \notin \overline{G}_i$. Let k be the earliest derivation step $\overline{G}_k \Rightarrow \overline{G}_{k+1}$, with $i < k$, where an element $x \in (\overline{G}_0 \setminus \overline{G}_i)$ was generated i.e., $x \in (\overline{G}_{k+1} \setminus \overline{G}_k)$. By definition of $\bowtie$, we know that $x \bowtie y$ for every $y \in \overline{G}_{k+1} \setminus \overline{G}_k$, and according to the definition of CMark, if x has not any of those marks, then y has not either. This means that $\overline{G}_{k+1} \setminus \overline{G}_k \subseteq \overline{G}_0$. Now, if $r : L \to R$ is the rule applied in the derivation step $\overline{G}_k \Rightarrow \overline{G}_{k+1}$ then there are two possibilities:

1. If the elements matched by $\overline{L}$ in $\overline{G}_k$ are already in $\overline{G}_i$, it would mean that this derivation step is sequentially independent from all derivation steps $\overline{G}_i \Rightarrow \cdots \Rightarrow \overline{G}_k$ and we would have $\overline{G}_i \overset{r}{\Rightarrow} \overline{G}_{i+1}$, with $\overline{G}_{i+1} \subseteq \overline{G}_0$, contradicting the hypothesis that $\overline{SG} \Rightarrow \overline{G}_1 \Rightarrow \cdots \Rightarrow \overline{G}_i$ was the longest subderivation such that $\overline{G}_i \subseteq \overline{G}_0$.
2. If the elements matched by $\overline{L}$ in $\overline{G}_k$ are not in $\overline{G}_i$, it would mean that x depends on elements added in the derivation $\overline{G}_i \Rightarrow \cdots \Rightarrow \overline{G}_k$. Moreover, we know that all the elements y generated in that derivation such that $y \trianglelefteq x$ are unmarked with $+$, ?, or x and therefore they are included in $\overline{G}_0$, because otherwise x would not be in $\overline{G}_0$. But this contradicts the hypothesis that x was an element in $\overline{G}_0 \setminus \overline{G}_i$ added in the earliest possible derivation step.

To prove that $\overline{H}$ is consistent, it is enough to notice that, because of how recreation rules are defined, if $\overline{G}_i$ is a consistent unmarked subgraph of a marked graph $\overline{G}_i'$, and $r' : L' \to R$ is a recreating rule associated to the rule $r : L \to R$, then if $\overline{G}_i' \overset{r'}{\Rightarrow} \overline{G}_{i+1}'$, we have that $\overline{G}_i \overset{r}{\Rightarrow} \overline{G}_{i+1}$ such that $\overline{G}_{i+1}$ is a consistent subgraph of $\overline{G}_{i+1}'$. In particular, if $\overline{G}_0'$ is the result obtained by applying the marking algorithm to $\overline{G}$ and $\overline{G}_0$ is its unmarked consistent subgraph, then applying the first step of CRepair leads to a sequence of recreation transformations $\overline{G}_0' \overset{*}{\Rightarrow} \overline{G}_k'$. This means that given the associated sequence of transformations $\overline{G}_0 \overset{*}{\Rightarrow} \overline{G}_k$, we have that $\overline{G}_k$ is a consistent subgraph of $\overline{G}_k'$. Finally the second step of CRepair leads to $\overline{H} = \overline{G}_k$, which is the final result of CSynch. ∎

Before showing the rest of the properties of CSynch, we must first define which is the subgraph $\overline{G}_0$ such any solution of CSynch is incremental with respect to it. In general, depending on the choices of CSynch, the consistent model $\overline{G}_0$ computed by CMark may be different, because the choice of rules used to add to $\overline{G}$ the elements added by $\overline{u}$ defines different markings. So, if we want that all solutions of CSynch are incremental over the same graph, we can take the intersection of all these $\overline{G}_0$.

Definition 6 (Set of Computed Solutions). *Given a consistent model $\overline{G} \in \mathcal{L}(\mathcal{G})$ and a concurrent update $\overline{u} : \overline{G} \leftarrow \overline{K} \to \overline{H}_0$, we denote by* CSynch$(\overline{G}, \overline{u})$ *the set of all possible solutions computed by the algorithm* CSynch *when $\overline{G}$ and $\overline{u}$ are given.*

If for every $\overline{w} : \overline{G} \leftarrow \overline{K} \to \overline{H}$, we denote by $\overline{G}_w$ the subgraph of $\overline{G}$ computed by CMark, *then we define $M(\overline{G}, \overline{u})$ as: $M(\overline{G}, \overline{u}) = \cap_{\overline{w} \in \mathrm{CSynch}(\overline{G}, \overline{u})} \overline{G}_w$.*

Obviously, if $\overline{w}$ is incremental over $\overline{G}_w$, then $\overline{w}$ is also incremental with respect to any submodel of $\overline{G}_w$.

Proposition 1. *If $\overline{w} \in \text{CSynch}(\overline{G}, \overline{u})$ then $\overline{w}$ is incremental over $M(\overline{G}, \overline{u})$.*

Finally, we can show that our algorithm is complete, i.e., that any consistent update that is incremental over $M(\overline{G}, \overline{u})$, and satisfies the required properties, can be found by CSynch.

Theorem 2. *Given a consistent model $\overline{G}$ and an update $\overline{u} : \overline{G} \Longrightarrow \overline{H}'$, if $\overline{w} : \overline{G} \leftarrow \overline{K} \rightarrow \overline{H}$ is consistent, it has no unrelated additions, it has maximal covering and minimal information loss, and it is incremental over $M(\overline{G}, \overline{u})$ then $\overline{w} \in \text{CSynch}(\overline{G}, \overline{u})$.*

Proof. If $\overline{w} : \overline{G} \leftarrow \overline{K} \rightarrow \overline{H}$ is a consistent update, such that it has no unrelated additions, it has maximal covering and minimal information loss, and it is incremental over $M(\overline{G}, \overline{u})$ this means that there is a derivation $d = \overline{SG} \Rightarrow \overline{H}_1 \Rightarrow \cdots \Rightarrow \overline{H}_k \Rightarrow \cdots \Rightarrow \overline{H}$ such that $\overline{M(G, u)} \subseteq H_k$ for some k. Then, if we make the right choices in CSynch we will compute the solution $\overline{w}$. In particular, if CMark uses the same rule applications that are used in d to generate the additions in $\overline{u}$, on the one hand, it will compute a model $\overline{G}_w$ that will be preserved by CRepair and that includes $\text{CSynch}(\overline{G}, \overline{u})$. On the other hand, CMark will mark the model in such a way that if CRepair chooses the same rule applications (and in the same order) as in d, it will compute $\overline{H}$. ∎

5   Related Work

The concurrent synchronization problem can be considered as a special case of the general problem of model (or graph) repair. In particular, in our case, a triple graph can be easily represented by a single graph, so the consistency problem for triple graphs can be seen as a special case of the consistency problem for graphs. The literature on model repair is quite large (see [23] for an excellent survey on this topic), so it does not make much sense to review all the existing approaches.

Concentrating on the problem of concurrent model synchronization, to our knowledge, the only works addressing the general problem[10] of concurrent synchronization are [38,14,11,24,34,35]. All these approaches are propagation-based, which means that synchronization is performed, first, propagating the updates in one model to the other model, then checking if there is any conflict between the propagated updates and the ones previously applied to that model and, if there are, solving the conflicts in some given way, and finally, propagating back the updates in the second model to the first one. That is, sequentializing concurrent synchronization. In all cases it is shown that the result obtained is correct, but no other properties are shown. In particular, in all these approaches, except in [38] the trivial solution obtained by backtracking all the updates would be considered a valid solution. On the other hand, the approach presented

---

[10] There is some work considering this problem in a more restrictive setting. For instance, in [26] models are restricted to tree-like structures and the target model is an abstract view of the source; and in [36] updates must be defined in terms of a given set of operations.

in [38] may be unable to find some existing solutions, as shown in [24]. Actually, that paper shows that propagation-based approaches have important limitations.

Our approach to incrementality is based on the ideas presented in [25], for the sequential synchronization case. Other approaches based on TGGs that propose incremental solutions to sequential model synchronization are [10,16,12,22] (and some variations on them) but all of them are, in our opinion, not completely satisfactory. In particular, even if the construction of the solution does not start from scratch but from the given consistent model $\overline{G}$, the approaches in [16,12,22] have to analyze the whole model $\overline{G}$ (for instance, to know what parts of $\overline{G}$ must be modified) so their cost depends on the size of the given model. This is not the case of [10], but their approach only works for the case when source and target models are bijective, which excludes the case where source models are views of target models (or vice versa). In addition, in [10,16,22] there may be information loss, which we avoid using the approach developed in [12] and also used in [25].

6 Conclusion

In this paper we have presented some properties that ensure the adequacy of solutions for a concurrent synchronization problem, together with an incremental nondeterministic algorithm that is able to return all possible sound solutions that, in addition, satisfy these properties.

Most existing algorithms for model synchronization return just one solution. We believe that this is not adequate, especially in the case of concurrent synchronization. In that context, one concrete solution corresponds to a specific way of solving the existing conflicts, which may not be the way that the user would have preferred. For this reason, we decided that completeness of the algorithm was an important issue. It is clear that, in practice, delivering to a user a relatively large set of solutions is not very convenient. However, we think that this is something to take into account at the implementation level, for instance, by showing conflicts in a stepwise way and, then, showing the different ways of solving each conflict.

From a theoretical viewpoint, our algorithm works for any kind of graphs. However, in practice, if the models have attributes, our algorithm would not be adequate. For example, let us suppose that we are working with a class of models where a certain attribute a_1 must be equal to the addition of attributes a_2 and a_3 and let us suppose that we are trying to synchronize a model $\overline{G}$, where $a1$ has some given value v_1, but a_2 and a_3 have no value, i.e., the synchronization algorithm should provide values to a_2 and a_3, such that their addition equals v_1. In this context, our algorithm would deliver infinite solutions, assigning to a_2 and a_3 all possible values v_2 and v_3 such that $v_1 = v_2 + v_3$. In general, dealing with attributed graphs in the context of sequential or concurrent model synchronization poses problems that are described in [1,21].

As future work, on the one hand, we plan to address the case of attributed models and, on the other hand, to extend our results to the multimodel case, i.e. when synchronizing more than two models. This case has specific complications, see, for instance [32,4]. It has already been approached in [34,35], but just as a straightforward generalization of [14], which means that it shares its limitations.

References

1. Anjorin, A., Varró, G., Schürr, A.: Complex Attribute Manipulation in TGGs with Constraint-Based Programming Techniques. ECEASST **49** (2012)
2. Dayal, U., Bernstein, P.A.: On the Correct Translation of Update Operations on Relational Views. ACM Trans. Database Syst. **7**(3), 381–416 (1982)
3. Diskin, Z.: Model Synchronization: Mappings, Tiles, and Categories. In: Generative and Transformational Techniques in Software Engineering III, vol. 6491, pp. 92–165. Springer (2011)
4. Diskin, Z., König, H., Lawford, M.: Multiple Model Synchronization with Multiary Delta Lenses. In: Fundamental Approaches to Software Engineering, 21st International Conference, FASE 2018. Lecture Notes in Computer Science, vol. 10802, pp. 21–37. Springer (2018)
5. Diskin, Z., Xiong, Y., Czarnecki, K., Ehrig, H., Hermann, F., Orejas, F.: From State- to Delta-Based Bidirectional Model Transformations: The Symmetric Case. In: Model Driven Engineering Languages and Systems, MODELS 2011. Lecture Notes in Computer Science, vol. 6981, pp. 304–318. Springer (2011)
6. Ehrig, H., Ehrig, K., Prange, U., Taentzer, G.: Fundamentals of Algebraic Graph Transformation. EATCS Monographs of Theoretical Comp. Sc., Springer (2006)
7. Ehrig, H., Ehrig, K., Hermann, F.: From Model Transformation to Model Integration based on the Algebraic Approach to Triple Graph Grammars. ECEASST **10** (2008)
8. Ehrig, H., Ermel, C., Taentzer, G.: A Formal Resolution Strategy for Operation-Based Conflicts in Model Versioning Using Graph Modifications. In: FASE 2011. Lecture Notes in Computer Science, vol. 6603, pp. 202–216. Springer (2011)
9. Fagin, R., Kolaitis, P.G., Popa, L., Tan, W.C.: Quasi-inverses of schema mappings. ACM Trans. Database Syst. **33**(2) (2008)
10. Giese, H., Wagner, R.: From model transformation to incremental bidirectional model synchronization. Software and System Modeling **8**(1), 21–43 (2009)
11. Gottmann, S., Hermann, F., Nachtigall, N., Braatz, B., Ermel, C., Ehrig, H., Engel, T.: Correctness and Completeness of Generalised Concurrent Model Synchronisation Based on Triple Graph Grammars. In: AMT@MoDELS. Lecture Notes in Computer Science, vol. 1077. Springer (2013)
12. Greenyer, J., Pook, S., Rieke, J.: Preventing Information Loss in Incremental Model Synchronization by Reusing Elements. In: ECMFA 2011. Lecture Notes in Computer Science, vol. 6698, pp. 144–159. Springer (2011)
13. Hearnden, D., Lawley, M., Raymond, K.: Incremental Model Transformation for the Evolution of Model-Driven Systems. In: MoDELS 2006. Lecture Notes in Computer Science, vol. 4199, pp. 321–335. Springer (2006)
14. Hermann, F., Ehrig, H., Ermel, C., Orejas, F.: Concurrent Model Synchronization with Conflict Resolution Based on Triple Graph Grammars. In: FASE 2012. Lecture Notes in Computer Science, vol. 7212, pp. 178–193. Springer (2012)
15. Hermann, F., Ehrig, H., Golas, U., Orejas, F.: Formal Analysis of Model Transformations based on Triple Graph Grammars. Math. Struct. in Comp. Sc. **24** (2014)
16. Hermann, F., Ehrig, H., Orejas, F., Czarnecki, K., Diskin, Z., Xiong, Y.: Correctness of Model Synchronization Based on Triple Graph Grammars. In: MODELS 2011. Lecture Notes in Computer Science, vol. 6981, pp. 668–682. Springer (2011)
17. Hermann, F., Ehrig, H., Orejas, F., Golas, U.: Formal Analysis of Functional Behaviour for Model Transformations Based on Triple Graph Grammars. In: ICGT 2010. Lecture Notes in Computer Science, vol. 6372, pp. 155–170. Springer (2010)

18. Hofmann, M., Pierce, B.C., Wagner, D.: Symmetric lenses. In: POPL 2011. pp. 371–384. ACM (2011)
19. Hofmann, M., Pierce, B.C., Wagner, D.: Edit lenses. In: Field, J., Hicks, M. (eds.) POPL'12. pp. 495–508. ACM (2012)
20. Lack, S., Sobocinski, P.: Adhesive and quasiadhesive categories. Theor. Inf. App. **39**, 511–545 (2005)
21. Lambers, L., Hildebrandt, S., Giese, H., Orejas, F.: Attribute Handling for Bidirectional Model Transformations: The Triple Graph Grammar Case. ECEASST **49** (2012)
22. Lauder, M., Anjorin, A., Varró, G., Schürr, A.: Efficient Model Synchronization with Precedence Triple Graph Grammars. In: ICGT 2012. Lecture Notes in Computer Science, vol. 7562, pp. 401–415. Springer (2012)
23. Macedo, N., Tiago, J., Cunha, A.: A Feature-Based Classification of Model Repair Approaches. IEEE Trans. Software Eng. **43**(7), 615–640 (2017)
24. Orejas, F., Boronat, A., Ehrig, H., Hermann, F., Schölzel, H.: On Propagation-Based Concurrent Model Synchronization. In: BX 2013. Electronic Communications of the EASST, vol. 57, pp. 1–20. European Association of Software Science and Technology (2013)
25. Orejas, F., Pino, E.: Correctness of Incremental Model Synchronization with Triple Graph Grammars. In: ICMT 2014. Lecture Notes in Computer Science, vol. 8568, pp. 74–90. Springer (2014)
26. Pierce, B.C.: Harmony: The Art of Reconciliation. In: TGC 2005. Lecture Notes in Computer Science, vol. 3705, p. 1. Springer (2005)
27. Schürr, A.: Specification of Graph Translators with Triple Graph Grammars. In: WG '94. Lecture Notes in Computer Science, vol. 903, pp. 151–163. Springer (1994)
28. Schürr, A., Klar, F.: 15 Years of Triple Graph Grammars. In: ICGT 2008. pp. 411–425 (2008)
29. Stevens, P.: Towards an Algebraic Theory of Bidirectional Transformations. In: ICGT'08. Lecture Notes in Computer Science, vol. 5214, pp. 1–17. Springer (2008)
30. Stevens, P.: Bidirectional model transformations in QVT: semantic issues and open questions. Software and System Modeling **9**(1), 7–20 (2010)
31. Stevens, P.: Observations relating to the equivalences induced on model sets by bidirectional transformations. ECEASST **49** (2012)
32. Stevens, P.: Towards sound, optimal, and flexible building from megamodels. In: Proceedings of the 21th ACM/IEEE International Conference on Model Driven Engineering Languages and Systems, MODELS 2018. pp. 301–311. ACM (2018)
33. Terwilliger, J.F., Cleve, A., Curino, C.: How Clean Is Your Sandbox? - Towards a Unified Theoretical Framework for Incremental Bidirectional Transformations. In: ICMT 2012. Lecture Notes in Computer Science, vol. 7307, pp. 1–23. Springer (2012)
34. Trollmann, F., Albayrak, S.: Extending Model to Model Transformation Results from Triple Graph Grammars to Multiple Models. In: ICMT 2015. Lecture Notes in Computer Science, vol. 9152, pp. 214–229. Springer (2015)
35. Trollmann, F., Albayrak, S.: Decision Points for Non-determinism in Concurrent Model Synchronization with Triple Graph Grammars. In: ICMT 2017. Lecture Notes in Computer Science, vol. 10374, pp. 35–50. Springer (2017)
36. Xiong, Y., Hu, Z., Zhao, H., Song, H., Takeichi, M., Mei, H.: Supporting automatic model inconsistency fixing. In: ESEC/FSE 2009. pp. 315–324 (2009)
37. Xiong, Y., Song, H., Hu, Z., Takeichi, M.: Supporting Parallel Updates with Bidirectional Model Transformations. In: ICMT 2009. Lecture Notes in Computer Science, vol. 5563, pp. 213–228. Springer (2009)
38. Xiong, Y., Song, H., Hu, Z., Takeichi, M.: Synchronizing concurrent model updates based on bidirectional transformation. Software and System Modeling **12**, 89–104 (2013)

Statistical Model Checking for Variability-Intensive Systems

Maxime Cordy[1] , Mike Papadakis[1], and Axel Legay[2]

[1] SnT, University of Luxembourg, Luxembourg
{maxime.cordy,michail.papadakis}@uni.lu
[2] Université Catholique de Louvain, Belgium
axel.legay@uclouvain.be

Abstract. We propose a new Statistical Model Checking (SMC) method to discover bugs in variability-intensive systems (VIS). The state-space of such systems is exponential in the number of variants, which makes the verification problem harder than for classical systems. To reduce verification time, we sample executions from a featured transition system – a model that represents jointly the state spaces of all variants. The combination of this compact representation and the inherent efficiency of SMC allows us to find bugs much faster (up to 16 times according to our experiments) than other methods. As any simulation-based approach, however, the risk of Type-1 error exists. We provide a lower bound and an upper bound for the number of simulations to perform to achieve the desired level of confidence. Our empirical study involving 59 properties over three case studies reveals that our method manages to discover all variants violating 41 of the properties. This indicates that SMC can act as a low-cost-high-reward method for verifying VIS.

1 Introduction

We consider the problem of bug detection in Variability Intensive Systems (VIS). This category of systems encompasses any system that can be derived into multiple variants (differing, e.g., in provided functionalities), including software product lines [12] and configurable systems [32]. Compared to traditional ("single") systems, the complexity of bug detection in VIS is increased: bugs can appear only in some variants, which requires analysing the peculiarities of each variant.

Among the number of techniques developed for bug detection, one finds testing and model checking. Testing [6] executes particular test inputs on the system and checks whether it triggers a bug. Albeit testing remains widely used in industry, the rise of concurrency and inherent system complexity has made system-level test case generation a hard problem. Also, testing is often limited to bounded reachability properties and cannot assess liveness properties.

Model checking [2] is a formal verification technique which checks that all behaviours of the system satisfy specified requirements. These behaviours are typically modelled as an automaton, whose each node represents a state of the

H. Wehrheim and J. Cabot (Eds.): FASE 2020, LNCS 12076, pp. 294–314, 2020.
https://doi.org/10.1007/978-3-030-45234-6_15

system (e.g. a valuation of the variables of a program and a location in this program's execution flow) and where each transition between two states expresses that the program can move from one state to the other by executing a single action (e.g. executing the next program statement). Requirements are often expressed in temporal logics, e.g. the Linear Temporal Logic (LTL) [31].

Such logics capture both safety and liveness properties of system behaviours. As an example, consider the LTL formula $\Box(command\_sleep \Rightarrow \Diamond system\_sleep)$. $command\_sleep$ and $system\_sleep$ are logic atoms and represent, respectively, a state where the $\texttt{sleep}$ command is input and another state where the system enters sleep mode. The symbols $\Box$ and $\Diamond$ means $always$ and $eventually$, respectively. Thus, the whole formula expresses that "it is always the case that when the $\texttt{sleep}$ command is input, the system eventually enters sleep mode".

Contrary to testing, model checking is exhaustive: if a bug exists then the checking algorithm outputs a $counterexample$, i.e. an execution trace of the system that violates the verified property. Exhaustiveness makes model checking an appealing solution to obtain strong guarantees that the system works as intended. It can also nicely complement testing (whose main advantage remains to be applied directly on the running system), e.g. by reasoning over liveness properties or by serving as oracle in test generation processes [1]. Those benefits, however, come at the cost of scalability issues, the most prominent being the $state\ explosion\ problem$. This term refers to the phenomenon where the state space to visit is so huge that an exhaustive search is intractable. As an illustration of this, let us remark that the theoretical complexity of the LTL model-checking problem is PSPACE-complete [37].

Model checking complexity is further exacerbated when it comes to VIS. Indeed, in this case, the model-checking problem requires verifying whether all the variants satisfy the requirements [11]. This means that, if the VIS comprises n variation points (n features in a software product line or n Boolean options in a configurable system), the number of different variants to represent and to check can reach 2^n. This exponential factor adds to the inherent complexity of model checking. Thus, checking each variant (or models thereof) separately – an approach known as $enumerative$ or $product$-$based$ [34] – is often intractable. To alleviate this, variability-aware models and companion algorithms were proposed to represent and check efficiently the behaviour of all variants at once. For instance, $Featured\ Transition\ Systems$ (FTS) [11] are transition systems where transitions are labelled with (a symbolic encoding of) the set of variants able to exercise this transition. The structure of FTS, if well constructed, allows one to capture in a compact manner commonalities between states and transitions of several variants. Exploiting that information, $family$-$based$ algorithms can check only once the executions that several variants can execute and explore the state space of an individual variant only when it differs from all the others. In spite of positive improvements over the enumerative approach, state space explosion remains a major challenge.

In this work, we propose an alternative technique for state-space exploration and bug detection in VIS. We use Statistical Model Checking (SMC) [26] as a trade-off between testing and model checking to verify properties (expressed in full LTL) on FTS. The core idea of SMC is to conduct some simulations (i.e. sample executions) of the system (or its model) and verify if these executions satisfy the property to check. The results are then used together with statistical tests to decide whether the system satisfies the property with some degree of confidence. Of course, in contrast with an exhaustive approach, a simulation-based solution does not guarantee a result with 100% confidence. Still, it is possible to bound the probability of making an error. Simulation-based methods are known to be far less memory- and time-consuming than exhaustive ones, and are sometimes the only viable option. Over the past years, SMC has been used to, e.g. assess the absence of errors in various areas from aeronautic to systems biology; measure cost average and energy consumption for complex applications such as nanosatellites; detect rare bugs in concurrent systems [10, 21, 25].

Given an LTL formula and an FTS, our *family-based* SMC method samples executions from all variants at the same time. Doing so, it avoids sampling twice (or more) executions that exist in multiple variants. Merging the individual state spaces biases the results, though, as it changes the probability distribution of the executions. This makes the problem different from previous methods intended for single systems (e.g. [20]) and obliges us to revisit the fundamentals of SMC in the light of VIS. In particular, we want to characterize the number of execution samples required to bound the probability of Type-1 error by a desired degree of confidence. We provide a lower bound and an upper bound for this number by reducing its computation to particular instances of the coupon problem [4]. We implemented our method within ProVeLines [17], a model checker for VIS. We provide empirical evidence, based on 3 case studies totalling 59 properties to check, that family-based SMC is a viable approach to verify VIS. Our study shows that our method manages to find all buggy variants in 41 properties and does so up to 16 times faster than state-of-the-art model-checking algorithms for VIS [11]. Moreover, our approach can achieve a median bug detection rate 3 times higher than classical SMC applied to each variant individually. The hardest cases arise when the state space of some variant is substantially smaller than the other. This leads to a reduced probability to find a bug in those variants.

2 Background on Model Checking

In model checking, the behaviour of the system is often represented as a transition system (S, Δ, AP, L) where S is a set of states, $\Delta \subseteq S \times S$ is the transition relation, AP is a set of atomic propositions[3] and $L : S \rightarrow 2^{AP}$ labels any state with the atomic propositions that the system satisfies when in such a state.

2.1 Linear Temporal Logic

LTL is a temporal logic that allows specifying desired properties over all future executions of some given system. Given a set AP of atomic propositions, an LTL

---

[3] Atomic propositions can be seen as basic observable properties of the system state.

formula ϕ is formed according to the following grammar: $\phi ::= \top \mid a \mid \phi_1 \wedge \phi_2 \mid \neg\phi_1 \mid \bigcirc\phi_1 \mid \phi_1 U \phi_2$ where ϕ_1 and ϕ_2 are LTL formulae, $a \in AP$, $\bigcirc$ is the next operator and U is the until operator. We also define $\Diamond\phi$ ("eventually" ϕ) and $\Box\phi$ ("always" ϕ) as a shortcut for $\top U \phi$ and $\neg\Diamond\neg\phi$, respectively.

Vardi and Wolper have presented an automata-based approach for checking that a system – modelled as a transition system ts – satisfies an LTL formula ϕ [37]. Their approach consists of, first, transforming ϕ into a Büchi automaton $\mathcal{B}_{\neg\phi}$ whose language is exactly the set of executions that violate ϕ, that is, those that visit infinitely often a so-called *accepting* state. Such execution σ takes the form of a *lasso*, i.e. $\sigma = q_0 \ldots q_n$ with $q_j = q_n$ for some j and where q_i is accepting for some $i : j \leq i \leq n$. We name *accepting* any such lasso whose cycle contains an accepting state.

The second step is to compute the synchronous product of ts and $\mathcal{B}_{\neg\phi}$, which results in another Büchi automaton $\mathcal{B}_{ts \otimes \neg\phi}$. Any accepting lasso in $\mathcal{B}_{ts \otimes \neg\phi}$ represents an execution of the system that violates ϕ. Thus, Vardi and Wolper's algorithm comes down to checking the absence of such accepting lasso in the whole state space of $\mathcal{B}_{ts \otimes \neg\phi}$. The size of this state space is $\mathcal{O}(|ts| \times |2^{|\phi|}|)$ and the complexity of this algorithm is PSPACE-complete.

2.2   Statistical Model Checking

Originally, SMC was used to compute the probability to satisfy a bounded LTL property for stochastic system [39]. The idea was to monitor the properties on bounded executions represented by Bernoulli variables and then use Monte Carlo to estimate the resulting property. SMC also applies to non-stochastic systems by assuming an implicit uniform probability distribution on each state successor.

Grosu and Smolka [20] lean on this and propose an SMC method to address the full LTL model-checking problem. Their sampling algorithm walks randomly through the state space of $\mathcal{B}_{ts \otimes \neg\phi}$ until it finds a lasso. They repeat the process M times and conclude that the system satisfies the property if and only if none of the M lassos is accepting. They also show that, given a confidence ratio δ and assuming that the probability p for an execution of the system exceeds an error margin ϵ, setting $M = \frac{\delta}{1-\epsilon}$ bounds the probability of a Type-1 error (rejecting the hypothesis that the system violates the property while it actually violates it) by δ. Thus, M can serve as a minimal number of samples to perform. Our work extends theirs in order to support VIS instead of single systems. Other work on applying SMC to the full LTL logic can be found in [18, 38].

2.3   Model Checking for VIS

Applying classical model checking to VIS requires iterating over all variants, construct their corresponding automata $\mathcal{B}_{ts \otimes \neg\phi}$ and search for accepting lasso in each of these. This enumerative method (also named *product-based* [34]) fails to exploit the fact that variants have behaviour in common.

As an alternative, researchers came up with models able to capture the behaviour of multiple variants and distinguish between the unique and common

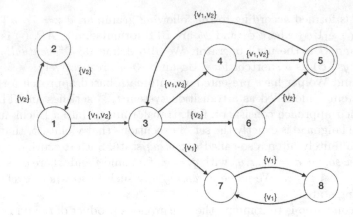

Fig. 1: An example of FBA with two variants.

behaviour of those variants [3, 8, 11]. Among such models, we focus on *featured transition systems* [11] as those can link an execution to the variants able to execute it more directly than the alternative formalisms. In a nutshell, FTS extend the standard transition system by labelling each transition with a symbolic encoding of the set of variants able to exercise this transition. Then, the set of variants that can produce an execution π is the intersection of all sets of variants associated with the transitions in π.

To check which variants violate a given LTL formula ϕ, one can adapt the procedure of Vardi and Wolper and build the synchronous product of the featured transition system with $\mathcal{B}_{\neg\phi}$ [11]. This product is similar to the Büchi automaton obtained in the single system case, except that its transitions are also labelled with a set of variants.[4] Then, the buggy variants are those that are able to execute the accepting lassos of this automaton. This generalized automaton is the fundamental formalism we work on in this paper.

Definition 1 *Let V be a set of variants. A* Featured Büchi Automaton *(FBA) over V is a tuple $(Q, \Delta, Q_0, A,, \Theta, \gamma)$ where Q is a set of states, $\Delta \subseteq Q \times Q$ is the transition relation, $Q_0 \subseteq Q$ is a set of initial states, $A \subseteq Q$ is the set of accepting states, Θ is the whole set of variants, and $\gamma : \Delta \to 2^{\Theta}$ associates each transition with the set of variants that can execute it.*

Figure 1 shows an FBA with two variants and eight states. State 5 as the only accepting state. Both variants can execute the transition from State 3 to State 4, whereas only variant v_2 can move from State 3 to State 6.

The Büchi automaton corresponding to one particular variant v is derived by removing the transitions not executable by v. That is, we remove all transitions $(q, q') \in \Delta$ such that $v \notin \gamma(q, q')$. The resulting automaton is named the *projection* of the FBA onto v. For example, one obtains the projection of the FBA in

---

[4] Those labels are equal to those found in the corresponding transitions of the featured transition system.

Figure 1 onto v_2 by removing the transition from State 3 to State 7 and those between State 7 to State 8.

2.4   Other Related Work

Recent work has applied SMC in the context of VIS. In [36], the authors proposed an algebraic language to describe (quantitative) behavioural variability in a dynamic manner. While their work shares some similarities with ours, there are fundamental differences. First, we seek for guaranteeing the absence of bugs in all variants of the family (applying family-based concepts), while they focus on dynamic feature interactions (on a product-based basis). The second difference is that they consider quantitative bounded properties, while we support the entire LTL verification problem by extending the multi-lasso concept of [20, 28].

Another related, yet different area is the sampling of VIS variants (e.g. [27, 30]). Such work considers the problem of sampling uniformly variants in order to study their characteristics (e.g. performance [22] and other quality requirements [15]) and infers those of the other variants. Recently, Thüm et al. [35] survey different strategies for the performance analysis of VIS, including the sampling of variants and family-based test generation, which is based on the same idea of executing test cases common to multiple variants. Contrary to us, such works do not consider temporal/behavioural properties and most of them perform the sampling based on a static representation of the variant space (i.e. a feature model [23]). An interesting direction for future work is to combine our family-based SMC with sampling techniques to check only representative variants of the family.

3   Family-Based Statistical Model Checking

The purpose of SMC is to reduce the verification effort (when visiting the state space of the system model) by sampling a given number of executions (i.e. lassos). This gain in efficiency, however, comes at the risk of Type-1 errors. Indeed, while the discovery of a counterexample leads with certainty to the conclusion that the variants able to execute it violate the property ϕ, the fact that the sampling did not find a counterexample for some variant v does not entail a 100% guarantee that v satisfies ϕ. The more lassos we sample, the more confident we can get that the variants without counterexamples satisfy ϕ. Thus, designing a family-based SMC method involves answering three questions: (1) how to sample executions; (2) how to choose a suitable number of executions; (3) what is the associated probability of Type-1 error.

3.1   Random Sampling in Featured Büchi Automata

One can sample a lasso in an FBA by randomly walking through its state space, starting from a randomly-chosen initial state and ending as soon as a cycle is found. A particular restriction is that this lasso should be executable by at least

Input: $fba = (Q, \Delta, Q_0, A, \Theta, \gamma)$
Output: $(\sigma, \Theta_\sigma, accept)$ where σ is a lasso of fba and Θ_σ is the set of the variants able to execute σ and $accept$ is true iff σ is accepting.

1 $q_0 \leftarrow$ pick from Q_0 with probability $\frac{1}{|Q_0|}$;
2 $q \leftarrow q_0$; $\sigma \leftarrow q_0$; $\Theta_\sigma \leftarrow \Theta$; $depth \leftarrow 0$; $a \leftarrow 0$;
3 **while** $hash(q) = \perp$ **do**
4 $\quad depth \leftarrow depth + 1$;
5 $\quad hash(q) \leftarrow depth$;
6 $\quad$ **if** $q \in A$ **then**
7 $\quad\quad a \leftarrow depth$;
8 $\quad$ **end**
9 $\quad Succ_\sigma \leftarrow \{q' \in Q | (q, q') \in \Delta \wedge (\gamma(q, q') \cap \Theta_\sigma) \neq \emptyset\}$;
10 $\quad q' \leftarrow$ pick from $Succ_\sigma$ with probability $\frac{1}{|Succ_\sigma|}$;
11 $\quad \sigma \leftarrow \sigma q'$;
12 $\quad \Theta_\sigma \leftarrow \Theta_\sigma \cap \gamma(q, q')$;
13 $\quad q \leftarrow q'$;
14 **end**
15 **return** $(\sigma, \Theta_\sigma, hash(q) \leq a)$

Algorithm 1: Random Lasso Sampling

one variant; otherwise, we would sample a behaviour that does not actually exist. The set of variants able to execute a given lasso are those that can execute all its transitions, i.e. the intersection of all $\gamma(q, q')$ met along the transitions of this lasso. More generally, we define the lasso sample space of an FBA as follows.

Definition 2 *Let $fba = (Q, \Delta, Q_0, A, \Theta, \gamma)$ be a featured Büchi automaton. The lasso sample space L of fba is the set of executions $\sigma = q_0 \ldots q_n$ such that $q_0 \in Q_0$, $(q_i, q_{i+1}) \in \Delta$ for all $0 \leq i \leq n - 1$, $(\bigcap_{0 \leq i \leq n-1} \gamma(q_i, q_{i+1})) \neq \emptyset$, $q_j = q_n$ for some $0 \leq j \leq n - 1$ and $a \neq b \Rightarrow q_a \neq q_b$ for all $0 \leq a, b \leq n - 1$. Moreover, σ is said to be an accepting lasso if $\exists q_a \in A$ for some $j \leq a \leq n$.*

Algorithm 1 formalizes the sampling of lassos in a deadlock-free FBA.[5] After randomly picking an initial state (Line 1), we walk through the state space by randomly choosing, at each iteration, a successor state among those available (Line 7–18). Throughout the search, we maintain the set of variants Θ_σ that can execute σ so far (Line 16). Then, we use this set as a filter when selecting successor states, so as to make sure that σ remains executable by at least one variant. At Line 13, $Succ_\sigma$ is the set of successors q' of q (last state of σ) that can be reached. We stop the search as soon as we reach a state that was previously visited (Line 7). If this state was visited before the last accepting state, it means that the sampled lasso is accepting (Line 19).

---

[5] We assume that no variant may remain stuck in a state without outgoing transition that this variant can execute. Should this happen, we assume that the variant self-loops in the state wherein it is stuck, yielding an immediate lasso.

A motivated criticism [28] of the use of random walk to sample lasso is that shorter lassos receive a higher probability to be sampled. To counterbalance this, we implemented a heuristic named *multi-lasso* [20]. It consists of ignoring backward transitions that do not lead to an accepting lasso if there are still forward transitions to explore. This is achieved by modifying Line 13 such that backward transitions leading to a non-accepting lasso are not considered in the successor set.

Assuming a uniform selection of outgoing transitions from each state, one can compute the probability that a random walk samples any given lasso from the sample space.

Definition 3 *The probability $P(\sigma)$ of a lasso $\sigma = q_0 \ldots q_n$ is inductively defined as follows: $P[q_0] = |Q_0|^{-1}$ and $P[q_0 \ldots q_j] = P[q_0 \ldots q_{j-1}] \times |Succ_{q_0 \ldots q_{j-1}}|^{-1}$.*

In the absence of deadlock, $(L, \mathcal{P}(\mathcal{L}), P)$ defines a probability space. Probability spaces on infinite executions are by no means a trivial construction (see e.g. [9]). Nevertheless, the proof of this proposition is similar to its counterpart in Büchi automata [20] and is therefore omitted. It derives from the observation that the lasso sample space is composed of non-subsuming finite prefixes of all infinite paths of the automaton.

Let us consider an example. In the FBA from Figure 1, there are two non-accepting lassos ($l_1 = (1,2,1)$ and $l_2 = (1,3,7,8,7)$) and two accepting lassos ($l_3 = (1,3,4,5,3)$ and $l_4 = (1,3,6,5,3)$). Both variants can execute lassos l_3, while only v_1 can execute l_2 and only v_2 can execute l_1 and l_4. The probability of sampling l_1 is $\frac{1}{2}$, whereas $P[l_2] = P[l_3] = P[l_4] = \frac{1}{6}$. Thus, the probability of sampling a counterexample executable by v_2 is $\frac{1}{3}$, whereas it is only $\frac{1}{6}$ for v_1.

Next, we characterize the relationship between this probability space and any individual variant v. Let L_v be the set of lassos executable by v. Since $L_v \subseteq L$, the probability p_v to sample such a lasso is $\sum_{\sigma_v \in L_v} P(\sigma)$. Note that p_v can be different from the probability $\hat{p}_v$ of sampling an accepting lasso from the automaton modelling the behaviour of v only (i.e. the projection of the FBA onto v). This is because, in the FBA, the probability of selecting an outgoing transition from a given state is assigned uniformly regardless of the number of variants able to execute that transition. This balance-breaking effect increases more as the variants have different numbers of unique executions.

Let $\sigma = q_0 \ldots q_n$ be a lasso in L_v. Then $P_v(\sigma)$ is inductively defined as follows: $P_v[q_0] = P[q_0]$ and $P_v[q_0 \ldots q_j] = P_v[q_0 \ldots q_{j-1}] \times |\{(q_{j-1}, q) \in \Delta_v : q \in Q\}|^{-1}$ where $\Delta_v = \{(q, q') \in \Delta : v \in \gamma(q, q')\}$. In our example, $P_{v_1}[l_3] = \frac{1}{2}$, as opposed to $P[l_3] = \frac{1}{6}$. This implies that it is more likely to sample an accepting lasso executable by v_1 from its projection in one trial than it is from the whole FBA in two trials. This illustrates the case where merging the state spaces of the variants can have a negative impact on the capability to find bugs specific to one variant.

Thus, sampling lassos from the FBA allows finding one counterexample executable by multiple products but it introduces a bias. Overall, it tends to decrease the probability of sampling lassos from variants that have a smaller state space.

This can impact the results and parameter choices of SMC, like the number of samples required to get confident results and the associated Type-1 error.

3.2   Hypothesis Testing

Remember that addressing the model checking problem for VIS requires to find a counterexample for every buggy variant v. Thus, one must sample a number M of lassos such that one gets an accepting lasso for each such buggy variant with a confidence ratio δ. Let fba be a featured Büchi automaton, v be a variant and $p_v = \sum \sigma \in L_v^\omega P(\sigma)$ where L_v^ω is the set of accepting lasso executable by v. Let Z_v denote a Bernoulli random variable such that $Z_v = 1$ with probability p_v and $Z_v = 0$ with probability $q_v = 1 - p_v$. Now, let X_v denote the geometric random variable with parameter p_v that encodes the number of independent samples required until $Z_v = 1$. For a set of variants $V = \{v_1 \dots v_{|V|}\}$, we have that $X_{v_1} \dots X_{v_{|V|}}$ are *not* independent since one may sample a lasso executable by more than one variant.

We define $X = \max_{i=1..|V|} X_{v_i}$. We aim to find a number of sample M such that $P[X \leq M] \geq 1 - \delta$ for a confidence ratio δ. This is analogous to the coupon collector's problem [4], which asks how many boxes are needed to collect one instance of every coupon placed randomly in the boxes. It differs from the standard formulation in that the probability of occurrence of coupons are neither independent nor uniform, and a single box can contain 0 to $|V|$ coupons. Even for simpler instances of the coupon problem, computing $P[X \leq M]$ analytically is known to be hard [33]. Thus, existing solutions rather characterise a lower bound and an upper bound. We follow this approach as well.

3.3   Lower Bound (Minimum Number of Samples)

To compute a lower bound for the number of samples to draw, we transform the family-based SMC problem to a simpler form (in terms of verification effort). We divide our developments into two parts. First, we show that assigning equal probabilities p_{v_i} to every variant v_i (obtained by averaging the original probability values) reduces the number M of required samples. As a second step, we show that assuming that all variants share all their executions also reduces M. Doing so, we reduce the family-based SMC problem to its single-system counterpart, which allows us to obtain the desired lower bound.

Averaged probabilities. Let $p_{avg} = \frac{1}{|V|} \sum_{v=1..|V|} p_v$ and X_{even} be the counterpart of X where all probabilities p_{v_i} have been replaced by p_{avg}.

Lemma 4 *For any number N, it holds that $P[X_{even} \leq N] \geq P[X \leq N]$.*

Intuitively, the value of X depends mainly on the variants whose accepting lassos are rarer. By averaging the probability of sampling accepting lassos, we raise the likelihood to get those rarer lassos and, thus, the number of samples required to get an accepting lasso for all variants. Shioda [33] proves a similar result for the coupon collector problem. He does so by showing that the vector $\mathbf{p_{even}}$ *majorizes* $\mathbf{p} = \{p_{v_1} \dots p_{v_1}\}$ and that the $ccdf$[6] of X is a Schur-concave function of the sampling probabilities. Even though our case is more general than the non-uniform coupon collector's problem, the result of Lemma 4 still holds. Indeed, we observe that the theoretical proof of [33] (a) does not assume the independence of the random variables Z_{v_i}; (b) still applies to the dependent case; and (c) supports the case where the sum of the probability values p_{v_i} is less than one.

Maximized commonalities. Next, let $X_{\mathbf{all}}$ be the particular case of $X_{\mathbf{even}}$ where all accepting lassos are executable by all variants and are sampled with probability p_{avg}. Thus, the number of samples to find an accepting lasso for every variant is reduced to the number of samples required to find any accepting lasso.

Lemma 5 *It holds that* $P[X_{all} \leq N] \geq P[X_{even} \leq N]$.

Moreover, let us note that $X_{\mathbf{all}}$ is a geometric random variable with parameter p_{avg}. This reduces our problem to sampling an accepting lasso in a classical Büchi automaton and allows us to reuse the results of Grosu and Smolka [20].

Lemma 6 *For a confidence ratio δ and an error margin ϵ, it holds that*

$$p_{avg} \geq \epsilon \Rightarrow P[X_{all} \leq M] \geq P[X_{all} \leq N] = 1 - \delta$$

where $M = \frac{ln(\delta)}{ln(1-\epsilon)}$ *and* $N = \frac{ln(\delta)}{ln(1-p_{avg})}$.

This leads us to the central result of this section.

Theorem 7 *Assuming that $p_{avg} \geq \epsilon_{avg}$ for a given error margin ϵ_{avg}, a lower bound for the number of samples required to find an accepting lasso for each buggy variant is $M = \frac{ln(\delta)}{ln(1-\epsilon_{avg})}$ with a Type-1 error bounded by δ.*

3.4   Upper Bound (Maximum Number of Samples)

We follow a similar two-step process to characterise an upper bound for M. In the first step, we replace the probabilities p_{v_i} of every variant by their minimum. In the second step, we alter the model so that the variants have no common behaviour. Then we show that, given a desired degree of confidence, the obtained model requires a higher number of samples than the original one.

Minimum probability. Let $p_{min} = \min_{v=1..|V|} p_v$ and $X_{\mathbf{min}}$ be the counterpart of X where all probabilities p_{v_i} have been replaced by p_{min}. The $ccdf$ of X being a decreasing function of the sampling probabilities, we have that $P[X_{\mathbf{min}} \leq N] \leq P[X \leq N]$.

---

[6] $ccdf$ stands for complementary cumulative distribution function

No common counterexamples. Let $\{(X_{\mathbf{indep}})_{v_i}\}$ be a set of independent geometric random variables with parameters p_{min} and let $X_{\mathbf{indep}} = \max(X_{\mathbf{indep}})_{v_i}$. $X_{\mathbf{indep}}$ actually encodes the number of samples required to get a counterexample for all buggy variants when those have no common counterexamples. We have that $P[X_{\mathbf{indep}} \leq N] \leq P[X_{\mathbf{min}} \leq N]$, since the number of samples to perform cannot be reduced by sampling a counterexample executable by multiple variants. Now, let us note that $X_{\mathbf{indep}}$ is an instance of the uniform coupon problem with $|V|$ coupons to collect. A lower bound for $P[X_{\mathbf{indep}} \leq M]$ is known to be $1 - |V| \times (1 - p_{min})^M$ [33]. Assuming p_{min} greater than some error margin ϵ_{min}, we have $P[X_{\mathbf{indep}} \leq M] \geq 1 - |V| \times (1 - \epsilon_{min})^M$. Setting a confidence ratio δ, we want to find a M such that $P[X_{\mathbf{indep}} \leq M] \geq 1 - \delta$. By solving $1 - |V|(1 - \epsilon_{min})^M = 1 - \delta$, we obtain $M = \frac{ln(\delta) - ln(|V|)}{ln(1 - \epsilon_{min})}$, which we can use as the upper bound for the number of samples to perform.

Theorem 8 *Assuming that $p_{min} \geq \epsilon_{min}$ for a given error margin ϵ_{min}, an upper bound for the number of samples required to find an accepting lasso for each buggy variant is $M = \frac{ln(\delta) - ln(|V|)}{ln(1 - \epsilon_{min})}$ with a Type-1 error is bounded by δ.*

4   Empirical Study

4.1   Objectives and Methodology

One can regard SMC as a means of speeding up verification while risking missing counterexamples. Our first question studies this trade-off and analyses the empirical Type-1 error rate. More precisely, we compute the detection rate of our family-based SMC method, expressed as the number of buggy variants that it detects over the total number of buggy variants.

RQ1 *What is the empirical buggy variant detection rate of family-based SMC?*

We compute the detection rate for different numbers M of samples lying between the lower and upper bounds as characterised in Section 3. To get the ground truth (i.e. the true set of all buggy variants), we execute the exhaustive LTL model checking algorithms for FTS designed by Classen et al. [11]. For the lower bound, we assume that the average probability to sample an accepting lasso for any variant is higher than $\epsilon_{avg} = 0.01$. Setting a confidence ratio $\delta = 0.05$ yields $\frac{ln(0.05)}{ln(0.99)} = 298$. We round up and set $M = 300$ as our lower bound. For the higher bound, we assume that the minimum probability to sample a counterexample in a buggy variant is higher than $\epsilon_{min} = 3.10^{-4}$ and also set $\delta = 0.05$. For a model with 256 variants[7], this yields $M = \frac{ln(0.05) - ln(256)}{ln(0.9997)} = 18478$. For convenience, we round it up to $19,200 = 300 \cdot 2^6$. In the end, we successively set M to $300, 600, \ldots, 19200$ and observe the detection rates.

Next, we investigate a complementary scenario where the engineer has a limited budget of samples to check. We study the smallest budget required by

---

[7] 256 is the maximum number of variants in our case studies

SMC to detect all buggy variants (in the cases where it can indeed detect all of them) and what is the incurred computation resources compared to an exhaustive search of the state space. Thus, our second question is:

RQ2 *How much efficient is SMC with a minimal sample budget compared to an exhaustive search?*

Finally, we compare family-based SMC with the alternative of sampling in each variant's state space separately. We name this alternative method *enumerative SMC*. Hence, our last research question is:

RQ3 *How does family-based SMC compares with enumerative SMC?*

As before, we compare the two techniques w.r.t. detection rate. We set M to the same values as in RQ1. In enumerative SMC, this means that each variant receives a budget of samples of $\frac{M}{|V|}$ where M is the number of samples used in family-based SMC and V is the set of variants.

4.2   Experimental Setup

Implementation. We implemented our SMC algorithms (family-based and enumerative-based) in a prototype tool. The tool takes as input an FTS, an LTL formula and a sample budget. Then it performs SMC until all samples are checked or until all variants are found to violate the formula. To compare with the exhaustive search we use ProVeLines [17], a state-of-the-art model checker for VIS.

Dataset. We consider three systems that were used in past research to evaluate VIS model checking algorithms [11,14,16]. Table 1 summarizes the characteristics of our case studies and their related properties. The first system is a minepump system [11,24] with 128 variants. The underlying FTS comprises 250,561 states, while the state space of all variants taken individually reaches 889,124 states. The second model is an elevator model inspired by Plath and Ryan [29]. It is composed of eight configuration options, which can be combined into 256 different variants, and its FTS has 58,945,690 states to explore. The third and last is a case study inspired by the CCSDS File Delivery Protocol (CFDP) [13], a real-world configurable spacecraft communication protocol [5]. The FTS modelling the protocol consists of 1,732,536 states to explore and 56 variants (individually totalling 2,890,399 states). We discarded the properties that are satisfied by all variants. Those are: Minepump #17, #33, #40; Elevator #13, CFDP #5. Indeed, these properties are not relevant for RQ1 and RQ3 since SMC is trivially correct in such cases. As for RQ2, any small sample budget would return correct results while being more efficient than the exhaustive search. This leaves us with 59 properties.

Infrastructure and repetitions. We run our experiments on a MacBook Pro 2018 with a 2.9 GHz Core-i7 processor and macOS 10.14.5. To account for random variations in the sampling, we execute 100 runs of each experiment and compute the average detection rates for each property.

Table 1: Models and LTL formulae used in our experiments.

Minepump (250,561 FTS states, 128 valid variants)	
#1	$\neg(\Box\Diamond(stateReady \land highWater \land userStart))$
#2	$\neg(\Box\Diamond stateReady)$
#3	$\neg(\Box\Diamond stateRunning)$
#4	$\neg(\Box\Diamond stateStopped)$
#5	$\neg(\Box\Diamond stateMethanestop)$
#6	$\neg(\Box\Diamond stateLowstop)$
#7	$\neg(\Box\Diamond readCommand)$
#8	$\neg(\Box\Diamond readAlarm)$
#9	$\neg(\Box\Diamond readLevel)$
#10	$\neg((\Box\Diamond readCommand) \land (\Box\Diamond readAlarm) \land (\Box\Diamond readLevel))$
#11	$\neg(\Box\Diamond pumpOn)$
#12	$\neg(\Box\Diamond\neg pumpOn)$
#13	$\neg((\Box\Diamond pumpOn) \land (\Box\Diamond\neg pumpOn))$
#14	$\neg(\Box\Diamond methane)$
#15	$\neg(\Box\Diamond\neg methane)$
#16	$\neg((\Box\Diamond methane) \land (\Box\Diamond\neg methane))$
#17	$\Box(\neg pumpOn \lor stateRunning)$
#18	$\Box(methane \Rightarrow (\Diamond stateMethanestop))$
#19	$\Box(methane \Rightarrow \neg(\Diamond stateMethanestop))$
#20	$\Box(pumpOn \lor \neg methane)$
#21	$\Box((pumpOn \land methane) \Rightarrow \Diamond\neg pumpOn)$
#22	$((\Box\Diamond readCommand) \land (\Box\Diamond readAlarm) \land (\Box\Diamond readLevel)) \Rightarrow \Box((pumpOn \land methane) \Rightarrow \Diamond\neg pumpOn)$
#23	$\neg\Diamond\Box(pumpOn \land methane)$
#24	$((\Box\Diamond readCommand) \land (\Box\Diamond readAlarm) \land (\Box\Diamond readLevel)) \Rightarrow \neg\Diamond\Box(pumpOn \land methane)$
#25	$\Box((\neg pumpOn \land methane \land \Diamond\neg methane) \Rightarrow ((\neg pumpOn)U\neg methane))$
#26	$\Box((highWater \land \neg methane) \Rightarrow \Diamond pumpOn)$
#27	$\neg(\Diamond(highWater \land \neg methane))$
#28	$((\Box\Diamond readCommand) \land (\Box\Diamond readAlarm) \land (\Box\Diamond readLevel)) \Rightarrow (\Box((highWater \land \neg methane) \Rightarrow \Diamond pumpOn))$
#29	$\Box((highWater \land \neg methane) \Rightarrow \neg\Diamond pumpOn)$
#30	$\neg\Diamond\Box(\neg pumpOn \land highWater)$
#31	$((\Box\Diamond readCommand) \land (\Box\Diamond readAlarm) \land (\Box\Diamond readLevel)) \Rightarrow (\neg\Diamond\Box(\neg pumpOn \land highWater))$
#32	$\neg\Diamond\Box(\neg pumpOn \land \neg methane \land highWater)$
#33	$((\Box\Diamond readCommand) \land (\Box\Diamond readAlarm) \land (\Box\Diamond readLevel)) \Rightarrow (\neg\Diamond\Box(\neg pumpOn \land \neg methane \land highWater))$
#34	$\Box((pumpOn \land highWater \land \Diamond lowWater) \Rightarrow (pumpOnUlowWater))$
#35	$\neg\Diamond(pumpOn \land highWater \land \Diamond lowWater)$
#36	$\Box(lowWater \Rightarrow (\Diamond\neg pumpOn))$
#37	$((\Box\Diamond readCommand) \land (\Box\Diamond readAlarm) \land (\Box\Diamond readLevel)) \Rightarrow (\Box(lowWater \Rightarrow (\Diamond\neg pumpOn)))$
#38	$\neg\Diamond\Box(pumpOn \land lowWater)$
#39	$((\Box\Diamond readCommand) \land (\Box\Diamond readAlarm) \land (\Box\Diamond readLevel)) \Rightarrow (\neg\Diamond\Box(pumpOn \land lowWater))$
#40	$\Box((\neg pumpOn \land lowWater \land \Diamond highWater) \Rightarrow ((\neg pumpOn)UhighWater))$
#41	$\neg\Diamond(\neg pumpOn \land lowWater \land \Diamond highWater)$

Elevator (58,945,690 FTS states, 256 valid variants)	
#1	$\neg\Box\Diamond progress$
#2	$\neg\Box\Diamond f0 \lor \neg\Box\Diamond f1 \lor \neg\Box\Diamond f2 \lor \neg\Box\Diamond f3$
#3	$\neg\Box\Diamond p0at0 \lor \neg\Box\Diamond p0at1 \lor \neg\Box\Diamond p0at2 \lor \neg\Box\Diamond p0at3$
#4	$\Box(fb2 \Rightarrow (\Diamond f2))$
#5	$\Box\Diamond progress \Rightarrow (\Box(fb2 \Rightarrow (\Diamond f2)))$
#6	$\Box\Diamond progress \Rightarrow (\Box(fb2 \Rightarrow (\Diamond(f2 \land dopen))))$
#7	$\Box\Diamond progress \Rightarrow (\neg\Diamond\Box f2)$
#8	$\Box\Diamond(progress \lor waiting) \Rightarrow (\neg\Diamond\Box f2)$
#9	$\Box\Diamond(progress \lor waiting) \Rightarrow (\neg\Diamond\Box f0)$
#10	$\neg\Diamond((cb0 \lor cb1 \lor cb2 \lor cb3) \land \neg(p0in \lor plin) \land dclosed)$
#11	$\Box\Diamond progress \Rightarrow (\neg\Diamond\Box dclosed)$
#12	$\Box\Diamond progress \Rightarrow (\neg\Diamond\Box(p0to3 \land dclosed))$
#13	$\Box\Diamond progress \Rightarrow (\neg\Diamond\Box dopen)$
#14	$\Box\Diamond(progress \lor waiting) \Rightarrow (\neg\Diamond\Box dopen)$
#15	$((\Box\Diamond(progress \lor waiting)) \land (\Box\Diamond(fb0 \lor fb1 \lor fb2 \lor fb3))) \Rightarrow (\neg\Diamond\Box dopen)$
#16	$\neg\Diamond(p0in \land plin \land dclosed)$
#17	$\neg\Diamond\Box(p0in \land dclosed)$
#18	$\Box\Diamond progress \Rightarrow (\neg\Diamond\Box(p0in \land dclosed))$

CFDP (1,801,581 FTS states, 56 valid variants)	
#1	$\Diamond fileReceived$
#2	$(\Diamond eofReceived) \Rightarrow \Diamond fileReceived$
#3	$((\Diamond eofReceived) \land (\Box\Diamond nakReceived)) \Rightarrow \Diamond fileReceived$
#4	$((\Diamond eofReceived) \land (\Box\Diamond nakReceived)) \Rightarrow \Diamond fileReceived$
#5	$\Box(finSend \Rightarrow fileReceived)$

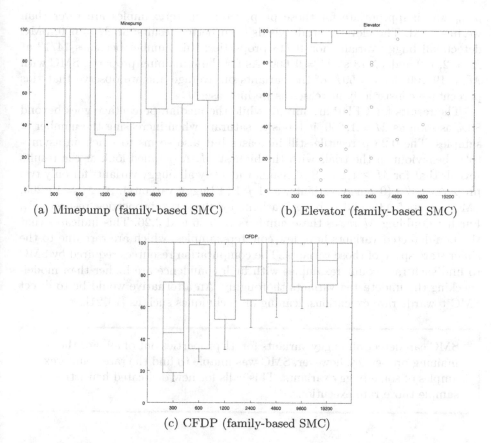

(a) Minepump (family-based SMC)   (b) Elevator (family-based SMC)

(c) CFDP (family-based SMC)

Fig. 2: Detection rate of the buggy variants achieved by our SMC method, in the three case studies and using different sample sizes. In each figure, the x-axis is the number of samples.

5 Results

5.1 RQ1: Detection Rate

Figure 2 shows as boxplots, for each case study and over all checked properties, the percentage of buggy variants for which family-based SMC found a counterexample. We provide those boxplots for different number M of samples.

In the case of Minepump and Elevator, the median detection percentage is 100% starting from $M = 1200$ and $M = 600$, respectively. Further increasing the number of samples raises the 0.25 percentile. In Minepump and for $M = 1200$, there are 18/41 properties for which SMC could not detect all buggy variants. Increasing M improves significantly the percentage of buggy variants detected by SMC for all these properties, although there remain undetected variants in 15 of them even with $M = 19,200$. This illustrates that our assumption regarding

p_{min} was inappropriate for those properties: counterexamples are rarer than we imagined. The elevator study yields even better results: at $M = 600$, SMC detects all buggy variants for 10/18 properties; this number becomes 14/18 at $M = 2,400$ and 17/18 at $M = 9,600$. As for the remaining property, SMC with $M = 19,200$ detects 50% of the variants on average and we observe that this percentage consistently increases as we increase M.

The results for CFDP are mixed: while the median percentage goes beyond 80% as soon as $M = 1,200$, it tends to saturate when increasing the number of samples. The 0.25 percentile still increases but also seems to reach an asymptotic behaviour in the trials with the highest M. A detailed look at the results reveals that for $M \geq 1,200$, SMC cannot identify all buggy variants for only two properties: #3 (9 buggy variants) and #4 (4 buggy variants). At $M = 19,200$, SMC detects 5.43 and 3.14 buggy variants for those two properties, respectively. Further doubling M raises these numbers to 6.36 and 3.26. This indicates that the non-detected variants have few counterexamples, which are rare due to the tinier state space of those variants. The computation resources required by SMC to find such rare counterexamples with high confidence are higher than model-checking the undetected variants thoroughly. An alternative would be to direct SMC towards rare executions, leaning on techniques such as [10,21].

SMC can detect all buggy variants for 41 properties out of 59. For the remaining properties, however, SMC was unable to find the rare counterexamples of some buggy variants. This calls for new dedicated heuristics to sample those rare executions.

5.2 RQ2: Efficiency

Next, we check how much execution time SMC can spare compared to the exhaustive search. Results are shown in Table 2. Overall, we see that SMC holds the potential to greatly accelerate the discovery of all buggy variants, achieving a total speedup of 526%, 1891% and 356% for Minepump, Elevator and CFDP, respectively. For more than half of the properties, the smallest number of samples we tried (i.e. 300) was sufficient for a thorough detection. Those properties are actually satisfied by all variants. The fact that SMC requires such a small number of samples means that the same bug lies in all the variants (as opposed to each variant violating the property in its own way). On the contrary, Minepump property #31 is also violated by all variants but requires a much higher sample number, which illustrates the presence of variant-specific bugs.

Interestingly, the benefits of SMC are higher in the Elevator case (the largest of the three models), achieving speedups of up to 16,575%. A likely explanation is that the execution paths of the Elevator model share many similarities, which means that a single bug can lead to multiple failed executions. By sampling randomly, SMC avoids exploring thoroughly a part of the state space that contains no bug and, instead, increases the likelihood to move to interesting

Table 2: Least numbers of samples (in our experiments) that allowed detecting all buggy variants and corresponding execution time. Full refers to an exhaustive search of the search space. Only properties that are violated by at least one variant and for which SMC found all buggy variants are shown.

Property	# Samples	SMC # States	Time	Full # States	Time	Speedup
Minepump #1	600	25332	0.18	92469	1.33	739%
Minepump #2	300	12553	0.10	24908	1.06	1060%
Minepump #4	300	2383	0.03	103933	3.10	10333%
Minepump #5	1200	48714	0.32	76040	1.03	322%
Minepump #7	300	2469	0.03	18482	0.21	700%
Minepump #8	300	2757	0.03	4646	0.05	167%
Minepump #9	300	2758	0.03	8263	0.08	267%
Minepump #10	600	15191	0.11	55936	0.58	527%
Minepump #12	300	2356	0.03	811	0.02	67%
Minepump #14	300	2915	0.04	989	0.02	50%
Minepump #15	300	2389	0.03	2673	0.05	167%
Minepump #16	300	4102	0.04	1917	0.03	75%
Minepump #18	300	2604	0.03	125	0.01	33%
Minepump #19	600	25027	0.18	143540	2.69	1494%
Minepump #20	300	3864	0.03	40	0.01	33%
Minepump #25	2400	67620	0.50	346935	6.12	1224%
Minepump #26	300	2708	0.03	4382	0.05	167%
Minepump #27	300	2450	0.03	3702	0.04	133%
Minepump #28	2400	58382	0.43	99780	1.28	298%
Minepump #30	300	300	0.03	3648	0.05	167%
Minepump #31	9600	165802	1.29	61185	1.03	80%
Minepump #32	300	2684	0.03	4110	0.05	167%
Minepump #41	300	5732	0.05	3886	0.04	80%
Total		**461092**	**3.60**	**1062400**	**18.93**	**526%**
Elevator #1	300	4371	0.03	105883	0.52	1733%
Elevator #2	600	226813	1.14	437252	2.48	218%
Elevator #3	4800	1736781	7.67	14822853	103.22	1346%
Elevator #4	300	4403	0.04	1194568	6.63	16575%
Elevator #5	300	7719	0.05	1305428	7.76	15520%
Elevator #6	300	7061	0.05	1202204	6.89	13780%
Elevator #7	600	25021	0.12	732684	4.33	3608%
Elevator #8	600	26120	0.13	204934	1.19	915%
Elevator #9	300	3142	0.03	39086	0.28	933%
Elevator #11	300	3278	0.03	91	0.02	67%
Elevator #12	9600	1502419	6.53	1954924	11.12	170%
Elevator #14	2400	141753	0.61	7889584	52.88	8669%
Elevator #15	2400	142405	0.69	7889753	57.64	8354%
Elevator #16	2400	955206	4.02	28551923	182.25	4534%
Elevator #17	1200	100755	0.38	516230	3.53	929%
Elevator #18	4800	510145	1.94	486694	3.00	155%
Total		**5397392**	**23.46**	**67334091**	**443.74**	**1891%**
CFDP #1	300	50206	0.20	87937	1.71	855%
CFDP #2	1200	117897	0.52	102842	0.85	163%
Total		**168103**	**0.72**	**190779.00**	**2.56**	**356%**

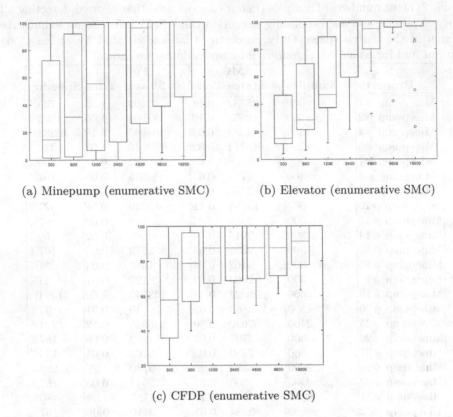

(a) Minepump (enumerative SMC)   (b) Elevator (enumerative SMC)

(c) CFDP (enumerative SMC)

Fig. 3: Detection rate of the buggy variants achieved by classical SMC applied variant by variant, in the three case studies and using different sample sizes. In each figure, the x-axis is the number of samples.

(likely-buggy) parts. A striking example is property #16 (satisfied by half of the variants), where SMC reduces the verification time from 3 minutes to 4 seconds.

> Where SMC can detect all buggy variants, it can do so with more efficiency compared to exhaustive search, for 33/41 properties, achieving speedups of multiple orders of magnitude.

5.3   RQ3: Family-based SMC versus Enumerative SMC

Figure 3 shows the detection rate achieved the enumerative SMC for the three case studies and different numbers of samples, while the results of the family-based SMC were shown in Figure 2. In the Minepump and Elevator cases, enumerative SMC achieves a lower detection rate than family-based SMC. In both cases, a Student t-test with $\alpha = 0.05$ rejects, with statistical significance, the hypothesis that the two SMC methods yield no difference in error rate. One can observe, for instance, that, with 600 samples, enumerative SMC achieves a median detection rate of 31.13%, while family-based SMC achieved 99.86%. This tends to validate our hypothesis that family-based SMC is more effective as the variants share more executions. Indeed, on average, one state of the Minepump is shared by 3.55 variants.

In the case of CFDP, however, enumerative SMC performs systematically better (up to 13.95% more). Still, the difference in median detection rate tends to disappear as more executions are sampled. Nevertheless, CFDP illustrates the main drawback of family-based SMC: it can overlook counterexamples in variants with fewer behaviours. In such cases, enumerative SMC might complement family-based SMC by sampling from the state space of specific variants.

Family-based SMC can detect significantly more buggy variants than enumerative SMC, especially when few lassos are sampled. Yet, enumerative SMC remains useful for variants that have a tiny state space compared to the others and can, thus, complement the family-based method.

---

6 Conclusion

We proposed a new simulation-based approach for finding bugs in VIS. It applies statistical model checking to FTS, an extension of transition systems designed to model concisely multiple VIS variants. Given an LTL formula, our method results in either collecting counterexamples for multiple variants at once or proving the absence of bugs. The algorithm always converges, up to some confidence error which we quantify on the FTS structure by relying on results for the coupon collector problem. After implementing the approach within a state-of-the-art tool, we study empirically its benefits and drawbacks. It turns out that a small number of samples is often sufficient to detect all variants, outperforming an exhaustive search by an order of magnitude. On the downside, we were unable to find counterexamples for some faulty variants and properties. This calls for future research, exploiting techniques to guide the simulation towards rare bugs/events [7,10,21] or towards uncovered variants relying, e.g., on distance-based sampling [22] or light-weight scheduling sampling [19]. Nevertheless, the positive outcome of our study is to show that SMC can act as a low-cost-high-reward alternative to exhaustive verification, which can provide thorough results in a majority of cases.

References

1. Ammann, P.E., Black, P.E., Majurski, W.: Using model checking to generate tests from specifications. In: Proceedings Second International Conference on Formal Engineering Methods (Cat.No.98EX241). pp. 46–54 (1998)

2. Baier, C., Katoen, J.: Principles of model checking. MIT Press (2008)
3. ter Beek, M.H., Fantechi, A., Gnesi, S., Mazzanti, F.: Modelling and analysing variability in product families: Model checking of modal transition systems with variability constraints. Journal of Logical and Algebraic Methods in Programming **85**(2), 287 – 315 (2016)
4. Boneh, A., Hofri, M.: The coupon-collector problem revisited — a survey of engineering problems and computational methods. Communications in Statistics. Stochastic Models **13**(1), 39–66 (1997)
5. Boucher, Q., Classen, A., Heymans, P., Bourdoux, A., Demonceau, L.: Tag and prune: A pragmatic approach to software product line implementation. In: ASE'10. pp. 333–336. ACM (2010)
6. Broy, M., Jonsson, B., Katoen, J., Leucker, M., Pretschner, A. (eds.): Model-Based Testing of Reactive Systems, Advanced Lectures [The volume is the outcome of a research seminar that was held in Schloss Dagstuhl in January 2004], Lecture Notes in Computer Science, vol. 3472. Springer (2005)
7. Budde, C.E., D'Argenio, P.R., Hermanns, H.: Rare event simulation with fully automated importance splitting. In: Beltrán, M., Knottenbelt, W.J., Bradley, J.T. (eds.) Computer Performance Engineering - 12th European Workshop, EPEW 2015, Madrid, Spain, August 31 - September 1, 2015, Proceedings. Lecture Notes in Computer Science, vol. 9272, pp. 275–290. Springer (2015)
8. Chechik, M., Devereux, B., Easterbrook, S.M., Gurfinkel, A.: Multi-valued symbolic model-checking. ACM Trans. Softw. Eng. Methodol. **12**(4), 371–408 (2003)
9. Cheung, L., Stoelinga, M., Vaandrager, F.W.: A testing scenario for probabilistic processes. J. ACM **54**(6), 29 (2007)
10. Chockler, H., Ivrii, A., Matsliah, A., Rollini, S.F., Sharygina, N.: Using cross-entropy for satisfiability. In: Shin, S.Y., Maldonado, J.C. (eds.) Proceedings of the 28th Annual ACM Symposium on Applied Computing, SAC '13, Coimbra, Portugal, March 18-22, 2013. pp. 1196–1203. ACM (2013)
11. Classen, A., Cordy, M., Schobbens, P.Y., Heymans, P., Legay, A., Raskin, J.F.: Featured transition systems: Foundations for verifying variability-intensive systems and their application to LTL model checking. Transactions on Software Engineering pp. 1069–1089 (2013)
12. Clements, P.C., Northrop, L.: Software Product Lines: Practices and Patterns. SEI Series in Software Engineering, Addison-Wesley (August 2001)
13. Consultative Committee for Space Data Systems (CCSDS): CCSDS File Delivery Protocol (CFDP): Blue Book, Issue 4. NASA (2007)
14. Cordy, M., Heymans, P., Legay, A., Schobbens, P.Y., Dawagne, B., Leucker, M.: Counterexample guided abstraction refinement of product-line behavioural models. In: FSE'14. ACM (2014)
15. Cordy, M., Legay, A., Lazreg, S., Collet, P.: Towards sampling and simulation-based analysis of featured weighted automata. In: Proceedings of the 7th International Workshop on Formal Methods in Software Engineering, FormaliSE@ICSE 2019, Montreal, QC, Canada, May 27, 2019. pp. 61–64 (2019)
16. Cordy, M., Schobbens, P.Y., Heymans, P., Legay, A.: Beyond Boolean product-line model checking: Dealing with feature attributes and multi-features. In: ICSE'13. pp. 472–481. IEEE (2013)
17. Cordy, M., Schobbens, P.Y., Heymans, P., Legay, A.: Provelines: A product-line of verifiers for software product lines. In: SPLC'13. pp. 141–146. ACM (2013)
18. Daca, P., Henzinger, T.A., Kretínský, J., Petrov, T.: Faster statistical model checking for unbounded temporal properties. ACM Trans. Comput. Log. **18**(2), 12:1–12:25 (2017)

19. D'Argenio, P.R., Hartmanns, A., Sedwards, S.: Lightweight statistical model checking in nondeterministic continuous time. In: Margaria, T., Steffen, B. (eds.) Leveraging Applications of Formal Methods, Verification and Validation. Verification - 8th International Symposium, ISoLA 2018, Limassol, Cyprus, November 5-9, 2018, Proceedings, Part II. Lecture Notes in Computer Science, vol. 11245, pp. 336–353. Springer (2018)
20. Grosu, R., Smolka, S.A.: Monte Carlo model checking. In: Halbwachs, N., Zuck, L.D. (eds.) Tools and Algorithms for the Construction and Analysis of Systems. pp. 271–286. Springer Berlin Heidelberg, Berlin, Heidelberg (2005)
21. Jégourel, C., Legay, A., Sedwards, S.: Importance splitting for statistical model checking rare properties. In: Sharygina, N., Veith, H. (eds.) Computer Aided Verification - 25th International Conference, CAV 2013, Saint Petersburg, Russia, July 13-19, 2013. Proceedings. Lecture Notes in Computer Science, vol. 8044, pp. 576–591. Springer (2013)
22. Kaltenecker, C., Grebhahn, A., Siegmund, N., Guo, J., Apel, S.: Distance-based sampling of software configuration spaces. In: Atlee, J.M., Bultan, T., Whittle, J. (eds.) Proceedings of the 41st International Conference on Software Engineering, ICSE 2019, Montreal, QC, Canada, May 25-31, 2019. pp. 1084–1094. IEEE / ACM (2019)
23. Kang, K., Cohen, S., Hess, J., Novak, W., Peterson, S.: Feature-oriented domain analysis (FODA) feasibility study. Tech. Rep. CMU/SEI-90-TR-21 (1990)
24. Kramer, J., Magee, J., Sloman, M., Lister, A.: Conic: an integrated approach to distributed computer control systems. Computers and Digital Techniques, IEE Proceedings E **130**(1), 1–10 (1983)
25. Larsen, K.G., Legay, A.: Statistical model checking the 2018 edition! In: Margaria, T., Steffen, B. (eds.) Leveraging Applications of Formal Methods, Verification and Validation. Verification - 8th International Symposium, ISoLA 2018, Limassol, Cyprus, November 5-9, 2018, Proceedings, Part II. Lecture Notes in Computer Science, vol. 11245, pp. 261–270. Springer (2018)
26. Legay, A., Delahaye, B., Bensalem, S.: Statistical model checking: An overview. In: Runtime Verification - First International Conference, RV 2010, St. Julians, Malta, November 1-4, 2010. Proceedings. pp. 122–135 (2010)
27. Oh, J., Gazzillo, P., Batory, D.S.: t-wise coverage by uniform sampling. In: Berger, T., Collet, P., Duchien, L., Fogdal, T., Heymans, P., Kehrer, T., Martinez, J., Mazo, R., Montalvillo, L., Salinesi, C., Tërnava, X., Thüm, T., Ziadi, T. (eds.) Proceedings of the 23rd International Systems and Software Product Line Conference, SPLC 2019, Volume A, Paris, France, September 9-13, 2019. pp. 15:1–15:4. ACM (2019)
28. Oudinet, J., Denise, A., Gaudel, M., Lassaigne, R., Peyronnet, S.: Uniform Monte-Carlo model checking. In: Giannakopoulou, D., Orejas, F. (eds.) Fundamental Approaches to Software Engineering - 14th International Conference, FASE 2011, Held as Part of the Joint European Conferences on Theory and Practice of Software, ETAPS 2011, Saarbrücken, Germany, March 26-April 3, 2011. Proceedings. Lecture Notes in Computer Science, vol. 6603, pp. 127–140. Springer (2011)
29. Plath, M., Ryan, M.: Feature integration using a feature construct. SCP **41**(1), 53–84 (2001)
30. Plazar, Q., Acher, M., Perrouin, G., Devroey, X., Cordy, M.: Uniform sampling of SAT solutions for configurable systems: Are we there yet? In: 12th IEEE Conference on Software Testing, Validation and Verification, ICST 2019, Xi'an, China, April 22-27, 2019. pp. 240–251. IEEE (2019)

31. Pnueli, A.: The temporal logic of programs. In: FOCS'77. pp. 46–57 (1977)
32. Sabin, D., Weigel, R.: Product configuration frameworks-a survey. IEEE Intelligent Systems and their Applications **13**(4), 42–49 (Jul 1998)
33. Shioda, S.: Some upper and lower bounds on the coupon collector problem. Journal of Computational and Applied Mathematics **200**(1), 154 – 167 (2007)
34. Thüm, T., Apel, S., Kästner, C., Schaefer, I., Saake, G.: A classification and survey of analysis strategies for software product lines. ACM Comput. Surv. **47**(1), 6:1–6:45 (2014)
35. Thüm, T., van Hoorn, A., Apel, S., Bürdek, J., Getir, S., Heinrich, R., Jung, R., Kowal, M., Lochau, M., Schaefer, I., Walter, J.: Performance analysis strategies for software variants and versions. In: Managed Software Evolution., pp. 175–206 (2019)
36. Vandin, A., ter Beek, M.H., Legay, A., Lluch-Lafuente, A.: Qflan: A tool for the quantitative analysis of highly reconfigurable systems. In: Havelund, K., Peleska, J., Roscoe, B., de Vink, E.P. (eds.) Formal Methods - 22nd International Symposium, FM 2018, Held as Part of the Federated Logic Conference, FloC 2018, Oxford, UK, July 15-17, 2018, Proceedings. Lecture Notes in Computer Science, vol. 10951, pp. 329–337. Springer (2018)
37. Vardi, M.Y., Wolper, P.: An automata-theoretic approach to automatic program verification. In: LICS'86. pp. 332–344. IEEE CS (1986)
38. Younes, H.L.S., Clarke, E.M., Zuliani, P.: Statistical verification of probabilistic properties with unbounded until. In: Davies, J., Silva, L., da Silva Simão, A. (eds.) Formal Methods: Foundations and Applications - 13th Brazilian Symposium on Formal Methods, SBMF 2010, Natal, Brazil, November 8-11, 2010, Revised Selected Papers. Lecture Notes in Computer Science, vol. 6527, pp. 144–160. Springer (2010)
39. Younes, H.L.S., Simmons, R.G.: Probabilistic verification of discrete event systems using acceptance sampling. In: Brinksma, E., Larsen, K.G. (eds.) Computer Aided Verification, 14th International Conference, CAV 2002,Copenhagen, Denmark, July 27-31, 2002, Proceedings. Lecture Notes in Computer Science, vol. 2404, pp. 223–235. Springer (2002)

Schema Compliant Consistency Management via Triple Graph Grammars and Integer Linear Programming *

Nils Weidmann[1] and Anthony Anjorin[1]

Paderborn University, Paderborn, Germany,
{nils.weidmann, anthony.anjorin}@upb.de

Abstract. Triple Graph Grammars (TGGs) are a declarative and rule-based approach to bidirectional model transformation. The key feature of TGGs is the automatic derivation of various operations such as unidirectional transformation, model synchronisation, and consistency checking. Application conditions can be used to increase the expressiveness of TGGs by guaranteeing schema compliance, i.e., that domain constraints are respected by the TGG. In recent years, a series of new TGG-based operations has been introduced leveraging Integer Linear Programming (ILP) solvers to flexible consistency maintenance even in cases where no strict solution exists. Schema compliance is not guaranteed, however, as application conditions from the original TGG cannot be directly transferred to these ILP-based operations. In this paper, we extend ILP-based TGG operations so as to guarantee schema compliance. We implement and evaluate the practical feasibility of our approach.

Keywords: Application conditions, Triple graph grammars, Integer linear programming

1 Introduction

In the context of Model-Driven Engineering (MDE), software systems are represented as a collection of different models. Often several semantically related models are involved and therefore have to be kept consistent to each other. The process of maintaining consistency among multiple models is called consistency management and involves various operations including (unidirectional) transformation, synchronisation, and consistency checking. Practical applications of consistency checking occur in the industry automation domain, where multiple domain-specific languages (DSLs) are used to describe complex systems [4].

Triple Graph Grammars (TGGs) are a declarative rule-based approach to specifying a bidirectional consistency relation between two modelling languages. The main advantage of TGGs is the possibility to derive multiple consistency management operations from the same formal specification. In their roadmap for

---

* This work was partially supported by the German Federal Ministry of Education and Research (BMBF) through the SPEAR project (01IS17024I).

H. Wehrheim and J. Cabot (Eds.): FASE 2020, LNCS 12076, pp. 315–334, 2020.
https://doi.org/10.1007/978-3-030-45234-6_16

future research on TGGs [2], Anjorin et al. name the *expressiveness* of the TGG language in use as one research dimension. One way of increasing the expressiveness [25] of TGGs is to ensure the satisfaction of certain *constraints*, such as multiplicities with lower and upper bounds, which are typically posed by each domain and should be respected by consistency maintainers. Using terminology from Ehrig et. al [9], so called graph constraints consist of a premise (if), and a set of conclusions (then). They are powerful enough to *forbid* certain situations (negative constraints), *demand* certain conditions (positive constraints), and *enforce* implications. One possible approach to handling constraints in the context of TGGs is the use of *application conditions (ACs)* to restrict the applicability of rules. The subset of ACs supported for operationalised TGGs is, however, still quite restricted. All approaches we are aware of only handle a subset of Negative Application Conditions (NACs) and mostly focus on model transformation and synchronisation rather than consistency checking.

Recent work [17, 18, 20, 24] has introduced TGG operations based on Integer Linear Programming (ILP). Such operations are advantageous because they implement a flexible and generic strategy for multiple consistency management operations, while still providing acceptable scalability for growing model sizes. Flexibility here means that the consistency management operations are able to handle cases where no strict solution exists by providing "optimal" partial results. Graph constraints, however, have not yet been integrated in this hybrid ILP-TGG framework and only basic TGG language features [25] are currently supported. We extend this line of work by the notion of *schema compliance* for TGGs, i.e., that all derived operations respect a set of constraints, as introduced by Anjorin et al. [3]. Instead of trying to integrate ACs into TGG rules, we propose to handle domain constraints directly in the ILP-based operations, thus achieving schema compliance in this manner. By directly encoding graph constraints as ILP constraints, we are able to handle a larger class of constraints than in previous work on schema compliance [3]. We apply our approach to consistency checking with given correspondence links: a basic operation that must be both flexible and efficient as it is often used as a "cheap" check in order to avoid unnecessary work and ensure hippocraticness [6]. An extension to other operations such as unidirectional transformation is straightforward and sketched at the end of this paper. Our approach can be regarded as a step towards tolerant consistency management, as the largest consistent sub-triple is computed in case of inconsistent input models. In this case, checking all domain constraints in advance is not helpful as the user is only informed about the violation of constraints and is not provided with a partial but optimal result.

The rest of the paper is organised as follows: Section 2 introduces a running example, which is used to explain the main ideas on an intuitive level in Sect. 3. Our contribution is compared with related work in Sect. 4. Basic definitions are provided in Sect. 5, and used to express the formal concepts in Sect. 6. A reference implementation together with an experimental evaluation is described in Sect. 7, before discussing extensions towards other operations in Sect. 8. Finally, Sect. 9 concludes the paper and provides some directions for future work.

2   Running Example

To illustrate our approach, a consistency relation between simplified data models of the social networks *Facebook* and *Instagram* is used
as a running example. The respective meta-
models are depicted in Fig. 1. A `Facebook-`
`Network` consists of multiple `FacebookUsers`,
who can share `Friendships` with each other.
Similarly, an `InstagramNetwork` is made up
of arbitrarily many `InstagramUsers`. In contrast to the `Facebook` metamodel, the social

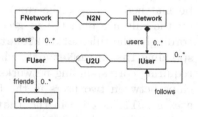

Fig. 1. Triple of Metamodels

interaction is not expressed via `Friendship` nodes but by a `follows` relation
between `InstagramUsers`. To complete the triple, a correspondence metamodel
connects the network and user classes of the two metamodels via correspondence
types, depicted as hexagons. In the following diagrams, the prefixes `Facebook`
and `Instagram` are abbreviated with `F` and `I`, respectively. A triple graph typed
according to Fig. 1 is consistent if (1) the correspondence links form a bijec-
tion between all networks and users of the two networks, and (2) the following
additional graph constraints are satisfied:

- We *forbid* two or more `Friendship` nodes connecting the same two `Facebook-`
  `Users` as depicted in Fig. 2. This is denoted as a *negative constraint*.
- There should be a `Friendship` between two `FacebookUsers` if the corresponding `InstagramUsers` follow each other. This means if the *premise* that
  two `InstagramUsers` follow each other holds, the *conclusion* that there is
  a corresponding `Friendship` on `Facebook` should also hold. The combination of premise and (possibly multiple) conclusions is denoted as *positive*
  constraint (as depicted in Fig. 3).

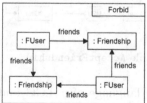

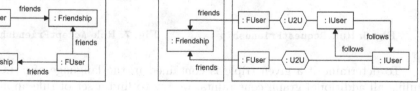

Fig. 2. `NoDoubleFriendship`   **Fig. 3.** `EnforceFriendship`

3   Main Ideas

In this section, we demonstrate our approach by formalising the consistency
relation from the running example as a TGG and deriving a consistency checker.
The novelty of our approach is that we are able to guarantee schema compliance,
i.e., that all additional graph constraints (two from the running example) are
respected by the consistency checker.

The consistency relation can be defined by four TGG rules depicted in Fig. 4, 5, 6, and 7. Nodes and edges required as context (i.e., they have to be matched to apply the rule) are depicted in black, while elements created by the rule are depicted in green and are annotated with a ++-markup. Accordingly, the rule NetworkToNetwork creates a FacebookNetwork and a corresponding InstagramNetwork, whereas UserToUser creates corresponding users, requiring corresponding networks as context. The other two rules add relationships between two users in the two social networks. RequestFriendship creates a follows edge in the Instagram model, while the Facebook model remains unchanged. A follows edge in the opposite direction is added between two InstagramUsers and a Friendship node is created for the corresponding FacebookUsers when the rule AcceptFriendship is applied. A triple graph is consistent if it can be generated using the four rules of the TGG and if it fulfils the two graph constraints.

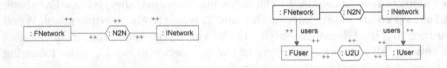

Fig. 4. Rule NetworkToNetwork   **Fig. 5.** Rule UserToUser

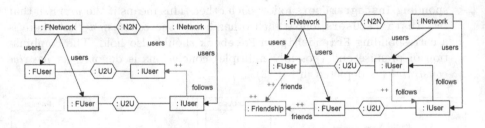

Fig. 6. Rule RequestFriendship   **Fig. 7.** Rule AcceptFriendship

To determine if a given triple is contained in the language of a TGG and fulfils all additional graph constraints, we try to find a set of rule applications that marks the input triple entirely while fulfilling all generated ILP constraints. If this is impossible, we conclude that the given triple is inconsistent and provide a consistent sub-triple with maximum number of elements as result. Five constraint types and the construction of the objective function are briefly introduced using the example instance depicted in Fig. 8 which can be generated by the TGG but violates the constraint NoDoubleFriendship. The elements are annotated with variables which correspond to those rules that potentially mark the respective element, i.e. NetworkToNetwork (d_1), UserToUser (d_2, d_3), Request-Friendship (d_4, d_5) and AcceptFriendship (d_6, d_7). A variable is set to 1 if the associated rule application is chosen to be applied to create the solution graph. Furthermore, Fig. 8 also depicts all matches for NoDoubleFriendship (p_8), the premise of EnforceFriendship (p_9)[1] and the conclusion for Enforce-Friendship (c_{10}, c_{11}). To allow for uniform handling, negative constraints are represented as graph constraints with a premise but no conclusions.

Context for rules: The applicability of rules that require elements as context depends on previous rule applications that have created these elements. In the example instance, the application of UserToUser (d_2, d_3) implies that the rule NetworkToNetwork (d_1) was applied already, because the INetwork is required as context. ILP implication constraints of the form $di \implies (d_{j_1} \vee \cdots \vee d_{j_m}) \wedge \cdots \wedge (d_{k_1} \vee \cdots \vee d_{k_n})$ are thus created for all rules applications d_i with required context elements $j, \ldots, k$, and rule applications $(d_{j_1}, \ldots, d_{j_m}, \ldots, d_{k_1}, \ldots d_{k_n})$ that can mark these elements.

Exclusions for rules: As elements should only be marked once, multiple rule applications that mark the same element exclude each other. The follows edges between two InstagramUsers can be marked both by applications of RequestFriendship (d_4, d_5) and AcceptFriendship (d_6, d_7). For each element that can be marked by multiple rule applications $d_i, \ldots, d_j$, an ILP exclusion constraint $d_i \oplus \cdots \oplus d_j$ is created.

Context for premises: Similar to ILP implication constraints for rules, matches for the premises of graph constraints also depend on context provided by other rule applications (whereas no elements are marked by those matches, so there are no context dependencies among them). However, as soon as the context is provided completely, the premise *is* fulfilled. The implication constraint is thus in the opposite direction: Choosing a subset of rule applications $d_i, \ldots, d_j$ that is sufficient to create the context for a premise match p_k implies that p_k has to be chosen.

Context for conclusions: For a conclusion of a graph constraint to hold, all required elements have to be marked, which is reflected in a constraint similar to the context constraint for rules. In the concrete example, there are two matches (c_{10}, c_{11}) for the conclusion of EnforceFriendship (differing in F1 and F2 as Friendship nodes).

Implications for graph constraints: The semantics of premise and conclusion(s) is reflected in the implications for graph constraints, which define that the presence of a premise match implies the existence of a corresponding conclusion match. p_8 as a negative constraint is represented as a graph constraint with a premise but no conclusions, whereas $p9$ implies c_{10} or c_{11} to be satisfied.

Objective function: In order to find a consistent solution for the given input, it is necessary to find a set of rule applications that marks the input models *entirely*. The objective function maximizes the number of marked elements, i.e. each variable associated with a rule application is weighted with the number of elements it marks, and the weighted sum is maximised. Variables associated with constraints need not be taken into account because they do not create elements.

---

[1] To simplify the solution, we omit symmetric matches that lead to more ILP constraints but neither change the result nor provide additional insight.

Context for rules:

- $d_2 \implies d_1$
- $d_3 \implies d_1$
- $d_4 \implies d_1 \wedge d_2 \wedge d_3$
- $d_5 \implies d_1 \wedge d_2 \wedge d_3$
- $d_6 \implies d_1 \wedge d_2 \wedge d_3 \wedge d_5$
- $d_7 \implies d_1 \wedge d_2 \wedge d_3 \wedge d_4$

Context for premises:

- $d_2 \wedge d_3 \wedge d_6 \wedge d_7 \implies p_8$
- $d_2 \wedge d_3 \wedge (d_4 \vee d_6) \wedge (d_5 \vee d_7) \implies p_9$

Context for conclusions:

- $c_{10} \implies d_2 \wedge d_3 \wedge (d_4 \vee d_6) \wedge (d_5 \vee d_7) \wedge d_6$
- $c_{11} \implies d_2 \wedge d_3 \wedge (d_4 \vee d_6) \wedge (d_5 \vee d_7) \wedge d_7$

Exclusions for rules:

- $d_4 \oplus d_6$
- $d_5 \oplus d_7$

Implications for graph constraints:

- $p_8 \implies \text{false}$
- $p_9 \implies c_{10} \vee c_{11}$

Objective Function: max. $3d_1 + 5d_2 + 5d_3 + d_4 + d_5 + 4d_6 + 4d_7$

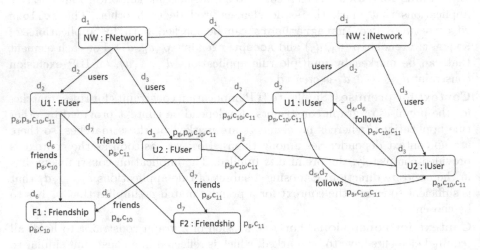

Fig. 8. Example instance with annotations for rule applications and constraint matches

All context elements in the example instance can be marked setting d_1, d_2, d_3, d_6 and d_7 to 1 and d_4 and d_5 to 0, leading to an objective function value of 21 equal to the total number of elements. This marking would however violate the constraint NoDoubleFriendship, as U1 and U2 are connected by two Friendship nodes. This violation is reflected in the ILP constraints as well: The first context constraint for premises enforces setting p_8 to 1, which immediately contradicts the first implication for graph constraints. As no other subset of rule applications is able to mark the input triple entirely, the consistency check fails. The optimal solution, representing the maximal consistent sub-triple, is achieved either by exchanging d_4 and d_6 or d_5 and d_7 in the set of chosen rule applications, decreasing the objective function value to 18 and leaving one Friendship node and the two connecting friends edges unmarked. Note that for this example, the objective function and hard constraints contradict each other, emphasising the fact that constraints must be taken into account when computing optimal partial solutions.

4   Related Work

Our contribution builds upon and extends the existing work on combining TGGs and ILP [17, 18, 20, 24]. This previous work covers the basic idea of modelling consistency checking without correspondence links as a search problem [17, 20], a proof for correctness and completeness [18], and a generalisation to include other operations such as unidirectional transformation and consistency checking with correspondence links [24]. Only basic TGG rules without graph constraints or ACs are handled, meaning that schema compliance cannot be guaranteed.

To the best of our knowledge, all existing TGG-based approaches ensure schema compliance by enriching a provided TGG with suitable ACs. Ehrig et al. introduce NACs to TGG and prove correctness and completeness for unidirectional model transformation [10]. Golas et al. [13] extend these results to more general ACs for TGGs but only cover the direct application of TGG rules, i.e., model triple generation. In both cases, the runtime efficiency and thus practical feasibility of the derived operations is beyond scope. With a focus on guaranteeing polynomial runtime, Klar et al. [16] present a translation algorithm with polynomial runtime for correct and complete TGG-based unidirectional model transformation. Klar et al. restrict the class of supported NACs to NACs that are only used to guarantee schema compliance, arguing that (i) such NACs can be supported efficiently, (ii) are still very useful in practice to guarantee schema compliance, and (iii) can also be efficiently supported by model synchronisation algorithms (as later demonstrated [19]). Anjorin et al. [3] show that this restricted class of "schema compliance" NACs can be automatically generated from negative constraints and is thus equivalent to providing negative constraints together with a TGG. All these approaches, however, can only handle negative constraints that are contained in a single domain, as the derivation of forward and backward transformations can only handle "domain separable" NACs.

Similar to our hybrid TGG/ILP-approch, Callow and Kalawski [5] combine model transformation and Mixed Integer Linear Programming (MILP) optimization techniques but focus on model compliance for forward transformations and not on deriving multiple consistency management operations. Xiong et al. [26] solve consistency management tasks using the Haskell-based language Beanbag. The approach considers implicit constraints and correspondences and is tailored to the application to Unified Modeling Language (UML) structures, though.

There are also purely constraint-based approaches [11, 14, 21] that encode both model structure and consistency relation into constraints and can easily handle schema compliance. This comes at a price, however, as the underlying constraint solvers do not scale with model-size and cannot compete with other approaches [1]. Our hybrid TGG/ILP approach is a compromise that leverages the flexibility of constraint solvers but still scales reasonably well [24] as the variables of the ILP problem are matches and not model elements.

There are also various constraint-based approaches that use bio-inspired meta-heuristics and could also handle schema compliance. The tool MOMoT [12] realises model transformation based on evolutionary algorithms as a search strategy for rule orchestration. Similarly, the multi-objective optimisation technique

Design Space Exploration (DSE) is used by Denil et al. [7] in combination with the T-core transformation framework [23]. In their tool *MOTOE* [15], Kessentini et al. extract transformation blocks from examples and use Particle Swarm Optimisation (PSO) as a search technique. In general, approaches that use metaheuristics can potentially scale better than exact search-based approaches, but have to sacrifice hard guarantees of correctness, completeness, and optimality of partial solutions.

5   Preliminary Definitions

Our basic definitions are adapted from Ehrig et al. [9], supplemented by the definition of schema compliance [3]. TGGs are a declarative rule-based approach which describes a language of triples of *graphs*. For that, we use the categorical definition of graphs, treating graphs as objects and *graph morphisms* as arrows, injectively mapping elements of one graph to those of another.

Definition 1 (Graph (Morphism)).
*A **graph** $G = (V, E, src, trg)$ consists of a set V of nodes (vertices), a set E of edges, and two functions $src, trg : E \to V$ that assign each edge a source and target node, respectively. The set $elem(G) = V \cup E$ denotes the union of vertices and edges. Given graphs $G = (V, E, src, trg)$, $G' = (V', E', src', trg')$, a **graph morphism** $f : G \to G'$ consists of two functions $f_V : V \to V'$ and $f_E : E \to E'$ such that $src \, ; f_V = f_E \, ; src'$ and $trg \, ; f_V = f_E \, ; trg'$. The ; operator denotes the composition of functions: $f \, ; g(x) := g(f(x))$.*

Based on Def. 1 triple graphs and triple morphisms can also be defined categorically. A *triple graph* consists of a correspondence graph with a unique morphism to a source graph and a target graph each. An example for such a triple graph is depicted in Fig. 8. Source and target graph are interchangeable, such that the choice for source and target between the Facebook model and the Instagram model is just a question of design.

Definition 2 (Triple Graph (Morphism)).
*A **triple graph** $G = G_S \xleftarrow{\gamma_S} G_C \xrightarrow{\gamma_T} G_T$ consists of graphs G_S, G_C, G_T and graph morphisms $\gamma_S : G_C \to G_S$ and $\gamma_T : G_C \to G_T$. $elem(G)$ denotes the union $elem(G_S) \cup elem(G_C) \cup elem(G_T)$. A **triple morphism** $f : G \to G'$ with $G' = G'_S \xleftarrow{\gamma'_S} G'_C \xrightarrow{\gamma'_T} G'_T$, is a triple $f = (f_S, f_C, f_T)$ of graph morphisms where $f_X : G_X \to G'_X, X \in \{S, C, T\}, \gamma_S \, ; f_S = f_C \, ; \gamma'_S$ and $\gamma_T \, ; f_T = f_C \, ; \gamma'_T$.*

In this setting, we introduce typing by demanding a type (triple) morphism to a chosen type (triple) graph. In Fig. 5, network nodes and user nodes can be distinguished by typing information, for instance. The language of a type (triple) graph TG is the set of (triple) graphs typed over TG.

Definition 3 (Typed Triple Graph (Morphism)).
*A **typed triple graph** $(G, type)$ is a triple graph G together with a triple morphism $type : G \to TG$ to a distinguished type triple graph TG. A **typed triple***

morphism $f : \hat{G} \to \hat{G}'$ *is a triple morphism* $f : G \to G'$ *with* type $= f;$type$',$ *where* $\hat{G} = (G, type), \hat{G}' = (G', type')$. $\mathcal{L}(TG) := \{G \mid \exists\ type : type(G) = TG\}$ *denotes the set of all triple graphs of type* TG.

In the following, all (triple) graphs and (triple) morphisms are assumed to be typed unless explicitly stated otherwise. A (triple) graph morphism can be viewed as a *monotonic (triple) rule*, such as depicted in Fig. 4, 5, 6 or 7 of the running example. By applying a (triple) rule on a concrete host graph, nodes and edges can be added to produce a new triple. (Triple) rules are applied by constructing a *pushout*, which can be interpreted as a generalised union of (triple) graphs R and G over a common sub-(triple)graph L:

Definition 4 (Triple Rule (Application)).
*A **triple rule** $r : L \to R$ is a monomorphic (injective) triple morphism. A direct derivation $G \overset{r@m}{\Longrightarrow} G'$ via a triple rule r, is constructed as depicted to the right by building a pushout over r and a triple monomorphism $m : L \to G$ called a match. A derivation $D : G \overset{*}{\Longrightarrow} G_n = G \overset{r_1@m_1}{\Longrightarrow} G_1 \overset{r_2@m_2}{\Longrightarrow} \cdots \overset{r_n@m_n}{\Longrightarrow}$ G_n is a sequence of direct derivations. We denote by $\mathcal{D} = \{d_1, \ldots, d_n\}$ the underlying set of direct derivations included in D.*

$$
\begin{array}{ccc}
L & \overset{r}{\longrightarrow} & R \\
\downarrow{\scriptstyle m} & PO & \downarrow{\scriptstyle m'} \\
G & \underset{r'}{\longrightarrow} & G'
\end{array}
$$

Starting off with the *empty triple graph*, all triples that can be produced by finitely many rule applications form the *language* of a TGG.

Definition 5 (Triple Graph Grammar (Language)).
*A **triple graph grammar** $TGG = (G, \mathcal{R})$ consists of a triple graph G, and a finite set $\mathcal{R}$ of triple rules. The **triple graph language** of TGG is defined as $L(TGG) = \{G_\emptyset\} \cup \{G \mid \exists\ D : G_\emptyset \overset{*}{\Longrightarrow} G\}$, where $G_\emptyset$ is the **empty triple graph**.*

While the formal definition of rule-based triple graph generation is completed at this point, we want to pose further restrictions on triples by introducing domain constraints. Therefore, we introduce graph conditions for triple graphs and graph constraints as a context-independent form of graph conditions. A graph constraint is either satisfied trivially, if there does not exist a match for the premise P, or if there exists at least one match for a conclusion C_i.

Definition 6 (Graph Constraint).
*A **graph constraint** is a pair $gc = (p_\emptyset : G_\emptyset \to P, \{c_i : P \to C_i \mid i \in I\})$, for some index set I. P is referred to as the **premise** and $\{C_i \mid i \in I\}$ as the **conclusions** of the graph constraint gc. A triple graph G **satisfies** gc, denoted by $G \models gc$, iff $\forall m_p : P \to G, \exists i \in I\ \exists m_{c_i} : C_i \to G, [m_p = c_i; m_{c_i}]$, where $m_p, (m_{c_i})_{i \in I}$ are monomorphisms.*

A type graph TG along with a set of graph constraints is denoted as *schema* for graphs. In the running example, the schema consist of the metamodel (Fig. 1) and the graph constraints depicted in Fig. 2 and 3. A (triple) graph *complies* to a schema if it is typed over TG and fulfils all graph constraints.

Definition 7 (Schema Compliance).
*A schema is a pair $(TG, \mathcal{GC})$ of a type triple graph TG and a set $\mathcal{GC} \subseteq \mathcal{L}(TG)$ of graph constraints. Let $\mathcal{L}(TG, \mathcal{GC}) := \{G \in \mathcal{L}(TG) \mid \forall gc \in \mathcal{GC}, \ G \models gc\}$ denote the set of all **schema-compliant** triple graphs.*

Finally, a triple graph is denoted as *consistent* with respect to a schema and a TGG if it is schema-compliant and contained in the language of the TGG.

Definition 8 (Consistency).
*Given a triple graph grammar TGG and a schema $(TG, \mathcal{GC})$, a triple graph G is said to be **consistent** iff $G \in \mathcal{L}(TGG) \cap \mathcal{L}(TG, \mathcal{GC})$.*

6   Correctness and Completeness

We now formalise our approach to guarantee *correctness* and *completeness*, i.e., the consistency check succeeds if and only if the input model is consistent. As our approach extends seminal work by Leblebici et al. [20], [18] and Weidmann et al. [24] towards graph constraints, large parts of the formalisation originate from these sources in an adapted version. The novelty of this section is the integration of graph constraints into this formal framework (Def. 10, 12, 15, 18), as well as showing that formal properties still hold in a setting with graph constraints (Def. 21 ff.), assuming that the TGG at hand is progressive (Def. 23), i.e. each rule application marks at least one element.

In the original definition of TGGs (Def. 5), triples are *generated* by creating elements in source, correspondence and target graph simultaneously. For consistency checking, a TGG can be *operationalised* to check if a given triple is contained in the language of a TGG. In this case, elements are *marked* by rule applications instead of being created. To determine if a concrete triple graph is a member of the language of a TGG, one searches for a derivation sequence starting with the empty triple graph (cf. Def. 5) and producing the triple graph. The consistency checking operation derived from a TGG does not modify the input triple but instead marks this graph by successive rule applications in the course of a derivation sequence. An operational rule, derived from a corresponding triple rule, requires its context elements to be marked already.

Definition 9 (Operational Rule and Marking Elements).

*Given a triple rule $r : L \to R$, the **operational rule** $cr : CL \to CR$ for r is constructed as depicted to the right. It holds $CL = CR = R$, and $cr : CL \to CR = id_{CR}$. An element $e \in elem(R)$ is a **marking element** of cr iff $\nexists e' \in elem(L)$ with $r_S(e') = e$ or $r_C(e') = e$ or $r_T(e') = e$.*

For operational rules, elements can be partitioned into those which are created by the original TGG rule (marked elements) and those which must be provided as context (required elements). Graph constraints do not mark elements and therefore, only a set for the elements required by premise and conclusion, respectively, are defined.

Definition 10 (Marked and Required Elements).
For a direct derivation $d : G \overset{cr@cm}{\Longrightarrow} G$ via an operational rule $cr : CL \to CR$, the following sets are defined:

- $mrk(d) = \{e \in elem(G) \mid \exists e' \in elem(CL), cm(e') = e$ where e' is a marking element of $cr\}$
- $req(d) = \{e \in elem(G) \mid \exists e' \in elem(CL), cm(e') = e$ where e' is not a marking element of $cr\}$

For a graph constraint $gc = (p_\emptyset : G_\emptyset \to P, \{c_i : P \to C_i \mid i \in I\})$, we define:

- $req(p_\emptyset) = \{e \in elem(G) \mid e' \in elem(P), m_p(e') = e\}$
- $req(c_i) = \{e \in elem(G) \mid e' \in elem(C_i), m_{c_i}(e') = e\}, i \in I$

All candidate rule applications are associated with a binary variable which indicates by its value (0 or 1) whether the candidate is considered within the final solution. To determine the variable assignment, all candidates are collected and handed over to an ILP solver to determine the optimal subset of rule applications (cf. Sect. 2) respecting all linear constraints.

Definition 11 (Constraints for Derivations).
Given a triple graph G, let $D : G \overset{*}{\Longrightarrow} G$ be a derivation via operational rules with the underlying set $\mathcal{D}$ of direct derivations. For each direct derivation $d_1, \ldots, d_n \in \mathcal{D}$, respective binary variables $\delta_1, \ldots, \delta_n$ with $\delta_1, \ldots, \delta_n \in \{0, 1\}$ are defined. A linear constraint $\mathcal{LC}$ for $\mathcal{D}$ is a conjunction of linear inequalities which involve $\delta_1, \ldots, \delta_n$. A set $\mathcal{D}' \subset \mathcal{D}$ fulfils $\mathcal{LC}$, denoted as $\mathcal{D}' \vdash \mathcal{LC}$, iff $\mathcal{LC}$ is satisfied for variable assignments $\delta_i = 1$ if $d_i \in \mathcal{D}'$ and $\delta_i = 0$ if $d_i \notin \mathcal{D}', 1 \leq i \leq n$.

Graph constraints are also associated to binary variables to ensure that only schema-compliant triples pass the consistency check, while premises and each of the corresponding conclusions are split into separate constraints. In contrast to the binary variables for rule applications, the value assignment cannot be chosen by the ILP solver. Instead, any variable assignment which does not violate the linear constraints is fine, as they ensure schema-compliance by the interrelations of rule applications and graph constraints.

Definition 12 (Constraints for Graph Constraints).
Let $\mathcal{GC} = \{(p_\emptyset : G_\emptyset \to P, \{c_i : P \to C_i \mid i \in I\})\}$ be a set of graph constraints. For each graph constraint $gc \in \mathcal{GC}$, respective binary variables $\pi_1 \ldots \pi_n$ for the premises and $\gamma_{1,1} \ldots \gamma_{1,m_1} \ldots \gamma_{n,1} \ldots \gamma_{n,m_n}$ for the conclusions are defined. A linear constraint $\mathcal{LC}$ for $\mathcal{GC}$ is a conjunction of linear inequalities which

involve $\pi_1 \ldots \pi_n$ *and* $\gamma_{1,1} \ldots \gamma_{1,m_1} \ldots \gamma_{n,1} \ldots \gamma_{n,m_n}$. *A triple graph G fulfils LC,* *denoted as* $G \models LC$, *iff LC is satisfied for any variable assignment* $\{\pi_1 \ldots \pi_n\} \to \{0,1\}, \{\gamma_{1,1} \ldots \gamma_{1,m_1} \ldots \gamma_{n,1} \ldots \gamma_{n,m_n}\} \to \{0,1\}$.

As the operational rules reflect the behaviour of the original rules of the underlying TGG, multiple markings for the same elements must be prohibited as this would mean that an element is created multiple times. For each node and edge, a linear constraint is created that ensures that this element is marked at most once in order to guarantee schema compliance and containment in the language of the TGG later on.

Definition 13 (Sum of Alternative Markings for an Element).
Given a triple graph G, let $D : G \stackrel{*}{\Longrightarrow} G$ *be a derivation via operational rules* *with the underlying set* $\mathcal{D}$ *of direct derivations. For each element* $e \in elem(G)$, *let* $\mathcal{E}(e) = \{d \in \mathcal{D} \mid e \in mrk(d)\}$. *The integer mrkSum(e) denotes the sum of the* *associated variable assignments for each* $d \in \mathcal{E}$:

$$mrkSum(e) = \sum_{d_i \in \mathcal{E}(e)} \delta_i$$

Definition 14 (Constraint 1: Mark Elements at Most Once).
Given a triple graph G, let $D : G \stackrel{*}{\Longrightarrow} G$ *be a derivation via operational rules:*

$$markedAtMostOnce(G) = \bigwedge_{e \in elem(G)} [\, mrkSum(e) \leq 1]$$

The reason for the sum of marked elements not being strictly equal to 1 is the desired treatment of inconsistent inputs: The system should still be feasible in case of inconsistent inputs and a maximal consistent sub-triple should be the result of the optimisation step.

The following constraint ensures that the required context elements for operational rule applications as well as premises and conclusions are provided in the final solution, such that the original TGG rule is guaranteed to be applicable in this situation and the marked part of the triple graph is schema-compliant.

Definition 15 (Constraint 2: Guarantee Context).
Given a triple graph G and a schema $(TG, \mathcal{GC})$, *let* $D : G \stackrel{*}{\Longrightarrow} G$ *be a deriva-* *tion via operational rules with the underlying set* $\mathcal{D}$ *of direct derivations. For* *each direct derivation* $d \in \mathcal{D}$ *and each graph constraint* $gc \in \mathcal{GC}$, *the following* *constraints are defined:*

$$con(d) = \bigwedge_{e \in req(d)} [\delta \leq mrkSum(e)]$$

$$con(p_\emptyset) = \bigvee_{e \in req(p_\emptyset)} [\, mrkSum(e) \leq \pi]$$

$$con(c_i) = \bigwedge_{e \in req(c_i)} [\gamma_i \leq mrkSum(e)], i \in I$$

$$context(D) = \bigwedge_{d \in \mathcal{D}} con(d) \wedge \bigwedge_{gc \in \mathcal{GC}} [con(p_\emptyset) \wedge \bigwedge_{i \in I} con(c_i)]$$

There are constellations in which rule application candidates mutually provide context for each other in a *dependency cycle*, such that parts of the graph could be potentially marked by these rules, but none of them can ever be applied first because the necessary context is not yet there. Therefore, we introduce a relation ▷ among rule applications to arrange them in a proper order.

Definition 16 (Dependency Cycles).
Let $D : G \overset{*}{\Longrightarrow} G$ be a derivation via operational rules with the underlying set $\mathcal{D}$ of direct derivations. A relation $\triangleright \subseteq \mathcal{D} \times \mathcal{D}$ between $d_i, d_j \in \mathcal{D}$ is defined as follows:

$$d_i \triangleright d_j \text{ iff } req(d_i) \cap mrk(d_j) \neq \emptyset$$

*A set $cy \subseteq \mathcal{D}$ with $cy = \{d_1, \ldots, d_n\}$ of direct derivations is a **dependency cycle** iff $d_1 \triangleright \cdots \triangleright d_n \triangleright d_1$.*

The following constraint breaks dependency cycles by forbidding to choose all of its member rule applications for the final solution.

Definition 17 (Constraint 3: Forbid Dependency Cycles).
Given a triple graph G, let $D : G \overset{*}{\Longrightarrow} G$ be a derivation via operational rules with the underlying set $\mathcal{D}$ of direct derivations, and let $\mathcal{CY}$ be the set of all dependency cycles $cy \in \mathcal{D}$. A linear constraint $acyclic(D)$ is defined as follows:

$$acyclic(D) = \bigwedge_{cy \in \mathcal{CY}, cy = \{d_1, \ldots, d_n\}} \sum_{i=1}^{n} \delta_i < n$$

While the previous constraint types guarantee containment in the language of the TGG at hand as well as context constraints for premises and conclusions, Constraint 4 expresses the semantics of graph constraints to achieve schema-compliance. Thereby, the linear constraint is very similar to the definition for satisfaction of graph constraints (Def. 6). It is possible to formulate this constraint independent of the concrete rule application because only graph constraints are supported instead of arbitrary graph conditions.

Definition 18 (Constraint 4: Satisfy Graph Constraints).
Let $(TG, \mathcal{C} = \{(p_\emptyset : G_\emptyset \to P, \{c_i : P \to C_i \mid i \in I\})\})$ be a schema. A linear constraint $sat(G)$ expressing that G fulfils all graph constraints of $\mathcal{C}$ is defined as follows:

$$sat(G) = \bigwedge_{C \in \mathcal{C}} [\neg \pi \vee \bigvee_{i \in I} \gamma_i]$$

Finally, the objective function can be defined to maximize the number of markings over the entire input triple, while ensuring that no correctness constraints are violated and the result is schema-compliant according to Def. 7.

Definition 19 (Optimisation Problem).
Given a triple graph G and a schema $(TG, \mathcal{C})$, let $D : G \stackrel{*}{\Longrightarrow} G$ be a derivation via operational rules. The ILP to be optimised is constructed as follows: max.

$$\sum_{d \in D} |mrk(d)| \ s.t. \ markedAtMostOnce(G) \wedge context(D) \wedge acyclic(D) \wedge sat(G)$$

The remainder of this section provides a proof sketch showing that the consistency check always terminates, and succeeds iff the input triple graph is consistent with respect to Def. 8. It is an extension of the proof for correctness and completeness in a setting without graph constraints [18,24], such that the focus of this version is set on schema compliance. In the following, let a TGG $TGG = (G_\emptyset, \mathcal{R})$, a schema $(TG, \mathcal{GC})$, a triple graph G, and a derivation via operational rules $D : G \stackrel{*}{\Longrightarrow} G$ with underlying set of direct derivations $\mathcal{D}$ be given for all definitions, lemmas and theorems.

First, we define a *proper subset* of operational rule applications as a set which is associated to a feasible solution for the ILP (Def. 14, 15, 17 and 18).

Definition 20 (Proper Subset of Rule Applications).
A subset $\mathcal{D}' \subseteq \mathcal{D}$ is a proper subset of $\mathcal{D}$ iff $\mathcal{D}' \vdash markedAtMostOnce(G) \wedge context(D) \wedge acyclic(D) \wedge sat(G)$.

Next, it is shown that there exists a sequence of the rule applications of a proper subset, such that the marked elements of the graph form a consistent triple. Furthermore, the marked part of the graph is schema-compliant.

Lemma 1 (Consistent Portions of a Triple Graph).
$\exists$ proper subset $\mathcal{D}' \subseteq \mathcal{D} \iff \exists G' \in L(TGG) \cap \mathcal{L}(TG, \mathcal{GC})$ such that:

$$elem(G') = \bigcup_{d' \in \mathcal{D}'} mrk(d')$$

Proof (Sketch). When all direct derivations $d \in \mathcal{D}'$ are sequenced over the $\triangleright$ relation (Def. 16), a proper subset according to Def. 20 is formed, resulting in a triple graph $G' \in L(TGG)$ consisting of the elements marked by D'. At the same time, G' will be schema-compliant iff $\mathcal{D}' \vdash sat(G')$ as this predicate ensures that all given graph constraints are satisfied.

We demand the property of *maximality* to avoid trivial solutions such as the empty triple graph:

Definition 21 (Maximal Proper Subset of Rule Applications).
A proper subset $\mathcal{D}'$ of $\mathcal{D}$ is maximal if there does not exist any other proper subset $\mathcal{D}''$ of $\mathcal{D}$ with a greater objective function value (cf. Def. 19).

The application of a sequenced maximal proper subset of rule applications on the empty triple graph is denoted as *maximally marked triple graph*.

Definition 22 (Maximally Marked Triple Graph).
Let $\mathcal{D}'$ be a maximal, proper subset of $\mathcal{D}$. The triple graph G' identified with $\mathcal{D}'$ according to Lemma 1 is denoted as a maximally marked triple graph with respect to D.

Theorem 1 guarantees that a triple graph that can be completely marked by rule applications of a maximal proper subset is indeed consistent.

Theorem 1 (Correctness).
For a maximally marked triple graph G' with respect to D, it holds:

$$\bigcup_{d \in \mathcal{D}} mrk(d) = elem(G) \implies G' \text{ is consistent}$$

Proof (Sketch). $G' \in L(TGG)$ immediately follows from Lemma 1: As D is a maximal proper subset, $G' \in L(TGG)$ holds, and the rule applications of D can be sequenced, such that they can mark G' entirely according to the premise of this theorem. $G' \in L(TG, \mathcal{GC})$ holds as well because the choice of any $d \in D'$ leading to a violation of any $gc \in \mathcal{GC}$ would make $sat(G')$ false. Therefore, G' is consistent according to Def. 8.

To guarantee completeness, it remains to show that the process of constructing the ILP terminates, which requires the set of possible rule applications to be finite. As all possible derivation sequences are collected, the ILP solver terminates with an optimum solution iff one exist. We therefore demand the underlying TGGs to be *progressive*, i.e., each operational rule is required to mark at least one element. In fact, operational rules that do not mark elements correspond to TGG rules that do not have any effect on the host graph they are applied on because they cannot add any elements, and are therefore irrelevant for practical use.

Definition 23 (Progressive TGGs).
TGG is progressive if each of its operational rules has at least one marking element.

Demanding the TGG at hand to be progressive, completeness can be concluded by showing that the consistency check cannot cycle.

Theorem 2 (Completeness).
Let TGG be progressive. A maximally marked triple graph G' with respect to D exist such that:

$$G' \text{ is consistent} \implies \bigcup_{d \in \mathcal{D}} mrk(d) = elem(G)$$

Proof (Sketch). As Lemma 1 guarantees the existence of a derivation D, and ILP solving always produces a maximally marked triple graph G', we only need to show the implication (equivalence follows from Thm. 1). To derive a contradiction, we now assume that G' is consistent, but that G' either contains unmarked elements or violates any constraint $gc \in \mathcal{GC}$. From G' being consistent, it follows from the decomposition and composition theorem for TGGs and operational rules [8, 18] that there exists a derivation sequence $D' : G \overset{*}{\Longrightarrow} G'$ with operational rules. This means that at least one rule application of D' is not contained in D or G' violates any $gc \in \mathcal{GC}$. The latter is impossible, as it would contradict to the assumption that G' is consistent. The former implies that the objective function value could be increased by using D' for marking G, which contradicts the optimality of the result found by ILP solving.

7   Implementation and Experimental Evaluation

We investigate the impact of graph constraints on runtime performance, considering scalability of consistency checking for growing model sizes with and without taking graph constraints into account, by two research questions:

(RQ1) By which factor does the number of variables and ILP constraints increase when introducing graph constraints to the ILP? How does this influence the runtime of pattern matching, ILP construction, and ILP solving?

(RQ2) How does the runtime performance relate to model size (number of nodes and edges) for consistency checking with and without graph constraints?

Setup: We implemented our approach within the tool eMoflon[2] using Neo4J[3] as an underlying graph pattern matcher and database for querying and storing the models. As a test example, we took the `FacebooktoInstagram` TGG as described in Sect. 2. To obtain synthetic models, we used the derived TGG-based model generator to produce random models with 1078 to 226,988 elements (roughly the same number of nodes and edges). We then executed the derived TGG-based consistency checker, once taking the negative graph constraint from Sect. 2 into account, and once without any graph constraints. For each configuration, the number of variables and constraints of the ILP, as well as the time needed for pattern matching, ILP construction, and ILP solving were measured for 10 repeated runs. As final values, the medians of the 10 test runs were taken to minimize the bias introduced by outliers. All performance tests were executed on a standard notebook with an Intel Core i7 (1.80 GHz), 16GB RAM, and Windows 10 64-bit as operating system. An installation of Eclipse IDE for Java and DSL Developers, version 2019-09 with Java Development Kit (JDK) version 13 was used. The JVM running the tests was allocated a maximum of 4GB memory, and 8GB were allocated to the graph database Neo4J.

Results:[4] Figure 9 shows the time needed for pattern matching, ILP construction, and ILP solving for different model sizes. One can observe that for both configurations (with and without graph constraints), the runtime of all components depends linearly on the number of model elements. Taking graph constraints into account for the consistency check makes the ILP construction roughly 20% - 40% slower. This is to be expected as the ILP problem is simply larger. For similar reasons, a difference can also be observed for the ILP solving step, whose runtime is negligible without constraints, but increases by a factor of 10 when including graph constraints. While this increase is substantial, ILP solving does not have a large overall impact on the runtime performance even for 200k elements. Interestingly, pattern matching gets faster when the additional negative graph constraint is included. This is surprising as additional pattern matching is required to determine matches of the negative constraint. The underlying graph database is heuristic-based, however, and also uses caching strategies to decide what data to keep in memory. Apparently the pattern matching strategy applied for the collection of patterns including the negative constraint seems to scale better for model sizes greater than 130k.

---

[2] `github.com/eMoflon/emoflon-neo`   [3] `neo4j.com`   [4] `bit.ly/2BFAutd`

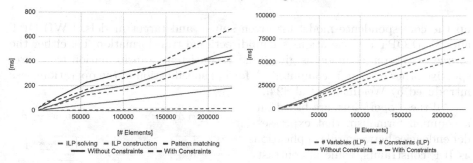

Fig. 9. Runtime Measurements   **Fig. 10.** #Variables and #Constraints

The number of binary variables and constraints grows linearly with model size for both settings, involving slightly more variables than constraints (cf. Fig. 10). With the negative graph constraint, this number increases by about 25%-50%.

Summary: Revisiting our research questions, one can state that the number of binary variables and constraints increases by a constant factor when introducing (negative) graph constraints, resulting in a constant increase of the overall runtime for consistency checking. While the ILP solving step increases substantially and could become problematic for large models, our measurements indicate that the ILP solving step is probably not the bottle neck for our example (RQ1). In both settings (with and without the negative graph constraint), the runtime for consistency checking increases linearly with growing model size (RQ2).

Threats to validity: The evaluation was performed with only one TGG consisting of only four rules, only the consistency checker (of all operations) was run on randomly generated synthetic instances, and we measured the additional price of taking only the negative graph constraint from Sect. 2 into account. While our initial results are positive and indicate that the additional price of guaranteeing schema compliance as we propose does not render the ILP-based TGG operations infeasible due to an explosion in runtime, extensive benchmarking with multiple TGGs, multiple graph constraints, larger model sizes, and multiple consistency management operations is required to transfer these results to practical, real-world applications.

8   Extension to Other Operations

The presented concepts are tailored to consistency checking with correspondences, i.e. source, target and correspondence model are given as inputs and are *marked* by operational rule applications, whereas all three models are simultaneously *created* by the original rule applications. There are also other operations which use a mixture of creating and marking elements to complement given input models to a complete triple. Figure 11 depicts the example instance of Fig. 8 annotated with the operations which require the respective model(s) as input. The previously presented CO (check only) operation gets all three models as input, whereas CC (correspondence creation) checks for consistency by building up the correspondence model for given source and target models. FWD_OPT and BWD_OPT are operations for unidirectional transformation, i.e. either the source or the target model is given and a consistent transformation to the respective other domain is computed. A formal specification of the operations was introduced by Weidmann et al. [24].

All these operations are based on a common formalism that expresses dependencies between rule applications as ILP constraints, while in contrast to the definitions of this paper, dependencies between created elements are also taken into account. As constraints for marked and created parts of the triple are formed almost the same way, it is possible to transfer the results for consistency checking respecting graph constraints to the other operations as well. However, the formal proof which guarantees the operations' correctness and completeness [18,24] has to be extended to take graph constraints into account.

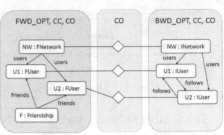

Fig. 11. Input models per operation

9   Conclusion and Future Work

We presented an extension of a seminal approach to combining TGGs and ILP by supporting graph constraints. For consistency checking with given correspondence links, we have shown correctness and completeness of the approach. The results can be generalised towards other operations such as unidirectional transformations as well. Additionally, the approach was implemented in a TGG tool, and an experimental evaluation indicated that the scalability of the approach is sufficient for practical use. For future work, we plan to extend the approach to cope with general AC as well, increasing the expressive power of the supported class of TGGs. As a proof of concept, we only implemented negative constraints until now, which should be extended towards general graph constraints. Using an incremental pattern matcher with extensible matches, it should be possible to collect matches for the premise and corresponding conclusions at once, which would keep the implementation efficient. Further performance tests with other (industrial) examples will also be necessary to underpin the validity of the evaluation results with respect to runtime performance, as both the metamodels and the rule set are very restricted, whereas the considered model sizes are realistic. Generating consistent models first and then mutate them slightly would further lead to a smaller and therefore more reasonable number of inconsistencies.

Acknowledgements

We like to thank Surbhi Verma, Shubhangi Salunkhe and Darya Zarkalam for contributing to large parts of the implementation.

References

1. Anjorin, A., Buchmann, T., Westfechtel, B., Diskin, Z., Ko, H.S., Eramo, R., Hinkel, G., Samimi-Dehkordi, L., Zündorf, A.: Benchmarking bidirectional transformations: theory, implementation, application, and assessment. Software and Systems Modeling (Sep 2019). https://doi.org/10.1007/s10270-019-00752-x
2. Anjorin, A., Leblebici, E., Schürr, A.: 20 Years of Triple Graph Grammars: A Roadmap for Future Research. ECEASST **73** (2015)
3. Anjorin, A., Schürr, A., Taentzer, G.: Construction of integrity preserving triple graph grammars. In: Ehrig, H., Engels, G., Kreowski, H.J., Rozenberg, G. (eds.) ICGT 2012. Springer, Berlin, Heidelberg (2012). https://doi.org/10.1007/978-3-642-33654-6_24
4. Anjorin, A., Yigitbas, E., Leblebici, E., Schürr, A., Lauder, M., Witte, M.: Description Languages for Consistency Management Scenarios Based on Examples from the Industry Automation Domain. Programming Journal **2**(3), 7 (2018)
5. Callow, G., Kalawsky, R.: A Satisficing Bi-Directional Model Transformation Engine using Mixed Integer Linear Programming. Journal of Object Technology **12**(1), 1:1–43 (2013). https://doi.org/10.5381/jot.2013.12.1.a1
6. Cheney, J., Gibbons, J., McKinna, J., Stevens, P.: On principles of least change and least surprise for bidirectional transformations. Journal of Object Technology **16**(1), 3:1–31 (2017)
7. Denil, J., Jukss, M., Verbrugge, C., Vangheluwe, H.: Search-Based Model Optimization Using Model Transformations. In: Amyot, D., Fonseca i Casas, P., Mussbacher, G. (eds.) SAM 2014. Springer, Cham (2014). https://doi.org/10.1007/978-3-319-11743-0_6
8. Ehrig, H., Ehrig, K., Ermel, C., Hermann, F., Taentzer, G.: Information Preserving Bidirectional Model Transformations. In: Dwyer, M.B., Lopes, A. (eds.) FASE 2007. Springer (2007)
9. Ehrig, H., Ehrig, K., Prange, U., Taentzer, G.: Fundamentals of Algebraic Graph Transformation. Springer-Verlag Berlin Heidelberg (2006)
10. Ehrig, H., Hermann, F., Sartorius, C.: Completeness and Correctness of Model Transformations based on Triple Graph Grammars with Negative Application Conditions. ECEASST **18** (2009)
11. Eramo, R., Pierantonio, A., Tucci, M.: Enhancing the JTL tool for bidirectional transformations. In: Marr, S., Sartor, J.B. (eds.) Programming 2018, Nice, France, April 09-12, 2018. ACM (2018)
12. Fleck, M., Troya, J., Wimmer, M.: Search-Based Model Transformations with MOMoT. In: Van Gorp, P., Engels, G. (eds.) ICMT 2016. Springer, Cham (2016). https://doi.org/10.1007/978-3-319-42064-6_6
13. Golas, U., Ehrig, H., Hermann, F.: Formal Specification of Model Transformations by Triple Graph Grammars with Application Conditions. ECEASST **39** (2011)
14. Horn, T.: Solving the TTC Families to Persons Case with FunnyQT. In: García-Domínguez, A., Hinkel, G., Krikava, F. (eds.) TTC 2017. CEUR Workshop Proceedings, vol. 2026. CEUR-WS.org (2017)
15. Kessentini, M., Sahraoui, H., Boukadoum, M.: Model Transformation as an Optimization Problem. In: Czarnecki, K., Ober, I., Bruel, J.M., Uhl, A., Völter, M (eds.) MoDELS 2008. Springer, Berlin, Heidelberg (2008). https://doi.org/10.1007/978-3-540-87875-9_12
16. Klar, F., Lauder, M., Königs, A., Schürr, A.: Extended Triple Graph Grammars with Efficient and Compatible Graph Translators, pp. 141–174. Springer, Berlin, Heidelberg (2010). https://doi.org/10.1007/978-3-642-17322-6_8

17. Leblebici, E.: Towards a graph grammar-based approach to inter-model consistency checks with traceability support. In: Anjorin, A., Gibbons, J. (eds.) Bx 2016. CEUR-WS.org (2016)
18. Leblebici, E.: Inter-Model Consistency Checking and Restoration with Triple Graph Grammars. Ph.D. thesis, Darmstadt University of Technology, Germany (2018)
19. Leblebici, E., Anjorin, A., Fritsche, L., Varró, G., Schürr, A.: Leveraging incremental pattern matching techniques for model synchronisation. In: de Lara, J., Plump, D. (eds.) ICGT 2017, Marburg, Germany, July 18-19, 2017, Proceedings (2017)
20. Leblebici, E., Anjorin, A., Schürr, A.: Inter-model Consistency Checking Using Triple Graph Grammars and Linear Optimization Techniques. In: Huisman, M., Rubin, J. (eds.) FASE 2017. Springer, Berlin, Heidelberg (2017). https://doi.org/10.1007/978-3-662-54494-5_11
21. Macedo, N., Cunha, A.: Implementing QVT-R Bidirectional Model Transformations Using Alloy. In: Cortellessa, V., Varró, D. (eds.) FASE 2013. Springer, Berlin, Heidelberg (2013). https://doi.org/10.1007/978-3-642-37057-1_22
22. Nierstrasz, O., Gray, J., d. S. Oliveira, B.C. (eds.): SLE 2019, Athens, Greece, October 20-22, 2019, Proceedings. ACM (2019)
23. Syriani, E., Vangheluwe, H., Lashomb, B.: T-Core: A Framework for Custom-built Model Transformation Engines. Softw. Syst. Model. **14**(3), 1215–1243 (2015)
24. Weidmann, N., Anjorin, A., Leblebici, E., Schürr, A.: Consistency management via a combination of triple graph grammars and linear programming. In: Nierstrasz et al. [22], pp. 29–41. https://doi.org/10.1145/3357766.3359544
25. Weidmann, N., Oppermann, R., Robrecht, P.: A feature-based classification of triple graph grammar variants. In: Nierstrasz et al. [22], pp. 1–14. https://doi.org/10.1145/3357766.3359529
26. Xiong, Y., Hu, Z., Zhao, H., Song, H., Takeichi, M., Mei, H.: Supporting automatic model inconsistency fixing. In: van Vliet, H., Issarny, V. (eds.) Proceedings of the 7th joint meeting of the European Software Engineering Conference and the ACM SIGSOFT International Symposium on Foundations of Software Engineering, 2009, Amsterdam, The Netherlands, August 24-28, 2009. pp. 315–324. ACM (2009)

Towards Multiple Model Synchronization with Comprehensive Systems

Patrick Stünkel[1] , Harald König[2] , Yngve Lamo[1], and Adrian Rutle[1]

[1] Høgskulen på Vestlandet, Bergen, Norway {past,yla,aru}@hvl.no
[2] University of Applied Sciences, FHDW, Hannover, Germany
Harald.Koenig@fhdw.de

Abstract. Model management is a central activity in Software Engineering. The most challenging aspect of model management is to keep models consistent with each other while they evolve. As a consequence, there has been increasing activity in this area, which has produced a number of approaches to address this synchronization challenge. The majority of these approaches, however, is limited to a binary setting; i.e. the synchronization of exactly two models with each other. A recent Dagstuhl seminar on multidirectional transformations made it clear that there is a need for further investigations in the domain of general multiple model synchronization simply because not every multiary consistency relation can be factored into binary ones. However, with the help of an auxiliary artifact, which provides a global view over all models, multiary synchronization can be achieved by existing binary model synchronization means. In this paper, we propose a novel *comprehensive system* construction to produce such an artifact using the same underlying base modelling language as the one used to define the models. Our approach is based on the definition of partial commonalities among a set of aligned models. Comprehensive systems can be shown to generalize the underlying categories of graph diagrams and triple graph grammars and can efficiently be implemented in existing tools.

Keywords: Model Synchronization · Multimodelling · Multidirectional Transformations (MX) · Inter-Model Consistency · Model Merging · Graph Diagrams · Triple Graph Grammars · Category Theory

1   Introduction

Conceptual *models*, i.e. abstract specifications of the system under development, are recognized to be of major importance in software engineering [52]. Representing the whole system in a single global model is generally unfeasible, hence, different teams design and maintain several models which focus on different aspects of the system. This collection of inter-related models is often referred to as a *multimodel*. A rigorous use of these models within the engineering process eventually requires consistency management of multimodels. This is because the collection of models must obey global consistency rules and as models are inevitably subject to change, global consistency becomes an issue [16].

H. Wehrheim and J. Cabot (Eds.): FASE 2020, LNCS 12076, pp. 335–356, 2020.
https://doi.org/10.1007/978-3-030-45234-6_17

Model Synchronization represents a means to maintain global consistency of inter-related models by combining consistency verification with (semi-)automatic consistency restoration. The cross-disciplinary research field *Bidirectional Transformations (BX)* [8] investigates such means within different communities and it provides a number of theoretical and practical results (see [2] for a recent survey). However, the majority of these approaches is limited to a binary setting, i.e. keeping pairs of models consistent. Stevens [44] recognized this limitation in her outreach to the modelling community that lead to an increased momentum in this area as evident from a recent Dagstuhl seminar on *Multidirectional Transformations (MX)* [7].

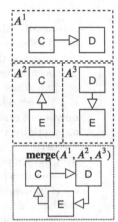

One way to address multiary synchronization is to consider it as a network of well-understood binary synchronization problems. However, not every multiary consistency rule can be factored into binary ones [9]; e.g. the class diagrams A^1, A^2 and A^3 in fig. 1 are pairwise consistent but not altogether—since class inheritance is acyclic. Thus, multiary model synchronization is needed to keep global consistency. Another approach to global consistency management is the *model merge* approach [6]: It constructs the union of all models wherein the related elements are identified, see lower half of fig. 1 (inter-relations given by sameness of class' names). Thus, global consistency can be verified within a single artifact, the merge. However, the major drawback of this approach, apart from requiring additional computational overhead, is that it forgets the origin of elements; e.g. that class C was contained in A^1 and A^2 but not in A^3. This is a problem if global consistency rules depend on this containment information.

Fig. 1. Inconsistent class diagrams

The most important information in multiary model synchronization are the inter-relations between models and their elements. We call the latter *commonalities* and cannot generally assume that they are always given by equality of names as it was the case in fig. 1. Thus, multimodels must be extended with such commonality information, which allows element traceability and global consistency verification. Aligning models via an additional commonality structure has some tradition, e.g. it is the foundation of *Triple Graph Grammars (TGGs)* [40], a formal and mature BX approach with a focus on Model Driven Engineering (MDE). In the TGG approach, models are considered to have a *graph based* structure, i.e. there is a common underlying *base modelling language* and we will also stick to this idea of a common base language.

In this paper, we propose a novel construction called *comprehensive system* which serves as a foundation for various ways of multiary model management. It is based on a simple, non-intrusive and easy-to-handle *linguistic extension* of the base modelling language with commonality specifications, which allows to work with an arbitrary number $n \geq 2$ of heterogeneously typed (*local*) models as one single (*global*) model. Moreover, we will show that we are still able to apply mature methods for model verification and restoration in the same way as for single local models. Furthermore, we show that this approach is more expressive than, and overcomes the obstacles of, the model merge approach, and that it generalizes TGGs and *graph diagrams* [48] – a recent generalization of TGGs.

Before defining comprehensive systems and their properties (sect. 5 and 6), we clarify terminology (sect. 2), introduce of a running example (sect. 3), and provide an overview of the state of the art (sect. 4). An extended version of the proofs in sect. 6 is given in the technical report [47].

2   Preliminaries: Multimodelling

Every fast moving research field is prone to produce separate terms for the same concepts. Thus, we begin with a short definition of the most important terms in multi-model consistency management. We will stick to the imperative of MDE [42] and consider all Software Engineering (SE) artifacts as models:

Model A model is an abstract specification of the system (or parts of it) under development. Models are atomic elements in the multimodel consistency management process. To be amenable for electronic processing, we assume them to be formal, i.e. following the format of a specific *modelling language*. We denote models by capital letters A, A', A^1, A^2 etc.

Metamodel and Conformance Every modelling language is specified by an artifact called *metamodel*. We denote metamodels by capital letters M, M', M^1, M^2 etc. Models must conform to their respective metamodel, i.e. the model must be well-structured w.r.t. the metamodel **and** fulfill all *constraints* imposed on the metamodel, thus further narrowing admissible model structure. The model is then called an *instance* of the metamodel. Conformance is also called *local* or *intra-model consistency*. We denote a single constraint by lowercase ϕ and a set of constraints by uppercase Φ. A metamodel with a set of constraints Φ imposed on it will be written M_Φ.

Correspondence is a relation among a set of models. It is a consequence of *commonalities* (common concepts) shared by these models. A collection of models together with a correspondence among them is called a *multimodel*. In the similar way as for local models, global *consistency rules* can be imposed on a multimodel. It is considered (*globally*) *consistent*, if all local constraints and global consistency rules are fulfilled. Consistency of a multimodel is also referred to as *inter-model consistency*.

Model Space A model space is a set of models together with changes among them. In an MDE setting it can be considered to be given by a metamodel M: The set of all instances of M together with M-respecting instance changes, which describe how an instance A' is the result of edits on A. We write $\mathbf{Mod}(M_\Phi)$ to denote the respective model space.

3   Use Case

We depict a *collaborative modelling* example within *healthcare*. More concretely, the task is to develop ICT support for a *patient referral* process. A referral is "the act of sending a patient to another physician for ongoing management of a specific problem with the expectation that the patient will continue seeing the original physician for co-ordination of total care" [41]. It is an important and recurring process in the healthcare domain. Hence, ICT-support is desirable [51].

At the same time, development remains tricky since it requires multiple actors (software vendors, government officials, hospitals and physicians) to agree on common data structures, processes and interfaces. For our example, let us assume that the design of the system follows a model-based approach and there are three different models, each covering a different aspect of the system: There is a *process* model A^1 denoted in *Business Process Model and Notation (BPMN)* [30], a *data* model A^2 denoted as a *Unified Modelling Language (UML) class diagram* [32], and a *decision* model A^3 denoted in *Decision Model and Notation (DMN)* [33].

These three models are depicted in fig. 2 (ignore the cyan lines for the moment). The central ingredient is the process model A^1. It represents a simplified version of the process developed in [51]. The process is triggered by a patient's appeal beginning with an introductory consultation. Afterwards the main part of the process begins: Information about the patient and its medical history is extracted while in parallel a consultant is selected via a `business-rule` activity. The patient information is then sent to the consultant. The consultant can either approve the referral or reject it. In the latter case, another consultant has to be found. If a consultant accepts the referral, the process is finished.

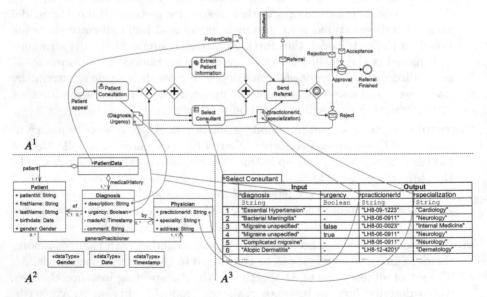

Fig. 2. Example models A^1, A^2 and A^3 and their commonalities

The other models in fig. 2 contain the respective data types (A^2) and specify the domain-specific behaviour of the "Select Consultant" activity (A^3). The latter is depicted as a table that assigns, for a given combination of values in input side columns, a combination of values in output side columns, i.e. based on diagnosis and urgency, an appropriate consultant is selected (which is identified by a practicionerId and specialization).

All models could be edited completely independent of each other would there not be a correspondence between them. It arises from the existence of abstractly "the same" information simultaneously contained in multiple models. Consider e.g. the column called diagnosis in A^3, which is reflected by a process variable in A^1 (visualized by a file symbol) and an attribute named description in A^2. We call these relations *commonalities* and depict them via cyan lines in fig. 2.

But the arising multimodel (models A^1, A^2, A^3 plus their commonalities) underlies *consistency rules* [11] (see sect. 2) which define consistency of a multimodel. For our example, assume the following consistency rules:

CR1 For every business-rule activity in A^1, there must exist a corresponding decision table in A^3 and vice versa.

CR2 Every column type in A^3 must refer to an existing data type in A^2 with the same name.

CR3 Every column in A^3 must have a corresponding public attribute (denoted by +) in A^2 and should be reflected by a process variable in A^1.

CR4 Every process variable in A^1 must either be reflected by a class or an attribute in A^2.

To actually maintain consistency of A^1, A^2 and A^3, w.r.t. CR1-CR4, we begin by a review of the state of the art how commonalities are identified, consistency is verified and if needed restored.

4   State of the Art

A seminal exposition of the process of *multimodel consistency management* is already given in [43]. It comprises four phases: (i) Detection of overlaps (we call them commonalities, see sect. 3, (ii) Detection of inconsistencies, (iii) Diagnosis of inconsistencies, and (iv) Handling of inconsistencies. The first step is also called *model alignment*. Many approaches do not consider an explicit diagnosis stage and combine (iii) and (iv) into a phase called *consistency restoration* a.k.a. *model repair* [28]. Hence, existing work can be grouped into these three categories:

Alignment The goal of model alignment is to identify relations between models, i.e. finding their commonalities. This procedure, a.k.a. *model matching*, has been studied in several domains: databases [35], ontologies [15], MDE [23], graph transformation [14] and software product lines [53]. Automatic model matching, in general, is NP-hard [36]. However, there may be domain specific heuristics [53] which exploit underlying global identification mechanisms, e.g. social security numbers for persons or the ICD-10 ontology [54] for diseases. Surveys on this topic can be found in [15] (focus on ontologies), [35] (focus on databases) and [23] (focus on MDE). Further, it is important to note that model element matching requires that elements are transferable between models. This is e.g. directly given within the UML or multi-viewpoint modelling as there is a *single underlying metamodel* [3]. If this is not given a priori, matching on the level of metamodels [38,10] has to preceed the matching of model elements.

Verification The goal of consistency verification is to find all consistency violations. A recent survey on this topic is found in [22]. The focus of the authors is on UML but the results are universal. They present four categories to classify verification approaches: *system model (SMV)*, *universal logic (ULV)*, *heterogeneous transformation (HTV)* and *dynamic metamodelling (DMV)*. In the SMV approach every model is translated into a comprehensive artifact where the verification is executed. ULV is a variant of the former where the translation is executed on the level of an underlying logic. HTV define translations between each pair of models and DMV considers extensions of each metamodel with elements from other metamodels or models to express global consistency.

Restoration A comprehensive survey about model repair approaches is found in [28], whereas [2] is a recent survey about BX based approaches. Insights from these surveys show that there are basically three categories of consistency restoration approaches: *programming based (PBR)* approaches where consistency and its restoration is explicitly defined simultaneously, *solver based (SBR)* approaches where consistency is abstractly posed as logic formula and restoration is implemented using a solver or search-based algorithm, and finally, *grammar based (GBR)* approaches such as TGGs [19], which place themselves somewhere in between. The big majority of these approaches, however, considers binary synchronization only. There are only few notable exceptions, e.g. the solver based *Echo* [29] and the *graph diagram* framework [48,49].

Architecture Analyzing the underlying system architecture of these approaches, there are, in principal, two designs: We call them the *network design* and the *span design*. Consider the multimodel as a graph where nodes represent models and edges represent correspondences (for alignment), consistency relations (for verification) or repair functions (for restoration). In the network design there are edges between each pair of models. In the span design the graph has a hub-and-spoke layout, i.e. there is an *additional* hub-node that has an edge towards every model. Approaches in the categories SMV, ULV and SBR are associated with a span design since they perform a translation into a an intermediate model, while approaches in the categories HTV, DMV and PBR are associated with the network design because they directly act on a pair of models. GBR approaches have used either of them.

Comparing the architecture, the network design puts the complexity on the edges whereas the span design puts complexity on the nodes (more specifically on a single node: the hub). The drawback of the network design is that the number of edges grows quadratically with the number of participating models and if consistency relations cannot be factored into binary relations, hyperedges are required, which further increase the complexity. Another issue with this design is the coordination of concurrent changes. The drawback of the span design is the additional overhead of the hub-node model, however, the hub-node provides a means to coordinate concurrent changes.

5 Comprehensive Systems

In this section, we introduce *comprehensive systems* (sect. 5.1 to 5.3), which follow a SMV-approach and mitigate the drawbacks of the span design. We will show in sect. 5.4 that comprehensive systems are a foundation for the PBR restoration approach and we conjecture that the same is true for SBR, because they do not fundamentally differ from the structure of local models, such that they can be fed into existing means for model verification and restoration. Moreover, sect. 5.5 shortly reports why our approach eliminates the model merge obstacles (see the discussion in the introduction and fig. 1).

Before introducing comprehensive systems concretely, we want to illustrate where they occur in typical conceptual workflows for multimodel consistency management. Fig. 3 depicts such a workflow which is more or less informally used in many approaches of multimodel management, e.g. [16]. It comprises the phases mentioned in sect. 4: alignment, verification and restoration. The result of the first stage are the comprehensive metamodel and global consistency rules imposed upon it, and metamodel element commonalities, which are stored persistently to avoid expensive re-computation and possible information loss, cf. motivation in [25]. These commonalities are then used to *compute* the comprehensive system under consideration, e.g. a model merge. It can be used in the subsequent phases shown in fig. 3.

In contrast to this *additional* computation, our definition of comprehensive system is based on a non-intrusive extension of existing models by commonalities *without extensive computations*. Furthermore, it enables natural internalizations of inter-relations between different local models into a single artifact. Our intention is to demonstrate this internalization informally in this section and formalize it in sect. 6, where we will also state that the resulting structure generalizes triple graphs [40] and graph diagrams [48]; hence it is ready to be used in GBR approaches, too.

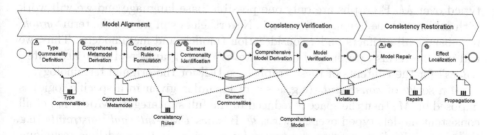

Fig. 3. General Multimodel Consistency Management Process

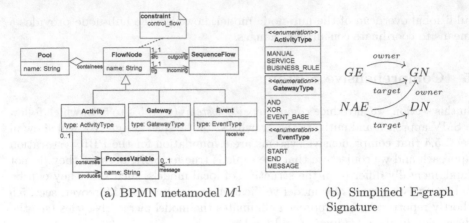

(a) BPMN metamodel M^1 (b) Simplified E-graph Signature

Fig. 4. Metamodel Example and Base Language

5.1 Typed Local Models

We begin on the level of metamodels: Fig. 4a depicts a simplified metamodel M^1 of BPMN for our example. We do not endorse any specific MDE-framework and denote metamodels in a UML class diagram-like style. Metamodels M^2 and M^3 for UML class diagram and DMN models can be defined in the same way as metamodel M^1 (excerpts of them are shown in fig. 5). E-graphs [12] (see fig. 4b) give a formal interpretation to the class diagram syntax, which may serve as an appropriate *base modelling language* $\mathbb{B}$ for our purposes, i.e. a shared *linguistic (meta-)metamodel* [26]. It consists of Graph Nodes GN and Data Nodes DN (complex and primitive types in the UML terminology), as well as Graph Edges GE (associations) and Node Attribute Edges NAE (attributes) together with appropriate owner and target functions. For the sake of simplicity we omitted edge attribute edges, which are usually included in E-graphs. Every model A must conform to a metamodel M. Since models and metamodels can be depicted as E-Graphs, the conformance relation is a *typing* homomorphisms $t : A \to M$ between the E-Graphs A and M. If, e.g. a is a flow node in A^1, see fig. 2, then $t(a) = \texttt{FlowNode} \in M^1$. Hence, model space $\mathbf{Mod}(M)$ is the category of E-graphs typed over M. E-graphs are only one possible base language and we will work with arbitrary base languages in sect. 6. Nevertheless will we use the term "*graph*" to subsume all artifacts under consideration (models and metamodels). Thus, we will use the terms (graph- and data-) "*nodes*" and (graph- and node attribute-) "*edges*" for the contents of these graphs, see [12] for the original terminology.

If a set Φ of *constraints* (e.g. a set of formulas given in a specific logic) is imposed on M, then the space is reduced to the full subcategory $\mathbf{Mod}(M_\Phi)$ of all consistent models typed over M w.r.t. Φ. Besides *UML-internal constraints* (e.g. the $1..1$-multiplicity on $\texttt{src}$ and $\texttt{tgt}$ in fig. 4a) given in the modelling technique, there are often *attached constraints* $\phi \in \Phi$. An example for an attached constraint is $\phi := \texttt{control\_flow}$, see the note at $\texttt{FlowNode}$ in fig. 4a. This constraint defines that every $\texttt{Start Event}$ must not have any incoming $\texttt{SequenceFlow}$ [30, p. 237], whereas an **End Event** must not have any outgoing **SequenceFlow** [30, p. 245]. Listing 1.1 shows an *Object Constraint Language (OCL)* [31] formulation of this constraint.

Listing 1.1. Constraint ϕ:=`control_flow` formulated in OCL

```
context FlowNode inv:
  self.oclIsTypeOf(Event) and self.eventType=EventType::START) implies
    self.incoming->count() = 0
  and (self.oclIsTypeOf(Event) and self.eventType=EventType::END) implies
    self.outgoing->count() = 0
```

OCL is just an example of a possible means for defining attached constraints. As we do not endorse a specific metamodelling framework and thus also not endorse a specific technique for the definition of attached constraints, we treat all constraints uniformly and assume that all internal and external constraints can be modelled as *diagrammatic constraints* [37]. A diagrammatic constraint ϕ imposed on a metamodel M possesses an "arity graph" S_ϕ and is imposed on M by a scope $d_\phi : S_\phi \to M$ (a homomorphism). The semantics is provided by a predicate $check_\phi : \mathbf{Mod}(S_\phi) \to Bool$, which verifies whether a given structure typed over the arity fulfills this constraint. The scope highlights a fragment (the image of d) of metamodel M, e.g. the blue coloured fragment in fig. 4a is the scope of the constraint ϕ from listing 1.1. For a typed graph $t : A \to M$, the verification procedure $verify(t) = check_\phi(query(t))$ comprises two steps: First, $query$ forgets all elements of A not typed over the scope, then it retypes the remaining elements w.r.t. d such that they are typed over S_ϕ. That is, $query$ implements the *pullback* of d and t. Finally, $check_\phi$ is invoked on the pullback result.

5.2 Extending the Base Language

As seen in sect. 3, consistency rules play a major role in multimodelling. However, we cannot directly formalize them via the diagrammatic constraints described above since their definition involves elements spanning multiple models. Note that inter-relations between models arise from models sharing abstractly the "same" real-world concepts (see the intuitive cyan lines in fig. 2). We name these structural relations *commonalities* and they are also well-known in practice as traceability links [16,39,1]. There are different interpretations of what such a link can mean, e.g. identity, subset, extension? etc. [16]. In our framework commonality semantics are kept abstract, i.e. considering them as any kind of structural relation allowing us to define diagrammatic constraints in multimodels.

For example, in order to formalize CR2, we need to declare a commonality between the terms **DataType** (in M^2) and **ColumnType** in M^3. In addition to these *binary* commonalities in which only two terms are matched, there are also ternary commonalities, e.g. **String** occurs in all three metamodels and it is necessary to relate BPMN-term **ProcessVariable** with UML-term **Attribute** and DMN-term **Column** together with their respective **name**- and **type**-features to express CR3. These declarations may be formulated in an intuitive domain-specific language (DSL) shown in listing 1.2.

Listing 1.2. Type Commonalities

```
1   commonalities (BPMN,UML,DMN) {
2    relate(BPMN.String,UML.String,DMN.String) as String;
3    relate(BPMN.Activity,DMN.Table) as Decision;
4    relate(BPMN.ProcessVariable,UML.Attribute,DMN.Column)
5     as Var with {
6      relate(BPMN.name,UML.name,DMN.name) as name;
7      relate(DMN.type,UML.type) as type; };
8    relate(UML.DataType,DMN.ColumnType) as Type
9     with { relate{UML.name,DMN.name} as name; };
10    relate(BPMN.ProcessVariable,UML.Class) as Entity; }
```

The specification in listing 1.2 *extends* the modelling artifacts M^1, M^2 and M^3 and we call its syntax a *linguistic extension*. Each `relate`-statement translates to an object, which is identified by an alias (keyword `as`) and which reifies the "tupling" of terms it relates. E.g. the object `Var` in lines 4-7 specifies a commonality of the triple `ProcessVariable` (M^1), `Attribute` (M^2), and `Column` (M^3). `Var` is an object in its own right and we call it a *(commonality) representative*.

However, not only the nodes (of the graphs) should be related: In listing 1.2 we see that the keyword `with` defines the two features, i.e. edges, `type` and `name` of the respective graphs to be related as well. Common edges require that their respective source and target nodes are also related, e.g. the `type`-commonality entails commonality of `Attribute` and `Column`, which is already given by the surrounding `relate`-statement, as well as commonality of `DataType` and `ColumnType` (see lines 8-9). Hence, commonality specifications must preserve edge-node-incidences.

Consequently, it is reasonable to use the same language $\mathbb{B}$ for commonality representatives. In such a way, a commonality specification is itself an E-graph: The semantic interpretation of listing 1.2 is depicted in cyan in fig. 5. The proper linguistic extension further comprises mappings, which assign to each commonality representative w the elements it relates. E.g. `Decision` is mapped to `Activity` and to `Table` in the respective metamodels. Since the assignment syntax in the above DSL also contains the target metamodel of the related elements (e.g. *BPMN* in `relate(BPMN.Activity...)`), these mappings decompose into 3 *projection mappings* $p_j : M^0 \rightarrow M^j$ ($j \in \{1, 2, 3\}$), depicted by dotted arrows in fig. 5, e.g. $p_1(\text{Decision}) = \text{Activity} \in M^1$, as well as $p_2(\text{Type}) = \text{DataType} \in M^2$, the target metamodel now encoded in p's index. Since the corresponding tuples can be of arbitrary arity, these mappings may be partial:

$$p_1(w') = \bot, p_2(w') = \text{DataType}, p_3(w') = \text{ColumnType}$$

if $w' = \text{Type}$. Finally, the above required edge-node-incidence means that definedness of $p_j(e)$ entails definedness of $p_j(v)$, where v is the source of e, and

$$p_j(v) = \text{source of } p_j(e) \tag{1}$$

for all edges e in M^0 (and likewise for targets).

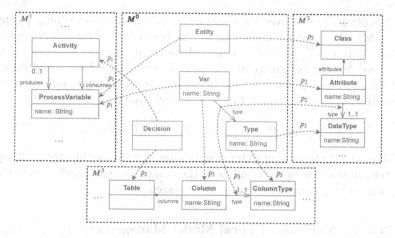

Fig. 5. Commonality representative metamodel M^0

5.3 Metamodel and Model Commonalities

The previous section showed that a linguistic extension of the base language with projection functions between commonality representatives and the elements they relate yields an alignment of metamodels $M^1, \ldots, M^n$. The result is a comprehensive metamodel, in which commonalities are accurately specified with the help of (a graph of) commonality representatives. Formally, we obtain a new graph M^0 and partial projections

$$M^0 \overset{p_i^M}{\rightharpoonup} M^i. \tag{2}$$

for all $i \in \{1, \ldots, n\}$. Since all artifacts under consideration (models and metamodels) conform to the base $\mathbb{B}$, see sect. 5.1, commonalities among models $A^1 \in \mathbf{Mod}(M^1), \ldots, A^n \in \mathbf{Mod}(M^n)$ can be encoded in the same way, i.e. there is a graph A^0 of commonality representatives together with partial projections

$$A^0 \overset{p_i^A}{\rightharpoonup} A^i. \tag{3}$$

for all $i \in \{1, \ldots, n\}$. Again they can be specified in the same language as in listing 1.2, and can be stored physically, given that the modelling technique offers means to identify elements, e.g. primary keys in a database, position in an XML document, Uniform Resource Identificators (URIs) [5], etc.

The alignment of models A^1, A^2, and A^3 together with their commonalities is shown in fig. 2. Each cyan line represents a commonality representative and each line ends at the value under the respective projection. Some of the lines are binary, some ternary. In general, we would expect any arity, especially when the number n of model spaces increases. The complete contents of fig. 2 is called a *comprehensive system*: the cyan connections its *commonalities* and models $A^1, \ldots, A^n$ its *components*.

Models A^i are typed over their metamodels, i.e. there are typing morphisms $t_i : A^i \to M^i$ which can be combined to one big typing of all components. This typing extends to A^0 as well because elements a_j and a_k $(j \neq k)$ of model components A^j and A^k are relatable only if their types $t_j(a_j)$ and $t_k(a_k)$ are related via a representative $w \in M^0$. Hence, a natural typing t_0 of a commonality representative v of a_j and a_k is $t_0(v) := w$, such that

$$p_j^M(t_0(v)) = p_j^M(w) = t_j(a_j) = t_j(p_j^A(v)), \tag{4}$$

which shows that the typing extension t_0 integrates smoothly (respecting commonalities) into a typing of all parts of the comprehensive model, such that we end up with a *single typed* comprehensive system: $t : A \to M$.

5.4 Reusing Methods of Local Model Management

Consider the OCL example and its generalization in terms of diagrammatic constraints in sect. 5.1. Theorem 1 in sect. 6 will show that comprehensive systems constitute a category basically with the same properties as the base language $\mathbb{B}$. Especially, pullbacks can be computed in a similar way, see Corollary 1 in sect. 6. Thus, we can define the consistency rules CR1-CR4 from sect. 3 as diagrammatic constraints $(\phi_i)_{i \in \{1,...,4\}}$, now imposed on the comprehensive metamodel, which treat the commonality witnesses and projections as regular nodes and edges. Local constraints can be encoded as global constraints as well [24], such that we obtain comprehensive system M_Φ with a set Φ of constraints spanning local model elements but also elements of the linguistic extension. Any typed system $t : A \to M$ can then be checked against a constraint ϕ imposed via scope $d : S_\phi \to M$ by pullback of d and t in the category of comprehensive systems, see Theorem 1 in sect. 6. Hence, *query* implementation by pullbacks carries over from local models to comprehensive systems and we can reuse the theory of *diagrammatic constraints* to verify global consistency, which e.g. can be implemented by a straightforward translation of a respective model fragment and constraint to *Alloy* [20]. This can be used to formally verify that Fig. 2 is consistent w.r.t. CR1-CR4.

5.5 Advantages over Model Merge

A merged model is an artifact which is computed *additionally* from local models A^i. Basically, it is the union of all elements of the A^i's modulo their commonalities, see fig. 1. E.g. in the merge of models A^1, A^2, A^3 in fig. 2 there remains a single node, say Diag/descr of type Var (a type in M^0, see fig. 5), which represents sameness of Diagnosis $\in A^1$, description $\in A^2$ and diagnosis $\in A^3$.

We could implement global consistency rules on the merge by including the merge computation in the *check*-function as described in the algorithm in [24]. However, this leads to problems if the verification of a global constraint depends on the knowledge of containment in local models. This can be seen with consistency rule CR3 which relies om the containment of elements (in this case containment in A^2 and A^3). After merging Diagnosis and description into the single node Diag/descr, distinguishing its original local model would no longer be possible. In contrast, we do not loose this differentiation in comprehensive systems and can successfully check the validity of this constraint.

6   Categorical Formalization

This section is devoted to the formalization of comprehensive systems from sect. 5. In order to relate comprehensive systems to the TGG framework we need to employ *category theory (CT)* because TGGs are usually formulated in terms of CT. We recall the central terminology in the following section and refer to the introductory textbooks [4,34,50] for further references about CT.

6.1   Theoretical Background and Notation

A *category* $\mathbb{C}$ is a collection of mathematical *objects* and of *morphisms*, which are means to compare objects. For a category $\mathbb{C}$, the set of objects is denoted $|\mathbb{C}|$ and for each pair $A, B \in |\mathbb{C}|$ the (hom-)set of morphisms from A to B is denoted by $Arr_{\mathbb{C}}(A, B)$. For each object $A \in |\mathbb{C}|$ there exists a special *identity* morphism $id_A : A \to A$. Moreover there is a neutral and associative *composition* operation $\circ : Arr_{\mathbb{C}}(A, B) \times Arr_{\mathbb{C}}(B, C) \to Arr_{\mathbb{C}}(A, C)$ for all $A, B, C \in |\mathbb{C}|$. The most prominent example is the base language of mathematics: $\mathbb{S}et$, the category of sets and total mappings. A category $\mathbb{C}$ is said to be *small*, if $|\mathbb{C}|$ is itself a set. *Equivalence* of two categories $\mathbb{C}$ and $\mathbb{D}$, written $\mathbb{C} \cong \mathbb{D}$, means that the network of objects and morphisms in $\mathbb{C}$ is identical to the one in $\mathbb{D}$ up to isomorphisms (e.g. bijections in $\mathbb{S}et$) between objects.

A *functor* provides the means to compare two categories $\mathbb{C}$ and $\mathbb{D}$: It is denoted $\mathbf{F} : \mathbb{C} \to \mathbb{D}$ and maps objects of $\mathbb{C}$ to objects of $\mathbb{D}$ and morphisms of each set $Arr_{\mathbb{C}}(A, B)$ to $Arr_{\mathbb{D}}(\mathbf{F}(A), \mathbf{F}(B))$. Moreover, it preserves identities and composition. $\mathbf{F}$ is called an *embedding*, if it is injective on objects of $\mathbb{C}$ and injective on $Arr_{\mathbb{C}}(A, B)$ for all $A, B \in |\mathbb{C}|$. For fixed categories $\mathbb{C}$ and $\mathbb{D}$ and functors $\mathbf{F}, \mathbf{F}' : \mathbb{C} \to \mathbb{D}$, a *natural transformation* $n : \mathbf{F} \Rightarrow \mathbf{F}'$ is a family $(n_A : \mathbf{F}(A) \to \mathbf{F}'(A))_{A \in |\mathbb{C}|}$ of $\mathbb{D}$-morphisms compatible with images of $\mathbf{F}$ and $\mathbf{F}'$, i.e. for all $\mathbb{C}$-arrows $f : A \to B$: $n_B \circ \mathbf{F}(f) = \mathbf{F}'(f) \circ n_A$. In such a way we get a new category, the *functor category* $\mathbb{D}^{\mathbb{C}}$ with objects all functors from $\mathbb{C}$ to $\mathbb{D}$ and arrows the natural transformations. Functors $\mathbf{F} : \mathbb{C} \to \mathbb{S}et$ where $\mathbb{C}$ is small play a special role: $\mathbf{F}$ assigns to each $S \in |\mathbb{C}|$ a *(carrier) set* $\mathbf{F}(S)$ and for every $op \in Arr_{\mathbb{C}}(S, S')$ a mapping $\mathbf{F}(op) : \mathbf{F}(S) \to \mathbf{F}(S')$, i.e. $\mathbb{C}$ is a signature (think metamodel) that is interpreted by $\mathbf{F}$ (think instantiated). Hence, this is also called *functorial* or *indexed semantics* and $\mathbb{S}et^{\mathbb{C}}$ corresponds to the class of algebras for a signature $\mathbb{C}$ (instance worlds for a metamodel). E.g. objects of $\mathbb{G} := \mathbb{S}et^{\mathbb{B}}$ are E-Graphs, if $\mathbb{B}$ is the category depicted in fig. 4b (identities are omitted) and E-Graph-homomorphisms are exactly the natural transformations. For set-based structures, we use the notation $A \hookrightarrow B$ to indicate included structures (A in B) such as subsets or subgraphs.

Universal constructions in categories have proven to be of importance in many software theoretical methods. Intuitively universal constructions can be described as a generalization of *meets* and *joins* in a preorder. Some well known examples for universal constructions in Set are cartesian products or disjoint unions (coproduct). It is important to note that Set possesses all these universal constructions and thus every category $\mathsf{Set}^\mathbb{C}$ does as well, where the computation of universal constructions is carried out "pointwise".

6.2   Comprehensive System

We begin the formalization of comprehensive systems by fixing a sufficiently large natural number n and considering a synchronization scenario with model spaces $(\mathbf{Mod}(M_{\Phi_j}^j))_{j \in \{1,\dots,n\}}$. E.g. UML class diagrams, BPMN process models and DMN tables.

Definition 1 (Base Modelling Language). *The base modelling language is a small category $\mathbb{B}$.*

In order to distinguish between the different system components, we will work with copies $\mathbb{B}_j$ of $\mathbb{B}$. We let $|\mathbb{B}_j| = \{s_j \mid s \in |\mathbb{B}|\}$ and similarly $op_j : s_j \to s_j'$ be an arrow in $Arr_{\mathbb{B}_j}$, if $op : s \to s'$ is an arrow of $Arr_\mathbb{B}$.[1]

Definition 2 (Comprehensive Systems, Components, Commonalities). *A comprehensive system C consists of*

- *Functors $C_j : \mathbb{B}_j \to \mathsf{Set}$ for each $j \in \{1,\dots,n\}$, called* Components
- *A functor $C_0 : \mathbb{B}_0 \to \mathsf{Set}$ determining the* Commonality *representatives, and*
- *A collection of* partial *functions $(C_0(s) \xrightarrow{p_{j,s}} C_j(s))_{s \in |\mathbb{B}|, 1 \leq j \leq n}$, called* projections, *establishing the* commonalities *of C,*

such that for all $op : s \to s' \in \mathbb{B}$ and $1 \leq j \leq n$ the following statement holds:

$$\text{If } p_{j,s}(x) \text{ is defined, then } p_{j,s'}(C_0(op_0)(x)) \text{ is defined} \tag{5}$$

$$\text{and } p_{j,s'}(C_0(op_0)(x)) = C_j(op_j)(p_{j,s}(x)). \tag{6}$$

Note that (5) and (6) generalize the edge-node-incidences, see sect. 5.2, which we already semi-formalized in (1). In the sequel, the index of functors C_i will be omitted, since it can be derived from the domain of definition. Hence, a comprehensive system is a *single* functor C with domain the $n + 1$ copies of $\mathbb{B}$ and $(n + 1)b$ carrier sets, if b is the cardinality of $|\mathbb{B}|$: In view of the introductory remarks on functors in sect. 6.1, $C_0, \dots, C_n$ can be seen as $n + 1$ instance worlds for metamodel $\mathbb{B}$, e.g. E-Graphs, each with $b = 4$ carrier sets.

The fundamental *linguistic extension* are the partial functions. They act according to our example in sect. 5.2: In the tuple $(p_1(w), \dots, p_n(w))$ the p_j determine sameness of its components based on representative w.

---

[1]   The abbreviation "op" for arrows of the base shall indicate that $\mathbb{B}$-arrows are certain operations constituting the structure of the base language, such as source and target operations of edges in graphs.

The next definition deals with different comprehensive systems. In this case, it is necessary to tell the respective partial mappings apart, such that we write $p_{j,s}^{C}$, if we depict the mappings in the particular system C.

Definition 3 (Homomorphisms between Comprehensive Systems). *Let C, C' be comprehensive systems as defined in Def.2. A homomorphism between comprehensive systems is a family*

$$(f_{i,s} : C(s_i) \to C'(s_i))_{s \in |\mathbb{B}|, 0 \leq i \leq n}$$

of mappings compatible with arrows, i.e. $\forall i \in \{0, \ldots, n\}, \forall op : s \to s' \in Arr_{\mathbb{B}}$: $f \circ C(op_i) = C'(op_i) \circ f$, and compatible with partial mappings: For all $j \in \{1, \ldots, n\}$, $s \in |\mathbb{B}|$ and $x \in C(s_0)$:

$$\text{If } p_{j,s}^{C}(x) \text{ is defined, then } p_{j,s}^{C'}(f(x)) \text{ is defined and } p_{j,s}^{C'}(f(x)) = f(p_{j,s}^{C}(x)) \quad (7)$$

where we write f instead of $f_{j,s}$, if the indexing becomes clear from the context.

A typical example is a typing morphism $t : A \to M$ for two comprehensive systems A and M. Then equation (7) reflects property (4), i.e. compatibility of commonalities and typing. This can be seen in fig. 2: The complete contents of it is a comprehensive system A typed over the comprehensive metamodel M partly depicted in fig. 5. A^0 consists of all cyan (binary or ternary) lines and $p_{j,s}$ assigns to a line its line end in model A^j, where s is the respective element type (node or edge).

Proposition 1. *Comprehensive Systems together with homomorphisms between them constitute a category $\mathbb{CS}$.*

Proof. An identity is a family of identities, composition is composition of mappings $f_{j,s}$. This yields neutrality and associativity. Moreover, composed homomorphisms are still compatible with arrows. Whereas this follows in the usual way for $op : s \to s'$, transitivity of the definedness implication in (7) also yields compatibility with partial functions.   □

6.3   Multimodel Equivalence

An alternative but closely related approach to our construction is to consider commonalities, i.e. commonality representatives A^0 together with projections $(p_j^A)_{1 \leq j \leq n}$, not represented *internally* by means of the modelling technique but *externally* as n spans of morphisms [24,46]. Let for this $\mathbb{G} := \mathbb{S}et^{\mathbb{B}}$, see the remarks on functor categories in sect. 6.1. The resulting artifacts of the category in [46] is a subcategory $\mathbb{M}$ of the functor category $\mathbb{G}^{\mathbb{I}}$, where $\mathbb{I}$ is defined as in fig. 6 (identity arrows of $\mathbb{I}$ are again omitted). It is a subcategory, because it only consists of those functors $\mathbf{M} : \mathbb{I} \to \mathbb{G}$, for which the images $\mathbf{M}(-j)$ of the top arrows in fig. 6 are monic (i.e. are monomorphisms).

The proof of the following theorem relies mainly on cartesian closedness of the category of small categories, i.e. $\mathbb{G}^\mathbb{I} \cong \mathbb{S}et^{\mathbb{B}\times\mathbb{I}}$ (internalization) and the fact that spans with one monic leg represent partial mappings, the middle object of the span being the domain of definition of the partial map. A detailed proof of the theorem is given in [47].

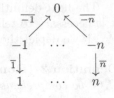

Fig. 6. Category $\mathbb{I}$

Theorem 1 (Equivalence of Categories). $\mathbb{CS} \cong \mathbb{M}$.

Corollary 1. $\mathbb{CS}$ *possesses all pullbacks and they are computed separately for the commonality representatives and for each component.*

Proof. Follows from Theorem 1 and the fact that functor categories possess all pullbacks, their pointwise construction guaranteeing that spans with one monic leg are preserved, because pullbacks preserve monomorphisms.   □

Auxiliary commonality structures have been used for model synchronization in the TGG framework [40]: Consistency relations between two model spaces are defined declaratively by a grammar. The grammar rules are defined over triple graphs, i.e. pairs of graphs connected by special *correspondence*-graphs, which resemble structural commonalities. From the grammar rules, procedures for consistency verification [27], model transformation [13] and (concurrent) model synchronization [19,18] can automatically be derived. The solution space, however, is limited to binary scenarios. Trollmann and Albayrak [48,49] generalized the TGG framework to cope with multiple models within a *graph diagram* (GD) framework. If we assume that the involved models are also objects of the graph-like category $\mathbb{G}$ (see above), then graph diagrams are the objects of a functor category $\mathbb{G}^\mathbb{X}$, but with a different schema category $\mathbb{X}$: It has objects $|\mathbb{X}| = R \sqcup N$ and all non-identity morphisms connect a source from R (relations) to a target from N (models). There is at most one arrow in $Arr_\mathbb{X}(r, m)$ for fixed $r \in R$ and $m \in N$. In such a way graph diagrams, i.e. functors $\mathbf{D} : \mathbb{X} \to \mathbb{G}$ can specify relations of different arities.

They are, however, *static*: If $r \in R$ has k outgoing morphisms with targets $m_1, ..., m_k \in N$, $\mathbf{D}(r)$ is a k-ary correspondence relation with representatives which relate exactly one element in each of the k models $\mathbf{D}(m_j)$. Consequently, the schema category has to change each time a new relation is added!

Graph diagrams (GD) subsume TGGs, which have schema $\mathbb{X}_{TGG} := 1 \xleftarrow{s} 0 \xrightarrow{t} 2$, i.e. $R = \{0\}$ and $N = \{1, 2\}$. Computations of triple graphs (and graph diagrams) during rule application as well as decomposing GD rules for forward and backward transformations are based on *pushout* constructions in $\mathbb{G}^\mathbb{X}$. In the rest of the section we show that our framework is more general than graph diagrams in that there is an embedding functor $\mathbf{T} : \mathbb{G}^\mathbb{X} \to \mathbb{CS}$, the *translation functor*, which preserves pushouts and hence is able to replay all GD computations in our framework, yet being able to cope with new relations *without* changing the schema category.

We use the following notations: For a morphism $f : A \to B$ in a category $\mathbb{C}$ we write $A = \mathrm{dom}(f)$ and $B = \mathrm{codom}(f)$ for its domain and codomain and we use the shorthand notation $Arr_{\mathbb{C}}(\_, B) := \{ f \in Arr_{\mathbb{C}} \mid codom(f) = B \}$. We write $\coprod_{i \in I} D_i$ to depict the coproduct of a collection $(D_i)_{i \in I}$ of $\mathbb{G}$-objects. Note that a collection $(D_i \xrightarrow{f_i} D)_{i \in I}$ of morphisms yields the morphism $\coprod_{i \in I} f_i : \coprod_{i \in I} D_i \to D$ by the universal property of coproducts, i.e. the morphism, which acts as f_i on each D_i.

By Theorem 1, it suffices to define a functor from $\mathbb{G}^{\mathbb{X}}$ to $\mathbb{M}$. The composition of this functor with the equivalence will yield the desired result. This functor will also be called $\mathbf{T}$. Let a schema category $\mathbb{X}$ for graph diagrams be given with $|\mathbb{X}| = R \uplus N$ and let n be the cardinality of N. Without loss of generality, we assume $N = \{1, \dots, n\}$. Let $\mathbf{D}$ be a graph diagram, then we define a multimodel $M := \mathbf{T}(\mathbf{D})$ intuitively as follows (recall the multimodel schema in fig. 6): The model components of N are the same as those of $\mathbf{D}$, the commonality specification $M(0)$ is the disjoint union of all relations in $\mathbf{D}$, the middle objects $M(-j)$ are the union of those relations, the model $\mathbf{D}(j)$ participates in:

$$M(j) := \mathbf{D}(j) \qquad \text{(Models are untouched)}$$
$$M(0) := \coprod_{r \in R} \mathbf{D}(r) \qquad \text{(Coproduct of all relations)}$$
$$M(-j) := \coprod_{f \in Arr_{\mathbb{X}}(\_, j)} \mathbf{D}(\mathrm{dom}(f)) \quad \text{(Participating Relations of } \mathbf{D}(j))$$

for all $j \in \{1, \dots, n\}$. Furthermore,

$$M(\overline{j}) = \coprod_{f \in Arr_{\mathbb{X}}(\_, j)} \mathbf{D}(f) \qquad \text{(Projections)}$$
$$M(\overline{-j}) : \coprod_{f \in Arr_{\mathbb{X}}(\_, j)} \mathbf{D}(\mathrm{dom}(f)) \hookrightarrow \coprod_{r \in R} \mathbf{D}(r) \quad \text{(Domains)}$$

Hence projections $M(\overline{j})$ are the unions of the domains of those relating morphisms that have target $\mathbf{D}(j)$ and inclusions arise from the fact that coproducts in the above definition of $M(-j)$ (taken over some relations) are always subgraphs of the complete coproduct $M(0)$ (which is taken over all relations).

The definition of $\mathbf{T}$ on arrows is straightforward and we give it only informally: If $n : \mathbf{D} \Rightarrow \mathbf{D}'$ is an arrow between graph diagrams, then (1) $\mathbf{T}(n)_i$ is a morphism which acts in the same way as n_i on $\mathbf{D}(i)$, if $i > 0$, (2) it amalgamates the actions of n on relations, if $i = 0$, which (3) naturally restricts to the respective actions, if $i < 0$. It is then easy to see, that $\nu := \mathbf{T}(n)$ is again a natural transformation.

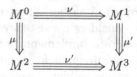

Fig. 7. Pushout in $\mathbb{M}$

Theorem 2. *Functor* $\mathbf{T} : \mathbb{G}^{\mathbb{X}} \to \mathbb{CS}$ *is an embedding and preserves pushouts.*

For a detailed proof of this theorem consult [47]. To sketch the idea, note that we cannot rely on pointwise pushout construction alone: Given a span (ν, μ) in $\mathbb{M}$ as in fig. 7, pointwise pushout construction may fail to belong to $\mathbb{M}$! E.g. if ν and μ are arbitrarily given, then M^3 in fig. 7 may not be admissible for $\mathbb{M}$ because the mapping $M^3(\overline{-j})$ may fail to be monic, an effect already studied in [25, Example 6]

Instead the proof uses the fact that naturality squares in ν are pullbacks, if ν is in the image of $\mathbf{T}$. Then *hereditariness* [17] of pushouts in $\mathbb{G}$ yields admissibility of M^3 and nevertheless allows for pointwise pushout construction. We obtain as a consequence:

Corollary 2. *Every sequence of rule applications in* $\mathbb{G}^X$ *has a unique representation of corresponding rule applications in* $\mathbb{CS}$ *and hence can be replayed in the general framework of comprehensive systems.*   □

7   Conclusion, Related Work and Future Plans

Our work can be summarized by the slogan "from many models to one model": Multimodelling is addressed by a construction that yields a single artifact, where existing means for consistency verification and restoration can be reused. Over many years such global artifacts were computed via merging [38,6,36,10], which poses several difficulties especially if the verification of a global constraint depends on the knowledge of which local model the elements came from. Hence, we proposed comprehensive systems that mitigate issues with the former and represent a generalization of graph diagrams and triple graphs—alternatives to our approach. Comprehensive systems stress the utility of *partial* mappings in commonality specifications, which have been promoted in [46] and were also picked up in [25].

Related work on multimodel consistency management was surveyed in sect. 4. Thus, at this point we mainly want to place our contribution in this landscape. Our approach can be considered as a *structural* one and is in tradition with other approaches based on *traceability links*. Recent other representatives in this line are [16], which uses binary links to relate different artifacts in a practical scenario, and [21], which develops a language, similar to ours, for expressing commonalities for global consistency restoration. All these works share the requirement for a common meta-metalanguage: In our case, given by graph-like structures (presheaf topoi). A rather different approach is the framework proposed by Stevens [45]: It considers consistency restoration to be performed locally by a builder. The concrete implementation of the builder is up to the user and thus there is no requirement for a common meta-metalanguage. The global coordination of multiple builder is handled by the framework, controlled by an orientation model. Comparing Stevens approach to structural approaches, the former is more abstract and thus allows more directions for tooling implementation, whereas structural approaches allow formal analysis of the nature of consistency rules. It will be worthwhile to investigate the relationship between both approaches in the future.

This paper provides the framework for performing multi model consistency management by reusing existing restoration techniques. We plan to address the momentary lack of practical evidence by investigating *model repair* [28] as the next step. Being conceptually close to TGGs, grammar-based approaches seem a natural fit but we plan to experiment with solver-based approaches as well, further taking into account: Human interaction and learning.

References

1. Aizenbud-Reshef, N., Nolan, B.T., Rubin, J., Shaham-Gafni, Y.: Model traceability. IBM Systems Journal **45**(3), 515–526 (2006). https://doi.org/10.1147/sj.453.0515
2. Anjorin, A., Buchmann, T., Westfechtel, B., Diskin, Z., Ko, H.S., Eramo, R., Hinkel, G., Samimi-Dehkordi, L., Zündorf, A.: Benchmarking bidirectional transformations: theory, implementation, application, and assessment. Software and Systems Modeling (Sep 2019). https://doi.org/10.1007/s10270-019-00752-x
3. Atkinson, C., Stoll, D., Bostan, P.: Orthographic Software Modeling: A Practical Approach to View-Based Development. In: Maciaszek, L.A., González-Pérez, C., Jablonski, S. (eds.) Evaluation of Novel Approaches to Software Engineering. pp. 206–219. Communications in Computer and Information Science, Springer Berlin Heidelberg (2010)
4. Barr, M., Wells, C.: Category theory for computing science. Prentice Hall (1990)
5. Berners-Lee, T., Fielding, R.T., Masinter, L.: Uniform resource identifiers (uri): Generic syntax. RFC 2396, IETF (August 1998), https://www.ietf.org/rfc/rfc2396.txt
6. Brunet, G., Chechik, M., Easterbrook, S., Nejati, S., Niu, N., Sabetzadeh, M.: A Manifesto for Model Merging. In: GaMMa '06 Workshop Proceedings. pp. 5–12. ACM, New York, NY, USA (2006). https://doi.org/10.1145/1138304.1138307
7. Cleve, A., Kindler, E., Stevens, P., Zaytsev, V.: Multidirectional Transformations and Synchronisations (Dagstuhl Seminar 18491). Dagstuhl Reports **8**(12), 1–48 (2019). https://doi.org/10.4230/DagRep.8.12.1
8. Czarnecki, K., Foster, N., Hu, Z., Lämmel, R., Schürr, A., Terwilliger, J.F.: Bidirectional Transformations: A Cross-Discipline Perspective. In: ICMT'09 Proceedings. pp. 193–204 (2009)
9. Diskin, Z., König, H., Lawford, M.: Multiple Model Synchronization with Multiary Delta Lenses. In: Russo, A., Schürr, A. (eds.) FASE'18 Proceedings. pp. 21–37. LNCS, Springer International Publishing (2018)
10. Diskin, Z., Xiong, Y., Czarnecki, K.: Specifying Overlaps of Heterogeneous Models for Global Consistency Checking. In: MDI@MODELS 2010. pp. 165–179 (2011)
11. Egyed, A.: Fixing inconsistencies in UML design models. Proceedings - International Conference on Software Engineering pp. 292–301 (2007). https://doi.org/10.1109/ICSE.2007.38
12. Ehrig, H., Ehrig, K., Prange, U., Taentzer, G.: Fundamentals of algebraic graph transformation. Springer (2006)
13. Ehrig, H., Ehrig, K., Ermel, C., Hermann, F., Taentzer, G.: Information Preserving Bidirectional Model Transformations. In: Dwyer, M.B., Lopes, A. (eds.) FASE'07 Proceedings. pp. 72–86. LNCS, Springer Berlin Heidelberg (2007)
14. Ehrig, H., Ehrig, K., Hermann, F.: From Model Transformation to Model Integration based on the Algebraic Approach to Triple Graph Grammars. Electronic Communications of the EASST **10**(0) (Jun 2008). https://doi.org/10.14279/tuj.eceasst.10.154
15. Euzenat, J., Shvaiko, P.: Ontology Matching. Springer-Verlag, Berlin Heidelberg, 2 edn. (2013)
16. Feldmann, S., Kernschmidt, K., Wimmer, M., Vogel-Heuser, B.: Managing inter-model inconsistencies in model-based systems engineering: Application in automated production systems engineering. Journal of Systems and Software **153**, 105–134 (Jul 2019). https://doi.org/10.1016/j.jss.2019.03.060
17. Hayman, J., Heindel, T.: On pushouts of partial maps. In: ICGT'14 Proceedings. pp. 177–191 (2014). https://doi.org/10.1007/978-3-319-09108-2_12

18. Hermann, F., Ehrig, H., Ermel, C., Orejas, F.: Concurrent Model Synchronization with Conflict Resolution Based on Triple Graph Grammars. In: de Lara, J., Zisman, A. (eds.) FASE'12 Proceedings. pp. 178–193. LNCS, Springer Berlin Heidelberg (2012)

19. Hermann, F., Ehrig, H., Orejas, F., Czarnecki, K., Diskin, Z., Xiong, Y.: Correctness of model synchronization based on triple graph grammars. In: Whittle, J., Clark, T., Kühne, T. (eds.) MODELS'11 Proceedings. pp. 668–682. Springer Berlin Heidelberg, Berlin, Heidelberg (2011)

20. Jackson, D.: Alloy: A Lightweight Object Modelling Notation. ACM Trans. Softw. Eng. Methodol. 11(2), 256–290 (Apr 2002)

21. Klare, H., Gleitze, J.: Commonalities for Preserving Consistency of Multiple Models. In: MODELS 2019 Companion. pp. 371–378 (Sep 2019). https://doi.org/10.1109/MODELS-C.2019.00058

22. Knapp, A., Mossakowski, T.: Multi-view Consistency in UML: A Survey. In: Graph Transformation, Specifications, and Nets, pp. 37–60. LNCS 10800, Springer, Cham (2018)

23. Kolovos, D.S., Ruscio, D.D., Pierantonio, A., Paige, R.F.: Different models for model matching: An analysis of approaches to support model differencing. In: CVSM@ICSE'09 Workshop Proceedings. pp. 1–6 (May 2009). https://doi.org/10.1109/CVSM.2009.5071714

24. König, H., Diskin, Z.: Efficient Consistency Checking of Interrelated Models. In: ECMFA 2017 Proceedings. pp. 161–178 (2017)

25. Kosiol, J., Fritsche, L., Schürr, A., Taentzer, G.: Adhesive Subcategories of Functor Categories with Instantiation to Partial Triple Graphs. In: Guerra, E., Orejas, F. (eds.) ICGT'19 Proceedings. pp. 38–54. LNCS, Springer International Publishing (2019)

26. Kühne, T.: Matters of (Meta-) Modeling. Software & Systems Modeling 5(4), 369–385 (Dec 2006). https://doi.org/10.1007/s10270-006-0017-9

27. Leblebici, E., Anjorin, A., Fritsche, L., Varró, G., Schürr, A.: Leveraging incremental pattern matching techniques for model synchronisation. In: ICGT'17 Proceedings. pp. 179–195 (2017). https://doi.org/10.1007/978-3-319-61470-0_11

28. Macedo, N., Jorge, T., Cunha, A.: A Feature-Based Classification of Model Repair Approaches. IEEE Transactions on Software Engineering 43(7), 615–640 (Jul 2017). https://doi.org/10.1109/TSE.2016.2620145

29. Macedo, N., Cunha, A.: Least-change bidirectional model transformation with QVT-R and ATL. Software & Systems Modeling 15(3), 783–810 (Jul 2016). https://doi.org/10.1007/s10270-014-0437-x

30. OMG: Business Process Model And Notation (BPMN) v.2.0 (2011), http://www.omg.org/spec/BPMN

31. OMG: Object Constraint Language (OCL) v.2.3.1 (2012), http://www.omg.org/spec/OCL/2.3.1/

32. OMG: Unified Modeling Language (UML) v.2.4.1 (2015), http://www.omg.org/spec/UML

33. OMG: Decision Model and Notation (DMN) v.1.2 (2019), https://www.omg.org/spec/DMN/About-DMN/

34. Pierce, B.C.: Basic Category Theory for Computer Scientists. MIT Press, Cambridge, MA, USA (1991)

35. Rahm, E., Bernstein, P.A.: A Survey of Approaches to Automatic Schema Matching. The VLDB Journal 10(4), 334–350 (2001)

36. Rubin, J., Chechik, M.: N-way Model Merging. In: ESEC/FSE'13 Proceedings. pp. 301–311. ACM, New York, NY, USA (2013). https://doi.org/10.1145/2491411.2491446
37. Rutle, A., Rossini, A., Lamo, Y., Wolter, U.: A Diagrammatic Formalisation of MOF-Based Modelling Languages. In: TOOLS EUROPE 2009, pp. 37–56. Springer, Berlin, Heidelberg (2009)
38. Sabetzadeh, M., Easterbrook, S.: An Algebraic Framework for Merging Incomplete and Inconsistent Views. In: RE 2005 Proceedings. pp. 306–315 (2005)
39. Samimi-Dehkordi, L., Zamani, B., Kolahdouz-Rahimi, S.: EVL+Strace: a novel bidirectional model transformation approach. Information and Software Technology **100**, 47–72 (Aug 2018). https://doi.org/10.1016/j.infsof.2018.03.011
40. Schürr, A.: Specification of Graph Translators with Triple Graph Grammars. In: WG '94. pp. 151–163 (1994)
41. Segen, J.C.: The Dictionary of Modern Medicine. CRC Press (Feb 1992)
42. Rodrigues da Silva, A.: Model-driven engineering: A survey supported by the unified conceptual model. Computer Languages, Systems & Structures **43**, 139–155 (Oct 2015)
43. Spanoudakis, G., Zisman, A.: Inconsistency Management in Software Engineering: Survey and Open Research Issues. In: Handbook of Software Engineering and Knowledge Engineering. pp. 329–380 (2000). https://doi.org/10.1142/9789812389718_0015
44. Stevens, P.: Bidirectional Transformations In The Large. In: MODELS 2017 Proceedings. pp. 1–11. IEEE Press, Piscataway, NJ, USA (Jun 2017). https://doi.org/10.1109/MODELS.2017.8
45. Stevens, P.: Towards Sound, Optimal, and Flexible Building from Megamodels. In: MODELS '18 Proceedings. pp. 301–311. ACM, New York, NY, USA (2018). https://doi.org/10.1145/3239372.3239378
46. Stünkel, P., König, H., Lamo, Y., Rutle, A.: Multimodel correspondence through inter-model constraints. In: BX@<Programming>2018. ACM (2 2018)
47. Stünkel, P., König, H., Lamo, Y., Rutle, A.: Towards multiple model synchronization with comprehensive systems: Extended version. Tech. Rep. 1, Fachhochschule für die Wirtschaft (FHDW) Hannover, https://fhdwdev.ha.bib.de/public/papers/02020-01.pdf (2020)
48. Trollmann, F., Albayrak, S.: Extending model to model transformation results from triple graph grammars to multiple models. In: ICMT '15 Proceedings. pp. 214–229 (2015)
49. Trollmann, F., Albayrak, S.: Extending Model Synchronization Results from Triple Graph Grammars to Multiple Models. In: Van Gorp, P., Engels, G. (eds.) ICMT'16 Proceedings. pp. 91–106. LNCS (2016)
50. Walters, R.F.C.: Categories and Computer Science. Cambridge University Press, New York, NY, USA (1992)
51. Weber, J.H., Kuziemsky, C.: Pragmatic Interoperability for Ehealth Systems: The Fallback Workflow Patterns. In: SEH '19. pp. 29–36. IEEE Press, Piscataway, NJ, USA (2019). https://doi.org/10.1109/SEH.2019.00013
52. Whittle, J., Hutchinson, J., Rouncefield, M.: The State of Practice in Model-Driven Engineering. IEEE Software **31**(3), 79–85 (may 2014). https://doi.org/10.1109/MS.2013.65
53. Wille, D., Wehling, K., Seidl, C., Pluchator, M., Schaefer, I.: Variability Mining of Technical Architectures. In: SPLC '17 Proceedings. pp. 39–48. ACM, New York, NY, USA (2017). https://doi.org/10.1145/3106195.3106202

54. World Health Organization: ICD-10 : international statistical classification of diseases and related health problems : tenth revision (2004)

Analysis and Refactoring of Software Systems Using Performance Antipattern Profiles*

Radu Calinescu[1] , Vittorio Cortellessa[2] ,
Ioannis Stefanakos[1] , and Catia Trubiani[3]

[1] University of York, York, United Kingdom
{radu.calinescu,is742}@york.ac.uk
[2] University of L'Aquila, L'Aquila, Italy
vittorio.cortellessa@univaq.it
[3] Gran Sasso Science Institute, L'Aquila, Italy
catia.trubiani@gssi.it

Abstract. Refactoring is often needed to ensure that software systems meet their performance requirements in deployments with different operational profiles, or when these operational profiles are not fully known or change over time. This is a complex activity in which software engineers have to choose from numerous combinations of refactoring actions. Our paper introduces a novel approach that uses performance antipatterns and stochastic modelling to support this activity. The new approach computes the performance antipatterns present across the operational profile space of a software system under development, enabling engineers to identify operational profiles likely to be problematic for the analysed design, and supporting the selection of refactoring actions when performance requirements are violated for an operational profile region of interest. We demonstrate the application of our approach for a software system comprising a combination of internal (i.e., in-house) components and external third-party services.

1 Introduction

Performance antipatterns [8,31] and stochastic modelling (e.g., using queueing networks, stochastic Petri nets, and Markov models [7,16,33]) have long been used in conjunction, to analyse performance of software systems and to drive system refactoring when requirements are violated. End-to-end approaches supporting this analysis and refinement processes have been developed (e.g., [4,9,20]), often using established tools for the simulation or formal verification of stochastic models of the software system under development (SUD).

While these approaches can significantly speed up the development of systems that meet their performance requirements, they are only applicable when the SUD operational profile is known and does not change over time. Both of these are strong assumptions. In practice, software systems are often used in

---

* This work has been partially supported by the PRIN project "SEDUCE" n. 2017TWRCNB and by Microsoft Research through its PhD Scholarship Programme.

H. Wehrheim and J. Cabot (Eds.): FASE 2020, LNCS 12076, pp. 357–377, 2020.
https://doi.org/10.1007/978-3-030-45234-6_18

applications affected by uncertainty, due both to incomplete knowledge of and to changes in workloads, availability of shared resources, etc.

In this paper, we introduce a novel performance analysis and refactoring approach that addresses this significant limitation of current solutions. The new approach considers the uncertainty in the SUD operational profile by identifying the performance antipatterns present in predefined *operational profile regions*. These regions capture aleatoric and epistemic operational profile uncertainties due to unavoidable changes in the environment (e.g., workload variations) and to insufficiently measured environment properties (e.g., CPU speed), respectively.

A few existing solutions [2,11,19] employ sensitivity analysis to assess the robustness of software to variations in its operational profile. However, these solutions are not interested in major operational profile changes like our approach, and therefore focus on establishing the effect of small operational profile variations on the performance of the SUD. In contrast, our new approach provides a global perspective on the performance antipatterns associated with a wide range of operational profiles. This perspective enables software engineers to identify operational profile regions in which their SUD is likely to require refactoring, and supports the selection of suitable refactoring actions for such regions. The main contributions of this paper are:

1. We introduce the concept of a *performance antipattern profile* (i.e., a "map" showing the antipatterns present in different regions from the operational profile space of a SUD), and a method for synthesising such profiles for systems comprising a mix of internal and external software components.
2. We present a tool-supported approach that uses our performance antipattern profile synthesis method, and we define best practices for refactoring the architecture of a SUD using performance antipattern profiles.
3. We demonstrate the application of our approach for a software system comprising a combination of internal (i.e., in-house) components and external (i.e., third-party) services.

The remainder of the paper is organized as follows. Section 2 introduces a software system that we use to illustrate the application of our approach throughout the paper. Section 3 presents the new approach for the performance analysis and refactoring of software systems, and Section 4 describes its application to the service-based system from our motivating example. Section 5 compares our solution with existing approaches. Finally, Section 6 summarises the benefits and limitations of our approach, and suggests directions for future work.

2   Running Example

To illustrate the application of our approach, we consider a heterogeneous software system comprising both internal components and external services. We assume that the internal components are deployed on the private servers of the organisation that owns the system. As such, the architecture and resources of these components can be modified if needed. In contrast, the external services are accessed remotely from third-party providers and cannot be modified. These services can only be replaced with (or can be used alongside) other services that are functionally equivalent but may induce different performance.

2.1 System description

The system we use as a running example is adapted from [14], and comes from the foreign currency trading domain. The workflow implemented by this "FOREX" system is shown in Figure 1, and involves handling requests sent by currency traders. Two types of requests are possible: requests that must be handled in a so-called "expert" mode, and requests handled in a "normal" mode. The request type determines whether the system starts with a "fundamental analysis" operation or a "market watch" operation. Both of these operations use external services. "Technical analysis" is an operation provided by an internal component. This operation follows the market watch, and determines whether the trader's objectives (specified in the request) are satisfied

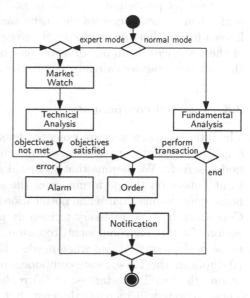

Fig. 1. Workflow of the foreign currency trading system (FOREX)

or not. If there is a conflict between these objectives and the results of the technical analysis, then the market watch is re-executed. Furthermore, the technical analysis may return an error, i.e., an internal "alarm" operation is triggered to inform the user about the erroneous result. The optimal results of either technical or fundamental analysis (satisfied objectives/trade acceptance) lead to the execution of an external "order" operation that completes the trade, and is followed by an internal "notification" operation that confirms the successful completion of the workflow.

2.2 External services

For the operations executed using external services, multiple services can be used as equivalent alternatives or in some combination deemed suitable. Given $n > 1$ functionally equivalent services, three options for combining them are possible:

- *Sequential* (SEQ): first invoke service 1; if the invocation succeeds, use its response; if it fails, then invoke service 2, etc., until service n is invoked, if needed.

– *Parallel* (PAR): invoke all n services at once, and use the first result that comes back.
– *Probabilistic* (PROB): invoke one of the n available services, selected based on a discrete probability distribution.

Therefore, we need to choose a "good" option (i.e., one that enables the system to satisfy its performance requirements) starting from information about the performance characteristics shown by each of these services, which we assume known from either the service-level agreement (SLA) published by the providers of these services, from our observations, or from both. Additionally, we assume that all these services already satisfy the functional requirements.

2.3 Internal components

The internal operations are executed by software components belonging to the organisation that "owns" the system, and running on their private hardware nodes/servers. We assume that technical analysis (TA) has a much more significant impact on the performance of the system compared to the other two in-house components (alarm and notification), which require only modest resources. Consequently, it is necessary to identify possible antipattern-driven refactoring actions for the TA component, to ensure that the system operates with an optimal performance. If and when needed, the refactoring actions we consider are: (i) duplicate the TA software component and load balance the incoming requests among the two TA instances; or (ii) replace the TA instance with a faster one. These actions will increase the cost, but may be needed to satisfy the performance requirements of the system.

2.4 Operational profile parameters

Several parameters of the system are outside the control of its developers. These parameters represent the *operational profile* of the system. For our FOREX system, they include the probability that a user request needs expert-mode handling, and the probability of a transactions being performed after the execution of the fundamental analysis operation (cf. Figure 1). The choice of these parameter ranges reflects, for instance, the engineers' expectation about a particular deployment of the system, numerical values will be provided in Section 4.

3 Approach

3.1 Overview

As shown in Figure 2, our approach to performance analysis and system refactoring comprises five steps. Starting for an initial system design proposed by a software engineer, step 1 involves modelling the performance characteristics of the system across its entire operational profile space (i.e., for all possible

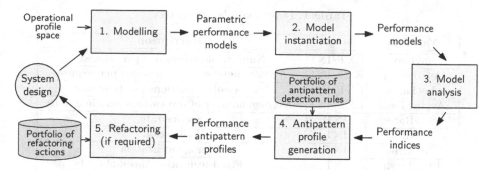

Fig. 2. Performance analysis and refactoring using antipattern profiles

values of the operational profile parameters). As such, the performance models produced by the modelling step are *parametric models*—models containing (uninstantiated) parameters like the probabilities of receiving different types of user requests. Our approach is not prescriptive about the type of performance models that can be used in its modelling step. However, these models must be able to capture the uncertainty associated with the operational profile of the system. Therefore, in this paper we will use parametric discrete-time and continuous-time Markov chains (parametric DTMCs and CTMCs).

Step 2 of the approach instantiates the parametric performance models for combinations of parameter values covering the entire operational profile space. A suitable discretization of the continuous parameters is used for this purpose.

The performance models are then analysed in step 3 to compute the performance indices corresponding to all considered combinations of operational profile parameter values. Existing analysis tools suitable for the adopted type of performance models need to be used in this step—in the case of our DTMC and CTMC models, a probabilistic model checker such as PRISM [24] or Storm [18]([1]).

Step 4 of the approach is using the performance indices and a portfolio of antipattern detection rules to identify the performance antipatterns that occur for different combinations of parameter values. This step produces a series of maps that show the distribution of such antipatterns across the operational profile space, thus to highlight problematic (from a performance viewpoint) areas.

Finally, step 5 assesses whether refactoring actions are required, because performance antipatterns occur in regions of the operational profile space where the deployed system is expected to operate. When refactoring is required, suitable refactoring actions (selected from a repository of such actions) are used to update the system design. Updated system designs are then further evaluated through re-executing the five steps of the approach, until a design with suitable performance antipattern profiles is obtained.

---

[1] An estimation of the effort required to create and solve performance models is out of this paper scope, as it may depend on the application domain complexity and the analysts' expertise.

Table 1. Detection rule parameters.

Variable	Scope	Description
InvReq	EXT/INT	Number of invocations per request
AvgInvReq	EXT/INT	Average number of invocations per request
InvTime	EXT/INT	Number of invocations per time unit
AvgInvTime	EXT/INT	Average number of invocations per time unit
ServRate	INT	Service rate
Util	INT	Utilization
AvgUtil	INT	Average utilization
UtilThresh	INT	Fixed utilization threshold
RespTime	EXT	Response time
AvgRespTime	EXT	Average response time
PathProb	EXT/INT	Probability of path execution
AvgPathProb	EXT/INT	Average probability of path execution
PathProbThresh	EXT/INT	Fixed threshold for probability of path execution

3.2 Detection rules

The concept of Performance Antipattern has been introduced several years ago [31] to define bad design practices that can induce performance problems in software systems. This concept has been later formalized in First-Order Logics [17] and then employed, in the context of Software Performance Engineering processes, for the purpose of automating the detection and solution of performance problems [29].

Inspired from the formalization provided in [17], we have here bounded the detection rules of three performance antipatterns to the modeling and analysis context of this paper. This binding is indeed required for any context, due to specificities and possible limitations of the notations adopted. In our case, Markov models of service-based software systems, on one side, offer the advantage of easy deduction of stochastic indices and, on the other side, suffer of lack of separation between software and hardware parameters. The latter are in fact implicitly taken into account in execution rates of operations.

Hereafter we report the formalization of the performance antipattern detection rules that we have used in this paper, while their parameters are defined in Table 1, where we also specify whether each parameter is available for external services ('EXT'), for internal components ('INT'), or for both ('EXT/INT').

- **BLOB**
  General description
  It occurs when a component performs most of the work of an application, thus resulting in excessive components' interactions that can degrade performance.
  Internal components
  $(InvReq > AvgInvReq) \land (Util > UtilThresh) \land (Util > AvgUtil)$
  External components
  $InvReq > AvgInvReq$

- **CONCURRENT PROCESSING SYSTEMS (CPS)**
  General description
  It occurs either when too many resources are dedicated to a component (MAX) or when a component does not make use of available resources (MIN).
  Internal components
  MAX - $(Util > UtilThresh) \wedge (Util > AvgUtil)$
  MIN - $(Util < UtilThresh) \wedge (Util < AvgUtil)$
  External components
  MAX - PAR pattern $\wedge (RespTime > AvgRespTime)$
  MIN - PAR pattern $\wedge (RespTime < AvgRespTime)$

- **PIPE AND FILTER (P&F)**
  General description
  It occurs when the slowest filter in a "pipe and filter" architecture causes the system to have unacceptable throughput.
  Internal and External components
  $(InvTime > AvgInvTime) \wedge (PathProb > PathProbThresh) \wedge$
  $\wedge (PathProb > AvgPathProb)$

We remark that, in our context, the rules for detecting a specific antipattern on internal components may differ from the ones defined for external services. This is because the parameters available for external services are obviously more limited than those of the internally developed components. For example, the whole response time (i.e., service plus waiting time) of an external service is usually negotiated in a service-level agreement, but it is difficult to isolate the net service time contribution to it, due to lack of control on the execution platform and the amount of resources dedicated to the service by the provider. Both indices can instead be estimated for internal components. As a consequence, wherever the service time (or any derived index like utilization) appears in a detection rule, the corresponding predicate has to be skipped/modified for external services. For this reason, in our case BLOB and CPS antipatterns present different rules when applied to internal components or external services because, as reported in Table 1, utilization cannot be estimated for the latter ones. In the BLOB case, the predicates including utilization for internal components are simply skipped in the external service formulation, because no other predicate would make sense there. Instead, in the CPS case, the predicates on utilization have been replaced with similar ones on response time for external services, because the CPS definition is compliant with this modification.

We highlight that all predicates include parameters that evidently change across different areas of the system operational profile (e.g., $InvReq$, $Util$), hence we expect that the occurrences of the corresponding antipatterns vary consequently. The only exceptions are the CPS rules for external services, because their parameters and thresholds do not depend on the operational profile. Such rules refer to the response time that, for these components, is based on service level agreement, and thus it cannot vary with the operational profile. This will evidently reflect on our experimental results, where CPS on external services will appear either everywhere or nowhere in the operational profile space.

3.3   Synthesis of antipattern profiles

The more software applications are being used worldwide from different types of users, the more difficult is to estimate a representative average behavior of users that induces a specific operational profile. In fact, not only users can have different operational profiles depending on their locations [15], but even in the same area the users behavior can (sometime radically) change over time [23].

Nevertheless, applications should show acceptable performance across different operational profiles. A motivation for our work is that different operational profiles can induce various performance problems, for example because a higher execution frequency of a path can overload components involved in that path. Hence, the idea is that, in order to identify the most appropriate refactoring actions to apply for overcoming performance problems, these problems must be identified across different operational profiles.

In this paper, we introduce the concept of *Performance Antipattern Profile*, which is a representation of performance antipattern occurrences while varying operational profile parameters. As discussed above, different antipattern occurrences are expected to appear in different areas of an operational profile, as shown in Figure 3, where two operational profile parameters vary (from 0 to 1) on the axes, and different coloured shapes in the graph indicate the occurrences of different antipatterns. Only with this information in hand, the performance experts can suggest appropriate refactoring actions when the system falls within a certain operational profile area, or even (in a proactive way) when the system is expected to enter a specific operational profile area.

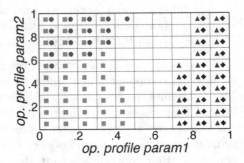

Fig. 3. Example of *antipattern profile*

3.4   Refactoring

The notational aspects outlined in the previous section for antipattern detection obviously reflect in the portfolio of refactoring actions aimed at removing performance antipatterns. In general, a refactoring action modifies some available *architectural knob* (e.g., the number of messages exchanged between two components, the list of operations provided by a component) to remove a source of the antipattern causes. The type and number of knobs depend on the adopted notation, so the portfolio of refactoring actions does the same.

Our notation distinguished between internal components and external services. The two types of system elements are characterized by a few common parameters and by parameters specific to each type (see Table 1). Therefore, our portfolio of refactoring actions is partitioned in two sets, as detailed below.

Actions for internal components

- Change service rate - The modification of a component service rate can be induced by several actions on the system, which could act on the hardware platform or on the software architecture, such as: (i) redeploy the component to a platform node with different hardware characteristics, (ii) replace some devices of the platform node where the component is currently allocated, (iii) redesign the software component so that its resource requests change, (iv) split a component into two (or more) components and re-deploy them.
- Change number of threads - This action is always possible where the control on the number of threads is on the designer's hands, and indeed for internal components this is guaranteed.

Actions for external services

- Change pattern - We have considered three combination patterns for external services, that are: SEQ, PAR, and PROB (see Section 2.2). They are used to combine (a subset of) the available instances of a certain external service. This action requires to modify the combination pattern, by keeping unchanged the set of combined services.
- Change the pattern parameters - Some patterns are regulated by parameters, in particular: PROB has a probability of each instance invocation, and SEQ has a failure probability for each instance. A change in the PROB probabilities is always feasible, because they are under full control of the designer. Instead, a change in the failure probabilities within a SEQ pattern implies that the designers are enabled for deeper modifications in the involved instances that can induce different reliability, and this is not often the case.
- Change combination of service instances - This action requires to replace some (or all) of service instances that are combined to provide a certain operation, by keeping unchanged the combination pattern.

Of course, the above actions can be combined together to study their joint effects on the performance improvement.

4   Evaluation

In this section, we first introduce the research questions that we intend to address (see Section 4.1). Thereafter, we describe the experimental scenarios (see Section 4.2) and discuss the obtained results (see Section 4.3). We finally report the threats to validity in Section 4.4. The implemented tool, the models and the experimental results are available at: https://github.com/Fase20/automated-antipattern-detection.

4.1   Research questions

The detection and solution of performance antipatterns largely depends on the operational profile, which is determined by the end-users behaviour, thus it can only be known after the system deployment. Naturally, some antipatterns are more affected than others by the operational profile that can have a considerable influence on the software system and, consequently, on its performance characteristics. Through our experimentation, we aim at answering the following two research questions:

- RQ_1: Does our approach provide insights on the performance antipattern profile of a specific design?

- RQ_2: Does our approach support performance-driven refactoring decisions on the basis of the performance antipattern profile?

In order to answer these questions, we apply our approach to the running example introduced in Section 2.

4.2   Experimental scenarios

Table 2 reports the system parameters of the default configuration we have used for our experiments. It is structured in three different groups. First, system settings, i.e., *ExtReqs-rate* (rate of external requests incoming to the system), and *QueueSize* (maximum number of queueing requests). These values are both set to 10. Second, the rate of internal components and external services, e.g., *TA-rate* = 3 is the execution rate of the Technical Analysis (TA) internal component. For external services, this rate corresponds to the inverse of the response time (as explained in Section 3.2), and it was obtained through

Table 2. System parameters.

Parameter	Values
ExtReqs-rate	$10s^{-1}$
QueueSize	10
TA-rate	$3s^{-1}$
Alarm-rate	$40s^{-1}$
Notif-rate	$55s^{-1}$
MW-rate	$19.92s^{-1}$
FA-rate	$24.99s^{-1}$
Order-rate	$19.09s^{-1}$
TA-threads	1

the analysis of discrete-time Markov chain (DTMC) models of the service combinations (i.e., SEQ, PAR or PROB) used for the external operations of the system. The model checker Storm was used to perform this analysis. Third, TA (as internal component) has a number of threads that is initially set to 1, but we provide a refactoring action that can change such number to modify the parallelism degree for such component.

The operational profile space of our running example (see Figure 1) is fully defined by the following branching point probabilities: (i) pExpertMode (p_{EM}), i.e., the probability of executing the workflow in expert mode; (ii) pPerformTransaction (p_{PT}), i.e., the probability of successfully performing a transaction; (iii) pObjectivesSatisfied (p_{OS}) and pObjectivesNotMet (p_{ON}), i.e., the probabilities of satisfying or not the objectives, respectively. As a consequence, $1 - (p_{OS} + p_{ON})$ is the resulting probability of an error occurring.

The experimental scenarios that we analyze in the next section include the variations of p_{EM} and p_{PT} within their full range $[0, 1]$ with a 0.1 step. Given the space constraints, we decided to bind (p_{OS}, p_{ON}) to three scenarios, namely: $\{(0.21, 0.78), (0.48, 0.01), (0.98, 0.01)\}$, which in the following we call $scenario_A$, $scenario_B$, and $scenario_C$, respectively.

We have considered the following design changes for refactoring purposes: (R_1) - the service rate of the TA internal component can be modified from 3 to 6 jobs per second (i.e., it becomes faster when performing computations) when TA is detected as an instance of a BLOB performance antipattern; (R_2) - a further thread of the TA component can be added to split the incoming load and manage users' requests, again as a solution of a BLOB performance antipattern on TA; (R_3) - change pattern (from SEQ to PAR) and service rate (from 50.21 to 500) of the MW external service, when MW has been detected as part of a Pipe and Filter antipattern; (R_4) - change service rate (from 40.02 to 400) of the FA external service while keeping the same pattern (i.e., PAR), and this is suggested as a solution of a Pipe and Filter antipattern that involves FA.

The results presented in the next section were obtained using the tool we developed to implement the analysis and refactoring process from Figure 2. This tool generates antipattern profiles using the antipattern detection rules from Section 3.2 and performance indices computed through the probabilistic model checking of a continuous-time Markov chain (CTMC) model of the entire FOREX system from Figure 1. The model checker Storm is automatically invoked by the tool for this purpose. The tool and the parametric CTMC models we used are available in our project's GitHub repository.

4.3   Experimental Results

In order to answer RQ_1, we have investigated the occurrence of performance antipatterns across different operational profiles, so to obtain performance antipattern profiles. Figures 4, 5, and 6 report the BLOB, CPS, and P&F detected antipatterns, respectively, across the operational profile space. Each figure shows the three considered scenarios for p_{OS} and p_{ON} and, for each scenario, p_{EM} varies from 0 to 1 (with a step size of 0.1) on the x-axis , while p_{PT} varies in the same range on the y-axis. Antipatterns occurring in each operational profile point are denoted by specific symbols.

We have here considered full ranges of the operational profile parameters, even though, in each instant of its runtime, the system will fall in a single point of the profile. Therefore, suitable refactoring actions depend on the area where the running system profile falls in the considered time. In particular, if it runs in an area where antipatterns do not occur, then no refactoring action is suggested.

In Figure 4(a) we can notice that in $scenario_A$ (i.e., $p_{OS} = 0.21$ and $p_{ON} = 0.78$) four different components are detected as BLOB antipatterns, specifically: (i) BLOB(FA) occurs for low values of p_{EM} only (i.e., up to 0.2); as opposite, (ii) BLOB(TA) occurs for larger values of p_{EM}; (iii) BLOB(MW) shows a very similar behaviour with respect to BLOB(TA) except in two corner cases where it occurs alone; (iv) BLOB(Order) occurs for low values of p_{EM} and high values of p_{PT} only.

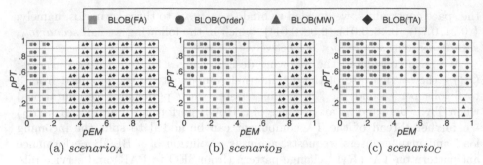

Fig. 4. BLOB antipattern instances while varying operational profiles.

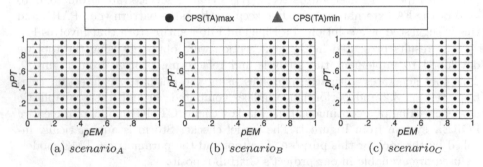

Fig. 5. CPS antipattern instances while varying operational profiles.

Figure 4(b) interestingly shows that in $scenario_B$ (i.e., $p_{OS} = 0.48$, and $p_{ON} = 0.01$), BLOB(TA) and BLOB(MW) occur in a smaller portion of the operational profile space, i.e., the right-most side (starting when $p_{EM} = 0.7$). Also the other antipatterns are subject to the probability changes, in fact both BLOB(FA) and BLOB(Order) occur in a larger portion of the space, i.e., the left-most side (up to $p_{EM} = 0.5$). This is because $scenario_B$ moves a consistent part of the workload far from the MW-TA loop, with respect to $scenario_A$.

Figure 4(c) illustrates the case of $scenario_C$ (i.e., $p_{OS} = 0.98$, and $p_{ON} = 0.01$), where further differences appear. In particular, BLOB(TA) antipattern does not occur anymore since the higher value of p_{OS} induces less computation in TA. BLOB(MW) is confined to three cases of large p_{EM} values and low p_{PT} values. This is because the major load is going here to FA and Order that in fact more widely are detected as BLOB antipatterns.

Figure 5 depicts the CPS antipattern profile that, as compared to the BLOB one, does not considerably vary across different scenarios. For readability reasons, CPS(FA)min is not reported in this figure, although it occurs across the whole operational space for all the three scenarios. We recall that this is due to the CPS detection rule that takes into account the response time for external services, which does not change with users' behaviour since it is a fixed value outcoming from service-level agreements. CPS(TA)min is not affected at all by the scenario variations, as it always occurs in the same operational profile area. Instead, the CPS(TA)max instances progressively decrease when increasing p_{OS}. A p_{OS}

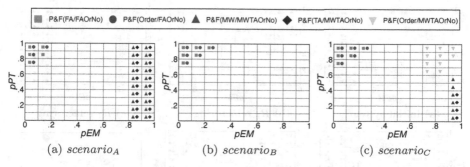

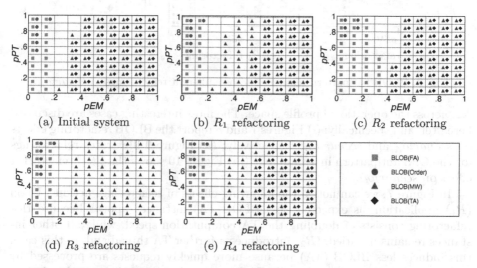

Fig. 6. P&F antipattern instances while varying operational profiles.

(a) Initial system   (b) R_1 refactoring   (c) R_2 refactoring

(d) R_3 refactoring   (e) R_4 refactoring

Fig. 7. BLOB antipattern instances across different refactorings - $scenario_A$.

growth, in fact, relieves the MW-TA loop, thus inducing less unbalancing in its components.

Figure 6 shows the P&F antipattern profile, where the antipattern instances obviously refer to execution paths instead of single components/services. Hence, different symbols represents different paths where one of the components/services is the slowest filter. For example, MW/MWTAOrNo means that MW is the slowest filter of the MW-TA-Order-Notification path. Interesting variations of this antipattern profile appear across scenarios, again driven by variations in the operational profile parameter values.

> *Summary for RQ_1:* Our approach provides insights on the performance antipattern profile of a specific design. In fact, we are able to identify considerable variations in the detected antipattern instances while varying the operational profile parameters.

In order to answer RQ_2, we have investigated the occurrence of performance antipatterns after applying refactoring actions that we have defined in Section

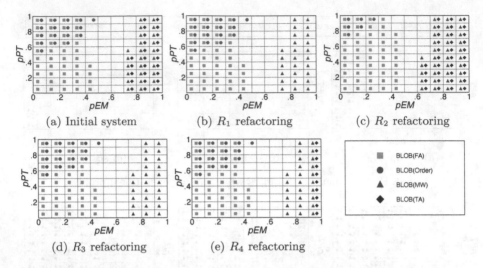

(a) Initial system   (b) R_1 refactoring   (c) R_2 refactoring

(d) R_3 refactoring   (e) R_4 refactoring

Fig. 8. BLOB antipattern instances across different refactorings - $scenario_B$.

4.2, across the operational profile space. The most interesting cases are discussed hereafter, and specifically: (i) Figures 7 and 8 report the BLOB refactoring effects on $scenario_A$ and $scenario_B$, respectively; (ii) Figure 9 illustrates refactorings for the CPS antipattern in $scenario_A$; (iii) Figure 10 shows the P&F refactoring effect on $scenario_C$.

In Figure 7, we can notice the following effects of refactorings actions. Upon (R_1) application, as expected, less BLOB(TA) instances appear because this refactoring consists of doubling the TA computation speed, while all other instances remains unvaried. (R_2) introduces a further TA thread and, in this case, this induces less BLOB (TA) because more quickly requests are processed by these two threads, and realistically FA becomes the overloaded one thus inducing more BLOB(FA) instances to appear. (R_3) modifies the rate of MW and makes it much slower, thus inducing the side effect of providing much less load to TA; in fact all the BLOB(TA) instances disappear, and all the other instances remain unvaried. (R_4) decreases the rate of FA and, similarly to above, it has the effect of providing less load to TA, in fact the number of BLOB(TA) instances decreases.

Figure 8 illustrates the effect of BLOB refactorings on $scenario_B$. (R_1) refactoring consists of making the TA component two times faster, hence the BLOB(TA) instance completely disappears from the operational space, while all the other antipatterns are not affected. (R_2), introduces a further TA thread, but in this case it occurs in a quite less stressed context with respect to $scenario_A$. This aspect, together with the fact that two threads allow to drop less requests, given that the queue length remains unvaried, in practice does not relieve TA itself. This is the reason for BLOB(TA) to not disappear. The decrease of BLOB(Order) instances is very likely due to the fact that, if performance indices change for some components/services, then their calculated average value change as well, hence inequalities in detection rules can change their results due

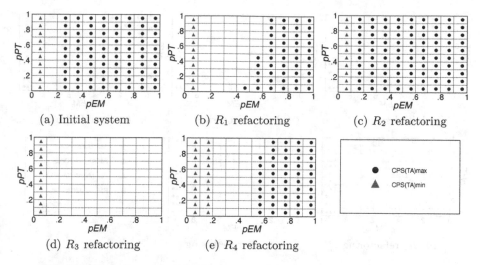

(a) Initial system   (b) R_1 refactoring   (c) R_2 refactoring

(d) R_3 refactoring   (e) R_4 refactoring

Fig. 9. CPS antipattern instances across different refactorings - $scenario_A$.

to changes in the right-hand-side targets. (R_3), similarly to Figure 7, modifies the MW rate and makes it much slower, thus having the effect of providing much less load to TA, in fact all BLOB(TA) instances disappear. Also (R_4) behaves similarly to Figure 7.

Figure 9 depicts $scenario_A$ (i.e., the $p_{OS} = 0.21$ and $p_{ON} = 0.78$ case) when considering CPS antipattern instances. We recall that the detection rule for CPS on external services operates on response time values that do not change with the operational profile. This leads that CPS(FA)min occurs in the whole operational space (not only for the initial system, but also after R_1, R_2, and R_3 refactorings). Instead, for R_4 refactoring, we found CPS(FA)max always occurring, and this is due to nature of this refactoring that modifies the FA rate. For R_3 refactoring, besides CPS(FA)min, we also found CPS(MW)max always occurring, and this is again due to the fact that R_3 modifies the MW rate.

In addition to this, we can make the following specific considerations. (R_1), makes the TA component two times faster, hence less CPS(TA)max instances appear, as expected. (R_2) introduces a further TA thread but it is not beneficial for the system, in fact the number of CPS(TA)max instances increase in the operational profile space. This effect is again very likely due to the fact that, with two threads, less requests are dropped than in the one thread case. Hence the work on TA in practice increases. This apparent anomaly would be mitigated whether, in the analysis, the number of dropped requests would be considered. (R_3), decreases the MW rate, so it has the effect of providing less load to TA; in fact CPS(TA)max instances disappear, and (as mentioned above) a CPS(MW)max instance appears in the whole operational profile space. (R_4) decreases the FA rate, thus having the effect of increasing the number of CPS(TA)min instances and decreasing the CPS(TA)max ones.

Figure 10 illustrates $scenario_C$ (i.e., the $p_{OS} = 0.98$ and $p_{ON} = 0.01$ case) when considering P&F antipattern instances. Quite small variations can be ob-

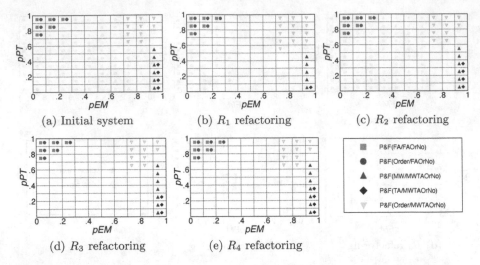

(a) Initial system   (b) R_1 refactoring   (c) R_2 refactoring

(d) R_3 refactoring   (e) R_4 refactoring

Fig. 10. P&F antipattern instances across different refactorings - *scenario$_C$*.

served here, as compared to other antipatterns and scenarios, always limitedly to single points of the operational profile space. Some specific comments follow. (R_1) induces less P&F instances where TA is the slowest filter and, on the same path, introduces more instances where Order is the slowest filter. This is an expected behavior due to the refactoring action that makes TA faster. (R_2) has no effect at all. (R_3) modifies the rate of MW component and makes it much slower, thus inducing less load to TA. The effect on the P&F antipattern is minimal and coherent, because one more P&F(MW) instance and one less P&F(TA) instance occur in the same path. (R_4) only introduces one more P&F(MW) on the same path as above, and this could be a side effect of changing the average values of performance indices.

Summary for RQ_2: The approach supports performance-driven refactoring decisions based on antipattern profiles, in that refactorings determine different effects on different regions of the operational profile space.

4.4   Threats to validity

Internal validity. In order to spot internal errors in our implementation for automatically detecting multiple performance antipatterns, we have thoroughly tested it. We verified that the detected performance antipatterns follow the given rules defined in their specification, along with the expected performance indicators. Note that the detection and solution of performance antipatterns relies on our previous experience in this domain [17], but in the future we are interested to involve external users that will be enabled to add their own rules for detection and refactoring.

External validity. We are aware that one case study is not enough to thoroughly validate the effectiveness of our approach. Nevertheless, several experiments have been performed beside the proposed experimental scenarios, in order to inspect the large number of variabilities in the operational profile space that may affect performance characteristics in unexpected ways. As future work, we would like to better investigate the effectiveness of our approach by applying it to further case studies (including industrial applications).

5   Related Work

In literature, the operational profile has been recognized as a very relevant factor in many domains, such as software reliability [27] and testing [30]. In the context of performance analysis of software systems, there are many techniques developed to act at: (i) design-time, i.e., providing model-based predictions [6,12,32]; (ii) run-time, i.e., actual measurements derived from system monitoring [10,13,35]. The refactoring, instead, is a more recent research direction, and many issues arise when modifying different system abstractions [3,26,5]. This paper contributes in demonstrating that both performance analysis and refactoring are affected by operational profiles, and in the following we review the related work aimed at pursuing this research direction.

In [22], a method for uncertainty analysis of the operational profile is presented, and the perturbation theory is used to evaluate how the execution rates of software components are affected by changes in the operational profile. Our approach also considers execution rates, but it is intended to support designers in the task of identifying performance-critical scenarios (i.e., when antipatterns occur and their evolution when refactoring actions are applied). In [34], performance antipatterns are used to isolate the problems' root causes, and facilitating their solutions; the TPC-W benchmark showed a relevant increase in the maximum throughput, thus to assess the usefulness of performance antipatterns. However, the choice of representative usage profiles is recognized by the authors as a limitation of the approach, since no directives are given for this scope. Our approach, instead, is intentionally focused on exploiting the performance antipatterns while considering the operational profile space as a first-class citizen of the conducted analysis.

The static technique proposed in [25] detects and fixes performance bugs (i.e., break out of the loop when a given condition becomes true). It is applied to real-world Java and C/C++ applications, and it resulted very promising since a large number of new performance bugs are discovered. Like [34], this approach neglects the operational profile that instead may trigger the presence of further performance problems. As opposite, our goal is to shed the light on the importance of the operational profile space, and our experimentation demonstrates that performance problems and solutions indeed vary across such a space.

In [21], performance anomalies in testing data are detected through a new metric, namely the transaction profile (TP), that is inferred from the testing data along with the queueing network model of the testing system. The key intuition is that TP is independent from the workload, it is sensitive to variations caused by software updates only. Our approach also investigates what are the refactorings that are more responsible of performance issues, along with the characteristics of the operational profile. In fact, refactorings produce regions of the operational profile space that are differently affected, and these differences can be used by the designers in the task of understanding the suitability of a specific design. The work more related to our approach is [28] where sequences of code refactorings (for Java-like programs) are driven by the avoidance of antipatterns (i.e., the BLOB only) and aimed at improving the system security. These refactorings consider the attack surface (i.e., how users/attackers access to software functionalities) as an additional optimization objective. Our approach shares the intuition that antipattern-based refactorings are beneficial for software quality (i.e., performance in our case) and that the operational profile needs to be part of the evaluation, but unlike [28] we target software design abstractions, and we provide a global view of the antipatterns encountered by software systems across their entire operational profile space. A systematic literature review on software architecture optimization methods is provided in [1], but users' operational profiles are neglected. This further motivates our work as promoter of a research line that should foster more attention on the role of users and their effects on the available software resources.

Summarizing, to the best of our knowledge, there is no approach that focuses on how the operational profile affects the performance analysis and refactoring of software systems, and the idea of adopting performance antipatterns for this scope seems to be promising according to our experimentation.

6   Conclusion

We presented a novel approach that considers the operational profile space of a system under development as a first class citizen in performance-driven analysis and refactoring of software systems. Performance antipatterns profiles have been used to support designers in the nontrivial task of identifying problematic (from a performance perspective) areas of the operational profile space, and refactoring actions are applied to improve the system performance in such areas. Experimental results confirm the usefulness of the approach, and show how it can be used to evaluate the suitability of a specific design in different regions of the operational profile space.

In addition to the areas of future work mentioned in Section 4.4, we plan to extend our approach with the ability to handle reliability and costs constraints, and thus to support trade-off analysis among multiple quality attributes. Finally, the applicability of the approach could be extended by a portfolio of generic refactoring actions (which need to be feasible with our modelling and analysis techniques), and methods that automate the selection of suitable actions from this portfolio.

References

1. Aldeida Aleti, Barbora Buhnova, Lars Grunske, Anne Koziolek, and Indika Meedeniya. Software architecture optimization methods: A systematic literature re-

view. *IEEE Transactions on Software Engineering*, 39(5):658–683, 2012.

2. Aldeida Aleti, Catia Trubiani, André van Hoorn, and Pooyan Jamshidi. An efficient method for uncertainty propagation in robust software performance estimation. *Journal of Systems and Software*, 138:222–235, 2018.

3. Vahid Alizadeh and Marouane Kessentini. Reducing interactive refactoring effort via clustering-based multi-objective search. In *ASE'18*, pages 464–474, 2018.

4. Davide Arcelli, Vittorio Cortellessa, and Catia Trubiani. Antipattern-based model refactoring for software performance improvement. In *QoSA'12*, pages 33–42, 2012.

5. Gabriele Bavota, Andrea De Lucia, Massimiliano Di Penta, Rocco Oliveto, and Fabio Palomba. An experimental investigation on the innate relationship between quality and refactoring. *Journal of Systems and Software*, 107:1–14, 2015.

6. Simona Bernardi, José Merseguer, and Dorina C. Petriu. Dependability modeling and analysis of software systems specified with UML. *ACM Comput. Surv.*, 45(1):2:1–2:48, 2012.

7. Gunter Bolch, Stefan Greiner, Hermann De Meer, and Kishor S Trivedi. *Queueing networks and Markov chains: modeling and performance evaluation with computer science applications*. John Wiley & Sons, 2006.

8. William H Brown, Raphael C Malveau, Hays W McCormick, and Thomas J Mowbray. *AntiPatterns: refactoring software, architectures, and projects in crisis*. John Wiley & Sons, 1998.

9. Axel Busch, Dominik Fuchss, and Anne Koziolek. Peropteryx: Automated improvement of software architectures. In *ICSA-C'19*, pages 162–165, 2019.

10. Radu Calinescu, Carlo Ghezzi, Marta Z. Kwiatkowska, and Raffaela Mirandola. Self-adaptive software needs quantitative verification at runtime. *Commun. ACM*, 55(9):69–77, 2012.

11. Radu Calinescu, Milan Ceska Jr., Simos Gerasimou, Marta Kwiatkowska, and Nicola Paoletti. Efficient synthesis of robust models for stochastic systems. *Journal of Systems and Software*, 143:140–158, 2018.

12. Radu Calinescu and Shinji Kikuchi. Formal methods @ runtime. In *Monterey Workshop*, pages 122–135. Springer, 2010.

13. Radu Calinescu and Marta Kwiatkowska. CADS*: Computer-aided development of self-* systems. In *FASE'09*, pages 421–424. Springer, 2009.

14. Radu Calinescu, Danny Weyns, Simos Gerasimou, Muhammad Usman Iftikhar, Ibrahim Habli, and Tim Kelly. Engineering trustworthy self-adaptive software with dynamic assurance cases. *IEEE Transactions on Software Engineering*, 44(11):1039–1069, 2018.

15. Xi Chen, Zibin Zheng, Qi Yu, and Michael R. Lyu. Web service recommendation via exploiting location and qos information. *IEEE Trans. Parallel Distrib. Syst.*, 25(7):1913–1924, 2014.

16. Vittorio Cortellessa, Antinisca Di Marco, and Paola Inverardi. *Model-Based Software Performance Analysis*. Springer, 2011.

17. Vittorio Cortellessa, Antinisca Di Marco, and Catia Trubiani. An approach for modeling and detecting software performance antipatterns based on first-order logics. *Software and Systems Modeling*, 13(1):391–432, 2014.

18. Christian Dehnert, Sebastian Junges, Joost-Pieter Katoen, and Matthias Volk. A storm is coming: A modern probabilistic model checker. In *Computer Aided Verification*, pages 592–600. Springer International Publishing, 2017.

19. Michalis Famelis and Marsha Chechik. Managing design-time uncertainty. *Software and Systems Modeling*, 18(2):1249–1284, 2019.

20. Simos Gerasimou, Radu Calinescu, and Giordano Tamburrelli. Synthesis of probabilistic models for quality-of-service software engineering. *Autom. Softw. Eng.*, 25(4):785–831, 2018.
21. Shadi Ghaith, Miao Wang, Philip Perry, Zhen Ming Jiang, Patrick O'Sullivan, and John Murphy. Anomaly detection in performance regression testing by transaction profile estimation. *Softw. Test., Verif. Reliab.*, 26(1):4–39, 2016.
22. Sunil Kamavaram and Katerina Goseva-Popstojanova. Sensitivity of software usage to changes in the operational profile. In *Annual Workshop of NASA Goddard Software Engineering*, pages 157–164, 2003.
23. Arijit Khan, Xifeng Yan, Shu Tao, and Nikos Anerousis. Workload characterization and prediction in the cloud: A multiple time series approach. In *NOMS'12*, pages 1287–1294, 2012.
24. M. Kwiatkowska, G. Norman, and D. Parker. PRISM 4.0: Verification of probabilistic real-time systems. In *CAV'11*, volume 6806 of *LNCS*, pages 585–591, 2011.
25. Adrian Nistor, Po-Chun Chang, Cosmin Radoi, and Shan Lu. Caramel: Detecting and fixing performance problems that have non-intrusive fixes. In *ICSE'15*, pages 902–912, 2015.
26. Ali Ouni, Marouane Kessentini, Mel Ó Cinnéide, Houari A. Sahraoui, Kalyanmoy Deb, and Katsuro Inoue. MORE: A multi-objective refactoring recommendation approach to introducing design patterns and fixing code smells. *Journal of Software: Evolution and Process*, 29(5), 2017.
27. Süleyman Özekici and Refik Soyer. Reliability of software with an operational profile. *European Journal of Operational Research*, 149(2):459–474, 2003.
28. Sebastian Ruland, Géza Kulcsár, Erhan Leblebici, Sven Peldszus, and Malte Lochau. Controlling the attack surface of object-oriented refactorings. In *FASE'18*, pages 38–55, 2018.
29. Martina De Sanctis, Catia Trubiani, Vittorio Cortellessa, Antinisca Di Marco, and Mirko Flamminj. A model-driven approach to catch performance antipatterns in ADL specifications. *Information & Software Technology*, 83:35–54, 2017.
30. Carol Smidts, Chetan Mutha, Manuel Rodríguez, and Matthew J Gerber. Software testing with an operational profile: Op definition. *ACM Computing Surveys (CSUR)*, 46(3):39, 2014.
31. Connie U. Smith and Lloyd G. Williams. Software performance antipatterns for identifying and correcting performance problems. In *CMG'12*, 2012.
32. Mirco Tribastone, Stephen Gilmore, and Jane Hillston. Scalable differential analysis of process algebra models. *IEEE Trans. Software Eng.*, 38(1):205–219, 2012.
33. Kishor S. Trivedi and Andrea Bobbio. *Reliability and Availability Engineering - Modeling, Analysis, and Applications*. Cambridge University Press, 2017.
34. Alexander Wert, Jens Happe, and Lucia Happe. Supporting swift reaction: automatically uncovering performance problems by systematic experiments. In *ICSE'13*, pages 552–561, 2013.
35. Xiao Yu, Shi Han, Dongmei Zhang, and Tao Xie. Comprehending performance from real-world execution traces: A device-driver case. In *ACM SIGPLAN Notices*, volume 49, pages 193–206, 2014.

Business Process Compliance using Reference Models of Law

Hugo A. López[1,3] , Søren Debois[2] , Tijs Slaats[1] , and Thomas T. Hildebrandt[1]

[1] Software, Data, People & Society Section
Department of Computer Science
Copenhagen University, Denmark
{hala,slaats,hilde}@di.ku.dk
[2] Computer Science Department, IT University of Copenhagen, Denmark
debois@itu.dk
[3] DCR Solutions A/S, Denmark

Abstract. Legal compliance is an important part of certifying the correct behaviour of a business process. To be compliant, organizations might hard-wire regulations into processes, limiting the discretion that workers have when choosing what activities should be executed in a case. Worse, hard-wired compliant processes are difficult to change when laws change, and this occurs very often. This paper proposes a model-driven approach to process compliance and combines a) reference models from laws, and b) business process models. Both reference and process models are expressed in a declarative process language, The Dynamic Condition Response (DCR) graphs. They are subject to testing and verification, allowing law practitioners to check consistency against the intent of the law. Compliance checking is a combination of alignments between events in laws and events in a process model. In this way, a reference model can be used to check different process variants. Moreover, changes in the reference model due to law changes do not necessarily invalidate existing processes, allowing their reuse and adaptation. We exemplify the framework via the alignment of laws and business rules and a real contract change management process, Finally, we show how compliance checking for declarative processes is decidable, and provide a polynomial time approximation that contrasts NP complexity algorithms used in compliance checking for imperative business processes. All-together, this paper presents technical and methodological steps that are being used by legal practitioners in municipal governments in their efforts towards digitalization of work practices in the public sector.

Keywords: Formal Models of Law, Dynamic Condition Response (DCR) graphs, Compliance Checking, Process Calculi, Refinement

1 Introduction

Ensuring that business processes comply with applicable laws and regulations has been a central concern with the arrival of regulatory technologies (RegTech),

© The Author(s) 2020
H. Wehrheim and J. Cabot (Eds.): FASE 2020, LNCS 12076, pp. 378–399, 2020.
https://doi.org/10.1007/978-3-030-45234-6_19

and bring together different disciplines ranging from legal theory to computer science. We understand compliance as the *"act/process to ensure that business operations, processes, and practices are in accordance with prescriptive (often legal) documents"* [15]. Checking compliance requires ways to compare artefacts coming from very different domains: the legal domain and the process domain. On the one hand, business processes have as a main criteria the fulfilment of a business goal. On the other hand, processes operate within a regulated context, that sets certain limitations on how to achieve the goals, and defines responsibilities for actors involved. In the public sector, being non-compliant is not an option, as regulations determine the rights and obligations of their citizens. In the private sector, the risk of being non-compliant equates to possible hefty fines for the organization[4].

Linking laws and processes have several challenges: First, how can we formally interpret ambiguous regulations written in natural language? Second, how to pair that formal interpretation of the law against a business process? Third, how to reuse legal specifications in different process domains?, and fourth, what will happen with compliance when the laws change? *Compliance checking* refers to the verification procedure that compares regulations and processes: In its most simple form, compliance checking can be expressed as the following problem: given a formal specification of a law L and a business process P, we say that the process is compliant if 1. Every action that P does is in accordance to the permissions allowed by L, and 2. Every execution of P meets the set of obligations established by L, and 3. Executions of P don't do anything prohibited by L. In any other case we will say that the process is not compliant.

In this paper we focus on the compliance checking problem from a modelling/programming language perspective. First, we explore how declarative process languages can describe the set of requirements expressed in legal documents. The challenge is both at the level of language expressiveness (can the language express the intended semantics of a legal text?), as well as understandability (can a non-expert understand the specification?). Second, we look at the process dimension: can we have a general framework that considers different process artefacts? Third, we look at the alignment between the legal and the process dimension: Can we provide an efficient algorithm to compute whether a process is compliant with the legislation?

In [20], a taxonomy of the requirements needed to formally express laws was presented. Overall, a formal language that expresses legal requirements should be able to describe what can be done (*permissions*), what must be done (*obligations*), and what should not happen (*violations*). Moreover, these so-called deontic constraints are *effectful* (e.g.: an obligation might grant certain permissions, e.g. "you must pay for delivery, but when you do so, you may decide whether to pay now or upon delivery" and vice-versa, a permission may impose certain obligations, e.g. "you may park here if you pay later"). The content of the laws might also influence the choice of the language. Laws might describe

---

[4] https://www.theverge.com/2019/1/21/18191591/google-gdpr-fine-50-million-euros-data-consent-cnil

constraints related to the control flow, temporal information, data, or resource constraints [39]. Finally, the language of choice should be able to describe *defeasible conditions* [18], that is, when parts of the law become irrelevant, and are superseded by other parts.

Compliance checking requires a formal representation of business goals and processes. Such a representation traditionally takes the shape of traces (c.f.: event-logs) at run-time, and of *imperative* process models at design-time. In the imperative paradigm, languages such as BPMN [35] and UML Activity Diagrams [34] describe processes as activities and composition operators that prescribe *how* the flow in the activities executed in the process. Rules and laws are not first-class citizens in imperative models, and they need to be encoded as annotations in the process language [13], or paired with additional languages, such as BPMN-Q [4]. In contrast, declarative process models focus in the description of circumstantial information of processes (e.g.: the *why* of the process). Languages such as Declare [37] and Dynamic Condition Response (DCR) Graphs [10, 22] are some exponents of these types of languages. They describe a process as a set of constraints between activities which can be translated to specific business rules or goals. Their semantics is usually characterised by either mapping the declarative model to a flow-based model (e.g. transition systems), or by introducing an operational semantics that reasons over the state of the different constraints and/or activities of the model.

The objective of this paper is two-fold. First, it explores whether existing declarative process languages are expressive enough to formalise regulations; second, it introduces compliance checking via declarative processes. The DCR graphs process notation has been developed for the formalisation and digitalisation of collaborative, adaptive case management processes. The visual notation is both supported by a range of formal techniques, and serves as the formal base for the industrial (www.dcrgraphs.net) modelling and simulation tool. In contrast to Declare, the DCR graphs technology has been succesfully employed in major industrial case management systems, and at the moment it supports 70% of the Danish Central Government institutions[5]. DCR graphs have been extended to include both data [43], time [5, 24], sub-processes [10], and choreographies [25]. In the present paper we consider the core notation with time, which is expressive enough to represent both regular and omega-regular languages [10] as well as so-called true concurrency [9]. In this work we only focus on laws describing control-flow and temporal constraints, leaving data, resource constraints or inter-law dependencies for future work.

Our approach for process compliance can be summarised as follows: both the legal domain and the business/organisational domain are defined as independent DCR graphs, and compliance checking is reduced to process refinement. These two independent models allow for a separation of concerns on what is legal and what is business/organisational requirements and goals, and it eases compliance checking when either laws or organisational processes change. It is worth to point out that at its core, the choice of a process language can be replaced to any

---

[5] https://www.kmd.dk/indsigter/fleksibilitet-og-dynamisk-sagsbehandling-i-staten

existing process language (including imperative ones), as compliance checking is mainly defined over traces. Changes in regulations might affect existing running processes: the typical example is governmental case work, where processes need to be revised every time a new regulation is signed. In addition, organisational changes or process optimisation efforts might modify a business process in a way that stops being compliant with existing laws. Finally, the separation of the legal and business domains supports different stages of the compliance life cycle: designing new processes that are compliant with the laws (e.g.: *Compliance-by-Design* (CbD) [14]), as well as the verification of existing or mined process models [33] becomes possible.

Contributions This paper presents the first compliance framework for declarative process models that 1) can represent safety and omega-regular liveness properties, 2) is supported by industrial design and simulation tools, and 3) is currently in use in the digitalization strategies of municipal governments, and 4) allows for a separation of concerns between what is legal and what is process-specific. Thanks to having the *same formal language* for laws and business processes, we can use efficient verification techniques based on process refinement, This comes in contrast to approaches based in annotated imperative business processes, where the complexity of compliance checking belongs to the non-polynomial complexity class [45].

Document Structure Section 2 introduces the compliance framework. Section 3 presents DCR graphs, and illustrates its use on a case study. Section 4 explains the construction of reference models. Section 5 describes our compliance checking technique. Results from validation with organizations are documented in Section 6. Related work is compared in 7. We conclude in Section 8.

2   Regulatory Compliance Framework

The overall components of our compliance framework are described in Fig. 1. It shows the interactions between two different type of roles: The compliance officer, with a background in law, identifies the applicable regulations, and for each law she generates a reference model. Laws might be abstract, e.g.: *"Any information relating to an identified or identifiable natural person ('data subject')"* (Art. 4 in GDPR [7]). Consequently, the officer might need to combine the law with implementation acts (e.g. the Danish Data Protection Act [8]). In this way, the specification must narrow down ambiguities such as: "What corresponds to any information"?, "in which ways will the process identify a person"? or "who constitutes a natural person"? While the disambiguation process is mostly a manual processes that depends on the expertise of the compliance officer, computer support might provide help in the elicitation phase. Dual-coding tools support lawyers in the generation of formal specifications [29], and NLP techniques can be used to speedup the identification of process-related information [30]. The output will be a collection of reference models, each of them describing a law. Each model describe roles, rights, obligations, and the relations between them.

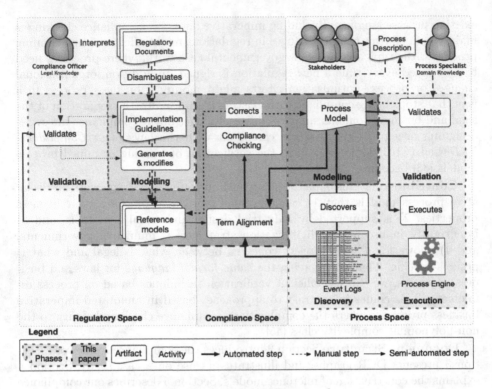

Fig. 1. Compliance Framework

Compliance checking assumes the existence of a process. This can be elicited from stakeholders via standard techniques [12] or, if the process already exists, via process mining [33]. Process models contain the activities performed, roles, and resource information (time & data) used. Alternatively, one can consider disregarding process discovery and perform compliance checking directly over event logs, as in classical process conformance approaches [1].

Both models and process models are subject to verification and validation phases. Scenario replays, reachability and deadlock-livelock checkers provide guarantees that both structural properties of the models are preserved.

The last dimension revolves compliance, and it constitutes the core of this paper. Since reference models are specific to a given regulation, they need to be instantiated in terms of the business process. This requires the alignment between events identified in the reference model, and activities in the business process. Compliance checking is then reduced to trace refinement: all traces in the process model are a subset of the traces in the reference model.

The separation between reference and compliance models allows for modular verification. When laws and processes change, their models can be changed separately, only needing to revise the alignment between events and activities.

$$T, U ::= e \xrightarrow{t_0} \bullet f \qquad \text{condition} \qquad | \; e \bullet \xrightarrow{t_\omega} f \qquad \text{response}$$
$$| \; e \rightarrow + f \qquad \text{inclusion} \qquad | \; e \rightarrow \% f \qquad \text{exclusion}$$
$$| \; e \rightarrow \diamond f \qquad \text{milestone} \qquad | \; T \parallel U \qquad \text{parallel composition}$$
$$| \; 0 \qquad \text{unit}$$

$$M, N ::= M, e : \Phi \mid \epsilon \qquad \text{marking} \qquad \Phi ::= (h, i, p) \qquad \text{event state}$$
$$\lambda ::= \lambda, e : l \mid \epsilon \qquad \text{labelling} \qquad h ::= f \mid t_0 \qquad \text{(h)appened } t_0 \text{ ticks in the past}$$
$$P, Q ::= [M] \; \lambda T \qquad \text{process} \qquad i ::= f \mid t \qquad \text{(i)ncluded}$$
$$p ::= f \mid 0 \mid t_\omega \qquad \text{(p)ending deadline}$$
$$t_0 \in \mathbb{N} \cup \{0\} \qquad \text{0-time} \qquad t_\omega \in \mathbb{N} \cup \{\omega\} \qquad \omega\text{-time}$$

Fig. 2. DCR Processes Syntax.

3   DCR Graphs

In this section, we recall the syntax and semantics of Dynamic Condition Response (DCR) processes. We use the core term-based definition with time, without bound events and subprocesses, following the original presentation in [5].

We assume a fixed universe of *events* $\mathcal{E}$ ranged over by e, f with a special symbol tick $\notin \mathcal{E}$. A DCR process $[M] \; T$ comprises a *marking* M, a *term* T. Its syntax is given in Figure 2.

A *term* represents a process model consisting of events (which may be activities, tasks, or the identification of the state of affairs) and their relations. In a DCR graph, events are the nodes and relations are the arcs. A *marking* represents the current state of a process by specifying for every event the event state (whether the event previously happened, is currently included, and/or is pending). A *process* is then represented by the process model (a term) and its current state (a marking). Relations can take the following shape:

- Condition $e \xrightarrow{t} \bullet f$: It defines a *prohibition*, or a precondition for f. Before f can occur, e must have happened at least t time units ago, or e must have been excluded. In the case that $t = 0$, we simply write $e \rightarrow \bullet f$.
- Response $e \bullet \xrightarrow{t} f$: It defines an *obligation* for e. If e has happened, then f must occur within t time units, or be excluded. In the case $t = \omega$, this will be treated as eventually in LTL, that is, not bounded by any time constraint. For such a case we can simply write $e \bullet \rightarrow f$.
- Dynamic Inclusion $e \rightarrow + f$: It defines *relevance* of an event. After executing event e, event f is included among the possible actions to take. Notice that the inclusion of f does not deem its necessity (captured by a response).
- Dynamic Exclusion $e \rightarrow \% f$: It defines *irrelevance* of an event. The result of executing e is that event f becomes excluded. Moreover, all conditions $f \rightarrow \bullet g$ and milestones $f \rightarrow \diamond g$ are ignored (unless f is included again).
- Milestone $e \rightarrow \diamond f$: A reaction chain. Initially f is included among the possible actions, but if e becomes pending, then f cannot occur until e has occurred.

Finally, term 0 denotes the null process. Note that it is possible to specify a relation twice, e.g., $e {\to} \%f \parallel e {\to} \%f$; this duplication has no additional effect.

All relations refer to a marking M, a finite map from events to triples of variables (h, i, p), referred to as the *event state* and indicating whether or not the event previously (h)appened, is currently (i)ncluded, and/or is (p)ending. A pending event represents an unfulfilled obligation, and the values it can take denote whether the event is not pending $(p = f)$, it has a finite deadline $(p \in \mathbb{N} \cup \{0\})$, or it should be eventually executed $(p = \omega)$. We write markings as finite lists of pairs of events and event states, e.g. $e_1 : \Phi_1, \ldots, e_k : \Phi_k$ but treat them as maps, writing $\mathsf{dom}(M)$ and $M(e)$, and understand $M, e : \Phi$ to be undefined when $e \in \mathsf{dom}(M)$. The *free events* $\mathsf{fe}(T)$ of a term T is simply the set of events appearing in it.

With respect to the original presentation [5], our syntax extends the process definition with labels. Labelling λ defines a total function from events to labels. However, we often omit the labelling function, as it rarely changes, writing $[M]\, T$ instead of $[M]\, \lambda T$. We assume that event labels are unique, e.g.: if $e, f \in \mathsf{fe}(T)$ then $\lambda(e) \neq \lambda(f)$ or $e = f$, therefore, λ has an inverse, which we will denote by λ^{-1}. A substitution $\sigma = \{e_1, \ldots, e_n / f_1, \ldots, f_n\}$ maps each event e_i and replaces it with f_i, being $1 \leq i \leq n$ and e_i pairwise distinct. The application of σ to a process term T is denoted by $T\sigma$, and it applies similarly for markings and for processes, being $([M]\, T)\sigma = [M\sigma]\, T\sigma$. We require of a process $P = [M]\, \lambda T$ that $\mathsf{fe}(T) \subseteq \mathsf{dom}(M) = \mathsf{dom}(\lambda)$, and so define $\mathsf{fe}(P) = \mathsf{dom}(M)$. The *alphabet* $\mathsf{alph}(P)$ is the set of labels of its free events.

Example 3.1. We use a contract change management process from the construction industry as our running example. The process model in Fig. 3 has been extracted from structured interviews with domain specialists, and then validated in a workshop. We will focus on the most salient aspects of the process, and direct to [2] for the complete specification. The process includes three significant roles: a subcontractor, a project manager and a trade package manager (TPM) –external to the organization–, collaborating via a document management system. The process starts when the subcontractor notices that additional work is required compared to an original construction contract. To be paid for the extra work, it is their responsibility to justify using supportive documentation $(A1)$. Hence, the subcontractor submits a change management request on the platform $(A2)$. Further, the TPM must notify the subcontractor that his request has been initiated $(A5)$, as well as checking the request specifications against the initial contract requirements and the technical documentation $(A4)$. Once the request is checked, the TPM can decide whether to accept the change request $(A7)$, to reject the request $(A8)$ or to ask for additional documents that support the subcontractors' claim $(A6)$. If the TPM decides to reject the claim, she must attach reasoning for the decision and communicate it to the subcontractor. Next, the subcontractor can evaluate the rejection $(A16)$. If there is need for further documentation to support the claim, the TPM must send a request for additional information $(A1)$. If the TPM agrees with the change, she must forward documentation describing what changes from the initial contract to the

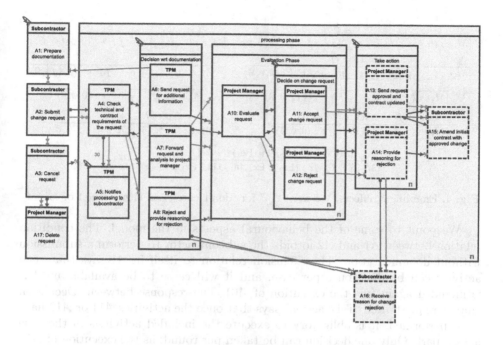

Fig. 3. Contract Change Management Process P_{spec}

project manager. The project manager must evaluate the request ($A10$). He is responsible for taking the final decision, whether to accept ($A11$) or reject ($A12$) the request. In case of rejection, the project manager must notify the subcontractor about the decision and substantiate with reasoning ($A14$). Besides, if the answer is an acceptance, the project manager is responsible for sending an updated contract form ($A13$). Once the new contract is received, the subcontractor must attach it to the old contract ($A15$). As part of the DMS capabilities, the subcontractor is allowed to cancel the change request ($A3$) at any point after submission, with the effects of deleting the application ($A17$).

The diagram in Fig. 3 provides a visual representation of process P_{spec} described above[6]. Events are denoted via boxes, and arrows describe the relations introduced in the previous section. Each event has a label presenting its description, as well as the role of the agent(s) that can execute the event. An included event is represented with a solid border, with a dashed line if it is excluded. Included events can be executed at any time (unless they become excluded), and, unless preceded by a response relation, they can also be left unexecuted. Relations can point to events or to events "collections" (boxes marked with "n"). As formalised in [23], such collections are referred to as "nestings" and are just a visual shorthand, understanding arrows to (from) nestings to represent arrows to (from) every event inside the nesting.

---

[6] The process is available for simulation and execution at https://www.dcrgraphs.net/tool/main/Graph?id=43ea382d-de1b-4278-8eff-591426244d90

$$\frac{i \Rightarrow h \geq k}{[M, e : (h, i, \_), f : (\_, \mathsf{t}, \_)] \, e \xrightarrow{k} \bullet f \vdash f : (\emptyset, \emptyset, \emptyset)} \qquad \frac{}{[M, e : (\_, \mathsf{t}, \_)] \, e \bullet \xrightarrow{k} f \vdash e : (\emptyset, \emptyset, \{f : k\})}$$

$$\frac{i \Rightarrow (p = \mathsf{f})}{[M, e : (\_, i, p), f : (\_, \mathsf{t}, \_)] \, e \rightarrow \diamond f \vdash f : (\emptyset, \emptyset, \emptyset)} \qquad \frac{}{[M, e : (\_, \mathsf{t}, \_)] \, e \rightarrow + f \vdash e : (\emptyset, \{f\}, \emptyset)}$$

$$\frac{}{[M, e : (\_, \mathsf{t}, \_)] \, e \rightarrow \% f \vdash e : (\{f\}, \emptyset, \emptyset)} \qquad \frac{}{[M, e : (\_, \mathsf{t}, \_)] \, 0 \vdash e : (\emptyset, \emptyset, \emptyset)}$$

$$\frac{e \neq f' \qquad \mathcal{R} \in \{\xrightarrow{k} \bullet, \rightarrow \diamond\}}{[M, e : (\_, \mathsf{t}, \_)] \, f \, \mathcal{R} \, f' \vdash e : (\emptyset, \emptyset, \emptyset)} \qquad \frac{e \neq f \qquad \mathcal{R} \in \{\bullet \xrightarrow{k}, \rightarrow +, \rightarrow \%\}}{[M, e : (\_, \mathsf{t}, \_)] \, f \, \mathcal{R} \, f' \vdash e : (\emptyset, \emptyset, \emptyset)}$$

$$\frac{[M] \, T_i \vdash e : (\mathsf{Ex}_i, \mathsf{In}_i, \mathsf{Pe}_i) \quad i = \{1, 2\}}{[M] \, T_1 \parallel T_2 \vdash e : (\mathsf{Ex}_1 \cup \mathsf{Ex}_2, \mathsf{In}_1 \cup \mathsf{In}_2, \mathsf{Pe}_1 \cup \mathsf{Pe}_2)}$$

Fig. 4. Enabling & effects. We write "$\_$" for "don't care", i.e., either true t or false f

We point to some of the behavioural aspects in the model. The condition relation between $A1$ and $A2$ forbids the subcontractor to perform a submission without documentation. The exclusion relation to itself in $A1$ says that such activity can be done once per case, and it will cease to be available until it is included again (via the execution of $A6$). The response between "Decide on change request" and "Take action" says that once the activities $A11$ or $A12$ have been performed, it is obligatory to execute the included activities in the take action part. Only one decision can be taken per round, as the execution of $A11$ and $A12$ exclude each other. The chain of milestones and responses between $A10$ and $A15$ ensures that the attached copy only corresponds to the most updated decision: every time a project manager executes $A10$, the activities inside "decide on change request" become pending. This will inhibit any action until the decision has been revised. Finally, the timed response between $A4$ and $A5$ says that notification must be done within 30 time units of the execution of $A4$.

3.1 Semantics

We first define when an event is *enabled* and what *effects* it has if executed. The judgement $[M] \, T \vdash e : (Exc, Inc, Pen)$, defined in Figure 4, should be read: "in the marking M, the term T allows the event e to happen, with the effects of excluding events Exc, including events Inc, and making events Pen pending."

The first rule says that if e is a condition for f, then f can happen only if (1) it is itself included, and (2) if e is included, then e happened at least k steps ago. The second rule says that if e is a milestone for f, then f can happen only if (1) it is itself included, and (2) if e is included, then e must not be pending. The third rule says that if f is a response to e and e is included, then e can happen with the effect of making f pending with a deadline of k. The fourth (respectively fifth) rule says that if f is included (respectively excluded) by e and e is included, then e can happen with the effect of including (respectively excluding) f. The sixth rule says that for an unconstrained process 0, an event e can happen if it is included. The seventh rule says that a relation allows any included event e to happen without effects when e is not the relation's right-hand-side event.

$$\frac{[M]\ T \vdash e : \delta}{T \vdash M \xrightarrow{e} \delta\langle e\langle M\rangle\rangle}\ [\text{EVENT}] \qquad\qquad \frac{\text{deadline}\langle M\rangle > 0}{T \vdash M \xrightarrow{\text{tick}} \text{tick}\langle M\rangle}\ [\text{TIME}]$$

Fig. 5. Transition semantics.

Finally, the last rule says that enabledness for parallel composition depends on its constituents (we omit symmetric rules for sake of clarity).

Given enabling and effects of events, we define the *action* of respectively an *event* e and an *effect* $\delta = (\text{Ex}, \text{In}, \text{Pe})$ on a marking M pointwise by the action on individual event states $f : (h, i, r)$ as follows. Assume e is enabled in the process $[M]\ T$ with effect $\delta = (\text{Ex}, \text{In}, \text{Pe})$. The state of e tracks that the event has happened now, setting its executed flag to 0. Similarly, we say that it is not longer pending. The effect of executing e in a marking M, written $e\langle M\rangle$, is inductively defined as follows:

$$e\langle M\rangle = \begin{cases} \epsilon & \text{if } M = \epsilon \\ e\langle N\rangle, f : (0, i, \mathsf{f}) & \text{if } M = N, f : (\_, i, \_) \wedge e = f \\ e\langle N\rangle, f : (h, i, r) & \text{if } M = N, f : (h, i, r) \wedge e \neq f. \end{cases}$$

The application of effect $\delta = (\text{Ex}, \text{In}, \text{Pe})$ over a marking M, denoted $\delta\langle M\rangle$, is inductively defined as follows:

$$\delta\langle M\rangle = \begin{cases} \epsilon & \text{if } M = \epsilon \\ \delta\langle N\rangle, f : (h, \underbrace{(i \wedge f \notin \text{Ex}) \vee f \in \text{In}}_{\text{included?}}, r') & \text{if } M = N, f : (h, i, r) \end{cases}$$

Where $r' = \min\{d \mid (f, d) \in \text{Pe}\}$ if $(f, d) \in \text{Pe}$ and $r' = r$ otherwise. That is, the event only stays included (second component) if $f \notin \text{Ex}$ (it is not excluded) or $f \in \text{In}$ (it is included). The pending flag takes the minimal deadline for which $f : d \in \text{Pe}$, otherwise, it keeps the flag unchanged. Note that an event can be both excluded and included by the effect, conceptually the exclusion happens first, followed by the inclusion.

The transition semantics requires us to account for the time that has passed between events. The deadline function is inductively defined over markings:

$$\text{deadline}\langle M\rangle = \begin{cases} \omega & \text{if } M = \epsilon \\ \min\{p', \text{deadline}\langle M'\rangle\} & \text{if } M = M', e : (h, i, p) \end{cases}$$

With p' taking the value of p if $i = \mathsf{t}$, otherwise $p' = \omega$. Basically, only deadlines of included events are considered. The deadline function sets a lower limit for events to happen. Moreover, we need to update the marking by incrementing the time after an event has fired. The tick function is inductively defined over markings with such purpose:

$$\text{tick}\langle M\rangle = \begin{cases} \epsilon & \text{if } M = \epsilon \\ \text{tick}\langle M'\rangle, e : (h + 1, i, \max\{0, p - 1\}) & \text{if } M = M', e : (h, i, p) \end{cases}$$

Extending the $+$ and $-$ operators such that $\mathsf{f} + 1 = \mathsf{f}$ and $\mathsf{f} - 1 = \mathsf{f}$, and $\omega - 1 = \omega$.

Figure 5 introduces the transition semantics of processes. In rule [EVENT], the marking M fires an enabled event e, generating as a result a marking M'.

Note that transitions are non-deterministic: more than one event can be enabled in M. In rule [TIME], the marking M is updated in one unit, generating M'. Intuitively, a transition $T \vdash M \xrightarrow{e} M'$ expresses that process $[M] \lambda T$ fires an event e and modifies its marking to M'. As customary, we denote with $\xrightarrow{e}{}^*$ the transitive closure of $\xrightarrow{e}$. Moreover, we define the state space of $[M] T$ as $\mathcal{P}([M] T) = \{[M'] T \mid T \vdash M \xrightarrow{e}{}^* M'\}$. Event transitions give rise to a labelled transition system $lts([M] \lambda T) = \langle \mathcal{P}(M), [M] T, \mathcal{E}', \longrightarrow, \Sigma, \lambda' \rangle$, where $[M] T \in \mathcal{P}([M] T)$ is the initial state, $\mathcal{E}' = \mathcal{E} \cup \{\text{tick}\}$ is the set of labels, $\longrightarrow \subseteq \mathcal{P}([M] T) \times \mathcal{E}' \times \mathcal{P}([M] T)$, Σ is an alphabet, and a labelling function $\lambda' \subseteq \mathcal{E} \times \Sigma$ defined by $\lambda(e) = \lambda(e)$ for $e \in \mathcal{E}$, and $\lambda'(\text{tick}) = \text{tick}$.

We equip with the LTS with notions of *accepting runs*, incorporating similar notions defined for DCR Graphs [6,32] to their timed setting:

Definition 1 (Runs, Accepting Runs). *A run of $[M] T$ is a finite or infinite sequence of transitions $[M] T = [M_0] T_0 \to e_0 \cdots$. A run is accepting iff for every state $[M_i] T_i$, when $M_i(e) = (\_, \text{t}, \text{t})$ then there exists $j \geq i$ s.t. either $M_j(e) = (\_, \text{f}, \_)$ or $[M_j] T_j \xrightarrow{e} [M_{j+1}] T_{j+1}$.*

In other words, an accepting run consider transitions that either execute pending events, or excludes them. Note that since an event e may happen more than once, even processes with only finitely many events may have infinite runs. Having defined the LTS and runs we can define the language defined by a DCR process to be its set of accepting runs.

Definition 2 (Traces). *A trace of a process $[M] \lambda T$ is a possibly infinite string $s = (s_i)_{i \in I}$ s.t. $[M] T$ has an accepting run $[M_i] T_i \xrightarrow{e_i} [M_{i+1}] T_{i+1}$ with $s_i = \lambda(e_i)$. Finally, the process $[M] T$ has the language $\mathsf{lang}([M] \lambda T) = \{s \mid s \text{ is a trace of } [M] \lambda T\}$.*

4 Compliance Rules

Not all law paragraphs are created equal. Different articles describe definitions, commencement periods, amendments, and other provisions. We focus on *self-contained* procedural articles, those paragraphs that do not depend on the state of affairs of events described in other paragraphs. One example is GDPR Art. 21 §1:

(Right to Object) §1. The data subject shall have the right to object, on grounds relating to his or her particular situation, at any time to processing of personal data concerning him or her [...]. The controller shall no longer process the personal data unless the controller demonstrates compelling legitimate grounds for the processing which override the interests, rights and freedoms of the data subject or for the establishment, exercise or defence of legal claims.

Legal Text	Policy	Compliance Rule
GDPR Art. 21 §1.	If the subcontractor submits a change request, he may cancel it afterwards. After cancellation, the project manager must eventually delete the request.	$RC1 = [e_1 : (f, t, f), e_2 : (f, t, f), e_3 : (f, t, f)] \lambda_1 T_1$ $T_1 = e_1 \rightarrow \bullet e_2 \parallel e_2 \rightarrow \bullet e_3 \parallel e_2 \bullet \rightarrow e_3$ $\lambda_1(e_1) = $ "A2: submit a change request" $\lambda_1(e_2) = $ "A3: cancel change request" $\lambda_1(e_3) = $ "A17: delete the request"
95/46/EC. Sect IV, Art. 11. §1. [...] The controller [...] must at the time of undertaking the recording of personal data [...] provide the data subject with at least the following information [...].	After the subcontractor submits a change request, eventually the TPM will notify the subcontractor about the processing of request, including the personal data used.	$RC2 = [e_4 : (f, t, f), e_5 : (f, t, f)] \lambda_2 T_2$ $T_2 = e_4 \bullet \rightarrow e_5 \parallel e_4 \rightarrow \bullet e_5$ $\lambda_2(e_4) = $ "A2: Submit change request" $\lambda_2(e_5) = $ "A5: Notifies processing to subcontractor"
Organization KPI. A change request should take a maximum amount of time, otherwise it becomes invalid.	The change request is valid for 60 working days and afterwards it is closed.	$RC3 = [e_6 : (f, t, f), e_7 : (f, f, f), e_8 : (f, t, f)] \lambda_3 T_3$ $T_3 = e_6 \rightarrow + e_7 \parallel e_6 \bullet \xrightarrow{60} e_7 \parallel e_6 \xrightarrow{60} \bullet e_8 \parallel e_8 \rightarrow \% e_7$ $\lambda_3(e_6) = $ "A2: Submit change request" $\lambda_3(e_7) = $ "Finish Processing request" $\lambda_3(e_8) = $ "Cancel Processing"

Fig. 7. Elicitation of Compliance Rules

We observe dependencies between two events, (B_1) processing of personal data, and (B_2) the right to object. We also observe the consequences of applying B_2. For the sake of clarity we assume "no longer process personal data" as the event (B_3) "stop processing". The process for Art. 21 §1 is:

Event in Legislation	Activity/event in Process Model
B_1: Process personal data	A2: Submit change request
B_2: Right to object	A3: Cancel request
B_3: Stop processing	A17: Delete request

Fig. 6. Instantiation of Art 21. GDPR for process in Fig. 3

$$RF_1 = [B_1 : (f, t, f), B_2 : (f, t, f), B_3 : (f, t, f)] \, B_1 \rightarrow \bullet B_2 \parallel B_2 \bullet \rightarrow B_3$$

The reference model requires a mapping from abstract rights such as "right to object" into activities/events in the business process. Further knowledge from implementation guidelines is used to determine the proper mapping for concepts such as "data subject", "controller" or "personal data". Fig. 6 presents a mapping between events Art. 21 §1 and and events in P_{spec} in Fig. 3.

The result of combining the dependencies from laws and business process information gives rise to compliance policies that are specific to the domain. A natural language policy such as *"in case (the subcontractor) submits a change request, (the subcontractor) may cancel the change request. If (the subcontractor) cancels the request, (the project manager) must eventually delete the request"*. These policies are formalized in terms of DCR processes. Fig. 7 present some exemplary policies. We will refer as *compliance rules* to the resulting DCR processes in this stage.

We capture event dependencies by relying on test-driven development [42, 46], which serves as means of validation when introducing constraints in the model. Interestingly, test-driven development aligns with current practices when introducing changes in a law. Scenarios correspond to legal precedents [27]. In common law, a legal precedent corresponds to a previous case that establishes a principle or rule. This principle is then used by judicial bodies when deciding later cases with similar issues or facts. Compliance rules can be tested against scenarios representing legal precedents, where valid rules should at least be able to reach the same decisions from earlier precedents.

The last step in the elicitation of compliance rules is the alignment between the compliance rules and the process model.

Definition 3 (Term Alignment & Target events). *Let* $L, L' \subseteq \mathcal{L}$.

A term alignment is the total function $g : L \to L'$. *If* P, Q *are DCR processes with labels* L, L' *respectively, we say that* g *is a term alignment from* P *to* Q *if* g *is a term alignment from* L *to* L'. *Moreover, we define the* target events *of* g *for* e *in* P *as* $tg(g, e, P) = \lambda^{-1}(g(\lambda(e)))$.

Although term alignment is an arbitrary function defined by the compliance officer, we require for simplicity of the exposition that there is exactly a *single* target event for each event.

Note that more than one g can be defined if the rules in the law applies to more than one set of events in the process. Also, g will typically be non-surjective since the business process might contain activities that do not map to any legal requirement.

Definition 4 (Instances of a Compliance Rule). *Let* $G = \{g_1, \ldots, g_n\}$ *be a set of term alignments from* P *to* Q. *An* instance of P under g in Q, *written* $P{\downarrow}_g Q$ *for* $g \in G$, *is* $P\sigma$ *with labelling* $\lambda'(e) = g(\lambda(e))$, *such that* $\sigma = \{f_1, \ldots, f_n / e_1, \ldots, e_n\}$ *where* $f_i = tg(g, e_i, P)$. *We denote by* $Inst(P, G, Q) = \{P{\downarrow}_g Q \mid g \in G\}$ *the set of all instances of* P *under* G *in* Q.

Example 4.2. The term alignments g_1, g_2 are built from the obvious maps from events in $RC1$ and $RC2$ to events with same labels in P_{spec} in Fig. 3. Two term alignments are required for $RC3$:

Term Alignment	Label Reference Model	Event P_{spec}	Label Process Model
g_3	A2: submit a change request	f_1	A2: submit a change request
	Finish Processing request	f_2	A15: Amend initial contract
	Cancel Processing	f_3	A3: Delete request
g_4	A2: submit a change request	f_1	A2: submit a change request
	Finish Processing request	f_4	A16: Receive reason for change rejection
	Cancel Processing	f_3	A15: Delete request

The set of term alignments for each compliance rule is respectively $G_1 = \{g_1\}$, $G_2 = \{g_2\}$, and $G_3 = \{g_3, g_4\}$. As can be seen from Def. 4, the set of instances substitute the events for the corresponding ones in P_{spec}, so

$Inst(RC3, G_3, P_{spec}) =$

$$\left\{ \begin{array}{l} [f_1 : (\mathsf{f,t,f}), f_2 : (\mathsf{f,f,f}), f_3 : (\mathsf{f,t,f})] \; \lambda_3 f_1 \to + f_2 \parallel f_1 \bullet \xrightarrow{60} f_2 \parallel f_1 \xrightarrow{60} \bullet f_3 \parallel f_3 \to \% f_2, \\ [f_1 : (\mathsf{f,t,f}), f_4 : (\mathsf{f,f,f}), f_3 : (\mathsf{f,t,f})] \; \lambda_3 f_1 \to + f_4 \parallel f_1 \bullet \xrightarrow{60} f_4 \parallel f_1 \xrightarrow{60} \bullet f_3 \parallel f_3 \to \% f_4 \end{array} \right\}$$

Moreover, labels have also changed, being $\lambda_3(f_2) =$ "A15: Amend initial contract with approved change", and $\lambda_3(f_4) =$ "A16: Receive reason for change rejection".

5   Compliance Checking by Refinement

In previous sections we showed how to use DCR processes for the specification of declarative workflows (c.f. Section 3), and the generation of compliance rules (c.f.: Section 4). In this section, we will consider compliance as a particular instance of DCR process refinement [10], between each of the instances generated by a compliance rule, and the process specification.

Abstractly, we take refinement to be just inclusion of languages (trace sets). Given a sequence s, write s_i for the i-th element of s, and $s|_\Sigma$ for the largest sub-sequence s' of s such that $s'_i \in \Sigma$ for $0 < i \le |s|$; e.g, if $s = AABC$ then $s|_{A,C} = AAC$. We lift projection to sets of sequences point-wise.

Definition 5 (Refinement [11]). *Let P, Q be processes. We say that Q is a refinement of P iff $\mathrm{lang}(Q)|_{\mathrm{alph}(P)} \subseteq \mathrm{lang}(P)$. We will write $R \sqsubseteq P$ whenever R is a refinement of P.*

In practice, we will use a notion of refinement by composition, as introduced in [11] to define a "refines" relation between a process and an instance of a compliance rule. To define composition, we need to merge parallel markings and effects. Merge on markings is *partial*, since it is only defined on markings that agree on their overlap:

$$(M_1, e : m) \oplus (M_2, e : m) = (M_1 \oplus M_2), e : m$$
$$(M_1, e : m) \oplus M_2 = (M_1 \oplus M_2), e : m \quad \text{when } e \notin \mathrm{dom}(M_2)$$
$$M_1 \oplus (M_2, e : m) = (M_1 \oplus M_2), e : m \quad \text{when } e \notin \mathrm{dom}(M_1).$$

The *merge of effects δ* is defined as the pointwise union of each of the sets of excluded/included/pending events: $(Exc_1, Inc_1, Pen_1) \oplus (Exc_2, Inc_2, Pen_2) = (Exc_1 \cup Exc_2, Inc_1 \cup Inc_2, Pen_1 \cup Pen_2)$.

Definition 6 (Merge & Marking Compatibility). *The merge of processes $[M]\ \lambda_1 T$ and $[N]\ \lambda_2 U$ is defined if the merge of markings $M \oplus N$ is defined and the labelling functions agree as well, in which case $[M]\ \lambda_1 T \oplus [N]\ \lambda_2 U = [M \oplus N]\ (\lambda_1 \cup \lambda_2)(T \parallel U)$. If the merge of two processes is defined, we say that they are* marking compatible.

We can now define the refines relation between an instance P of a compliance rule and a marking compatible process Q (i.e.: the process model) as follows.

Definition 7 (Refines). *Let P, Q be marking compatible processes. We say that Q refines P iff $P \oplus Q \sqsubseteq P$.*

Note that even though $P \oplus Q = Q \oplus P$, it may still be the case that $P \oplus Q \sqsubseteq P$ but not of $P \oplus Q \not\sqsubseteq Q$.

Definition 8 (Compliance). *Let P, R be DCR processes, and G be a set of term alignments from R to P. We say that P is strongly (resp. weakly) compliant with R under G, written $P \le^s_G R$ (resp. $P \le^w_G R$) if $\forall R_i \in Inst(R, G, P)$, P refines R_i (resp. if $\exists R_i \in Inst(R, G, P)$, P refines R_i).*

That is, take rule R, a process P and a term alignment mapping labels in R to P. (Strong) compliance requires us to 1) generate all instances of R in P and 2) check whether the merge of each instance with the P is compatible (i.e. refines) the instance. Notice that while instances and the process will have their merge defined, P might have different constraints that might affect refinement.

We close this section stating results regarding the decidability and tractability of compliance checking for DCR processes.

Theorem 1 (Compliance checking is decidable). *Let P, R be DCR processes, and let G be a set of term alignments from R to P. Then checking $P \leq_G^w R$ and $P \leq_G^s R$ is decidable.*

Proof. We know from [11] that refinement of DCR processes is known to be decidable; this fact relies on the state space of a DCR process being finite. Time does not change this; see [24] for details. It is therefore sufficient to prove that for any R and G, the set $Inst(R, G, P)$ is finite. By Definition 3, this set is bounded by the size of G and the number of possible substitutions σ. But G is finite by definition, and σ is clearly uniquely determined given a $g \in G$. $\qquad\square$

While generally checking refinement for DCR processes is NP-hard already in the absence of time, [11] showed that the refines relation can be approximated by a static property, the non-invasiveness on the graphs recalled below.

Definition 9 (Non-invasiveness [11]). *Let $P = [M_P] \lambda_P T_P$ and R be marking compatible processes. We say that P is* non-invasive *for R iff*

1. *For every context $C[-]$, such that $T_P = C[e \rightarrow\% f]$ or $T_P = C[e \rightarrow+ f]$, $f \notin \mathsf{fe}(R)$; and*
2. *For every label $l \in \mathsf{alph}(P) \cap \mathsf{alph}(R)$, if $e \in \mathsf{fe}(P)$ is labelled l, then $e \in \mathsf{fe}(R)$.*

.

That is, a process P is non-invasive for a process R if it does not introduce inclusion or exclusion relations on the events of R. We note that this property can straightforwardly be determined in polynomial time.

Lemma 1. *Non-invasiveness is decidable in polynomial time.*

Proof. Follows from Definition 9: an algorithm only needs to check for each inclusion and exclusion relation in P if the target event exists in R.

In [11] it was also shown that non-invasiveness guarantees the refine relation. This can be extended to timed processes.

Theorem 2. *If P is non-invasive for R then P refines R.*

Proof (sketch). We need to extend the proof in [11] to timed processes observing the following: 1) in the case of conflicting deadlines the most strict deadlines always take precedence, 2) therefore after composition of a R and P which share a timed relation with a different deadline, the most strict deadline will be followed, and 3) the composed process will not allow for traces which were forbidden under the strictest deadline. $\qquad\square$

We can apply this result to compliance, and show that a process is compliant with a compliance rule, if it is non-invasive for all term alignments.

Lemma 2. *Let P, R be DCR processes, and G be a set of term alignments from R to P, P is strongly (resp. weakly) compliant with R under G if $\forall R_i \in Inst(R, G, P)$, P is non-invasive for R_i.*

Proof. Follows directly from Definition 8 and Theorem 2.

Correspondingly, this means that compliance checking is a polynomial time task if P is non-invasive for R for all term alignments.

Theorem 3. *If P is non-invasive $\forall R_i \in Inst(R, G, P)$, then checking $P \leq_G^w R$ and $P \leq_G^s R$ is polynomial in R, G, P.*

Proof. Follows directly from Lemmas 1 and 2.

We conclude that through careful construction of the process model, in particular by avoiding the unnecessary introduction of exclusion and inclusion relations on events which may be governed by compliance rules, we can significantly reduce the time complexity of checking the compliance of the process. This comes in contrast to approaches based in annotated imperative business processes, which to a great extent belong to the non-polynomial complexity class [45].

Corollary 1. $P_{spec} \leq_{G_1} RC1$, $P_{spec} \leq_{G_2} RC2$, and $P_{spec} \nleq_{G_3} RC3$

6   Adoption considerations

We describe two uses of the compliance framework: one at the municipality of Syddjurs (DK), and another at the municipality of Genoa (IT). The municipalities selected processes in different domains: the provision of benefits offered to young persons with special needs (DK), and the release of construction permits (IT). They were regulated by different laws, for which reference models of selected articles were created by compliance specialists. The reference models of articles in the Danish Consolidation for Social Services [44] and the Construction Law of the Liguria region [40] vary on size and complexity, ranging from a minimum of 4 events and 12 relations, up to 86 events and 125 relations in a single article. The intended use of the framework varied: while Syddjurs aims at driving a new implementation of their processes, Genoa wanted to verify their current implementations with respect to the law. The work was carried out by case workers within the municipality (DK), and a consultancy house (IT). We collected feedback from users generating reference models of law about their use, benefits and challenges. Both organisations commented that the pairing of laws and models provide them traceability, and allowed lawyers to be part in the co-creation of process implementations using their domain knowledge. Moreover, law-process pairings helped them to understand the legislation, making evident bottlenecks in a process (an activity that for which many other events depend on), and showed them previously unknown paths for achieving goal, while still be in accordance to the law. This aligns with previous studies on comprehension of hybrid artefacts combining texts and declarative models [3]. On their use, both organisations agreed that some laws are too general, and they required implementation guidelines to complete their models. A challenge concerned the writing style of the guidelines: if guidelines have been written in an imperative style, there is a risk of over-constraining the model. When asked about the understandability of the models, they reported that after an initial training, generated models were understandable for compliance specialist, and they could be used as communication artefacts. However, they also reported challenges on the understandability of large models, and suggested the inclusion of abstractions to increase model comprehension. With respect to compliance, the main challenge concerned term alignment, as it currently needs to be hard-coded (no tool support). In some cases, an event in the law had a 1-to-many correspondence with the process. Another suggestion was to extend feedback support to reasons for non-compliance, rather than yes/no outputs.

7   Related Work

We can divide related approaches into four categories:

Model Checking techniques: Most model checking techniques for compliance [19] represent the process as a finite state machine and the laws in a temporal logic. We differ from such approaches in that we use a declarative process language both for defining the process and laws. The reasons are threefold: First, it is known that some of these languages present technical difficulties when modelling permissions, obligations and defeasible (i.e.: exceptional) conditions [16]. These concepts are straightforward in DCR graphs: permissions are encoded as enabled events, obligations are the composition of events using a response relation, and defeasible conditions are represented by mutual exclusion relations between events. The second advantage is the possibility of combining process narratives and visual notations: our work puts forward the recommendations from [36] that states that higher cognitive loads can be achieved when combining process descriptions with graphical notations. This is particularly important in our case, as compliance specialists in local governments do not have prior training in using verification techniques using temporal logics. Finally, verification is efficient: it relies on refinement of transition systems with responses [6,28], and although the complexity process refinement belongs to the category of NP-hard problems [11], we have shown that we can use syntactic restrictions to check compliance in polynomial time.

Compliance Refinement: Seaflows [31] proposes an alignment of compliance requirements into business processes. Laws are modelled in terms of constraints over event traces that can be verified at design-time and monitored at run-time. However, no specific constraint specification language is provided. The work in [41] presents a refinement-based approach where abstract business processes representing laws are incrementally refined until executable processes can be generated. The nature of such abstract business processes is imperative, given in BPMN diagrams, which imposes rigidity on how to achieve certain rights.

Compliance-by-design (CbD): FCL/PCL & Regorous [13,14,17,18,21] treats compliance as a property of the process to execute while not violating the laws in a regulation. Compliance checking requires to 1. identify the deontic effects of the set of modelled regulations, 2. determine the tasks and the obligations in force for each task, and 3. check whether the obligations have been fulfilled or postponed after the execution of a task. While we subscribe to CbD as a methodology, our approach differs in the fact that there is no need to map a declarative language (such as PCL and FCL) into an imperative specification.

Visual Languages for Compliance: The work in [26] introduces eCRG, a visual modelling notation for compliance rules including control flow, interaction, time, data, and resource perspectives. eCRG rules are then paired with event logs to determine whether completed or running process instances are compliant. While our approach is mostly tailored to design stages, [26] focuses on after-the-fact compliance. Finally, the BPMN-Q language [4] provides a visual notation to CTL, and the language describes compliance rules including control and data flow aspects, that are later model-checked against BPMN models. Declare [38] is LTL based and in principle, the compliance checking approach presented here could also be used. However, its LTL-semantics has been shown to present technical difficulties when modelling obligations and defeasible conditions [16].

8   Concluding Remarks

We presented a verification framework for the design of process models that are compliant with regulations. This work exploits the similarities of declarative process languages with logical languages to be able to express models of law. In this manner, both process models and models of law are described in the same declarative notation, and it becomes straightforward to verify whether compliance is achievable. We show that compliance can be checked efficiently in polynomial time, given careful construction of the models.

While the focus of this paper is centred on CbD approaches, it accommodates after-the-fact compliance. In future work we will explore other variants of compliance, such as process conformance based on event logs. Our results rely on the choice of DCR as language for reference and process models, and in this paper we have restricted ourselves to a version of DCR graphs without subprocesses and locality. The decidability results in Thm. 1 will not hold with the inclusion of these operators. We have not needed to consider such constructs in the construction of compliance rules so far, but it would be interesting to revisit them in future work, as well as multi-dimensional compliance policies [39].

Acknowledgments: Thanks to Nicklas Healy from Syddjurs Kommune, and Paolo Gangemi from MAPS Group for their evaluations on the compliance framework. This work has been financially supported by the Innovation Fund Denmark project EcoKnow.org (7050-00034A), and the European Union Marie Sklodowska-Curie grant agreement BehAPI No.778233.

References

1. Aalst, van der, W.: Process mining: discovery, conformance and enhancement of business processes. Springer, Germany (2011). https://doi.org/10.1007/978-3-642-19345-3
2. Agafitei, S.: Usability and understandability studies of business process notations within the construction industry. Master's thesis, IT University of Copenhagen (August 2019)
3. Andaloussi, A.A., Buch-Lorentsen, J., López, H.A., Slaats, T., Weber, B.: Exploring the modeling of declarative processes using a hybrid approach. In: Laender, A.H.F., Pernici, B., Lim, E.P. (eds.) Intl. Conference on Conceptual Modelling (ER). Lecture Notes in Computer Science, vol. 11788. Springer (4 2019)
4. Awad, A., Weidlich, M., Weske, M.: Visually specifying compliance rules and explaining their violations for business processes. Journal of Visual Languages & Computing **22**(1), 30–55 (Feb 2011)
5. Basin, D.A., Debois, S., Hildebrandt, T.T.: In the nick of time: Proactive prevention of obligation violations. In: IEEE 29th Computer Security Foundations Symposium, CSF 2016, Lisbon, Portugal, June 27 - July 1, 2016. pp. 120–134. IEEE Computer Society (2016). https://doi.org/10.1109/CSF.2016.16
6. Carbone, M., Hildebrandt, T.T., Perrone, G., Wasowski, A.: Refinement for transition systems with responses. In: Bauer, S.S., Raclet, J. (eds.) Proceedings Fourth Workshop on Foundations of Interface Technologies, FIT 2012, Tallinn, Estonia, 25th March 2012. EPTCS, vol. 87, pp. 48–55 (2012). https://doi.org/10.4204/EPTCS.87.5
7. Council of European Union: Regulation (eu) 2016/679 of the european parliament and of the council of 27 april 2016 on the protection of natural persons with regard to the processing of personal data and on the free movement of such data. https://publications.europa.eu/s/llVw (May 2016)
8. Danish Parliament (Folketinget): Act on supplementary provisions to the regulation on the protection of natural persons with regard to the processing of personal data and on the free movement of such data (the data protection act). https://www.datatilsynet.dk/media/6894/danish-data-protection-act.pdf (May 2018)
9. Debois, S., Hildebrandt, T., Slaats, T.: Concurrency and asynchrony in declarative workflows. In: Business Process Management (BPM). LNCS, vol. 9253. Springer, Cham (2016)
10. Debois, S., Hildebrandt, T.T., Slaats, T.: Safety, liveness and run-time refinement for modular process-aware information systems with dynamic sub processes. In: Bjørner, N., de Boer, F.S. (eds.) FM. LNCS, vol. 9109, pp. 143–160. Springer (2015). https://doi.org/10.1007/978-3-319-19249-9_10
11. Debois, S., Hildebrandt, T.T., Slaats, T.: Replication, refinement & reachability: complexity in dynamic condition-response graphs. Acta Informatica pp. 1–32 (2017). https://doi.org/10.1007/s00236-017-0303-8
12. Dumas, M., La Rosa, M., Mendling, J., Reijers, H.A., et al.: Fundamentals of business process management, vol. 1. Springer (2013)
13. Governatori, G.: The regorous approach to process compliance. In: Proceedings of the 2015 IEEE 19th International Enterprise Distributed Object Computing Conference Workshops and Demonstrations, EDOCW 2015. pp. 33–40 (2015)
14. Governatori, G., Sadiq, S.: The journey to business process compliance. Handbook of Research on Business Process Modeling pp. 426–454 (2009). https://doi.org/10.4018/978-1-60566-288-6.ch020

15. Governatori, G.: Representing business contracts in ruleml. International Journal of Cooperative Information Systems **14**(02n03), 181–216 (2005)
16. Governatori, G.: Thou shalt is not you will. In: Proceedings of the 15th International Conference on Artificial Intelligence and Law. pp. 63–68. ICAIL '15, ACM, New York, NY, USA (2015). https://doi.org/10.1145/2746090.2746105
17. Governatori, G., Rotolo, A.: How do agents comply with norms? In: Proceedings of the 2009 IEEE/WIC/ACM International Joint Conference on Web Intelligence and Intelligent Agent Technology-Volume 03. pp. 488–491. IEEE Computer Society (2009)
18. Governatori, G., Rotolo, A.: Norm Compliance in Business Process Modeling. In: Semantic Web Rules. pp. 194–209. Lecture Notes in Computer Science, Springer, Berlin, Heidelberg (Oct 2010). https://doi.org/10.1007/978-3-642-16289-3_17
19. Hashmi, M., Governatori, G., Lam, H.P., Wynn, M.T.: Are we done with business process compliance: state of the art and challenges ahead. Knowledge and Information Systems pp. 1–55 (2018)
20. Hashmi, M., Governatori, G., Wynn, M.T.: Normative requirements for business process compliance. In: Australian Symposium on Service Research and Innovation. pp. 100–116. Springer (2013)
21. Hashmi, M., Governatori, G., Wynn, M.T.: Normative requirements for regulatory compliance: An abstract formal framework. Information Systems Frontiers **18**(3), 429–455 (2016)
22. Hildebrandt, T.T., Mukkamala, R.R.: Declarative event-based workflow as distributed dynamic condition response graphs. In: PLACES. vol. 69, pp. 59–73 (2010)
23. Hildebrandt, T.T., Mukkamala, R.R., Slaats, T.: Nested dynamic condition response graphs. In: FSEN. LNCS, vol. 7141, pp. 343–350. Springer (2011)
24. Hildebrandt, T.T., Mukkamala, R.R., Slaats, T., Zanitti, F.: Contracts for cross-organizational workflows as timed dynamic condition response graphs. Journal of Logic and Algebraic Programming **82**(5-7), 164–185 (2013)
25. Hildebrandt, T.T., Slaats, T., López, H.A., Debois, S., Carbone, M.: Declarative choreographies and liveness. In: Formal Techniques for Distributed Objects, Components, and Systems, FORTE. LNCS, Springer, Accepted for Publication (February 2019)
26. Knuplesch, D., Reichert, M.: A visual language for modeling multiple perspectives of business process compliance rules. Software & Systems Modeling **16**(3), 715–736 (2017)
27. Legal Information Institute, Cornell Law School: Stare decisis. https://www.law.cornell.edu/wex/stare_decisis (May 2019)
28. López, H.A.: Foundations of Communication-Centred Programming. Ph.D. thesis, IT University of Copenhagen (2012)
29. López, H.A., Debois, S., Hildebrandt, T.T., Marquard, M.: The process highlighter: From texts to declarative processes and back. In: BPM (Dissertation/Demos/Industry). CEUR Workshop Proceedings, vol. 2196, pp. 66–70. CEUR-WS.org (2018)
30. López, H.A., Marquard, M., Muttenhaler, L., Strømsted, R.: Assisted declarative process creation from natural language descriptions. In: Franke, U., Kornyshova, E., Lê, L.S. (eds.) 23rd IEEE International Enterprise Distributed Object Computing (EDOC). vol. 2325-6605, pp. 96–99. IEEE (10 2019)
31. Ly, L.T., Rinderle-Ma, S., Göser, K., Dadam, P.: On enabling integrated process compliance with semantic constraints in process management systems. Information Systems Frontiers **14**(2), 195–219 (Apr 2012). https://doi.org/10.1007/s10796-009-9185-9

32. Mukkamala, R.R., Hildebrandt, T.T., Slaats, T.: Towards trustworthy adaptive case management with dynamic condition response graphs. In: EDOC. pp. 127–136. IEEE Computer Society (2013)

33. Nekrasaite, V., Parli, A.T., Back, C.O., Slaats, T.: Discovering responsibilities with dynamic condition response graphs. In: Conference on Advanced Information Systems Engineering (CAiSE) (2019)

34. Object Management Group UML Technical Committee: Unified Modeling Language, version 2.5.1 (2017), http://www.omg.org/spec/UML/2.5.1/

35. OMG: Business Process Model and Notation (BPMN), Version 2.0 (January 2011), http://www.omg.org/spec/BPMN/2.0

36. Ottensooser, A., Fekete, A., Reijers, H.A., Mendling, J., Menictas, C.: Making sense of business process descriptions: An experimental comparison of graphical and textual notations. Journal of Systems and Software **85**(3), 596 – 606 (2012). https://doi.org/https://doi.org/10.1016/j.jss.2011.09.023, novel approaches in the design and implementation of systems/software architecture

37. Pesic, M., van der Aalst, W.: A Declarative Approach for Flexible Business Processes Management. Lecture Notes in Computer Science **4103**, 169 (2006)

38. Pesic, M., Schonenberg, H., Aalst, W.M.P.v.d.: DECLARE: Full Support for Loosely-Structured Processes. In: EDOC. pp. 287–287 (Oct 2007). https://doi.org/10.1109/EDOC.2007.14

39. Ramezani, E., Fahland, D., Aalst, W.M.P.v.d.: Where Did I Misbehave? Diagnostic Information in Compliance Checking. In: Business Process Management. pp. 262–278. Lecture Notes in Computer Science, Springer, Berlin, Heidelberg (Sep 2012). https://doi.org/10.1007/978-3-642-32885-5_21

40. Regione Liguria: Legge regionale n.16 del 6 giugno 2008 e successive modifiche (2008), https://www.regione.liguria.it/components/com_publiccompetitions/includes/download.php?id=9145:legge-regionale-n-16-del-6-giugno-2008-e-successive-modifiche.pdf

41. Schleicher, D., Anstett, T., Leymann, F., Schumm, D.: Compliant Business Process Design Using Refinement Layers. In: On the Move to Meaningful Internet Systems: OTM 2010. pp. 114–131. Lecture Notes in Computer Science, Springer, Berlin, Heidelberg (Oct 2010). https://doi.org/10.1007/978-3-642-16934-2_11

42. Slaats, T., Debois, S., Hildebrandt, T.T.: Open to change: A theory for iterative test-driven modelling. In: BPM. Lecture Notes in Computer Science, vol. 11080, pp. 31–47. Springer (2018)

43. Strømsted, R., López, H.A., Debois, S., Marquard, M.: Dynamic evaluation forms using declarative modeling. In: BPM (Dissertation/Demos/Industry). CEUR Workshop Proceedings, vol. 2196, pp. 172–179. CEUR-WS.org (2018)

44. The Danish Ministry of Social Affairs and the Interior: Consolidation Act on Social Services (Sep 2015), http://english.sm.dk/media/14900/consolidation-act-on-social-services.pdf, Executive Order no. 1053 of 8 September 2015; File no. 2015-4958

45. Tosatto, S.C., Governatori, G., van Beest, N.: Checking regulatory compliance: Will we live to see it? In: International Conference on Business Process Management. pp. 119–138. Springer (2019)

46. Zugal, S., Pinggera, J., Weber, B.: Creating declarative process models using test driven modeling suite. In: International Conference on Advanced Information Systems Engineering. pp. 16–32. Springer (2011)

Algorithmic Analysis of Blockchain Efficiency with Communication Delay

Carlos Pinzón, Camilo Rocha, Jorge Finke

Pontificia Universidad Javeriana, Cali, Colombia

Abstract. A blockchain is a distributed hierarchical data structure. Widely-used applications of blockchain include digital currencies such as Bitcoin and Ethereum. This paper proposes an algorithmic approach to analyze the efficiency of a blockchain as a function of the number of blocks and the average synchronization delay. The proposed algorithms consider a random network model that characterizes the growth of a tree of blocks by adhering to a standard protocol. The model is parametric on two probability distribution functions governing block production and communication delay. Both distributions determine the synchronization efficiency of the distributed copies of the blockchain among the so-called workers and, therefore, are key for capturing the overall stochastic growth. Moreover, the algorithms consider scenarios with a fixed or an unbounded number of workers in the network. The main result illustrates how the algorithms can be used to evaluate different types of blockchain designs, e.g., systems in which the average time of block production can match the average time of message broadcasting required for synchronization. In particular, this algorithmic approach provides insight into efficiency criteria for identifying conditions under which increasing block production has a negative impact on the stability of a blockchain. The model and algorithms are agnostic of the blockchain's final use, and they serve as a formal framework for specifying and analyzing a variety of non-functional properties of current and future blockchains.

1   Introduction

A blockchain is a distributed hierarchical data structure that cannot be modified (retroactively) without alteration of all subsequent blocks and the consensus of a majority. It was invented to serve as the public transaction ledger of Bitcoin [22]. Instead relying on a trusted third party, this digital currency is based on the concept of 'proof-of-work', which allows users to execute payments by signing transactions using hashes through a distributed time-stamping service. Resistance to modifications, decentralized consensus, and robustness for supporting cryptocurrency transactions, unleashes the potential of blockchain technology for uses in various industries, including financial services [12,26,3], distributed data models [5], markets [25], government systems [15,23], healthcare [13,1,18], IoT [16], and video games [21].

H. Wehrheim and J. Cabot (Eds.): FASE 2020, LNCS 12076, pp. 400–419, 2020.
https://doi.org/10.1007/978-3-030-45234-6_20

Technically, a blockchain is a distributed append-only data structure comprising a linear collection of blocks, shared among so-called *workers*, also referred often as *miners*. These miners generally represent computational nodes responsible for working on extending the blockchain with new blocks. Since the blockchain is decentralized, each worker possesses a local copy of the blockchain, meaning that two workers can build blocks at the same time on unsynchronized local copies of the blockchain. In the typical peer-to-peer network implementation of blockchain systems, workers adhere to a consensus protocol for inter-node communication and validation of new blocks. Specifically, workers build on top of the largest blockchain. If they encounter two blockchains of equal length, then workers select the chain whose last produced block was first observed. This protocol generally guarantees an effective synchronization mechanism, provided that the task of producing new blocks is hard to achieve in comparison to the time it takes for inter-node communication. The effort of producing a block relative to that of communicating among nodes is known in the literature as 'proof of work'. If several workers extend different versions of the blockchain, the consensus mechanism enables the network to eventually select only one of them, while the others are discarded (including the data they carry) when local copies are synchronized. The synchronization process persistently carries on upon the creation of new blocks.

The scenario of discarding blocks massively, which can be seen as an efficiency issue in a blockchain implementation, is rarely present in "slow" block-producing blockchains. The reason is that the time it takes to produce a new block is long enough for workers to synchronize their local copies of the blockchain. Slow blockchain systems avert workers from wasting resources and time in producing blocks that are likely to be discarded in an upcoming synchronization. In Bitcoin, for example, it takes on average 10 minutes for a block to be produced and only 12.6 seconds to communicate an update [8]. The theoretical fork-rate of Bitcoin in 2013 was approximately 1.78% [8]. However, as the blockchain technology finds new uses, it is being argued that block production needs to be faster [6,7]. Broadly speaking, understanding how speed-ups in block production can negatively impact blockchains, in terms of the number of blocks discarded due to race conditions among the workers, is important for designing new fast and yet efficient blockchains.

This paper introduces a framework to formally study blockchains as a particular class of random networks with emphasis in two key aspects: the speed of block production and the network synchronization delays. As such, it is parametric on the number of workers under consideration (possibly infinite), the probability distribution function that specifies the time for producing new blocks, and the probability distribution function that specifies the communication delay between any pair of randomly selected workers. The model is equipped with probabilistic algorithms to simulate and formally analyze blockchains concurrently producing blocks over a network with varying communication delays. These algorithms focus on the analysis of the continuous process of block production in *fast* and highly distributed systems, in which inter-node communication delays are crucial. The framework enables the study of scenarios with fast block production, in which blocks tend to be discarded at a high rate. In particular, it captures the trade-off between speed and efficiency. Experiments are presented to understand how this trade-off can be analyzed for different scenarios. As fast blockchain systems tend to spread to novel applications, the algorithmic approach provides mathematical tools for specifying, simulating, and analyzing blockchain systems.

It is important to highlight that the proposed model and algorithms are agnostic of the concrete implementation and final use of the blockchain system. For instance, the 'rewards' for mining blocks such as the ones present in the Bitcoin network are not part of the model and are not considered in the analysis algorithms. On the one hand, this sort of features can be seen as particular mechanisms of a blockchain implementation that are not explicitly required for the system to evolve as a blockchain. Thus, including them as part of the framework can narrow its intended aim as a general specification, design, and analysis tool. On the other hand, such features may be abstracted away into the proposed model by tuning the probability distribution functions that are parameters of the model, or by considering a more refined base of choices among the many probability distribution functions at hand for a specific analysis. Therefore, the proposed model and algorithms are general enough to encompass a wide variety of blockchain systems and their analysis.

The contribution of this work is threefold. First, a random network model is introduced (in the spirit of, e.g., Barabasi-Albert [4] and Erdös-Renyi [9]) for specifying blockchains in terms of the speed of block production and communication delays for synchronization among workers. Second, exact and approximation algorithms for the analysis of blockchain efficiency are made available. Third, based on the proposed model and algorithms, empirical observations about the tensions between production speed and synchronization delay are provided.

The remaining sections of the paper are organized as follows. Section 2 summarizes basic notions of proof-of-work blockchains. Sections 3 and 4 introduce the proposed network model and algorithms. Section 5 presents experimental results on the analysis of fast blockchains. Section 6 relates these results to existing research, and draws some concluding remarks and future research directions.

2   An Overview of Proof-of-work Blockchains

This section overviews the concept of proof-of-work distributed blockchain systems and introduces basic definitions, which are illustrated with the help of an example.

A *blockchain* is a distributed hierarchical data structure of blocks that cannot be modified (retroactively) without alteration of all subsequent blocks and the consensus of the network majority. The nodes in the network, called *workers*, use their computational power to generate *blocks* with the goal of extending the blockchain. The adjective 'proof-of-work' comes from the fact that producing a single block for the blockchain tends to be a computationally hard task for the workers, e.g., a partial hash inversion.

Definition 1. *A block is a digital document containing: (i) a digital signature of the worker who produced it; (ii) an easy to verify proof-of-work witness in the form of a nonce; and (iii) a hash pointer to the previous block in the sequence (except for the first block, called the* origin, *that has no previous block and is unique).*

Technical definitions of blockchain as a data structure have been proposed by different authors (see, e.g., [27]). Most of them coincide on it being an immutable, transparent, and decentralized data structure shared by all workers in the network. For the purpose of this paper, it is important to distinguish between the *local* copy, independently owned by each worker, and the abstract *global* blockchain, shared by all workers. The latter holds the complete history of the blockchain.

Definition 2. *The* local blockchain *of a worker w is a non-empty sequence of blocks stored in the local memory of w. The* global blockchain *(or,* blockchain*) is the minimal rooted tree containing all workers' local blockchains as branches.*

Under the assumption that the origin is unique (Definition 1), the (global) blockchain is well-defined for any number of workers present in the network. If there is at least one worker, then the blockchain is non-empty. Definition 2 allows for local blockchains to be either synchronized or unsynchronized. The latter is common in systems with long communication delays or in the presence of anomalous situations (e.g., if a malicious group of workers is holding a fork intentionally). As a consequence, the global blockchain cannot simply be defined as a unique sequence of blocks, but rather as a distributed data structure against which workers are assumed to be partly synchronized to.

Figure 1 presents an example of a blockchain with five workers, where blocks are represented by natural numbers. On the left, the local blockchains are depicted as linked lists; on the right, the corresponding global blockchain is depicted as a rooted tree. Some of the blocks in the rooted tree representation in Figure 1 are labeled with the identifier of a worker, which indicates the position of each worker in the global blockchain. For modeling, the rooted tree representation of a blockchain is preferred. On the one hand, it can reduce the amount of memory needed for storage and, on the other hand, it visually simplifies the inspection of the data structure. Furthermore, storing a global blockchain with m workers containing n unique blocks as a collection of lists requires in the worst-case scenario $O(mn)$ memory (i.e., with perfect synchronization). In contrast, the rooted tree representation of the same blockchain with m workers and n unique blocks requires $O(n)$ memory for the rooted tree (e.g., using parent pointers) and an $O(m)$ map for assigning each worker its position in the tree, totaling $O(n + m)$ memory.

A blockchain tends to achieve synchronization among the workers due to the following reasons. First, workers follow a *standard protocol* in which they are constantly trying to produce new blocks and broadcasting their achievements to the entire network. In the case of cryptocurrencies, for instance, this behavior is motivated by paying a reward. Second, workers can easily verify (i.e., with

$$w_0 : 0 \leftarrow 1 \leftarrow 5 \qquad\qquad 0 \leftarrow 1 \leftarrow 5^{w_0}$$
$$w_1 : 0 \leftarrow 2 \leftarrow 3 \leftarrow 6 \qquad\qquad 2 \leftarrow 3^{w_3} \leftarrow 6^{w_1,w_4}$$
$$w_2 : 0 \leftarrow 2 \leftarrow 4 \qquad\qquad 4^{w_2}$$
$$w_3 : 0 \leftarrow 2 \leftarrow 3$$
$$w_4 : 0 \leftarrow 2 \leftarrow 3 \leftarrow 6$$

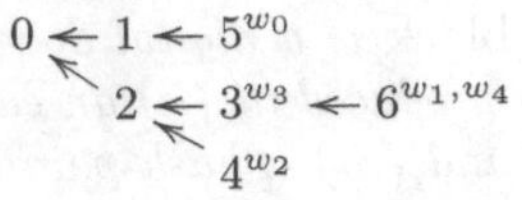

Fig. 1: A blockchain network of five workers with their local blockchains (left) and the corresponding global blockchain (right); blocks are represented by natural numbers. Workers w_0, w_2, and w_3 are not yet synchronized with the longest sequence of blocks.

a fast algorithm) the authenticity of any block. If a malicious worker (i.e., an *attacker*) changes the information of one block, that worker is forced to repeat the extensive proof-of-work process for that block and all its subsequent blocks in the blockchain. Otherwise, its malicious modification cannot become part of the global blockchain. Since repeating the proof-of-work process requires that the attacker spends a prohibitively high amount of resources (e.g., electricity, time, and/or machine rental), such a situation is unlikely to occur. Third, the standard protocol forces any malicious worker to confront the computational power of the whole network, assumed to have mostly honest nodes.

Algorithm 1 presents a definition of the above-mentioned standard protocol, which is followed by each worker in the network. When a worker produces a new block, it is appended to the block it is standing on, moves to it, and notifies the network about its current position and new distance to the root. Upon reception of a notification, a worker compares its current distance to the root with the incoming position. Such a worker switches to the incoming position whenever it represents a greater distance. To illustrate the use of the standard protocol with a simple example, consider the blockchains depicted in figures 1 and 2. In the former, either w_1 or w_4 produced block 6, but the other workers are not yet aware of its existence. In the latter, most of the workers are synchronized with the longest branch, which is typical of a slow blockchain system, and results in a tree with few and short branches.

$$0 \leftarrow 1 \leftarrow 2 \leftarrow 4 \leftarrow 5^{w_7} \leftarrow 6^{w_0,\dots,w_6}$$
$$3$$

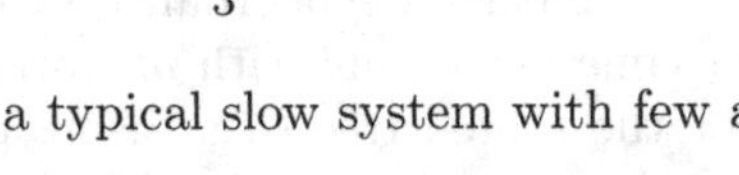

Fig. 2: Example of a typical slow system with few and short branches.

Some final remarks on inter-node communication and implementations for enforcing the standard protocol are due. Note that message communication in the standard protocol is required to include enough information about the position of a worker to be located in the tree. The detail degree of this information depends, generally, on the design of the particular blockchain system. On the one hand,

---

Algorithm 1: Standard protocol for each worker w_i in a blockchain.

```
1  B_i ← [origin]
2  do forever
3  |  do in parallel, stop on first to occur
4  |  |   Task 1: b ← produce a subsequent block for B_i
5  |  |   Task 2: B' ← notification from another worker
6  |  end
7  |  if Task 1 has been completed then
8  |  |   append b to B_i
9  |  |   notify workers in the network about B_i
10 |  else if B' is longer than B_i then
11 |  |   B_i ← B'
12 |  endif
```

---

sending the complete sequence from root to end as part of such a message is an accurate, but also expensive approach, in terms of bandwidth, computation, and time. On the other hand, sending only the last block as part of the message is modest on resources, but can represent a communication conundrum whenever the worker being notified about a new block x is not yet aware of the parent block of x. In contrast to slow systems, this situation may frequently occur in fast systems. The workaround is to use subsequent messages to query the previous blocks of x, as needed, thus extending the average duration of inter-working communication.

3   A Random Network Model for Blockchains

The network model generates a rooted tree representing a global blockchain from a collection of linked lists representing local blockchains (see Definition 2). It consists of three mechanisms, namely, growth, attachment, and broadcast. By growth it is meant that the number of blocks in the network increases by one at each time step. Attachment refers to the fact that new blocks connect to an existing block, while broadcast refers to the fact that the newly connected block is announced to the entire network. The model is parametric in a natural number m specifying the number of workers, and two probability distributions α and β governing the growth, attachment, and broadcast mechanisms. Internally, the growth mechanism creates a new block to be assigned at random among the m workers by taking a sample from α (the time it takes to produce such a block) and broadcasts a synchronization message, whose reception time is sampled from β (the time it takes the other workers to update their local blockchains with the new block).

A network at a given discrete step n is represented as a rooted tree $T_n = (V_n, E_n)$, with nodes $V_n \subseteq \mathbb{N}$ and edges $E_n \subseteq V_n \times V_n$, and a map $w_n : \{0, 1, \ldots, m-1\} \to V_n$. A node $u \in V_n$ represents a block u in the network and an edge $(u, v) \in E_n$ represents a directed edge from block u to its *parent* block v. The assignment $w_n(w)$ denotes the position (i.e., the last block in the local blockchain) of worker w in T_n.

Definition 3. *(Growth model) Let α and β be positive and non-negative probability distributions. The algorithm used in the network model starts with $V_0 = \{b_0\}$, $E_0 = \{\}$ and $w_0(w) = b_0$ for all workers w, being $b_0 = 0$ the root block (origin). At each step $n > 0$, T_n evolves as follows:*

Growth. *A new block b_n (or, simply, n) is created with production time α_n sampled from α. That is, $V_n = V_{n-1} \cup \{n\}$.*

Attachment. *Uniformly at random, a worker $w \in \{0, 1, \ldots, m-1\}$ is chosen for the new block to extend its local blockchain. A new edge appears so that $E_n = E_{n-1} \cup \{(w_{n-1}(w), n)\}$, and w_{n-1} is updated to form w_n with the new assignment $w \mapsto n$, that is, $w_n(w) = n$ and $w_n(z) = w_{n-1}(z)$ for any $z \neq w$.*

Broadcast. *Worker w broadcasts the extension of its local blockchain with the new block n to any other worker z with time $\beta_{n,z}$ sampled from β.*

The rooted tree generated by the model in Definition 3 begins with block 0 (the root) and adds new blocks $n = 1, 2, \ldots$ to some of the workers. At each step $n > 0$, a worker w is selected at random and its local blockchain, $0 \leftarrow \cdots \leftarrow w_{n-1}(w)$, is extended to $0 \leftarrow \cdots \leftarrow w_{n-1}(w) \leftarrow n = w_n(w)$. This results in a concurrent random global behavior, inherent to distributed blockchain systems, not only because the workers are chosen randomly due to the proof-of-work scheme, but also because the communication delays bring some workers out of sync. It is important to note that the steps $n = 0, 1, 2, \ldots$ are logical time steps, not to be confused with the sort of time units sampled from the variables α and β. More precisely, although the model does not mention explicitly the time advancement, it assumes implicitly that workers are synchronized at the corresponding point in the logical future. For instance, if w sends a synchronization message of a newly created block n to another worker z, at the end of logical step n and taking $\beta_{n,z}$ time, the message will be received by z during the logical step $n' \geq n$ that satisfies $\sum_{i=n+1}^{n'} \alpha_i \leq \beta_{n,z} < \sum_{i=n+1}^{n'+1} \alpha_i$.

Another two reasonable assumptions are implicitly made in the model, namely: (i) the computational power of all workers is similar; and (ii) any broadcasting message includes enough information about the new and previous blocks, so that no re-transmission is required to fill block gaps (or, equivalently, that these re-transmission times are included in the delay sampled from β). Assumption (i) justifies why the worker producing the new block is chosen uniformly at random. Thus, instead of simulating the proof-of-work of the workers to know who will produce the next block and at what time, it is enough to select a worker uniformly and take a sample time from α. Assumption (ii) helps in keeping the model description simple. Without Assumption (ii), it would be mandatory to explicitly define how to proceed when a worker is severely out of date and requires several messages to get synchronized.

In practice, the distribution α that governs the time it takes for the network, as a single entity, to produce a block is exponential with mean $\bar{\alpha}$. Since proof-of-work is based on finding a nonce that makes a hashing function fall into a specific set of targets, the process of producing a block is statistically equivalent to waiting for a success in a sequence of Bernoulli trials. Such waiting times would correspond –at first– to a discrete geometric distribution. However, because the time between trials is very small compared to the average time between successes (usually fractions of microseconds against several seconds or minutes), the discrete geometric distribution can be approximated by a continuous exponential distribution function. Finally, note that the choice of the distribution function β that governs the communication delay, and whose mean is denoted by $\bar{\beta}$, heavily depends on the system under consideration and its communication details (e.g., its hardware and protocol).

4   Algorithmic Analysis of Blockchain Efficiency

This section presents an algorithmic approach to the analysis of blockchain efficiency. The algorithms are used to estimate the proportion of valid blocks that are produced during a fixed number of growth steps, based on the network model introduced in Section 3, for blockchains with fixed and unbounded number of workers. In general, although presented in this section for the specific purpose of measuring blockchain efficiency, these algorithms can be easily adapted to compute other metrics of interest, such as the speed of growth of the longest branch, the relation between confirmations of a block and the probability of being valid in the long term, or the average length of forks.

Definition 4. *Let $T_n = (V_n, E_n)$ be a blockchain that satisfies Definition 3. The proportion of valid blocks p_n in T_n is defined as the random variable:*

$$p_n = \frac{\max\{\mathrm{dist}(0, u) \mid u \in V_n\}}{|V_n|}.$$

The proportion of valid blocks p produced for a blockchain (in the limit) is defined as the random variable:

$$p = \lim_{n \to \infty} p_n.$$

Their expected values are denoted with $\bar{p}_n$ and $\bar{p}$, respectively.

Note that $\bar{p}_n$ and $\bar{p}$ are random variables particularly useful to determine some important properties of blockchains. For instance, the probability that a newly produced block becomes valid in the long run is $\bar{p}$. The average rate at which the longest branch grows is approximated by $\bar{p}/\bar{\alpha}$. Moreover, the rate at which invalid blocks are produced is approximately $(1 - \bar{p})/\bar{\alpha}$ and the expected time for a block to receive a confirmation is $\bar{\alpha}/\bar{p}$. Although p_n and p are random for any single simulation, their expected values $\bar{p}_n$ and $\bar{p}$ can be approximated by averaging several Monte Carlo simulations.

The three algorithms presented in the following subsections are sequential and single threaded[1], designed to compute the value of p_n under the standard

---

[1] This would be mitigated by the fact that parallelization may be available for the Monte-Carlo simulations.

protocol (Algorithm 1). They can be used for computing $\bar{p}_n$ and, thus, for approximating $\bar{p}$ for large values of n. The first and second algorithms compute the *exact* value of p_n for a bounded number of workers. While the first algorithm simulates the three mechanisms present in the network model (i.e., growth, attachment, and broadcast –see Definition 3), the second one takes a more time-efficient approach for computing p_n. The third algorithm is a fast approximation algorithm for p_n, useful in the context of an *unbounded* number of workers. It is of special interest for studying the efficiency of large and fast blockchain systems because its time complexity does not depend on the number of workers in the network.

4.1   Network Simulation with a Priority Queue

Algorithm 2 simulates the model with m workers running concurrently under the standard protocol for up to n logical steps. It uses a list B of m block sequences that reflect the local copy of each worker. The sequences are initially limited to the origin block 0 and can be randomly extended during the simulation. Each iteration of the main loop consists of four stages: (i) the wait for a new block to be produced, (ii) the reception of messages within a given waiting period, (iii) the addition of a block to the blockchain of a randomly selected worker, and (iv) the broadcasting of the new position of the selected worker in the shared blockchain to the other workers. The priority queue pq is used to queue messages for future delivery, thus simulating the communication delays. Messages have the form (t', i, B'), where t' represents the arrival time of the message, i is the recipient worker, and B' the content that informs that a (non-specified) worker has the sequence of blocks B'. The statements $\alpha()$ and $\beta()$ draw samples from α and β, respectively.

The overall complexity of Algorithm 2 depends, as usual, on specific assumptions on its concrete implementation. First, let the time complexity to query $\alpha()$ and $\beta()$ be $O(1)$, which is a reasonable assumption in most computer programming languages. Second, note that the following time complexity estimates may be higher depending on their specific implementations (e.g., if a histogram is used instead of a continuous function for sampling these variables). In particular, consider two implementation variants. For both variants, the average length of the priority queue with arbitrarily large n is expected to be $O(m)$, more precisely, $m\bar{\beta}/\bar{\alpha}$. Consider a scenario in which the statement $B_i \leftarrow B'$ is implemented by creating a copy in $O(n)$ time and the append statement is $O(1)$ time. The overall time complexity of the algorithm is $O(mn^2)$. Now consider a scenario in which $B_i \leftarrow B'$ merely copies the list reference in $O(1)$ time and the append statement creates a copy in $O(n)$ time. For the case where $n \gg m$, under the assumption that the priority queue has log-time insertion and removal, the time complexity is brought down to $O(n^2)$. In either case, the spatial complexity is $O(mn)$.

A key advantage of Algorithm 2 is that with a slight modification it can return the blockchain s instead of the proportion p_n, which enables a richer analysis in the form of additional metrics different than p. For example, assume

---

Algorithm 2: Simulation of m workers using a priority queue.

```
 1  t ← 0
 2  B ← [ [0], [0], ..., [0] ]   (m block sequences, 0 is the origin)
 3  pq ← empty priority queue
 4  for k ← 1, ..., n − 1 do
 5      t ← t + α()
 6      for (t', i, B') ∈ pq with t' < t  do   (receive notifications)
 7          pop (t', i, B') from pq
 8          if B' is longer than B_i then B_i ← B' endif
 9      end
10      j ← random_worker()   (block producer)
11      append a new block (k) to B_j
12      for i ∈ {0, ..., m − 1} \ {j} do   (publish notifications)
13          push (t + β(), i, B_j) to pq
14      end
15  end
16  s ← arg max |s|   (longest sequence)
        s∈B
17  return |s|/n
```

---

that I denotes the random variable that describes the quantity of invalid blocks that are created between consecutive blocks. The expected value $E[I]$ can be estimated from $\bar{p}$ as $E[I] \approx (1 - \bar{p})/\bar{\alpha}$. Building a complete blockchain can be used to estimate not only $E[I]$, but also a complete histogram of I and various properties it may possess.

4.2   A Faster Simulation Algorithm

Algorithm 3: Simulation of m workers using a matrix d

```
 1  t_0, h_0, z_0 ← 0, 1, 0
 2  d_0 ← ⟨0, 0, ..., 0⟩   (m elements)
 3  for k ← 1, ..., n − 1 do
 4      j ← random_worker()
 5      t_k ← t_{k−1} + α()
 6      h_k ← 1 + max {h_i | i < k ∧ t_i + d_{i,j} < t_k}   (Algorithm 4)
 7      z_k ← max(z_{k−1}, h_k)
 8      d_k ← ⟨β(), ..., β(), 0, β(), ..., β()⟩
                      ⎵⎵⎵⎵⎵⎵⎵⎵⎵⎵
                        j'th position
 9  end
10  return z_{n−1}
```

Algorithm 3 is a faster alternative to Algorithm 2. It uses a different encoding for the collection of local blockchains. In particular, Algorithm 3 stores the length of the blockchains instead of the sequences themselves. Thereby, it suppresses the need for a priority queue. Algorithm 4 offers an optimized routine that can be called from Algorithm 3.

Algorithm 4: Fast computation of h_k given t_i, z_i, h_i and d_i for all $i < k$

---

1 $x, i \leftarrow 1, k - 1$
2 **while** $i \geq 0$ and $x < z_i$ **do**
3   **if** $t_i \leq t_k - d_{i,j}$ and $h_i > x$ **then**
4 $x = h_i$
5   **endif**
6 $i \leftarrow i - 1$
7 **end**
8 **return** $1 + x$ (compute $h_k := 1 + \max \{h_i \mid i < k \wedge t_i + d_{i,j} < t_k\} \cup \{1\}$)

Let t_k represent the (absolute) time at which block k is created, h_k the length of the local blockchain after being extended with block k, and z_k the cumulative maximum given by

$$z_k := \max \{h_i \mid i \leq k\}.$$

The spatial complexity of Algorithm 3 is $O(mn)$ due to the computation of matrix d and its time complexity is $O(nm + n^2)$ when Algorithm 4 is not used. Note that there are n iterations, each requiring $O(n)$ and $O(m)$ time for computing h_k and d_k, respectively. However, if Algorithm 4 is used for computing h_k, the average overall complexity is reduced. In the worst-case scenario, the complexity of Algorithm 4 is $O(k)$. However, the experimental evaluations suggest an average below $O(\bar{\beta}/\bar{\alpha})$ (constant with respect to k). Thus, the average runtime complexity of Algorithm 3 is bounded by $O\left(nm + \min\{n^2, n + n\bar{\beta}/\bar{\alpha}\}\right)$, and this corresponds to $O(nm)$, unless the blockchain system is extremely fast ($\bar{\beta} \gg \bar{\alpha}$).

4.3 An Approximation Algorithm for Unbounded Number of Workers

Algorithms 2 and 3 compute the value of p_n for a *fixed* number m of workers. Both algorithms can be used to compute p_n for different values of m. However, the time complexity of these two algorithms heavily depends on the value of m, which presents a practical limitation when faced with the task of analyzing large blockchain systems. This section introduces an algorithm for approximating p_n for an unbounded number of workers. It also presents formal observations that support the proposed approximation.

Recall that p_n can be used as a measure of efficiency in terms of the proportion of valid blocks that have been produced up to step n in the blockchain

$T_n = (V_n, E_n)$. Formally:

$$p_n = \frac{\max\{\text{dist}(0, u) \mid u \in V_n\}}{|V_n|}.$$

This definition assumes a fixed number of workers. That is, p_n can be written as $p_{m,n}$ to represent the proportion of valid blocks in T_n *with* m workers. For the analysis of large blockchains, the challenge is to find an efficient way to estimate $p_{m,n}$ for large values of m and n. In other words, to find an efficient algorithm for approximating the random variables p_n^* and p^* defined as:

$$p_n^* = \lim_{m \to \infty} p_{m,n} \qquad \text{and} \qquad p^* = \lim_{n \to \infty} p_n^* = \lim_{m,n \to \infty} p_{m,n}.$$

The proposed approach modifies Algorithm 3 by suppressing the matrix d. The idea is to replace the need for computing $d_{i,j}$ by an approximation based on the random variable β and the length of the blockchain h_k in each iteration of the main loop. Note that the first row can be assumed to be 0 wherever it appears because $d_{0,j} = 0$ for all j. For the remaining rows, an approximation is introduced by observing that if an element X_m is chosen at random from the matrix d of size $(n-1) \times m$ (i.e., matrix d without the first row), then the cumulative distribution function of X_m is given by

$$P(X_m \leq r) = \begin{cases} 0 & , r < 0 \\ \frac{1}{m} + \frac{m-1}{m} P(\beta() \leq r) & , r \geq 0, \end{cases}$$

where $\beta()$ is a sample from β. This is because the elements X_m of d are either samples from β, whose domain is $\mathbb{R}_{\geq 0}$, or 0 with a probability of $1/m$ since there is one zero per row. Therefore, given that the following functional limit converges uniformly (see Theorem 1 below),

$$\lim_{m \to \infty} \left(r \overset{f_m}{\mapsto} P(X_m \leq r) \right) = \left(r \overset{f}{\mapsto} P(\beta() \leq r) \right),$$

each $d_{i,j}$ can be approximated by directly sampling the distribution β. As a result, Algorithm 4 can be used for computing h_k by replacing $d_{i,j}$ with $\beta()$.

Theorem 1. *Let* $f_k(r) := P(X_k \leq r)$ *and* $g(r) := P(\beta() \leq r)$. *The functional sequence* $\{f_k\}_{k=1}^{\infty}$ *converges uniformly to* g.

Proof. Let $\epsilon > 0$. Define $n := \lceil \frac{1}{2\epsilon} \rceil$ and let k be any integer $k > n$. Then

$$\sup |f_k - g| = \sup \left\{ \left| \frac{1}{k} + \left(\frac{k-1}{k} - 1 \right) P(\beta() \leq r) \right| : r \geq 0 \right\}$$

$$\leq \frac{1}{k} + \frac{1}{k} \sup \{ P(\beta() \leq r) : r \geq 0 \}$$

$$= \frac{1}{k} + \frac{1}{k}$$

$$< \frac{2}{n} \leq \epsilon.$$

$\square$

Using Theorem 1, the need for the bookkeeping matrix d and the selection of a random worker j are discarded from Algorithm 3, resulting in Algorithm 5. The proposed algorithm computes p_n^*, an approximation of $\lim_{m\to\infty} p_{m,n}$ in which the matrix entries $d_{i,j}$ are replaced by samples from β, each time they are needed, thus ignoring the arguably negligible hysteresis effects.

Algorithm 5: Approximation for $\lim_{m\to\infty} p_{m,n}$ simulation

---

1 $t_0, h_0, z_0 \leftarrow 0, 0, 0$
2 **for** $k \leftarrow 1, ..., n-1$ **do**
3       $t_k \leftarrow t_{k-1} + \alpha()$
4       $h_k \leftarrow 1 + \max\{h_i \mid i < k \wedge t_i + \beta() < t_k\} \cup \{1\}$ (Algorithm 4*)
5       $z_k \leftarrow \max(z_{k-1}, h_k)$
6 **end**
7 **return** z_{n-1}
   Algorithm 4* stands for Algorithm 4 with $\beta()$ instead of $d_{i,j}$ (approximation)

The time complexity of Algorithm 5 implemented by using Algorithm 4 with $\beta()$ instead of $d_{i,j}$ is $O(n^2)$ and its space complexity is $O(n)$. If the pruning algorithm is used, the time complexity drops below $O(n + n\bar{\beta}/\bar{\alpha})$ according to experimentation. This complexity can be considered $O(n)$ as long as $\bar{\beta} \not\gg \bar{\alpha}$.

5   Empirical Evaluation of Blockchain Efficiency

This section presents an experimental evaluation of blockchain efficiency in terms of the proportion of valid blocks produced by the workers for the global blockchain. The model in Section 3 is used as the mathematical framework, while the algorithms in Section 4 are used for experimental evaluation on that framework. The main claim is that, under certain conditions, the efficiency of a blockchain can be expressed as a ratio between $\bar{\alpha}$ and $\bar{\beta}$. Experimental evaluations provide evidence on why Algorithm 5 –the approximation algorithm for computing the proportion of valid blocks in a blockchain system with an unbounded number of workers– is an accurate tool for computing the measure of efficiency p^*.

Note that the speed of a blockchain can be characterized by the relationship between the expected values of α and β.

Definition 5. *Let α and β be the distributions according to Definition 3. A blockchain is classified as:*

- slow *if $\bar{\alpha} \gg \bar{\beta}$,*
- chaotic *if $\bar{\alpha} \ll \bar{\beta}$, and*
- fast *if $\bar{\alpha} \approx \bar{\beta}$.*

Definition 5 captures the intuition about the behavior of a global blockchain in terms of how alike are the times required for producing a block and for local block synchronization. Note that the Bitcoin implementation is classified as a slow blockchain system because the time between the creation of two consecutive blocks is much larger than the time it takes for local blockchains to synchronize. In chaotic blockchains, a dwarfing synchronization time means that basically no (or relatively little) synchronization is possible, resulting in a blockchain in which rarely any block would be part of "the" valid chain of blocks. A fast blockchain, however, is one in which both the times for producing a block and broadcasting a message are similar. The two-fold goal of this section is first, to analyze the behavior of $\bar{p}^*$ for the three classes of blockchains, and second, to understand how the trade-off between production speed and communication time affects the efficiency of the data structure by means of a formula.

In favor of readability, the experiments presented next identify algorithms 3 and 5 as A_m and A_∞, respectively. Furthermore, the claims and experiments assume that the distribution α is exponential, which holds true for proof-of-work systems.

Claim 1 *Unless the system is chaotic, the hysteresis effect of the matrix entries $d_{i,j}$ in A_m is negligible. Moreover, $\lim_{m\to\infty} A_m(n) = A_\infty(n)$.*

Note that Theorem 1 implies that if the hysteresis effect of the random variables $d_{i,j}$ is negligible, then Algorithm 5 is a good enough approximation of Algorithm 3. However, it does not prove that this assertion holds in general. Experimental evaluation suggests that this is indeed the case, as stated in Claim 1.

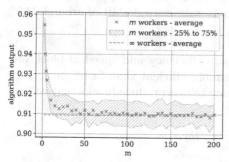

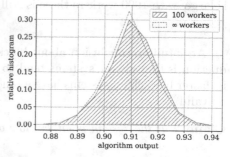

(a) Evolution of A_m to A_∞ as m grows. Simulation runs contain at least 100 samples per point.

(b) High similarity between the p.d.f. of A_{100} and A_∞. Simulation runs contain at least 1000 samples in total.

Fig. 3: Algorithmic simulation of $n = 1000$ blocks with $\bar{\alpha} = 1$, $\bar{\beta} = 0.1$, and β exponential. The number of samples and the size of the blockchain n are chosen such that the execution time on a standard cpu lies below a few seconds.

Figure 3 summarizes the average output of A_m and the region that contains half of these outputs, for several values of m. All outputs seem to approach that of A_∞, not only for the expected value (Figure 3.(a)), but also in terms of the generated p.d.f. (Figure 3.(b)). Similar results were obtained with several distribution functions for β. In particular, the exponential, chi-squared, and gamma probability distribution functions were used (with $k \in \{1, 1.5, 2, 3, 5, 10\}$), all with different mean values. The resulting plots are similar to the ones depicted in Figure 3.

As the quotient $\bar{\beta}/\bar{\alpha}$ grows beyond 1, the convergence of A_m becomes much slower and the approximation error is noticeable. An example is depicted in Figure 4, where a blockchain system produces on average 10 blocks during the transmission of a synchronization message (i.e., the system is classified as chaotic). Even after considering 1000 workers, the shape of the p.d.f. is shifted considerably. The error can be due to: (i) the hysteresis effect that is ignored by A_∞; or (ii) the slow rate of convergence. In any case, the output of this class of systems is very low, making them unstable and useless in practice.

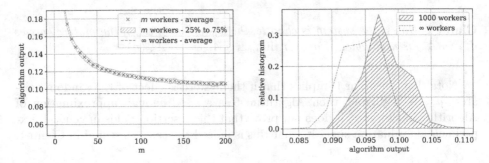

Fig. 4: For chaotic systems, the convergence is slow and the approximation error is large: with 1000 workers there is still an average output shift of around 0.005.

An intuitive conclusion about blockchain efficiency and speed of block production is that slower systems tend to be more efficient than faster ones. That is, faster blockchain systems have a tendency to overproduce blocks that will not be valid.

Claim 2 *If the system is either slow or fast, then*

$$\bar{p}^* = \frac{\bar{\alpha}}{\bar{\alpha} + \bar{\beta}}.$$

Figure 5 presents an experimental evaluation of the proportion of valid blocks in a blockchain in terms of the ratio $\bar{\beta}/\bar{\alpha}$. For the left and right plots, the horizontal axis represents how fast blocks are produced in comparison with how slow synchronization is achieved. If the system is slow, then efficiency is high because most newly produced blocks tend to be valid. If the system is fast, however, then efficiency is balanced because the newly produced blocks are likely to either become valid or invalid with equal likelihood. Finally, note that for fast and chaotic blockchains, say for $10^{-1} \leq \bar{\beta}/\bar{\alpha}$, there is still a region in which efficiency is arguably high. As a matter of fact, even if synchronization of local blockchains takes on average a tenth of the time it takes to produce a block, in general, the proportion of blocks that become valid is almost 90%. In practice, this observation can bridge the gap between the current use of blockchains as slow systems and the need for faster blockchains.

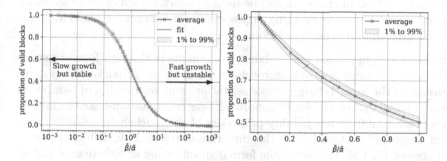

Fig. 5: Effect of speed on the proportion of valid blocks.

6 Related Work and Concluding Remarks

A comprehensive account of the vast literature on complex networks is beyond the scope of this work. The aim here is more modest, namely, the focus is on related work proposing and using formal and semi-formal algorithmic approaches to evaluate properties of blockchain systems. There are a number of recent studies that focus on the analysis of blockchain properties with respect to meta-parameters. Some of them are based on network and node simulators. Other studies conceptualize different metrics and models that aim to reduce the analysis to the essential parts of the system.

In [10], A. Gervais et al. introduce a quantitative framework to analyze the security and performance implications of various consensus and network parameters of proof-of-work blockchains. They devise optimal adversarial strategies for several attack scenarios while taking into account network propagation. Ultimately, their approach can be used to compare the tradeoffs between blockchain performance and its security provisions. Y. Aoki et al. [2] propose SimBlock, a blockchain network simulator in which blocks, nodes, and the network itself can be instantiated by using a comprehensive collection of parameters, including the propagation delay between nodes. Towards a similar goal, J. Kreku et al. [19] show how to use the Absolut simulation tool [28] for prototyping blockchains in different environments and finding optimal performance, given some parameters, in constrained platforms such as Raspberry Pi and Nvidia Jetson Tk1.

R. Zhang and B. Preneel [29] introduce a multi-metric evaluation framework to quantitatively analyze proof-of-work protocols. Their systemic security analysis in seven of the most representative and influential alternative blockchain designs concludes that none of them outperforms the so-called Nakamoto Consensus in terms of either the chain quality or attack resistance. All these efforts have in common that simulation-based analysis is used to understand non-functional requirements of blockchain designs such as performance and security, up to a high degree of confidence. However, in most of the cases the concluding results are tied to a specific implementation of the blockchain architecture. The model and algorithms presented in this work can be used to analyze each of these scenarios in a more abstract fashion by using appropriate parameters for simulating the blockchain growth and synchronization.

An alternative approach for studying blockchains is through formal semantics. G. Rosu [24] takes a novel approach to the analysis of blockchain systems by focusing on the formal design, implementation, and verification of blockchain languages and virtual machines. His approach uses continuation-based formal semantics to later analyze reachability properties of the blockchain evolution with different degrees of abstraction. In this direction of research, E. Hildenbrandt et al. [14] present KEVM, an executable formal specification of Ethereum's virtual machine that can be used for rapid prototyping, as well as a formal interpreter of Ethereum's programming languages. C. Kaligotla and C. Macal [17] present an agent-based model of a blockchain systems in which the behavior and decisions made by agents are detailed. They are able to implement a generalized simulation and a measure of blockchain efficiency from an agent choice and energy cost perspective. Finally, J. Göbel et al. [11] use Markov models to establish that some attack strategies, such as selfish-mine, causes the rate of production of orphan blocks to increase. The research presented in this manuscript uses random networks to model the behavior of blockchain systems. As future work, the proposed model and algorithms can be specified in a rewrite-based framework such as rewriting logic [20], so that the rule-based approach in [24,14] and the agent-based approach in [17] can both be extended to the automatic analysis of (probabilistic) temporal properties of blockchains. Moreover, as it is usual in a random network approach, topological properties of blockchain systems can be studied with the help of the model proposed in this manuscript.

In general, this paper differs from the above studies in the following aspects. The proposed analysis is not based on an explicit low-level simulation of a network or protocol; it does not explore the behavior of blockchain systems under the presence attackers. Instead, this work simulates the behavior of blockchain efficiency from a meta-level perspective and investigates the strength of the system with respect to shortcomings inherent in its design. Therefore, the proposed analysis differs from [10,2,19,29] and is rather closely related to studies which consider the core properties of blockchain systems prior to attacks [17,29]. The bounds for the meta-parameters are more conservative and less secure, compared to scenarios in which the presence of attackers is taken into account. Finally, with respect to studying blockchains through formal semantics, the proposed analysis is able to consider an artificial but convenient scenario of having an infinite number of concurrent workers. Formal semantics, as well as other related simulation tools, cannot currently handle such scenarios.

This paper presented a network model for blockchains and showed how the proposed simulation algorithms can be used to analyze the efficiency (in terms of production of valid blocks) of blockchain systems. The model is parametric on: (i) the number of workers (or nodes); and (ii) two probability distributions governing the time it takes to produce a new block and the time it takes the workers to synchronize their local copies of the blockchain. The simulation algorithms are probabilistic in nature and can be used to compute the expected value of several metrics of interest, both for a fixed and unbounded number of workers, via Monte Carlo simulations. It is proven, under reasonable assumptions, that the fast approximation algorithm for an unbounded number of workers yields accurate estimates in relation to the other two exact (but much slower) algorithms. Claims –supported by extensive experimentation– have been proposed, including a formula to measure the proportion of valid blocks produced in a blockchain in terms of the two probability distributions of the model. The model, algorithms, and experiments provide insights and useful mathematical tools for specifying, simulating, and analyzing the design of fast blockchain systems in the years to come.

Future work on the analytic analysis of the experimental observations contributed in this work should be pursued. This includes proving the two claims in Section 5. First, that hysteresis effects are negligible unless the system is extremely fast. Second, that the expected proportion of valid blocks in a blockchain system is given by $\bar{\alpha}/(\bar{\alpha} + \bar{\beta})$, being $\bar{\alpha}$ and $\bar{\beta}$ the mean of the probability distributions governing block production and communication times, respectively. Furthermore, the generalization of the claims to non-proof-of-work schemes, i.e. to different probability distribution functions for specifying the time it takes to produce a new block may also be considered. Finally, the study of different forms of attack on blockchain systems can be pursued with the help of the proposed model.

Acknowledgments. This research was supported by the Center of Excellence and Appropriation in Big Data and Data Analytics (CAOBA), founded by the Ministry of Information Technologies and Telecommunications of Colombia (MinTIC) and the Colombian Administrative Department of Science, Technology and Innovation (COLCIENCIAS) under grant no. FP44842-anex46-2015.

References

1. Z. Alhadhrami, S. Alghfeli, M. Alghfeli, J. A. Abedlla, and K. Shuaib. Introducing blockchains for healthcare. In *International Conference on Electrical and Computing Technologies and Applications (ICECTA)*, pages 1–4. IEEE, 2017.
2. Y. Aoki, K. Otsuki, T. Kaneko, R. Banno, and K. Shudo. Simblock: A blockchain network simulator. In *IEEE INFOCOM 2019-IEEE Conference on Computer Communications Workshops (INFOCOM WKSHPS)*, pages 325–329. IEEE, 2019.

3. T. Aste, P. Tasca, and T. Di Matteo. Blockchain technologies: The foreseeable impact on society and industry. *Computer*, 50(9):18–28, 2017.
4. A.-L. Barabasi and R. Albert. Emergence of scaling in random networks. *Science*, 286(5439):509–512, 1999.
5. T. Bui and T. Aura. Application of public ledgers to revocation in distributed access control. In *International Conference on Information and Communications Security*, pages 781–792. Springer, 2018.
6. U. W. Chohan. The limits to blockchain? Scaling vs. Decentralization. 2019.
7. K. Croman, C. Decker, I. Eyal, A. E. Gencer, A. Juels, A. Kosba, A. Miller, P. Saxena, E. Shi, E. G. Sirer, et al. On scaling decentralized blockchains. In *International Conference on Financial Cryptography and Data Security*, pages 106–125. Springer, 2016.
8. C. Decker and R. Wattenhofer. Information propagation in the Bitcoin network. In *P2P*, pages 1–10. IEEE, 2013.
9. P. Erdö and A. Rényi. On random graphs. *Publicationes Mathematicae*, 6:290–297, 1959.
10. A. Gervais, G. O. Karame, K. Wüst, V. Glykantzis, H. Ritzdorf, and S. Capkun. On the security and performance of proof of work blockchains. In *SIGSAC conference on computer and communications security*, pages 3–16. ACM, 2016.
11. J. Göbel, H. P. Keeler, A. E. Krzesinski, and P. G. Taylor. Bitcoin blockchain dynamics: The selfish-mine strategy in the presence of propagation delay. *Performance Evaluation*, 104:23–41, 2016.
12. Y. Guo and C. Liang. Blockchain application and outlook in the banking industry. *Financial Innovation*, 2(1):24, 2016.
13. O. Gutiérrez, J. J. Saavedra, P. M. Wightman, and A. Salazar. Bc-med: Plataforma de registros médicos electrónicos sobre tecnología blockchain. In *Colombian Conference on Communications and Computing (COLCOM)*, pages 1–6. IEEE, 2018.
14. E. Hildenbrandt, M. Saxena, N. Rodrigues, X. Zhu, P. Daian, D. Guth, B. Moore, D. Park, Y. Zhang, A. Stefanescu, et al. KEVM: A complete formal semantics of the Ethereum virtual machine. In *Computer Security Foundations Symposium (CSF)*, pages 204–217. IEEE, 2018.
15. H. Hou. The application of blockchain technology in E-government in China. In *International Conference on Computer Communication and Networks (ICCCN)*, pages 1–4. IEEE, 2017.
16. S. Huh, S. Cho, and S. Kim. Managing IoT devices using blockchain platform. In *International Conference on Advanced Communication Technology (ICACT)*, pages 464–467. IEEE, 2017.
17. C. Kaligotla and C. M. Macal. A generalized agent based framework for modeling a blockchain system. In *2018 Winter Simulation Conference (WSC)*, pages 1001–1012. IEEE, 2018.
18. E. Karafiloski and A. Mishev. Blockchain solutions for big data challenges: A literature review. In *17th International Conference on Smart Technologies*, pages 763–768. IEEE, 2017.
19. J. Kreku, V. A. Vallivaara, K. Halunen, J. Suomalainen, M. Ramachandran, V. Muñoz, V. Kantere, G. Wills, and R. Walters. Evaluating the efficiency of blockchains in iot with simulations. In *IoTBDS*, pages 216–223, 2017.
20. J. Meseguer. Conditional rewriting logic as a unified model of concurrency. *Theoretical Computer Science*, 96:73–155, 1992.
21. S. Munir and M. S. I. Baig. Challenges and security aspects of blockchain based on online multiplayer games, 2019.

22. S. Nakamoto et al. Bitcoin: A peer-to-peer electronic cash system. 2008.
23. S. Ølnes, J. Ubacht, and M. Janssen. Blockchain in government: Benefits and implications of distributed ledger technology for information sharing, 2017.
24. G. Rosu. Formal design, implementation and verification of blockchain languages. In *International Conference on Formal Structures for Computation and Deduction*, 2018.
25. J. J. Sikorski, J. Haughton, and M. Kraft. Blockchain technology in the chemical industry: Machine-to-machine electricity market. *Applied Energy*, 195:234–246, 2017.
26. A. Tapscott and D. Tapscott. How blockchain is changing finance. *Harvard Business Review*, 1(9):2–5, 2017.
27. H. Treiblmaier. Toward more rigorous blockchain research: Recommendations for writing blockchain case studies. *Frontiers in Blockchain*, 2:3, 2019.
28. J. Vatjus-Anttila, J. Kreku, J. Korpi, S. Khan, J. Saastamoinen, and K. Tiensyrjä. Early-phase performance exploration of embedded systems with ABSOLUT framework. *Journal of Systems Architecture*, 59(10, Part D):1128 – 1143, 2013.
29. R. Zhang and B. Preneel. Lay down the common metrics: Evaluating proof-of-work consensus protocols' security. In *Symposium on Security and Privacy (SP)*, pages 175–192. IEEE, 2019.

Holistic Specifications for Robust Programs

Sophia Drossopoulou[1][3] , James Noble[2] ,
Julian Mackay[2] , and Susan Eisenbach[1]

[1] Imperial College London, United Kingdom
{scd,susan}@imperial.ac.uk
[2] Victoria University of Wellington, New Zealand
{julian.mackay,kjx}@ecs.vuw.ac.nz
[3] Microsoft Research Cambridge

Abstract Functional specifications describe what program components *can* do: the *sufficient* conditions to invoke components' operations. They allow us to reason about the use of components in a *closed world* setting, where components interact with known client code, and where the client code must establish the appropriate pre-conditions before calling into a component.

Sufficient conditions are not enough to reason about the use of components in an *open world* setting, where components interact with external code, possibly of unknown provenance, and where components may evolve over time. In this open world setting, we must also consider the *necessary* conditions, *i.e.* what are the conditions without which an effect will *not* happen.

In this paper we propose the $Chainmail$ specification language for writing *holistic* specifications that focus on necessary conditions (as well as sufficient conditions). We give a formal semantics for $Chainmail$, and discuss several examples. The core of $Chainmail$ has been mechanised in the Coq proof assistant.

1 Introduction

Software guards our secrets, our money, our intellectual property, our reputation [47]. We entrust personal and corporate information to software which works in an *open* world, where it interacts with third party software of unknown provenance, possibly buggy and potentially malicious.

This means we need our software to be *robust*: to behave correctly even if used by erroneous or malicious third parties. We expect that our bank will only make payments from our account if instructed by us, or by somebody we have authorised, that space on a web page given to an advertiser will not be used to obtain access to our bank details [43], or that a concert hall will not book the same seat more than once.

While language mechanisms such as constants, invariants, object capabilities [40], and ownership [14] make it *possible* to write robust programs, they cannot *ensure* that programs are robust. Ensuring robustness is difficult because it means different things for different systems: perhaps that critical operations should only be invoked with the requisite authority; perhaps that sensitive personal information should not be leaked; or perhaps that a resource belonging to one user should not be consumed by another. To ensure robustness, we need ways to specify what robustness means for a particular

H. Wehrheim and J. Cabot (Eds.): FASE 2020, LNCS 12076, pp. 420–440, 2020.
https://doi.org/10.1007/978-3-030-45234-6_21

```
class Safe{                          class Safe{
    field treasure                       field treasure
    field secret                         field secret
    method take(scr){                    method take(scr){
        if (secret==scr) then                ...as version 1...
        {                                }
            t=treasure                   method set(scr){
            treasure = null                  secret=scr  }
            return t }  }            }
}
```

Figure 1. Two Versions of the class `Safe`

program, and ways to demonstrate that the particular program adheres to its specific robustness requirements.

Consider the code snippets from Fig. 1. Objects of class `Safe` hold a `treasure` and a `secret`, and only the holder of the secret can remove the treasure from the safe. We show the code in two versions; both have the same method `take`, and the second version has an additional method `set`. We assume a dynamically typed language (so that our results are applicable to both statically and dynamically typed settings)[4]; that fields are private in the sense of Java (*i.e.* only methods of that class may read or write these fields); and that addresses are unforgeable (so there is no way to guess a secret). A classical Hoare triple describing the behaviour of `take` would be:

(ClassicSpec) $\triangleq$
method take(scr)
PRE: this:Safe
POST: scr=this.secret$_{pre}$ $\longrightarrow$ this.treasure=null
        $\wedge$
        scr$\neq$this.secret$_{pre}$ $\longrightarrow$ $\forall$s:Safe. s.treasure=s.treasure$_{pre}$

(ClassicSpec) expresses that knowledge of the `secret` is *sufficient* to remove the treasure, and that `take` cannot remove the treasure unless the secret is provided. But it cannot preclude that `Safe` – or some other class, for that matter – contains more methods which might make it possible to remove the treasure without knowledge of the secret. This is the problem with the second version of `Safe`: it satisfies (ClassicSpec), but is not robust, as it is possible to overwrite the `secret` of the `Safe` and then use it to remove the treasure. To express robustness requirements, we introduce *holistic specifications*, and require that:

(HolisticSpec) $\triangleq$
$\forall$s.[s : Safe $\wedge$ s.treasure $\neq$ null $\wedge$ will$\langle$ s.treasure = null $\rangle$
        $\longrightarrow$ $\exists$o.[external$\langle$ o $\rangle$ $\wedge$ $\langle$ o access s.secret $\rangle$]]

(HolisticSpec) mandates that for any safe s whose treasure is not null, if some time in the future its treasure were to become null, then at least one external object (*i.e.* an object whose class is not `Safe`) in the current configuration has direct access

---

[4] We do not depend on the additional safety static typing provides, so we assume only a dynamically typed language.

to s's secret. This external object need not have caused the change in s.treasure but it would have (transitively) passed access to the secret which ultimately did cause that change. Both classes in Fig. 1 satisfy (ClassicSpec), but the second version does not satisfy (HolisticSpec).

In this paper we propose $Chainmail$, a specification language to express holistic specifications. The design of $Chainmail$ was guided by the study of a sequence of examples from the object-capability literature and the smart contracts world: the membrane [17], the DOM [20,59], the Mint/Purse [40], the Escrow [18], the DAO [12,15] and ERC20 [61]. As we worked through the examples, we found a small set of language constructs that let us write holistic specifications across a range of different contexts. $Chainmail$ extends traditional program specification languages [31,37] with features which talk about:

Permission: Which objects may have access to which other objects; this is central since access to an object grants access to the functions it provides.
Control: Which objects called functions on other objects; this is useful in identifying the causes of certain effects - eg funds can only be reduced if the owner called a payment function.
Time: What holds some time in the past, the future, and what changes with time,
Space: Which parts of the heap are considered when establishing some property, or when performing program execution; a concept related to, but different from, memory footprints and separation logics,
Viewpoint: Which objects and which configurations are internal to our component, and which are external to it; a concept related to the open world setting.

While many individual features of $Chainmail$ can be found in other work, their power and novelty for specifying open systems lies in their careful combination. The contributions of this paper are:

- the design of the holistic specification language $Chainmail$,
- the semantics of $Chainmail$,
- a Coq mechanisation of the core of $Chainmail$.

The rest of the paper is organised as follows: Section 2 gives an example from the literature which we will use to elucidate key points of $Chainmail$. 3 presents the $Chainmail$ specification language. Section 4 introduces the formal model underlying $Chainmail$, and then section 5 defines the semantics of $Chainmail$'s assertions. Section 6 discusses our design, 7 considers related work, and section 8 concludes. We relegate key points of exemplar problems and various details to appendices which are available at [1].

2   Motivating Example: The Bank

As a motivating example, we consider a simplified banking application taken from the object capabilities literature [41]: Accounts belong to Banks and hold money (balances); with access to two Accounts of the same Bank one can transfer any amount of money from one to the other. This example has the advantage that it requires several objects and classes.

We will not show the code here (see appendix C), but suffice it to say that class `Account` has methods `deposit(src, amt)` and `makeAccount(amt)` (*i.e.* a method called `deposit` with two arguments, and a method called `makeAccount` with one argument). Similarly, `Bank` has method `newAccount(amt)`. Moreover, `deposit` requires that the receiver and first argument (`this` and `src`) are `Account`s and belong to the same bank, that the second argument (`amt`) is a number, and that `src`'s balance is at least `amt`. If this condition holds, then `amt` gets transferred from `src` to the receiver. The function `makeNewAccount` returns a fresh `Account` with the same bank, and transfers `amt` from the receiver `Account` to the new `Account`. Finally, the function `newAccount` when run by a `Bank` creates a new `Account` with corresponding amount of money in it.[5] It is not difficult to give formal specifications of these methods in terms of pre- and post-conditions.

However, what if the bank provided a `steal` method that emptied out every account in the bank into a thief's account? The critical problem is that a bank implementation including a `steal` method could meet the functional specifications of `deposit`, `makeAccount`, and `newAccount`, and still allow the clients' money to be stolen.

One obvious solution would be to adopt a closed-world interpretation of specifications: we interpret functional specifications as *exact* in the sense that only implementations that meet the functional specification exactly, *with no extra methods or behaviour*, are considered as suitable implementations of the functional specification. The problem is that this solution is far too strong: it would for example rule out a bank that during software maintenance was given a new method `count` that simply counted the number of deposits that had taken place, or a method `notify` to enable the bank to occasionally send notifications to its customers.

What we need is some way to permit bank implementations that send notifications to customers, but to forbid implementations of `steal`. The key here is to capture the (implicit) assumptions underlying the design of the banking application. We provide additional specifications that capture those assumptions. The following three informal requirements prevent methods like `steal`:

1. An account's balance can be changed only if a client calls the `deposit` method with the account as the receiver or as an argument.
2. An account's balance can be changed only if a client has access to that particular account.
3. The `Bank/Account` component does not leak access to existing accounts or banks.

Compared with the functional specification we have seen so far, these requirements capture *necessary* rather than *sufficient* conditions: Calling the `deposit` method to gain access to an account is necessary for any change to that account taking place. The function `steal` is inconsistent with requirement (1), as it reduces the balance of an `Account` without calling the function `deposit`. However, requirement (1) is not enough to protect our money. We need (2) to avoid an `Account`'s balance getting

---

[5] Note that our very limited bank specification doesn't even have the concept of an account owner.

modified without access to the particular Account, and (3) to ensure that such accesses are not leaked.

We can express these requirements through $\mathcal{C}hainmail$ assertions. Rather than specifying the behaviour of particular methods when they are called, we write assertions that range across the entire behaviour of the Bank/Account module:

(1) $\triangleq$ ∀a.[a : Account ∧ changes⟨ a.balance ⟩ $\longrightarrow$
         ∃o.[⟨ o calls a.deposit(_,_) ⟩ ∨ ⟨ o calls _.deposit(a,_) ⟩]]

(2) $\triangleq$ ∀a.∀S : Set. [a : Account ∧ ⟨ will⟨ changes⟨ a.balance ⟩⟩ in S ⟩
         $\longrightarrow$ ∃o. [o ∈ S ∧ external⟨ o ⟩ ∧ ⟨ o access a ⟩]]

(3) $\triangleq$ ∀a.∀S : Set. [a : Account ∧
         ⟨ will⟨ ∃o.[external⟨ o ⟩ ∧ ⟨ o access a ⟩]⟩⟩ in S ⟩
         $\longrightarrow$ ∃o'. [o' ∈ S ∧ external⟨ o' ⟩ ∧ ⟨ o' access a ⟩]]

In the above and throughout the paper, we use an underscore (_) to indicate an existentially bound variable whose value is of no interest.

Assertion (1) says that if an account's balance changes (changes⟨ a.balance ⟩), then there must be some client object o that called the deposit method with a as a receiver or as an argument (⟨ o calls _.deposit(_) ⟩).

Assertion (2) similarly constrains any possible change to an account's balance. If at some future point the balance changes (will⟨ changes⟨ ... ⟩ ⟩), and if this future change is observed with the state restricted to the objects from S (*i.e.* ⟨ ... in S ⟩), then at least one of these objects (o ∈ S) is external to the Bank/Account system (external⟨ o ⟩) and has direct access to that account object (⟨ o access a ⟩). Notice that while the change in the balance happens some time in the future, the external object o has access to a in the *current* state. Notice also that the object which makes the call to deposit described in (1), and the object which has access to a in the current state described in (2), need not be the same: it may well be that the latter passes a reference to a to the former (indirectly), which then makes the call to deposit.

It remains to think about how access to an Account may be obtained. This is the remit of assertion (3), which says that if at some time in the future of the state restricted to S, some object o which is external has access to some account a, and if a exists in the current state, then in the current state some object from S has access to a. Where o and o' may, but need not, be the same object. And where o' has to exist and have access to a in the *current* state, but o need not exist in the current state – it may be allocated later. Assertion (3) thus gives essential protection when dealing with foreign, untrusted code. When an Account is given out to untrusted third parties, assertion (3) guarantees that this Account cannot be used to obtain access to further Accounts.

A holistic specification for the bank account, then, would be a sufficient functional specification plus the necessary specifications (1)-(3) from above. This holistic specification permits an implementation of the bank that also provides count and notify methods, even though the specification does not mention either method. Critically, though, the holistic $\mathcal{C}hainmail$ specification does not permit an implementation that includes a steal method.

3 *Chainmail* **Overview**

In this Section we give a brief and informal overview of some of the most salient features of *Chainmail*— a full exposition appears in Section 5.

Example Configurations We will illustrate these features using the Bank/Account example from the previous section. We use the runtime configurations σ_1 and σ_2 shown in the left and right diagrams in Figure 2. In both diagrams the rounded boxes depict objects: green for those from the Bank/Account component, and grey for the "external", "client" objects. The transparent green rectangle shows which objects are contained by the Bank/Account component. The object at 1 is a Bank, those at 2, 3 and 4 are Accounts, and those at 91, 92, 93 and 94 are "client" objects which belong to classes different from those from the Bank/Account module.

Each configuration represents one alternative implementation of the Bank object. Configuration σ_1 may arise from execution using a module M_{BA1}, where Account objects have a field myBank pointing to their Bank, and an integer field balance – the code can be found in appendix C Fig. 3. Configuration σ_2 may arise from execution using a module M_{BA2}, where Accounts have a myBank field, Bank objects have a ledger implemented though a sequence of Nodes, each of which has a field pointing to an Account, a field balance, and a field next – the code can be found in appendix C Figs. 6 and 4.

σ_1 σ_2

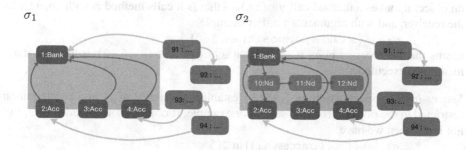

Figure 2. Two runtime configurations for the Bank/Account example.

For the rest, assume variable identifiers b_1, and a_2–a_4, and u_{91}–u_{94} denoting objects 1, 2–4, and 91–94 respectively for both σ_1 and σ_2. That is, for $i=1$ or $i=2$, $\sigma_i(b_1)=1$, $\sigma_i(a_2)=2$, $\sigma_i(a_3)=3$, $\sigma_i(a_4)=4$, $\sigma_i(u_{91})=91$, $\sigma_i(u_{92})=92$, $\sigma_i(u_{93})=93$, and $\sigma_i(u_{94})=94$.

Classical Assertions talk about the contents of the local variables (*i.e.* the topmost stack frame), and the fields of the various objects (*i.e.* the heap). For example, the assertion $a_2.myBank=a_3.myBank$, says that a_2 and a_3 have the same bank. In fact, this assertion is satisfied in both σ_1 and σ_2, written formally as

$$..., \sigma_1 \models a_2.myBank = a_3.myBank$$
$$..., \sigma_2 \models a_2.myBank = a_3.myBank.$$

The term x:ClassId says that x is an object of class ClassId. For example

$$\ldots, \sigma_1 \models \texttt{a}_2.\texttt{myBank} : \texttt{Bank}.$$

We support ghost fields [11,31], *e.g.* $\texttt{a}_1.\texttt{balance}$ is a physical field in σ_1 and a ghost field in σ_2 since in MBA2 an Account does not store its balance (as can be seen in appendix C Fig. 6). We also support the usual logical connectives, and so, we can express assertions such as

$$\forall \texttt{a}.[\ \texttt{a} : \texttt{Account} \longrightarrow \texttt{a.myBank} : \texttt{Bank} \land \texttt{a.balance} \geq 0\ ].$$

Permission: Access Our first holistic assertion, $\langle \texttt{x access y} \rangle$, asserts that object x has a direct reference to another object y: either one of x's fields contains a reference to y, or the receiver of the currently executing method is x, and y is one of the arguments or a local variable. For example:

$$\ldots, \sigma_1 \models \langle \texttt{a}_2 \texttt{ access } \texttt{b}_1 \rangle$$

If σ_1 were executing the method body corresponding to the call $\texttt{a}_2.\texttt{deposit}(\texttt{a}_3, 360)$, then we would have

$$\ldots, \sigma_1 \models \langle \texttt{a}_2 \texttt{ access } \texttt{a}_3 \rangle,$$

That is, during execution of deposit, the object at $\texttt{a}_2$ has access to the object at $\texttt{a}_3$, and could, if the method body chose to, call a method on $\texttt{a}_3$, or store a reference to $\texttt{a}_3$ in its own fields. Access is not symmetric, nor transitive:

$$\ldots, \sigma_1 \not\models \langle \texttt{a}_3 \texttt{ access } \texttt{a}_2 \rangle,$$
$$\ldots, \sigma_2 \models \langle \texttt{a}_2 \texttt{ access}^* \texttt{ a}_3 \rangle, \qquad \ldots, \sigma_2 \not\models \langle \texttt{a}_2 \texttt{ access } \texttt{a}_3 \rangle.$$

Control: Calls The assertion $\langle \texttt{x calls m.y}(\texttt{z s}) \rangle$ holds in configurations where a method on object x makes a method call $\texttt{y.m}(\texttt{z s})$ — that is it calls method m with object y as the receiver, and with arguments $\texttt{z s}$. For example,

$$\ldots, \sigma_3 \models \langle \texttt{x calls } \texttt{a}_2.\texttt{deposit}(\texttt{a}_3, 360) \rangle.$$

means that the receiver in σ_3 is x, and that $\texttt{a}_2.\texttt{deposit}(\texttt{a}_3, 360)$ is the next statement to be executed.

Space: In The space assertion $\langle A \texttt{ in } \texttt{S} \rangle$ establishes validity of A in a configuration restricted to the objects from the set S. For example, if object 94 is included in S_1 but not in S_2, then we have

$$\ldots, \sigma_1 \models \langle (\exists \texttt{o}. \langle \texttt{o access } \texttt{a}_4 \rangle) \texttt{ in } S_1 \rangle$$
$$\ldots, \sigma_1 \not\models \langle (\exists \texttt{o}. \langle \texttt{o access } \texttt{a}_4 \rangle) \texttt{ in } S_2 \rangle.$$

The set S in the assertion $\langle A \texttt{ in } \texttt{S} \rangle$ is therefore *not* the footprint of A; it is more like the *fuel* [2] given to establish that assertion. Note that $\ldots, \sigma \models \langle A \texttt{ in } \texttt{S} \rangle$ does not imply $\ldots, \sigma \models A$ nor does it imply $\ldots, \sigma \models \langle A \texttt{ in } \texttt{S} \cup \texttt{S}' \rangle$. The other direction of the implication does not hold either.

Time: Next, Will, Prev, Was We support several operators from temporal logic: ($\texttt{next}\langle A \rangle$, $\texttt{will}\langle A \rangle$, $\texttt{prev}\langle A \rangle$, and $\texttt{was}\langle A \rangle$) to talk about the future or the past in one or more steps. The assertion $\texttt{will}\langle A \rangle$ expresses that A will hold in one or more steps. For example, taking σ_4 to be similar to σ_2, the next statement to be executed to be $\texttt{a}_2.\texttt{deposit}(\texttt{a}_3, 360)$, and $M_{BA2} \,\mathbf{\mathring{,}}\, \ldots, \sigma_4 \models \texttt{a}_2.\texttt{balance} = 60$, and that $M_{BA2} \,\mathbf{\mathring{,}}\, \ldots, \sigma_4 \models \texttt{a}_4.\texttt{balance} \geq 360$, then

$$M_{BA2} \,\mathbf{\mathring{,}}\, \ldots, \sigma_4 \models \texttt{will}\langle \texttt{a}_2.\texttt{balance} = 420 \rangle.$$

The *internal* module, M_{BA2} is needed for looking up the method body of deposit.

Viewpoint: – *External* The assertion external$\langle\, x\,\rangle$ expresses that the object at x does not belong to the module under consideration. For example,

$$M_{AB2}\,\mathring{\,}\,...,\sigma_2 \models \text{external}\langle\, u_{92}\,\rangle, \qquad M_{AB2}\,\mathring{\,}\,...,\sigma_2 \not\models \text{external}\langle\, a_2\,\rangle,$$
$$M_{AB2}\,\mathring{\,}\,...,\sigma_2 \not\models \text{external}\langle\, b_1.\texttt{ledger}\,\rangle$$

The *internal* module, M_{BA2}, is needed to judge which objects are internal or external.

Change and Authority: We have used changes$\langle\,...\,\rangle$ in our $Chainmail$ assertions in section 2, as in changes$\langle\, a.\texttt{balance}\,\rangle$. Assertions that talk about change, or give conditions for change to happen are fundamental for security; the ability to cause change is called *authority* in [40]. We can encode change using the other features of $Chainmail$, namely, for any expression e:

$$\text{changes}\langle\, e\,\rangle \equiv \exists v.[\, e = v \wedge \text{next}\langle\, \neg(e = v)\,\rangle\,].$$

and similarly for assertions.

Putting these together We now look at some composite assertions which use several features from above. For example, the assertion below says that if the statement to be executed is $a_2.\texttt{deposit}\,(a_3, 60)$, then the balance of a_2 will eventually change:

$$M_{BA2}\,\mathring{\,}\,...,\sigma_2 \models \langle\, .. \text{calls}\, a_2.\texttt{deposit}(\, a_3, 60)\,\rangle \longrightarrow \text{will}\langle\, \text{changes}\langle\, a_2.\texttt{balance}\,\rangle\rangle.$$

Now look deeper into space assertions, $\langle\, A \text{ in } S\,\rangle$, which allow us to characterise the set of objects which have authority over certain effects (here A). In particular, the assertion $\langle\, \text{will}\langle\, A\,\rangle \text{ in } S\,\rangle$ requires two things: i) that A will hold in the future, and ii) that all the objects which cause the effect which will make A valid are included in S. Knowing who has, and who has not, authority over properties or data is a fundamental concern of robustness [40]. Notice that the authority is a set, rather than a single object: quite often it takes *several objects in concert* to achieve an effect.

Consider assertions (2) and (3) from the previous section. They both have the form "will$\langle\langle\, A \text{ in } S\,\rangle\rangle \longrightarrow P(S)$", where P is some property over a set. These assertions say that if ever in the future A becomes valid, and if the objects involved in making A valid are included in S, then S must satisfy P. Such assertions can be used to restrict whether A will become valid. If we have some execution which only involves objects which do not satisfy P, then we know that the execution will not ever make A valid.

In summary, in addition to classical logical connectors and classical assertions over the contents of the heap and the stack, our holistic assertions draw from some concepts from object capabilities ($\langle\, \_\, \text{access}\, \_\,\rangle$ for permission; $\langle\, \_\, \text{calls}\, \_.\_(\, \_)\,\rangle$ and changes$\langle\, \_\,\rangle$ for authority) as well as temporal logic (will$\langle\, A\,\rangle$, was$\langle\, A\,\rangle$ and friends), and the relation of our spatial connective ($\langle\, A \text{ in } S\,\rangle$) with ownership and effect systems [60,14,13].

The next two sections discuss the semantics of $Chainmail$. Section 4 contains an overview of the formal model and section 5 focuses on the most important part of $Chainmail$: assertions.

4 Overview of the Formal foundations

We now give an overview of the formal model for $Chainmail$. In section 4.1 we introduce the shape of the judgments used to give semantics to $Chainmail$, while in section

4.2 we describe the most salient aspects of an underlying programming language used in $Chainmail$.

4.1 $Chainmail$ judgments

Having outlined the ingredients of our holistic specification language, the next question to ask is: When does a module M satisfy a holistic assertion A? More formally: when does M $\models A$ hold?

Our answer has to reflect the fact that we are dealing with an *open world*, where M, our module, may be linked with *arbitrary untrusted code*. To model the open world, we consider pairs of modules, M $\S$ M$'$, where M is the module whose code is supposed to satisfy the assertion, and M$'$ is another module which exercises the functionality of M. We call our module M the *internal* module, and M$'$ the *external* module, which represents potential attackers or adversaries.

We can now answer the question: M $\models A$ holds if for all further, *potentially adversarial*, modules M$'$ and in all runtime configurations σ which may be observed as arising from the execution of the code of M combined with that of M$'$, the assertion A is satisfied. More formally, we define:

$$M \models A \qquad \text{if} \qquad \forall M'. \forall \sigma \in \mathit{Arising}(M \S M').[\, M \S M', \sigma \models A\,].$$

Module M$'$ represents all possible clients of M. As it is arbitrarily chosen, it reflects the open world nature of our specifications.

The judgement M $\S$ M$'$, $\sigma \models A$ means that assertion A is satisfied by M $\S$ M$'$ and σ. As in traditional specification languages [31,37], satisfaction is judged in the context of a runtime configuration σ; but in addition, it is judged in the context of the internal and external modules. These are used to find abstract functions defining ghost fields as well as method bodies needed when judging validity of temporal assertions such as will$\langle \_ \rangle$.

We distinguish between internal and external modules. This has two uses: First, $Chainmail$ includes the "external$\langle \circ \rangle$" assertion to require that an object belongs to the external module, as in the Bank Account's assertion (2) and (3) in section 2. Second, we adopt a version of visible states semantics [45,25,38], treating all executions within a module as atomic. We only record runtime configurations which are *external* to module M, *i.e.* those where the executing object (*i.e.* the current receiver) comes from module M$'$. Execution has the form

$$M \S M', \sigma \rightsquigarrow \sigma'$$

where we ignore all intermediate steps with receivers internal to M. In the next section we shall outline the underlying programming language, and define the judgment M $\S$ M$'$, $\sigma \rightsquigarrow \sigma'$ and the set $\mathit{Arising}(M \S M')$.

4.2 An underlying programming language, $\mathcal{L}_{oo}$

The meaning of $Chainmail$ assertions is parametric with an underlying object-oriented programming language, with modules as repositories of code, classes with fields, methods and ghostfields, objects described by classes, a way to link modules into larger ones, and a concept of program execution[6].

---

[6] We believe that $Chainmail$ can be applied to any language with these features.

We have developed $\mathcal{L}_{oo}$, a minimal such object-oriented language, which we outline in this section. We describe the novel aspects of $\mathcal{L}_{oo}$, and summarise the more conventional parts, relegating full, and mostly unsurprising, definitions to Appendix A.

Modules are central to $\mathcal{L}_{oo}$, as they are to $Chainmail$. As modules are repositories of code, we adopt the common formalisation of modules as maps from class identifiers to class definitions, c.f. Appendix, Def. 1. We use the terms module and component in an analogous manner to class and object respectively. $\mathcal{L}_{oo}$ is untyped for several reasons. Many popular programming languages are untyped. The external module might be untyped, and so it is more general to consider everything as untyped. Finally, a solution that works for an untyped language will also apply to a typed language, while the converse is not true.

Class definitions consist of field, method and ghost field declarations, c.f. Appendix, Def. 2. Method bodies are sequences of statements, which can be field reads or field assignments, object creation, method calls, and return statements. Fields are private in the sense of C++: they can only be read or written by methods of the current class. This is enforced by the operational semantics, *c.f.* Fig. 1. We discuss ghost fields in the next section.

Runtime configurations, σ, contain all the usual information about execution snapshots: the heap, and a stack of frames. Each frame consists of a continuation, contn, describing the remaining code to be executed by the frame, and a map from variables to values. Values are either addresses or sets of addresses; sets are needed to deal with assertions which quantify over sets of objects, such as assertions (1) and (2) from section 2. We define *one-module* execution through a judgment of the form $M, \sigma \rightsquigarrow \sigma'$ in the Appendix, Fig. 1.

We define a module linking operator $\circ$ so that $M \circ M'$ is the union of the two modules, provided that their domains are disjoint, c.f. Appendix, Def. 8. As we said in section 4.1, we distinguish between the internal and external module. We consider execution from the view of the external module, and treat execution of methods from the internal module as atomic. For this, we define *two-module execution* based on one-module execution as follows:

Definition 1. *Given runtime configurations* σ, σ', *and a module-pair* $M \, \mathring{,} \, M'$ *we define execution where* M *is the internal, and* M' *is the external module as below:*

- $M \, \mathring{,} \, M', \sigma \rightsquigarrow \sigma'$ *if there exist* $n \geq 2$ *and runtime configurations* $\sigma_1, \dots \sigma_n$, *such that*
  - $\sigma = \sigma_1$, *and* $\sigma_n = \sigma'$.
  - $M \circ M', \sigma_i \rightsquigarrow \sigma'_{i+1}$, *for* $1 \leq i \leq n-1$
  - $Class(\text{this})_\sigma \notin dom(M)$, *and* $Class(\text{this})_{\sigma'} \notin dom(M)$,
  - $Class(\text{this})_{\sigma_i} \in dom(M)$, *for* $2 \leq i \leq n-2$

In the definition above, $Class(x)_\sigma$ looks up the class of the object stored at x, c.f. Appendix, Def. 5. For example, for σ_4 as in Section 3 whose next statement to be executed is $a_2.\text{deposit}(a_3, 360)$, we would have a sequence of configurations σ_{41}, ... σ_{4n}, σ_5 so that the one-module execution gives $M_{BA2}, \sigma_4 \rightsquigarrow \sigma_{41} \rightsquigarrow \sigma_{42} \dots \rightsquigarrow$

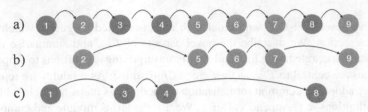

Figure 3. Two Module Execution (Def. 1). a) $M_1 \circ M_2$ b) $M_1 \,\S\, M_2$ c) $M_2 \,\S\, M_1$

$\sigma_{4n} \rightsquigarrow \sigma_5$. This would correspond to an atomic evaluation in the two-module execution: $M_{BA2} \,\S\, M', \sigma_4 \rightsquigarrow \sigma_5$ (see Fig.3; where blue stands for $\sigma(this) \in M_1$, and orange for $\sigma(this) \in M_2$).

Two-module execution is related to visible states semantics [45] as they both filter configurations, with the difference that in visible states semantics execution is unfiltered and configurations are only filtered when it comes to the consideration of class invariants while two-module execution filters execution. The lemma below says that linking is associative and commutative, and preserves both one-module and two-module execution.

Lemma 1 (Properties of linking). *For any modules* M, M′, M″, *and* M‴ *and runtime configurations* σ, *and* σ' *we have*:

- $(M \circ M') \circ M'' = M \circ (M' \circ M'')$ *and* $M \circ M' = M' \circ M$.
- $M, \sigma \rightsquigarrow \sigma'$, *and* $M \circ M'$ *is defined,* *implies* $M \circ M', \sigma \rightsquigarrow \sigma'$.
- $M \,\S\, M', \sigma \rightsquigarrow \sigma'$ *implies* $(M \circ M'') \,\S\, (M' \circ M'''), \sigma \rightsquigarrow \sigma'$.

We can now answer the question as to which runtime configurations are pertinent when judging a module's adherence to an assertion. *Initial configurations* are those whose heap have only one object, of class Object, and whose stack have one frame, with arbitrary continuation. *Arising* configurations are those that can be reached by two-module execution, starting from any initial configuration.

Definition 2 (Initial and Arising Configurations). *are defined as follows*:

- *Initial*$\langle (\psi, \chi) \rangle$, *if* ψ *consists of a single frame* ϕ *with* $dom(\phi) = \{\text{this}\}$, *and there exists some address* α, *such that* $\lfloor \text{this} \rfloor_\phi = \alpha$, *and* $dom(\chi) = \alpha$, *and* $\chi(\alpha) = (\text{Object}, \emptyset)$.
- *Arising*$(M \,\S\, M') = \{\ \sigma \mid \exists \sigma_0. [\textit{Initial}\langle \sigma_0 \rangle \ \wedge\ M \,\S\, M', \sigma_0 \rightsquigarrow^* \sigma\ ]\ \}$

5 Assertions

$\mathcal{C}hainmail$ assertions (details in appendix B.3) consist of (pure) expressions e, comparisons between expressions, classical assertions about the contents of heap and stack, the usual logical connectives, as well as our holistic concepts. In this section we focus on the novel, holistic, features of $\mathcal{C}hainmail$ (permission, control, time, space, and viewpoint), as well as our wish to support some form of recursion while keeping the logic of assertions classical.

5.1   Satisfaction of Assertions - Access, Control, Space, Viewpoint

Permission expresses that an object has the potential to call methods on another object, and to do so directly, without help from any intermediary object. This is the case when the two objects are aliases, or the first object has a field pointing to the second object, or the first object is the receiver of the currently executing method and the second object is one of the arguments or a local variable. Interpretations of variables and paths, $\lfloor ... \rfloor_\sigma$, are defined in the usual way (appendix Def. 5).

Definition 3 (Permission). *For any modules* M, M', *variables* x *and* y, *we define*

- $M \,\mathring{,}\, M', \sigma \models \langle x \text{ access } y \rangle$ *if* $\lfloor x \rfloor_\sigma$ *and* $\lfloor y \rfloor_\sigma$ *are defined, and*
  - $\lfloor x \rfloor_\sigma = \lfloor y \rfloor_\sigma$, *or*
  - $\lfloor x.f \rfloor_\sigma = \lfloor y \rfloor_\sigma$, *for some field* f, *or*
  - $\lfloor x \rfloor_\sigma = \lfloor this \rfloor_\sigma$ *and* $\lfloor y \rfloor_\sigma = \lfloor z \rfloor_\sigma$, *for some variable* z *and* z *appears in* σ.contn.

In the last disjunct, where z is a parameter or local variable, we ask that z appears in the code being executed (σ.contn). This requirement ensures that variables which were introduced into the variable map in order to give meaning to existentially quantified assertions, are not considered.

Control expresses which object is the process of making a function call on another object and with what arguments. The relevant information is stored in the continuation (cont) on the top frame.

Definition 4 (Control). *For any modules* M, M', *variables* x, y, $z_1, ... z_n$, *we define*:

- $M \,\mathring{,}\, M', \sigma \models \langle x \text{ calls } y.m(\, z_1, ... z_n) \,\rangle$ *if* $\lfloor x \rfloor_\sigma, \lfloor y \rfloor_\sigma, \lfloor z_1 \rfloor_\sigma, \; ... \; \lfloor z_n \rfloor_\sigma$ *are defined, and*
  - $\lfloor this \rfloor_\sigma = \lfloor x \rfloor_\sigma$, *and*
  - σ.contn=u.m($v_1, ..v_n$);__ *for some* u,$v_1, ... v_n$, *and*
  - $\lfloor y \rfloor_\sigma = \lfloor u \rfloor_\sigma$, *and* $\lfloor z_i \rfloor_\sigma = \lfloor v_i \rfloor_\sigma$, *for all* i.

Thus, $\langle x \text{ calls } y.m(\, z_1, ... z_n) \,\rangle$ expresses the call $y.m(z_1, ... z_n)$ will be executed next, and that the caller is x.

Viewpoint is about whether an object is viewed as belonging to the internal mode; this is determined by the class of the object.

Definition 5 (Viewpoint). *For any modules* M, M', *and variable* x, *we define*

- $M \,\mathring{,}\, M', \sigma \models \text{external}\langle x \rangle$ *if* $\lfloor x \rfloor_\sigma$ *is defined and* $Class(\lfloor x \rfloor_\sigma)_\sigma \notin dom(M)$
- $M \,\mathring{,}\, M', \sigma \models \text{internal}\langle x \rangle$ *if* $\lfloor x \rfloor_\sigma$ *is defined and* $Class(\lfloor x \rfloor_\sigma)_\sigma \in dom(M)$

Space is about asserting that some property A holds in a configuration whose objects are restricted to those from a given set S. This way we can express that the objects from the set S have authority over the assertion A. In order to define validity of $\langle A \text{ in } S \rangle$ in a configuration σ, we first define a restriction operation, $\sigma \!\downarrow_S$ which restricts the objects from σ to only those from S.

Definition 6 (Restriction of Runtime Configurations). *The restriction operator* $\downarrow$ *applied to a runtime configuration* σ *and a variable* S *is defined as follows:*

- $\sigma\downarrow_S \triangleq (\psi,\chi')$, *if* $\sigma=(\psi,\chi)$, $dom(\chi') = \lfloor S \rfloor_\sigma$, *and* $\forall\alpha\in dom(\chi').\chi(\alpha) = \chi'(\alpha)$.

For example, if we take σ_2 from Fig. 2 in Section 2, and restrict it with some set S_4 such that $\lfloor S_4\rfloor_{\sigma_2} = \{91,1,2,3,4,11\}$, then the restriction $\sigma_2\downarrow_{S_4}$ will look as on the right.

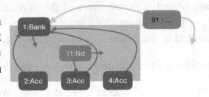

Note in the diagram above the dangling pointers at objects 1, 11, and 91 - reminiscent of the separation of heaps into disjoint subheaps, as provided by the $*$ operator in separation logic [53]. The difference is that in separation logic, the separation is provided through the assertions, where $A * A'$ holds in any heap which can be split into disjoint χ and χ' where χ satisfies A and χ' satisfies A'. That is, in $A*A'$ the split of the heap is determined by the assertions A and A' and there is an implicit requirement of disjointness, while in $\sigma\downarrow_S$ the split is determined by S, and no disjointness is required.

We now define the semantics of $\langle A \text{ in } S \rangle$.

Definition 7 (Space). *For any modules* M, M', *assertions* A *and variable* S, *we define*:

- $M \, \text{\textsemicolon} \, M', \sigma \models \langle A \text{ in } S \rangle$ *if* $M \, \text{\textsemicolon} \, M', \sigma\downarrow_S \models A$.

The set S in the assertion $\langle A \text{ in } S \rangle$ is related to framing from implicit dynamic frames [57]: in an implicit dynamic frames assertion **acc** x.f $* A$, the frame x.f prescribes which locations may be used to determine validity of A. The difference is that frames are sets of locations (pairs of address and field), while our S-es are sets of addresses. More importantly, implicit dynamic frames assertions whose frames are not large enough are badly formed, while in our work, such assertions are allowed and may hold or not, *e.g.* $M_{BA2} \, \text{\textsemicolon} \, M', \sigma \models \neg \langle (\exists n.a_2.\texttt{balance} = n) \text{ in } S_4 \rangle$.

5.2 Satisfaction of Assertions - Time

To deal with time, we are faced with four challenges: a) validity of assertions in the future or the past needs to be judged in the future configuration, but using the bindings from the current one, b) the current configuration needs to store the code being executed, so as to be able to calculate future configurations, c) when considering the future, we do not want to observe configurations which go beyond the frame currently at the top of the stack, d) there is no "undo" operator to deterministically enumerate all the previous configurations.

Consider challenge a) in some more detail: the assertion will$\langle$ x.f $= 3 \rangle$ is satisfied in the *current* configuration σ_1, if in some *future* configuration σ_2, the field f of the object that is pointed at by x in the *current* configuration (σ_1) has the value 3, that is, if $\lfloor\lfloor x\rfloor_{\sigma_1}.f\rfloor_{\sigma_2} = 3$, even if in that future configuration x denotes a different object (i.e. if $\lfloor x\rfloor_{\sigma_1} \neq \lfloor x\rfloor_{\sigma_2}$). To address this, we define an auxiliary concept: the operator$\triangleleft$, where

$\sigma_1 \triangleleft \sigma_2$ adapts the second configuration to the top frame's view of the former: it returns a new configuration whose stack comes from σ_2 but is augmented with the view from the top frame from σ_1 and where the continuation has been consistently renamed. This allows us to interpret expressions in σ_2 but with the variables bound according to σ_1; *e.g.* we can obtain that value of x in configuration σ_2 even if x was out of scope in σ_2.

Definition 8 (Adaptation). *For runtime configurations σ_1, σ_2.:*

- $\sigma_1 \triangleleft \sigma_2 \triangleq (\phi_3 \cdot \psi_2, \chi_2)$ *if*
  - $\phi_3 = (\,\texttt{contn}_2[\texttt{zs}_2/\texttt{zs}'], \beta_2[\texttt{zs}' \mapsto \beta_2(\texttt{zs}_2)][\texttt{zs}_1 \mapsto \beta_1(\texttt{zs}_1)]\,)$, *where*
  - $\sigma_1 = (\phi_1 \cdot \_, \_)$, $\sigma_2 = (\phi_2 \cdot \psi_2, \chi_2)$, $\phi_1 = (\_, \beta_1)$, $\phi_2 = (\texttt{contn}_2, \beta_2)$, *and*
  - $\texttt{zs}_1 = dom(\beta_1)$, $\texttt{zs}_2 = dom(\beta_2)$,   *and*
  - $\texttt{zs}'$ *is a set of variables with the same cardinality as* $\texttt{zs}_2$, *and all variables in* $\texttt{zs}'$ *are fresh in* β_1 *and in* β_2.

That is, in the new frame ϕ_2 from above, we keep the same continuation as from σ_2 but rename all variables with fresh names $\texttt{zs}'$, and combine the variable map β_1 from σ_1 with the variable map β_2 from σ_2 while avoiding names clashes through the renaming $[\texttt{zs}' \mapsto \beta_2(\texttt{zs}_2)]$. The consistent renaming of the continuation allows the correct modelling of execution, as needed for the semantics of nested time assertions, as *e.g.* in $\text{will}\langle\, \texttt{x.f} = 3 \wedge \text{will}\langle\, \texttt{x.f} = 5 \,\rangle \,\rangle$.

Having addressed challenge a) we turn our attention to the remaining challenges: We address challenge b) by storing the remaining code to be executed in $\texttt{cntn}$ in each frame. We address challenge c) by only taking the top of the frame when considering future executions. Finally, we address challenge d) by considering only configurations which arise from initial configurations, and which lead to the current configuration.

Definition 9 (Time Assertions). *For any modules* M, M', *and assertion* A *we define*

- $\text{M}\,\mathring{}\,\text{M}', \sigma \models \text{next}\langle\, A \,\rangle$ *if* $\exists \sigma'.[\; \text{M}\,\mathring{}\,\text{M}', \phi \rightsquigarrow \sigma' \wedge \text{M}\,\mathring{}\,\text{M}', \sigma \triangleleft \sigma' \models A\;]$,
  and where ϕ is so that $\sigma = (\phi \cdot \_, \_)$.
- $\text{M}\,\mathring{}\,\text{M}', \sigma \models \text{will}\langle\, A \,\rangle$ *if* $\exists \sigma'.[\; \text{M}\,\mathring{}\,\text{M}', \phi \rightsquigarrow^* \sigma' \wedge \text{M}\,\mathring{}\,\text{M}', \sigma \triangleleft \sigma' \models A\;]$,
  and where ϕ is so that $\sigma = (\phi \cdot \_, \_)$.
- $\text{M}\,\mathring{}\,\text{M}', \sigma \models \text{prev}\langle\, A \,\rangle$ *if* $\forall \sigma_1, \sigma_2.[\; \mathit{Initial}\langle \sigma_1 \rangle \wedge \text{M}\,\mathring{}\,\text{M}', \sigma_1 \rightsquigarrow^* \sigma_2$
  $\wedge \text{M}\,\mathring{}\,\text{M}', \sigma_2 \rightsquigarrow \sigma \;\longrightarrow\; \text{M}\,\mathring{}\,\text{M}', \sigma \triangleleft \sigma_2 \models A\;]$
- $\text{M}\,\mathring{}\,\text{M}', \sigma \models \text{was}\langle\, A \,\rangle$ *if* $\forall \sigma_1.[\; \mathit{Initial}\langle \sigma_1 \rangle \wedge \text{M}\,\mathring{}\,\text{M}', \sigma_1 \rightsquigarrow^* \sigma \longrightarrow$
  $(\; \exists \sigma_2. \text{M}\,\mathring{}\,\text{M}', \sigma_1 \rightsquigarrow^* \sigma_2 \wedge \text{M}\,\mathring{}\,\text{M}', \sigma_2 \rightsquigarrow^* \sigma \wedge \text{M}\,\mathring{}\,\text{M}', \sigma \triangleleft \sigma_2 \models A \;)]$

In general, $\text{will}\langle\,\langle\, A \text{ in } \text{S} \,\rangle\,\rangle$ is different from $\langle\, \text{will}\langle\, A \,\rangle \text{ in } \text{S} \,\rangle$. In the former assertion, S must contain the objects involved in reaching the future configuration as well as the objects needed to then establish validity of A in that future configuration. In the latter assertion, S need only contain the objects needed to establish A in that future configuration. For example, revisit Fig. 2, and take S_1 to consist of objects $1, 2, 4, 93$, and 94, and S_2 to consist of objects $1, 2, 4$. Assume that σ_5 is like σ_1, that the next call in σ_5 is a method on $\texttt{u}_{94}$, whose body obtains the address of $\texttt{a}_4$ (by making a call on 93 to which it has access), and the address of $\texttt{a}_2$ (to which it has access), and then makes the call $\texttt{a}_2.\texttt{deposit}(\texttt{a}_4, 360)$. Assume also that $\texttt{a}_4$'s balance is 380. Then

$$M_{BA1}\,\mathring{}\,..., \sigma_5 \models \langle\, \text{will}\langle\, \text{changes}\langle\, \texttt{a}_2.\texttt{balance} \,\rangle \,\rangle \text{ in } \text{S}_1 \,\rangle$$
$$M_{BA1}\,\mathring{}\,..., \sigma_5 \not\models \langle\, \text{will}\langle\, \text{changes}\langle\, \texttt{a}_2.\texttt{balance} \,\rangle \,\rangle \text{ in } \text{S}_2 \,\rangle$$
$$M_{BA1}\,\mathring{}\,..., \sigma_5 \models \text{will}\langle\,\langle\, \text{changes}\langle\, \texttt{a}_2.\texttt{balance} \,\rangle \text{ in } \text{S}_2 \,\rangle\,\rangle$$

5.3 Properties of Assertions

We define equivalence of assertions in the usual way: assertions A and A' are equivalent
if they are satisfied in the context of the same configurations and module pairs – *i.e.*

$$A \equiv A' \quad \text{if} \quad \forall \sigma. \forall \text{M}, \text{M}'. \ [\ \text{M} \,\text{\textreferencemark}\, \text{M}', \sigma \models A \text{ if and only if } \text{M} \,\text{\textreferencemark}\, \text{M}', \sigma \models A' \ ].$$

We can then prove that the usual equivalences hold, *e.g.* $A \vee A' \equiv A' \vee A$, and
$\neg(\exists \text{x}.A) \equiv \forall \text{x}.(\neg A)$. Our assertions are classical, *e.g.* $A \wedge \neg A \equiv$ `false`, and
$\text{M} \,\text{\textreferencemark}\, \text{M}', \sigma \models A$ and $\text{M} \,\text{\textreferencemark}\, \text{M}', \sigma \models A \to A'$ implies $\text{M} \,\text{\textreferencemark}\, \text{M}', \sigma \models A'$. This desirable property
comes at the loss of some expected equivalences, *e.g.*, in general, e = `false` and ¬e
are not equivalent. More in Appendix B.

5.4 Modules satisfying assertions

Finally, we define satisfaction of assertions by modules: a module M satisfies an assertion A if for all other potential modules M', in all configurations arising from executions
of $\text{M} \,\text{\textreferencemark}\, \text{M}'$, the assertion A holds.

Definition 10. *For any module* M, *and assertion* A, *we define:*

– $\text{M} \models A \quad \text{if} \quad \forall \text{M}'. \forall \sigma \in \mathit{Arising}(\text{M} \,\text{\textreferencemark}\, \text{M}'). \ \text{M} \,\text{\textreferencemark}\, \text{M}', \sigma \models A$

6 Examplar Driven Design

Examplars The design of $\mathcal{C}hainmail$ was guided by the study of a sequence of exemplars taken from the object-capability literature and the smart contracts world:

1. **Bank** [49] - Bank and Account as in Section 2 with two different implementations.
2. **ERC20** [61] - Ethereum-based token contract.
3. **DAO** [12,15] - Ethereum contract for Decentralised Autonomous Organisation.
4. **DOM** [20,59] - Restricting access to browser Domain Object Model

We present these exemplars as appendices [1]. Our design was also driven by work on
other examples such as the membrane [17], the Mint/Purse [40], and Escrow [18,24].

Model We have constructed a Coq model[7] [23] of the core of the Chainmail specification language, along with the underlying $\mathcal{L}_{oo}$ language. Our formalism is organised as
follows:

1. The $\mathcal{L}_{oo}$ Language: a class based, object oriented language with mutable references.
2. Chainmail: The full assertion syntax and semantics defined in Definitions 1, 2, 3,
   4, 5, 6, 7, 8, 9 and 10.
3. $\mathcal{L}_{oo}$ Properties: Secondary properties of the loo language that aid in reasoning about
   its semantics.
4. Chainmail Properties: The core properties defined on the semantics of Chainmail.

---

[7] A current model can be found at: https://github.com/sophiaIC/HolisticSpecifications

In the associated appendix (see Appendix G) we list and present the properties of Chainmail we have formalised in Coq. We have proven that Chainmail obeys much of the properties of classical logic. While we formalise most of the underlying semantics, we make several assumptions in our Coq formalism: (i) the law of the excluded middle, a property that is well known to be unprovable in constructive logics, and (ii) the equality of variable maps and heaps down to renaming. Coq formalisms often require fairly verbose definitions and proofs of properties involving variable substitution and renaming, and assuming equality down to renaming saves much effort.

More details of the formal foundations of *Chainmail*, and the model, are also in appendices [1].

7 Related Work

Behavioural Specification Languages Hatcliff et al. [26] provide an excellent survey of contemporary specification approaches. With a lineage back to Hoare logic [28], Meyer's Design by Contract [38] was the first popular attempt to bring verification techniques to object-oriented programs as a "whole cloth" language design in Eiffel. Several more recent specification languages are now making their way into practical and educational use, including JML [31], Spec♯ [4], Dafny [32] and Whiley [51]. Our approach builds upon these fundamentals, particularly Leino & Shulte's formulation of two-state invariants [33], and Summers and Drossopoulou's Considerate Reasoning [58]. In general, these approaches assume a closed system, where modules can be trusted to coöperate. In this paper we aim to work in an open system where modules' invariants must be protected irrespective of the behaviour of the rest of the system.

Defensive Consistency In an open world, we cannot rely on the kindness of strangers: rather we have to ensure our code is correct regardless of whether it interacts with friends or foes. Attackers *"only have to be lucky once"* while secure systems *"have to be lucky always"* [5]. Miller [39,40] defines the necessary approach as **defensive consistency**: *"An object is defensively consistent when it can defend its own invariants and provide correct service to its well behaved clients, despite arbitrary or malicious misbehaviour by its other clients."* Defensively consistent modules are particularly hard to design, to write, to understand, and to verify: but they make it much easier to make guarantees about systems composed of multiple components [46].

Object Capabilities and Sandboxes. *Capabilities* as a means to support the development of concurrent and distributed system were developed in the 60's by Dennis and Van Horn [19], and were adapted to the programming languages setting in the 70's [44]. *Object capabilities* were first introduced [40] in the early 2000s, and many recent studies manage to verify safety or correctness of object capability programs. Google's Caja [42] applies sandboxes, proxies, and wrappers to limit components' access to *ambient authority*. Sandboxing has been validated formally. Maffeis et al. [35] develop a model of JavaScript, demonstrate that it obeys two principles of object capability systems and show how untrusted applications can be prevented from interfering with the rest of the system. Recent programming languages [27,10,54] including Newspeak [9], Dart [8], Grace [7,30] and Wyvern [36] have adopted the object capability model.

Verification of Object Capability Programs Murray made the first attempt to formalise defensive consistency and correctness [46]. Murray's model was rooted in counterfactual causation [34]: an object is defensively consistent when the addition of untrustworthy clients cannot cause well-behaved clients to be given incorrect service. Murray formalised defensive consistency very abstractly, over models of (concurrent) object-capability systems in the process algebra CSP [29], without a specification language for describing effects, such as what it means for an object to provide incorrect service. Both Miller and Murray's definitions are intensional, describing what it means for an object to be defensively consistent.

Drossopoulou and Noble [21,48] have analysed Miller's Mint and Purse example [40] and discussed the six capability policies as proposed in [40]. In [22], they sketched a specification language, used it to specify the six policies from [40], showed that several possible interpretations were possible, and uncovered the need for another four further policies. They also sketched how a trust-sensitive example (the escrow exchange) could be verified in an open world [24]. Their work does not support the concepts of control, time, or space, as in $Chainmail$, but it offers a primitive expressing trust.

Devriese et al. [20] have deployed powerful theoretical techniques to address similar problems: They show how step-indexing, Kripke worlds, and representing objects as state machines with public and private transitions can be used to reason about object capabilities. Devriese have demonstrated solutions to a range of exemplar problems, including the DOM wrapper (replicated in our section F) and a mashup application. Their distinction between public and private transitions is similar to the distinction between internal and external objects.

More recently, Swasey et al. [59] designed OCPL, a logic for object capability patterns, that supports specifications and proofs for object-oriented systems in an open world. They draw on verification techniques for security and information flow: separating internal implementations ("high values" which must not be exposed to attacking code) from interface objects ("low values" which may be exposed). OCPL supports defensive consistency (they use the term "robust safety" from the security community [6]) via a proof system that ensures low values can never leak high values to external attackers. This means that low values *can* be exposed to external code, and the behaviour of the system is described by considering attacks only on low values. They use that logic to prove a number of object-capability patterns, including sealer/unsealer pairs, the caretaker, and a general membrane.

Schaefer et al. [55] have recently added support for information-flow security using refinement to ensure correctness (in this case confidentiality) by construction. By enforcing encapsulation, all these approaches share similarity with techniques such as ownership types [14,50], which also protect internal implementation objects from accesses that cross encapsulation boundaries. Banerjee and Naumann demonstrated that by ensuring confinement, ownership systems can enforce representation independence (a property close to "robust safety") some time ago [3].

$Chainmail$ differs from Swasey, Schaefer's, and Devriese's work in a number of ways: They are primarily concerned with mechanisms that ensure encapsulation (aka confinement) while we abstract away from any mechanism via the external⟨ ⟩ predicate. They use powerful mathematical techniques which the users need to understand in order to write their specifications, while $Chainmail$ users only need to understand first order logic and the holistic operators presented in this paper. Finally, none of these systems offer the kinds of holistic assertions addressing control flow, change, or temporal operations that are at the core of $Chainmail$'s approach.

Scilla [56] is a minimalistic typed functional language for writing smart contracts that compiles to the Ethereum bytecode. Scilla's semantic model is restricted, assuming actor based communication and restricting recursion, thus facilitating static analysis of Scilla contracts and ensuring termination. Scilla is able to demonstrate that a number of popular Ethereum contracts avoid type errors, out-of-gas resource failures, and preservation of virtual currency. Scilla's semantics are defined formally, but have not yet been represented in a mechanised model.

Finally, the recent VerX tool is able to verify a range of specifications for solidity contracts automatically [52]. Similar to $Chainmail$, VerX has a specification language based on temporal logic. VerX offers three temporal operators (always, once, prev) but only within a past modality, while $Chainmail$ has two temporal operators, both existential, but with both past and future modalities. VerX specifications can also include predicates that model the current invocation on a contract (similar to $Chainmail$'s "calls"), can access variables, and compute sums (only) over collections. $Chainmail$ is strictly more expressive as a specification language, including quantification over objects and sets (so can compute arbitrary reductions on collections) and of course specifications for permission ("access"), space ("in") and viewpoint ("external") which have no analogues in VerX. Unlike $Chainmail$, VerX includes a practical tool that has been used to verify a hundred properties across case studies of twelve Solidity contracts.

8 Conclusions

In this paper we have motivated the need for holistic specifications, presented the specification language $Chainmail$ for writing such specifications, and outlined the formal foundations of the language. To focus on the key attributes of a holistic specification language, we have kept $Chainmail$ simple, only requiring an understanding of first order logic. We believe that the holistic features (permission, control, time, space and viewpoint) are intuitive concepts when reasoning informally, and were pleased to have been able to provide their formal semantics in what we argue is a simple manner.

9 Acknowledgments

This work is based on a long-standing collaboration with Mark S. Miller and Toby Murray. We have received invaluable feedback from Alex Summers, Bart Jacobs, Chris Hawblitzel, Michael Jackson, Lucius G. Meredith, Mike Stay, Shuh Peng Loh, Emil Klasan, members of WG 2.3, and the FASE 2020 reviewers. The work has been supported by the Royal Society of New Zealand (Te Apārangi) Marsden Fund (Te Pūtea Rangahau a Marsden) grants VUW-1318 and VUW-1815, and research gifts from Agoric, the Ethereum Foundation, and Facebook.

References

1. Holistic specifications paper with appendices. https://arxiv.org/abs/2002.08334, accessed: 2020-02-21
2. Ahmed, A., Dreyer, D., Rossberg, A.: State-dependent representation independence. In: POPL (2009)
3. Banerjee, A., Naumann, D.A.: Ownership confinement ensures representation independence for object-oriented programs. J. ACM 52(6), 894–960 (Nov 2005)
4. Barnett, M., Leino, K.R.M., Schulte, W.: The Spec# programming system: An overview. In: CASSIS. pp. 49–69. LNCS, Springer (2005)
5. BBC: On This Day: 1984: Tory cabinet in Brighton bomb blast (2015), [Online; accessed 15-October-2015]
6. Bengtson, J., Bhargavan, K., Fournet, C., Gordon, A.D., Maffeis, S.: Refinement types for secure implementations. ACM Trans. Program. Lang. Syst. 33(2), 8:1–8:45 (Feb 2011)
7. Black, A., Bruce, K., Homer, M., Noble, J.: Grace: the Absence of (Inessential) Difficulty. In: Onwards (2012)
8. Bracha, G.: The Dart Programming Language (Dec 2015)
9. Bracha, G.: The Newspeak language specification version 0.1 (Feb 2017), newspeaklanguage.org/
10. Burtsev, A., Johnson, D., Kunz, J., Eide, E., van der Merwe, J.E.: Capnet: security and least authority in a capability-enabled cloud. In: Proceedings of the 2017 Symposium on Cloud Computing, SoCC 2017, Santa Clara, CA, USA, September 24 - 27, 2017. pp. 128–141 (2017)
11. Chalin, P., Kiniry, J.R., Leavens, G.T., Poll, E.: Beyond assertions: Advanced specification and verification with JML and esc/java2. In: Formal Methods for Components and Objects, 4th International Symposium, FMCO 2005, Amsterdam, The Netherlands, November 1-4, 2005, Revised Lectures. pp. 342–363 (2005), https://doi.org/10.1007/11804192_16
12. Christoph Jentsch: Decentralized autonomous organization to automate governance (Mar 2016), https://download.slock.it/public/DAO/WhitePaper.pdf
13. Clarke, D., Drossopoulou, S.: Ownership, encapsulation and the disjointness of type and effectr. In: OOPSLA. ACM (2002)
14. Clarke, D.G., Potter, J.M., James Noble: Ownership types for flexible alias protection. In: OOPSLA. ACM (1998)
15. Coindesk: Understanding the DAO attack (2016), www.coindesk.com/understanding-dao-hack-journalists/
16. Community, S.: Solidity, https://solidity.readthedocs.io/en/develop/
17. van Cutsem, T.: Membranes in Javascript (2012), available from prog.vub.ac.be/~tvcutsem/invokedynamic/js-membranes
18. Cutsem, T.V., S, M.: Trustworthy proxies: Virtualizing objects with invariants. In: ECOOP (2013)
19. Dennis, J.B., Horn, E.C.V.: Programming Semantics for Multiprogrammed Computations. Comm. ACM 9(3) (1966)
20. Devriese, D., Birkedal, L., Piessens, F.: Reasoning about object capabilities with logical relations and effect parametricity. In: IEEE EuroS&P. pp. 147–162 (2016). https://doi.org/10.1109/EuroSP.2016.22
21. Drossopoulou, S., Noble, J.: The need for capability policies. In: (FTfJP) (2013)
22. Drossopoulou, S., Noble, J.: Towards capability policy specification and verification (May 2014), ecs.victoria.ac.nz/Main/TechnicalReportSeries
23. Drossopoulou, S., Noble, J., Mackay, J., Eisenbach, S.: Holisitic Specifications for Robust Programs - Coq Model (2020). https://doi.org/10.5281/zenodo.3677621

24. Drossopoulou, S., Noble, J., Miller, M.: Swapsies on the internet: First steps towards reasoning about risk and trust in an open world. In: (PLAS) (2015)
25. Guttag, J.V., Horning, J.J.: Larch: Languages and Tools for Formal Specification. Springer (1993)
26. Hatcliff, J., Leavens, G.T., Leino, K.R.M., Müller, P., Parkinson, M.J.: Behavioral interface specification languages. ACM Comput.Surv. **44**(3), 16 (2012)
27. Hayes, I.J., Wu, X., Meinicke, L.A.: Capabilities for Java: Secure access to resources. In: APLAS. pp. 67–84 (2017)
28. Hoare, C.A.R.: An axiomatic basis for computer programming. Comm. ACM **12**, 576–580 (1969)
29. Hoare, C.A.R.: Communicating Sequential Processes. Prentice Hall (1985)
30. Jones, T., Homer, M., James Noble, Bruce, K.B.: Object inheritance without classes. In: ECOOP. pp. 13:1–13:26 (2016)
31. Leavens, G.T., Poll, E., Clifton, C., Cheon, Y., Ruby, C., Cok, D.R., Müller, P., Kiniry, J., Chalin, P.: JML Reference Manual (February 2007), iowa State Univ. www.jmlspecs.org
32. Leino, K.R.: Dafny: An automatic program verifier for functional correctness. In: LPAR16. Springer (April 2010)
33. Leino, K.R.M., Schulte, W.: Using history invariants to verify observers. In: ESOP (2007)
34. Lewis, D.: Causation. Journal of Philosophy **70**(17) (1973)
35. Maffeis, S., Mitchell, J., Taly, A.: Object capabilities and isolation of untrusted web applications. In: Proc of IEEE Security and Privacy (2010)
36. Melicher, D., Shi, Y., Potanin, A., Aldrich, J.: A capability-based module system for authority control. In: ECOOP. pp. 20:1–20:27 (2017)
37. Meyer, B.: Eiffel: The Language. Prentice Hall (1992)
38. Meyer, B.: Object-Oriented Software Construction, Second Edition. Prentice Hall, second edn. (1997)
39. Miller, M.S., Cutsem, T.V., Tulloh, B.: Distributed electronic rights in JavaScript. In: ESOP (2013)
40. Miller, M.S.: Robust Composition: Towards a Unified Approach to Access Control and Concurrency Control. Ph.D. thesis, Baltimore, Maryland (2006)
41. Miller, M.S., Morningstar, C., Frantz, B.: Capability-based Financial Instruments: From Object to Capabilities. In: Financial Cryptography. Springer (2000)
42. Miller, M.S., Samuel, M., Laurie, B., Awad, I., Stay, M.: Safe active content in sanitized JavaScript (2008), code.google.com/p/google-caja/
43. Mitre Organisation: CWE-830: Inclusion of Web Functionality from an Untrusted Source (2019), https://cwe.mitre.org/data/definitions/830.html
44. Morris Jr., J.H.: Protection in programming languages. CACM **16**(1) (1973)
45. Müller, P., Poetzsch-Heffter, A., Leavens, G.T.: Modular invariants for layered object structures. Science of Computer Programming **62**, 253–286 (2006)
46. Murray, T.: Analysing the Security Properties of Object-Capability Patterns. Ph.D. thesis, University of Oxford (2010)
47. Murray, T., Sison, R., Engelhardt, K.: COVERN: A logic for compositional verification of information flow control. In: EuroS&P (2018)
48. Noble, J., Drossopoulou, S.: Rationally reconstructing the escrow example. In: FTfJP (2014)
49. Noble, J., Potanin, A., Murray, T., Miller, M.S.: Abstract and concrete data types vs object capabilities. In: Müller, P., Schaefer, I. (eds.) Principled Software Development (2018)
50. Noble, J., Potter, J., Vitek, J.: Flexible alias protection. In: ECOOP (Jul 1998)
51. Pearce, D., Groves, L.: Designing a verifying compiler: Lessons learned from developing Whiley. Sci. Comput. Prog. (2015)
52. Permenev, A., Dimitrov, D., Tsankov, P., Drachsler-Cohen, D., Vechev, M.: VerX: Safety verification of smart contracts. In: IEEE Symp. on Security and Privacy (2020)

53. Reynolds, J.C.: Separation logic: A logic for shared mutable data structures. In: LICS. pp. 55–74. IEEE Computer Society (2002)
54. Rhodes, D., Disney, T., Flanagan, C.: Dynamic detection of object capability violations through model checking. In: DLS. pp. 103–112 (2014)
55. Schaefer, I., Runge, T., Knüppel, A., Cleophas, L., Kourie, D.G., Watson, B.W.: Towards confidentiality-by-construction. In: Leveraging Applications of Formal Methods, Verification and Validation. Modeling - 8th International Symposium, ISoLA 2018, Limassol, Cyprus, November 5-9, 2018, Proceedings, Part I. pp. 502–515 (2018)
56. Sergey, I., Nagaraj, V., Johannsen, J., Kumar, A., Trunov, A., Chan, K.: Safer smart contract programming with Scilla. In: OOPSLA (2019)
57. Smans, J., Jacobs, B., Piessens, F.: Implicit Dynamic Frames. ToPLAS (2012)
58. Summers, A.J., Drossopoulou, S.: Considerate Reasoning and the Composite Pattern. In: VMCAI (2010)
59. Swasey, D., Garg, D., Dreyer, D.: Robust and Compositional Verification of Object Capability Patterns. In: OOPSLA (2017)
60. Talpin, J.P., Jouvelot, P.: The Type and Effect Discipline. In: LICS. pp. 162–173 (1992)
61. The Ethereum Wiki: ERC20 Token Standard (Dec 2018), https://theethereum.wiki/w/index.php/ERC20_Token_Standard

Automated Generation of Consistent Graph Models with First-Order Logic Theorem Provers

Aren A. Babikian[1], Oszkár Semeráth[2,3], and Dániel Varró[1,2,3]

[1] McGill University, Montreal, Canada
[2] MTA-BME Lendület Cyber-Physical Systems Research Group, Budapest, Hungary
[3] Budapest University of Technology and Economics, Budapest, Hungary
aren.babikian@mail.mcgill.ca, semerath@mit.bme.hu, daniel.varro@mcgill.ca

Abstract. The automated generation of graph models has become an enabler in several testing scenarios, including the testing of modeling environments used in the design of critical systems, or the synthesis of test contexts for autonomous vehicles. Those approaches rely on the automated construction of consistent graph models, where each model satisfies complex structural properties of the target domain captured in first-order logic predicates. In this paper, we propose a transformation technique to map such graph generation tasks to a problem consisting of first-order logic formulae, which can be solved by state-of-the-art TPTP-compliant theorem provers, producing valid graph models as outputs. We conducted performance measurements over all 73 theorem provers available in the TPTP library, and compared our approach with other solver-based approaches like Alloy and VIATRA Solver.

Keywords: Domain-Specific Modeling Languages · Model Generation · Theorem Provers

1 Introduction

Motivation. Synthetic graph models have been in use for many challenges of software engineering including the testing of object-oriented programs [18, 20], quality assurance of domain-specific languages [28], validation of model transformations [7] or performance benchmarks of model repositories [5]. In particular, various lines of research in model-driven engineering rely upon such graph models. Network science also heavily depends on the availability of graph models with designated distribution of nodes and edges.

Active research in automated graph model generation [10,25,30,31] has been focusing on deriving graphs with desirable properties like consistency, diversity, scalability or realistic nature [37]. A particularly challenging task of domain-specific model generators is to ensure *consistency*, i.e. to guarantee that synthetic models are not only compliant with the metamodel of the domain, but they also satisfy additional well-formedness constraints captured in popular high-level languages like OCL or graph patterns.

H. Wehrheim and J. Cabot (Eds.): FASE 2020, LNCS 12076, pp. 441–461, 2020.
https://doi.org/10.1007/978-3-030-45234-6_22

Problem statement. Consistent graph generators frequently rely on back-end solvers by mapping model generation problems into logic formulae with different levels of expressiveness. For example, SAT-solvers are used by Kodkod [34] that map high-level languages to propositional logic, CSP-solvers are exploited in EMF2CSP [10], while SMT-solvers were applied in [12, 15, 28]. Consistent model generators may rely on custom search-based techniques [31], symbolic techniques [25] or custom decision procedures [9, 30] to improve scalability.

Automated theorem proving techniques have been developed within the automated reasoning community for decades with a wide range of supporting tools such as HOL [11] and Vampire [19]. In particular, first-order theorem provers have an extensive tool competition where each participating tool takes logic problems using a unified representation of first-order logic (FOL) formulae. This suggests that, despite not being designed for model generation, theorem provers may provide interesting results within the domain considering the success of other general-purpose approaches.

Interestingly, while theorem provers have been used in model-driven engineering to prove the consistency specifications (e.g. HOL-OCL [6], Maude, KeY), their performance has not been investigated in depth for model generation purposes. Since FOL theorem provers already have to face undecidability issues, they are typically optimized to quickly find inconsistencies in formal specifications, while generating a model as a proof of consistency may be less of a priority. As such, existing mappings to FOL formulae may not be reusable in their entirety when theorem provers are used for consistent model generation.

Objectives. In this paper, we aim to systematically investigate and evaluate the *use of first-order logic theorem provers for model generation purposes*. In particular, we present a mapping of domain specifications consisting of a *metamodel, well-formedness constraints* and an optional initial seed model to FOL formulae. Using the standard Thousands of Problems for Theorem Provers (TPTP) format for representing FOL formulae, we used 73 different theorem provers and solvers in a total of 87 different configurations to generate instance models of various size in the context of an industrial domain-specific modeling tool (Yakindu Statecharts) for a scalability evaluation of those solvers. Finally, model results can be transformed to instance models of the domain that can be opened in their native editor - although implementing this step turned out to be solver-specific.

Added value. While various back-end solvers have been used in related mappings, the integration and inclusion of an entire family of first-order logic theorem provers is a novel practical result. Furthermore, our paper provides the first evaluation of a wide range of theorem provers for model generation purposes. As an important technical side effect, thanks to a novel use of constants as object identifiers incorporated in the mapping to FOL formulae, we managed to significantly improve the scalability of the Z3 SMT-solver for model generation purposes compared to existing approaches [28, 32], which relied upon the native support of decision procedures in SMT-solvers.

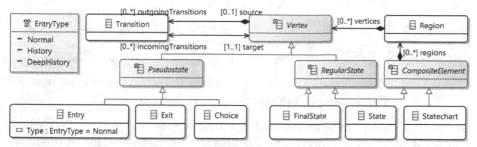

Fig. 1: Metamodel extract of Yakindu Statecharts

2   Preliminaries

The core concepts of domain-specific languages (DSL) and tools are illustrated in the context of Yakindu Statecharts [39], which is an industrial DSL for developing reactive, event-driven systems, and supports validation and code generation.

2.1   Models and metamodels

In this paper we use EMF as a metamodeling technique which is widely used in the modeling community. Formally [28], an (EMF) metamodel defines a vocabulary $\Sigma = \{C_1, \ldots, C_n, R_1, \ldots, R_m, c_1, \ldots, c_o\}$, where a unary predicate symbol C_i is defined for each *EClass* and *EDataType* (like *EInteger* or *EEnums*), a binary predicate symbol R_j is derived for each *EReference* and *EAttribute*, and constant symbols c_k for *EEnum* literals.

Example 1. A simplified metamodel for Yakindu Statecharts is illustrated in Figure 1. A **Statechart** consists of **Regions**, which contain states (**Vertex**) and **Transitions**. The abstract state **Vertex** is further refined into **RegularStates** (like **State** or **FinalState**) and **PseudoStates** (like **Entry**, **Exit** or **Choice**). **Entry** states have a **Type** attribute of type **EntryType**.

Additionally, a metamodel also imposes several *structural constraints*:
1. *Type Hierarchy (TH)* expresses the correct combination of classes (e.g. if an object is an **Entry** then it must be a **Vertex**, but it cannot be a **Region**);
2. *Type Compliance (TC)* requires that for any relation $R(o, t)$, its source and target objects o and t must have compliant types (e.g. the target of a reference **target** must be an instance of **Vertex**);
3. *Abstract (ABS)*: If a class is defined as abstract, it is not allowed to have direct instances (like **CompositeElement**);
4. *Multiplicity (MUL)* of structural features can be limited with upper and lower bound in the form of "lower..upper" (e.g. 1..1 for reference **target**);
5. *Inverse (INV)* states that two parallel references of opposite direction always occur in pairs (e.g. **outgoingTransitions** and **source**).
6. *Containment (CON)*: Instance models in EMF are expected to be arranged into a containment hierarchy, which is a directed tree along relations marked in the metamodel as containment (e.g., **vertices** or **outgoingTransitions**).

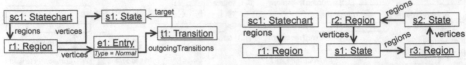

(a) Valid Yakindu instance model   (b) Invalid, cyclic Yakindu instance model

Fig. 2: Sample Yakindu Statechart instance models

An *instance model* can be represented as a logic structure $M = \langle \mathcal{O}_M, \mathcal{I}_M \rangle$, where $\mathcal{O}_M$ is the finite set of objects, and $\mathcal{I}_M$ provides interpretation for all predicate symbols in Σ as follows:

- The interpretation of a unary predicate symbol C_i is defined in accordance with the types of the EMF model: $\mathcal{I}_M(C_i) : \mathcal{O}_M \to \{1, 0\}$. An object $o \in \mathcal{O}_M$ is an instance of (more precisely, conforms to) a class C_i in a model M if $\mathcal{I}_M(C_i)(o) = 1$. It is possible for an object to conform to multiple types, e.g. in case of inheritance or abstract classes.
- The interpretation of a binary predicate symbol R_j is defined in accordance with the links in the EMF model: $\mathcal{I}_M(R_j) : \mathcal{O}_M \times \mathcal{O}_M \to \{1, 0\}$. There is a reference R_j between $o_1, o_2 \in \mathcal{O}_M$ in model M if $\mathcal{I}_M(R_j)(o_1, o_2) = 1$.
- The interpretation assigns each constant symbol c_k: $\mathcal{I}_M : c_k \to \mathcal{O}_M$.

Example 2. Figure 2a illustrates an instance model M with objects $\mathcal{O}_M = \{sc1, r1, s1, t1, e1\}$. Classes of the object are added as labels (e.g. label sc1: Statechart denotes $\mathcal{I}_M(\texttt{Statechart})(sc1) = 1$), attribute values are illustrated as attribute=value labels (e.g. Type = Normal as $\mathcal{I}_M(\texttt{Type})(e1, \texttt{Normal}) = 1$), and reference predicates as labelled edges (e.g. regions edge from $sc1$ to $r1$ as $\mathcal{I}_M(\texttt{regions})(sc1, r1) = 1$).

2.2   Model predicates and Well-formedness constraints

In many industrial modeling tools, domain-specific WF constraints are defined by *error predicates* captured either as OCL constraints [24] or as graph patterns [35]. A major practical subclass of such constraints can be formalized using first-order logic predicates [28].

A graph predicate φ is defined inductively over a vocabulary Σ of a metamodel and an infinite set of (object) variables $\{v_1, v_2, \ldots\}$ and the constant symbols as seen in Figure 3a. A graph predicate φ with free variables $param = \{v_1, \ldots, v_n\}$ can be evaluated over a model M with variable binding $Z : param \to \mathcal{O}_M$ (denoted with $[\![\varphi(v_1, \ldots, v_n)]\!]_Z^M$) using the rules of Figure 3b.

Therefore, if a domain defines error patterns $\varphi_1, \ldots, \varphi_n$, a model is considered consistent (valid), if it does not satisfy any error predicates $\varphi_i(v_1, \ldots, v_m)$ $(1 \le i \le n)$, i.e. $\forall v_1, \ldots, v_m : \neg\varphi_i(v_1, \ldots, v_m)$. Since a formalization of these structural restrictions as WF constraints is provided in [28], the predicate language of Figure 3b can uniformly be used for both kinds of structural constraints.

Example 3. Figure 4 illustrates three graph patterns defined in both graphical and textual syntax. Pattern `transition(t,src,trg)` defines a relation

	Logic Syntax	TPTP Syntax	
$\varphi :=$	c	c	*constant*
$\vert$	$\mathtt{C}(v)$	C(v)	*type predicate*
$\vert$	$\mathtt{R}(v_1, v_2)$	R(v1,v2)	*reference predicate*
$\vert$	$v_1 = v_2$	v1=v2	*equivalence*
$\vert$	$dist(v_1, ..., v_n)$	v1!=v2 &...&vn-1!=vn	*n-ary inequality (distinctness)*
$\vert$	$\neg\varphi \mid \varphi_1 \wedge \varphi_2 \mid \varphi_1 \vee \varphi_2$	~p | p1&p2 | p1|p2	*logic connectives*
$\vert$	$\exists v : \varphi \mid \forall v : \varphi$	?[v]:p | ![v]:p	*quantified expression*

(a) Syntax of graph predicates

$$\llbracket c \rrbracket_Z^M := \mathcal{I}_M(c)$$
$$\llbracket \mathtt{C}(v) \rrbracket_Z^M := \mathcal{I}_M(\mathtt{C})(Z(v)) \qquad \llbracket \varphi_1 \wedge \varphi_2 \rrbracket_Z^M := min(\llbracket \varphi_1 \rrbracket_Z^M, \llbracket \varphi_2 \rrbracket_Z^M)$$
$$\llbracket \mathtt{R}(v_1, v_2) \rrbracket_Z^M := \mathcal{I}_M(\mathtt{R})(Z(v_1), Z(v_2)) \qquad \llbracket \varphi_1 \vee \varphi_2 \rrbracket_Z^M := max(\llbracket \varphi_1 \rrbracket_Z^M, \llbracket \varphi_2 \rrbracket_Z^M)$$
$$\llbracket v_1 = v_2 \rrbracket_Z^M := Z(v_1) = Z(v_2) \qquad \llbracket \exists v : \varphi \rrbracket_Z^M := max_{o \in \mathcal{O}_M} \{\llbracket \varphi_1 \rrbracket_{Z, v \mapsto o}^M\}$$
$$\llbracket \neg\varphi \rrbracket_Z^M := 1 - \llbracket \varphi \rrbracket_Z^M \qquad \llbracket \forall v : \varphi \rrbracket_Z^M := min_{o \in \mathcal{O}_M} \{\llbracket \varphi_1 \rrbracket_{Z, v \mapsto o}^M\}$$

(b) Semantic rules for graph predicates

Fig. 3: Syntax and semantics for graph predicates

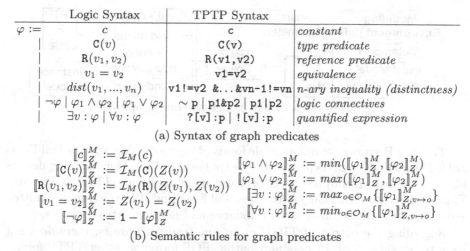

```
pattern transition(t,src,trg) {
    Transition.source(t,src);
    Transition.target(t,trg); }
```

$$transition(t, src, trg) = \mathbf{source}(t, src) \wedge \mathbf{target}(t, trg)$$

```
@Constraint
pattern incomingToEntry(t, e:Entry) {
    find transition(t,_,e); }
```

$$ite(t, e) = \exists s : transition(t, s, e) \wedge \mathbf{Entry}(e)$$

```
@Constraint
pattern noOutgoing(e:Entry) {
    neg find transition(_,e,_); }
```

$$no(e) = \forall t, trg : \neg transition(t, e, trg) \wedge \mathbf{Entry}(e)$$

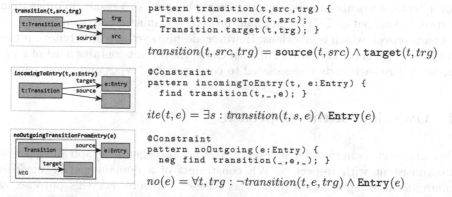

Fig. 4: Example graph patterns defined with graphical and VIATRA syntax

between two **Vertices** which are connected via a **Transition** using **source** and **target** references. Reusing this pattern, two WF constraints are defined concerning **Entry** states: if any of them has a match, then the model is malformed. First, `incomingToEntry(t, e)` selects invalid **Transitions** that are leading to an **Entry** (by reusing the previously defined **transition** pattern). Next, `noOutgoingTransitionFromEntry(e)` matches to **Entry** states that does not have any outgoing **Transition** (by negatively using **transition** pattern).

2.3 First-Order Logic Theorem Provers

Our approach to model generation involves using a back-end FOL theorem prover to generate finite models according to input constraints. The theorem prover is treated as a black-box component in our model generation workflow, thus it takes input formulae and generates an output formula. Logic formulae are given using the TPTP Syntax [33] as it is a standard within the theorem prover community.

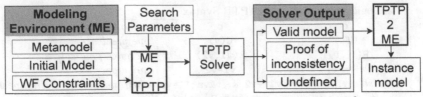

Fig. 5: Overview of our model generation approach

The TPTP syntax defines multiple forms of logic formulae, such as Full First-order Form (FOF) and Typed Higher-order Form (THF). Our mapping derives FOF formulae defined by a subsyntax that can handle standard FOL statements. This is sufficient for modeling most aspects of EMF and WF constraints. Omitted aspects include containment cycle avoidance and numeric attributes

Regarding the output of TPTP-compliant theorem provers, there does not seem to be a standard. Provers may output FOF formulae, other TPTP formulae, or TPTP non-compliant formulae. This is not surprising, as many TPTP-compliant solvers also handle various other syntaxes. As a result, in order to interpret the output of TPTP-compliant provers, one must create a custom parser for each prover, which is laborious. However, despite syntactic differences, prover outputs are structurally similar: in most cases, the output contains a list of graph nodes, where each node is associated to corresponding types and graph edges.

3   Overview of the Approach

Our approach (summarized in Figure 5) aims to generate graph models that are consistent with respect to WF constraints of a domain-specific *modeling environment* using theorem provers as back-end solvers. For this purpose, we map the high-level specifications of the input DSL into equivalent FOL formulae written in TPTP-compliant syntax [33]. We implement our approach as part of the VIATRA Model Generation Framework [1].

The specification of the DSL (or modeling environment) consists of a *meta-model* specified in EMF augmented with *well-formedness constraints* captured by model queries (using the VIATRA framework [36]). Additionally, our generator can take an optional *initial instance model* that acts as a seed for model generation. Our model generation framework can also take various *search parameters* such as type scope (requested size) and containment cycle avoidance specifications as input to guide model generation towards desired characteristics.

The input modeling environment and the search parameters are mapped to FOL formulae using the novel *ME2TPTP* model-to-text transformation detailed in section 4. The FOL-formula is then fed into a TPTP-compliant theorem prover (*TPTP Solver*). The solver may output a *valid model* if all input constraints are satisfiable. In this case, the output is transformed into a domain-compliant *instance model* through a *TPTP2ME* backwards mapping. Otherwise, if input constraints are inconsistent, the solver can either identify its *inconsistency*, or provides an *undefined* output (if it cannot decide by its decision procedures or due to lack of computational resources).

Our approach is designed to generate a finite model rather than a finite counterexample of the input specifications. Such a task is facilitated by including size requirements for the desired model a priori. However, if size requirements are not provided, the theorem prover could easily check for inconsistencies in the input formulae due to the small-model theorem [14].

In addition to generating graph models from scratch, our approach is also capable of completing initial seed models. An initial model may be inconsistent (i.e. it may violate some metamodel or WF constraints), thus it is the task of the TPTP solver to extend the input model into a consistent instance model. Another use case is to validate the consistency of DSLs and modeling environments [16, 28]. Our approach is capable of detecting when constraints derived from a modeling environment are contradictory with each other. In this case, our approach can prove the unsatisfiability of the input constraints.

4   From Domain-Specific Languages to First-Order Logic

We discuss how the various components of a modeling language are mapped into a set $\varphi = \varphi^{MM} \wedge \varphi^{IM} \wedge \varphi^{WF}$ of TPTP-compliant FOL formulae. The formula φ^{MM} is derived from the metamodel types (in section 4.1) and relations (in section 4.2) , as defined in section 2.1 , along with additional constraints and search parameters. φ^{IM} describes the mapping for initial instance models (in section 4.3). Finally, φ^{WF} describes how additional WF constraints defined as VIATRA queries are mapped into FOL formulae (in section 4.4). All components of our mapping with the exception of lower multiplicities and WF constraints output Essentially Propositional Logic formulae. Proof systems for such formulae [23] do exist, but cannot be fully exploited on the output of our mapping.

4.1   Mapping Types in the Metamodel

The various types in the input EMF metamodel are mapped to FOL formulae as described below.

Objects: A key idea in our mapping is that we use FOL constants (instead of other data types such as TPTP distinct objects) to represent the generated graph nodes. Constants are preferred due to their compatibility with our presented encoding (distinct objects cannot be used as arguments for FOL predicates).

These constants are separated into two categories: first, nodes defined prior to theorem proving are denoted with a set of constant symbols $Obj^O = \{old_1, \ldots, old_n\}$. This set includes known objects such as enum literals and elements of the initial partial model. Additionally, the logic solver will add new objects to the generated model, some of which are denoted with constant symbols $Obj^N = \{new_1, \ldots, new_m\}$. We also introduce a unary predicate $object(o)$ that selects all nodes of the graph model (including attribute values, enum literals and objects). The $object(o)$ predicate holds for all constants o in Obj^O and for some in Obj^N.

448   A. A. Babikian et al.

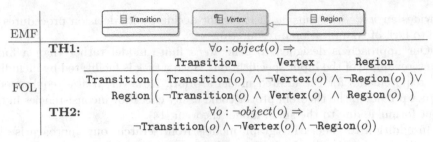

Fig. 6: Mapping type hierarchy

Type Hierarchy (TH): To handle complex generalization relations (e.g multiple inheritance) in the type hierarchy, we introduce formulae to control the potential combinations of the type predicates. For this purpose, we map each *EClass* of the input metamodel to a FOL predicate $C_i(o)$. A sample mapping is shown in Figure 6 for an extract of the domain metamodel.

To express the *mutual exclusiveness* of (non-abstract) classes in the type hierarchy, we construct a formula $d_0 = \bigvee_{C_i \in s_{na}} t_i(C_i)$ in disjunctive normal form (DNF) for the set s_{na} of all non-abstract classes in the metamodel. For each non-abstract type C_i, a conjunction $t_i(C_i)$ is created for all class predicates such that a predicate C_j is positive if and only if it is a member of set $s(C_i)$ containing C_i and its superclasses, formally $t_i(C_i) = \bigwedge_{C_j \in s(C_i)} C_j(o) \wedge \bigwedge_{C_j \notin s(C_i)} \neg C_j(o)$. We must ensure that any constant satisfying the $object(o)$ predicate also satisfies the type hierarchy described in d_0. Thus, we generate the following FOL formula: $\varphi_{\mathbf{TH1}}^{MM} = \forall o : object(o) \Rightarrow d_0$. This is a *filtered-types* approach to type hierarchy transformations used in the context of Object-Relation Mapping [17].

We also generate a formula to handle the negative case for the *object* predicate. We specify that any constants o that is not compliant with the $object(o)$ predicate must not be an instance of any class in the metamodel. Formally, the negation of $object(o)$ implies a conjunction t_{no} of the negations of all class predicates C_i in the metamodel (MM): $t_{no} = \bigwedge_{C_i \in MM} \neg C_i$. The generated FOL formula is as follows: $\varphi_{\mathbf{TH2}}^{MM} = \forall o : \neg object(o) \Rightarrow t_{no}$.

Enumerations and Literals (EN) Mapping for enumerations is carried out similarly to that of types. A unary predicate is created for each enum class $E_i(o)$ in the input metamodel, and a distinct unary predicate $l_i(o)$ is created for each literal of the enum class. The mapping of an enum class creates a disjunction $d_1 = \bigvee_{l_i} t_i(l_i)$. For each literal l_i, a conjunction t_i is created, where only the predicate corresponding to l_i is positive and all others are negative, formally $t_i(l_i) = l_i(o) \wedge \bigwedge_{l_j \neq l_i} \neg l_j(o)$. To ensure that generated enum instances are part of the output model and that each literal is unique, a FOL constraint is generated for each enum class stating that objects satisfy the corresponding predicate E_i if and only if they also satisfy the $object(o)$ predicate and the disjunction d_1:

$$\varphi_{\mathbf{EN1}}^{MM} = \forall o : E_i(o) \Leftrightarrow object(o) \wedge \bigvee_{l_i} \left(l_i(o) \wedge \bigwedge_{l_j \neq l_i} \neg l_j(o) \right)$$

$$\textbf{EN1:} \quad \forall o : \texttt{EntryType}(o) \Leftrightarrow (object(o) \wedge$$
$$((\texttt{Normal}(o) \wedge \neg\texttt{History}(o)) \vee (\neg\texttt{Normal}(o) \wedge \texttt{History}(o))))$$
$$\textbf{EN2-N:} \quad \forall o : (o = eo_1 \Leftrightarrow \texttt{Normal}(o))$$
$$\textbf{EN2-H:} \quad \forall o : (o = eo_2 \Leftrightarrow \texttt{History}(o))$$

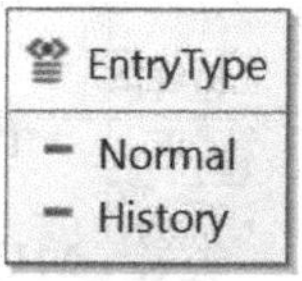

☰ EntryType

– Normal

– History

Fig. 7: Mapping enumerations

Each enum literal is also transformed into an individual FOL constraint that instantiates a constant eo_i to define an enum object for each l_i that is associated with E_i. The generated FOL constraint ensures that the output model contains a constant eo_i corresponding to each enum literal: $\varphi_{\textbf{EN2}}^{MM} = \forall o : (o = eo_i \Leftrightarrow l_i(o))$.

Example 4. To better understand this mapping, we consider the `EntryType` enum in Figure 1. We omit the `DeepHistory` literal for the sake of conciseness. This enum is mapped into the 3 FOL statements shown in Figure 7.

Model Scope: Our mapping also allows for users to specify a scope (size) for the generated model as a search parameter. A scope may contain an upper bound u and a lower bound l for the number of generated objects in the output model. For an upper bound specification u, we define $Obj^N = \{new_1, \ldots, new_{u-|Obj^O|}\}$, where Obj^O is the set of nodes defined prior to theorem proving. If $u - |Obj^O|$ is negative then the problem is surely inconsistent. We then generate a FOL expression which specifies that any constant o satisfying $object(o)$ must be contained in either Obj^O or Obj^N, to ensure that the theorem prover does not generate any further constants (that satisfy $object(o)$) as part of the output finite model.

$$\varphi_{\textbf{MUB}}^{MM} = \forall o : object(o) \Rightarrow \left(\bigvee_{old_i \in Obj^O} (o = old_i) \vee \bigvee_{new_i \in Obj^N} (o = new_i) \right)$$

For a lower bound specification l, we define $m' = l - |Obj^O|$ and we create a set $Obj_{lb}^N \subseteq Obj^N$ containing m' constants that are also in Obj^N. In the case where Obj^N is not defined (an upper bound value has not been specified), we define $Obj_{lb}^N = \{new_1, \ldots, new_{l-|Obj^O|}\}$. We then generate a FOL formula to specify that any object o that is either in Obj^O or in Obj_{lb}^N must also satisfy $object(o)$ to ensure that these constants are part of the output finite model:

$$\varphi_{\textbf{MLB}}^{MM} = \forall o : \left(\bigvee_{old_i \in Obj^O} (o = old_i) \vee \bigvee_{new_i \in Obj_{lb}^N} (o = new_i) \right) \Rightarrow object(o)$$

Example 5. To generate a model that contains from 4 to 6 objects, 2 of which are already defined (e.g. enum literals), the following FOL statements are derived:

MUB: $\quad \forall o : object(o) \Rightarrow ((o = old_1) \vee (o = old_2) \vee (o = new_1) \vee$
$$(o = new_3) \vee (o = new_4) \vee (o = new_2))$$

MLB: $\quad \forall o : ((o = old_1) \vee (o = old_2) \vee (o = new_1) \vee (o = new_2)) \Rightarrow object(o)$

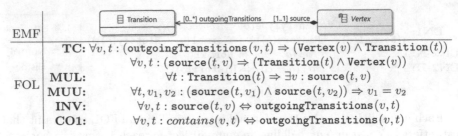

$$\textbf{TC:} \ \forall v,t : (\textbf{outgoingTransitions}(v,t) \Rightarrow (\textbf{Vertex}(v) \wedge \textbf{Transition}(t))$$
$$\forall v,t : (\textbf{source}(t,v) \Rightarrow (\textbf{Transition}(t) \wedge \textbf{Vertex}(v)))$$

MUL: $\qquad \forall t : \textbf{Transition}(t) \Rightarrow \exists v : \textbf{source}(t,v)$

MUU: $\quad \forall t, v_1, v_2 : (\textbf{source}(t,v_1) \wedge \textbf{source}(t,v_2)) \Rightarrow v_1 = v_2$

INV: $\qquad \forall v,t : \textbf{source}(t,v) \Leftrightarrow \textbf{outgoingTransitions}(v,t)$

CO1: $\qquad \forall v,t : contains(v,t) \Leftrightarrow \textbf{outgoingTransitions}(v,t)$

EMF / FOL labels at left.

Fig. 8: Mapping relations

Type Scope: A scope may be specified for each particular type C. In the case of an upper bound u_t, we define a set Obj^N_{ut} such that $u_t = |Obj^N_{ut}|$. If a model upper bound has been defined, then $Obj^N_{ut} \subseteq Obj^N$ holds, and we specify that any constant o satisfying $object(o)$ and $C_i(o)$ must be contained in Obj^N_{ut}:

$$\varphi^{MM}_{\textbf{TUB}} = \forall o : (object(o) \wedge C_i(o)) \Rightarrow \bigvee_{new_i \in Obj^N_{ut}} (o = new_i)$$

In case of a lower bound l_t, we select a set $Obj^N_{lt} \subseteq Obj^N_{ut}$ (if Obj^N_{ut} is defined) such that $l_t = |Obj^N_{lt}|$. We then generate a FOL expression which specifies that all constants in Obj^N_{lt} must also satisfy $object(o)$ and $C_i(o)$:

$$\varphi^{MM}_{\textbf{TLB}} = \forall o : \bigvee_{new_i \in Obj^N_{lt}} (o = new_i) \Rightarrow (object(o) \wedge C_i(o))$$

Uniqueness: For every model object mapped to a FOL constant c_i, we must generate formulae to ensure that it is distinct from other objects. These formulae are only generated in the case where a scope is defined. Assuming that an ordering is defined for all n constants c_i, we generate $n-1$ FOL constraints with increasing value of $j < n$: $\varphi^{MM}_{\textbf{Un}}(j,n) = \bigwedge^n_{c_i:i=j+1} c_j \neq c_i$.

4.2 Mapping Relations Between Metamodel Types

Once type-related constraints are mapped into FOL formulae, relations between these types are mapped as binary predicates.

Type Compliance (TC) Relations between classes and class attributes are mapped into FOL in the same way (see section 2). Each relation and attribute is mapped to a FOL predicate $R_i(o_1, o_2)$. When mapping relations, we must ensure that the endpoint objects are type-compliant with the metamodel: for each $R_i(o_1, o_2)$ that points from a class C_1 to a type C_2, we generate a formula

$$\varphi^{MM}_{\textbf{TC}} = \forall o_1, o_2 : R_i(o_1, o_2) \Rightarrow (C_1(o_1) \wedge C_2(o_2)).$$

Note that for the purpose of this specific mapping, inverse relations are considered as two separate unidirectional relations. Figure 8 contains an example of such a case, with the corresponding TC mapping.

Multiplicities (MUL) As the multiplicity of a unidirectional relation has a lower and an upper bound, at most two FOL formulae will be generated. Lower multiplicities of 0 and upper multiplicities of $*$ do not generate any formulae.

Lower Multiplicity : Consider the relation $R_i(a, b)$ from $C_i(a)$ to $C_j(b)$ which has a lower multiplicity $m \neq 0$. We generate the constraint that for all objects a of type $C_i(a)$, there must exist at least m unique constants $b_0 \ldots b_m$ connected to $C_i(a)$ through a $R_i(a, b_i)$ relation. The generated FOL constraint is:

$$\varphi_{\mathbf{MUL}}^{MM} = \forall a : \left(C_i(a) \Rightarrow \left(\exists b_0 \ldots b_m : \left(\bigwedge_{b_i :: i=0}^{m} R_i(a, b_i) \right) \wedge distinct(b_0 \ldots b_m) \right) \right)$$

Upper Multiplicity : Given the relation $R_i(a, b)$ introduced previously, let us consider an upper multiplicity of $n \neq *$. We generate the constraint that if there are $n + 1$ objects $b_0 \ldots b_{n+1}$ connected to an object a through $R_i(a, b_i)$ relations, then there are at least 2 identical b_i constants among $b_0 \ldots b_{n+1}$. This means that $b_0 \ldots b_{n+1}$ are not pairwise distinct, formally $\neg distinct(b_0 \ldots b_{n+1})$.

$$\varphi_{\mathbf{MUU}}^{MM} = \forall a, b_0 \ldots b_{n+1} : \left(\bigwedge_{b_i :: i=0}^{n+1} R_i(a, b_i) \right) \Rightarrow \neg distinct(b_0 \ldots b_{n+1})$$

Multiplicity formulae derived from a relation in Figure 1 are shown in Figure 8. Note the asymmetric nature of the two formulae: lower multiplicities are more difficult to satisfy for the prover as that might introduce an infinite model.

Inverse Relations (INV) As mentioned earlier, we consider inverse relations as two separate (unidirectional) relations. The bidirectional nature of such relations implies that both of their corresponding unidirectional relations cannot exist without each other. Thus, we must ensure that for two objects a and b are connected by inverse relations $R_i(a, b)$ and $R_j(b, a)$ simultaneously: $\varphi_{\mathbf{INV}}^{MM} = \forall a, b : R_i(a, b) \Leftrightarrow R_j(b, a)$. An example can be seen in Figure 8.

Containment Hierarchy (CON) Containment hierarchy is enforced by the following constraints (see Figure 8 for examples):

- *Union of containment edges:* We first define a disjunction $contains(o_1, o_2)$ of all containment relations $R_{c-i}(o_1, o_2)$ in the metamodel. The generated FOL formula is $\varphi_{\mathbf{CO1}}^{MM} = \forall o_1, o_2 : contains(o_1, o_2) \Leftrightarrow \bigvee_{R_{c-i}} R_{c-i}(o_1, o_2)$.
- *Existence of a unique root constant:* We define a unique constant **root** as an object that is not contained: $\varphi_{\mathbf{CO2}}^{MM} = \forall r, o : (r = \mathbf{root} \Leftrightarrow \neg contains(o, r))$.
- *Container Object:* We must ensure that every non-root object in the generated model is contained by another object. Thus, any constant o that satisfies $object(o)$ is either the root constant **root** or is contained by another constant. Formally, $\varphi_{\mathbf{CO3}}^{MM} = \forall o : object(o) \Rightarrow (o = \mathbf{root} \vee \exists p : contains(p, o))$.
- *Single Container:* We must also ensure that any constant o is contained by at most one other constant. Thus, if o is contained by two constants p_1 and p_2, then p_1 and p_2 are identical. Formally, $\varphi_{\mathbf{CO4}}^{MM} = \forall o, p_1, p_2 : (contains(p_1, o) \wedge contains(p_2, o)) \Rightarrow (p_1 = p_2)$.

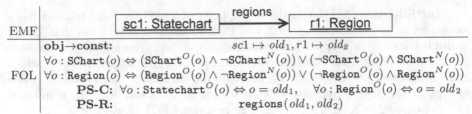

$$\text{obj} \rightarrow \text{const:} \qquad\qquad sc1 \mapsto old_1, r1 \mapsto old_2$$

$$\text{FOL} \quad \forall o : \text{SChart}(o) \Leftrightarrow (\text{SChart}^O(o) \land \neg\text{SChart}^N(o)) \lor (\neg\text{SChart}^O(o) \land \text{SChart}^N(o))$$

$$\forall o : \text{Region}(o) \Leftrightarrow (\text{Region}^O(o) \land \neg\text{Region}^N(o)) \lor (\neg\text{Region}^O(o) \land \text{Region}^N(o))$$

$$\textbf{PS-C:} \quad \forall o : \text{Statechart}^O(o) \Leftrightarrow o = old_1, \quad \forall o : \text{Region}^O(o) \Leftrightarrow o = old_2$$

$$\textbf{PS-R:} \qquad\qquad \text{regions}(old_1, old_2)$$

Fig. 9: Mapping instance models

Avoidance of Cyclic Containment (CYC) Unfortunately, FOL is not expressive enough to capture formulae required to avoid cyclic containment relations (an example is shown in Figure 2b) in the output models. Therefore, we generate approximated constraints to avoid cycles up to length n given as an input parameter. For that purpose, we derive separate formulae for each length x (with $0 < x \le n$) using the $contains(o_1, o_2)$ predicate defined in $\varphi_{\textbf{CO1}}^{MM}$. Formally,

$$\varphi_{\textbf{CYC}}^{MM}(x) = \neg\exists o_1 \ldots o_x : \left(\bigwedge_{i=0}^{x-1} contains(o_i, o_{i+1}) \right) \land contains(o_x, o_0).$$

4.3   Instance model mapping

When mapping an instance model $P = \langle \mathcal{O}_P, \mathcal{I}_P \rangle$ as a partial snapshot, we transform its objects $\mathcal{O}_P = \{o_1, \ldots, o_n\}$ to a set of constants $Const_P = \{old_1, \ldots, old_n\}$ while maintaining a trace map $t : \mathcal{O}_P \to Const_P$. Additionally, all classes C which have an instance in the instance model are split into two categories: C^O and C^N that differentiate the old (i.e. $old_1, \ldots, old_n$) and new objects (generated by the solver). Finally, if a class predicate C_i is true in the partial model $\mathcal{I}_P(C_i)(o) = 1$, then it must be true in the generated model too, which is enforced by formula $C_i^O(t(o))$. Similarly, if a reference predicate R_j is true in the partial model $\mathcal{I}_M(R_j)(o_1, o_2) = 1$, then it also must be true in the generated model, which is enforced by formula $R_j(t(o_1), t(o_2))$.

A sample generated FOL formulae for an instance model is shown in Figure 9.

4.4   Mapping additional constraints

The modeling environment of our approach may contain additional FOL patterns and WF constraints defined in the Viatra Query Language (VQL). The header of each VQL pattern taking n parameters as input is mapped to a predicate $\text{ph}_i(v_1 \ldots v_n)$. The pattern body is mapped into a FOL statement $\varphi_{pci}(v_1 \ldots v_n)$ according to its FOL content such that if a set of n variables satisfy the associated pattern header predicate, it must also satisfy the specifications described in $\varphi_{pci}(v_1 \ldots v_n)$: $\varphi_{\textbf{WF1}}^{WF} = \forall v_1 \ldots v_n : \text{ph}_i(v_1 \ldots v_n) \Rightarrow \varphi_{pci}(v_1 \ldots v_n)$.

For patterns that are specified as WF constraint, an additional FOL formula is generated to ensure that such patterns does not matching in the generated model. Structurally, the corresponding FOL formula checks that no objects $v_1 \ldots v_n$ satisfies the condition of the pattern: $\varphi_{\textbf{WF2}}^{WF} = \forall v_1 \ldots v_n : \neg\text{ph}_i(v_1 \ldots v_n)$. Figure 10 shows the mapping for patterns specified in Figure 4.

VQL	`pattern transition(t,src,trg){`
	`  Transition.source(t,src);`
	`  Transition.target(t,trg); }`
		`@Constraint`
		`pattern incomingToEntry(t, e:Entry){`
		`  find transition(t,_,e); }`

FOL	**WF1-TRA.:**	$\forall t, src, trg : transition(t, src, trg) \Rightarrow$ $\textbf{source}(t, src) \wedge \textbf{target}(t, trg)$
	WF1-ITE: $\forall t, e : ite(t, e) \Rightarrow (\textbf{Entry}(e) \wedge (\exists s : transition(t, s, e)))$	
	WF2-ITE: $\forall t, e : (\textbf{Transition}(t) \wedge \textbf{Entry}(e)) \Rightarrow \neg ite(t, e)$	

Fig. 10: Mapping VQL patterns and WF constraints

5   Evaluation

We conduct several measurements to address the following research questions:

RQ1: Which TPTP-compliant theorem provers are most scalable wrt. model size and runtime of model generation?

RQ2: How do theorem provers scale compared to other logic solvers for a model generation scenario?

Target domain: To address these questions, we perform model generation scenarios and analyze the results in the context of the *Yakindu Statecharts* industrial modeling environment introduced in section 2.1. We use the metamodel shown in Figure 1, which contains 13 classes, including an enum class, and 6 references. Moreover, the Yakindu metamodel covers all mapping rules introduced in section 4. We also formalize 17 WF constraints as graph predicates to further restrict the model generation scope. Finally, we provide an initial instance model as a seed for model generation which contains only a single root node, thus the underlying solvers have full responsibility in model generation. Examples of input and output files as well as our measurement results are on GitHub[4]. Altogether, *Yakindu Statecharts* provide a sufficiently complex case to assess the proposed mapping and the underlying theorem provers, and it has been used as a case study in existing papers of model generation [27, 30].

5.1   Research Question 1 (RQ1)

Measurement setup: We compare the scalability of all TPTP-compliant theorem provers available on the *System on TPTP*[5] website, which is the official TPTP web interface for solving FOL problems for theorem proving competitions. *System on TPTP* lists 73 solvers and 87 different solver configurations that can be called directly on their servers[6] through HTTP requests.

Our experimentation consists of three phases. For all three phases, we generate constraints to avoid containment cycles of up to 5 objects, which is a parameter used in existing research such as [28].

PHASE I: As a *preliminary step*, we attempt to generate a small model containing 9-10 nodes within a time limit of 1 minute with each listed TPTP-prover.

---

[4] https://github.com/ArenBabikian/publication-pages/wiki/
Automated-Generation-of-Consistent-Graph-Models-with-Theorem-Provers
[5] http://tptp.cs.miami.edu/cgi-bin/SystemOnTPTP
[6] Intel Xeon CPU E5-4610 2.40GHz, 128GB RAM, Linux 3.10.0

Note that from the 9-10 output nodes, 3 nodes are enforced by the enum mapping, 1 node is defined in the initial model and 5-6 nodes must be generated by the theorem prover. We perform this experimentation three times and we manually analyze the output. If a theorem prover is unable to read the input TPTP problem or is incapable of generating a finite model according to the specifications, it is disqualified for the subsequent two steps of our workflow.

PHASE II: This phase involves *small-size model generation* to further eliminate weak TPTP solvers. For each qualified solver, we generate finite models with increasing size (starting from 5 objects as a lower bound, with a step size of 5 objects). We set a timeout of 1 minute for each generation run. We execute each generation run 10 times and take the median of the execution times of successful runs (i.e. that provide a finite model as result within the given timeout).

We also measure the ratio of failed runs for each model size. We end the sequence of model generations for a given solver if all 10 runs at a same size specification fail to output a finite model. Considering that we are running the measurements on a server, we cannot influence warm-up effects and memory handling. After this second phase, we keep the (four) best performing solvers.

PHASE III: We complete our experimentation by performing *large-scale model generation*. For this phase, we perform the same data collection as for PHASE II. However, we begin model generation at a size of 30 objects and use step size of 10 objects. Furthermore, we use a timeout of 5 minutes and we perform each generation run 20 times.

Scalability in model size: We compare model size derived by TPTP solvers.

PHASE I: Among the 87 prover configurations provided on the TPTP server, only 8 configurations were able to generate models with 9-10 objects, namely CVC4 (SAT-1.7), DarwinFM (1.4.5), E-Darwin (1.5), Geo-III (2018C), iProver (SAT-3.0), Paradox (4.0), Vampire (SAT-4.4) and Z3 (4.4.1). The MACE2 (2.2) prover also claimed generating a finite model for the given inputs. However, after manual analysis of the output, no generated finite model was found. As a result, we decided to drop MACE2 from the following measurement phases.

PHASE II: Figure 11a presents the complete measurements for scalability analysis of the 4 least scalable remaining solver configurations. PHASE II results for the 4 more scalable solver configurations are included in Figure 11b, along with their results for PHASE III. Figure 11a contains the median runtime (as provided by the server) of successful model generations wrt the size of the generated model while the runtime required for the mapping itself is excluded (as it is negligible). Measurements for PHASE II are performed for models of up to 25 objects, while measurements for larger models correspond to PHASE III.

Figure 11c presents the ratio of failed model generation runs wrt. model size. When all runs fail in generating models, the failure ratio becomes 1 and no further model generation runs are performed. Notice that solvers CVC4, DarwinFM, E-Darwin and Geo-III are unable to generate models of 30 objects within the 1-minute timeout period, thus they are excluded from further experiments.

PHASE III: Figure 11b shows that iProver and Z3 dominate in terms of scalability. There exists a steady increase in runtime with respect to generated model

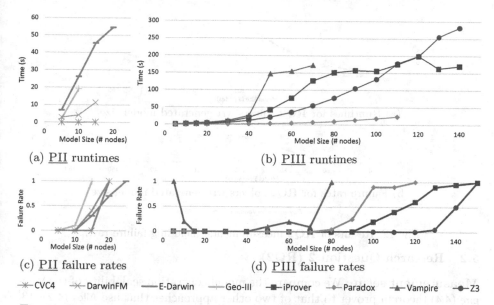

(a) PII runtimes

(b) PIII runtimes

(c) PII failure rates

(d) PIII failure rates

Fig. 11: Results of PHASE II and PHASE III measurements (incl. failure rates)

size, however, we notice certain inconsistencies when failure rates increase as the generated models become larger. Both solvers can generate models of 140 objects: iProver can do so at a faster rate, however, Z3 does so more consistently with respect to failures. Moreover, it is interesting to see that existing model generation approaches that used Z3 as an underlying solver [28, 32] report inferior results with respect to the size of generated (fully connected) models.

The Paradox solver provides very fast model generation for models of up to 110 objects. Although failure rates are high for large models, by inspecting the measurement data, we notice that Paradox explicitly reports (within timeout) that it is unknown if a model can be generated for the given input.

Scalability of the Vampire solver lacks in comparison to the other solvers. We observe an interesting pattern in failure rates for Vampire: the solver fails often when generating not only large models, but also very small models. In fact, analysis of measurement data shows that in these cases, Vampire states that the input constraints are satisfiable, but it does not generate a finite model. This behavior is similar to that of Paradox, since failures are not caused by timeouts.

Runtime of solvers: Runtime differences between solvers are negligible for generated models of size 20 and under. For models larger than 20 nodes, Paradox was the fastest solver as highlighted in Figure 11b. For models with 120 objects or more, iProver is slightly faster than Z3. However, increased failure rates for iProver make the measured median values less reliable than those of Z3.

RQ1: *Only 9% (8/87) of theorem prover configurations presented in the System on TPTP website are able to generate small models. Only 4 configurations can generate larger models containing 30 nodes. iProver and Z3 are the most scalable provers and are able to generate models of 140 nodes, while Paradox is significantly faster than other solvers for models of up to 110 nodes.*

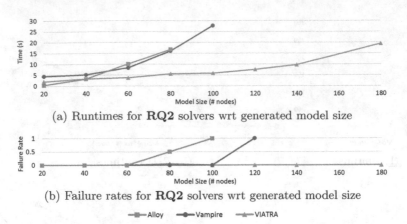

(a) Runtimes for **RQ2** solvers wrt generated model size

(b) Failure rates for **RQ2** solvers wrt generated model size

Fig. 12: Results of **RQ2** measurements, including failure rates.

5.2   Research Question 2 (RQ2)

Measurement setup: We compare the model generation scalability of the Vampire (4.4) theorem prover to that of two other approaches that use Alloy (4.2) [13] and VIATRA Solver [27, 30] as back-end solvers, respectively. We select Vampire for our experimentation as it is the most scalable theorem prover that we are able to run locally using generated TPTP files as input. We use the most recent stable releases of the solvers to generate graphs of increasing size (starting from models with *exactly* 20 objects, and an increment of *exactly* 20 objects).

We generate constraints to avoid containment cycles of up to 5 objects and we set a timeout of 5 minutes. We execute 20 runs per generated graph size and take the median of the execution times of successful runs (i.e. that provide a finite model as result within the given timeout). To account for warm-up effects and memory handling of the Java 8 VM, we add an extra 5 runs before the actual measurements and call the garbage collector explicitly between runs. We perform measurements on an average personal computer[7] with local installation of solvers. We end the sequence of model generations if none of the 20 runs at a same size specification provide a generated finite model.

Scalability in model size: Figure 12a presents the scalability measurements for the Vampire, Alloy and VIATRA solvers. Figure 12b presents the corresponding failure rates. VIATRA was able to generate models of up to 1380 objects, but data points are shown in Figure 12a and Figure 12b for models only up to 180 nodes. We notice that our mapping using the Vampire solver slightly outperforms Alloy, but both approaches are significantly outperformed by the VIATRA-solver, which is coherent with previous research results [30]. The variation in Vampire performance (cf. Figure 11b and Figure 12a) is attributed to the different measurement environments and Vampire versions used to assess each research question.

> **RQ2:** *Using Vampire as a back-end solver, our approach scales for 20% larger models with less failures compared to an Alloy-based approach, but it is outperformed by the VIATRA-based approach.*

---

[7] Intel Core i7-8550U CPU@1.80GHz, 16 GB RAM, Windows 10, Java 1.8, 8 GB Heap

5.3   Threats to validity

Internal Validity: The measurements for **RQ1** are performed on a server that acts as a black box with regards to our experimentation. We mitigate this threat by using the same server for the entirety of **RQ1** experimentation. Nevertheless, we take the server runtime output as is for our experimentation. We cannot perform further analysis regarding potential warm-up time and garbage collection, which is mitigated for the experimentation of **RQ2**. Furthermore, we make comparison between our approach and others that use the same back-end solvers (namely, Z3) for model generation. However, we must be aware of the different measurement setups used for each implementation.

External Validity: Our approach is limited to a single domain selected based on its past use in related lines of existing research [27, 29, 30, 37]. The domain of Yakindu Statecharts is sufficiently complex to cover all features of our mapping, thus we expect similar scalability results in other domains.

Construct Validity: For **RQ1**, we specify a scope ranging from 9 to 10 objects for PHASE I, while we only provide a lower-bound scope specification for the other phases. As for **RQ2**, we ask for an exact number of generated objects. These scope specifications may be disadvantageous for certain solvers (e.g. Alloy, if no upper bound is specified). We mitigate this threat by staying consistent in scope specifications throughout a research question or phase.

6   Related work

We provide an overview of various graph generation approaches that derive *consistent* graphs.

Model generators using back-end logic solvers: These approaches translate graphs and WF constraints into logic formulae and use a logic solver to generate graphs that satisfy them. EMF2CSP/UML2CSP [8, 10] translates model generation to a constraint programming problem, and solves it by use of an underlying CSP solver. ASMIG [38] uses the Z3 SMT solver [22] to generate typed and attributed graphs with inheritance. An advanced model generation approach is presented in the Formula framework [15] also using the Z3 SMT solver. AutoGraph [26] generates consistent attributed multidimensional graphs by separating the generation of the graph structure and the attributes. Graph generation is driven by a tableau approach, while attribute handling uses the Z3 SMT-solver. [28] proposes a mapping of EMF models enriched with derived features for the formal validation of DSLs. Model generation for this purpose is performed by using Z3 and Alloy as backend solvers.

Logic-solver based generators do ensure consistency and they can also detect inconsistencies in a specification. However, their scalability is comparable to our approach. In fact, we managed to improve scalability of model generation compared to results reported in [28] using Z3 as a back-end solver.

Custom consistent model generators: Cartesian genetic programming (CGP) [21] encodes graphs with linear or grid-based genotypes and produces new ones by evolving the initial graph, originally used to produce electronic circuits. Recent work [3, 4] introduces evolving graphs by graph programming, CGP's generalization to arbitrary graphs. However, consistency of models is addressed only on a best-effort basis, i.e. there is no formal guarantee of consistency.

SDG [31] proposes an approach that uses a search-based custom OCL solver to generate synthetic data for statistical testing. Generated models are multi-dimensional and consistent. The study claims scalability by generating a large set of small models. Research in [32] proposes a hybrid approach that uses both a meta-heuristic search-based OCL solver [2] for structural constraints and an SMT solver for attribute constraints, based on the snapshot generator of the USE framework [9]. Generated typed models are (locally) consistent and large, but not fully connected (a large family of small models are generated). The VIA-TRA graph solver [30] is able to generate large and consistent (fully connected) models by lifting SAT solving algorithms to the level of graphs, and exploiting partial modeling techniques.

Custom approaches are more scalable than our approach, but the inconsistency of a DSL specification cannot be detected, thus, there is no graceful degradation in the case when no consistent models can be derived.

7   Conclusion and Future Work

In this paper, we provided a mapping of DSL specifications consisting of an EMF metamodel and well-formedness constraints into first-order logic formulae to be fed into TPTP-compliant theorem provers. As such, we successfully integrated more than 70 different theorem provers for model generation purposes. However, our scalability evaluation of these theorem provers carried out in the scope of an industrial DSL tool revealed that most of those provers cannot be effectively used for model generation purposes – not even for very small models. While these solvers can potentially be efficient in detecting inconsistencies of FOL specifications, our experiments revealed that a different solver profile would be beneficial for model generation purposes despite the similarity in the underlying logic formalization. On the positive side, our mapping improved scalability when using Z3 as a back-end theorem prover for model generation purposes.

As we obtained negative scalability results for the vast majority of theorem provers, we believe that *our case study can serve as an interesting benchmark case for future TPTP competitions* as part of future work. Moreover, we plan to better exploit that theorem provers when no models can exist due to inconsistencies regardless of model size by combining calls to TPTP solvers with custom graph model generation techniques. In this case, TPTP solvers may be able to highlight a minimal set of unsatisfiable elements, which can be checked subsequently during the exploration to prevent inconsistent dead ends.

Acknowledgements The first author was partially supported by the Fonds de recherche du Québec - Nature et technologies (FRQNT) B1X scholarship (file number: 272709). This paper is partially supported by MTA-BME Lendület Research Group on Cyber-Physical Systems, and NSERC RGPIN-04573-16 project.

References

1. Viatra solver project. https://github.com/viatra/VIATRA-Generator
2. Ali, S., Iqbal, M.Z., Khalid, M., Arcuri, A.: Improving the performance of OCL constraint solving with novel heuristics for logical operations: a search-based approach. Empirical Software Engineering **21**(6), 2459–2502 (Dec 2016). https://doi.org/10.1007/s10664-015-9392-6
3. Atkinson, T., Plump, D., Stepney, S.: Evolving graphs by graph programming. In: Genetic Programming - 21st European Conference, EuroGP 2018, Parma, Italy, April 4-6, 2018, Proceedings. LNCS, vol. 10781, pp. 35–51. Springer (2018). https://doi.org/10.1007/978-3-319-77553-1_3
4. Atkinson, T., Plump, D., Stepney, S.: Evolving graphs with horizontal gene transfer. In: Proceedings of the Genetic and Evolutionary Computation Conference, GECCO 2019, Prague, Czech Republic, July 13-17, 2019. pp. 968–976. ACM (2019). https://doi.org/10.1145/3321707.3321788
5. Bagan, G., Bonifati, A., Ciucanu, R., Fletcher, G.H.L., Lemay, A., Advokaat, N.: gmark: Schema-driven generation of graphs and queries. IEEE Trans. Knowl. Data Eng. **29**(4), 856–869 (2017). https://doi.org/10.1109/TKDE.2016.2633993
6. Brucker, A.D., Wolff, B.: HOL-OCL: A formal proof environment for UML/OCL. In: Fiadeiro, J.L., Inverardi, P. (eds.) Fundamental Approaches to Software Engineering. pp. 97–100. Springer, Berlin, Heidelberg (2008)
7. Büttner, F., Egea, M., Cabot, J., Gogolla, M.: Verification of ATL transformations using transformation models and model finders. In: ICFEM. pp. 198–213. Springer (2012)
8. Cabot, J., Clarisó, R., Riera, D.: On the verification of UML/OCL class diagrams using constraint programming. Journal of Systems and Software (Mar 2014). https://doi.org/10.1016/j.jss.2014.03.023
9. Gogolla, M., Büttner, F., Richters, M.: USE: A UML-based specification environment for validating UML and OCL. Science of Computer Programming **69**(1), 27 – 34 (2007). https://doi.org/10.1016/j.scico.2007.01.013
10. González Pérez, C.A., Buettner, F., Clarisó, R., Cabot, J.: EMFtoCSP: A Tool for the Lightweight Verification of EMF Models. In: Formal Methods in Software Engineering: Rigorous and Agile Approaches (FormSERA). Zurich, Switzerland (Jun 2012), https://hal.inria.fr/hal-00688039
11. Gordon, M.J.C., Melham, T.F. (eds.): Introduction to HOL: A Theorem Proving Environment for Higher Order Logic. Cambridge University Press, New York, NY, USA (1993)
12. Hao, W.: Automated metamodel instance generation satisfying quantitative constraints. Ph.D. thesis, National University of Ireland Maynooth (2013)
13. Jackson, D.: Alloy: a lightweight object modelling notation. Trans. Softw. Eng. Methodol. **11**(2), 256–290 (2002). https://doi.org/10.1145/505145.505149
14. Jackson, D.: Software Abstractions: logic, language, and analysis. MIT press (2012)
15. Jackson, E.K., Levendovszky, T., Balasubramanian, D.: Reasoning about metamodeling with formal specifications and automatic proofs. In: Model Driven Engineering Languages and Systems, pp. 653–667. Springer (2011)
16. Jackson, E.K., Sztipanovits, J.: Towards a formal foundation for domain specific modeling languages. In: EMSOFT. pp. 53–62. ACM, New York, NY, USA (2006)
17. Juneau, J.: Object Relational Mapping and JPA, pp. 55–72. Apress, Berkeley, CA (2013)

18. Khurshid, S., Marinov, D.: Testera: Specification-based testing of java programs using SAT. Autom. Softw. Eng. **11**(4), 403–434 (2004). https://doi.org/10.1023/B:AUSE.0000038938.10589.b9
19. Kovács, L., Voronkov, A.: First-order theorem proving and Vampire. In: Proceedings of the 25th International Conference on Computer Aided Verification - Volume 8044. pp. 1–35. CAV 2013, Springer-Verlag, New York, NY, USA (2013)
20. Milicevic, A., Misailovic, S., Marinov, D., Khurshid, S.: Korat: A tool for generating structurally complex test inputs. In: ICSE. pp. 771–774. IEEE Computer Society (2007). https://doi.org/10.1109/ICSE.2007.48
21. Miller, J.F.: Cartesian genetic programming: its status and future. Genetic Programming and Evolvable Machines (2019). https://doi.org/10.1007/s10710-019-09360-6
22. de Moura, L.M., Bjørner, N.: Z3: an efficient SMT solver. In: Tools and Algorithms for the Construction and Analysis of Systems, 14th International Conference, TACAS 2008, Held as Part of the Joint European Conferences on Theory and Practice of Software, ETAPS 2008, Budapest, Hungary, March 29-April 6, 2008. Proceedings. pp. 337–340 (2008). https://doi.org/10.1007/978-3-540-78800-3_24
23. Navarro, J.A., Voronkov, A.: Proof systems for effectively propositional logic. In: Armando, A., Baumgartner, P., Dowek, G. (eds.) Automated Reasoning. pp. 426–440. Springer Berlin Heidelberg, Berlin, Heidelberg (2008)
24. The Object Management Group: Object Constraint Language, v2.4 (February 2014)
25. Schneider, S., Lambers, L., Orejas, F.: Symbolic model generation for graph properties. In: Fundamental Approaches to Software Engineering - 20th International Conference, FASE 2017, Held as Part of the European Joint Conferences on Theory and Practice of Software, ETAPS 2017, Uppsala, Sweden, April 22-29, 2017, Proceedings. pp. 226–243 (2017). https://doi.org/10.1007/978-3-662-54494-5_13
26. Schneider, S., Lambers, L., Orejas, F.: Automated reasoning for attributed graph properties. STTT **20**(6), 705–737 (2018). https://doi.org/10.1007/s10009-018-0496-3
27. Semeráth, O., Babikian, A.A., Pilarski, S., Varró, D.: VIATRA Solver: a framework for the automated generation of consistent domain-specific models. In: ICSE. pp. 43–46 (2019), https://dl.acm.org/citation.cfm?id=3339687
28. Semeráth, O., Barta, Á., Horváth, Á., Szatmári, Z., Varró, D.: Formal validation of domain-specific languages with derived features and well-formedness constraints. Software and Systems Modeling pp. 357–392 (2017). https://doi.org/10.1016/j.entcs.2008.04.038
29. Semeráth, O., Farkas, R., Bergmann, G., Varró, D.: Diversity of graph models and graph generators in mutation testing. STTT **22**(1), 57–78 (2020). https://doi.org/10.1007/s10009-019-00530-6
30. Semeráth, O., Nagy, A.S., Varró, D.: A graph solver for the automated generation of consistent domain-specific models. In: ICSE. pp. 969–980. ACM (2018). https://doi.org/10.1145/3180155.3180186
31. Soltana, G., Sabetzadeh, M., Briand, L.C.: Synthetic data generation for statistical testing. In: ASE. pp. 872–882 (2017). https://doi.org/10.1109/ASE.2017.8115698
32. Soltana, G., Sabetzadeh, M., Briand, L.C.: Practical model-driven data generation for system testing. CoRR **abs/1902.00397** (2019)
33. Sutcliffe, G.: The TPTP problem library and associated infrastructure. Journal of Automated Reasoning **59**(4), 483–502 (Dec 2017). https://doi.org/10.1007/s10817-017-9407-7

34. Torlak, E., Jackson, D.: Kodkod: A relational model finder. In: TACAS. LNCS, vol. 4424, pp. 632–647. Springer (2007). https://doi.org/10.1007/978-3-540-71209-1_49
35. Ujhelyi, Z., Bergmann, G., Hegedüs, Á., Horváth, Á., Izsó, B., Ráth, I., Szatmári, Z., Varró, D.: EMF-IncQuery: An integrated development environment for live model queries. Sci. Comput. Program. **98**, 80–99 (2015). https://doi.org/10.1016/j.scico.2014.01.004
36. Varró, D., Bergmann, G., Hegedüs, Á., Horváth, Á., Ráth, I., Ujhelyi, Z.: Road to a reactive and incremental model transformation platform: three generations of the VIATRA framework. Software and Systems Modeling **15**(3), 609–629 (2016)
37. Varró, D., Semeráth, O., Szárnyas, G., Horváth, Á.: Towards the automated generation of consistent, diverse, scalable and realistic graph models. In: Graph Transformation, Specifications, and Nets - In Memory of Hartmut Ehrig. LNCS, vol. 10800, pp. 285–312. Springer (2018). https://doi.org/10.1007/978-3-319-75396-6_16
38. Wu, H., Monahan, R., Power, J.F.: Exploiting attributed type graphs to generate metamodel instances using an SMT solver. In: TASE. pp. 175–182 (July 2013). https://doi.org/10.1109/TASE.2013.31
39. Yakindu Statechart Tools: Yakindu (2019), http://statecharts.org/

Combining Partial Specifications using Alternating Interface Automata*

Ramon Janssen

Radboud University, Nijmegen, the Netherlands
ramonjanssen@cs.ru.nl

Abstract. To model real-world software systems, modelling paradigms should support a form of compositionality. In interface theory and model-based testing with inputs and outputs, *conjunctive* operators have been introduced: the behaviour allowed by composed specification $s_1 \wedge s_2$ is the behaviour allowed by both partial models s_1 and s_2. The models at hand are non-deterministic *interface automata*, but the interaction between non-determinism and conjunction is not yet well understood. On the other hand, in the theory of *alternating automata*, conjunction and non-determinism are core aspects. Alternating automata have not been considered in the context of inputs and outputs, making them less suitable for modelling software interfaces. In this paper, we combine the two modelling paradigms to define *alternating interface automata* (AIA). We equip these automata with an observational, trace-based semantics, and define testers, to establish correctness of black-box interfaces with respect to an AIA specification.

1 Introduction

The challenge of software verification is to ensure that software systems are correct, using techniques such as model checking and model-based testing. To use these techniques, we assume that we have an abstract specification of a system, which serves as a description of what the system should do. A popular approach is to model a specification as an automaton. However, the huge number of states in typical real-world software systems quickly makes modelling with explicit automata infeasible. A form of compositionality is therefore usually required for scalability, so that a specification can be decomposed into smaller and understandable parts. Parallel composition is based on a structural decomposition of the modelled system into components, and it thus relies on the assumption that components themselves are small and simple enough to be modelled. This assumption is not required for logical composition, in which partial specification models of the same component or system are combined in the manner of logical conjunction. Formally, for a composition to be conjunctive, the behaviour allowed by $s_1 \wedge s_2$ is the behaviour allowed by both partial specifications s_1 and

---

* Funded by the Netherlands Organisation of Scientific Research (NWO-TTW), project 13859: SUMBAT - SUpersizing Model-BAsed Testing

H. Wehrheim and J. Cabot (Eds.): FASE 2020, LNCS 12076, pp. 462–481, 2020.
https://doi.org/10.1007/978-3-030-45234-6_23

s_2. Such a composition is important for scalability of modelling, as it allows writing independent partial specifications, sometimes called view modelling [3]. On a fundamental level, specifications can be seen as logical statements about software, and the existence of conjunction on such statements is only natural. Conjunctive operators have been defined in many language-theoretic modelling frameworks, such as for regular expressions [12] and process algebras [5].

1.1 Conjunction for Inputs and Outputs

A conjunctive operator $\wedge$ has also been introduced in many automata frameworks for formal verification and testing, such as interface theory [8], ioco theory [3] and the theory of substitutivity refinement [7]. Within these theories, systems are modelled as *labelled transition systems* [15] or *interface automata* [1] (IA), and actions are divided into inputs and outputs.

An informal example of some (partial) specification models, as could be expressed in these theories, is shown by the automata in Figure 1, in which inputs are labelled with question marks, and outputs with exclamation marks. The specifications represent a vending machine with two input buttons (?a and ?b), which provides coffee (!c) and tea (!t) as outputs, optionally with milk (!c+m and !t+m). The first model, p, specifies that after pressing button ?a, the machine dispenses coffee. The second model, q, specifies that after pressing button ?b, the machine has a choice between dispensing tea, or tea with milk. The third model, r, is similar, but uses non-determinism to specify that button ?b results in coffee with milk or tea with milk.

The fourth model, $p \wedge q \wedge r$, states that all former three partial models should hold. Here, we use the definition of $\wedge$ from [3], but the definition from [7] is similar. An input is specified in the combined model if it is specified in any partial model, making both buttons ?a and ?b specified. Additionally, an output is allowed in the combined model if it is allowed by all partial models, meaning that after button ?b, only tea with milk is allowed.

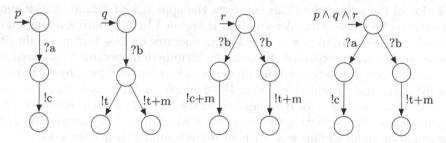

Fig. 1. Three independent specifications for a vending machine, and their conjunction.

1.2 Conjunctions of states

This form of conjunctive composition acts as an operator on entire models. However, a partial specification could also describe the expected behaviour of a particular state of the system, other than the initial state. For example, suppose that the input ?on turns the vending machine on, after which the machine should behave as specified by p, q and r from Figure 1. This, by itself, is also a specification, illustrated by s in Figure 2. However, the formal meaning of this model is unclear: transitions connect states, whereas $p \wedge q \wedge r$ is not a state but an entire automaton. A less trivial case is partial specification t, also in Figure 2: after obtaining any drink by input ?take, we should move to a state where we can obtain a drink as described by specifications p, q, r and t. Thus, we combine conjunctions with a form of recursion. This cannot easily be formalized using $\wedge$ as an operator on automata, like in [3,7,8]. Defining conjunction as a composition on individual states would provide a formal basis for these informal examples.

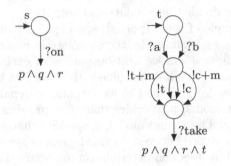

Fig. 2. Two specifications with transitions to a conjunction.

Conjunctions of states are a main ingredient of *alternating automata* [6], in which conjunctions and non-determinism alternate. Here, non-determism acts as logical disjunction, dually to conjunction. Because of this duality, both conjunction and disjunction are treated analogously: both are encoded in the transition relation of the automaton. This contrasts the approach of defining conjunction directly on IAs, where non-determinism is encoded in the transition relation of the IA, whereas conjunction is added as an operator on IAs, leaving the duality between the two unexploited. In fact, the conjunction-operator in [3] even requires that any non-determinism in its operands is removed first, by performing an exponential determinization step. For example, model r in Figure 1 is non-deterministic, and must be determinized to the form of model q before $p \wedge q \wedge r$ is computed. This indicates that it is hard to combine conjunction and non-determinism in an elegant way, without understanding their interaction.

Despite their inherent support for conjunction, alternating automata are not entirely suitable for modeling the behaviour of software systems, since they lack the distinction between inputs and outputs. In this respect, alternating automata are similar to deterministic finite automata (DFAs). Distinguishing inputs and outputs in an IA allows modelling of software systems in a less abstract way than with the homogeneous alphabet of actions of DFAs and alternating automata.

1.3 Contributions

We combine concepts from the worlds of interface theory and alternating automata, leading to Alternating Interface Automata (AIAs), and show how these can be used in the setting of a trace semantics for observable inputs and outputs. We provide a solid formal basis of AIAs, by

- combining alternation with inputs and outputs (Section 3.1),
- defining a trace semantics for AIAs (Section 3.2), by lifting the *input-failure refinement* semantics for non-deterministic interface automata [11] to AIAs,
- providing insight into the semantics of an AIA, by defining a determinization operator (Section 3.3) and a transformation between IAs and AIAs (Section 3.4), and
- defining testers (Section 4), which represent practical testing scenarios for establishing input-failure refinement between a black-box implementation IA and a specification AIA, analogously to ioco test case generation [15].

The definition of input-failure refinement [11] is based upon the observation that, for a non-deterministically reached set of states Q, the observable outputs of that set are the union of the outputs of the individual states in Q, whereas the specified inputs for Q are the intersection of the inputs specified in individual states in Q. For conjunction, we invert this: outputs allowed by a conjunction of states are captured by the intersection, whereas specified inputs are captured by the union. In this way, our AIAs seamlessly combine the duality between conjunction and non-determinism with the duality between inputs and outputs.

Proofs can be found in the extended technical report [10].

2 Preliminaries

We first recall the definition of interface automata [1] and input-failure refinement [11]. The original definition of IAs [1] allows at most one initial state, but we generalize this to sets of states. Moreover, [1] supports internal actions, which we do not need. Transitions are commonly encoded by a relation, whereas we use a function.

Definition 1. *An Interface Automaton (IA) is a 5-tuple* (Q, I, O, T, Q^0), *where*

- Q *is a set of states,*
- I *and* O *are disjoint sets of input and output actions, respectively,*
- $T : Q \times (I \cup O\}) \to \mathcal{P}(Q)$ *is an image-finite transition function (meaning that* $T(q, \ell)$ *is finite for all* q *and* ℓ*), and*
- $Q^0 \subset Q$ *is a finite set of initial states.*

The domain of IAs is denoted $\mathcal{IA}$. *For* $s \in \mathcal{IA}$, *we refer to its respective elements by* $Q_s, I_s, O_s, T_s, Q_s^0$. *For* $s_1, s_2, \ldots, s_A, s_B, \ldots$ *a family of IAs, we write* Q_j, I_j, O_j, T_j *and* Q_j^0 *to refer to the respective elements, for* $j = 1, 2, \ldots, A, B, \ldots$.

In examples, we represent IAs graphically as in Figure 1. For the remainder of this paper, we assume fixed input and output alphabets I and O for IAs, with $L = I \cup O$. For (sets of) sequences of actions, $*$ denotes the Kleene star, and ϵ denotes the empty sequence. We define auxiliary notation in the style of [15].

Definition 2. *Let $s \in \mathcal{IA}$, $Q \subseteq Q_s$, $q, q' \in Q_s$, $\ell \in L$ and $\sigma \in L^*$. We define*

$$q \xrightarrow{\epsilon}_s q' \Leftrightarrow q = q' \qquad\qquad q \xrightarrow{\sigma \ell}_s q' \Leftrightarrow \exists r \in Q_s : q \xrightarrow{\sigma}_s r \wedge q' \in T_s(r, \ell)$$

$$q \xrightarrow{\sigma}_s \Leftrightarrow \exists r \in Q_s : q \xrightarrow{\sigma}_s r \qquad\qquad q \not\xrightarrow{\sigma}_s \Leftrightarrow \neg(q \xrightarrow{\sigma}_s)$$

$$\text{traces}_s(q) = \{\sigma \in L^* \mid q \xrightarrow{\sigma}_s\} \qquad Q \text{ after}_s \sigma = \{r \in Q_s \mid \exists r' \in Q : r' \xrightarrow{\sigma}_s r\}$$

$$\text{traces}(s) = \bigcup_{q \in Q_s^0} \text{traces}_s(q) \qquad\qquad s \text{ after } \sigma = Q_s^0 \text{ after}_s \sigma$$

$$\text{out}_s(Q) = \{x \in O \mid \exists q \in Q : q \xrightarrow{x}_s\} \quad \text{in}_s(Q) = \{a \in I \mid \forall q \in Q : q \xrightarrow{a}_s\}$$

$$q \text{ is a sink-state of } s \iff \forall \ell \in L : T_s(q, \ell) \subseteq \{q\}$$

$$s \text{ is input-enabled} \iff \forall q \in Q_s : \text{in}_s(q) = I$$

$$s \text{ is deterministic} \iff \forall \sigma \in L^*, |s \text{ after } \sigma| \leq 1$$

We omit the subscript for interface automaton s when clear from the context.

We use IAs to represent black-box systems, which can produce outputs, and consume or refuse inputs from the environment. This entails a notion of observable behaviour, which we define in terms of *input-failure traces* [11].

Definition 3. *For any input action a, we denote the input-failure of a as $\bar{a}$. Likewise, for any set of inputs A, we define $\bar{A} = \{\bar{a} \mid a \in A\}$. The domain of input-failure traces is defined as $\mathcal{FT}_{I,O} = L^* \cup L^* \cdot \bar{I}$. For $s \in \mathcal{IA}$, we define*

$$\text{Ftraces}(s) = \text{traces}(s) \cup \{\sigma \bar{a} \mid \sigma \in L^*, a \in I, a \notin \text{in}(s \text{ after } \sigma)\}$$

Thus, a trace $\sigma \bar{a}$ indicates that σ leads to a state where a is not accepted, e.g. a greyed-out button which cannot be clicked.

Any such set of input-failure traces is prefix-closed. Input-failure traces are the basis of *input-failure refinement*, which we will now explain briefly. This refinement relation was introduced in [11] to bridge the gap between alternating refinements [1,2] and ioco theory [15]. Similarly to normal trace inclusion, the idea is that an implementation may only show a trace if a specification also shows this trace. Moreover, the most permissive treatment of an input is to fail it, so if a specification allows an input failure, then it also must allow acceptance of that input, as expressed by the *input-failure closure*.

Definition 4. *Set $S \subseteq \mathcal{FT}_{I,O}$ of input-failure traces is input-failure closed if, for all $\sigma \in L^*$, $a \in I$ and $\rho \in \mathcal{FT}_{I,O}$, $\sigma \bar{a} \in S \implies \sigma a \rho \in S$. The input-failure closure of S is the smallest input-failure closed superset of S, that is, $\text{fcl}(S) = S \cup \{\sigma a \rho \mid \sigma \bar{a} \in S, \rho \in \mathcal{FT}_{I,O}\}$.*

Input-failure refinement *and* input-failure equivalence *on IAs are respectively defined as*

$$s_1 \leq_{if} s_2 \iff \text{Ftraces}(s_1) \subseteq \text{fcl}(\text{Ftraces}(s_2)), \text{ and}$$
$$s_1 \equiv_{if} s_2 \iff s_1 \leq_{if} s_2 \wedge s_2 \leq_{if} s_1.$$

The input-failure closure of the Ftraces serves as a canonical representation of the behaviour of an IA. That is, two models are input-failure equivalent if and only if the closure of their input-failure traces is the same, as stated in Proposition 5.

Proposition 5. *[11] Let $s_1, s_2 \in \mathcal{IA}$. Then*

$$s_1 \leq_{if} s_2 \iff \text{fcl}(\text{Ftraces}(s_1)) \subseteq \text{fcl}(\text{Ftraces}(s_2))$$
$$s_1 \equiv_{if} s_2 \iff \text{fcl}(\text{Ftraces}(s_1)) = \text{fcl}(\text{Ftraces}(s_2))$$

Proposition 5 implies that relation $\leq_{if}$ is reflexive ($s \leq_{if} s$) and transitive ($s_1 \leq_{if} s_2 \wedge s_2 \leq_{if} s_3 \implies s_1 \leq_{if} s_3$). Formally, it is thus a preorder, making it suitable for stepwise refinement.

3   Alternating Interface Automata

Real software systems are always in a single state, but the precise state of a system cannot always be derived from an observed trace. Due to non-determinism, a trace may lead to multiple states. In IAs, this is modelled as a set of states, such as the set of initial states, the set $T(q, \ell)$ for state q and action ℓ, and the set s after σ for IA s and trace σ. The domain of such non-deterministic views on an IA with states Q is thus the powerset of states, $\mathcal{P}(Q)$. In set of states Q, traces from any individual state in Q may be observed.

3.1   Alternation

Alternation generalizes this view on automata: a system may not only be non-deterministically in multiple states, but also conjunctively. When conjunctively in multiple states, only traces which are in *all* these states may be observed. Alternation is formalized by exchanging the domain $\mathcal{P}(Q)$ for the domain $\mathcal{D}(Q)$. Formally, $\mathcal{D}(Q)$ is the *free distributive lattice*, which exist for any set Q [14].

Definition 6. *For any set Q, $\mathcal{D}(Q)$ denotes the* free distributive lattice *generated by Q. That is, $\mathcal{D}(Q)$ is the domain of equivalence classes of terms, inductively defined by the the grammar*

$$e \quad = \quad \top \mid \bot \mid \langle q \rangle \mid e_1 \vee e_2 \mid e_1 \wedge e_2 \qquad \text{with } q \in Q,$$

where equivalence of terms is completely defined by the following axioms:

$$e_1 \vee e_2 = e_2 \vee e_1 \qquad\qquad e_1 \wedge e_2 = e_2 \wedge e_1 \qquad \textit{[Commutativity]}$$
$$e_1 \vee (e_2 \vee e_3) = (e_1 \vee e_2) \vee e_3 \quad e_1 \wedge (e_2 \wedge e_3) = (e_1 \wedge e_2) \wedge e_3 \ \textit{[Associativity]}$$
$$e_1 \vee (e_1 \wedge e_2) = e_1 \qquad\qquad e_1 \wedge (e_1 \vee e_2) = e_1 \qquad \textit{[Absorption]}$$
$$e \vee e = e \qquad\qquad e \wedge e = e \qquad \textit{[Idempotence]}$$
$$e_1 \vee (e_2 \wedge e_3) = (e_1 \vee e_2) \wedge (e_1 \vee e_3) \qquad e_1 \wedge (e_2 \vee e_3) = (e_1 \wedge e_2) \vee (e_1 \wedge e_3)$$
$$\textit{[Distributivity]}$$
$$e \vee \top = \top \qquad\qquad e \wedge \bot = \bot \qquad \textit{[Identity]}$$

In short, $(\mathcal{D}(Q), \vee, \wedge, \bot, \top)$ forms a distributive lattice. Expression $\langle q \rangle$ is named the embedding of q in $\mathcal{D}(Q)$, and operators $\vee$ and $\wedge$ are named disjunction and conjunction, respectively. For the remainder of this paper, we make no distinction between expressions and their equivalence classes.

For finite n, we introduce the shorthand n-ary operators $\bigvee$ and $\bigwedge$, as follows:

$$\bigvee\{e_1, e_2, \ldots e_n\} = e_1 \vee e_2 \vee \ldots e_n \qquad \bigvee \emptyset = \bot$$
$$\bigwedge\{e_1, e_2, \ldots e_n\} = e_1 \wedge e_2 \wedge \ldots e_n \qquad \bigwedge \emptyset = \top$$

We distinguish the embedding $\langle q \rangle \in \mathcal{D}(Q)$ from q itself. We require this distinction only in Definition 18, where we will point this out. Otherwise, we do not need this distinction, so we write q instead of $\langle q \rangle$.

Intuitively, disjunction $q_1 \vee q_2$ replaces the non-deterministic set $\{q_1, q_2\}$. This is formalized by extending IAs with alternation.

Definition 7. *An* alternating interface automaton *(AIA) is defined as a 5-tuple (Q, I, O, T, e^0) where*

- *Q is a set of states, and elements of $\mathcal{D}(Q)$ are referred to as configurations,*
- *I and O are disjoint sets of input and output actions, respectively,*
- *$T : Q \times (I \cup O) \to \mathcal{D}(Q)$ is a transition function, with $T(q, a) \neq \bot$ for all $a \in I$, and*
- *$e^0 \in \mathcal{D}(Q)$ is the initial configuration.*

The domain of AIAs is denoted by $\mathcal{AIA}$. Notations for IAs are reused for AIAs, if this causes no ambiguity. For $\ell \in L$, we define $T_\ell : Q \to \mathcal{D}(Q)$ by $T_\ell(q) = T(q, \ell)$.

Configurations $\top$ and $\bot$ are analogous to the empty set of states in an IA s: if $T_s(q, \ell) = \emptyset$, this means that state q does not have a transition for ℓ. In terms of input-failure refinement, not having a transition for an input means that the input is underspecified, whereas not having a transition for an output means that the output is forbidden. This distinction is made explicit in AIA by using $\top$ to represent underspecification and $\bot$ to represent forbidden behaviour. We will formalize this in Section 3.2. Definition 7 also allows output transitions to $\top$, meaning that the behaviour is unspecified after that output. Automata models which do not allow distinct configurations $\top$ and $\bot$ commonly represent such underspecified behaviour with an explicit chaotic state [3,4] instead.

We graphically represent AIAs in a similar way as IAs, with some additional rules. A transition $T(q^0, \ell) = \langle q^1 \rangle$ is represented by a single arrow from q^0 to q^1. We represent $T(q^0, \ell) = q^1 \vee q^2$ by two arrows $q^0 \overset{\ell}{\to} q^1$ and $q^0 \overset{\ell}{\to} q^2$, analogous to non-determinism in IAs. Conjunction $T(q^0, \ell) = q^1 \wedge q^2$ is shown by adding an arc between the arrows. Nested expressions are represented by successive splits, as shown in Example 8. A state q without outgoing arrow for an output $\ell \in O$ represents $T(q, \ell) = \bot$, and a state without input transitions for input ℓ indicates $T(q, \ell) = \top$. For $\ell \in O$, a transitions $T(q, \ell) = \top$ is shown with an arrow to $\top$, denoting underspecification, but note that $\top$ is a configuration, not a state.

Example 8. Figure 3 shows AIA s_A, with $Q_A = \{q_A^0, q_A^1, q_A^2\}$, $I = \{?a, ?b\}$, $O = \{!x, !y\}$, $e_A^0 = q_A^0$ and T given by the following table:

action state	?a	?b	!x	!y
q_A^0	$q_A^0 \wedge (q_A^1 \vee q_A^2)$	$\top$	q_A^0	q_A^0
q_A^1	$\top$	$\top$	$\top$	$\bot$
q_A^2	$\top$	q_A^0	$\bot$	q_A^2

Moreover, AIA s_B combines the partial specifications from Section 1.

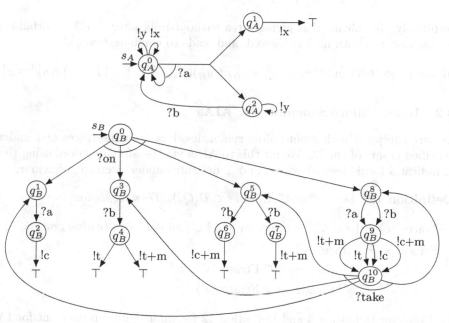

Fig. 3. Example AIAs s_A and s_B.

Before defining trace semantics for AIAs, we extend the transition function from single actions to sequences of actions, by defining an after-function on AIAs. This function transforms configurations by substituting every state according to the transition function, similarly to the approach for alternating automata in [6].

Definition 9. *Let $f : Q \to \mathcal{D}(Q)$ and $e \in \mathcal{D}(Q)$. Then substitution $e[f]$ is equal to e with all atomic propositions replaced by $f(e)$. Formally, $[f] : \mathcal{D}(Q) \to \mathcal{D}(Q)$ is a postfix operator defined by*

$$(e_1 \vee e_2)[f] = e_1[f] \vee e_2[f] \quad (e_1 \wedge e_2)[f] = e_1[f] \wedge e_2[f]$$
$$\top[f] = \top \quad \perp[f] = \perp \quad \langle q \rangle[f] = f(q)$$

Definition 10. *Let $s \in \mathcal{AIA}$. We define after: $\mathcal{D}(Q_s) \times L^* \to \mathcal{D}(Q_s)$ as*

$$e \text{ after}_s \, \epsilon = e \qquad e \text{ after}_s \, (\ell \cdot \sigma) = e[T_\ell] \text{ after}_s \, \sigma$$

Like before, we omit the subscript if clear from the context. We also define $(s \text{ after } \sigma) = e_s^0 \text{ after}_s \, \sigma$.

Example 11. Consider s_B in Figure 3. We evaluate s_B after ?on ?b !t, as follows:

$$q_B^0 \text{ after } ?\text{on } ?\text{b} !\text{t} = q_B^0[T_{?\text{on}}] \text{ after } ?\text{b} !\text{t} = T(q_B^0, ?\text{on}) \text{ after } ?\text{b} !\text{t}$$
$$= (q_B^1 \wedge q_B^3 \wedge q_B^5 \wedge q_B^8) \text{ after } ?\text{b} !\text{t} = (q_B^1 \wedge q_B^3 \wedge q_B^5 \wedge q_B^8)[T_{?\text{b}}] \text{ after } !\text{t}$$
$$= (\top \wedge q_B^4 \wedge (q_B^6 \vee q_B^7) \wedge q_B^9) \text{ after } !\text{t} = (q_B^4 \wedge (q_B^6 \vee q_B^7) \wedge q_B^9)[T_{!\text{t}}]$$
$$= (\top \wedge (\perp \vee \perp) \wedge q_B^{10}) = \perp$$

Intuitively, this means that giving a tea without milk after ?on ?b is forbidden. In contrast, tea with milk is allowed, and leads to configuration q_B^{10}:

$$q_B^0 \text{ after } ?\text{on } ?\text{b} !\text{t+m} = (q_B^4 \wedge (q_B^6 \vee q_B^7) \wedge q_B^9)[T_{!\text{t+m}}] = \top \wedge (\perp \vee \top) \wedge q_B^{10} = q_B^{10}$$

3.2   Input-Failure Semantics for AIAs

IAs are equipped with input-failure semantics, based on the traces and under-specified inputs of the IA. We lift this to AIAs via the after-function, using that $\perp$ indicates forbidden behaviour, and $\top$ indicates underspecified behaviour.

Definition 12. *Let $s, s' \in \mathcal{AIA}$, and $e \in \mathcal{D}(Q_s)$. Then we define*

$$\text{Ftraces}_s(e) = \{\sigma \in L^* \mid (e \text{ after}_s \, \sigma) \neq \perp\} \cup \{\sigma\bar{a} \in L^* \cdot \bar{I} \mid (e \text{ after}_s \, \sigma a) = \top\}$$
$$\text{Ftraces}(s) = \text{Ftraces}_s(e_s^0)$$
$$s \leq_{if} s' \iff \text{Ftraces}(s) \subseteq \text{Ftraces}(s')$$
$$s \equiv_{if} s' \iff \text{Ftraces}(s) = \text{Ftraces}(s')$$

Compare Definition 4 and Definition 12 for input-failure refinement for IAs and for AIAs. For AIAs, refinement is defined directly over their Ftraces, whereas for IA, the input-failure closure of the Ftraces is used for the right-hand model (and optionally for the left-hand model, according to Proposition 5). In this regard, AIAs are a more direct and natural representation of input-failure traces, since the input-failure closure is not needed.

Proposition 13. *For $s \in \mathcal{AIA}$, Ftraces(s) is input-failure closed.*

Another motivation to represent input-failure traces with AIAs is the connection between the distributive lattice $\mathcal{D}(Q)$ and the lattice of sets of input-failure traces: $\wedge$ and $\vee$ are connected to intersection and union of input-failure traces, respectively, and $\top$ and $\bot$ represent the largest and smallest possible input-failure trace sets.

Proposition 14. *Let* $s \in \mathcal{AIA}$, *and* $e, e' \in \mathcal{D}(Q_s)$. *Then*

1. $\text{Ftraces}(e \wedge e') = \text{Ftraces}(e) \cap \text{Ftraces}(e')$
2. $\text{Ftraces}(e \vee e') = \text{Ftraces}(e) \cup \text{Ftraces}(e')$
3. $\text{Ftraces}(\bot) = \emptyset$
4. $\text{Ftraces}(\top) = \mathcal{FT}_{I,O}$
5. $\text{Ftraces}(e) = \{\epsilon\} \cup \{\overline{a} \in \overline{I_s} \mid e \text{ after } a = \top\}$
$$\cup \left(\bigcup_{\ell \in L_s} \ell \cdot \text{Ftraces}(e \text{ after } \ell) \right) \qquad \textit{if } e \neq \bot$$

Propositions 14.3 and 14.5 show why Definition 7 does not allow transitions to $T(q, a) = \bot$ for an input a: in that case, $\text{Ftraces}(q)$ would contain trace ϵ, but it would not contain extension a nor $\overline{a}$ of ϵ, meaning that after trace ϵ it is not allowed to accept nor to refuse a.

We can lift configurations $\top$ and $\bot$, as well as $\wedge$ and $\vee$, to the level of AIAs. This provides the building blocks to compose specifications. Specifications $s_\top$ and $s_\bot$ can be used to specify that any or no behaviour is considered correct, respectively. The operators $\wedge$ and $\vee$ on specifications fulfill the same role as existing operators in substitutivity refinement [7], and have similar properties, described in Proposition 14.

Definition 15. *Let* $s_1, s_2 \in \mathcal{AIA}$. *Without loss of generality[1], assume that* Q_1 *and* Q_2 *are disjoint. We define*

$$s_\top = (\emptyset, I, O, \emptyset, \top) \qquad s_1 \wedge s_2 = (Q_1 \cup Q_2, I, O, T_1 \cup T_2, e_1^0 \wedge e_2^0)$$
$$s_\bot = (\emptyset, I, O, \emptyset, \bot) \qquad s_1 \vee s_2 = (Q_1 \cup Q_2, I, O, T_1 \cup T_2, e_1^0 \vee e_2^0)$$

Proposition 16. *Let* $i, i', s, s' \in \mathcal{AIA}$. *Then*

$$i \leq_{if} s \text{ and } i \leq_{if} s' \iff i \leq_{if} (s \wedge s')$$
$$i \leq_{if} s \text{ or } i \leq_{if} s' \implies i \leq_{if} (s \vee s')$$
$$i \leq_{if} s \text{ and } i' \leq_{if} s \iff (i \vee i') \leq_{if} s$$
$$i \leq_{if} s \text{ or } i' \leq_{if} s \implies (i \wedge i') \leq_{if} s$$
$$i \leq_{if} s_\top$$
$$i \not\leq_{if} s_\bot \qquad \textit{if } e_i^0 \neq \bot$$

The converse of statement (2) does not hold. As a counter-example, choose $\text{Ftraces}(i) = \{\epsilon, x, y\}$, $\text{Ftraces}(s_1) = \{\epsilon, x\}$ and $\text{Ftraces}(s_2) = \{\epsilon, y\}$. In that case, $i \leq_{if} s_1 \vee s_2$ holds, but $i \not\leq_{if} s_1$ and $i \not\leq_{if} s_2$. The converse of statement (4) can be disproven similarly.

---

[1] If Q_1 and Q_2 are not disjoint, the disjoint union $Q_1 \uplus Q_2$ can be used instead of $Q_1 \cup Q_2$. The transition functions of $s_1 \wedge s_2$ and $s_1 \vee s_2$ should be adjusted accordingly.

3.3 AIA Determinization

In case of nestings of $\wedge$ and $\vee$, the after-set s after σ may not be clear immediately, so a transition function producing configurations without $\wedge$ and $\vee$ is easier to interpret. For this reason, we lift the notions of determinism and determinization from IAs [11] to the alternating setting.

Definition 17. *Let $s \in \mathcal{AIA}$ and $e \in \mathcal{D}(Q_s)$. Then e is deterministic if $e = \top$ or $e = \bot$ or $e = \langle q \rangle$ for some $q \in Q_s$. Furthermore, s is deterministic if for all $\sigma \in L^*$, configuration s after σ is deterministic.*

Compare the notions of determinism for IAs and AIAs. For every trace σ, a deterministic IA s is in a singleton state $(s \text{ after } \sigma) = \{q\}$, unless $(s \text{ after } \sigma) = \emptyset$ (that is, σ is not a trace of s). For AIAs, this singleton set $\{q\}$ is replaced by the embedding $\langle q \rangle$, and $\emptyset$ is replaced by $\top$ or $\bot$, depending on whether this set was reached by an undespecified action or a forbidden action.

We now define determinization, where we require the distinction between $\langle q \rangle$ and q to avoid ambiguity.

Definition 18. *Let $s \in \mathcal{AIA}$. We define* $\det : \mathcal{D}(Q_s) \to \mathcal{D}(\mathcal{D}(Q_s) \setminus \{\top, \bot\})$ *as*

$$
\det(e) = \begin{cases} \top & \text{if } e = \top \\ \bot & \text{if } e = \bot \\ \langle e \rangle & \text{otherwise} \end{cases}
$$

The determinization of s, or $\det(s) \in \mathcal{AIA}$, is defined as

$$
\det(s) = (\mathcal{D}(Q_s) \setminus \{\top, \bot\}, I, O, T_{\det(s)}, \det(e_s^0)), \text{ with}
$$
$$
T_{\det(s)}(e, \ell) = \det(e \text{ after}_s \ell) \quad \text{for } \ell \in L
$$

Proposition 19. *For $s \in \mathcal{AIA}$, $\det(s)$ is deterministic.*

Example 20. Figure 4 shows (the reachable part of) the determinizations of s_A and s_B from Figure 3. In $\det(s_A)$, state $q_A^0 \wedge q_A^2$ has no outgoing !x-transition. This expresses $T_{\det(s_A)}(q_A^0 \wedge q_A^2, !\text{x}) = \bot$, which is because q_A^2 has no x-transition, so $T_A(q_A^0, !\text{x}) = \bot$. In contrast, state $q_A^0 \wedge q_A^2$ has an outgoing ?a-transition, $T_{\det(s_A)}(q_A^0 \wedge q_A^2, ?\text{a}) \neq \top$, because q_A^0 has an ?a-transition, $T_A(q_A^0, ?\text{a}) \neq \top$.

Example 20 shows that an input is specified by a conjunction of states in the determinization if *any* of the individual state specify this input, whereas an output is allowed by a conjunction of states only if *all* of the individual state allow this output. In the setting of IA, [11] already established that this works in a reversed way for non-determinism, following their definition of determinization: *all* individual states of a disjunction should specify an input to specify it in the determinization, and *any* individual state should allow an output to allow it in the determinization. Their so-called *input-universal determinization* is an instance of the determinization from Definition 18, using only disjunctions.

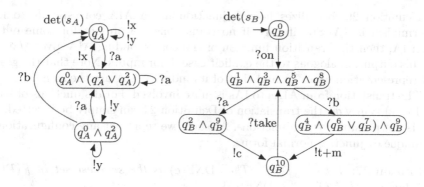

Fig. 4. Examples of determinization.

This duality arises from Definition 10 of *after*, since the determinization directly represents the after-function: the determinizations in Example 20 correspond to the after-sets such as those derived in Example 11. This correspondence is formalized in Proposition 21.

Proposition 21. *Let $s \in \mathcal{AIA}$ and $\sigma \in L^*$. Then*

$$(\det(s) \text{ after } \sigma) = \det(s \text{ after } \sigma).$$

Proposition 22. *Let $s \in \mathcal{AIA}$. Then $\mathrm{Ftraces}(s) = \mathrm{Ftraces}(\det(s))$.*

Corollary 23. *Let $s \in \mathcal{AIA}$. Then $s \equiv_{if} \det(s)$.*

A known result [6] is that alternating automata are exponentially more succinct than non-deterministic automata, and double exponentially more succinct than deterministic automata. Although alternating automata are not a special case of AIAs (as AIAs lack the accepting and non-accepting states of alternating automata), we expect AIAs to be exponentially more succinct than IAs, as well.

3.4   Connections between IAs and AIAs

IAs and AIAs are used to represent sets of input-failure traces, and are in that sense interchangeable. First, we show that any IA can be translated to an AIA.

Definition 24. *For $s \in \mathcal{IA}$, the AIA induced by s is defined as $\mathrm{AIA}(s) = (Q_s, I_s, O_s, T, \bigvee Q_s^0) \in \mathcal{AIA}$, where for all $q \in Q_s$ and $\ell \in L$:*

$$T(q, \ell) = \begin{cases} \top & \text{if } \ell \in I \text{ and } q \overset{\ell}{\not\rightarrow} \\ \bigvee T_s(q, \ell) & \text{otherwise} \end{cases}$$

Proposition 25. *Let $s \in \mathcal{IA}$. Then $\mathrm{Ftraces}(\mathrm{AIA}(s)) = \mathrm{fcl}(\mathrm{Ftraces}(s))$.*

Corollary 26. *Let $s_1, s_2 \in \mathcal{IA}$. Then $s_1 \leq_{if} s_2 \iff \mathrm{AIA}(s_1) \leq_{if} \mathrm{AIA}(s_2)$*

Definition 29 formalizes how disjunction in an AIA corresponds to non-determinism in IA. Specifically, if no transitions are present for some output in an IA, then the transition function of the corresponding AIA gives $\bigvee \emptyset = \bot$ for this output, analogous to the explicit case $\top$ for inputs. Note that the graphical representation of an IA and that of its induced AIA are the same.

The translation from AIAs to IAs is more involved. For disjunctions of states $(q \text{ after } \ell) = q_1 \vee q_2$, the translation of Definition 24 can simply be inverted, but this is not possible for conjunctions. As such, we represent any configuration by its unique disjunctive normal form.

Definition 27. *Let* $e \in \mathcal{D}(Q)$. *Then* $\mathrm{DNF}(e)$ *is the smallest set in* $\mathcal{P}(\mathcal{P}(Q))$ *such that* $e = \bigvee \{ \bigwedge Q' \mid Q' \in \mathrm{DNF}(e) \}$.

The set $\mathrm{DNF}(e)$ can be constructed by using the axioms from Definition 6.

Example 28. To find $\mathrm{DNF}(q^1 \vee (q^2 \wedge (q^1 \vee q^3)))$, we first rewrite the expression by using distributivity, associativity, commutativity and absorbtion, as follows:

$$q^1 \vee (q^2 \wedge (q^1 \vee q^3)) = q^1 \vee (q^2 \wedge q^1) \vee (q^2 \wedge q^3) = q^1 \vee (q^2 \wedge q^3)$$

So we find $\mathrm{DNF}(q^1 \vee (q^2 \wedge (q^1 \vee q^3))) = \{\{q^1\}, \{q^2, q^3\}\}$. Two other examples are $\mathrm{DNF}(\bot) = \mathrm{DNF}(\bigvee \emptyset) = \emptyset$ and $\mathrm{DNF}(\top) = \mathrm{DNF}(\bigvee \{\bigwedge \emptyset\}) = \{\emptyset\}$.

Definition 29. *Let* $s \in \mathcal{AIA}$. *Then the* induced IA *of* s *is defined as*

$$\mathrm{IA}(s) = (\mathcal{P}(Q_s), I, O, T, \mathrm{DNF}(e_s^0)) \in \mathcal{IA}, \text{ with for } Q \subseteq Q_s \text{ and } \ell \in L:$$

$$T(Q, \ell) = \begin{cases} \mathrm{DNF}((\bigwedge Q)[T_{s\ell}]) \setminus \{\emptyset\} & \text{if } \ell \in I \\ \mathrm{DNF}((\bigwedge Q)[T_{s\ell}]) & \text{if } \ell \in O \end{cases}$$

A state of $\mathrm{IA}(s)$ acts as the conjunction of the corresponding states in s. In particular, a singleton state $\{q\}$ in $\mathrm{IA}(s)$ acts as the contained state q in s, and state $\emptyset$ in $\mathrm{IA}(s)$ acts as a chaotic state, having $\mathrm{Ftraces}_{\mathrm{IA}(s)}(\emptyset) = \mathcal{FT}_{I,O}$.

Proposition 30. *Let* $s \in \mathcal{AIA}$. *Then* $\mathrm{Ftraces}(s) = \mathrm{fcl}(\mathrm{Ftraces}(\mathrm{IA}(s)))$.

Corollary 31. *Let* $s_1, s_2 \in \mathcal{AIA}$. *Then* $s_1 \leq_{if} s_2 \iff \mathrm{IA}(s_1) \leq_{if} \mathrm{IA}(s_2)$

4   Testing Input-Failure Refinement

So far, we have introduced refinement as a way of specifying correctness of one model with respect to another. Often, a specification is indeed a model, but we use it to ensure correctness of a real-world software implementation. To this end, we assume that this implementation behaves like a IA. We cannot see the actual states and transitions of this IA, but we can provide inputs to it and observe its outputs. We assume that this IA must have an initial state, i.e. it is *non-empty*.

Definition 32. *[1] An IA* i *is* empty *if* $Q_i^0 = \emptyset$.

In this section, we introduce a basis for *model-based testing* with AIAs, analogously to ioco test case generation [15]. Given a specification AIA, we derive a testing experiment on non-empty implementation IAs, in order to observe whether input-failure refinement holds with respect to the specification. This requires an extension of input-failure refinement to these domains.

Definition 33. *Let* $i \in \mathcal{IA}$ *and* $s \in \mathcal{AIA}$. *Then*

$$i \leq_{if} s \iff \mathrm{Ftraces}(i) \subseteq \mathrm{Ftraces}(s).$$

4.1 Testers for AIA Specifications

From a given specification AIA, we derive a tester. We model this tester as an IA as well, which can communicate with an implementation IA through a form of parallel composition. The tester eventually concludes a verdict, indicating whether the observed behaviour is allowed. To communicate, the inputs of the implementation must be outputs for the tester, and vice versa (note that I and O denote the inputs and outputs for the *implementation*, respectively). The tester should not block or ignore outputs from the implementation, meaning that the tester should be input-enabled. If the tester intends to supply an input to the implementation, it should also be prepared for a refusal of that input. A verdict is given by means of special states **pass** or **fail**. Lastly, to give consistent verdicts, a tester should be deterministic. This leads to the following definition of testers.

Definition 34. *A tester for (an IA or AIA with) inputs* I *and outputs* O *is a deterministic, input-enabled IA* $t = (Q_t, O, I \cup \overline{I}, T, q_t^0)$ *with* **pass**, **fail** $\in Q_t$, *such that* **pass** *and* **fail** *are sink-states with* $\mathrm{out}(\mathbf{pass}) = \mathrm{out}(\mathbf{fail}) = \emptyset$, *and* $a \in \mathrm{out}(q) \iff \overline{a} \in \mathrm{out}(q)$ *for all* $q \in Q_t$ *and* $a \in I$.

Testing is performed by a special form of parallel composition of a tester and an implementation. If the tester chooses to perform an input while the implementation also chooses to produce an output, this results in a race condition. In such a case, both the input or the output can occur during test execution. We assume a synchronous setting, in which the implementation and specification agree on the order in which observed actions are performed (in contrast to e.g. a queue-based setting [13], in which all possible orders are accounted for). These assumptions are in line with the assumptions in e.g. ioco-theory [15], and lead to the following definition of test execution.

Definition 35. *Let* $i \in \mathcal{IA}$ *be non-empty, and let* t *be a tester for* i. *We write* $q_t \,\|\, q_i$ *for* $(q_t, q_i) \in Q_t \times Q_i$. *Then test execution of* i *against* t, *denoted* $t \,\|\, i$, *is defined as* $(Q_t \times Q_i, \emptyset, I \cup \overline{I} \cup O, T, q_t^0 \,\|\, q_i^0) \in \mathcal{IA}$, *with*

$$T(q_t \,\|\, q_i, \ell) = \{q_t' \,\|\, q_i' \mid q_t \xrightarrow{\ell} q_t', \ q_i \xrightarrow{\ell} q_i'\} \qquad \textit{for } \ell \in I,$$

$$T(q_t \,\|\, q_i, \overline{a}) = \{q_t' \,\|\, q_i \mid q_t \xrightarrow{\overline{a}} q_t', \ q_i \xrightarrow{a} \} \qquad \textit{for } a \in I$$

We say that i **fails** t *if* $q_t^0 \,\|\, q_i^0 \xrightarrow{\sigma} \mathbf{fail} \,\|\, q_i$ *for some* σ *and* q_i, *and* i **passes** t *otherwise.*

We reuse the notions of *soundness* and *exhaustiveness* from [15], to express whether a tester properly tests for a given specification.

Definition 36. *Let $s \in \mathcal{AIA}$ and let t be a tester for s. Then t is* sound *for s if for all $i \in \mathcal{IA}$ with inputs I and outputs O, i* fails *t implies $i \not\leq_{if} s$. Moreover, t is* exhaustive *for s if for all $i \in \mathcal{IA}$, i* passes *t implies $i \leq_{if} s$.*

A simple attempt to translate specification AIA s to a sound and exhaustive tester would be similar to the determinization of s, but replacing every occurence of $\bot$ and $\top$ by **fail** and **pass**, respectively.

$$f_t(e) = \begin{cases} \textbf{fail} & \text{if } e = \bot \\ \textbf{pass} & \text{if } e = \top \\ e & \text{otherwise} \end{cases}$$

Taking special care of input failures, the function f_t then induces a tester $(\mathcal{D}(Q_s) \cup \{\textbf{pass}, \textbf{fail}\}, O, I \cup \overline{I}, T, f_t(e_s^0))$, with

$$T(e, \ell) = \{f_t(e \text{ after}_s \ell)\} \qquad \text{for } e \in \mathcal{D}(Q_s), \ell \in L$$

$$T(v, \ell) = \begin{cases} \{v\} & \text{if } \ell \in O \\ \emptyset & \text{if } \ell \in I \end{cases} \qquad \text{for } v \in \{\textbf{pass}, \textbf{fail}\}$$

$$T(e, \overline{a}) = \begin{cases} \{\textbf{pass}\} & \text{if } (e \text{ after}_s a) = \top \\ \{\textbf{fail}\} & \text{otherwise} \end{cases} \qquad \text{for } e \in \mathcal{D}(Q_s), a \in I$$

This tester is sound and complete for s: each possible input-failure trace is in Ftraces(s) if and only if it does not lead to **fail**, by construction. Here, we make use of the fact that Ftraces($\bot$) = $\emptyset$, meaning that $\bot$ cannot be implemented correctly by a non-empty IA and can thus be replaced by **fail**. Likewise, Ftraces($\top$) = $\mathcal{FT}_{I,O}$ means that $\top$ is always implemented correctly, and can be replaced by **pass**.

However, this tester is quite inefficient. If a tester reaches **pass** after both σa and $\sigma \overline{a}$, then this input a does not need to be tested after σ. Specifically, this is the case if and only if trace σa leads to specification configuration $\top$. We thus improve the tester for a given specifications as follows.

Definition 37. *Let $s \in \mathcal{AIA}$. Then* tester(s) $\in \mathcal{IA}$ *is defined as*

$$\text{tester}(s) = (\mathcal{D}(Q_s) \cup \{\textbf{pass}, \textbf{fail}\}, O, I \cup \overline{I}, T, f_t(e_s^0)), \text{ with } f_t \text{ as before, and}$$

$$T(e, \ell) = \begin{cases} \{f_t(e \text{ after}_s \ell)\} & \text{if } \ell \in O, \text{ or } \ell \in I \text{ and } (e \text{ after}_s \ell) \neq \top \\ \emptyset & \text{if } \ell \in I \text{ and } (e \text{ after}_s \ell) = \top \end{cases} \qquad \text{for } \ell \in L$$

$$T(e, \overline{a}) = \begin{cases} \emptyset & \text{if } (e \text{ after}_s a) = \top \\ \{\textbf{fail}\} & \text{otherwise} \end{cases} \qquad \text{for } e \in \mathcal{D}(Q_s), a \in I$$

$$T(v, \ell) = \begin{cases} \{v\} & \text{if } \ell \in O \\ \emptyset & \text{if } \ell \in I \end{cases} \qquad \text{for } v \in \{\textbf{pass}, \textbf{fail}\}, \ell \in L$$

Example 38. The tester for s_B in Figure 3 is shown in Figure 5.

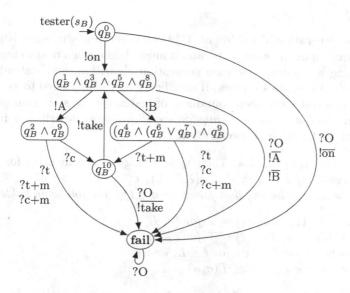

Fig. 5. The tester for the vending machine. The label ?O denotes a transition for every label in O. Remark that inputs for s_B are outputs for tester(s_B), and vice versa.

Theorem 39 shows that soundness and exhaustiveness of a tester corresponds to refinement of the corresponding AIA.

Theorem 39. *Let* $s_1, s_2 \in \mathcal{AIA}$. *Then*

1 tester(s_1) *is sound and exhaustive for* $\mathrm{IA}(s_1)$

2   tester(s_1) *is sound for* s_2 $\iff$ $s_2 \leq_{if} s_1$

3 tester(s_1) *is exhaustive for* s_2 $\iff$ $s_1 \leq_{if} s_2$

4.2   Test Cases for AIA Specifications

In [15], an algorithm was introduced to generate *test cases*. These are testers as in Definition 34 with additional restrictions, so that they can be used as unambiguous instructions to test a system. In particular, states of a test case should have at most one outgoing input transition. This ensures that no choice between different inputs has to be resolved during test execution. Additionaly, all paths of a test case lead to **pass** or **fail** in a finite number of steps, to ensure that test execution terminates with a verdict.

Definition 40. *A tester t for I and O is a* test case *if*

- *for all $q_t \in Q_t$, $|\mathrm{out}(q_t)| \leq 1$, and*
- *there are no infinite sequences $q_t^0, q_t^1, \ldots$ for $q_t^0, q_t^1, \ldots \in Q_t \setminus \{\mathbf{pass}, \mathbf{fail}\}$ such that $q_t^0 \xrightarrow{\ell^0} q_t^1 \xrightarrow{\ell^1} \ldots$*

The test case generation algorithm of [15] is non-deterministic, since it must choose at most one inputs in every state, and it must choose when to stop testing. We avoid defining a separate test case generation algorithm, and instead use Theorem 39 to obtain sound test cases. If specification s_1 is weakened to s_2, such that tester(s_2) is a test case, then soundness of tester(s_2) for s_1 is guaranteed by the theorem. Such a weakened *singular specification* s_2 describes a finite, tree-shaped part of the original specification s_1.

Definition 41. *Let $s_1, s_2 \in \mathcal{AIA}$. Then s_2 is a* singular specification *for s_1 if Q_2 is a finite subset of L^*, with $e_2^0 \in \{\epsilon, \top, \bot\}$, $e_1^0 = \top \implies e_2^0 = \top$ and $e_2^0 = \bot \implies e_1^0 = \bot$, and having that for every $\sigma \in Q_2$, the following holds:*

1. *$T_2(\sigma, \ell) = \bot \implies (s_1 \text{ after } \sigma\ell) = \bot \text{ for } \ell \in L$,*
2. *$(s_1 \text{ after } \sigma\ell) = \top \implies T_2(\sigma, \ell) = \top \text{ for } \ell \in L$*
3. *$T_2(\sigma, \ell)$ is either $\bot$ or $\top$ or $\sigma\ell$ for $\ell \in L$, and*
4. *there is at most one $a \in I$ with $T(\sigma, a) \neq \top$.*

It can be created from s_1 similarly to test case generation in [15]. In every state σ of the tree s_1, we either decide to pick one input specified in s_1 and also specify that in s_2; or we do not specify any input, but only outputs; or we leave any successive behaviour unspecified ($\top$).

Test cases based on singular specifications are inherently sound, and for any incorrect implementation, it is possible to find a singular specification which induces a test case to detects this incorrectness.

Theorem 42. *If s_2 is a singular specification for s_1, then tester(s_2) is a sound test case for s_1.*

Theorem 43. *Let $i \in \mathcal{IA}$ and $s_1 \in \mathcal{AIA}$. If $i \not\leq_{if} s_1$, then there is a singular specification s_2 for s_1 such that i **fails** tester(s_2).*

Example 44. Specification s_B in Figure 3 can be weakened to singular specification s_C shown in Figure 6. Indeed, $s_B \leq_{if} s_C$ holds, which can be established by comparing s_C with $\det(s_B)$ in Figure 4. Therefore tester(s_C) is a sound test case for s_B.

5   Conclusion and Future Work

Alternating interface automata serve as a natural and direct representation for sets of input-failure traces, and therefore also for refinement of systems with inputs, outputs, non-determinism and conjunction. We have used the observational nature of input-failure traces to define testers, describing an experiment to observationally establish refinement of a black-box system.

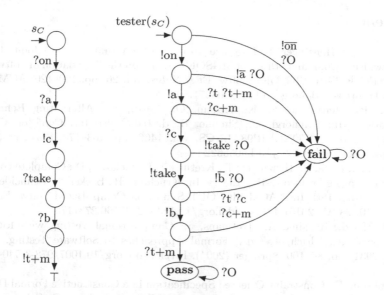

Fig. 6. A weakened version s_C of the vending machine, and the test case tester(s_C). Question and exclamation marks are interchanged in tester(s_C) to indicate that the input and output alphabets have been interchanged with respect to s_C.

The disjunction and conjunction of alternation brings interface automata specifications closer to the realm of logic and lattice theory. On the theoretical side, a possible direction is to extend configurations from distributive lattices to a full logic. On the practical side, classical testing techniques acting on logical expressions, such as combinatorial testing, could be translated to our black-box configurations of states.

Possible criticism on our running example of a vending machine s_B in Figure 3 may be that its representation as an AIA is not concise, since the determinization $det(s_B)$ is much smaller and more understandable than s_B itself. This is because the individual specifications offer a choice between outputs, such as tea with or without milk, whereas the intersection of all choices is singleton. A more natural encoding for this example is to express the types of drink with data data parameters, and the restrictions on them by logical constraints. This requires an automaton model in style of symbolic transition systems [9], which could be enriched with the concepts of alternation of AIAs.

Interface automata typically contain internal transitions, and the interaction between internal behaviour and alternation is not immediately clear. A possible approach to extend AIAs with internal behaviour is to lift the ϵ-closure of [1], the set of states reachable via internal transitions, to the level of configurations.

Acknowledgement.

We thank Jan Tretmans and Frits Vaandrager for their valuable feedback.

References

1. Alfaro, L.d., Henzinger, T.: Interface Automata. In: Gruhn, V. (ed.) Joint 8th Eur. Softw. Eng. Conf. and 9th ACM SIGSOFT Symp. on the Foundation of Softw. Eng. – ESEC/FSE-01. SIGSOFT Softw. Eng. Notes, vol. 26, pp. 109–120. ACM Press (2001). https://doi.org/10.1145/503271.503226
2. Alur, R., Henzinger, T., Kupferman, O., Vardi, M.: Alternating Refinement Relations. In: Sangiorgi, D., Simone, R, d. (eds.) 9th Int. Conf. on Concurrency Theory – CONCUR'98. LNCS, vol. 1466, pp. 163–178. Springer (1998). https://doi.org/10.1007/BFb0055622
3. Beneš, N., Daca, P., Henzinger, T., Křetínský, J., Ničković, D.: Complete composition operators for ioco-testing theory. In: Kruchten, P., Becker, S., Schneider, J.G. (eds.) Proc. 18th Int'l ACM SIGSOFT Symp. on Comp.-Based Softw. Eng. pp. 101–110. ACM (2015). https://doi.org/10.1145/2737166.2737175
4. Bijl, M.v.d., Rensink, A., Tretmans, J.: Compositional Testing with IOCO. In: Petrenko, A., Ulrich, A. (eds.) Formal Approaches to Software Testing. LNCS, vol. 2931, pp. 86–100. Springer (2004). https://doi.org/10.1007/978-3-540-24617-6_7
5. Brinksma, E.: Constraint-Oriented Specification in a Constructive Formal Description technique. In: de Bakker, J., Roever, W.P.d., Rozenberg, G. (eds.) Stepwise Refinement of Distributed Systems Models, Formalisms, Correctness: REX Workshop, Mook, The Netherlands. pp. 130–152. Springer Berlin Heidelberg (1990). https://doi.org/10.1007/3-540-52559-9_63
6. Chandra, A.K., Kozen, D.C., Stockmeyer, L.J.: Alternation. J. ACM **28**(1), 114–133 (Jan 1981). https://doi.org/10.1145/322234.322243
7. Chilton, C., Jonsson, B., Kwiatkowska, M.: An algebraic theory of interface automata. Theoretical Computer Science **549**, 146–174 (2014). https://doi.org/10.1016/j.tcs.2014.07.018
8. Doyen, L., Henzinger, T.A., Jobstmann, B., Petrov, T.: Interface theories with component reuse. In: Proceedings of the 8th ACM International Conference on Embedded Software. pp. 79–88. EMSOFT '08, ACM, New York, NY, USA (2008). https://doi.org/10.1145/1450058.1450070
9. Frantzen, L., Tretmans, J.: Model-based testing of environmental conformance of components. In: de Boer, F.S., Bonsangue, M.M., Graf, S., de Roever, W. (eds.) Formal Methods for Components and Objects. pp. 1–25. Springer (2007). https://doi.org/10.1007/978-3-540-74792-5_1
10. Janssen, R.: Combining partial specifications using alternating interface automata. Report, Radboud University, Nijmegen (2020), `https://arxiv.org/abs/2002.08754`
11. Janssen, R., Vaandrager, F., Tretmans, J.: Relating alternating relations for conformance and refinement. In: Ahrendt, W., Tapia Tarifa, S. (eds.) Integrated Formal Methods. pp. 246–264. LNCS, Springer (2019). https://doi.org/10.1007/978-3-030-34968-4_14
12. McNaughton, R., Yamada, H.: Regular expressions and state graphs for automata. IRE Transactions on Electronic Computers **EC-9**(1), 39–47 (1960). https://doi.org/10.1109/TEC.1960.5221603
13. Petrenko, A., Yevtushenko, N., Huo, J.L.: Testing transition systems with input and output testers. In: Hogrefe, D., Wiles, A. (eds.) Testing of Communicating Systems. pp. 129–145. Springer Berlin Heidelberg, Berlin, Heidelberg (2003). https://doi.org/10.1007/3-540-44830-6_11

14. Priestly, H., Davey, B.: Introduction to lattices and order. Cambridge University Press, England (1990)
15. Tretmans, J.: Model Based Testing with Labelled Transition Systems. In: Hierons, R., Bowen, J., Harman, M. (eds.) Formal Methods and Testing. LNCS, vol. 4949, pp. 1–38. Springer (2008). https://doi.org/10.1007/978-3-540-78917-8_1

Revisiting Semantics of Interactions for Trace Validity Analysis

Erwan Mahe[1], Christophe Gaston[2], and Pascale Le Gall[1]

[1] Laboratoire de Mathématiques et Informatique pour la Complexité et les Systèmes
CentraleSupélec - Plateau de Moulon
9 rue Joliot-Curie, F-91192 Gif-sur-Yvette Cedex
[2] CEA, LIST, Laboratory of Systems Requirements and Conformity Engineering,
P.C. 174, Gif-sur-Yvette, 91191, France

Abstract. Interaction languages such as MSC are often associated with formal semantics by means of translations into distinct behavioral formalisms such as automatas or Petri nets. In contrast to translational approaches we propose an operational approach. Its principle is to identify which elementary communication actions can be immediately executed, and then to compute, for every such action, a new interaction representing the possible continuations to its execution. We also define an algorithm for checking the validity of execution traces (i.e. whether or not they belong to an interaction's semantics). Algorithms for semantic computation and trace validity are analyzed by means of experiments.

Keywords: Interaction Language · Scenario · Sequence Diagram · Semantics · Causal Order · Trace Analysis

1 Introduction

Interaction Languages (IL) are powerful mechanisms to express behavioral requirements in the form of scenarios called *interactions*. ILs include several recognized standards such as MSC and LSC [6], HMSC [25], MSD [13], UML-Sequence Diagrams [21] (UML-SD), etc. These graphical languages represent parts involved in a communication scheme as vertical lines, called lifelines. Each one highlights a succession of instants where actions (emissions or receptions of messages) may occur. These instants are conventionally ordered from top to bottom as illustrated (in the style of UML-SD) in Fig.1-a, where the emission of m_1 occurs before that of m_2. However, this sequencing does not order actions occurring on different lifelines; in Fig.1-b, even though the reception of m occurs graphically below the emission of m, no order is enforced. As such, this specificity is called 'weak sequencing'. In order to enforce a causality relation between such uncorrelated actions, we

(a) Default sequencing
$i = seq(a!m1, a!m2)$

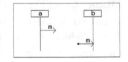

(b) Uncorrelated instants
$i = seq(a!m, b?m)$

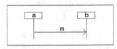

(c) Message passing
$i = strict(a!m, b?m)$

Fig. 1: UML-SD style

H. Wehrheim and J. Cabot (Eds.): FASE 2020, LNCS 12076, pp. 482–501, 2020.
https://doi.org/10.1007/978-3-030-45234-6_24

use a different 'strict sequencing' operator. In Fig.1-c, it is used to express a message m passing between lifelines a and b. Here, m cannot be received before being emitted; the origin of the arrow denoting an instant preceding the one depicted by its target. Additional operators (e.g. UML-SD combined fragments) enable the expression of various concepts to order actions such as parallelisation, repetition, alternatives (illustrated in Fig.2), etc. They structure interactions and specify relative scheduling for subscenarii.

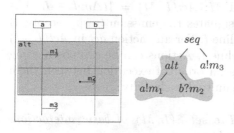

whole interaction $i = i_{|\epsilon}$

subinteraction $i_{|1}$ in blue

Fig. 2: Syntax and Positions

When ILs are fitted with formal semantics, requirements can be processed using formal techniques, such as model-checking [1] or model-based testing [19]. As pointed out earlier, the key semantic concept here is the causality relation between actions that the interaction's structure induce. Valid traces are those respecting the subsequent partial order [27,19]. The authors of [17] define a simple IL as a set of terms built above basic actions and provide it with a denotational semantics which associates each interaction term with a set of traces. This kind of formal framework can serve as a reference for stating theorems about interactions (e.g. the 'satisfaction condition' proven in [17]).

In this paper, we consider an IL which includes several distinct *loop* operators and provide it with a denotational semantics, directly comparable to that given by [17]. The semantics of an interaction with *loops* is defined by considering any finite number of loop unfolding combinations. Then, we introduce a second semantics, which can be qualified as operational, as we aim at presenting it in the style advocated in [24]. Here, accepted traces of an interaction i are defined by identifying its initial actions act, and for each of those the subsequent interaction i' that will express the remainder of the trace. This operational semantics can therefore be thought of as a set of rules of the form $i \xrightarrow{act} i'$. Doing so is however challenging as we need to keep track of possible conflicts between actions occurring on the same lifeline. While the operational semantics is particularly suitable to be adapted into concrete trace analysis algorithms, the denotational semantics serves as a mathematical foundation, revealing interesting algebraic properties. Both semantics have been implemented for semantic computation and conducted experiments indicate identical results. A trace analysis tool has also been adapted from the operational semantics and experimented on for correctness and performances.

The paper is organized as follows: Sec.2 introduces the IL and the denotational semantics. Sec.3 and Sec.5 resp. introduce the operational semantics and the subsequent trace analysis algorithm while Sec.4 reports experimental results about the consistency of both semantics w.r.t. one another. Finally, Sec.6 and Sec.7 resp. discuss related works and provide concluding remarks.

2   Interaction language and denotational semantics

2.1   Base syntax

This section provides a textual denotation of our basic IL (i.e. without loops). Interactions are defined up to a given signature (L, M) where L and M resp. are sets of lifelines and messages. Their base building blocks are a set of communication actions (actions) over L and M: $Act(L, M) = \{l\Delta m | l \in L, \Delta \in \{!, ?\}, m \in M\}$ where $l!m$ (resp. $l?m$) designates the emission (resp. reception) of the message m from (resp. on) the lifeline l. For any action act in $Act(L, M)$ of the form $l\Delta m$, $\Theta(act)$ denotes the lifeline l. Actions can be composed using different binary operators that introduce an order of execution between them (weak or strict sequentiality, parallelism, mutual exclusivity).

Definition 1 (Basic Interactions). *The set $\mathbb{B}(L, M)$ of basic interactions over L and M is inductively defined as follows:*

- *$\varnothing \in \mathbb{B}(L, M)$ and $Act(L, M) \subset \mathbb{B}(L, M)$,*
- *$\forall (i_1, i_2) \in \mathbb{B}(L, M)^2$ and $\forall f \in \{strict, seq, alt, par\}, f(i_1, i_2) \in \mathbb{B}(L, M)$.*

The empty interaction $\varnothing$ and actions of $Act(L, M)$ are elementary interactions. The *strict* and *seq* operators are sequential operators: in $strict(i_1, i_2)$, all the actions in i_1 must take place before any action in i_2 while in $seq(i_1, i_2)$ sequentiality is only enforced between actions that share the same lifeline. In Fig.1-b, $b?m$ may precede[3] $a!m$ (because $a \neq b$) while in Fig.1-c $b?m$ cannot precedes $a!m$. Hence we use *strict* to encode the emission and reception of the same message object e.g. $strict(a!m, b?m)$ on Fig.1-c[4]. In $alt(i_1, i_2)$, the behaviors specified by i_1 and i_2 are both acceptable albeit mutually exclusive[5]. In Fig.2 if $a!m_1$ happens then $b?m_2$ cannot happen and vice-versa. In $par(i_1, i_2)$, the executions of i_1 and i_2 are interleaved. For instance, in $par(a!m_1, a!m_2)$, actions $a!m_1$ and $a!m_2$ can happen in any order.

Interactions being defined as usual terms, we use positions expressed in Dewey decimal notation to refer to subinteractions [7]. A position p of i is a sequence of positive integers denoting a path leading from the root node of i to the subterm of i at position p. Interactions are defined with operations whose arity is at most 2. Hence, positions are words of $\{1, 2\}^*$ i.e. words built over the empty word ϵ, the words 1 and 2 and the concatenation law ".". In the following, we will use simplified notations without dots, e.g. "11" for the position "1.1".

In Def.2, the functions ST and pos resp. associate to any interaction the set of all its subinteractions and the set of its positions. Moreover, we use the usual notation $i_{|p}$ [7] to designate unambiguously the subinteraction of i at position p for $p \in pos(i)$ (cf. example in Fig.2).

---

[3] Note that we omit depicting *seq* on diagrams as is classically done in UML-SD.

[4] drawn by convention as a plain arrow between a and b

[5] note that we handle the UML-SD *opt* operator as $opt(i) = alt(i, \varnothing) = alt(\varnothing, i)$

Definition 2 (Positions and subinteractions of a basic interaction). *We define* $ST : \mathbb{B}(L,M) \to \mathcal{P}(\mathbb{B}(L,M))$, $pos : \mathbb{B}(L,M) \to \mathcal{P}(\{1,2\}^*)$ *and*[6] $\_|\_ : \mathbb{B}(L,M) \times \{1,2\}^* \to \mathbb{B}(L,M)$ *such that* $\forall i \in \mathbb{B}(L,M)$:

- *if* $i = \varnothing$ *or* $i \in Act(L,M)$ *then* $ST(i) = \{i\}$, $pos(i) = \{\epsilon\}$ *and* $i_{|\epsilon} = i$
- *if* $i = f(i_1, i_2)$ *with* $f \in \{strict, seq, par, alt\}$ *then:*
  - $ST(i) = \{i\} \cup ST(i_1) \cup ST(i_2)$
  - $pos(i) = \{\epsilon\} \cup 1.pos(i_1) \cup 2.pos(i_2)$
  - $i_{|\epsilon} = i$ *and for* $p = 1.p'$ *(resp.* $2.p'$*) in* $pos(i)$, $i_{|p} = i_{1|p'}$ *(resp.* $i_{2|p'}$*).*

2.2 Denotational semantics for basic interactions

As explained in Sec.2.1, operators occurring in an interaction induce relations of precedence between the actions of the interaction. In the example of Fig.2, if the left branch of the *alt* is chosen (i.e. $a!m_1$ at position 11) then the action $a!m_3$ at position 2 must occur after it. However if the other branch were chosen (i.e. $b?m_2$ at position 12), there would be no precedence order between actions $b?m_2$ and $a!m_3$ as their common ancestor is a *seq* operator which only orders actions sharing the same lifeline. As a result, several orderings can be defined, depending, among others, on the choice of *alt* branches. These possible orderings can be encoded as a set $ord(i)$ (defined in Def.4) which contains elements of the form (e, o) where e is the set of positions of the involved actions and o reflects the precedence relations between those. In the example of Fig.2, we have $ord(i) = \{(\{11, 2\}, \{(11, 2)\}), (\{12, 2\}, \emptyset)\}$. Indeed, as explained earlier, if the 11 branch is chosen then the only two actions to be considered are $a!m_1$ and $a!m_3$ on resp. positions 11 and 2 (therefore $e = \{11, 2\}$) and they are ordered because of both the *seq* operator and their common lifeline, so that the associated precedence relation is modelled by $o = \{(11, 2)\}$ meaning that $a!m_1$ at position 11 should occur before $a!m_3$ at position 2. The only other possible ordering occurs when branch 12 is chosen and likewise we would have $e = \{12, 2\}$ with $o = \emptyset$ because the *seq* does not constrain the order of actions $b?m_2$ and $a!m_3$ with different lifelines.

Definition 3 (Ordering type). *Given i in $\mathbb{B}(L,M)$. The set $\mathbb{O}(i)$ of candidate orderings of i contains all couples (e, o) such that (1) $e \subseteq pos(i)$, (2) for any p in e, $i_{|p} \in Act(L,M)$ and (3) $o \subseteq e \times e$. $\mathbb{O}$ is then the set $\bigcup_{i \in \mathbb{B}(L,M)} \mathbb{O}(i)$.*

In Def.4, for a given interaction i, $ord(i)$ precisely defines which orderings are to be considered among the candidate orderings $\mathbb{O}(i)$. For an ordering (e, o) in $\mathbb{O}$ and $p \in \{1, 2\}$, we use the notation $p.e = \{p.p' | p' \in e\}$, $p.o = \{(p.p_1, p.p_2) | (p_1, p_2) \in o\}$ and $p.(e, o) = (p.e, p.o)$. The notation is canonically extended to any set O of orderings, by $p.O = \{p.(e, o) | (e, o) \in O\}$.

For the interaction $\varnothing$, there is no associated action and therefore we have a single $(e, o) = (\emptyset, \emptyset)$. For $a \in Act(L,M)$, there is a single action a (at position ϵ) and as a result, $ord(a)$ contains a single $(e, o) = (\{\epsilon\}, \emptyset)$. For $i = alt(i_1, i_2)$,

---

[6] $\_|\_$ is a partial function so that $i_{|p}$ is only defined for positions occurring in $pos(i)$.

either i_1 or i_2 is executed. Thus any ordering in $ord(i)$ is simply an ordering from $ord(i_1)$ or from $ord(i_2)$ but correctly prefixed. Concretely, for any orderings $(e_1, o_1) \in ord(i_1)$ and $(e_2, o_2) \in ord(i_2)$, $ord(i)$ contains both $1.(e_1, o_1)$ and $2.(e_2, o_2)$. For $i = par(i_1, i_2)$, both i_1 and i_2 have to be executed but no order is enforced between actions of either child branch. Thus, for any ordering $(e_1, o_1) \in ord(i_1)$ and $(e_2, o_2) \in ord(i_2)$, $ord(i)$ contains $(1.e_1 \cup 2.e_2, 1.o_1 \cup 2.o_2)$. For $i = strict(i_1, i_2)$ both i_1 and i_2 have to be executed and all actions from i_1 must occur before actions from i_2. Thus for any orderings $(e_1, o_1) \in ord(i_1)$ and $(e_2, o_2) \in ord(i_2)$, $ord(i)$ contains an ordering (e, o) that concerns all actions from both children i.e. $e = 1.e_1 \cup 2.e_2$ and such that o keeps track of all initial precedence relations while incorporating those induced by the *strict* operator i.e. $o = 1.o_1 \cup 2.o_2 \cup \{(p_1, p_2) | p_1 \in 1.e_1, p_2 \in 2.e_2\}$. For $i = seq(i_1, i_2)$ the same reasoning can be applied, with the exception that additional precedence relations only concern actions that share the same lifelines. Using the same notations, $e = 1.e_1 \cup 2.e_2$ and $o = 1.o_1 \cup 2.o_2 \cup \{(p_1, p_2) | p_1 \in 1.e_1, p_2 \in 2.e_2, \Theta(i_{|p_1}) = \Theta(i_{|p_2})\}$.

Definition 4 (Orderings of a basic interaction). *We define the function* $ord : \mathbb{B}(L, M) \to \mathcal{P}(\mathbb{O})$ *as follows:*

$$ord(\varnothing) = \emptyset \quad and \quad \forall act \in Act(L, M), \ ord(act) = \{(\{\epsilon\}, \emptyset)\}$$

For any i_1 and i_2 in $\mathbb{B}(L, M)$:

$$ord(alt(i_1, i_2)) = 1.ord(i_1) \cup 2.ord(i_2)$$

$$ord(par(i_1, i_2)) = \bigcup_{\substack{(e_1, o_1) \in ord(i_1) \\ (e_2, o_2) \in ord(i_2)}} \{(1.e_1 \cup 2.e_2, 1.o_1 \cup 2.o_2)\}$$

$$ord(strict(i_1, i_2)) = \bigcup_{\substack{(e_1, o_1) \in ord(i_1) \\ (e_2, o_2) \in ord(i_2)}} \left\{ (e, o) \left| \begin{array}{l} e = (1.e_1 \cup 2.e_2) , \ o = 1.o_1 \cup 2.o_2 \cup o' \\ o' = \{(p_1, p_2) \mid p_1 \in 1.e_1 , \ p_2 \in 2.e_2\} \end{array} \right. \right\}$$

$$ord(seq(i_1, i_2)) = \bigcup_{\substack{(e_1, o_1) \in ord(i_1) \\ (e_2, o_2) \in ord(i_2)}} \left\{ (e, o) \left| \begin{array}{l} e = (1.e_1 \cup 2.e_2) , \ o = 1.o_1 \cup 2.o_2 \cup o' \\ o' = \left\{ (p_1, p_2) \left| \begin{array}{l} p_1 \in 1.e_1 , \ p_2 \in 2.e_2 \\ \Theta(i_{|p_1}) = \Theta(i_{|p_2}) \end{array} \right. \right\} \end{array} \right. \right\}$$

A given ordering (e, o) with $e = \{e_1, ..., e_n\}$ characterizes a set of behaviors that expresses every action whose position belongs to e exactly once. Such a behavior is thus given under the form of an execution trace $i_{|e_{\alpha(1)}} ... i_{|e_{\alpha(n)}}$ where α is a permutation of $[1, n]$. Obviously, not all of those permutations are acceptable as they must not contradict the partial order specified by o. If we note $p_j = e_{\alpha(j)}$ for j in $[1, n]$, we have $\forall j, k \in [1, n]^2 \ j > k \Rightarrow (p_j, p_k) \notin o$.

The semantics $\sigma(i)$ of an interaction i then comes naturally as the union of all sets $sem(i, e, o)$ of execution traces of i compatible with $(e, o) \in ord(i)$. When considering the example from Fig.2, we have $sem(i, \{11, 2\}, \{(11, 2)\}) = \{a!m_1.a!m_3\}$ and $sem(i, \{12, 2\}, \emptyset) = \{b?m_2.a!m_3, a!m_3.b?m_2\}$.

Definition 5 (Denotational semantics for basic interactions). *For $i \in$ $\mathbb{B}(L,M)$ and $(e,o) \in ord(i)$ with $n \in \mathbb{N}$ being the cardinal of e, we note:*

$$sem(i,e,o) = \{i_{|p_1}...i_{|p_n}|\forall(p_j,p_k) \in e^2, \ j > k \Rightarrow p_j \neq p_k \wedge (p_j,p_k) \notin o\}$$

$$\sigma : \mathbb{B}(L,M) \to \mathcal{P}(Act(L,M)^*) \text{ is s. t. } \forall i \in \mathbb{B}(L,M), \sigma(i) = \bigcup_{(e,o)\in ord(i)} sem(i,e,o)$$

2.3   Extension of the language with loops

A loop is a repetition operator. Its content can be instantiated any finite number of times i.e multiple copies of it are inserted into the interaction. For UML-SD, the norm [23] states that "*the loop construct represents a recursive application of the seq operator where the loop operand is sequenced after the result of earlier iterations*". The UML-SD loop is hence associated with the *seq* operator. When instantiated, the loop content is ordered using *seq* this means for example that $loop(a!m)$ becomes $seq(a!m, loop(a!m))$ then $seq(a!m, seq(a!m, loop(a!m)))$ and so on. In line with this explanation, let's consider the 4 types of loops that can be characterized according to the operator ordering the instantiated content (*seq, strict, par* or *alt*). We can discard *alt* as instantiating $loop(i)$ would lead to $alt(i, loop(i))$ meaning that the content can be read at most once and is therefore equivalent to $opt(i)$ (i.e. $alt(i, \varnothing)$). We will here consider 3 operators denoted $loop_{seq}$ (the classical loop), $loop_{strict}$ and $loop_{par}$.

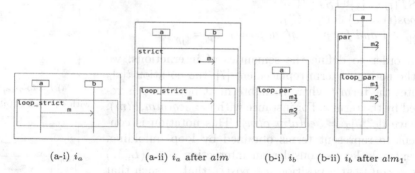

(a-i) i_a (a-ii) i_a after $a!m$ (b-i) i_b (b-ii) i_b after $a!m_1$

Fig. 3: Examples showcasing the pertinence of $loop_{strict}$ and $loop_{par}$

In Fig.3-a-i, $i_{a|11} = a!m$ is the only immediately executable action and its execution leads to the interaction $i'_a = strict(b?m, i_a)$ drawn on Fig.3-a-ii. Because of the *strict* operator, $i'_{a|211} = a!m$ is not immediately executable (preceded by $i'_{a|1} = b?m$). As a result $t_a = a!m.a!m.b?m.b?m$ is not an accepted trace for i_a. However, if there was a *seq* operator instead of the *strict*, $i'_{a|211}$ would be immediately executable and t_a an accepted trace.

Similarly, in Fig.3-b-i, $i_{b|11} = a!m_1$ is the only immediately executable action and its execution leads to $i'_b = par(a!m_2, i_b)$ drawn on Fig.3-b-ii. Because of the *par* operator, $i'_{b|211} = a!m_1$ is immediately executable. As a result $t_b = a!m_1.a!m_1.a!m_2.a!m_2$ is an accepted trace for i_b. However, if there was a *seq* instead of the *par*, $i'_{b|211}$ would not be immediately executable and t_b not an accepted trace.

Consequently, considering $loop_{par}$ and $loop_{strict}$ in addition to the classic $loop_{seq}$ improves expressiveness. In rough terms, $loop_{par}$ always allows new instantiations as each instance is executed in parallel w.r.t each others and the loop itself. $loop_{strict}$ on the contrary does not allow new instantiations as long as the previous instance has not been entirely executed. The behavior of $loop_{seq}$ is somewhat in the middle, instantiations being allowed depending on the current structure of actions preceding and within the loop.

In the following, we'll extend our IL to loops and adapt previous definitions (from $\mathbb{B}(L, M)$ to $\mathbb{I}(L, M)$). As in Def.6, any time we do so, we will only define the missing cases concerning loop terms.

Definition 6 (Interactions). *The set $\mathbb{I}(L, M)$ of interactions over L and M is inductively defined as follows:*

- *$\varnothing \in \mathbb{I}(L, M)$ and $Act(L, M) \subset \mathbb{I}(L, M)$,*
- *$\forall (i_1, i_2) \in \mathbb{I}(L, M)^2$ and $\forall f \in \{strict, seq, alt, par\}$, $f(i_1, i_2) \in \mathbb{I}(L, M)$,*
- *$\forall i \in \mathbb{I}(L, M)$ and $\forall f \in \{strict, seq, par\}$, $loop_f(i) \in \mathbb{I}(L, M)$.*

The functions $ST : \mathbb{I}(L, M) \to \mathcal{P}(\mathbb{I}(L, M))$, $pos : \mathbb{I}(L, M) \to \mathcal{P}(\{1, 2\}^*)$ and $\_|\_ : \mathbb{I}(L, M) \times \{1, 2\}^* \to \mathbb{I}(L, M)$ are defined by extending to loop terms the corresponding functions of Def.2:
For all i in $\mathbb{I}(L, M)$ of the form $loop_f(i')$ with $f \in \{strict, seq, par\}$:

- *$ST(i) = \{i\} \cup ST(i')$*
- *$pos(i) = \{\epsilon\} \cup 1.pos(i')$,*
- *$i_{|\epsilon} = i$ and for $p = 1.p'$ in $pos(i)$, $i_{|p} = i'_{|p'}$.*

In order to define the semantics of interactions, we use the notion of term replacement [7]: the notation $t[s]_p$ denotes the term t where its subterm at position p is replaced by the term s. For instance with $i = seq(a!m, b?m)$, we have $i[c?m]_2 = seq(a!m, c?m)$. This notation is convenient to represent terms obtained by loop unfolding. For example let us consider an interaction $i \in \mathbb{I}(L, M)$ with a $loop_{seq}$ at a position $p \in pos(i)$, that is, such that $i_{|p} = loop_{seq}(i_{|p.1})$. The interaction is then obtained from i by unfolding once the loop at position p is $i[seq(i_{|p.1}, i_{|p})]_p$. In Def.7, the set $\Upsilon(i, n)$ of all n-unfoldings of an interaction i (i.e. the set of all interactions resulting from n instantiations of *any* loop from i) is defined recursively. On Fig.4 loop unfolding is illustrated with $\Upsilon(i, 0) = \{i\}$ and $\Upsilon(i, 1) = \{i'\}$.

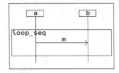

(a) $i = loop_{seq}(i_{|1})$ with $i_{|1} = strict(a!m, b?m)$

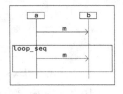

(b) $i' = seq(i_{|1}, i)$

Fig. 4: Unfolding

Definition 7 (n-unfoldings). *We define $\Upsilon : \mathbb{I}(L, M) \times \mathbb{N} \to \mathcal{P}(\mathbb{I}(L, M))$ such that $\forall i \in \mathbb{I}(L, M)$ $\Upsilon(i, 0) = \{i\}$ and $\forall n \in \mathbb{N}^+$:*

$$\Upsilon(i, n) = \bigcup_{p \in pos(i) \text{ s.t. } i_{|p} = loop_f(i_{|p.1})} \Upsilon(i[f(i_{|p.1}, i_{|p})]_p, n - 1)$$

We define a function $F : \mathbb{I}(L, M) \to \mathbb{B}(L, M)$ that flattens interactions with loops i.e. that replaces all loop subterms with the empty interaction $\varnothing$. For instance, in Fig.4 we have $F(i) = \varnothing$ and $F(i') = seq(i_{|1}, \varnothing)$. As $F(\mathbb{I}(L, M)) \subset \mathbb{B}(L, M)$, we can define an unfolding-based semantics[7] for $i \in \mathbb{I}(L, M)$ by simply considering the union of semantics obtained from flattened unfoldings of i.

Definition 8 (Denotational semantics for interactions).
We define $\sigma_u : \mathbb{I}(L, M) \to \mathcal{P}(Act(L, M)^*)$ such that for all i in $\mathbb{I}(L, M)$:

$$\sigma_u(i) = \bigcup_{n \in \mathbb{N}} \bigcup_{i' \in \Upsilon(i,n)} \sigma(F(i'))$$

3   Operational Semantics

We aim to define algorithms that can determine whether or not a trace t is accepted by an interaction i. This amounts to ascertaining whether or not $t \in \sigma_u(i)$. Naturally, being able to do so without having to compute $\sigma_u(i)$ is preferable. In the following we'll refer to this problem as 'trace analysis'.

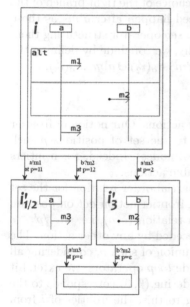

Fig. 5: Operational Semantics

As per Sec.2.3, asserting $t \in \sigma_u(i)$ equates to finding a combination of loop unfoldings $i^\star \in \bigcup_{k=0}^{\infty} \Upsilon(i, k)$ such that $t \in \sigma(F(i^\star))$. Even if feasible, this would be time and space consuming[8]. As for non acceptation, it equates to proving that $\forall i^\star \in \bigcup_{k=0}^{\infty} \Upsilon(i, k)$ we have $t \notin \sigma(F(i^\star))$. In this case, a termination in finite time would not even be guaranteed and would require defining some stopping criterion on the unfolding.

Consequently, we investigate another approach, in which traces are analyzed action by action. Here, instead of systematically unfolding loops, we do so on demand (when executing an *act* that is found within a loop). This approach is based on a different semantics (σ_o) whose description is the purpose of Sec.3.

σ_o is presented in the style of operational semantics, i.e. consisting in: **(1)** identifying from the structure of i which *act* can be immediately executed (coined 'frontier actions') and **(2)** deriving for each such *act* a new interaction i' specifying all the possible continuations of *act* within the set of execution traces specified by i (noted as $i \xrightarrow{act} i'$).

Intuitively, an action is in the frontier iff no structural operators (parent nodes) coerce it to be preceded by another action (sibling leaf). Accepted traces

---

[7] coined σ_u, u standing for 'unfolding-based'
[8] and would not be adaptable if one considers an extension to monitoring as new combinations $i^\star$ may be needed every time a new action is observed

are then built recursively through the successive consumption of actions. Let's consider a trace $t = act_1.(...).act_n$ with $\forall k \in [1, n]$ $i_{k-1} \xrightarrow{act_k} i_k$ and such that $i_0 = i$ (by extension we may note $i \xrightarrow{t} i_n$).

• If the last interaction i_n can express the empty trace ϵ (i.e. $\epsilon \in \sigma_u(i_n)$) - which can be statically analysed - then t is accepted by i i.e. $t \in \sigma_o(i)$.

• In any case, for all frontier actions act_{n+1} of i_n, we have $i_n \xrightarrow{act_{n+1}} i_{n+1}$, meaning that t can be extended by act_{n+1} and is a prefix of given trace(s) accepted by i.

To illustrate this, let's consider the example from Fig.5. The initial interaction is $i = seq(alt(a!m_1, b?m_2), a!m_3)$. There are 3 frontier actions that may play the role of act: $i_{|11} = a!m_1$, $i_{|12} = b?m_2$ and $i_{|2} = a!m_3$. The interactions remaining after the execution of $i_{|11}$ and $i_{|12}$ (resp. referred to as i'_1 and i'_2), which happen to be the same, are depicted below on the left, while the one remaining after the execution of $i_{|2}$ (noted i'_3) is depicted on the right. The cases leading to i'_1 and i'_2 are self-evident. As for the one leading to i'_3, the execution of $a!m_3$ is contingent to the choice of the branch 12 of the alt hence the elimination of branch 11 in the remaining interaction. Indeed, if branch 11 were to be chosen, the execution of $a!m_3$ would not be possible as $a!m_1$ should have been executed before. This illustrates that $a!m_3$ is a frontier action up to the choice of the right branch of the alt operator. Let us remark that $b?m_2$ may indeed happen after $a!m_3$ as those two actions occur on different lifelines and the top seq operator structuring them does not constrain their order of execution. Finally, we conclude by defining the operational semantics as $\sigma_o(i) = a!m_1.\sigma_o(i'_1) \cup b?m_2.\sigma_o(i'_2) \cup a!m_3.\sigma_o(i'_3)$.

3.1 Frontier actions

In this section we explain how to identify frontier actions. Our notion of frontier differs slightly from that of [4], where it refers to the set of positions p such that $\forall j \in \{1, 2\}^*$, $p.j \notin pos(i)$ (i.e. positions of leaf nodes). Indeed, our frontiers contain only leaves that are immediately executable actions.

Any ordering as defined in Def.4 provides a partial order relation for the set of (positions of) actions of a basic interaction. A frontier action act on position p is then simply a minimal element given such a relation (e, o), i.e. s.t. $\forall p' \in e$ we have $(p', p) \notin o$ i.e. act does not have to be preceded by any other action. The frontier of an interaction i is then defined as the union of such p, considering all the orderings from $ord(i)$. As Def.4 did not include $loop$ operators, we extend it in the following definition, in which the empty ordering $(\emptyset, \emptyset)$ corresponds to the case where the loop has not unfolded. According to this, the frontier of i from Fig.5 is then $front(i) = \{11, 12, 2\}$.

Definition 9 (Ordering). *We define* $ord : \mathbb{I}(L, M) \to \mathcal{P}(\mathbb{O})$ *as an extension to* $\mathbb{I}(L, M)$ *of its counterpart from Def.4. For all* f *in* $\{strict, seq, par\}$:

$$\forall i \in \mathbb{I}(L, M), \ ord(loop_f(i)) = 1.ord(i) \cup \{(\emptyset, \emptyset)\}$$

Definition 10 (Frontier). $front : \mathbb{I}(L, M) \to \mathcal{P}(\{1, 2\}^*)$ *is the function s.t.:*

$$\forall i \in \mathbb{I}(L, M), \ front(i) = \bigcup_{(e, o) \in ord(i)} \{p \in e \mid \forall p' \in e, (p', p) \notin o\}$$

3.2   Pruning

The design of the rules $i \xrightarrow{act} i'$ hinted at earlier is made operational thanks to 2 mechanisms: pruning and execution. Given an action $act \in front(i)$, branches preventing its execution are detected and eliminated with pruning. However, this is not done on the whole interaction i but rather on specific neighboring (w.r.t. act) subinteractions. Execution orchestrates the calls to pruning, eliminates act and constructs the remaining interaction i'.

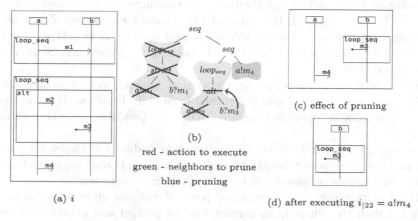

(a) i

(b)

red - action to execute

green - neighbors to prune

blue - pruning

(c) effect of pruning

(d) after executing $i_{|22} = a!m_4$

Fig. 6: Example showcasing pruning

We first define the pruning mechanism which consists in removing from an interaction all the actions which occur on a given lifeline. For instance, on Fig.6-b, let us consider the interactions $i_1 = i_{|1} = loop_{seq}(strict(a!m_1, b?m_1))$ and $i_2 = i_{|21} = loop_{seq}(alt(a!m_2, b?m_3))$ highlighted in green. We want to remove actions occurring on the lifeline a (so as to allow the execution of $i_{|22} = a!m_4$). We find that $i_{1|11} = a!m_1$ (resp. $i_{2|11} = a!m_2$) needs to be removed from i_1 (resp. i_2). If we do not want to get an interaction which is inconsistent or outwardly contradicts the original semantics, we can only prune subinteractions at positions where branching choices are made i.e. in alt and $loop$ nodes. Indeed, by definition, eliminating a subinteraction at one such node would lead to a semantics that is included in the original.

In i_2, eliminating $i_{2|11}$ is easily done given that its parent node is an alt and that its brother node does not need to be eliminated. Indeed, it suffices to operate the replacement $i_2[i_{2|12}]_1$ i.e. replacing the alt node with its right child $b?m_3$.

In i_1, eliminating $i_{1|11}$ is more delicate: its parent node is a $strict$ and as such, behaviors from its left and right children must both happen (there is no branching choice). Thus, if we want to eliminate $i_{1|11}$ we must also eliminate the whole $i_{1|1}$. The problem is hence forwarded upwards in the syntax. The parent $i_{1|\epsilon}$ is a loop operator, which characterizes a branching choice. We can eliminate the problematic branch by choosing not to instantiate the loop i.e. via the replacement $i_1[\varnothing]_\epsilon$.

The pruning mechanism is given in Def.11 as the recursive *prune* function, which takes as arguments an interaction i and a lifeline l. *prune* eliminates from i branching choices hosting actions that occur on l.

In a first descending phase, *prune* goes down the syntax of i through recursive calls (from root to leaves). When reaching a leaf, *prune* returns an interaction i' and a boolean b. $b = \top$ signifies that the current branch needs to be eliminated (pruned) while i' is the interaction that will be used to reconstruct i in the ascending phase (only used if $b = \bot$). Leaves are either actions or empty interactions. For an action act, if $\Theta(act) = l$, the current branch must be pruned so $prune(act, l) = (\varnothing, \top)$: the value of the returned interaction i' has no importance here because a parent will be pruned anyway. If $\Theta(act) \neq l$ we have $prune(act, l) = (act, \bot)$ because there is nothing to prune here. Similarly, we have $prune(\varnothing, l) = (\varnothing, \bot)$.

In the second, ascending phase, the pruned interaction is reconstructed according to the values of i' and b returned from child branches. If at any point $b = \top$, this value is forwarded upwards until an expendable branching choice is reached.

$prune(i, l)$ is recursively called on the child nodes of i. Depending on the operator in i, the return values of $prune(i_{|1}, l) = (i'_1, b_1)$ (and also $prune(i_{|2}, l) = (i'_2, b_2)$ for binary operators) will be used differently to determine i' and b.

For the operators $f \in \{strict, seq, par\}$, if any one child must be pruned ($b_1 \vee b_2$) then the whole branch must also be pruned and otherwise a reconstructed $f(i'_1, i'_2)$ is returned. For the exclusive alternative alt, if no branch needs pruning, $alt(i'_1, i'_2)$ is returned; if any single branch needs pruning, *prune* returns the one that does not need to be pruned and if both branches need pruning, then the whole interaction is pruned. For the repetition operators, if the loop content needs pruning then the choice of 'never taking the loop' is made meaning that $\varnothing$ is returned with $b = \bot$, signifying a successful pruning. If there is no needed pruning, it simply returns the loop with an already pruned loop content $loop_f(i'_1)$.

Definition 11 (Pruning). $prune : \mathbb{I}(L, M) \times L \to \mathbb{I}(L, M) \times bool$ *is the function such that for all* $i \in \mathbb{I}(L, M)$ *and* $l \in L$:

- $prune(\varnothing, l) = (\varnothing, \bot)$
- *for* $act \in Act(L, M)$: *if* $\Theta(i_{|p}) = l$ *then* $prune(act, l) = (\varnothing, \top)$ *(else* $(act, \bot)$*)*
- *if* $i = f(i_1, i_2)$ *with* $f \in \{strict, seq, par\}$, *given* $prune(i_1, l) = (i'_1, b_1)$ *and* $prune(i_2, l) = (i'_2, b_2)$:
  if $b_1 \vee b_2$ *then* $prune(i, l) = (\varnothing, \top)$ *(else* $(f(i'_1, i'_2), \bot)$*)*
- *if* $i = alt(i_1, i_2)$, *given* $prune(i_1, l) = (i'_1, b_1)$ *and* $prune(i_2, l) = (i'_2, b_2)$:
  - *if* $b_1 \wedge b_2$ *then* $prune(i, l) = (\varnothing, \top)$
  - *if* $b_1 \wedge \neg b_2$ *then* $prune(i, l) = (i'_2, \bot)$
  - *if* $\neg b_1 \wedge b_2$ *then* $prune(i, l) = (i'_1, \bot)$
  - *if* $\neg b_1 \wedge \neg b_2$ *then* $prune(i, l) = (alt(i'_1, i'_2), \bot)$
- *if* $i = loop_f(i_1)$ *with* $f \in \{strict, seq, par\}$, *given* $prune(i_1, l) = (i'_1, b_1)$:
  if b_1 *then* $prune(i, l) = (\varnothing, \bot)$ *(else* $(loop_f(i'_1), \bot)$*)*

3.3 Execute function and operational semantics

Let us consider the example i from Fig.6. We wish to execute the frontier action $i_{|22} = a!m_4$ (highlighted in red). To allow this execution we need at first to remove the actions occurring on the same lifeline (i.e. on a) from the neighbors highlighted in green. To do so, we use the *prune* function from Def.11. More generally, the nature of our syntax is such that, for the execution of a frontier action at position p, we only need to prune subinteractions at positions $p_0.1$ s.t. $\exists p' \in \{1,2\}^*$ s.t. $p = p_0.2.p'$ and s.t. $i_{|p_0} = seq(i_{|p_0.1}, i_{|p_0.2})$. Those are exactly the left cousins of $i_{|p}$ that are scheduled sequentially (i.e. with *seq*) w.r.t. $i_{|p}$.

We now define the execution function χ (Def.12), which takes as arguments an interaction i and a frontier position p and returns the remaining interaction i'. As explained earlier, χ orchestrates the use of *prune*. In the example from Fig.6 this first cleaning feature would result in the transformation of i from the diagram on Fig.6-a to the one on Fig.6-c. The only thing left to do is then to remove the executed action s.t. the result is the interaction from Fig.6-d.

χ is defined inductively on both the structure of the interaction i and the position $p = d_1...d_n \in \{1,2\}^n$. The execution of $\chi(i,p)$ traverses recursively the syntactic structure of i guided by the path defined by the position p, that is, from $\chi(i_{|\epsilon}, d_1...d_n)$ (root node), ..., up to $\chi(i_{|p}, \epsilon)$ (target action leaf to execute). Here, $\chi(i_{|p}, \epsilon) = \varnothing$ constitutes the stopping criterion and i' is then constructed when the algorithm goes back up through the syntactic structure of i. Assigning $\varnothing$ to $\chi(i_{|p}, \epsilon)$ ensures that the action $i_{|p}$ is removed in the construction of i'.

When a *par* node is encountered during the upward traversal, i.e. for $j \in [1,n]$, $i_{|d_1...d_j} = par(i_{|d_1...d_j.1}, i_{|d_1...d_j.2})$ then $\chi(i_{|d_1...d_j}, d_{j+1}...d_n)$ is simply:
$par(\chi(i_{|d_1...d_j.1}, d_{j+2}...d_n), i_{|d_1...d_j.2})$ if $d_{j+1} = 1$ or,
$par(i_{|d_1...d_j.1}, \chi(i_{|d_1...d_j.2}, d_{j+2}...d_n))$ if $d_{j+1} = 2$.
Indeed, as *par* specifies parallel executions, there is no need for pruning.

When an *alt* node is reached, using the same notations, we would have:
$\chi(i_{|d_1...d_j}, d_{j+1}...d_n) = \chi(i_{|d_1...d_{j+1}}, d_{j+2}...d_n)$.
Indeed, we can 'skip' the *alt* node itself and replace it directly with the interaction resulting from the execution of the chosen branch.

When a *loop* is reached, i.e. $i_{|d_1...d_j} = loop_f(i_{|d_1...d_j.1})$ (with a mandatory $d_{j+1} = 1$), we have :
$\chi(i_{|d_1...d_j}, d_{j+1}...d_n) = f(\chi(i_{|d_1...d_{j+1}}, d_{j+2}...d_n), i_{|d_1...d_j})$.
Indeed, the execution is done on a copy of the loop content that precedes (with f operator) the loop $i_{|d_1...d_j}$ itself, that is, on an unfolding of the loop.

For the sequential operators, pruning needs to be considered only if the executing action is situated on the right branch of the *seq* or *strict* node (if the action is on the left branch, we have the same transformation as in the *par* case). Given $i_{|d_1...d_j} = seq(i_{|d_1...d_j.1}, i_{|d_1...d_j.2})$ and $d_{j+1} = 2$, when constructing $\chi(i_{|d_1...d_j}, d_{j+1}...d_n)$ we must prune in $i_{|d_1...d_j.1}$ all the actions that could interfere with $i_{|p}$ i.e. those taking place on $\Theta(i_{|p})$. As such, given $(i'_1, b_1) = prune(i_{|d_1...d_j.1}, \Theta(i_{|p}))$, we'll replace the left branch of the *seq* with i'_1 and reconstruct:
$\chi(i_{|d_1...d_j}, d_{j+1}...d_n) = seq(i'_1, \chi(i_{|d_1...d_{j+1}}, d_{j+2}...d_n))$.

Given that the *strict* operator won't allow any action from the left branch to occur after an action on the right has occurred, we can simply prune the whole left branch i.e. given $i_{|d_1...d_j} = strict(i_{|d_1...d_j.1}, i_{|d_1...d_j.2})$ and $d_{j+1} = 2$:
$$\chi(i_{|d_1...d_j}, d_{j+1}...d_n) = \chi(i_{|d_1...d_{j+1}}, d_{j+2}...d_n).$$

Definition 12 (Execution). *The function* $\chi : \mathbb{I}(L, M) \times \{1, 2\}^* \to \mathbb{I}(L, M)$ *is defined for couples* (i, p) *with* $i \in \mathbb{I}(L, M)$ *and* $p \in front(i)$ *as follows:*

- *if* $p = \epsilon$ *then* $\chi(i, p) = \varnothing$
- *if* $p = 1.p_1$ *then*
  - *if* $i = f(i_1, i_2)$ *with* $f \in \{strict, seq, par\}$ *then* $\chi(i, p) = f(\chi(i_1, p_1), i_2)$
  - *if* $i = alt(i_1, i_2)$ *then* $\chi(i, p) = \chi(i_1, p_1)$
  - *if* $i = loop_f(i_1)$ *with* $f \in \{strict, seq, par\}$ *then* $\chi(i, p) = f(\chi(i_1, p_1), i)$
- *if* $p = 2.p_2$ *then*
  - *if* $i = seq(i_1, i_2)$ *then* $\chi(i, p) = seq(i_1', \chi(i_2, p_2))$
    where $prune(i_1, \Theta(i_{|p})) = (i_1', b)$
  - *if* $i = strict(i_1, i_2)$ *then* $\chi(i, p) = \chi(i_2, p_2)$
  - *if* $i = par(i_1, i_2)$ *then* $\chi(i, p) = par(i_1, \chi(i_2, p_2))$
  - *if* $i = alt(i_1, i_2)$ *then* $\chi(i, p) = \chi(i_2, p_2)$

In Def.13 below, we now define the operational semantics. Note that interactions that can express the empty trace ϵ are identified with the predicate exp_ϵ. This semantics expresses rules of the form $i \xrightarrow{i_{|p}} \chi(i, p)$ where $p \in front(i)$.

Definition 13 (Operational semantics for interactions).
We define $\sigma_o : \mathbb{I}(L, M) \to \mathcal{P}(Act(L, M)^*)$ *as:*

$$\sigma_o(i) = empty(i) \cup \bigcup_{p \in front(i)} i_{|p}.\sigma_o(\chi(i, p))$$

with $empty(i) = \{\epsilon\}$ *(resp.$\emptyset$) if* $exp_\epsilon(i) = \top$ *(resp.* $\bot$*)*
where $exp_\epsilon : \mathbb{I}(L, M) \to bool$ *is defined as:*

- $exp_\epsilon(\varnothing) = \top$
- $exp_\epsilon(l \Delta m) = \bot$
- $exp_\epsilon(f(i_1, i_2)) = exp_\epsilon(i_1) \wedge exp_\epsilon(i_2)$ *for* $f \in \{strict, seq, par\}$
- $exp_\epsilon(alt(i_1, i_2)) = exp_\epsilon(i_1) \vee exp_\epsilon(i_2)$
- $exp_\epsilon(loop_f(i_1)) = \top$ *for* $f \in \{strict, seq, par\}$

4   Back-to-back comparison of both semantics

Dataset. The recursive definition of interactions as syntactic terms allows to characterize them by their depth. Interactions of depth 1 include the empty interaction $\varnothing$ and all actions from $Act(L, M)$. Depending on the cardinals $n_l = Card(L)$ and $n_m = Card(M)$, those interactions can all be enumerated and computed. Given a signature, interactions of depth 2 can be deduced from those of depth 1 and exhaustively computed via the application of the binary and unary operators (e.g. $seq(\varnothing, a!m)$). Likewise, interactions of depth 3 can be computed from those of depths 1 and 2 and so on. To illustrate this, Fig.7 presents for each couple (n_l, n_m) the numbers of interactions of depths 1, 2 and 3 in each cell. For instance, we have 3 interactions of depth 1 for $n_l = n_m = 1$.

Experiments. We implemented both semantics (σ_u from Def.8 and σ_o from Def.13) and compared the set of traces $\sigma_u(i)$ and $\sigma_o(i)$ they generate (with a stopping criterion on the maximum number of loop unfolding - 4 in our experiments) on a significant set of interactions of depth 3 with $n_l = n_m = 3$. For all of the 234175 selected interactions i from our dataset, the tests systematically concluded on the equality $\sigma_u(i) = \sigma_o(i)$. Although not a proof, our successful back-to-back comparison comforts our confidence in both semantics, all the more so because of the exhaustivity of the subject data set up to maximum numbers of lifelines, messages types, interaction depth (up to 3), number of loop unfolding (up to 4), allowing covering all 2 by 2 combinations of operators.

n_m \ n_l	1	2	3
1	3	5	7
	45	115	217
	9315	57845	201159
2	5	9	13
	115	351	715
	57845	519129	2121405
3	7	13	19
	217	715	1501
	201159	2121405	9244659

Fig. 7: Numbers of interactions per n_l, n_m and d

5   Trace analysis

The definition of the execution function χ (Def.12) that comes with the operational nature of the σ_o semantics (Def.13) allows us to solve the 'trace analysis' problem hinted at earlier. Indeed, analysing a trace $t = act_1...act_n$ w.r.t. an interaction i_0 equates to verifying whether or not there exists transformations $i_0 \xrightarrow{act_1} \chi(i_0,p_1) = i_1, \ ..., \ i_{n-1} \xrightarrow{act_n} \chi(i_{n-1},p_n) = i_n$ s.t. i_n accepts the empty trace.

We define an ω function (Def.14) which takes as arguments an interaction i and a trace t and checks whether or not t is a trace of i. Additional traceability information is provided using four distinct verdicts:

- *Covered* is returned when t is a trace of i i.e. $t \in \sigma_o(i)$;
- *TooShort* is returned when $t \notin \sigma_o(i)$ is a strict prefix of a trace of i i.e. $\exists t' \in Act(L,M)^*$ s.t. $t.t' \in \sigma_o(i)$;
- *TooLong* is returned when neither *Covered* nor *TooShort* can be, and given $t = act_1...act_n$ $\exists k < n$ s.t. $act_1...act_k \in \sigma_o(i)$ i.e. t extends a trace of i;
- *Out* is returned when none of the others can be.

We define the enumerated type $Verdict$ and provide it with a total order $Out \prec TooLong \prec TooShort \prec Covered$.

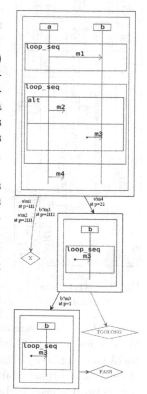

Fig. 8: Application of ω

- If t is empty then: either i accepts the empty trace in its semantics and in this case $\omega(i,t)$ returns *Covered*, or it returns *TooShort*.
- If t is of the form $act.t'$ (i.e. not empty and starts with act) then, for all matching actions $i_{|p}$ in the frontier of i, recursive calls are performed on $\omega(\chi(i,p),t')$ and $\omega(i,t)$ returns the strongest ($max_\prec$ function) verdict among those and either *TooLong* if i expresses the empty trace ϵ or *Out* if not.

Definition 14 (Trace Analysis). *We define* $\omega : \mathbb{I}(L,M) \times Act(L,M)^* \to Verdict$ *such that* $\forall i, t \in \mathbb{I}(L,M) \times Act(L,M)^*$:

- $\omega(i,\epsilon) = Covered$ *(resp. TooShort) if* $exp_\epsilon(i) = \top$ *(resp. $\bot$)*
- *if t is of the form $act.t'$ then:*

$$\omega(i,t) = max_\prec \left(out_\epsilon(i) \cup \left\{ \omega(\chi(i,p),t') \,\middle|\, \begin{array}{l} p \in front(i) \\ i_{|p} = act \end{array} \right\} \right)$$

with $out_\epsilon(i) = \{TooLong\}$ *(resp. $\{Out\}$) if* $exp_\epsilon(i) = \top$ *(resp. $\bot$)*

Fig.8 is a graphical representation of the ω process when applied to the interaction from Fig.6-a and the trace $a!m_4.b?m_3$.

Verdict	trc	act	prf	add	rep	Total
COV	3231	352	0	0	0	3583
SHORT	0	1705	4618	358	3246	9927
LONG	0	864	0	50242	10443	61549
OUT	0	15079	0	0	66138	81217
Total	3231	18000	4618	50600	79827	156276

Fig. 9: Correctness of ω experiments

Fig.9 presents a synthesis of experiments conducted to assess the correctness of ω and of our implementation of it. We randomly sampled 1000 interactions from the set of 234175 interactions mentioned in Sec.4. Each of them were tested with the 18 single action traces from $Act(L,M)$ and we sampled 15 traces from their semantics (computed with 3 loop unfolds). Each of those traces were tested as well as a random selection of their prefixes and of interesting mutants. Addition (resp. replacement) mutants consists in adding an action to a trace (resp. prefix). By construction we could classify all those traces according to the verdicts they are expected to obtain. Fig.9 details those results, showing a systematic concordance between the expected and obtained verdicts. Those results reinforce our confidence on ω, the more so that they were done on a panel of traces and interactions which covers all 2 by 2 combinations of operators.

To provide an evaluation of performances (plotting time vs. length), we needed a large model and long correct traces. Indeed, the time required by the analysis is not always correlated to trace length e.g. an arbitrarily long trace starting with an action act of position $p \notin front(i)$ is analyzed immediately, whatever length it may be. There is however a correlation for correct traces and their prefixes. We defined a partial high-level model of the MQTT [22] telecommunication protocol (see Fig.10-a). This model states that a communication session between a client and a broker starts (resp. ends) with a sequential connection (resp. disconnection) phase. In between, at any time, any number of instances of one of the 5 proposed subinteractions can be run concurrently. Hence, we used a multi-threaded Python script to generate 100 traces, each of those corresponding to the concurrent activation and execution at random time intervals of 20 instances of the $loop_{par}$ from Fig.10-a. All those traces (resp. prefixes) have the verdict $Covered$ (resp. $TooShort$); we evaluated computation times and plotted some of them on Fig.10-b.

The linear regression shows curves with a great variability (some traces need 4 seconds while others only 0.06). In this precise model, it is explained by the presence of *par* (via $loop_{par}$) operators and by the fact that messages are not uniquely identified. For instance analyzing $t = a!m.b?m$ on $i = par(a!m, strict(a!m, b?m))$ would give rise to 2 branches: $i' = strict(a!m, b?m)$ (resp. $i' = par(a!m, b?m)$) with $t' = b?m$ which ends with *Out* (resp. *Covered*) because m is not uniquely identified. This number of branches can quickly explode when *par* operators are stacked which happens when the trace describes an execution where many

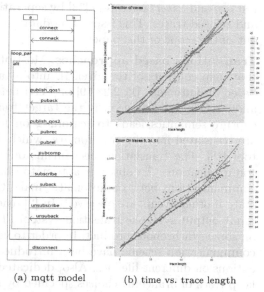

(a) mqtt model   (b) time vs. trace length

Fig. 10: Performances

loop content instances overlap. An applicable solution is to treat message data arguments, given that communication protocols provide unique ids e.g. $m(id1) \neq m(id2)$. In Fig.10-b, on the plot below, we magnified on traces 9, 34 & 61 which have a very short analysis time. We can surmise here that minimal (perhaps no) loop overlap occurred as the derivatives are almost constants (especially for trace 61). In conclusion, performance highly depends on the model and input trace, but treating data which specifies unique ids for messages would generalize the best case scenario. In this case, the algorithm could be applied to monitoring within the limits of an input frequency that is inferior to the time required to analyze a trace of length 1.

6 Related work

For classical IL such as UML-SD or HMSC, many authors have proposed their own takes on formal semantics (see the survey [21] for UML-SD).

Denotational Semantics. Most existing semantics based on term interpretations are given in a denotational style [27,14,3,17] and do not follow-up with algorithmic tools. In [27], the authors propose a denotational semantics similar to ours (Def.5) as far as the *strict*, *alt* and *par* operators are concerned. [14] proposes a semantics that is a detailed version of the one from [27]. In [17] there is a distinction $(snd(s,r,m)|snd(s,m)|rcv(s,r,m)|rcv(r,m))$ between basic actions whether or not the intended receiver or original sender is the environment. Apart from that, and the absence of *loops*, the denotational semantics proposed by [17] is similar to ours. In [3], an institutional approach, likened to that of [17] is proposed. However it includes *loops* and deals with modalities associated to the *neg* and *assert* operators [23] by separating the semantics in sets of accepted and refused traces. This issue of modality is also raised in [21] and [13] but it is out of the scope of this paper.

Translations based approaches. Most other approaches rely on translations that map concepts of the given IL into a target formal framework, most often based on automata [11,2,28,19] or Petri nets [8,5,10]. Albeit those translations allow reusing advantageously the target framework's tools, relying on them to capture semantics leads to reasoning on foreign concepts. In [11], UML-SDs are translated into timed automata, which are then verified with the UPPAAL tool [18]. The translation mechanisms only concern models with synchronous communications. An observer automaton has to be designed so as to intercept communications between automata, make them observable, and enter an error state if other events are observed. In [2], each lifeline is translated into a timed input output symbolic transition system (TIOSTS) and message passing relies on some synchronous product. In order to cope with asynchronism, FIFO based communication schema have been introduced to ensure the consistency of executions on different lifelines. Also, dedicated variables have to be introduced to keep track of branching choices specified by *alt* or *loop* operators. In [28], a symbolic automaton is built from UML-SD specifications in the goal of analyzing traces by means of valid, invalid or inconclusive verdicts. [19] focuses on how to test Message Sequence Charts when the system is only partially observed. A translation into a network of asynchronous concurrent automata allows to define semantics through a product automaton as in [2]. In [8], UML-SD specifications are translated into multivalued nets (M-nets). The translation is compositional, entry and exit places of the M-nets corresponding to subinteractions being connected differently according to the parent combined fragment. However this process is complicated by the tracking of actions that are completely unordered w.r.t. one another. [8] also treats data in the form of variables, message parameters and guards. In [5], the authors propose an approach to automatically translate UML-SDs designed with the Papyrus tool [12] to Coloured Petri Nets (CPNs) in a format compatible with CPNTools [16]. CPNs come with an execution semantics that is particularly adapted for the description and analysis of distributed and concurrent systems. In [5], the translation revolves around a list of 11 rules with different priorities and which are applied to translate different concepts (lifelines, message occurrences, combined fragments, etc.) while iterating sequentially through the UML-SD's elements. In [10] a set of UML-SDs are translated into Extended Petri Nets. Input execution traces can then be checked against the EPNs.

Operational approach. The literature contains few attempts at defining operational semantics for ILs. In [26], the authors build formal expressions over a process algebra signature. Starting from axioms such as $\epsilon \downarrow$ (the empty process ϵ terminates) and $a \xrightarrow{a} \epsilon$ (a being an atomic action), an expression describing a MSC is build using rules such as $(x \xrightarrow{a} x') \wedge (y \not\xrightarrow{a}) \Rightarrow (x \mp y \xrightarrow{a} x')$. Such an expression is then associated with a transition graph. The contribution in [26] does not however deal with *loop* operator and it is quite different from ours as the proposed transformations operate on process-algebraic expressions and not on syntactic terms. In contrast, the semantics proposed in [20] relies on syntactic term transformations. Still, it also requires a communication medium as it is defined as the output of a combination of two transitions systems: an execution system which keeps track of communications, and a projection system which selects the next action to execute and provide the resulting interaction. As explained in [9], communication models keep track of emitted messages and messages pending receptions. They can for instance take the form of a set of dedicated buffers (e.g. FIFO). Our approach has the advantage of making such communication models implicit.

Discussions. Despite interaction languages specifying no synchronisation mechanisms between lifelines, several approaches that aim to implement tools, impose synchronisation points when entering and exiting combined operators and at decision points (*alt, opt, loop*) [28,2,8,21] (although more recent works such as [10,20] do not). Although translation-based approaches have the benefit of allowing the use of the many existing analysis tools (UPPAAL [18], DIVERSITY [15], CPNTools [16] etc.) we postulate that direct operational approaches such as ours facilitate features such as animation and debugging, becoming for the most part free-of-charge by-products of the analysis process.

7   Conclusion

In this paper we proposed an operational semantics for ILs, aimed at trace validity analysis. This semantic is built upon a formal syntax for interaction terms and validated back-to-back w.r.t. a reference denotational semantics. Our semantics is built on partial order relations induced on messages by the syntax. Those relations allow the identification of immediately executable actions. Pruning techniques then ensure a consistent semantics based on successive transformations of the form $i \xrightarrow{act} i'$. On this principle, we have defined and implemented algorithms to compute semantics and to analyze the validity of traces. Experiments were successfully conducted in order to evaluate the correctness of each.

We intend to enrich our formalism: **(1)** by expanding trace analysis to a distributed context, where a set of traces (multi-trace) may be analyzed concurrently on a subset of observed lifelines; **(2)** by investigating whether or not our algorithmic treatments are fast enough to deal with traces on-the-fly so as to adapt them to monitoring. **(3)** by extending our IL to include modality operators such as *assert* or *negate*. **(4)** by allowing the use of message arguments, variables, clocks and constraints within models.

Additionally, it would be interesting to perform a comparison with translation-based approaches. This may consist in a comparison of formal semantics and/or in benchmarking implementations according to a certain performance metric.

500   E. Mahe et al.

References

1. Alur, R., Yannakakis, M.: Model checking of message sequence charts. In: CON-CUR '99: Concurrency Theory. Lecture Notes in Computer Science, vol. 1664, pp. 114–129. Springer (1999)
2. Bannour, B., Gaston, C., Servat, D.: Eliciting unitary constraints from timed sequence diagram with symbolic techniques: Application to testing. In: 2011 18th Asia-Pacific Software Engineering Conference. pp. 219–226 (2011)
3. Cengarle, M., Knapp, A.: An institution for uml 2.0 interactions (01 2008)
4. Comon, H., Dauchet, M., Gilleron, R., Löding, C., Jacquemard, F., Lugiez, D., Tison, S., Tommasi, M.: Tree automata techniques and applications (10 2007)
5. Custódio Soares, J.a.A., Lima, B., Pascoal Faria, J.a.: Automatic model transformation from uml sequence diagrams to coloured petri nets. In: Proceedings of the 6th International Conference on Model-Driven Engineering and Software Development. p. 668–679. MODELSWARD 2018, SCITEPRESS - Science and Technology Publications, Lda, Setubal, PRT (2018). https://doi.org/10.5220/0006731806680679
6. Damm, W., Harel, D.: Lscs: Breathing life into message sequence charts. Formal Methods in System Design 19(1), 45–80 (2001)
7. Dershowitz, N., Jouannaud, J.P.: Handbook of theoretical computer science (vol. b). chap. Rewrite Systems, pp. 243–320. MIT Press, Cambridge, MA, USA (1990)
8. Eichner, C., Fleischhack, H., Meyer, R., Schrimpf, U., Stehno, C.: Compositional semantics for uml 2.0 sequence diagrams using petri nets. In: Prinz, A., Reed, R., Reed, J. (eds.) SDL 2005: Model Driven. pp. 133–148. Springer Berlin Heidelberg, Berlin, Heidelberg (2005)
9. Engels, A., Mauw, S., Reniers, M.: A hierarchy of communication models for message sequence charts. Science of Computer Programming 44(3), 253 – 292 (2002). https://doi.org/10.1016/S0167-6423(02)00022-9
10. Faria, J.P., Paiva, A.C.R.: A toolset for conformance testing against uml sequence diagrams based on event-driven colored petri nets. International Journal on Software Tools for Technology Transfer 18(3), 285–304 (2016)
11. Firley, T., Huhn, M., Diethers, K., Gehrke, T., Goltz, U.: Timed sequence diagrams and tool-based analysis - A case study. In: UML'99: The Unified Modeling Language - Beyond the Standard. Lecture Notes in Computer Science, vol. 1723, pp. 645–660. Springer (1999)
12. Gérard, S., Dumoulin, C., Tessier, P., Selic, B.: Papyrus: A UML2 Tool for Domain-Specific Language Modeling, pp. 361–368. Springer Berlin Heidelberg, Berlin, Heidelberg (2010). https://doi.org/10.1007/978-3-642-16277-0_19
13. Harel, D., Maoz, S.: Assert and negate revisited: Modal semantics for UML sequence diagrams. Software and Systems Modeling 7(2), 237–252 (2008)
14. Haugen, O., Husa, K.E., Runde, R.K., Stølen, K.: STAIRS towards formal design with sequence diagrams. Software and Systems Modeling 4(4), 355–367 (2005)
15. Hussein, M., Nouacer, R., Radermacher, A., Puccetti, A., Gaston, C., Rapin, N.: An end-to-end framework for safe software development. Microprocessors and Microsystems 62, 41 – 49 (2018). https://doi.org/10.1016/j.micpro.2018.07.004
16. Jensen, K., Kristensen, L.M., Wells, L.: Coloured Petri Nets and CPN Tools for modelling and validation of concurrent systems. International Journal on Software Tools for Technology Transfer 9(3), 213–254 (Jun 2007). https://doi.org/10.1007/s10009-007-0038-x

17. Knapp, A., Mossakowski, T.: UML Interactions Meet State Machines - An Institutional Approach. In: 7th Conf. on Algebra and Coalgebra in Computer Science (CALCO 2017). Leibniz International Proceedings in Informatics (LIPIcs), vol. 72, pp. 15:1–15:15. Schloss Dagstuhl–Leibniz-Zentrum fuer Informatik (2017)
18. Larsen, K.G., Pettersson, P., Yi, W.: Uppaal in a nutshell. International Journal on Software Tools for Technology Transfer **1**(1), 134–152 (Dec 1997). https://doi.org/10.1007/s100090050010
19. Longuet, D.: Global and local testing from message sequence charts. In: Proceedings of the ACM Symposium on Applied Computing, SAC 2012. pp. 1332–1338. ACM (2012)
20. Lund, M.S., Stølen, K.: A fully general operational semantics for uml 2.0 sequence diagrams with potential and mandatory choice. In: Misra, J., Nipkow, T., Sekerinski, E. (eds.) FM 2006: Formal Methods. pp. 380–395. Springer Berlin Heidelberg, Berlin, Heidelberg (2006)
21. Micskei, Z., Waeselynck, H.: The many meanings of uml 2 sequence diagrams: a survey. Software & Systems Modeling **10**(4), 489–514 (2011)
22. OASIS: Mqtt version 3.1.1 (12 2015)
23. OMG: Unified Modeling Language v2.5.1 (12 2017)
24. Plotkin, G.D.: An operational semantics for CSP. In: Formal Description of Programming Concepts : Proceedings of the IFIP Working Conference on Formal Description of Programming Concepts- II. pp. 199–226. North-Holland (1983)
25. S., M., M. A., R.: High-level message sequence charts. In: SDL '97 Time for Testing, SDL, MSC and Trends - 8th International SDL Forum, Proceedings. pp. 291–306. Elsevier (1997)
26. S., M., M. A., R.: Operational semantics for msc. Computer Networks **31**(17), 1785–1799 (1999)
27. Storrle, H.: Semantics of interactions in uml 2.0. In: IEEE Symposium on Human Centric Computing Languages and Environments, 2003. Proceedings. 2003. pp. 129–136 (Oct 2003). https://doi.org/10.1109/HCC.2003.1260216
28. Waeselynck, H., Micskei, Z., Rivière, N., Hamvas, Á., Nitu, I.: Termos: A formal language for scenarios in mobile computing systems. In: Sénac, P., Ott, M., Seneviratne, A. (eds.) Mobile and Ubiquitous Systems: Computing, Networking, and Services. pp. 285–296. Springer Berlin Heidelberg, Berlin, Heidelberg (2012)

Test-Comp Contributions

Second Competition on Software Testing: Test-Comp 2020

Dirk Beyer [ID]

LMU Munich, Germany

Abstract. This report describes the 2020 Competition on Software Testing (Test-Comp), the 2nd edition of a series of comparative evaluations of fully automatic software test-case generators for C programs. The competition provides a snapshot of the current state of the art in the area, and has a strong focus on replicability of its results. The competition was based on 3 230 test tasks for C programs. Each test task consisted of a program and a test specification (error coverage, branch coverage). Test-Comp 2020 had 10 participating test-generation systems.

Keywords: Software Testing · Test-Case Generation · Competition · Software Analysis · Software Validation · Test Validation · Test-Comp · Benchmarking · Test Coverage · Bug Finding · BENCHEXEC · TESTCOV

1 Introduction

Software testing is as old as software development itself, because the most straightforward way to find out if the software works is to execute it. In the last few decades the tremendous breakthrough of fuzzers[1], theorem provers [40], and satisfiability-modulo-theory (SMT) solvers [21] have led to the development of efficient tools for automatic test-case generation. For example, symbolic execution and the idea to use it for test-case generation [33] exists for more than 40 years, yet, efficient implementations (e.g., KLEE [16]) had to wait for the availability of mature constraint solvers. Also, with the advent of automatic software model checking, the opportunity to extract test cases from counterexamples arose (see BLAST [9] and JPF [41]). In the following years, many techniques from the areas of model checking and program analysis were adapted for the purpose of test-case generation and several strong hybrid combinations have been developed [24].

There are several powerful software test generators available [24], but they were difficult to compare. For example, a recent study [11] first had to develop a framework that supports to run test-generation tools on the same program source code and to deliver test cases in a common format for validation. Furthermore, there was no widely distributed benchmark suite available and neither input programs nor output test suites followed a standard format. In software verification, the competition SV-COMP [3] helped to overcome the problem: the competition community developed standards for defining nondeterministic functions and a

---

[1] http://lcamtuf.coredump.cx/afl/

H. Wehrheim and J. Cabot (Eds.): FASE 2020, LNCS 12076, pp. 505–519, 2020.
https://doi.org/10.1007/978-3-030-45234-6_25

language to write specifications (so far for C and Java programs) and established a standard exchange format for the output (witnesses). A competition event with high visibility can foster the transfer of theoretical and conceptual advancements in the area of software testing into practical tools.

The annual Competition on Software Testing (Test-Comp) [4, 5] [2] is the showcase of the state of the art in the area, in particular, of the effectiveness and efficiency that is currently achieved by tool implementations of the most recent ideas, concepts, and algorithms for fully automatic test-case generation. Test-Comp uses the benchmarking framework BENCHEXEC [12], which is already successfully used in other competitions, most prominently, all competitions that run on the STAREXEC infrastructure [39]. Similar to SV-COMP, the test generators in Test-Comp are applied to programs in a fully automatic way. The results are collected via BENCHEXEC's XML results format, and transformed into tables and plots in several formats. [3] All results are available in artifacts at Zenodo (Table 3).

Competition Goals. In summary, the goals of Test-Comp are the following:

- Establish *standards* for software test generation. This means, most prominently, to develop a standard for marking input values in programs, define an exchange format for test suites, and agree on a specification language for test-coverage criteria, and define how to validate the resulting test suites.
- Establish a set of *benchmarks* for software testing in the community. This means to create and maintain a set of programs together with coverage criteria, and to make those publicly available for researchers to be used in performance comparisons when evaluating a new technique.
- Provide an overview of *available tools* for test-case generation and a snapshot of the state-of-the-art in software testing to the community. This means to compare, independently from particular paper projects and specific techniques, different test-generation tools in terms of effectiveness and performance.
- Increase the visibility and credits that *tool developers* receive. This means to provide a forum for presentation of tools and discussion of the latest technologies, and to give the students the opportunity to publish about the development work that they have done.
- Educate PhD students and other participants on how to set up performance experiments, packaging tools in a way that supports replication, and how to perform *robust and accurate research experiments*.
- Provide *resources* to development teams that do not have sufficient computing resources and give them the opportunity to obtain results from experiments on large benchmark sets.

Related Competitions. In other areas, there are several established competitions. For example, there are three competitions in the area of software verification: (i) a competition on automatic verifiers under controlled resources (SV-COMP [3]), (ii) a competition on verifiers with arbitrary environments (RERS [27]), and (iii) a competition on interactive verification (VerifyThis [28]). An overview of

---

[2] https://test-comp.sosy-lab.org
[3] https://test-comp.sosy-lab.org/2020/results/

16 competitions in the area of formal methods was presented at the TOOLympics events at the conference TACAS in 2019 [1]. In software testing, there are several competition-like events, for example, the DARPA Cyber Grand Challenge [38] [4], the IEEE International Contest on Software Testing [5], the Software Testing World Cup [6], and the Israel Software Testing World Cup [7]. Those contests are organized as on-site events, where teams of people interact with certain testing platforms in order to achieve a certain coverage of the software under test. There are two competitions for automatic and off-site testing: Rode0day [8] is a competition that is meant as a continuously running evaluation on bug-finding in binaries (currently Grep and SQLite). The unit-testing tool competition [32] [9] is part of the SBST workshop and compares tools for unit-test generation on Java programs. There was no comparative evaluation of automatic test-generation tools for whole C programs in source-code, in a controlled environment, and Test-Comp was founded to close this gap [4]. The results of the first edition of Test-Comp were presented as part of the TOOLympics 2019 event [1] and in the Test-Comp 2019 competition report [5].

2   Definitions, Formats, and Rules

Organizational aspects such as the classification (automatic, off-site, reproducible, jury, traning) and the competition schedule is given in the initial competition definition [4]. In the following we repeat some important definitions that are necessary to understand the results.

Test Task. A *test task* is a pair of an input program (program under test) and a test specification. A *test run* is a non-interactive execution of a test generator on a single test task, in order to generate a test suite according to the test specification. A *test suite* is a sequence of test cases, given as a directory of files according to the format for exchangeable test-suites.[10]

Execution of a Test Generator. Figure 1 illustrates the process of executing one test generator on the benchmark suite. One test run for a test generator gets as input (i) a program from the benchmark suite and (ii) a test specification (find bug, or coverage criterion), and returns as output a test suite (i.e., a set of test cases). The test generator is contributed by a competition participant. The test runs are executed centrally by the competition organizer. The test validator takes as input the test suite from the test generator and validates it by executing the program on all test cases: for bug finding it checks if the bug is exposed and for coverage it reports the coverage. We use the tool TESTCOV [14] [11] as test-suite validator.

---

[4] https://www.darpa.mil/program/cyber-grand-challenge/
[5] http://paris.utdallas.edu/qrs18/contest.html
[6] http://www.softwaretestingworldcup.com/
[7] https://www.inflectra.com/Company/Article/480.aspx
[8] https://rode0day.mit.edu/
[9] https://sbst19.github.io/tools/
[10] https://gitlab.com/sosy-lab/software/test-format/
[11] https://gitlab.com/sosy-lab/software/test-suite-validator

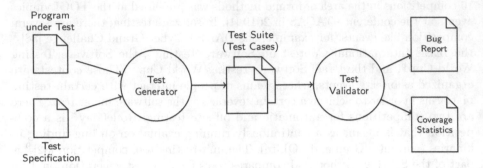

Fig. 1: Flow of the Test-Comp execution for one test generator

Table 1: Coverage specifications used in Test-Comp 2020 (same as in 2019)

Formula	Interpretation
COVER EDGES(@CALL(__VERIFIER_error))	The test suite contains at least one test that executes function __VERIFIER_error.
COVER EDGES(@DECISIONEDGE)	The test suite contains tests such that all branches of the program are executed.

Test Specification. The specification for testing a program is given to the test generator as input file (either `properties/coverage-error-call.prp` or `properties/coverage-branches.prp` for Test-Comp 2020).

The definition `init(main())` is used to define the initial states of the program under test by a call of function `main` (with no parameters). The definition `FQL(f)` specifies that coverage definition `f` should be achieved. The FQL (FSHELL query language [26]) coverage definition `COVER EDGES(@DECISIONEDGE)` means that all branches should be covered, `COVER EDGES(@BASICBLOCKENTRY)` means that all statements should be covered, and `COVER EDGES(@CALL(__VERIFIER_error))` means that calls to function `__VERIFIER_error` should be covered. A complete specification looks like: `COVER( init(main()), FQL(COVER EDGES(@DECISIONEDGE)) )`.

Table 1 lists the two FQL formulas that are used in test specifications of Test-Comp 2020; there was no change from 2019. The first describes a formula that is typically used for bug finding: the test generator should find a test case that executes a certain error function. The second describes a formula that is used to obtain a standard test suite for quality assurance: the test generator should find a test suite for branch coverage.

License and Qualification. The license of each participating test generator must allow its free use for replication of the competition experiments. Details on qualification criteria can be found in the competition report of Test-Comp 2019 [5].

3   Categories and Scoring Schema

Benchmark Programs. The input programs were taken from the largest and most diverse open-source repository of software verification tasks [12], which is also used by SV-COMP [3]. As in 2019, we selected all programs for which the following properties were satisfied (see issue on GitHub [13] and report [5]):

1. compiles with `gcc`, if a harness for the special methods [14] is provided,
2. should contain at least one call to a nondeterministic function,
3. does not rely on nondeterministic pointers,
4. does not have expected result 'false' for property 'termination', and
5. has expected result 'false' for property 'unreach-call' (only for category *Error Coverage*).

This selection yielded a total of 3 230 test tasks, namely 699 test tasks for category *Error Coverage* and 2 531 test tasks for category *Code Coverage*. The test tasks are partitioned into categories, which are listed in Tables 6 and 7 and described in detail on the competition web site.[15] Figure 2 illustrates the category composition.

Category Error-Coverage. The first category is to show the abilities to discover bugs. The programs in the benchmark set contain programs that contain a bug. Every run will be started by a batch script, which produces for every tool and every test task (a C program together with the test specification) one of the following scores: 1 point, if the validator succeeds in executing the program under test on a generated test case that explores the bug (i.e., the specified function was called), and 0 points, otherwise.

Category Branch-Coverage. The second category is to cover as many branches of the program as possible. The coverage criterion was chosen because many test-generation tools support this standard criterion by default. Other coverage criteria can be reduced to branch coverage by transformation [25]. Every run will be started by a batch script, which produces for every tool and every test task (a C program together with the test specification) the coverage of branches of the program (as reported by TESTCOV [14]; a value between 0 and 1) that are executed for the generated test cases. The score is the returned coverage.

Ranking. The ranking was decided based on the sum of points (normalized for meta categories). In case of a tie, the ranking was decided based on the run time, which is the total CPU time over all test tasks. Opt-out from categories was possible and scores for categories were normalized based on the number of tasks per category (see competition report of SV-COMP 2013 [2], page 597).

---

[12] https://github.com/sosy-lab/sv-benchmarks
[13] https://github.com/sosy-lab/sv-benchmarks/pull/774
[14] https://test-comp.sosy-lab.org/2020/rules.php
[15] https://test-comp.sosy-lab.org/2020/benchmarks.php

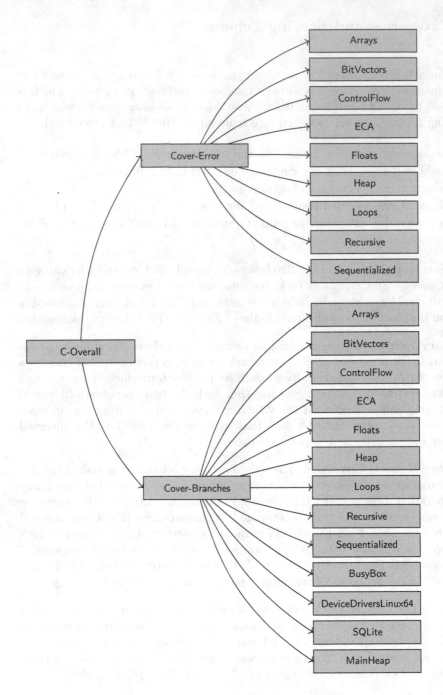

Fig. 2: Category structure for Test-Comp 2020

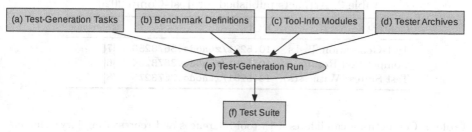

Fig. 3: Test-Comp components and the execution flow

Table 2: Publicly available components for replicating Test-Comp 2020

Component	Fig. 3	Repository	Version
Test-Generation Tasks	(a)	github.com/sosy-lab/sv-benchmarks	testcomp20
Benchmark Definitions	(b)	gitlab.com/sosy-lab/test-comp/bench-defs	testcomp20
Tool-Info Modules	(c)	github.com/sosy-lab/benchexec	2.5.1
Tester Archives	(d)	gitlab.com/sosy-lab/test-comp/archives-2020	testcomp20
Benchmarking	(e)	github.com/sosy-lab/benchexec	2.5.1
Test-Suite Format	(f)	gitlab.com/sosy-lab/software/test-format	testcomp20

4 Reproducibility

In order to support independent replication of the Test-Comp experiments, we made all major components that are used for the competition available in public version repositories. An overview of the components that contribute to the reproducible setup of Test-Comp is provided in Fig. 3, and the details are given in Table 2. We refer to the report of Test-Comp 2019 [5] for a thorough description of all components of the Test-Comp organization and how we ensure that all parts are publicly available for maximal replicability.

In order to guarantee long-term availability and immutability of the test-generation tasks, the produced competition results, and the produced test suites, we also packaged the material and published it at Zenodo. The DOIs and references are listed in Table 3. The archive for the competition results includes the raw results in BENCHEXEC's XML exchange format, the log output of the test generators and validator, and a mapping from files names to SHA-256 hashes. The hashes of the files are useful for validating the exact contents of a file, and accessing the files inside the archive that contains the test suites.

To provide transparent access to the exact versions of the test generators that were used in the competition, all tester archives are stored in a public Git repository. GITLAB was used to host the repository for the tester archives due to its generous repository size limit of 10 GB. The final size of the Git repository is 1.47 GB.

Table 3: Artifacts published for Test-Comp 2020

Content	DOI	Reference
Test-Generation Tasks	`10.5281/zenodo.3678250`	[7]
Competition Results	`10.5281/zenodo.3678264`	[6]
Test Suites (Witnesses)	`10.5281/zenodo.3678275`	[8]

Table 4: Competition candidates with tool references and representing jury members

Participant	Ref.	Jury member	Affiliation
CoVeriTest	[10, 31]	Marie-Christine Jakobs	TU Darmstadt, Germany
Esbmc	[22, 23]	Lucas Cordeiro	U. of Manchester, UK
HybridTiger	[15, 37]	Sebastian Ruland	TU Darmstadt, Germany
Klee	[17]	Martin Nowack	Imperial College London, UK
Legion	[36]	Gidon Ernst	LMU Munich, Germany
LibKluzzer	[34]	Hoang M. Le	U. of Bremen, Germany
PRTest	[35]	Thomas Lemberger	LMU Munich, Germany
Symbiotic	[18, 19]	Marek Chalupa	Masaryk U., Czechia
TracerX	[29, 30]	Joxan Jaffar	Nat. U. of Singapore, Singapore
VeriFuzz	[20]	Raveendra Kumar M.	Tata Consultancy Services, India

5   Results and Discussion

For the second time, the competition experiments represent the state of the art in fully automatic test-generation for whole C programs. The report helps in understanding the improvements compared to last year, in terms of effectiveness (test coverage, as accumulated in the score) and efficiency (resource consumption in terms of CPU time). All results mentioned in this article were inspected and approved by the participants.

Participating Test Generators. Table 4 provides an overview of the participating test-generation systems and references to publications, as well as the team representatives of the jury of Test-Comp 2020. (The competition jury consists of the chair and one member of each participating team.) Table 5 lists the features and technologies that are used in the test-generation tools. An online table with information about all participating systems is provided on the competition web site.[16]

Computing Resources. The computing environment and the resource limits were mainly the same as for Test-Comp 2019 [5]: Each test run was limited to 8 processing units (cores), 15 GB of memory, and 15 min of CPU time. The test-suite validation was limited to 2 processing units, 7 GB of memory, and 5 h of CPU time (was 3 h for Test-Comp 2019). The machines for running the experiments are part of a compute cluster that consists of 168 machines; each test-generation run was executed on an otherwise completely unloaded, dedicated machine, in order

---

[16] https://sv-comp.sosy-lab.org/2020/systems.php

Table 5: Technologies and features that the competition candidates offer

Participant	Bounded Model Checking	CEGAR	Evolutionary Algorithms	Explicit-Value Analysis	Floating-Point Arithmetics	Guidance by Coverage Measures	Predicate Abstraction	Random Execution	Symbolic Execution	Targeted Input Generation
CoVeriTest		✓		✓	✓		✓			
Esbmc	✓				✓					
HybridTiger		✓		✓	✓		✓			
Klee									✓	✓
Legion						✓		✓	✓	✓
LibKluzzer						✓			✓	✓
PRTest								✓		
Symbiotic						✓			✓	✓
TracerX	✓								✓	✓
VeriFuzz	✓		✓	✓		✓		✓		

to achieve precise measurements. Each machine had one Intel Xeon E3-1230 v5 CPU, with 8 processing units each, a frequency of 3.4 GHz, 33 GB of RAM, and a GNU/Linux operating system (x86_64-linux, Ubuntu 18.04 with Linux kernel 4.15). We used BenchExec [12] to measure and control computing resources (CPU time, memory, CPU energy) and VerifierCloud [17] to distribute, install, run, and clean-up test-case generation runs, and to collect the results. The values for time and energy are accumulated over all cores of the CPU. To measure the CPU energy, we use CPU Energy Meter [13] (integrated in BenchExec [12]). Further technical parameters of the competition machines are available in the repository that also contains the benchmark definitions. [18]

One complete test-generation execution of the competition consisted of 20 800 single test-generation runs. The total CPU time was 178 days and the consumed energy 49.9 kWh for one complete competition run for test-generation (without validation). Test-suite validation consisted of 29 899 single test-suite

---

[17] https://vcloud.sosy-lab.org
[18] https://gitlab.com/sosy-lab/test-comp/bench-defs/tree/testcomp20

Table 6: Quantitative overview over all results; empty cells mark opt-outs

Participant	Cover-Error 699 tasks	Cover-Branches 2531 tasks	Overall 3230 tasks
CoVeriTest	405	**1412**	1836
Esbmc	**506**		
HybridTiger	394	1351	1772
Klee	502	1342	**2017**
Legion	302	1257	1501
LibKluzzer	**630**	**1597**	**2474**
PRTest	66	545	500
Symbiotic	435	849	1548
TracerX	373	1244	1654
VeriFuzz	**636**	**1577**	**2476**

validation runs. The total consumed CPU time was 632 days. Each tool was executed several times, in order to make sure no installation issues occur during the execution. Including preruns, the infrastructure managed a total of 401 156 test-generation runs (consuming 1.8 years of CPU time) and 527 805 test-suite validation runs (consuming 6.5 years of CPU time). We did not measure the CPU energy during preruns.

Quantitative Results. Table 6 presents the quantitative overview of all tools and all categories. The head row mentions the category and the number of test tasks in that category. The tools are listed in alphabetical order; every table row lists the scores of one test generator. We indicate the top three candidates by formatting their scores in bold face and in larger font size. An empty table cell means that the tester opted-out from the respective main category (perhaps participating in subcategories only, restricting the evaluation to a specific topic). More information (including interactive tables, quantile plots for every category, and also the raw data in XML format) is available on the competition web site [19] and in the results artifact (see Table 3). Table 7 reports the top three testers for each category. The consumed run time (column 'CPU Time') is given in hours and the consumed energy (column 'Energy') is given in kWh.

Score-Based Quantile Functions for Quality Assessment. We use score-based quantile functions [12] because these visualizations make it easier to understand the results of the comparative evaluation. The web site [19] and the

---

[19] https://test-comp.sosy-lab.org/2020/results

Table 7: Overview of the top-three test generators for each category (measurement values for CPU time and energy rounded to two significant digits)

Rank	Verifier	Score	CPU Time (in h)	Energy (in kWh)
Cover-Error				
1	VERIFUZZ	**636**	17	.22
2	LIBKLUZZER	630	130	1.3
3	ESBMC	506	9.5	.11
Cover-Branches				
1	LIBKLUZZER	**1597**	540	5.6
2	VERIFUZZ	1577	590	7.5
3	COVERITEST	1412	430	4.4
Overall				
1	VERIFUZZ	**2476**	610	7.7
2	LIBKLUZZER	2474	670	6.9
3	KLEE	2017	460	5.2

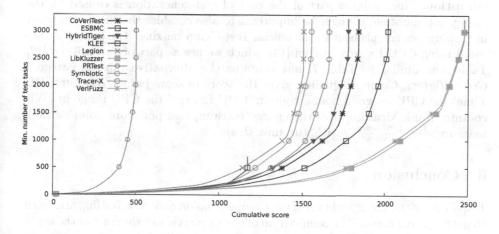

Fig. 4: Quantile functions for category *Overall*. Each quantile function illustrates the quantile (x-coordinate) of the scores obtained by test-generation runs below a certain number of test tasks (y-coordinate). More details were given previously [5]. A logarithmic scale is used for the time range from 1 s to 1000 s, and a linear scale is used for the time range between 0 s and 1 s.

Table 8: Alternative rankings; quality is given in score points (sp), CPU time in hours (h), energy in kilo-watt-hours (kWh), the rank measure in joule per score point (J/sp); measurement values are rounded to 2 significant digits

Rank	Verifier	Quality (sp)	CPU Time (h)	CPU Energy (kWh)	Rank Measure (J/sp)
Green Testers					
1	Symbiotic	1 548	41	0.50	1.2
2	Legion	1 501	160	1.8	4.4
3	TracerX	1 654	310	3.8	8.3
worst					53

results artifact (Table 3) include such a plot for each category; as example, we show the plot for category *Overall* (all test tasks) in Fig. 4. A total of 9 testers (all except Esbmc) participated in category *Overall*, for which the quantile plot shows the overall performance over all categories (scores for meta categories are normalized [2]). A more detailed discussion of score-based quantile plots for testing is provided in the previous competition report [5].

Alternative Ranking: Green Test Generation — Low Energy Consumption. Since a large part of the cost of test-generation is caused by the energy consumption, it might be important to also consider the energy efficiency in rankings, as complement to the official Test-Comp ranking. The energy is measured using CPU Energy Meter [13], which we use as part of BenchExec [12]. Table 8 is similar to Table 7, but contains the alternative ranking category *Green Testers*. Column 'Quality' gives the score in score points, column 'CPU Time' the CPU usage in hours, column 'CPU Energy' the CPU usage in kWh, column 'Rank Measure' uses the energy consumption per score point as rank measure: $\frac{\text{total CPU energy}}{\text{total score}}$, with the unit *J/sp*.

6 Conclusion

Test-Comp 2020, the 2nd edition of the Competition on Software Testing, attracted 10 participating teams. The competition offers an overview of the state of the art in automatic software testing for C programs. The competition does not only execute the test generators and collect results, but also validates the achieved coverage of the test suites, based on the latest version of the test-suite validator TestCov. The number of test tasks was increased to 3 230 (from 2 356 in Test-Comp 2019). As before, the jury and the organizer made sure that the competition follows the high quality standards of the FASE conference, in particular with respect to the important principles of fairness, community support, and transparency.

References

1. Bartocci, E., Beyer, D., Black, P.E., Fedyukovich, G., Garavel, H., Hartmanns, A., Huisman, M., Kordon, F., Nagele, J., Sighireanu, M., Steffen, B., Suda, M., Sutcliffe, G., Weber, T., Yamada, A.: TOOLympics 2019: An overview of competitions in formal methods. In: Proc. TACAS (3). pp. 3–24. LNCS 11429, Springer (2019). https://doi.org/10.1007/978-3-030-17502-3_1
2. Beyer, D.: Second competition on software verification (Summary of SV-COMP 2013). In: Proc. TACAS. pp. 594–609. LNCS 7795, Springer (2013). https://doi.org/10.1007/978-3-642-36742-7_43
3. Beyer, D.: Automatic verification of C and Java programs: SV-COMP 2019. In: Proc. TACAS (3). pp. 133–155. LNCS 11429, Springer (2019). https://doi.org/10.1007/978-3-030-17502-3_9
4. Beyer, D.: Competition on software testing (Test-Comp). In: Proc. TACAS (3). pp. 167–175. LNCS 11429, Springer (2019). https://doi.org/10.1007/978-3-030-17502-3_11
5. Beyer, D.: First international competition on software testing (Test-Comp 2019). Int. J. Softw. Tools Technol. Transf. (2020)
6. Beyer, D.: Results of the 2nd International Competition on Software Testing (Test-Comp 2020). Zenodo (2020). https://doi.org/10.5281/zenodo.3678264
7. Beyer, D.: SV-Benchmarks: Benchmark set of the 2nd Intl. Competition on Software Testing (Test-Comp 2020). Zenodo (2020). https://doi.org/10.5281/zenodo.3678250
8. Beyer, D.: Test suites from Test-Comp 2020 test-generation tools. Zenodo (2020). https://doi.org/10.5281/zenodo.3678275
9. Beyer, D., Chlipala, A.J., Henzinger, T.A., Jhala, R., Majumdar, R.: Generating tests from counterexamples. In: Proc. ICSE. pp. 326–335. IEEE (2004). https://doi.org/10.1109/ICSE.2004.1317455
10. Beyer, D., Jakobs, M.C.: CoVeriTest: Cooperative verifier-based testing. In: Proc. FASE. pp. 389–408. LNCS 11424, Springer (2019). https://doi.org/10.1007/978-3-030-16722-6_23
11. Beyer, D., Lemberger, T.: Software verification: Testing vs. model checking. In: Proc. HVC. pp. 99–114. LNCS 10629, Springer (2017). https://doi.org/10.1007/978-3-319-70389-3_7
12. Beyer, D., Löwe, S., Wendler, P.: Reliable benchmarking: Requirements and solutions. Int. J. Softw. Tools Technol. Transfer 21(1), 1–29 (2019). https://doi.org/10.1007/s10009-017-0469-y
13. Beyer, D., Wendler, P.: CPU Energy Meter: A tool for energy-aware algorithms engineering. In: Proc. TACAS (2). LNCS 12079, Springer (2020)
14. Beyer, D., Lemberger, T.: TestCov: Robust test-suite execution and coverage measurement. In: Proc. ASE. pp. 1074–1077. IEEE (2019). https://doi.org/10.1109/ASE.2019.00105
15. Bürdek, J., Lochau, M., Bauregger, S., Holzer, A., von Rhein, A., Apel, S., Beyer, D.: Facilitating reuse in multi-goal test-suite generation for software product lines. In: Proc. FASE. pp. 84–99. LNCS 9033, Springer (2015). https://doi.org/10.1007/978-3-662-46675-9_6
16. Cadar, C., Dunbar, D., Engler, D.R.: Klee: Unassisted and automatic generation of high-coverage tests for complex systems programs. In: Proc. OSDI. pp. 209–224. USENIX Association (2008)
17. Cadar, C., Nowack, M.: Klee symbolic execution engine (competition contribution). Int. J. Softw. Tools Technol. Transf. (2020)

18. Chalupa, M., Vitovska, M., Jašek, T., Šimáček, M., Strejček, J.: Symbiotic 6: Generating test-cases (competition contribution). Int. J. Softw. Tools Technol. Transf. (2020)

19. Chalupa, M., Strejček, J., Vitovská, M.: Joint forces for memory safety checking. In: Proc. SPIN. pp. 115–132. Springer (2018). https://doi.org/10.1007/978-3-319-94111-0_7

20. Chowdhury, A.B., Medicherla, R.K., Venkatesh, R.: VeriFuzz: Program-aware fuzzing (competition contribution). In: Proc. TACAS (3). pp. 244–249. LNCS 11429, Springer (2019). https://doi.org/10.1007/978-3-030-17502-3_22

21. Cok, D.R., Déharbe, D., Weber, T.: The 2014 SMT competition. JSAT **9**, 207–242 (2016)

22. Gadelha, M.R., Menezes, R., Monteiro, F.R., Cordeiro, L., Nicole, D.: Esbmc: Scalable and precise test generation based on the floating-point theory (competition contribution). In: Proc. FASE. LNCS 12076, Springer (2020)

23. Gadelha, M.Y., Ismail, H.I., Cordeiro, L.C.: Handling loops in bounded model checking of C programs via k-induction. Int. J. Softw. Tools Technol. Transf. **19**(1), 97–114 (Feb 2017). https://doi.org/10.1007/s10009-015-0407-9

24. Godefroid, P., Sen, K.: Combining model checking and testing. In: Handbook of Model Checking, pp. 613–649. Springer (2018). https://doi.org/10.1007/978-3-319-10575-8_19

25. Harman, M., Hu, L., Hierons, R.M., Wegener, J., Sthamer, H., Baresel, A., Roper, M.: Testability transformation. IEEE Trans. Software Eng. **30**(1), 3–16 (2004). https://doi.org/10.1109/TSE.2004.1265732

26. Holzer, A., Schallhart, C., Tautschnig, M., Veith, H.: How did you specify your test suite. In: Proc. ASE. pp. 407–416. ACM (2010). https://doi.org/10.1145/1858996.1859084

27. Howar, F., Isberner, M., Merten, M., Steffen, B., Beyer, D., Păsăreanu, C.S.: Rigorous examination of reactive systems. The RERS challenges 2012 and 2013. Int. J. Softw. Tools Technol. Transfer **16**(5), 457–464 (2014). https://doi.org/10.1007/s10009-014-0337-y

28. Huisman, M., Klebanov, V., Monahan, R.: VerifyThis 2012: A program verification competition. STTT **17**(6), 647–657 (2015). https://doi.org/10.1007/s10009-015-0396-8

29. Jaffar, J., Maghareh, R., Godboley, S., Ha, X.L.: TracerX: Dynamic symbolic execution with interpolation (competition contribution). In: Proc. FASE. LNCS 12076, Springer (2020)

30. Jaffar, J., Murali, V., Navas, J.A., Santosa, A.E.: Tracer: A symbolic execution tool for verification. In: Proc. CAV. pp. 758–766. LNCS 7358, Springer (2012). https://doi.org/10.1007/978-3-642-31424-7_61

31. Jakobs, M.C.: CoVeriTest with dynamic partitioning of the iteration time limit (competition contribution). In: Proc. FASE. LNCS 12076, Springer (2020)

32. Kifetew, F.M., Devroey, X., Rueda, U.: Java unit-testing tool competition: Seventh round. In: Proc. SBST. pp. 15–20. IEEE (2019). https://doi.org/10.1109/SBST.2019.00014

33. King, J.C.: Symbolic execution and program testing. Commun. ACM **19**(7), 385–394 (1976). https://doi.org/10.1145/360248.360252

34. Le, H.M.: Llvm-based hybrid fuzzing with LibKluzzer (competition contribution). In: Proc. FASE. LNCS 12076, Springer (2020)

35. Lemberger, T.: Plain random test generation with PRTest (competition contribution). Int. J. Softw. Tools Technol. Transf. (2020)

36. Liu, D., Ernst, G., Murray, T., Rubinstein, B.: LEGION: Best-first concolic testing (competition contribution). In: Proc. FASE. LNCS 12076, Springer (2020)
37. Ruland, S., Lochau, M., Jakobs, M.C.: HYBRIDTIGER: Hybrid model checking and domination-based partitioning for efficient multi-goal test-suite generation (competition contribution). In: Proc. FASE. LNCS 12076, Springer (2020)
38. Song, J., Alves-Foss, J.: The DARPA cyber grand challenge: A competitor's perspective, part 2. IEEE Security and Privacy **14**(1), 76–81 (2016). https://doi.org/10.1109/MSP.2016.14
39. Stump, A., Sutcliffe, G., Tinelli, C.: STAREXEC: A cross-community infrastructure for logic solving. In: Proc. IJCAR, pp. 367–373. LNCS 8562, Springer (2014). https://doi.org/10.1007/978-3-319-08587-6_28
40. Sutcliffe, G.: The CADE ATP system competition: CASC. AI Magazine **37**(2), 99–101 (2016)
41. Visser, W., Păsăreanu, C.S., Khurshid, S.: Test-input generation with Java PATHFINDER. In: Proc. ISSTA. pp. 97–107. ACM (2004). https://doi.org/10.1145/1007512.1007526

HybridTiger: Hybrid Model Checking and Domination-based Partitioning for Efficient Multi-Goal Test-Suite Generation (Competition Contribution)

Sebastian Ruland[1], Malte Lochau[1], and Marie-Christine Jakobs[2]

[1] Technical University of Darmstadt, Department of Electrical Engineering and Information Technology, Real-Time Systems Lab, Darmstadt, Germany
{sebastian.ruland,malte.lochau}@es.tu-darmstadt.de
[2] Technical University of Darmstadt, Department of Computer Science, Semantics and Verification of Parallel Systems, Darmstadt, Germany
jakobs@cs.tu-darmstadt.de

Abstract. In theory, software model checkers are well-suited for auto-mated test-case generation. The idea is to perform (non-)reachability queries for the test goals and extract test cases from resulting counter-examples. However, in case of realistic programs, even simple coverage criteria (e.g., branch coverage) force model checkers to deal with several hundreds or even thousands of test goals. Processing each of these test goals in isolation with model checking techniques does not scale. Therefore, our tool HybridTiger builds on recent ideas on multi-property verification. However, since every additional property (i.e., test goal) re-duces the model checker's abstraction possibilities, we split the set of all test goals into different partitions. In Test-Comp 2019, we applied a random partitioning strategy and used predicate analysis as model checking technique. In Test-Comp 2020, we improved our technique in two ways. First, we exploit domination information among control-flow locations in our partitioning strategy to group test goals being located on (preferably) similar paths. Second, we account to inherent weaknesses of the predicate analysis by applying a hybrid software model-checking approach that switches between explicit model checking and predicate-based model checking on-the-fly. Our tool HybridTiger is integrated into the software analysis framework CPACHECKER.

Keywords: CPAchecker · Test-Goal Set Partitioning · Hybrid Model-Checking Cooperation

1 Software Architecture

The HybridTiger algorithm is implemented within the software verification framework CPACHECKER [4]. CPACHECKER utilizes the Eclipse CDT C-parser[3].

---

[3] https://www.eclipse.org/cdt/

© The Author(s) 2020
H. Wehrheim and J. Cabot (Eds.): FASE 2020, LNCS 12076, pp. 520–524, 2020.
https://doi.org/10.1007/978-3-030-45234-6_26

```
1   int fib(int n){
2       if(n <= 0) return -1;
3       if(n == 1) return 1;
4       if(n == 2) return 1;
5       return fib(n-1)
6              +fib(n-2);
7   }
```

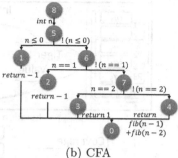

(a) C-Program	(b) CFA

Fig. 1. C Program to calculate the Fibonacci number of n and corresponding CFA

CPACHECKER allows developers to easily integrate new algorithms like Hybrid-Tiger, which may use other algorithms implemented in CPACHECKER, such as counterexample-guided abstraction refinement (CEGAR) [5]. Additionally, new reachability analyses can be integrated as CONFIGURABLE PROGRAM ANALYSES (CPAs) [2]. Each CPA consist of an abstract domain with the operators *post*, *merge*, and *stop*. Multiple CPAs can also be combined into one CPA.

HybridTiger uses the CoVeriTest [3] algorithm to sequentially combine test-case generation runs utilizing different verification techniques. Each test-case generation run applies the CPA/Tiger-MGP[4](Tiger Multi-Goal-Partitioning) algorithm, which utilizes the CEGAR algorithm.

2   Test-Generation Approach

HybridTiger first extracts test goals from input programs and repeatedly executes reachability analyses provided by CPACHECKER until every reachable test goal is covered by at least one test case. To this end, test goals are encoded into (non-)reachability properties. If a test goal has been reached, CPACHECKER thus returns a counterexample and HybridTiger extracts a test case (i.e., a vector of input values), writes the test case to disk and marks the test goal as covered.

Hybrid Test-Case Generation. HybridTiger receives as inputs a C program and a property specification (i.e., a set of test goals). Next, HybridTiger transforms the C program into a control-flow automaton (CFA) [1]. Figure 1 shows an example C program and the corresponding CFA. After CFA generation, the CoVeriTest algorithm as configured in HybridTiger (see Fig. 2) is executed. In every new iteration, each analysis of our configuration first (re-)partitions the set of uncovered test goals (e.g., partitions P1, P2, P3 and P4 for CPA/-Tiger-MGP-Value and P1 and P2 for CPA/Tiger-MGP-Predicate in Fig. 2). In each iteration, CPA/Tiger-MGP-Value is performed first using explicit model checking and is stopped after 120s. After that, CPA/Tiger-MGP-Predicate is

---

[4] https://www.es.tu-darmstadt.de/es/team/sebastian-ruland/testcomp19/

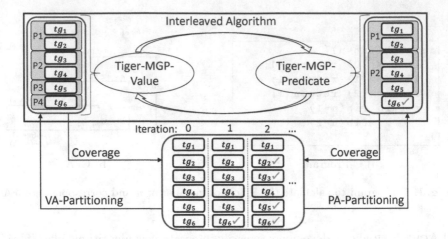

Fig. 2. Overview of HybridTiger

executed using predicate model checking for 780s, where the overall iteration stops after reaching the global time limit.

Partitioning. HybridTiger utilizes domination information of test-goal locations according to the respective CFA paths. This meta-information is retrieved from the generated CFA: each CFA node (i.e., basic block of program locations) in Fig. 1 is annotated with a *post-order ID* such that a node will only be reached *after* all nodes on the same path with a larger ID have been reached at least once. Hence, we use the IDs of predecessor nodes related to the CFA edges of test goals as sorting criterion for the overall set of test goals before splitting this set into partitions of predefined sizes. In this way, test goals sharing similar paths are more likely to be assigned to the same partition thus facilitating reuse potentials of reachability-information during reachability analysis.

3   Strengths and Weaknesses

HybridTiger has three main strengths. First, the *directed* generation of test cases aiming at covering particular test goals significantly reduces the overall number of test cases. Additionally, most test cases produced by HybridTiger effectively increase the overall coverage (i.e., HybridTiger produces mostly correct and non-redundant test cases). Second, HybridTiger uses control-flow information to partition test goals which potentially enhances efficiency of test-case generation due to information reuse among similar test goals. Lastly, HybridTiger uses combinations of different analysis strategies (i.e., value analysis and predicate analysis) to cope with structural diversity of input programs. One weakness of HybridTiger is that the partitioning approach does not improve performance of a goal-by-goal approach if being applied to programs with a small number of test goals (e.g., reaching one single error location as demanded in the Cover-Error category).

Results. In Test-Comp 2020, HybridTiger has participated in all categories and managed to reach the 4th rank in *Code Coverage* and the 6th rank in *Finding Bugs*, where HybridTiger performed better on tasks with many test goals.

4 Setup and Configuration

The version of HybridTiger submitted to Test-Comp 2020 is built from the tigerIntegration2[5] branch revision 32283 of the CPACHECKER repository and is archived at https://gitlab.com/sosy-lab/test-comp/archives-2020. HybridTiger can be applied to a single file using the command

```
1    scripts/cpa.sh −benchmark −heap 10000M −tigertestcomp20
        −spec spec.prp file
```

where *spec* is the property file (e.g., *coverage-error-call* or *coverage-branches*) and *file* is the input C program. Statistics of the analyses are printed to console and meta data on generated test cases as well as the test suite are written to files in the output folder. In order to run HybridTiger for the Test-Comp 2020 benchmarks a Linux system with Java 8, BenchExec[6] and the SV-benchmarks[7] is required. Finally, run *BenchExec* with:

- the benchmark definition *cpa-tiger.xml* (archived at https://gitlab.com/sosy-lab/test-comp/bench-defs/tree/master/benchmark-defs), and
- the tool-info module *cpachecker.py* (archived at https://github.com/sosy-lab/benchexec/tree/master/benchexec/tools).

5 Project and Contributors

CPACHECKER is maintained by the Software Systems Lab at LMU Munich as open-source project, contributed by an international group of researchers from LMU Munich, University of Passau, Technical University of Darmstadt and the Institute for System Programming of the Russian Academy of Sciences. The branch *tigerIntegration2* from which HybridTiger is built is mainly developed at the Technical University of Darmstadt. Additional information is available at https://cpachecker.sosy-lab.org/.

Acknowledgement. This work was funded by the Hessian LOEWE initiative within the Software-Factory 4.0 project.

---

[5] https://svn.sosy-lab.org/software/cpachecker/branches/tigerIntegration2
[6] https://github.com/sosy-lab/benchexec
[7] https://github.com/sosy-lab/sv-benchmarks

References

1. Beyer, D., Cimatti, A., Griggio, A., Keremoglu, M., Sebastiani, R.: Software model checking via large-block encoding. In: 2009 Formal Methods in Computer-Aided Design. pp. 25 – 32 (12 2009)
2. Beyer, D., Henzinger, T.A., Théoduloz, G.: Configurable Software Verification: Concretizing the Convergence of Model Checking and Program Analysis. In: Proc. CAV, LNCS 4590. pp. 504–518. Springer Berlin Heidelberg (2007)
3. Beyer, D., Jakobs, M.C.: CoVeriTest: Cooperative Verifier-Based Testing. In: Proc. FASE. pp. 389–408. Springer International Publishing (2019)
4. Beyer, D., Keremoglu, M.E.: CPAchecker: A Tool for Configurable Software Verification. In: Proc. CAV, LNCS 6806. pp. 184–190. Springer Berlin Heidelberg (2011)
5. Clarke, E., Grumberg, O., Jha, S., Lu, Y., Veith, H.: Counterexample-guided Abstraction Refinement for Symbolic Model Checking. J. ACM 50(5), 752–794 (2003)

ESBMC: Scalable and Precise Test Generation based on the Floating-Point Theory
(Competition Contribution)

Mikhail R. Gadelha[1], Rafael Menezes[2], Felipe R. Monteiro[2],
Lucas C. Cordeiro[3]*, and Denis Nicole[4]

[1] SIDIA Instituto de Ciência e Tecnologia, Manaus, Brazil
[2] Federal University of Amazonas, Manaus, Brazil
[3] University of Manchester, Manchester, UK
lucas.cordeiro@manchester.ac.uk
[4] University of Southampton, Southampton, UK

Abstract. ESBMC is an SMT-based bounded model checker for real-world C programs. Such programs often represent real numbers using the floating-points, most commonly, the IEEE floating-point standard (IEEE 754-2008). Thus, ESBMC now includes a new floating-point arithmetic encoding layer in our SMT backend, that encodes floating-point operations into bit-vector operations. In particular, ESBMC can use off-the-shelf SMT solvers that offer support for bit-vectors only to encode floating-point arithmetic.

Keywords: Automated Test Generation · Bounded Model Checking · Software Testing · Satisfiability Modulo Theories.

1 Test Generation Approach

ESBMC [3,7] is an SMT-based bounded model checker for the verification of safety properties and assertions in both sequential and multi-threaded C programs. ESBMC primarily aims to help software developers by finding subtle bugs in their code (e.g., array bounds violation, null-pointer dereference, arithmetic overflow, and deadlock). It also implements k-induction [5,10] and can be used to prove the absence of property violations, i.e., program correctness. In Test-Comp'20 [1], ESBMC produces test cases using the falsification mode, which is an iterative bounded model checking (BMC) approach that repeatedly unwinds the program until it either finds a property violation or exhausts time or memory limits. Intuitively, ESBMC aims to find a counterexample with up to k loop unwindings. The algorithm relies on the symbolic execution engine to increasingly unwind the loop after each iteration. ESBMC uses the falsification mode because it is known that there exist property violations in all programs in the Test-Comp, so there exists no need to prove correctness. From the counterexample produced by ESBMC, we define the test specification required by the competition using an external Python script.

---

* Jury member

© The Author(s) 2020
H. Wehrheim and J. Cabot (Eds.): FASE 2020, LNCS 12076, pp. 525–529, 2020.
https://doi.org/10.1007/978-3-030-45234-6_27

ESBMC runs with an improved SMT backend for test-case generation, which includes a floating-point encoding layer that converts all floating-point operations into bit-vector operations (a process called *bit-blasting*) when encoding the program into an SMT formula. Previous ESBMC versions [8] were only able to encode and verify programs using a fixed-point representation for floating-points. This particular encoding is a valid approximation since fixed-points are used in a large number of applications in the embedded world; however, it restricted ESBMC from verifying the broad set of programs that relied on processors that implement floating-point arithmetic.

There exist various strategies to solve SMT formulae with floating-point arithmetic. It is tempting to use a real arithmetic strategy to tackle these formulae; however, the floating-point arithmetic is an approximation of the real one and introduces a new set of values (e.g., NaNs). ESBMC follows the same approach as CBMC [2] and 2LS [15], which also bit-blast all operations, including floating-point operations, before checking satisfiability using SAT solvers. The bit-blasting algorithm in ESBMC is based on the bit-blasting performed by Z3, which is an improved version of the algorithms described by Muller et al. [12]. A floating-point is encoded into SMT using a single bit-vector and follows the IEEE–754 [11] standard for the size of the exponent and significand. For instance, a half-precision floating-point (16 bits) has 1 bit for the sign, 5 bits for the exponent and 11 bits for the significand (1 hidden bit) [11]. Thus, the floating-point encoding layer in ESBMC performs the operations in the bit-vectors representing the floating-points, e.g., the formula to check if a bit-vector is a NaN checks if the exponent is all 1's and if the significand is not zero. The resulting SMT formulae are the translation of the floating-point arithmetic digital circuits to SMT [12].

The improved SMT backend is an extension of our previous work on floating-point arithmetic encoding [9]. Previously, we extended ESBMC to encode floating-point arithmetic into SMT, however, we were restricted to SMT solvers that supported the FP theory natively (i.e., Z3, MathSAT and CVC4) [9]. Now, the floating-point encoding layer extends the FP theory support to all solvers supported by ESBMC, including Boolector [13] and Yices [4], which do not natively support that FP theory. In Test-Comp'20, ESBMC uses Boolector 3.0.1 and produces 470 confirmed test specifications. In particular, ESBMC achieved the the highest score in the ReachSafety-Floats, a category focused on programs with floating-point arithmetics, correctly verifying 30 out of the 32 test cases and outperforming all other tools in this category. The results in this category demonstrates the effectiveness of the floating-point bit-blasting: Boolector does not support the FP theory natively and yet was able to reason about almost all the test cases in the competition that involved floating-point arithmetic.

2   Strengths and Weaknesses

The falsification mode allows ESBMC to keep unwinding the program until a property violation is found, or until it exhausts time or memory limits. Its BMC approach, however, stops after it has found a property violation and prevents the generation of tests specifications for multiple property violations or coverage testing. This approach, however, is an advantage in the `Cover-Error` category as finding one error is the primary goal.

Encoding programs using the SMT FP theory has several advantages over the fixed-point approach. ESBMC can now accurately model C programs that use the IEEE floating-point arithmetic [11]. In particular, ESBMC ships with models for most of the current C11 standard functions. Furthermore, the floating-point encoding layer in ESBMC extends the support for the SMT FP theory to solvers that do not support it natively. ESBMC can verify programs with floating-point arithmetic using all currently supported solvers – including Boolector and Yices, which do not support the SMT FP theory.

In Test-Comp'20 results, 470 tests were confirmed while 13 tests were unconfirmed, where 11 were due to bugs in the script that generates the test specification (e.g., non-deterministic unions or duplication of non-deterministic values)[5], 1 was due to a bug in ESBMC that caused the tool to fail[6], and 1 was due to undefined behavior in the test case[7]. We chose Boolector for the competition because it outperforms all other SMT solvers supported by ESBMC. In the ReachSafety-Floats category, Boolector even outperforms all other SMT solvers that natively support FP theory. We believe that Boolector employs more abstract and less expensive techniques (e.g., algebraic reduction rules and contextual simplification) before bit-blasting SMT formulae into SAT.

The drawback of the floating-point encoding is that they are very complex; it is not uncommon to see the SMT solvers struggling to support every corner case [6,14]. The maintenance of our floating-point encoding layer is hard, and we do not yet have proof that it is entirely correct, even though empirical evidence [9] points in that direction and suggests that the approach is efficient in finding bugs as shown by Test-Comp'20 results. The complex bit-vector formulae also prevent high-level reasoning about the problem by the SMT solver, however, this is not a significant issue for ESBMC as all high-level simplifications are performed before encoding the program into SMT formulae.

3 Tool Setup and Configuration

In order to run our `esbmc-wrapper.py` script[8], one must set the architecture (*i.e.*, 32 or 64-bit), the competition strategy (i.e., k-induction, falsification, or incremental BMC), the property file path, and the benchmark path, as:

```
esbmc-wrapper.py [-a {32, 64}] [-p PROPERTY_FILE]
                 [-s {kinduction,falsi,incr,fixed}]
                 [BENCHMARK_PATH]
```

---

[5] https://github.com/esbmc/esbmc/issues/142
[6] https://github.com/esbmc/esbmc/issues/143
[7] https://github.com/sosy-lab/sv-benchmarks/pull/1073
[8] https://gitlab.com/sosy-lab/test-comp/archives-2020/blob/master/2020/esbmc-falsi.zip

where -a sets the architecture, -p sets the property file path, and -s sets the strategy (e.g., `kinduction`, `falsi`, `incr`, or `fixed`). In Test-Comp'20, ESBMC uses `falsi` for falsification.

Internally, by choosing the falsification strategy, the following options are set when executing ESBMC: `--no-div-by-zero-check`, disables the division by zero check (required by Test-Comp); `--force-malloc-success`, sets that all dynamic allocations succeed (a Test-Comp requirement); `--floatbv`, enables floating-point SMT encoding; `--falsification`, enables the falsification mode; `--unlimited-k-steps`, removes the upper limit of iteration steps in the falsification algorithm; `--witness-output`, sets the witness output path; `--no-bounds-check` and `--no-pointer-check` disable bounds check and pointer safety checks, resp., since we are only interested in finding reachability bugs; `--k-step 5`, sets the falsification increment to 5; `--no-allign-check`, disables pointer alignment checks; and `--no-slice`, disables slicing of unnecessary instructions. The Benchexec tool info module is named `esbmc.py` and the benchmark definition file is `esbmc-falsi.xml`.

4   Software Project

The ESBMC source code is written in C++ and it is available for downloading at GitHub[9], which include self-contained binaries for ESBMC v6.1 64-bit. ESBMC is publicly available under the terms of the Apache License 2.0. Instructions for building ESBMC from the source code are given in the file `BUILDING` (including the description of all dependencies). ESBMC is an international-joint project with the SIDIA Instituto de Ciência e Tecnologia, Federal University of Amazonas, University of Southampton, University of Manchester, and the University of Stellenbosch.

References

1. Beyer, D.: Second competition on software testing: Test-comp 2020. In: Proc. FASE. LNCS , Springer (2020)
2. Clarke, E., Kroening, D., Lerda, F.: A tool for checking ANSI-C programs. In: Tools And Algorithms For The Construction And Analysis Of Systems. LNCS, vol. 2988, pp. 168–176 (2004)
3. Cordeiro, L.C., Fischer, B.: Verifying multi-threaded software using SMT-based context-bounded model checking. In: International Conference on Software Engineering. pp. 331–340 (2011)
4. Dutertre, B.: Yices 2.2. In: Computer-Aided Verification. LNCS, vol. 8559, pp. 737–744 (2014)
5. Eén, N., Sörensson, N.: Temporal induction by incremental SAT solving. Electronic Notes in Theoretical Computer Science **89**(4), 543–560 (2003)
6. Erkk, L.: Bug in floating-point conversions. https://github.com/Z3Prover/z3/issues/1564 (2018), [Online; accessed January-2020]

---

[9] https://github.com/esbmc/esbmc

7. Gadelha, M.R., Monteiro, F., Cordeiro, L., Nicole, D.: ESBMC v6.0: Verifying C programs using k-induction and invariant inference. In: Tools And Algorithms For The Construction And Analysis Of Systems. LNCS, vol. 11429, pp. 209–213 (2019)
8. Gadelha, M.R., Monteiro, F.R., Morse, J., Cordeiro, L.C., Fischer, B., Nicole, D.A.: ESBMC 5.0: An industrial-strength C model checker. In: Automated Software Engineering. pp. 888–891 (2018)
9. Gadelha, M.Y.R., Cordeiro, L.C., Nicole, D.A.: Encoding floating-point numbers using the SMT theory in ESBMC: An empirical evaluation over the SV-COMP benchmarks. In: Simpósio Brasileiro De Métodos Formais. LNCS, vol. 10623, pp. 91–106 (2017)
10. Gadelha, M.Y.R., Ismail, H.I., Cordeiro, L.C.: Handling loops in bounded model checking of C programs via k-induction. Software Tools for Technology Transfer **19**(1), 97–114 (2017)
11. IEEE: IEEE Standard For Floating-Point Arithmetic (2008), IEEE 754-2008
12. Muller, J.M., Brisebarre, N., Dinechin, F., Jeannerod, C.P., Lefe, V., Melquiond, G., Revol, N., Stehl., Torres, S.: Handbook of Floating-Point Arithmetic. Birkher Boston, 1st edn. (2010)
13. Niemetz, A., Preiner, M., Biere, A.: Boolector 2.0 system description. Journal on Satisfiability, Boolean Modeling and Computation **9**, 53–58 (2014)
14. Noetzli, A.: Failing precondition when multiplying 4-bit significand/4-bit exponent floats. https://github.com/CVC4/CVC4/issues/2182 (2018), [Online; accessed January-2020]
15. Schrammel, P., Kroening, D., Brain, M., Martins, R., Teige, T., Bienmüller, T.: Incremental bounded model checking for embedded software (extended version). Formal Aspects of Computing **29**(5), 911–931 (2017)

TracerX: Dynamic Symbolic Execution with Interpolation (Competition Contribution)

Joxan Jaffar ⓘ, Rasool Maghareh ⓘ, Sangharatna Godboley ⓘ, and
Xuan-Linh Ha ⓘ

National University of Singapore, Singapore, Singapore
{joxan,rasool,sanghara,haxl}@comp.nus.edu.sg
http://www.springer.com/gp/computer-science/lncs

Abstract. Dynamic Symbolic Execution (DSE) is an important method
for testing of programs. An important system on DSE is KLEE [1] which
inputs a C/C++ program annotated with symbolic variables, compiles
it into LLVM, and then emulates the execution paths of LLVM using
a specified backtracking strategy. The major challenge in symbolic execution is *path explosion*. The method of *abstraction learning* [7] has
been used to address this. The key step here is the computation of an
interpolant to represent the learned abstraction.
TracerX, our tool, is built on top of KLEE and it implements and utilizes *abstraction learning*. The core feature in abstraction learning is *sub-
sumption* of paths whose traversals are deemed to no longer be necessary
due to similarity with already-traversed paths. Despite the overhead of
computing interpolants, the *pruning* of the symbolic execution tree that
interpolants provide often brings significant overall benefits. In particular, TracerX can *fully* explore many programs that would be impossible
for any non-pruning system like KLEE to do so.

Keywords: Dynamic Symbolic Execution, Interpolation, Testing, Code
Coverage

1 Overview and Software Architecture

Symbolic execution has emerged as an important method to reason about programs, in both verification and testing. By reasoning about inputs as symbolic
entities, its fundamental advantage over traditional black-box testing, which uses
concrete inputs, is simply that it has better *coverage* of *program paths*. In particular, *dynamic symbolic execution* (DSE), where the execution space is explored *path-by-path*, has been shown effective in systems such as DART [4] and
KLEE [1]. A key advantage of DSE is that by examining a single path, the analysis can be both precise, and efficient. However, the key disadvantage of DSE is
that the number of program paths is in general *exponential* in the program size,
and most available implementations of DSE do not employ a general technique
to prune away some paths.

In TracerX, our primary objective is to address the path explosion problem in
DSE. More specifically, we wish to perform path-by-path exploration of DSE to

ⓒ The Author(s) 2020
H. Wehrheim and J. Cabot (Eds.): FASE 2020, LNCS 12076, pp. 530–534, 2020.
https://doi.org/10.1007/978-3-030-45234-6_28

enjoy its benefits, but we include a *pruning mechanism* so that a generated path can be eliminated if it is guaranteed not to violate the stated safety conditions. Toward this goal, we employ the method of *abstraction learning* [7], which is more popularly known as *lazy annotations* [8,9].

The software architecture of TracerX is presented in Fig. 1. The core feature of TracerX is the use of *interpolation*, which serves to generalize the context of a node in the symbolic execution

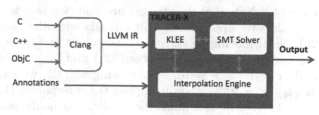

Fig. 1. TracerX Framework

tree (SET) with an approximation of the weakest precondition of the node. This method was implemented in the TRACER system [6], which was the first system to demonstrate DSE with pruning. TRACER was primarily used to evaluate new algorithms in verification, analysis and testing, e.g., [2,3,5]. While TRACER was able to perform bounded verification and testing on many examples, it could not accommodate industrial programs which often dynamically manipulate the heap memory. TracerX combines the state-of-the-art DSE technology used in KLEE with the pruning technology in TRACER to address this issue.

Now we explain *interpolation* in more detail. While exploring the SET, an *interpolant* of a state is an *abstraction* of it which ensures the safety of the subtree rooted at that state. In other words, if we continue the execution with the interpolant instead of the state we will *not* reach any error. Thus, upon

```
x = 0;
if ( b1 ) x += 12;
if ( b2 ) x += 15;
assert (x != 28);
```

Fig. 2. A Sample Program

encountering another state of the same program point, if the context of the state *implies* the interpolant formula, then continuing the execution from the new state will not lead to any error. Consequently, we can prune the subtree rooted at the new state.

Example 1. Consider the program in Fig. 2 and its SET explored by SE with interpolation in Fig. 3. The variables b1, b2 are symbolic and all combinations of the boolean conditions are satisfiable. The final statement assert($x \neq 28$) is the target. The path condition for every path is shown in the set in black color.

We traverse the SET in a left-right depth-first manner. In the end of the first path $x = 27$ which does not violate the assertion. Consider-

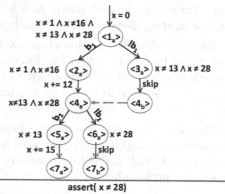

Fig. 3. SET with Interpolation of Program in Fig. 2

ing the target and the update on variable x between $\langle 5_a \rangle$ and $\langle 7_a \rangle$, we generate an interpolant which store the weakest precondition at $\langle 5_a \rangle$: $x \neq 13$ (Shown in purple color). Similarly, an interpolant is also computed at $\langle 6_a \rangle$: $x \neq 28$.

Now, combining these two interpolants, we generate an interpolant for the node $\langle 4_a \rangle$. Note that the weakest precondition here is $b_2 \longrightarrow (x \neq 13) \wedge !b_2 \longrightarrow (x \neq 28)$. We approximate this formula with the conjunction $(x \neq 13) \wedge (x \neq 28)$. Next, moving to $\langle 2_a \rangle$, the interpolant at $\langle 4_a \rangle$ is received and considering the update on variable x between $\langle 2_a \rangle$ and $\langle 4_a \rangle$, an interpolant is generated at $\langle 2_a \rangle$: $x \neq 1 \wedge x \neq 16$. Now moving to $\langle 4_b \rangle$, we check if the path condition at $\langle 4_b \rangle$ $(x = 0 \wedge !b_1 \wedge skip)$ implies the interpolant that was generated at $\langle 4_a \rangle$ $(x \neq 13 \wedge x \neq 28)$. Since the implication holds, node $\langle 4_b \rangle$ is subsumed with node $\langle 4_a \rangle$ (indicated by orange arrow) and the subtree below $\langle 4_b \rangle$ is pruned. The SET traversal continues by computing the interpolant at $\langle 3_a \rangle$ which is computed from $x \neq 13 \wedge x \neq 28$ subsuming $\langle 4_b \rangle$ and the updates between $\langle 3_a \rangle$ and $\langle 4_b \rangle$ (which is skip). The interpolants at $\langle 2_a \rangle$ and $\langle 3_a \rangle$ are then combined to generate an interpolant at $\langle 1_a \rangle$: $x \neq 1 \wedge x \neq 16 \wedge x \neq 13 \wedge x \neq 28$. Note that KLEE would explore the 4 paths in the SET while TracerX explores only two paths to the end. $\square$

2   Discussion on Strengths and Weaknesses

In Test-Comp 2020, TracerX stood at 6th rank in overall. Inspecting the results, TracerX was one of the teams having the highest score in: `cover-branches.BitVectors` and `cover-error.ControlFlow`. Moreover, TracerX was one of the top 3 scorers in: `cover-branches.DeviceDriversLinux64`, `cover-branches.ControlFlow`, and `cover-error.BitVectors`.

TracerX also accomplished more tasks by a meaningful margin compared to KLEE in: `cover-branches.BusyBox` and `cover-branches.MainHeap`. On the other hand, TracerX performed poorly in 3 sub-categories: `cover-error.ReachSafety-ECA`, `ReachSafety-Sequentialized` (both branches) and `cover-error.Floats`[1].

We should emphasize that TracerX in general requires symbolic execution trees to be bounded. Otherwise, interpolants cannot be computed. Moreover, TracerX is a heavy-weight approach and the overhead pays off as the problems gets harder. As a result it is expected for other light-weight approaches to have better results compared to TracerX in short timeout and memory limits.

Moreover, it appears that the configuration we used to explore unbounded programs (max-depth=1000) and also in the *benchexec tool-info* (wrongly running TracerX with the default memory (2GB) instead of 15GB RAM) might have had a profound effect in reaching timeout on the test programs.

---

[1] TracerX does not support symbolic expressions over floating point arithmetic.

3 Tool Setup and Configuration

The TracerX version used in TEST-COMP 2020 is available at https://gitlab. com/sosy-lab/test-comp/archives-2020/blob/testcomp20/2020/tracerx.zip[2]. The configuration/setting and running of TracerX is similar to KLEE. TracerX has some extra command line arguments. Firstly, the argument "solver-backend=z3" should be provided to run TracerX with interpolation. Without this option TracerX will run similar to KLEE. TracerX can do exploration in both the Random and DFS modes. However, the DFS exploration mode (using "-search=dfs") is preferred since it naturally increases the chance of generating interpolants. Furthermore, the option "-subsumed-test" should be used to generate a test-case from the subsumed nodes. This option is required for the coverage competition. The following is a sample full command line after compiling and running tracerx.py:

"../tracerx-svcomp/bin/../tracerx_build/Release+Asserts/bin/klee -max-memory=14305 -output-dir=../tracerx-svcomp/bin/../test-suite -search=dfs -solver-backend=z3 -write-xml-tests -tc-orig=s3_clnt_3.BV.c.cil-2a.c -tc-hash=acd2272114f13977ea7bdc712c7567ec2e43dc8e07ef033eb67487bab7f66d59 --dump-states-on-halt=false -exit-on-error-type=Assert -max-depth=1000 -max-time=900 /tmp/tmpvwkb459r/s3_clnt_3.BV.c.cil-2a.c.bc"

The two command line options, "-max-memory" and "-max-time" are used to set the maximum memory and time budget. The options "-write-xml-tests", "-tc-orig", and "-tc-hash" are to record the test input information. Once the halt instruction is invoked, "-dump-states-on-halt" creates a test case from all active states[3]. The option "-exit-on-error-type=Assert" terminates the search as soon as a bug is found (used only for coverage categories). The command line option "-max-depth=1000" is used to bound the maximum number of branches explored in unbounded paths.

4 Software Project and Contributors

The information about TracerX with self-contained binary is publicly available at https://www.comp.nus.edu.sg/~tracerx/. Also, the source code can be accessed at https://github.com/tracer-x/klee repository. Authors of this paper and other colleagues have contributed and developed TracerX at National University of Singapore, Singapore. The authors of this paper acknowledge the direct and indirect support of their students, former researchers, and colleagues.

---

[2] The *benchexec* tool-info file is https://github.com/sosy-lab/benchexec/blob/master/ benchexec/tools/tracerx.py and the benchmark description file is https://gitlab. com/sosy-lab/test-comp/bench-defs/blob/master/benchmark-defs/tracerx.xml.

[3] This was disabled to save execution time. However, it would have been better to enable this option for maximum coverage.

References

1. Cadar, C., Dunbar, D., Engler, D.R., et al.: KLEE: unassisted and automatic generation of high-coverage tests for complex systems programs. In: Proceedings of the 8th OSDI. pp. 209–224 (2008)
2. Chu, D.H., Jaffar, J.: A complete method for symmetry reduction in safety verification. In: 24th International Conference on Computer Aided Verification (CAV). pp. 616–633, USA. Springer (2012)
3. Chu, D.H., Jaffar, J., Maghareh, R.: Precise cache timing analysis via symbolic execution. In: 22nd IEEE Real-Time and Embedded Technology and Applications Symposium (RTAS). pp. 1–12 (2016)
4. Godefroid, P., Klarlund, N., Sen, K.: DART: Directed automated random testing. In: Proceedings of the 2005 ACM SIGPLAN conference on Programming language design and implementation (PLDI). pp. 213–223 (2005)
5. Jaffar, J., Murali, V., Navas, J.A.: Boosting concolic testing via interpolation. In: Proceedings of the 9th Conference on Foundations of Software Engineering (FSE). pp. 48–58 (2013)
6. Jaffar, J., Murali, V., Navas, J.A., Santosa, A.E.: TRACER: a symbolic execution tool for verification. In: 24th International Conference on Computer Aided Verification (CAV). pp. 758–766. Springer (2012)
7. Jaffar, J., Santosa, A.E., Voicu, R.: An interpolation method for CLP traversal. In: 15th International Conference on Principles and Practice of Constraint Programming (CP). pp. 454–469. Springer (2009)
8. McMillan, K.L.: Lazy annotation for program testing and verification. In: 22nd International Conference on Computer Aided Verification (CAV). pp. 104–118 (2010)
9. Mcmillan, K.L.: Lazy annotation revisited. In: 26th International Conference on Computer Aided Verification (CAV). pp. 243–259 (2014)

LLVM-based Hybrid Fuzzing with LibKluzzer (Competition Contribution)

Hoang M. Le(iD)

Insitute of Computer Science
University of Bremen, Germany
hle@uni-bremen.de

Abstract. LibKluzzer is a novel implementation of hybrid fuzzing, which combines the strengths of coverage-guided fuzzing and dynamic symbolic execution (a.k.a. whitebox fuzzing). While coverage-guided fuzzing can discover new execution paths at nearly native speed, whitebox fuzzing is capable of getting through complex branch conditions. In contrast to existing hybrid fuzzers, that operate directly on binaries, LibKluzzer leverages the LLVM compiler framework to work at the source code level. It employs LibFuzzer as the coverage-guided fuzzing component and KLUZZER, an extension of KLEE, as the whitebox fuzzing component.

Keywords: Hybrid Fuzzing · Coverage-guided Fuzzing · Symbolic Execution · LLVM.

1 Test Generation Approach

LibKluzzer is based on hybrid fuzzing which tries to combine the strengths of coverage-guided fuzzing and whitebox fuzzing. Most existing advanced hybrid fuzzers, e.g. [6,7,8], employ coverage-guided fuzzing as the main search algorithm and only apply whitebox fuzzing selectively on the most promising inputs. While such advanced approach is also being under development and evaluation for LibKluzzer, for simplicity and given the short time frame available for adapting to Test-Comp, the participating version of LibKluzzer combines coverage-guided fuzzing and whitebox fuzzing in a very simple way. Without any intrinsic integration, multiple instances of coverage-guided fuzzing and whitebox fuzzing are scripted to run in parallel in their own OS process. They operate on a common corpus to enable sharing the individual progresses. Each instance keeps an in-memory set of inputs it has generated, together with the code coverage achieved so far. Whenever an instance discovers an input that covers new code, it writes this input as a file to the common corpus. The corpus is scanned periodically by the instances to check for newly added files. Despite of (or thanks to) its simplicity, LibKluzzer managed to perform very well in Test-Comp 2020.

© The Author(s) 2020
H. Wehrheim and J. Cabot (Eds.): FASE 2020, LNCS 12076, pp. 535–539, 2020.
https://doi.org/10.1007/978-3-030-45234-6_29

2   Software Architecture

Two major components of LibKluzzer are LibFuzzer [1] for coverage-guided fuzzing and KLUZZER [5] for whitebox fuzzing. As mentioned earlier, KLUZZER is an extension of KLEE [2]. While it uses most of the KLEE infrastructure including the underlying SMT solver STP [3], KLUZZER provides several signicant enhancements that make it more suitable for hybrid fuzzing (see [5] for more details). For Test-Comp, both LibFuzzer and KLUZZER have been extended to support its specific requirements. The extension involves writing test cases in XML format, glue logic to convert the random byte array needed for the fuzzers into a sequence of calls to *nondet* functions, and implementing a fuzzing target as described later.

Workflow First, the C program under test undergoes a set of source-to-source program transformations to enable *in-process* coverage-guided fuzzing. The transformed program is then compiled using Clang to create an LLVM bitcode file and an executable. The compilation involves, among others, code coverage instrumentation and linking with LibFuzzer. Finally, the LLVM bitcode file is fed to KLUZZER to perform whitebox fuzzing, while the executable is started in two instances to perform coverage-guided fuzzing. These three fuzzing instances run concurrently until terminated by the Test-Comp BenchExec runner due to time limit exceeded. They share generated inputs via a common corpus of files as mentioned earlier and write XML test cases to the test suite on-the-fly.

Transformations for in-process fuzzing While the main components of LibKluzzer are implemented in C++, the program transformations, that are required to enable *in-process* coverage-guided fuzzing, consist of a set of Bash and Python scripts. This form of fuzzing is much faster than traditional out-of-process fuzzing, which forks a new process for each execution of the *main* function, but requires the global state of the fuzzing target to remain largely unchanged or to be resetted between executions. The transformations esssentially perform the following steps for each benchmark:

1. rename the existing *main* function to *FuzzMe*;
2. identify and duplicate global variables;
3. insert additional functions: *FuzzerSaveCtx* to capture the initial global state into the duplicated variables and *FuzzerRestoreCtx* to restore this state before each new execution of the *FuzzMe* function;
4. redirect calls to *exit* and *abort* to custom functions to prevent unwanted early exit from the fuzzing loop.

The current script-based implementation of these transformations is very fragile and might not work out-of-the-box for non-Test-Comp benchmarks. The next version of LibKluzzer will replace these with proper Clang-based source-to-source transformations.

```
int nondet_int() {                      int LLVMFuzzerTestOneInput(
  int Value = 0;                          uint8_t *Data, size_t Size) {
  if (Used + 4 <= Size) {                 FuzzerRestoreCtx();
    memcpy(&Value, Data + Used, 4);       MakeGlobalCopy(Data, Size);
    Used += 4;                            Used = 0;
  }                                       FuzzMe();
  return Value;                         }
}
```

Fig. 1. Implementation of *nondet* functions and fuzzing target for Test-Comp

Test-Comp fuzzing target and *nondet* functions Both KLUZZER and
LibFuzzer require the definition of a fuzzing target, i.e. an implementation of
the declared *LLVMFuzzerTestOneInput* function. The *main* function provided
by the fuzzers will repeatedly call *LLVMFuzzerTestOneInput* with fuzz inputs
in a loop to perform fuzzing. Each fuzz input consists of an array of random
bytes and its size. Fig. 1 shows a conceptual implementation of *LLVMFuzzerTestOneInput* on the right hand side. First, the initial global execution state is
restored. Then, the given fuzz input is copied into a global array and the number
of bytes already consumed for fuzzing is set to zero; Finally, *FuzzMe* is invoked.
During its execution, each time a *nondet* function is called to provide input, a
corresponding number of bytes from the global byte array will be consumed to
create the requested value, as exemplarily shown on the left hand side of Fig. 1
for *int*. With this conversion from random bytes, no changes are needed in the
core algorithms of KLUZZER and LibFuzzer for Test-Comp.

3 Strengths and Weaknesses

The main strength of LibKluzzer lies in achieving high code coverage as demonstrated by winning the branch coverage category of Test-Comp. Multiple factors
contribute to this success including the extremely high throughput of in-process
coverage-guided fuzzing implemented by LibFuzzer and the use of generational
search in KLUZZER, a coverage-maximizing search heuristic for dynamic symbolic execution/whitebox fuzzing first proposed by SAGE [4]. The individual
contribution of each single component is to be analyzed more thoroughly in a
further detailed study.

The main conceptual weakness of LibKluzzer is that the same coverage-
maximizing search strategy is used for reaching error calls. It is a big surprise
that LibKluzzer has still achieved the second place in the corresponding category.
We expect that adapting the search heuristics of both LibFuzzer and KLUZZER
to be directed by the distance to the location of error calls should improve the
performance significantly

Especially, the big ECA benchmarks have proven to be problematic for both
LibFuzzer and KLUZZER and hence also for LibKluzzer. The sequence of *nondet*
values required to reach the error calls is very specific and nearly impossible to
find with coverage-guided fuzzing, while KLUZZER suffers from path explosion.

In addition to error-directed search, path/state merging might be required to efficiently deal with these benchmarks.

A further weakness is that LibKluzzer makes little effort on minimizing the test suite with respect to both the size of the test suite and the size of each test case. Too many redundant test cases might cause the validator to timeout. Furthermore, some produced test cases are too big hitting a corner case in the validator and forcing it to exceed the given memory limit. In these cases, the validator crashes prematurely, leaving the remaining test cases uncounted.

4   Tool Setup and Configuration

Installation The LibKluzzer archive submitted to Test-Comp 2020 (version 0.6) can be downloaded from https://gitlab.com/sosy-lab/test-comp/archives-2020/ blob/testcomp20/2020/libkluzzer.zip. After unpacking, the main executable script LibKluzzer can be found in the *bin* folder.

Configuration The main script has been configured to reflect the resource restrictions of Test-Comp 2020. LibKluzzer treats every benchmark as 64-bit and always tries to maximize code coverage, and thus is agnostic to the property and architecture specification. The only meaningful parameter is the path to the source code file of the benchmark.

Participation LibKluzzer participates in both available categories of Test-Comp 2020: *Finding Bugs* and *Code Coverage*.

5   Software Project and Contributors

LibKluzzer and KLUZZER are being developed by the author at University of Bremen, Germany. This research and development are supported by the Central Research Development Fund, University of Bremen, Germany within the project SYMVIR. The source code of LibKluzzer will be made available at https:// github.com/hoangmle/LibKluzzerTestComp2020Submission. Much of the credits should go to the respective development teams of LibFuzzer and KLEE, which lay the foundation for LibKluzzer.

References

1. LibFuzzer - a library for coverage-guided fuzz testing. Available at https://llvm. org/docs/LibFuzzer.html.
2. C. Cadar, D. Dunbar, and D. R. Engler. KLEE: unassisted and automatic generation of high-coverage tests for complex systems programs. In *USENIX OSDI*, pages 209–224, 2008.
3. V. Ganesh and D. L. Dill. A decision procedure for bit-vectors and arrays. In *CAV*, pages 519–531, 2007.

4. P. Godefroid, M. Y. Levin, and D. A. Molnar. Automated whitebox fuzz testing. In *NDSS*, 2008.
5. H. M. Le. KLUZZER: Whitebox fuzzing on top of LLVM. In *ATVA*, pages 246–252.
6. N. Stephens, J. Grosen, C. Salls, A. Dutcher, R. Wang, J. Corbetta, Y. Shoshitaishvili, C. Kruegel, and G. Vigna. Driller: Augmenting fuzzing through selective symbolic execution. In *NDSS*, 2016.
7. I. Yun, S. Lee, M. Xu, Y. Jang, and T. Kim. QSYM : A practical concolic execution engine tailored for hybrid fuzzing. In *USENIX Security*, pages 745–761, 2018.
8. L. Zhao, Y. Duan, H. Yin, and J. Xuan. Send hardest problems my way: Probabilistic path prioritization for hybrid fuzzing. In *NDSS*, 2019.

CoVeriTest with Dynamic Partitioning of the Iteration Time Limit* (Competition Contribution)

Marie-Christine Jakobs**

Technical University of Darmstadt, Department of Computer Science, Darmstadt, Germany

Abstract. Our CoVeriTest submission, which is implemented in the analysis framework CPAchecker, uses verification techniques for automatic test-case generation. To this end, it checks the reachability of every test goal and generates one test case per reachable goal. Instead of checking the reachability of every test goal individually, which is too expensive, CoVeriTest considers all test goals at once and removes already covered goals from future reachability queries. To deal with the diverse set of Test-Comp tasks, CoVeriTest uses a hybrid approach that interleaves value and predicate analysis. In contrast to Test-Comp'19, the time limit per iteration is no longer fixed for an analysis. Instead, we fix the iteration time limit and split it dynamically among the analyses, rewarding analyses that previously covered more test goals per time unit.

Keywords: Test-case generation · Cooperative verification · CPAchecker

1 Test-Generation Approach

Test-case generation approaches have different strengths and weaknesses. To deal with the diverse Test-Comp benchmark, we therefore use an hybrid approach. More concrete, our Test-Comp'20 submission CoVeriTest combines different verification approaches using the idea of **co**operative, **veri**fier-based **test**ing [6].

Figure 1 shows the workflow of our CoVeriTest submission. Like in Test-Comp'19, CoVeriTest iteratively combines a value analysis [5], which only tracks the explicit values of those variables stored in its precision, and a predicate analysis, which applies adjustable block encoding [4] and abstracts at loop heads only. Both analyses use counterexample-guided abstraction refinement [8] to adjust their precision (the set of tracked variables or the set of predicates) and check which open test goals can be reached. Whenever one analysis reaches a test goal, i.e., it finds a real counterexample, a test case adhering to the Test-Comp exchange format[1] is constructed from that counterexample [1] and the test goal

---

* This work was funded by the Hessian LOEWE initiative within the Software-Factory 4.0 project.

** jury-member

[1] https://gitlab.com/sosy-lab/software/test-format/tree/master

H. Wehrheim and J. Cabot (Eds.): FASE 2020, LNCS 12076, pp. 540–544, 2020.
https://doi.org/10.1007/978-3-030-45234-6_30

is removed from the set of open test goals. Depending on the Test-Comp'20 property, the set of test goals is initialized to the set of all `__VERIFIER_error()` calls or the set of all branches.

Like in Test-Comp'19, both analyses resume their exploration from the previous round and do not exchange any further information. The novelty for Test-Comp'20 is the dynamic adjustment of the analyses' time limits. To better adjust to the program, we redistribute the iteration time limit among the analyses after each iteration round. Initially, we grant the

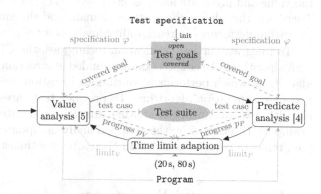

Fig. 1: CoVeriTest workflow for Test-Comp'20

value analysis 20 s and the predicate analysis 80 s. Thereafter, we use the normalized progresses p_V and p_P reported by the analyses to compute the new time limits. The normalized progress is the number of test goals covered by the analysis in the round divided by the total number of test goals. If no analysis made progress ($p_V \leq 0$ and $p_P \leq 0$), we will reuse the time limits from the current round. Otherwise, we adjust the limits according to Eq. 1 ($i \in \{V, P\}$). Each analysis gets at least 10 s to avoid to turn it off. The remaining 80 s of the iteration limit are redistributed according to the relative contribution of each analysis. The relative contribution of an analysis is its progress per time limit related to the sum of the progresses per time limit.

$$\text{limit}_i^{\text{new}} = 10\,\text{s} + \frac{\dfrac{p_i}{\text{limit}_i}}{\dfrac{p_V}{\text{limit}_V} + \dfrac{p_P}{\text{limit}_P}} * 80\,\text{s} \qquad (1)$$

The main differences to HybridTiger [11], which also applies cooperative, verifier-based testing, are that HybridTiger uses multi-goal partitioning [10] and that HybridTiger uses fixed time limits 120 s and 720 s for value and predicate analysis.

2   Tool Architecture

CoVeriTest is implemented within the Java-based software-analysis framework CPAchecker [3], which uses the Eclipse CDT parser[2] and integrates different SMT solvers via the JavaSMT [9] interface. For Test-Comp'20, we rely on CPAchecker's default SMT solver MathSAT5 [7].

---

[2] https://www.eclipse.org/cdt/

CPACHECKER's core is the configurable program analysis framework [2], which defines the basis for the verification approaches. The framework consists of two parts: configurable program analyses (CPAs) and the CPA algorithm. CPAs like the value and predicate analysis used by CoVERITEST describe program analyses. Therefore, they define the abstract domain and the analysis operators. The CPA algorithm performs the reachability analysis for a given CPA and program.

To integrate further verification techniques, the CPA framework is enhanced with algorithms like counterexample-guided abstraction refinement [8], the circular algorithm, which performs a continuous iteration over a set of analyses, or the test-case generation algorithm. To produce test cases, the test-case generation algorithm wraps and runs another analysis, generates test cases from counter-examples [1] returned by the wrapped analysis, updates the analysis specification (i.e., removes covered goals), and thereafter continues the wrapped analysis.

3 Strengths and Weaknesses

CoVERITEST won the third place in the category Cover-Branches and in contrast to Test-Comp'19, became better than KLEE in this category.

The major change of CoVERITEST from Test-Comp'19 to Test-Comp'20 is the dynamic adjustment of the iteration time limits. Thus, many strength and weaknesses are still the same as in Test-Comp'19. CoVERITEST's iterative combination of predicate and value analysis helped to adapt to the diverse set of Test-Comp tasks and its direct search of the test goals lead to few test cases. Also, CoVERITEST has still problems with tasks that contain large arrays because these are not supported by the underlying analyses. Furthermore, CoVERITEST has problems with the new subcategory BusyBox-Memsafety and fails to parse the programs in the new subcategory SQLite-MemSafety.

Now, let us discuss the effect of the adjustment of the time limits. For the time limit adjustment, we use the progress of the analyses measured in number of covered goals. Since there only exists one (reachable) test goal per task in the Cover-Error category, either both analyses make no progress in an iteration ($p_V \leq 0$ and $p_P \leq 0$) or one analysis covered the goal and CoVERITEST stops. Thus, the time limit adjustment has no effect on the Cover-Error category.

Next, let us consider the Cover-Branches category. Our own comparison of the CoVERITEST submissions for Test-Comp'19 and Test-Comp'20 revealed that the time limit adjustment mainly affects tasks of the ECA subcategory. In total, the coverage value for 320 tasks decreased and the coverage value for 591 tasks increased. Moreover, the increase is typically significantly larger than the decrease (on average 6.3 percent points increase compared to 1.5 percent points decrease). Furthermore, most of the tasks with a difference in the coverage value belong to the ECA subcategory. Therefore, the time limit adjustment pays off. Nevertheless, CoVERITEST could still perform better on the ECA subcategory. We believe that one problem in the ECA subcategory are redundant test goals, which lead to the same or similar test case generated multiple times and, thus, a waste of time.

4   Setup and Configuration

CoVeriTest is distributed as part of CPAchecker[3], which requires a Java 8 runtime environment. Our Test-Comp'20 submission, with which we participated in all categories, uses CPAchecker in revision 32236. After the environmental setup, one can run CoVeriTest on program `program.i` with the following command. The file `property.prp` is a placeholder for the test specification, either `coverage-error-call.prp` or `coverage-branches.prp`.

```
scripts/cpa.sh -testcomp20 -benchmark -heap 10000m
        -spec property.prp program.i
```

The command above assumes that `program.i` runs in a 32-bit environment. When requiring a 64-bit environment, one needs to add the parameter `-64` to the above command. Moreover, if the machine has not enough RAM to handle the specified Java heap memory, one can decrease the value passed with `-heap`.

The test suite generated during the execution of CoVeriTest is written to the directory `test-suite`, which is a subdirectory within the output directory of CPAchecker. As defined by the Test-Comp rules, the test suite contains a metadata file and test-case files adhering to the required XML format.

5   Project and Contributors

CoVeriTest is a component of the open-source project CPAchecker [3], which is hosted by Dirk Beyer's group at LMU Munich under Apache 2.0. Currently, also members of the Institute for System Programming of the Russian Academy of Sciences, Masaryk University, and Technical University of Darmstadt contribute to CPAchecker. We would like to thank all contributors.

References

1. Beyer, D., Chlipala, A.J., Henzinger, T.A., Jhala, R., Majumdar, R.: Generating tests from counterexamples. In: Proc. ICSE. pp. 326–335. IEEE (2004)
2. Beyer, D., Henzinger, T.A., Théoduloz, G.: Configurable software verification: Concretizing the convergence of model checking and program analysis. In: Proc. CAV. pp. 504–518. LNCS 4590, Springer (2007)
3. Beyer, D., Keremoglu, M.E.: CPAchecker: A tool for configurable software verification. In: Proc. CAV. pp. 184–190. LNCS 6806, Springer (2011)
4. Beyer, D., Keremoglu, M.E., Wendler, P.: Predicate abstraction with adjustable-block encoding. In: Proc. FMCAD. pp. 189–197. FMCAD (2010)
5. Beyer, D., Löwe, S.: Explicit-state software model checking based on CEGAR and interpolation. In: Proc. FASE. pp. 146–162. LNCS 7793, Springer (2013)
6. Beyer, D., Jakobs, M.: CoVeriTest: Cooperative verifier-based testing. In: Proc. FASE. pp. 389–408. LNCS 11424, Springer (2019)

---

[3] https://cpachecker.sosy-lab.org

7. Cimatti, A., Griggio, A., Schaafsma, B.J., Sebastiani, R.: The MathSAT5 SMT solver. In: Proc. TACAS. pp. 93–107. LNCS 7795, Springer (2013)
8. Clarke, E.M., Grumberg, O., Jha, S., Lu, Y., Veith, H.: Counterexample-guided abstraction refinement for symbolic model checking. J. ACM **50**(5), 752–794 (2003)
9. Karpenkov, E.G., Friedberger, K., Beyer, D.: JavaSMT: A unified interface for SMT solvers in Java. In: Proc. VSTTE. pp. 139–148. LNCS 9971, Springer (2016)
10. Ruland, S., Lochau, M., Fehse, O., Schürr, A.: Configurable test-goal set partitioning for multi-goal test-suite generation. STTT Competitions and Challenges Track - Test-Comp 2019 To appear
11. Ruland, S., Lochau, M., Jakobs, M.C.: HybridTiger: Hybrid model checking and domination-based partitioning for efficient multi-goal test-suite generation (competition contribution). In: Proc. FASE. LNCS, Springer (2020)

LEGION: Best-First Concolic Testing (Competition Contribution)

Dongge Liu[*1], Gidon Ernst[**2], Toby Murray[1], and Benjamin I.P. Rubinstein[1]

[1] University of Melbourne, Australia
donggel@student.unimelb.edu.au
[2] LMU Munich, Germany
gidon.ernst@lmu.de

Abstract. LEGION is a grey-box coverage-based concolic tool that aims to balance the complementary nature of fuzzing and symbolic execution to achieve the best of both worlds. It proposes a variation of *Monte Carlo tree search (MCTS)* that formulates program exploration as sequential decision-making under uncertainty guided by the best-first search strategy. It relies on *approximate path-preserving fuzzing*, a novel instance of constrained random testing, which quickly generates many diverse inputs that likely target program parts of interest. In Test-Comp 2020 [1], the prototype performed within 90% of the best score in 9 of 22 categories.

Keywords: Symbolic Execution, Fuzzing, Monte Carlo Search

1 Test-Generation Approach

Coverage testing aims to traverse all execution paths of the program under test to verify its correctness. Two traditional techniques for this task, *symbolic execution* [6] and *fuzzing* [7] are complementary in nature [5].

Consider exploring the program `Ackermann02` in Fig. 1 from the Test-Comp benchmarks as an example. Symbolic execution can compute inputs to penetrate the choke point (line 10) to reach the "rare branch" (lines 14/15), but then becomes unnecessarily expensive in solving the exponentially growing constraints from repeatedly unfolding the recursive function `ackermann`. By comparison, even though very few random fuzzer-generated inputs pass the choke point, the high speed of fuzzing means the "rare branch" will be quickly reached.

The following research question arises when exploring the program space in a conditional branch: Will it be more efficient to focus on the space under the constraint, or to flood both branches with unconstrained inputs, to target the internals of `log(m,n)` in line 11 at the same time?

LEGION[3] introduces *MCTS-guided program exploration* as a principled answer to this question, tailored to each program under test. For a program like

---

[*] This research was supported by Data61 under the Defence Science and Technology Group's Next Generation Technologies Program.

[**] Jury Member

[3] The name LEGION comes from the Marvel fictional character who changes personalities for different needs, to reflect the strategy adaption depending on the program.

© The Author(s) 2020
H. Wehrheim and J. Cabot (Eds.): FASE 2020, LNCS 12076, pp. 545–549, 2020.
https://doi.org/10.1007/978-3-030-45234-6_31

```
1   int ackermann(int m, int n) {
2     if (m==0) return n+1;
3     if (n==0) return ackermann(m-1,1);
4     return ackermann(m-1,ackermann(m,n-1));
5   }
6
7   void main() {
8     int m = input(), n = input();
9     // choke point
10    if (m < 0 || m > 3) || (n < 0 || n > 23) {
11      log(n,m);            // common branch
12      return;
13    } else {
14      int r = ackermann(m,n); // rare branch
15      assert(m < 2 || r >= 4);
16    }
17  }
```

Program entry state

Program path selected for fuzzing

A concrete execution trace

Unknown paths

Observed paths

Score: estimate the likelihood of finding new paths

Fig. 1: `Ackermann02.c`   Fig. 2: MCTS-guided fuzzing in LEGION

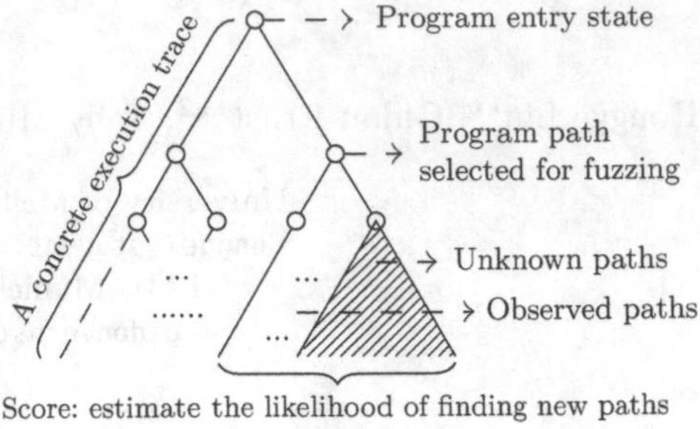

Fig. 2, LEGION estimates the expectation of finding new paths by the UCT score (upper confidence bound for trees), a successful approach for games [3], aiming to balance *exploration* of program space (where success is still uncertain) against *exploitation* of partial results (that appear promising already). Code behind rare branches is targeted by *approximate path-preserving fuzzing* to efficiently generate diverse inputs for a specific sub-part of the program.

LEGION's MCTS iteratively explores a tree-structured search space, whose nodes represent partial execution paths. On each iteration, LEGION selects a *target* node by recursively descending from the root along the highest scoring child, stopping when a parent's score exceeds its childrens'. A node's score is based on the ratio of the number of distinct vs. all paths observed passing through it, but nodes selected less often in the past are more likely to be chosen. Then, approximate path-preserving fuzzing is applied to explore the target node. The resulting execution traces are recorded and integrated into the tree.

Approximate path-preserving fuzzing (APPF) quickly generates inputs that likely follow the target program path, and therefore is crucial for LEGION's efficiency. LEGION's APPF implementation extends the QUICKSAMPLER [4] technique, which is a recent mutation-based algorithm that expands a small set of constraint solutions to a larger suite of likely solutions. LEGION extends QUICKSAMPLER from propositional logic to bitvector path constraints.

2 Tool Description & Configuration

We implemented LEGION as a prototype in `Python 3` on top of the symbolic execution engine `angr` [8]. We have extended its solver backend, `claripy`, by the approximate path-preserving fuzzing algorithm, relying on the optimizer component of Z3 [2]. Binaries are instrumented to record execution traces.

Installation. Download and unpack the competition archive (commit `b2fc8430`):
`https://gitlab.com/sosy-lab/test-comp/archives-2020/blob/master/2020/legion.zip`

LEGION requires `Python 3` with `python-setuptools` installed, and `gcc-multilib` for the compilation of C sources. Necessary libraries compiled for Ubuntu 18.04

are included in the subfolder `lib` (modified versions of `angr`, `claripy` and their dependencies). The archive contains the main executable, `Legion.py`, and a wrapper script, `legion-sv` that includes `lib` into `PYTHONPATH`. The version tag is `0.1-testcomp2020`, options can be shown with `python3 ./Legion.py --help`.

Configuration. In the competition, we ran `./legion-sv` with these parameters:

`--save-tests`	save test cases as `xml` files in Test-Comp format
`--persistent`	keep running when no more symbolic solutions are found (mitigates issue with dynamic memory allocations)
`--time-penalty 0`	do not penalise a node for expensive constraint-solving (experimental feature, not yet evaluated)
`--random-seed 0`	fix the random seed for deterministic result
`--symex-timeout 10`	limit symbolic execution and constraint solving to 10s
`--conex-timeout 10`	limit concrete binary execution to 10s

In the category `cover-branches`, we additionally use this flag:

`--coverage-only`	don't stop when finding an error

Finally, `-32` and `-64` indicate whether to use 32 or 64 bits (this affects binary compilation and the sizes for nondeterministic values of types `int`, . . .).

Participation. LEGION participates in all categories of Test-Comp 2020.

Software Project and Contributors. LEGION is principally developed by Dongge Liu, with technical and conceptual contributions by all authors of this paper. LEGION will be made available at `https://github.com/Alan32Liu/Legion`.

3   Discussion

LEGION is competitive in many categories of Test-Comp 2020, achieving within 90% of the best score in 2 of 9 error categories and 7 of 13 coverage categories.

```
1  void main( ) {
2    int N=100000, a1[N], a2[N], a3[N], i;
3    for (i=0; i<N; i++)
4      a1[i] = input(); a2[i] = input();
5    for(i=0; i<N; i++) a3[i] = a1[i];
6    for(i=0; i<N; i++) a3[i] = a2[i];
7    for(i=0; i<N; i++) assert(a1[i] == a3[i]);
8  }
```

Fig. 3: `standard_copy2_ground-1.c`

LEGION's instrumentation and exploration algorithm can accurately model the program. Consider the benchmark `standard_copy2_ground-1.c` in Fig. 3. With a single symbolic execution through the entire program over a trace found via initial random inputs, LEGION understands that all guards of the `for` loops can only evaluate in one way, and so omits them from the selection phase. It does discover that the assertion inside the last loop contributes interesting decisions, however, and will come up with two different ways to evaluate the comparison `a1[i] == a3[i]`, one of which triggers the error. With such an accurate model in combination with its principled MCTS search strategy, LEGION is particularly good at covering corner cases in deep loops: All other tools failed to score full marks in `standard_copy*_ground-*.c` benchmarks, but LEGION succeeded in 9 out of 18. We can furthermore solve benchmarks where pure constraint solving fails, e.g., when the solver times out on hard constraints of complex paths we label the respective branches for pure random exploration.

While instrumentation provides accurate information on the program, its currently naive implementation significantly slows down the concrete execution of programs with long execution traces. We mitigate this weakness by setting a time limit on the concrete executions. As a consequence, inputs that correspond to long concrete execution are not saved. In the future, we plan to explore Intel's PIN tool, which offloads binary tracing into the CPU with negligible overhead.

LEGION inherits some limitations from angr as a symbolic execution backend. Some benchmarks, such as array-tiling/mbpr5.c, dynamically allocate memory with a symbolic size that depends on the input. angr eagerly concretises this value, producing unsatisfiable path constraints for a feasible execution path. LEGION detects this inconsistency as soon as it encounters the feasible path and omits the erroneous node from selection. This helps e.g. on bubblesort-alloca-1.c where LEGION achieved full coverage (in contrast to most other participants) despite the dynamic allocations.

LEGION performed poorly on benchmark sets bitvector and ssh-simplified. These programs have long sequences of equality constraint that are hard to satisfy with fuzzing. This happens to be an extreme example of the parent-child trade-off that LEGION intends to balance where fuzzing the parent gives nearly no reward. This could potentially be mitigated by decreasing LEGION's exploration ratio in the UCT score, but we have not attempted such fine-tuning.

Another problem is allocations when loop counters or array sizes are randomly chosen very large in 64 bit mode, leading to excessively long concrete execution traces that cause timeouts or memory exhaustion. We plan to periodically prune the in-memory representation of the tree in the future.

References

1. Beyer, D.: Second competition on software testing: Test-comp 2020. In: Proc. of Fundamental Aspects of Software Engineering (FASE). LNCS, Springer (2020), https://www.sosy-lab.org/research/pub/2020-FASE.Second_Competition_on_Software_Testing_Test-Comp_2020.pdf
2. Bjørner, N., Phan, A.D., Fleckenstein, L.: νZ-an optimizing SMT solver. In: Proc. of Tools and Algorithms for the Construction and Analysis of Systems (TACAS). LNCS, vol. 9035, pp. 194–199. Springer (2015). https://doi.org/10.1007/978-3-662-46681-0_14
3. Browne, C.B., Powley, E., Whitehouse, D., Lucas, S.M., Cowling, P.I., Rohlfshagen, P., Tavener, S., Perez, D., Samothrakis, S., Colton, S.: A survey of monte carlo tree search methods. IEEE Transactions on Computational Intelligence and AI in Games 4(1), 1–43 (2012). https://doi.org/10.1109/TCIAIG.2012.2186810
4. Dutra, R., Laeufer, K., Bachrach, J., Sen, K.: Efficient sampling of SAT solutions for testing. In: Proc. of the International Conference on Software Engineering (ICSE). pp. 549–559. ACM (2018). https://doi.org/10.1145/3180155.3180248
5. Godefroid, P., Levin, M.Y., Molnar, D.A., et al.: Automated whitebox fuzz testing. In: Proc. of Network and Distributed Systems Security (NDSS). vol. 8, pp. 151–166. The Internet Society (2008)
6. King, J.C.: Symbolic execution and program testing. Communications of the ACM 19(7), 385–394 (1976). https://doi.org/10.1145/360248.360252

7. Takanen, A., Demott, J.D., Miller, C., Kettunen, A.: Fuzzing for software security testing and quality assurance. Artech House (2018)
8. Wang, F., Shoshitaishvili, Y.: Angr - the next generation of binary analysis. In: Proc. of Cybersecurity Development (SecDev). pp. 8–9. IEEE (2017). https://doi.org/10.1109/SecDev.2017.14

Author Index

Printed in the United States
By Bookmasters